Keira
curtis

COMPACT
WORLD
ATLAS

D0544148

LONDON, NEW YORK, MUNICH,
MELBOURNE, DELHI

A DORLING KINDERSLEY BOOK
www.dk.com

EDITOR-IN-CHIEF
Andrew Heritage

SENIOR MANAGING ART EDITOR
Philip Lord

SENIOR CARTOGRAPHIC MANAGER
David Roberts

SENIOR CARTOGRAPHIC EDITOR
Simon Mumford

PROJECT CARTOGRAPHER
Iorwerth Watkins

PROJECT DESIGNER
Karen Gregory

PROJECT EDITOR
Debra Clapson

SYSTEMS CO-ORDINATOR
Philip Rowles

PRODUCTION
Wendy Penn

First published in Great Britain in 2001
by Dorling Kindersley Limited
80 Strand, London WC2R 0RL

A CIP catalogue record for this book is available from the British Library

ISBN 0-7513-4883-X

Reproduced by GRB, Italy

Printed and bound in China by Toppan Printing Co. (Shenzhen) Ltd.

For the very latest information, visit:
www.dk.com and click on the Maps & Atlases icon

KEY TO MAP SYMBOLS

PHYSICAL FEATURES

Elevation

- 4,000m / 13,124ft
- 2,000m / 6,562ft
- 1,000m / 3,281ft
- 500m / 1,640ft
- 250m / 820ft
- 100m / 328ft
- 0
- Below sea level

△ Mountain

▽ Depression

◮ Volcano

)(Pass/tunnel

Sandy desert

DRAINAGE FEATURES

Major perennial river

Minor perennial river

- - - Seasonal river

Canal

| Waterfall

Perennial lake

Seasonal lake

Wetland

ICE FEATURES

Permanent ice cap/ice shelf

Winter limit of pack ice

Summer limit of pack ice

BORDERS

Full international border

- - - - Disputed *de facto* border

· · · · · Territorial claim border

x—x—x Cease-fire line

— — — Undefined boundary

Internal administrative boundary

COMMUNICATIONS

Major road

Minor road

Rail

✈ International airport

SETTLEMENTS

▣ Over 500,000

◉ 100,000 - 500,000

○ 50,000 - 100,000

○ Less than 50,000

● National capital

● Internal administrative capital

MISCELLANEOUS FEATURES

+ Site of interest

ⵀⵀⵀ Ancient wall

GRATICULE FEATURES

Line of latitude/longitude/ Equator

- - - Tropic/Polar circle

25° Degrees of latitude/ longitude

NAMES

Physical features

Andes

Sahara   Landscape features

Ardennes

Land's End   Headland

Mont Blanc 4,807m   Elevation/volcano/pass

Blue Nile   River/canal/waterfall

Ross Ice Shelf   Ice feature

PACIFIC OCEAN

Sulu Sea   Sea features

Palk Strait

Chile Rise   Undersea feature

Regions

FRANCE   Country

JERSEY (to UK)   Dependent territory

KANSAS   Administrative region

Dordogne   Cultural region

Settlements

PARIS   Capital city

SAN JUAN   Dependent territory capital city

Chicago

Kettering   Other settlements

Burke

INSET MAP SYMBOLS

Urban area

City

Park

▪ Place of interest

▫ Suburb/district

CONTENTS

THE WORLD ATLAS

NORTH & CENTRAL AMERICA

SOUTH AMERICA

AFRICA

EUROPE

THE POLITICAL WORLD

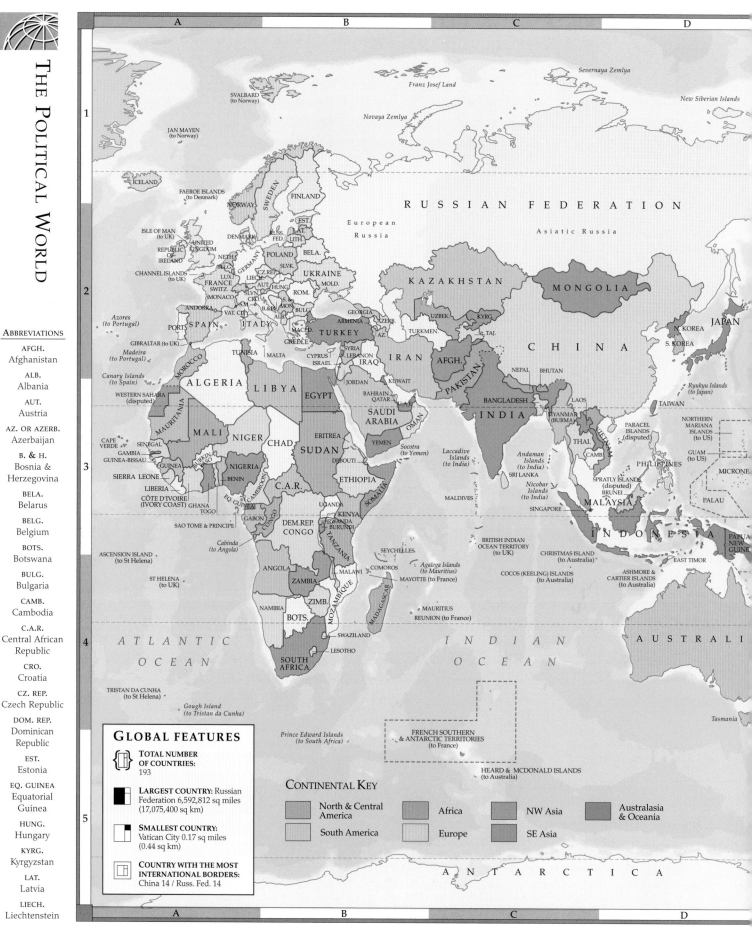

ABBREVIATIONS

AFGH.
Afghanistan

ALB.
Albania

AUT.
Austria

AZ. OR AZERB.
Azerbaijan

B. & H.
Bosnia &
Herzegovina

BELA.
Belarus

BELG.
Belgium

BOTS.
Botswana

BULG.
Bulgaria

CAMB.
Cambodia

C.A.R.
Central African
Republic

CRO.
Croatia

CZ. REP.
Czech Republic

DOM. REP.
Dominican
Republic

EST.
Estonia

EQ. GUINEA
Equatorial
Guinea

HUNG.
Hungary

KYRG.
Kyrgyzstan

LAT.
Latvia

LIECH.
Liechtenstein

GLOBAL FEATURES

**TOTAL NUMBER
OF COUNTRIES:**
193

LARGEST COUNTRY: Russian
Federation 6,592,812 sq miles
(17,075,400 sq km)

SMALLEST COUNTRY:
Vatican City 0.17 sq miles
(0.44 sq km)

**COUNTRY WITH THE MOST
INTERNATIONAL BORDERS:**
China 14 / Russ. Fed. 14

CONTINENTAL KEY

North & Central
America

South America

Africa

Europe

NW Asia

SE Asia

Australasia
& Oceania

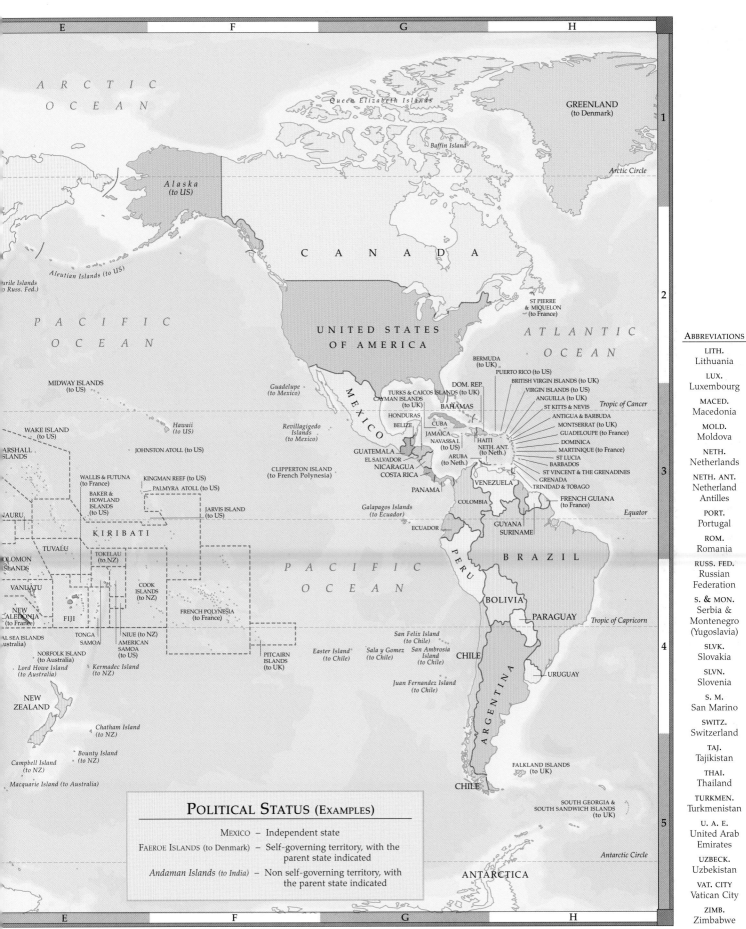

A R C T I C
O C E A N

Queen Elizabeth Islands

GREENLAND
(to Denmark)

1

Baffin Island

Arctic Circle

*Alaska
(to US)*

Aleutian Islands (to US)

*Kurile Islands
(to Russ. Fed.)*

C A N A D A

2

P A C I F I C

O C E A N

UNITED STATES
OF AMERICA

ST PIERRE
& MIQUELON
(to France)

A T L A N T I C

O C E A N

BERMUDA
(to UK)

LITH.
Lithuania

MIDWAY ISLANDS
(to US)

*Guadelupe
(to Mexico)*

PUERTO RICO (to US)

BRITISH VIRGIN ISLANDS (to UK)

VIRGIN ISLANDS (to US)

ANGUILLA (to UK)

ST KITTS & NEVIS

Tropic of Cancer

LUX.
Luxembourg

TURKS & CAICOS ISLANDS (to UK)

CAYMAN ISLANDS
(to UK)

BAHAMAS

ANTIGUA & BARBUDA

MACED.
Macedonia

*Hawaii
(to US)*

HONDURAS

CUBA

BELIZE

*Revillagigedo
Islands
(to Mexico)*

JAMAICA

MONTSERRAT (to UK)

GUADELOUPE (to France)

DOMINICA

MOLD.
Moldova

WAKE ISLAND
(to US)

JOHNSTON ATOLL (to US)

NAVASSA I.
(to US)

HAITI

NETH. ANT.
(to Neth.)

MARTINIQUE (to France)

ST LUCIA

NETH.
Netherlands

MARSHALL
ISLANDS

GUATEMALA

EL SALVADOR

ARUBA
(to Neth.)

BARBADOS

ST VINCENT & THE GRENADINES

NETH. ANT.
Netherland
Antilles

WALLIS & FUTUNA
(to France)

KINGMAN REEF (to US)

PALMYRA ATOLL (to US)

*Clipperton Island
(to French Polynesia)*

NICARAGUA

COSTA RICA

VENEZUELA

GRENADA

TRINIDAD & TOBAGO

3

PORT.
Portugal

BAKER &
HOWLAND
ISLANDS
(to US)

JARVIS ISLAND
(to US)

PANAMA

COLOMBIA

FRENCH GUIANA
(to France)

ROM.
Romania

NAURU

*Galapagos Islands
(to Ecuador)*

GUYANA

SURINAME

Equator

RUSS. FED.
Russian
Federation

KIRIBATI

ECUADOR

TUVALU

S. & MON.
Serbia &
Montenegro
(Yugoslavia)

SOLOMON
ISLANDS

P E R U

B R A Z I L

VANUATU

P A C I F I C

SLVK.
Slovakia

O C E A N

BOLIVIA

NEW
CALEDONIA
(to France)

FIJI

COOK
ISLANDS
(to NZ)

FRENCH POLYNESIA
(to France)

PARAGUAY

Tropic of Capricorn

SLVN.
Slovenia

CORAL SEA ISLANDS
(to Australia)

TONGA

SAMOA

NIUE (to NZ)

AMERICAN
SAMOA
(to US)

*San Felix Island
(to Chile)*

S. M.
San Marino

NORFOLK ISLAND
(to Australia)

PITCAIRN
ISLANDS
(to UK)

*Easter Island
(to Chile)*

*Sala y Gomez
(to Chile)*

*San Ambrosia
Island
(to Chile)*

CHILE

4

SWITZ.
Switzerland

*Lord Howe Island
(to Australia)*

*Kermadec Island
(to NZ)*

URUGUAY

TAJ.
Tajikistan

*Juan Fernandez Island
(to Chile)*

NEW
ZEALAND

A R G E N T I N A

THAI.
Thailand

*Chatham Island
(to NZ)*

TURKMEN.
Turkmenistan

*Bounty Island
(to NZ)*

*Campbell Island
(to NZ)*

FALKLAND ISLANDS
(to UK)

U. A. E.
United Arab
Emirates

Macquarie Island (to Australia)

CHILE

UZBECK.
Uzbekistan

SOUTH GEORGIA &
SOUTH SANDWICH ISLANDS
(to UK)

5

POLITICAL STATUS (EXAMPLES)

MEXICO — Independent state

FAEROE ISLANDS (to Denmark) — Self-governing territory, with the
parent state indicated

Andaman Islands (to India) — Non self-governing territory, with
the parent state indicated

Antarctic Circle

ANTARCTICA

VAT. CITY
Vatican City

ZIMB.
Zimbabwe

THE PHYSICAL WORLD

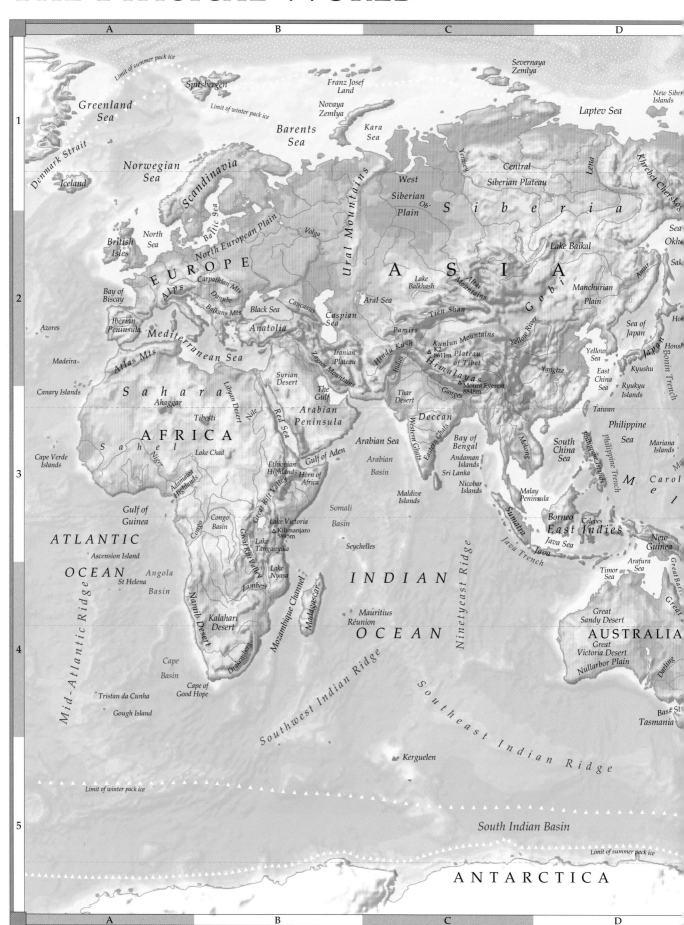

A | B | C | D

1

Limit of summer pack ice
Limit of winter pack ice
Spitsbergen
Franz Josef Land
Severnaya Zemlya
Greenland Sea
Novaya Zemlya
Kara Sea
New Siberian Islands
Barents Sea
Laptev Sea
Denmark Strait
Norwegian Sea
Iceland
Scandinavia
West Siberian Plain
Ob'
Central Siberian Plateau
Lena
Khrebet Cherskog
Sea Okh
Sak
British Isles
North Sea
Baltic Sea
North European Plain
Volga
Ural Mountains
S i b e r i a
Lake Baikal
Amur
A S I A
Bay of Biscay
EUROPE
Carpathian Mts
Danube
Alps
Balkans Mts
Black Sea
Caucasus
Aral Sea
Lake Balkhash
Altai Mountains
Gobi
Manchurian Plain
Sea of Japan
Hon
Azores
Iberian Peninsula
Anatolia
Caspian Sea
Pamirs
Tien Shan
Yellow River
Yangtze
Japan
Kyushu
Madeira
Mediterranean Sea
Iranian Plateau
Zagros Mountains
Hindu Kush
Indus
Kunlun Mountains
K2 8611m
Plateau of Tibet
Himalayas
Mount Everest 8848m
Yellow Sea
East China Sea
Ryukyu Islands
Bonin Trench
Honsi
Canary Islands
Atlas Mts
S a h a r a
Ahaggar
Libyan Desert
Syrian Desert
The Gulf
Arabian Peninsula
Thar Desert
Deccan
Ganges
Taiwan
Philippine Sea
Cape Verde Islands
Tibesti
Nile
Red Sea
Arabian Sea
Western Ghats
Eastern Ghats
Bay of Bengal
Andaman Islands
Mekong
South China Sea
Mariana Islands
Mi
Car o l
3
AFRICA
S a h e l
Niger
Lake Chad
Ethiopian Highlands
Gulf of Aden
Horn of Africa
Arabian Basin
Sri Lanka
Nicobar Islands
Malay Peninsula
philippine Trench
Philippine Islands
Adamaoua Highlands
Gulf of Guinea
Congo
Congo Basin
Great Rift Valley
Lake Victoria
Kilimanjaro 5895m
Somali Basin
Maldive Islands
Sumatra
Borneo
Celebes
East Indies
New Guinea
ATLANTIC
Ascension Island
St Helena
Angola Basin
Great Rift Valley
Lake Tanganyika
Lake Nyasa
Zambezi
Seychelles
INDIAN
Java Trench
Java
Java Sea
Arafura Sea
Timor Sea
Great Barri
Great
OCEAN
Mid-Atlantic Ridge
Namib Desert
Kalahari Desert
Mozambique Channel
Madagascar
Mauritius
Réunion
OCEAN
Ninetyeast Ridge
Great Sandy Desert
AUSTRALIA
4
Cape Basin
Drakensberg
Cape of Good Hope
Tristan da Cunha
Gough Island
Southwest Indian Ridge
Southeast Indian Ridge
Kerguelen
Great Victoria Desert
Nullarbor Plain
Darling
Bass St
Tasmania
Limit of winter pack ice
5
South Indian Basin
Limit of summer pack ice
A N T A R C T I C A

A | B | C | D

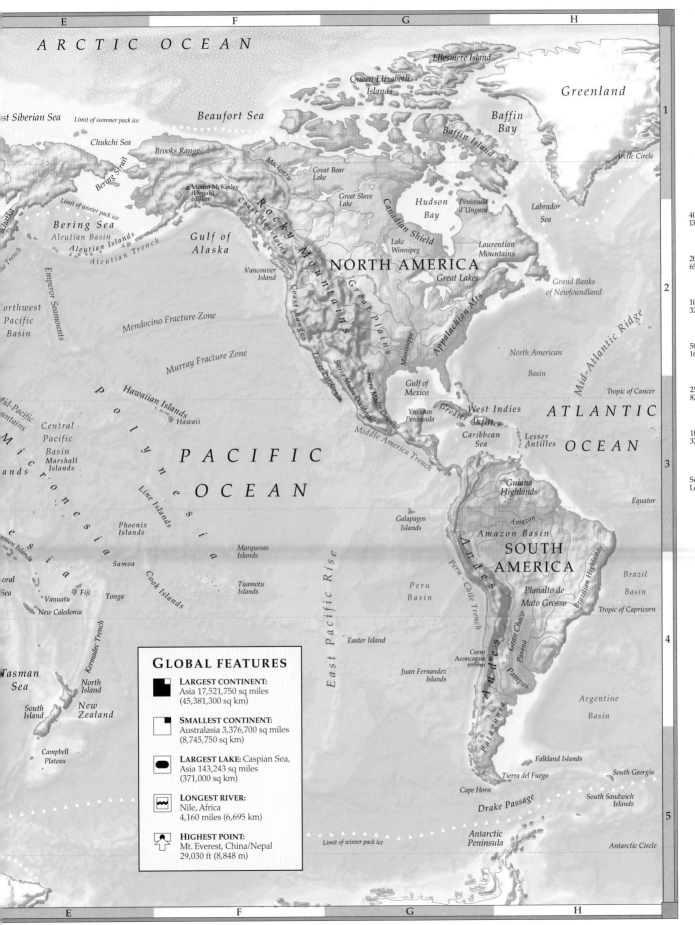

E   F   G   H

ARCTIC OCEAN

Ellesmere Island

Queen Elizabeth
Islands

Greenland

st Siberian Sea   Limit of summer pack ice   Beaufort Sea   Baffin
Bay

Chukchi Sea   Baffin Island   1

Brooks Range   Mackenzie

Bering Strait   Great Bear
Lake

△ Mount McKinley
(Denali)
6194m   Great Slave
Lake   Hudson
Bay   Péninsula
d'Ungava   Labrador
Sea   Arctic Circle

Limit of winter pack ice   Canadian Shield

Bering Sea   Aleutian Basin   Gulf of
Alaska   Lake
Winnipeg   NORTH AMERICA   Laurentian
Mountains

Aleutian Islands   Vancouver
Island   Great Lakes   Grand Banks
of Newfoundland   2

Aleutian Trench   Coast Ranges

Emperor Seamounts   Mendocino Fracture Zone   Great Plains   Appalachian Mts.   North American
Basin   Mid-Atlantic Ridge

orthwest
Pacific
Basin   Murray Fracture Zone   Sierra Madre Occidental   Mississippi   Tropic of Cancer

Hawaiian Islands   Lower California   Gulf of
Mexico   ATLANTIC

Central
Pacific
Basin   Hawaii   Yucatán
Peninsula   Sierra Madre Oriental   West Indies   Lesser
Antilles   OCEAN

Marshall
Islands   Greater
Antilles   100 m
328 ft

PACIFIC   Middle America Trench   Caribbean
Sea   3

OCEAN   Guiana
Highlands   Equator

Galapagos
Islands   Amazon

Phoenix
Islands   Amazon Basin   SOUTH
AMERICA

Marquesas
Islands   Peru
Basin   Brazil
Basin

East Pacific Rise   Andes   Planalto de
Mato Grosso   Brazilian Highlands   Tropic of Capricorn

Samoa   Tuamotu
Islands   Peru-Chile Trench

Vanuatu   Fiji   Tonga   Cook Islands   Gran Chaco   Paraná

New Caledonia   Easter Island   Pampas   4

Tasman
Sea   North
Island   Juan Fernandez
Islands   Cerro
Aconcagua
6959m   Argentine
Basin

South
Island   New
Zealand

Campbell
Plateau   Patagonia   Falkland Islands   South Georgia

Tierra del Fuego   South Sandwich
Islands

Cape Horn   South Sandwich
Islands

Drake Passage

Antarctic
Peninsula   Antarctic Circle   5

Limit of winter pack ice

E   F   G   H

ELEVATION

4000 m
13 124 ft

2000 m
6562 ft

1000 m
3281 ft

500 m
1640 ft

250 m
820 ft

100 m
328 ft

Sea Level   Sea Level

-250 m
-820 ft

-500 m
-1640 ft

-1000 m
-3281 ft

-2000 m
-6562 ft

-3000 m
-9843 ft

-4000 m
-13 124 ft

GLOBAL FEATURES

LARGEST CONTINENT:
Asia 17,521,750 sq miles
(45,381,300 sq km)

SMALLEST CONTINENT:
Australasia 3,376,700 sq miles
(8,745,750 sq km)

LARGEST LAKE: Caspian Sea,
Asia 143,243 sq miles
(371,000 sq km)

LONGEST RIVER:
Nile, Africa
4,160 miles (6,695 km)

HIGHEST POINT:
Mt. Everest, China/Nepal
29,030 ft (8,848 m)

TIME ZONES

The numbers represented thus: +2/-2, indicate the number of hours ahead or behind GMT (Greenwich Mean Time) of each time zone.

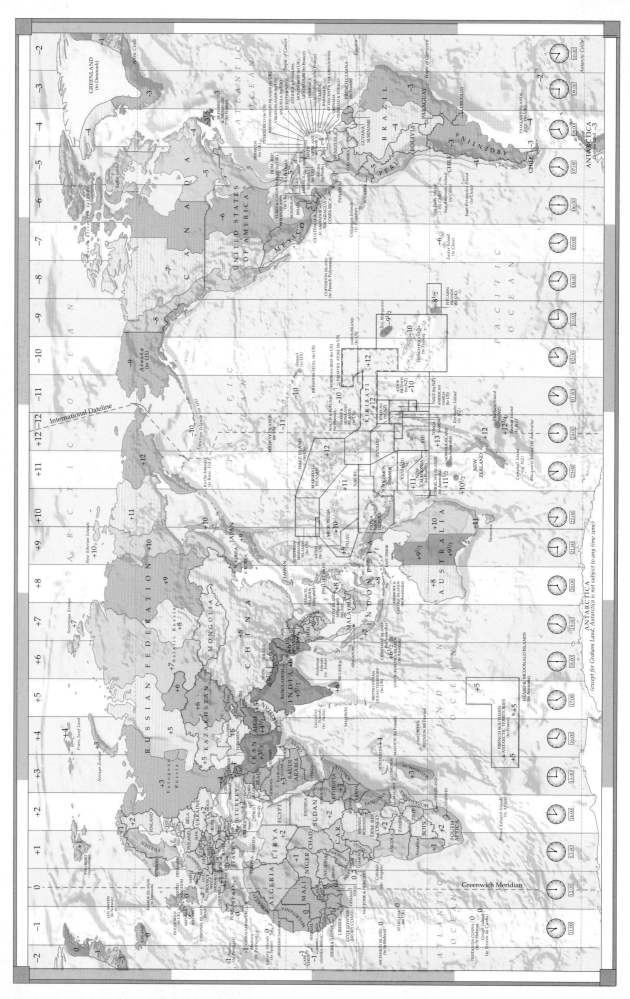

The
WORLD
ATLAS

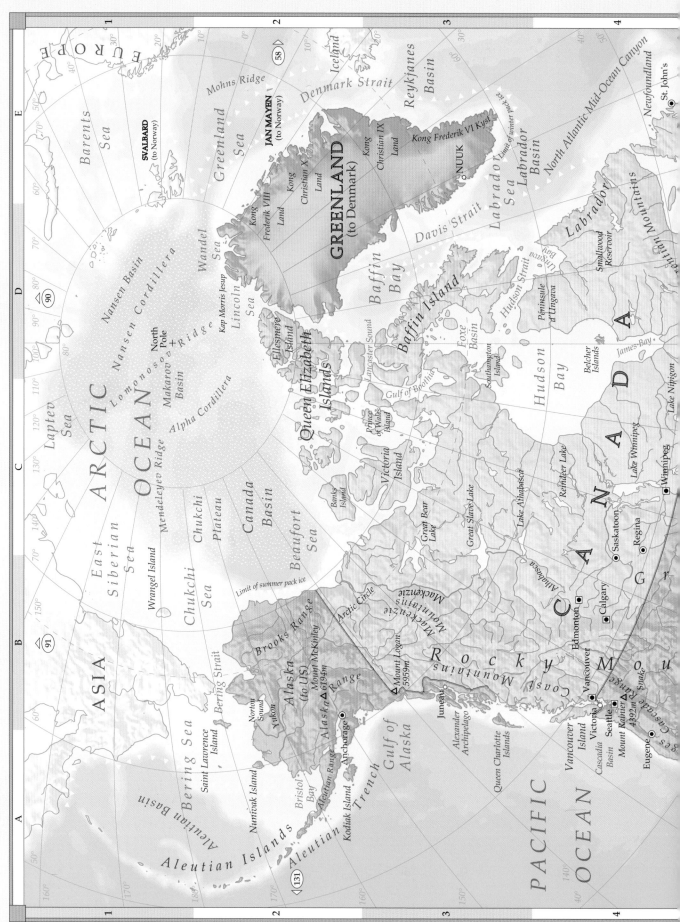

POPULATION

- Over 500,000
- 100,000 – 500,000
- 50,000 – 100,000
- Less than 50,000
- National capital

ATLANTIC OCEAN

SOUTH AMERICA

Andes

PACIFIC OCEAN

Gulf of Mexico

Caribbean Sea

UNITED STATES OF AMERICA

MEXICO

Sargasso Sea

Halifax
Montreal
OTTAWA
Boston
Cape Cod
New York
Philadelphia
Baltimore
WASHINGTON DC
Richmond
Raleigh
Columbia
Jacksonville
Miami
Tampa
New Orleans
Houston
San Antonio
Dallas
Austin
Baton Rouge
Jackson
Montgomery
Atlanta
Nashville
Memphis
Little Rock
Oklahoma City
Topeka
Kansas City
Lincoln
Des Moines
Denver
Salt Lake City
Phoenix
San Diego
Los Angeles
San Jose
San Francisco
Saint Paul
Madison
Milwaukee
Chicago
Indianapolis
Springfield
Columbus
Cleveland
Detroit
Lansing
Toronto
Buffalo
Niagara Falls
Albany

Lake Ontario
Lake Erie
Lake Huron
Lake Michigan
Lake Superior

Great Lakes
Appalachian Mountains
Georges Bank
Blake Plateau
Hatteras Plain
Nares Plain
Bermuda Rise

BERMUDA (to UK)

Tropic of Cancer

BAHAMAS
NASSAU
HAVANA
CUBA
Greater Antilles
Straits of Florida
CAYMAN ISLANDS (to UK)
JAMAICA
KINGSTON
HAITI
PORT-AU-PRINCE
SANTO DOMINGO
DOMINICAN REPUBLIC
PUERTO RICO (to US)
TURKS & CAICOS ISLANDS (to UK)
VIRGIN ISLANDS (to US)
BRITISH VIRGIN ISLANDS (to UK)
ANGUILLA (to UK)
ST KITTS & NEVIS
ANTIGUA & BARBUDA
MONTSERRAT (to UK)
GUADELOUPE (to France)
DOMINICA
MARTINIQUE (to France)
ST LUCIA
ST VINCENT & THE GRENADINES
BARBADOS
GRENADA
Lesser Antilles
TRINIDAD & TOBAGO
PORT-OF-SPAIN
NETHERLANDS ANTILLES (to Neth.)
ARUBA (to Neth.)
Colombian Basin
Panama Basin
Cocos Ridge
Colón Ridge
Galapagos Islands (to Ecuador)
PANAMA
PANAMA CITY
COSTA RICA
SAN JOSÉ
NICARAGUA
MANAGUA
Lake Nicaragua
TEGUCIGALPA
HONDURAS
BELIZE
BELMOPAN
GUATEMALA
GUATEMALA CITY
EL SALVADOR
SAN SALVADOR
Guatemala Basin
Middle America Trench
Yucatan Peninsula
MEXICO CITY
Volcán Pico de Orizaba 5700m
Acapulco
Guadalajara
Monterrey
Rio Grande
El Paso
Sierra Madre Oriental
Sierra Madre Occidental
Gulf of California
Lower California
East Pacific Rise
Great Basin
Coast Ranges
Mount Whitney 4418m
Grand Canyon
Colorado
Murray Fracture Zone
Tropic of Cancer
Equator

Mississippi Delta
Mississippi
Missouri
Arkansas
Red River
Ohio

POLITICAL FEATURES

TOTAL AREA:
9,400,000 sq miles
(24,346,000 sq km)

TOTAL NUMBER OF COUNTRIES:
23

TOTAL POPULATION:
466.2 million

LARGEST CITY WITH POPULATION:
Mexico City, Mexico 18 million

COUNTRY WITH HIGHEST POPULATION DENSITY:
Barbados 1,626 people per sq mile
(628 people per sq km)

LARGEST COUNTRY:
Canada 3,851,788 sq miles
(9,976,140 sq km)

SMALLEST COUNTRY:
Grenada 131 sq miles
(340 sq km)

PHYSICAL FEATURES

LARGEST LAKE:
Lake Superior, Canada/ USA
32,150 sq miles (83,270 sq km)

LONGEST RIVER:
Mississippi-Missouri, USA
3,740 miles (6,019 km)

HIGHEST POINT:
Mt. McKinley (Denali), Alaska, USA
20,322 ft (6,194 m)

LOWEST POINT:
Death Valley, California, USA
282 ft (86 m) below sea level

WESTERN CANADA & ALASKA

Poluostrov Kamchatka

⬆ 93

Arctic Circle

RUSSIAN FEDERATION

Ostrov Vrangelya

A R C T I

Chukchi Sea

Near Islands

Attu Island

◁ 130

Rat Islands

Amchitka Island

Bering Strait

Wevok   Point Lay
                          Barrow
Kivalina

Gambell   Wales

B e r i n g

S e a

Saint Lawrence Island

Deering

Prudhoe Bay

Umiat

Kaktov

Colville River

Brooks Range

Norton Sound

Alakanuk

Nunivak Island

Grayling   Yukon River   Kokrines

Pribilof Islands

Kwigillingok

A L A S K A (to US)

Fort Yukon

Aklavi

Andreanof Islands

Atka

A l e u t i a n   I s l a n d s

Platinum

Kuskokwim Mts

Fairbanks

Fort McPherson

Umnak Island

Unalaska Island

Dutch Harbor

Unimak Island

Belkofski

Bristol Bay

Iliamna Lake

Alaska Range

Mount McKinley 6194m

McKinley Park

Susitna

Y U K O N

Mackel

Anchorage

Hope

Gulkana

Alaska Peninsula

Shumagin Islands

Kodiak

Valdez

Cordova

Chitina

T E R R I T O R

Katalla

Mount Logan 5959m

Kodiak Island

Whitehorse

Gulf of Alaska

Yakutat

Haines

Atlin

Gustavus

Juneau

◁ 131

Kake

B R I T I S

Alexander Archipelago

Port Alexander

P A C I F I C

Ketchikan

Prince Rupert

Kitimat

O C E A N

Queen Charlotte Islands

Ocean Falls

Queen Charlotte Sound

Mount Waddington 4016m

Port Hardy

Campbell River

Vancouver Island

Nanaim

Victor

POPULATION

- ⬛ Over 500,000
- ◉ 100,000 – 500,000
- ○ 50,000 – 100,000
- ○ Less than 50,000
- ⚫ Internal administrative capital

0 km   400

0 miles   400

131

GREENLAND
(to Denmark)

Knud Rasmussen Land

Arctic Circle

Baffin Bay

Davis Strait

Alert

133

60

Ellesmere Island

Axel Heiberg Island

Nares Strait

Ellef Ringnes Island
Isachsen

Amund Ringnes Island

Prince Patrick Island

Queen Elizabeth Islands

Devon Island

Mould Bay

Bathurst Island

Cornwallis Island

Lancaster Sound

Cumberland Sound

OCEAN

Melville Island

Resolute

Baffin Island

Banks Island

Viscount Melville Sound

McClintock Channel

Somerset Island

Brodeur Peninsula

Gulf of Boothia

aufort Sea

chs Harbour

Prince of Wales Island

Boothia Peninsula

Iglooloik

Nettilling Lake

ktoyaktuk

Amundsen Gulf

Holman

Victoria Island

King William Island

Pelly Bay

Melville Peninsula

Foxe Basin

Amadjuak Lake

Iqaluit

rik

Paulatuk

Cambridge Bay

Gjoa Haven

Fort Good Hope

Kugluktuk

Repulse Bay

Southampton Island

Hudson Strait

Great Bear Lake

Echo Bay

Burnside

Back

Garry Lake

Baker Lake

Coral Harbour

Péninsule d'Ungava

Mackenzie

NUNAVUT

Coats Island

Mansel Island

NORTHWEST TERRITORIES

gsten

Dubawnt

Rankin Inlet

Whale Cove

QUEBEC

Edzo

Yellowknife

Reliance

Łutselk'e

Arviat

Hudson Bay

Fort Simpson

Great Slave Lake

Fort Providence

Fort Liard

Hay River

Fort Smith

Lake Athabasca

Churchill

Belcher Islands

16

Fort Nelson

James Bay

LUMBIA

Fort Vermilion

Wollaston Lake

Reindeer Lake

Nelson

re

C

Fort St. John

Fort McMurray

Fox Mine

Southern Indian Lake

A

A L B E R T A

Buffalo Narrows

Thompson

N

O N T A R I O

Grande Prairie

D

rince George

Athabasca

Athabasca

SASKATCHEWAN

Flin Flon

Edmonton

North Saskatchewan

Saskatchewan

The Pas

Lake Winnipeg

Mount Robson 3954m

Leduc

Prince Albert

Saskatoon

MANITOBA

Red Deer

Kindersley

Yorkton

Lake Manitoba

Kamloops

Calgary

Regina

Qu'Appelle

Lake Winnipeg

Winnipeg

Kelowna

Medicine Hat

Brandon

Weyburn

Lake of the Woods

Lake Superior

Lake Huron

ncouver

Cranbrook

Lethbridge

Estevan

Melita

23

Lake Michigan

Milk River

U N I T E D   S T A T E S   O F   A M E R I C A

ELEVATION

4000 m	13 124 ft
2000 m	6562 ft
1000 m	3281 ft
500 m	1640 ft
250 m	820 ft
100 m	328 ft
Sea Level	Sea Level
-250 m	-820 ft
-500 m	-1640 ft
-1000 m	-3281 ft
-2000 m	-6562 ft
-3000 m	-9843 ft
-4000 m	-13 124 ft

EASTERN CANADA

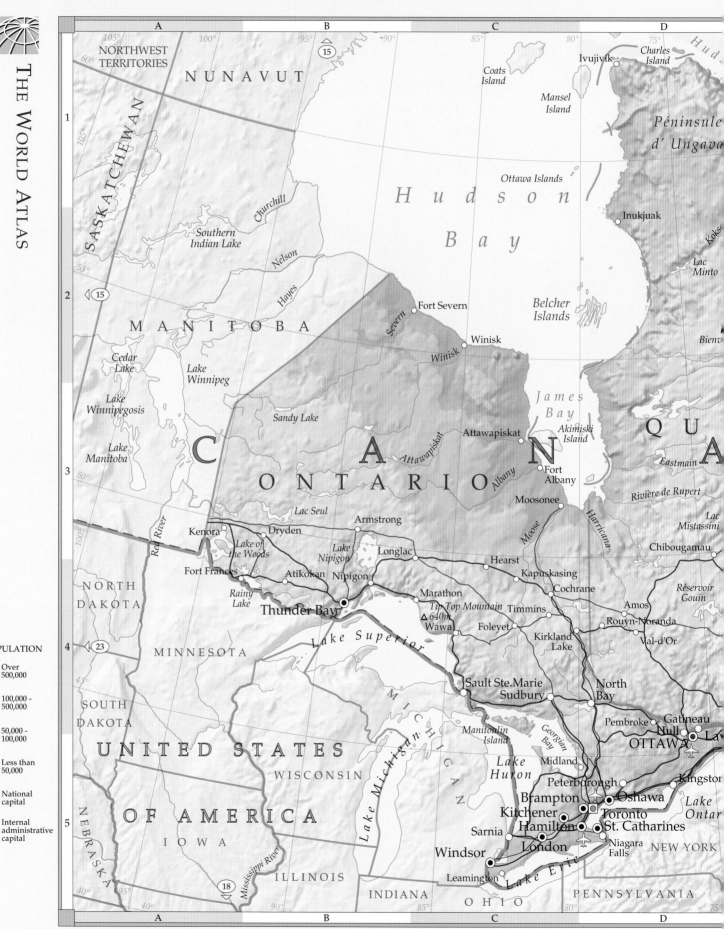

NORTHWEST TERRITORIES

NUNAVUT

SASKATCHEWAN

MANITOBA

ONTARIO

CANADA

QUA

Coats Island

Mansel Island

Ivujivik

Charles Island

Péninsule d' Ungava

HUDSON BAY

Ottawa Islands

Inukjuak

Lac Minto

Churchill

Southern Indian Lake

Nelson

Hayes

Severn

Fort Severn

Winisk

Winisk

Belcher Islands

Bienv

Cedar Lake

Lake Winnipeg

James Bay

Lake Winnipegosis

Sandy Lake

Attawapiskat

Attawapiskat

Akimiski Island

Lake Manitoba

Albany

Fort Albany

Eastmain

Rivière de Rupert

Moosonee

Lac Mistassini

Lac Seul

Armstrong

Harricana

Chibougamau

Red River

Kenora

Dryden

Lake Nipigon

Longlac

Hearst

Moose

Kapuskasing

Réservoir Gouin

Fort Frances

Lake of the Woods

Atikokan

Nipigon

Marathon

Tip Top Mountain
△ 640m
Wawa

Timmins

Cochrane

Amos

Rouyn-Noranda

NORTH DAKOTA

Rainy Lake

Thunder Bay

Lake Superior

Foleyet

Kirkland Lake

Val-d'Or

MINNESOTA

Sault Ste.Marie

Sudbury

North Bay

SOUTH DAKOTA

MICHIGAN

Pembroke

Gatineau
Hull

OTTAWA

La

UNITED STATES

Manitoulin Island

Georgian Bay

Midland

Lake Huron

Peterborough

Oshawa

Kingston

Lake Ontar

OF AMERICA

WISCONSIN

Lake Michigan

Brampton

Kitchener

Toronto

St. Catharines

NEBRASKA

IOWA

Sarnia

Hamilton

London

Niagara Falls

NEW YORK

Windsor

Mississippi River

Leamington

Lake Erie

ILLINOIS

INDIANA

OHIO

PENNSYLVANIA

POPULATION

- Over 500,000
- 100,000 - 500,000
- 50,000 - 100,000
- Less than 50,000
- National capital
- Internal administrative capital

ELEVATION

4000 m	13 124 ft
2000 m	6562 ft
1000 m	3281 ft
500 m	1640 ft
250 m	820 ft
100 m	328 ft
Sea Level	Sea Level
-250 m	-820 ft
-500 m	-1640 ft
-1000 m	-3281 ft
-2000 m	-6562 ft
-3000 m	-9843 ft
-4000 m	-13 124 ft

Baffin Island

Resolution Island

Button Islands

Akpatok Island

Ungava Bay

Kuujjuaq

Rivière à la Baleine

Caniapiscau

Nain

Hopedale

Makkovik

Cape Harrison

Labrador Sea

Scheffferville

NEWFOUNDLAND & LABRADOR

Labrador

Cartwright

Smallwood Reservoir

Lake Melville

Churchill

Réservoir de Caniapiscau

St.Anthony

Strait of Belle Isle

Laurentian Mountains

Réservoir Manicouagan

Havre-St-Pierre

Corner Brook

Gander

Grand Falls

St.John's

E C D A

Newfoundland

Sept-Îles

Île d'Anticosti

Cape Race

Baie-Comeau

St.Lawrence

Péninsule de Gaspé

Gaspé

Gulf of St. Lawrence

Channel-Port aux Basques

Cabot Strait

ST PIERRE & MIQUELON (to France)

Lac t-Jean

Chicoutimi

quière

Matane

Rimouski

Rivière-du-Loup

Edmundston

Îles de la Madeleine

PRINCE EDWARD ISLAND

Glace Bay

Sydney

Cape Breton Island

la Tuque

Charlesbourg

NEW BRUNSWICK

Bathurst

Charlottetown

Québec

Trois-Rivières

St-Georges

Moncton

Oromocto

Amherst

New Glasgow

Truro

Drummondville

Fredericton

NOVA SCOTIA

ntréal

MAINE

Saint John

Bay of Fundy

Dartmouth

Halifax

Sable Island

Sherbrooke

Liverpool

Yarmouth

VERMONT

NEW HAMPSHIRE

Cape Cod

MASSACHUSETTS

ATLANTIC

OCEAN

CONNECTICUT   RHODE ISLAND

N

USA: The Northeast

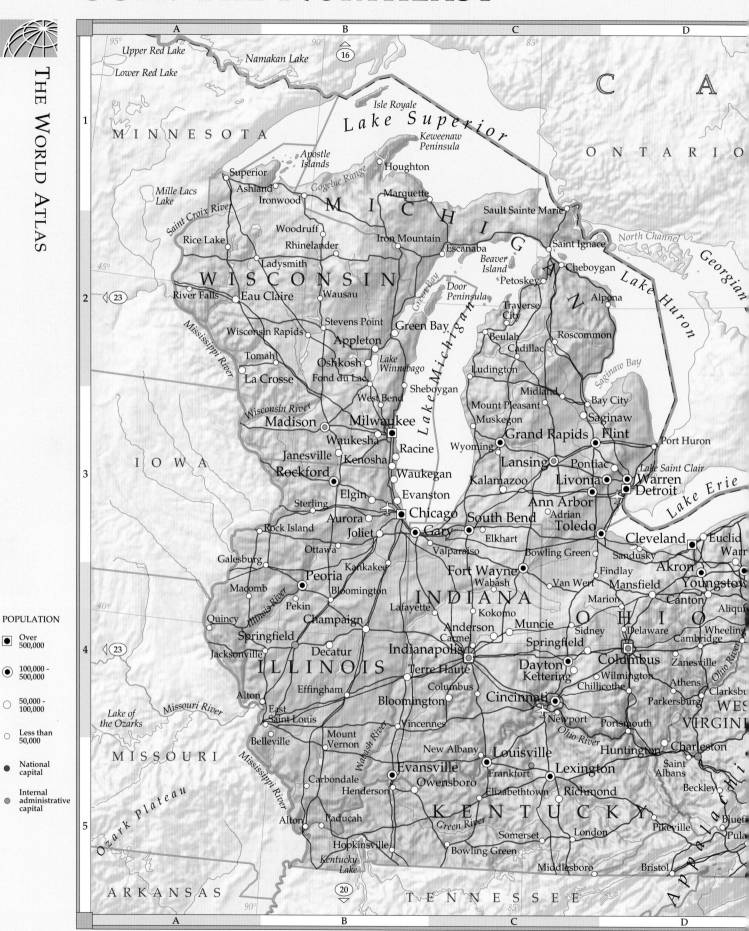

POPULATION

- Over 500,000
- 100,000 – 500,000
- 50,000 – 100,000
- Less than 50,000
- National capital
- Internal administrative capital

Upper Red Lake
Lower Red Lake
Namakan Lake
16
MINNESOTA
Isle Royale
Lake Superior
Keweenaw Peninsula
ONTARIO
C A N A
Superior
Ashland
Ironwood
Mille Lacs Lake
Apostle Islands
Houghton
Gogebic Range
Marquette
MICHIGAN
Sault Sainte Marie
North Channel
Georgian
Saint Croix River
Woodruff
Rhinelander
Rice Lake
Ladysmith
WISCONSIN
Iron Mountain
Escanaba
Saint Ignace
Beaver Island
Cheboygan
Petoskey
Alpena
Lake Huron
River Falls
Eau Claire
Wausau
Stevens Point
Green Bay
Traverse City
Roscommon
23
Wisconsin Rapids
Appleton
Beulah
Cadillac
Saginaw Bay
Tomah
Oshkosh
Lake Winnebago
Ludington
Midland
Bay City
La Crosse
Fond du Lac
Sheboygan
Mount Pleasant
Muskegon
Saginaw
Wisconsin River
West Bend
Madison
Milwaukee
Grand Rapids
Flint
Port Huron
Waukesha
Racine
Wyoming
Lansing
Pontiac
Lake Saint Clair
IOWA
Janesville
Kenosha
Kalamazoo
Livonia
Warren
Rockford
Waukegan
Ann Arbor
Detroit
Lake Erie
Elgin
Evanston
Adrian
Sterling
Chicago
South Bend
Toledo
Cleveland
Euclid
Aurora
Gary
Elkhart
Warr
Rock Island
Joliet
Valparaiso
Bowling Green
Sandusky
Akron
Ottawa
Kankakee
Findlay
Youngstow
Galesburg
Fort Wayne
Mansfield
Canton
Peoria
Bloomington
Wabash
Van Wert
Marion
OHIO
Aliqu
Macomb
Pekin
INDIANA
Lafayette
Kokomo
Sidney
Delaware
Wheeling
Quincy
Champaign
Anderson
Muncie
Springfield
Cambridge
Springfield
Carmel
Dayton
Columbus
Zanesville
Jacksonville
Decatur
Indianapolis
Kettering
Wilmington
Athens
Clarksbu
Alton
ILLINOIS
Terre Haute
Chillicothe
WES
Effingham
Columbus
Cincinnati
Parkersburg
VIRGINI
East Saint Louis
Bloomington
Newport
Portsmouth
Belleville
Vincennes
Ohio River
Huntington
Charleston
Mount Vernon
New Albany
Louisville
Saint Albans
MISSOURI
Lake of the Ozarks
Missouri River
Carbondale
Evansville
Owensboro
Frankfort
Lexington
Richmond
Beckley
Henderson
Elizabethtown
Alton
KENTUCKY
Paducah
Green River
Somerset
London
Pikeville
Bluefi
Pula
Ozark Plateau
Mississippi River
Hopkinsville
Bowling Green
Middlesboro
Bristol
Appalachi
Kentucky Lake
20
ARKANSAS
TENNESSEE

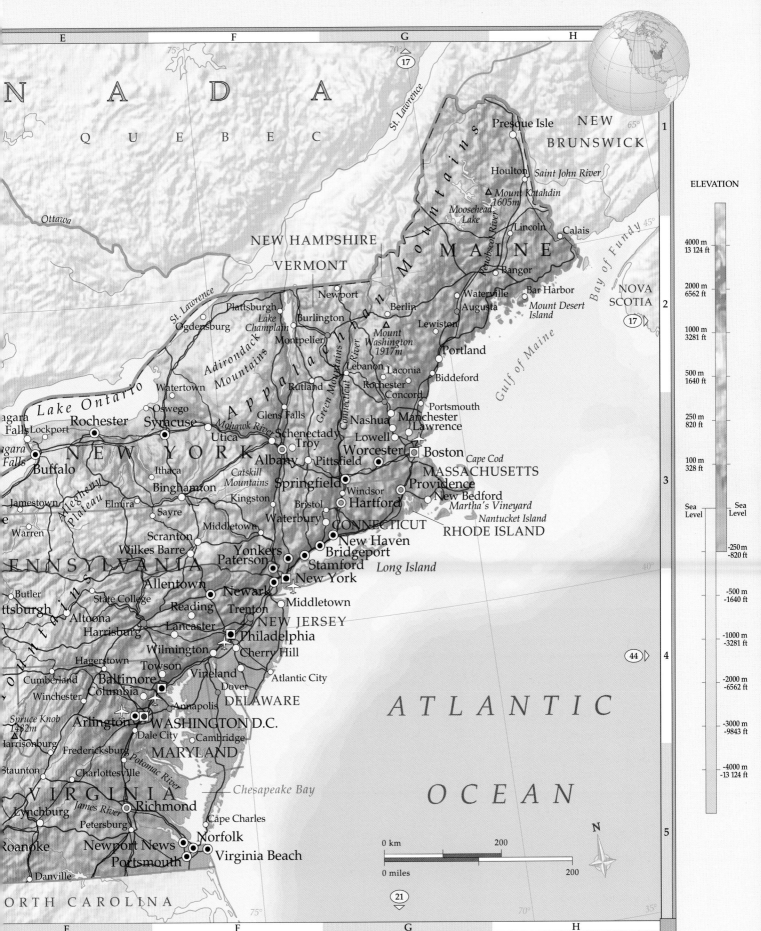

E F G H

ELEVATION

| 4000 m
13 124 ft |
| 2000 m
6562 ft |
| 1000 m
3281 ft |
| 500 m
1640 ft |
| 250 m
820 ft |
| 100 m
328 ft |
| Sea Level | Sea Level |
| -250 m
-820 ft |
| -500 m
-1640 ft |
| -1000 m
-3281 ft |
| -2000 m
-6562 ft |
| -3000 m
-9843 ft |
| -4000 m
-13 124 ft |

CANADA

QUEBEC

Ottawa

St. Lawrence

NEW BRUNSWICK

NEW HAMPSHIRE

VERMONT

Presque Isle

Houlton Saint John River

Mount Katahdin 1605m

Moosehead Lake

Penobscot River

Lincoln Calais

MAINE

Bangor

NOVA SCOTIA

St. Lawrence
Plattsburgh
Ogdensburg
Burlington
Montpelier
Lake Champlain
Newport
Berlin
Mount Washington 1917m
Waterville
Augusta
Lewiston
Bar Harbor
Mount Desert Island
Bay of Fundy

Adirondack Mountains

Appalachian Mountains

Green Mountains

Connecticut River

Lebanon
Rochester
Concord
Laconia
Portland
Biddeford
Portsmouth

Gulf of Maine

Niagara Falls
Lockport
Rochester
Watertown
Oswego
Syracuse
Utica
Schenectady
Troy
Albany
Mohawk River
Glens Falls
Rutland
Pittsfield
Nashua
Lowell
Lawrence
Manchester
Worcester
Boston

Niagara Falls
Buffalo
NEW YORK
Ithaca
Binghamton
Catskill Mountains
Springfield
Windsor
Bristol
Hartford
Providence
New Bedford
Cape Cod

MASSACHUSETTS

Martha's Vineyard
Nantucket Island

RHODE ISLAND

Jamestown
Warren
Allegheny Plateau
Elmira
Sayre
Kingston
Waterbury
Middletown
CONNECTICUT
New Haven
Bridgeport
Stamford
Long Island

PENNSYLVANIA

Scranton
Wilkes Barre
Yonkers
Paterson
Newark
New York

Butler
State College
Allentown
Reading
Trenton
Middletown

Pittsburgh
Altoona
Harrisburg
Lancaster
NEW JERSEY
Philadelphia
Cherry Hill

Mountains

Cumberland
Winchester
Hagerstown
Towson
Baltimore
Columbia
Wilmington
Vineland
Dover
DELAWARE
Atlantic City

Spruce Knob 1482m
Harrisonburg
Arlington
WASHINGTON D.C.
Dale City
Cambridge
Annapolis
MARYLAND

ATLANTIC

Staunton
Fredericksburg
Charlottesville
Potomac River
Chesapeake Bay

OCEAN

VIRGINIA
Lynchburg
James River
Richmond
Petersburg
Cape Charles
Roanoke
Newport News
Portsmouth
Norfolk
Virginia Beach
Danville

NORTH CAROLINA

0 km 200
0 miles 200

N

USA: The Southeast

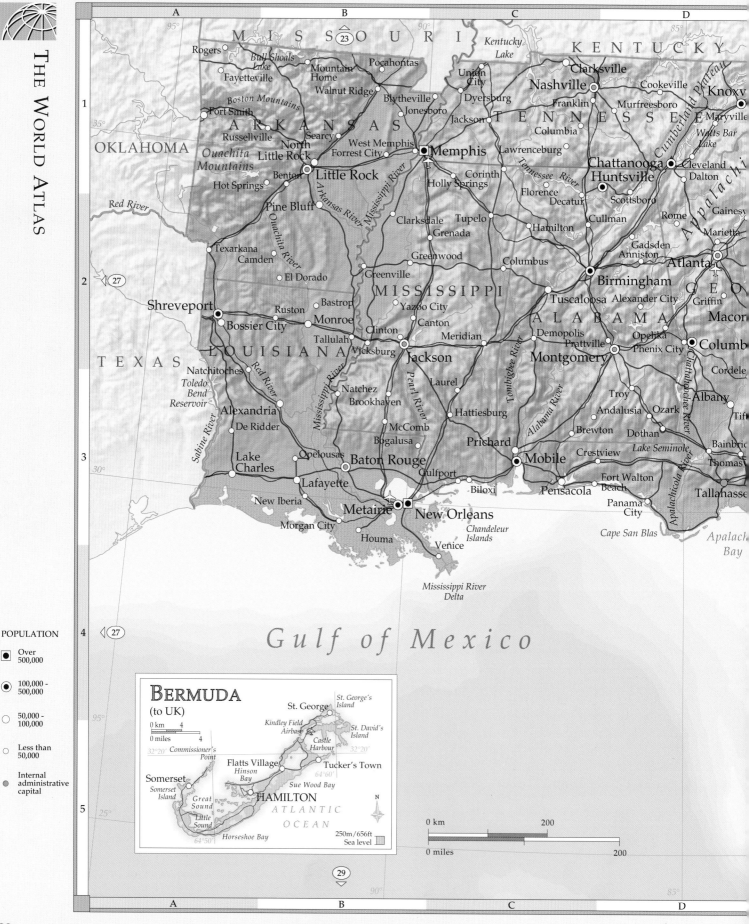

MISSOURI

Rogers
Bull Shoals Lake
Fayetteville
Mountain Home
Pocahontas
Walnut Ridge
Boston Mountains
Fort Smith
Blytheville
Jonesboro
Kentucky Lake
Union City
Dyersburg
Clarksville
Cookeville
Nashville
Franklin
Murfreesboro
Knoxv
Maryville
Watts Bar Lake

OKLAHOMA
ARKANSAS
Russellville
Searcy
West Memphis
Forrest City
Jackson
Columbia
Lawrenceburg
Chattanooga
Cleveland
Dalton
North Little Rock
Little Rock
Ouachita Mountains
Memphis
Corinth
Holly Springs
Florence
Decatur
Huntsville
Scottsboro
Rome
Gainesv
Benton
Hot Springs
Clarksdale
Tupelo
Grenada
Hamilton
Cullman
Gadsden
Anniston
Marietta
Pine Bluff
Arkansas River
Mississippi River
Tennessee River

Red River
Texarkana
Camden
El Dorado
Greenwood
Columbus
Atlanta
MISSISSIPPI
Birmingham
Tuscaloosa
Alexander City
Griffin
GEO
Macon

Shreveport
Bossier City
Ruston
Bastrop
Monroe
Yazoo City
Canton
Meridian
ALABAMA
Demopolis
Opelika
Phenix City
Columb

Tallulah
Vicksburg
Clinton
Prattville
Montgomery
Cordele

LOUISIANA
Natchitoches
Toledo Bend Reservoir
Red River
Jackson
Laurel
Troy
Andalusia
Ozark
Albany
Tif

Alexandria
De Ridder
Natchez
Brookhaven
Pearl River
Hattiesburg
Tombigbee River
Alabama River
Brewton
Dothan
Lake Seminole
Bainbri

Lake Charles
Opelousas
Baton Rouge
Bogalusa
McComb
Prichard
Mobile
Crestview
Fort Walton Beach
Pensacola
Apalachicola River
Thomas

Lafayette
Gulfport
Biloxi
Panama City
Tallahasse

New Iberia
Metairie
New Orleans
Chandeleur Islands
Cape San Blas
Apalach Bay

Morgan City
Houma
Venice

Mississippi River Delta

Gulf of Mexico

BERMUDA
(to UK)

0 km 4
0 miles 4

St. George
St. George's Island
Kindley Field Airbase
St. David's Island
Commissioner's Point
Castle Harbour
Flatts Village
Tucker's Town
Hinson Bay
Sue Wood Bay
Somerset
Somerset Island
Great Sound
HAMILTON
Little Sound
ATLANTIC OCEAN
Horseshoe Bay

250m/656ft
Sea level

0 km 200
0 miles 200

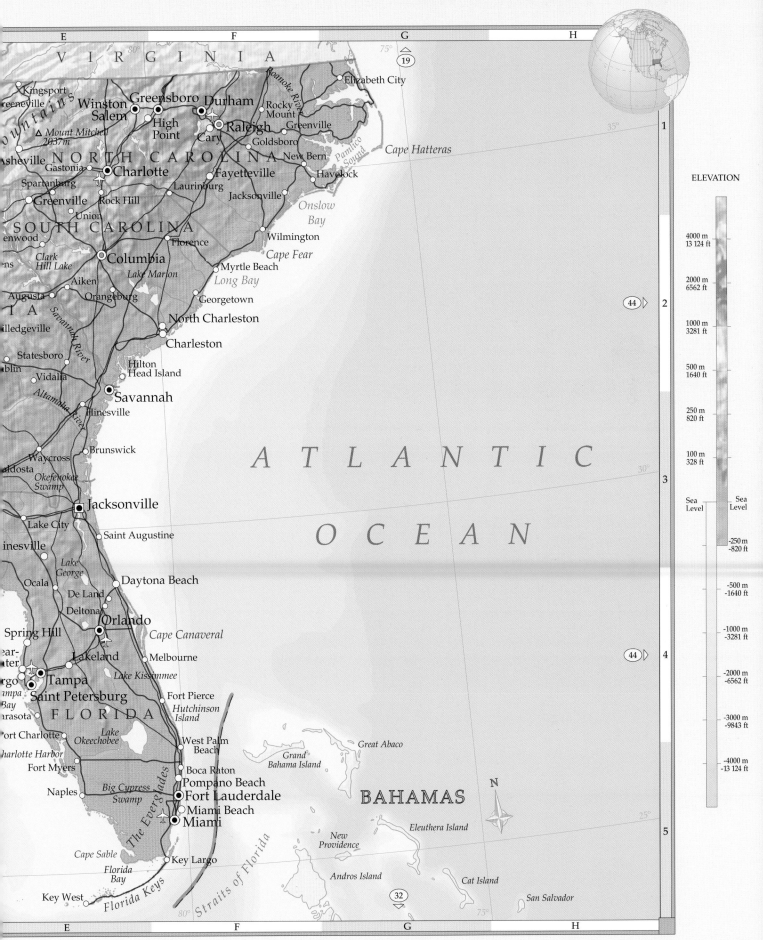

ELEVATION

4000 m 13 124 ft	
2000 m 6562 ft	
1000 m 3281 ft	
500 m 1640 ft	
250 m 820 ft	
100 m 328 ft	
Sea Level	Sea Level
	−250 m −820 ft
	−500 m −1640 ft
	−1000 m −3281 ft
	−2000 m −6562 ft
	−3000 m −9843 ft
	−4000 m −13 124 ft

VIRGINIA

Kingsport
Greeneville
Mountains
Winston Salem
Greensboro
Durham
Rocky Mount
Elizabeth City
Roanoke River
High Point
Cary
Raleigh
Goldsboro
Greenville
NORTH CAROLINA
Mount Mitchell 2037m
Asheville
Gastonia
Charlotte
Fayetteville
New Bern
Havelock
Pamlico Sound
Cape Hatteras
Spartanburg
Laurinburg
Jacksonville
Greenville
Rock Hill
Union
SOUTH CAROLINA
enwood
Florence
Wilmington
Onslow Bay
Clark Hill Lake
Columbia
Lake Marion
Myrtle Beach
Cape Fear
Aiken
Orangeburg
Long Bay
Augusta
Georgetown
illedgeville
North Charleston
TA
Savannah River
Charleston
Statesboro
Hilton Head Island
ublin
Vidalia
Altamaha River
Savannah
Hinesville

ATLANTIC

Waycross
Brunswick
aldosta
Okefenokee Swamp

OCEAN

Jacksonville
Lake City
Saint Augustine
inesville
Lake George
Ocala
Daytona Beach
De Land
Deltona
Orlando
Cape Canaveral
Spring Hill
Lakeland
Melbourne
ear-ter
argo
Tampa
Lake Kissimmee
Fort Pierce
ampa Bay
Saint Petersburg
Hutchinson Island
FLORIDA
arasota
ort Charlotte
Lake Okeechobee
West Palm Beach
Great Abaco
harlotte Harbor
Fort Myers
Boca Raton
Grand Bahama Island
Naples
Big Cypress Swamp
Pompano Beach
Fort Lauderdale
The Everglades
Miami Beach
BAHAMAS
Miami
Eleuthera Island
Cape Sable
Florida Bay
Key Largo
New Providence
25°
Florida Keys
Straits of Florida
Andros Island
Cat Island
Key West
San Salvador

USA: Central States

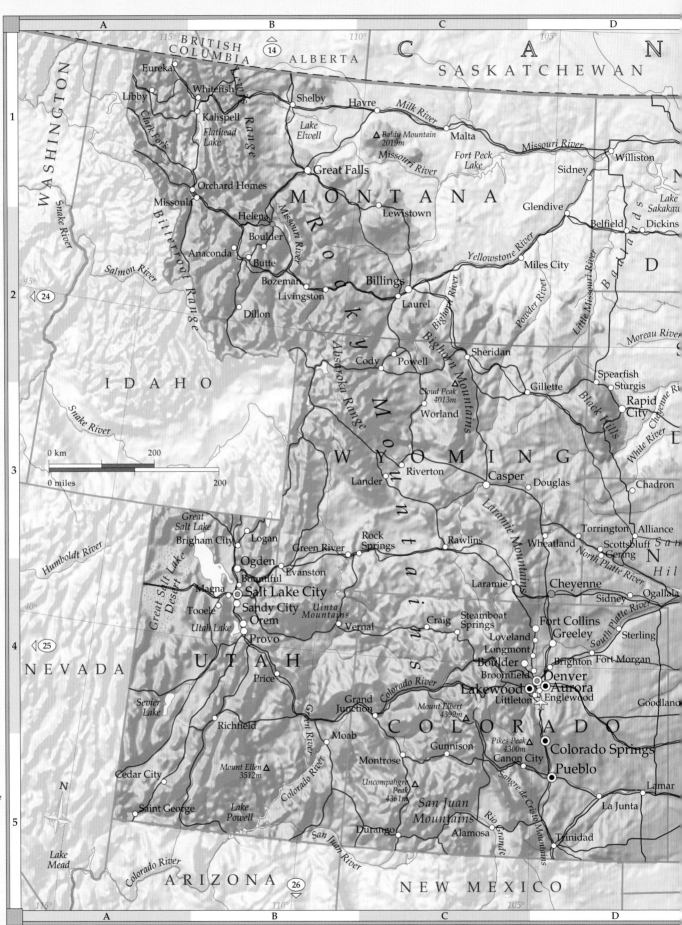

POPULATION

● Over 500,000

◉ 100,000 - 500,000

○ 50,000 - 100,000

○ Less than 50,000

● Internal administrative capital

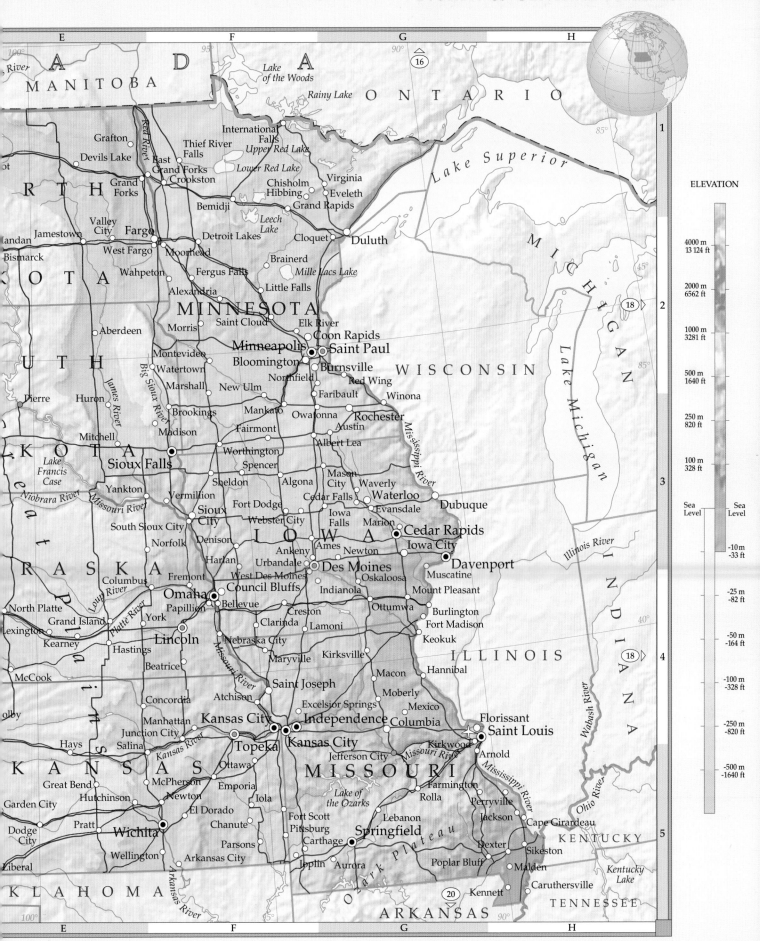

4000 m 13 124 ft	
2000 m 6562 ft	
1000 m 3281 ft	
500 m 1640 ft	
250 m 820 ft	
100 m 328 ft	
Sea Level	Sea Level
-10 m -33 ft	
	-25 m -82 ft
	-50 m -164 ft
	-100 m -328 ft
	-250 m -820 ft
	-500 m -1640 ft

MANITOBA

Lake of the Woods

Rainy Lake

ONTARIO

Lake Superior

MICHIGAN

Lake Michigan

NORTH DAKOTA

Grafton
Devils Lake
East Grand Forks
Grand Forks
Crookston
Valley City
Jamestown
Mandan
Bismarck
Fargo
West Fargo
Moorhead
Wahpeton
Aberdeen

International Falls
Thief River Falls
Upper Red Lake
Lower Red Lake
Bemidji
Chisholm
Hibbing
Virginia
Eveleth
Grand Rapids
Leech Lake
Detroit Lakes
Cloquet
Duluth
Brainerd
Mille Lacs Lake
Fergus Falls
Little Falls
Alexandria

MINNESOTA

Morris
Saint Cloud
Elk River
Coon Rapids
Minneapolis
Saint Paul
Bloomington
Burnsville
Montevideo
Watertown
Northfield
Red Wing
Marshall
New Ulm
Faribault
Winona
Mankato
Owatonna
Rochester
Austin

WISCONSIN

SOUTH DAKOTA

Pierre
Huron
Aberdeen
Mitchell
Brookings
Madison
Fairmont
Albert Lea
Sioux Falls
Lake Francis Case
Yankton
Vermillion
Sioux City
Worthington
Spencer
Sheldon
Algona
Mason City
Waverly
Cedar Falls
Waterloo
Evansdale
Dubuque
Niobrara River
James River
Big Sioux River
Missouri River

South Sioux City
Norfolk
Denison
Iowa Falls
Marion
Cedar Rapids
Iowa City
Davenport

IOWA

Ames
Newton
Ankeny
Urbandale
West Des Moines
Des Moines
Oskaloosa
Muscatine
Mount Pleasant

NEBRASKA

North Platte
Grand Island
Lexington
Kearney
McCook
Colby

Columbus
Loup River
Fremont
Omaha
Bellevue
Papillion
Council Bluffs
Indianola
Creston
Clarinda
Lamoni
Ottumwa
Burlington
Fort Madison
Keokuk
Hannibal

ILLINOIS

Platte River
York
Lincoln
Hastings
Beatrice
Nebraska City
Maryville
Kirksville
Macon
Moberly
Mexico
Columbia

Illinois River

INDIANA

Wabash River

Saint Joseph
Atchison
Excelsior Springs
Independence
Florissant
Saint Louis
Kirkwood
Arnold

KANSAS

Hays
Manhattan
Junction City
Salina
Concordia
Kansas City
Kansas City
Topeka
Jefferson City
Ottawa
MISSOURI
Great Bend
McPherson
Emporia
Garden City
Hutchinson
Newton
Iola
El Dorado
Chanute
Lake of the Ozarks
Lebanon
Rolla
Farmington
Perryville
Jackson
Cape Girardeau
Dodge City
Pratt
Wichita
Wellington
Parsons
Arkansas City
Fort Scott
Pittsburg
Carthage
Springfield
Dexter
Sikeston
Liberal
Joplin
Aurora
Ozark Plateau
Poplar Bluff
Malden
Caruthersville
Kennett

Kansas River
Arkansas River
Missouri River
Mississippi River
Ohio River

KENTUCKY

Kentucky Lake

OKLAHOMA

ARKANSAS

TENNESSEE

USA: THE WEST

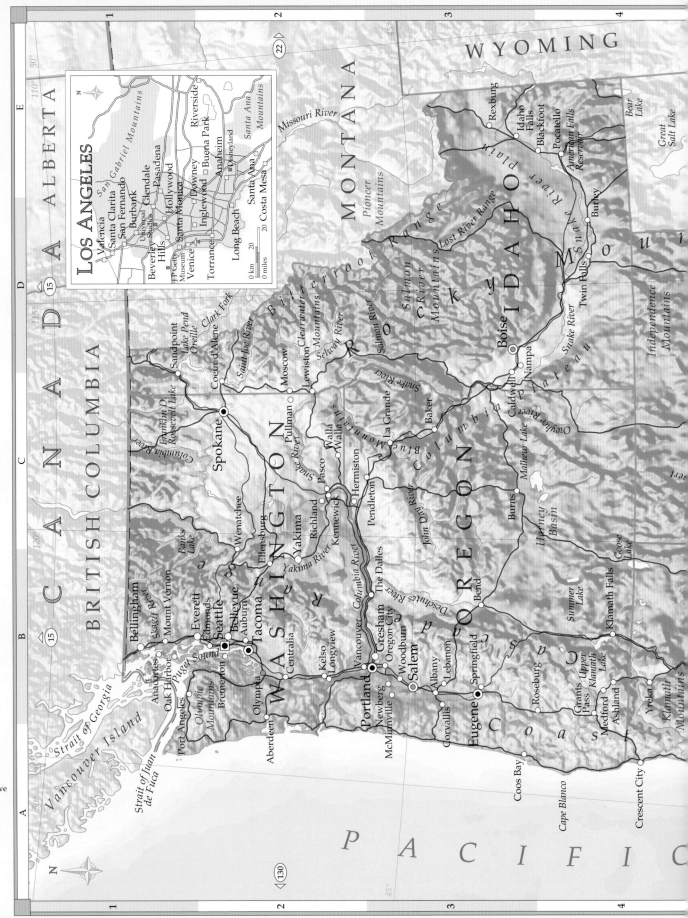

LOS ANGELES

Valencia
Santa Clarita
San Fernando
San Gabriel Mountains
Burbank
Universal Studios
Hollywood
Glendale
Pasadena
Beverley Hills
Santa Monica
Inglewood
Downey
Riverside
Buena Park
Anaheim
Disneyland
Santa Ana Mountains
J. P. Getty Museum
Venice
Santa Ana
Torrance
Costa Mesa
Long Beach

0 km 20
0 miles 20

POPULATION

- ● Over 500,000
- ◉ 100,000 – 500,000
- ○ 50,000 – 100,000
- ○ Less than 50,000
- ● Internal administrative capital

WYOMING

MONTANA

Pioneer Mountains

Missouri River

Rexburg
Idaho Falls
Blackfoot
Pocatello
American Falls Reservoir
Burley
Bear Lake
Great Salt Lake

IDAHO

Snake River Plain
Lost River Range
Salmon River
Mountains

ROCKY MOUNTAINS

Boise
Nampa
Caldwell
Snake River
Twin Falls

Independence Mountains

Owyhee River

CANADA

ALBERTA

BRITISH COLUMBIA

Franklin D. Roosevelt Lake
Columbia River

Sandpoint
Lake Pend Oreille
Clark Fork
Saint Joe River
Coeur d'Alene

Bitterroot Range

Moscow
Lewiston
Clearwater Mountains
Selway River
Salmon River
Snake River

La Grande
Baker

OREGON

Malheur Lake

Burns

Harney Basin

Summer Lake
Goose Lake

Klamath Falls

WASHINGTON

Spokane
Banks Lake
Wenatchee
Ellensburg
Pullman
Walla Walla
Pasco
Richland
Kennewick
Hermiston
Pendleton

Blue Mountains
Columbia River

Bellingham
Skagit River
Mount Vernon
Everett
Edmonds
Seattle
Bellevue
Auburn
Tacoma
Centralia
Kelso
Longview
Vancouver

Anacortes
Oak Harbor
Port Angeles
Puget Sound
Bremerton
Olympia
Aberdeen

Olympic Mountains

Strait of Georgia
Vancouver Island
Strait of Juan de Fuca

Cascade Range
Yakima
Yakima River

The Dalles
Deschutes River
John Day River

Gresham
Oregon City
Woodburn
Salem
Albany
Lebanon
Corvallis
Portland
Newberg
McMinnville

Bend

Springfield
Eugene

Roseburg

Grants Pass
Upper Klamath Lake
Medford
Ashland
Yreka

Klamath Mountains

Coos Bay
Cape Blanco
Crescent City

Coast

PACIFIC

24

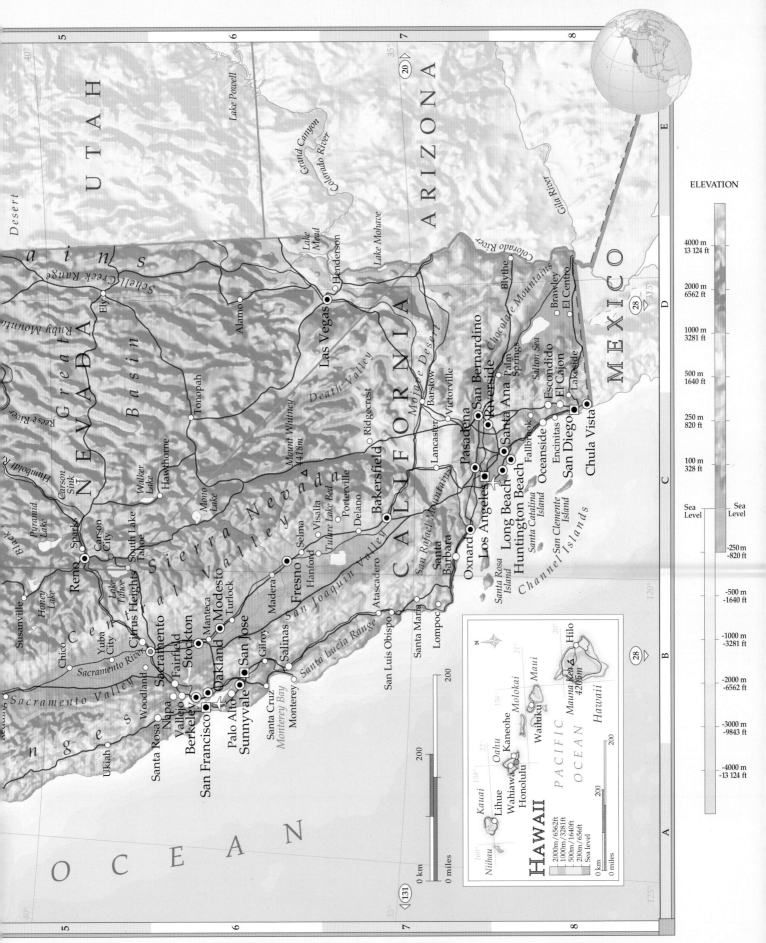

ELEVATION

4000 m	13 124 ft
2000 m	6562 ft
1000 m	3281 ft
500 m	1640 ft
250 m	820 ft
100 m	328 ft
Sea Level	Sea Level
-250 m	-820 ft
-500 m	-1640 ft
-1000 m	-3281 ft
-2000 m	-6562 ft
-3000 m	-9843 ft
-4000 m	-13 124 ft

UTAH

ARIZONA

MEXICO

NEVADA

CALIFORNIA

Great Basin

Sierra Nevada

Central Valley

San Joaquin Valley

Sacramento Valley

Death Valley

Mojave Desert

Schell Creek Range

Ruby Mountains

Desert

Chocolate Mountains

San Rafael Mountains

Santa Lucia Range

Channel Islands

PACIFIC OCEAN

Colorado River
Grand Canyon
Gila River
Lake Powell
Lake Mead
Lake Mohave
Salton Sea
Reese River
Humboldt R.
Carson Sink
Sacramento River
Mono Lake
Tulare Lake Bed
Walker Lake
Honey Lake
Pyramid Lake
Black R.
Lake Tahoe

Las Vegas
Henderson
Alamo
Ely
Tonopah
Hawthorne
Reno
Sparks
Carson City
Susanville
Chico
Yuba City
Citrus Heights
Sacramento
Woodland
Napa
Santa Rosa
Vallejo
Fairfield
Stockton
Oakland
Berkeley
San Francisco
Palo Alto
Sunnyvale
San Jose
Gilroy
Salinas
Santa Cruz
Monterey Bay
Monterey
Modesto
Manteca
Turlock
Madera
Fresno
Selma
Hanford
Visalia
Porterville
Delano
Bakersfield
Atascadero
Santa Maria
Lompoc
San Luis Obispo
Santa Barbara
Oxnard
Los Angeles
Pasadena
San Bernardino
Riverside
Santa Ana
Long Beach
Huntington Beach
Lancaster
Victorville
Barstow
Ridgecrest
Santa Catalina Island
Santa Rosa Island
San Clemente Island
Oceanside
Encinitas
Fallbrook
Escondido
El Cajon
Lakeside
San Diego
Chula Vista
Palm Springs
Brawley
El Centro
Blythe
Ukiah
South Lake Tahoe
Mount Whitney 4418m

HAWAII

N

PACIFIC OCEAN

Kauai
Niihau
Lihue
Wahiawa
Honolulu
Oahu
Kaneohe
Wailuku
Molokai
Maui
Hilo
Mauna Kea 4205m
Hawaii

2000m / 6562ft
1000m / 3281ft
500m / 1640ft
200m / 656ft
Sea level

0 km   200
0 miles   200

0 km   200
0 miles   200

0 km   200
0 miles   200

USA: THE SOUTHWEST

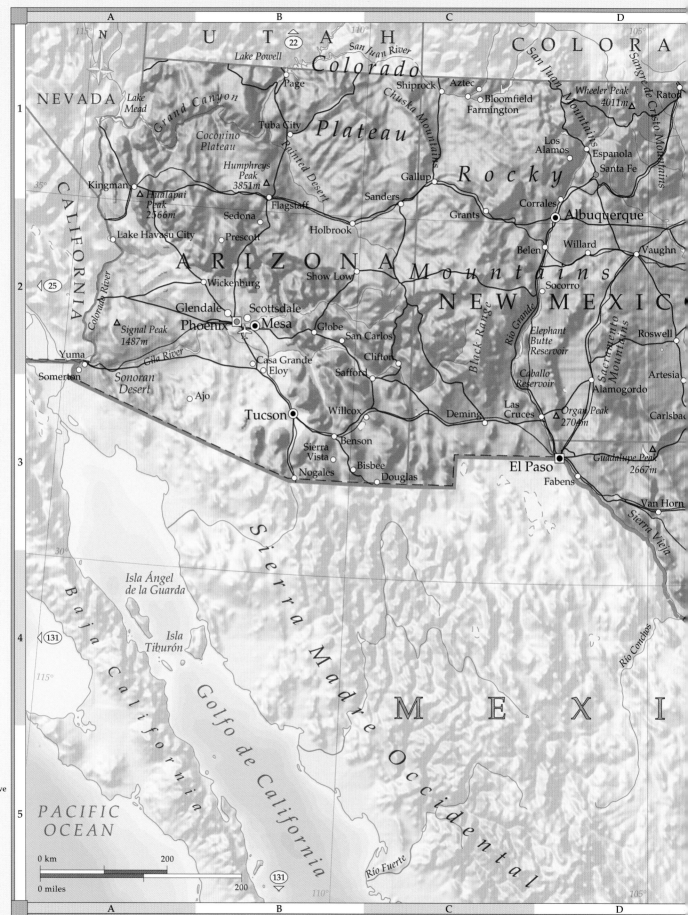

POPULATION

- Over 500,000
- 100,000 – 500,000
- 50,000 – 100,000
- Less than 50,000
- Internal administrative capital

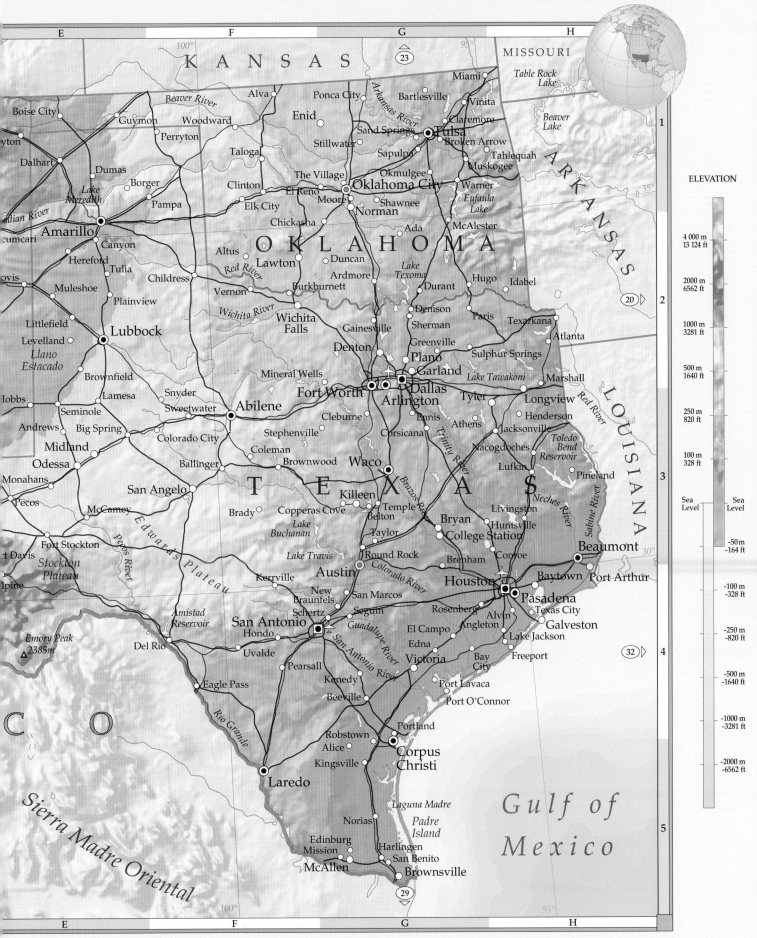

MEXICO

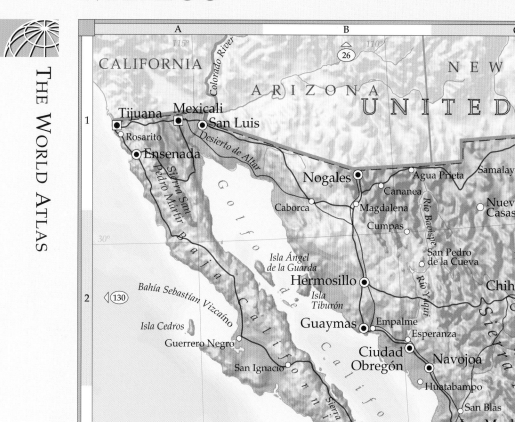

POPULATION

◉	Over 500,000
◉	100,000 - 500,000
○	50,000 - 100,000
○	Less than 50,000
●	National capital

CALIFORNIA

ARIZONA

NEW MEXICO

UNITED STATES O

Tijuana
Mexicali
San Luis
Rosarito
Ensenada
Nogales
Ciudad Juárez
Agua Prieta
Samalayuca
Pecos River
Rio Grande
Rio Bravo del Norte
Cananea
Magdalena
Caborca
Cumpas
Nuevo Casas Grandes
El Sueco
Ojinaga
Villa Acu
San Pedro de la Cueva
El Sáuz
San Miguel
Boquillas
Nueva Ros
Hermosillo
Chihuahua
Delicias
Sabi
Cuauhtémoc
Ciudad Camargo
Monclov
Guaymas
Empalme
Esperanza
Jiménez
San Francisco del Oro
Hidalgo del Parral
Ciudad Obregón
Navojoa
Santa Barbara
Huatabampo
Gómez Palacio
San Ped
San Blas
Torreón
Parra
Los Mochis
Ciudad Lerdo
Matamoros
Guasave
Guamúchil
Culiacán
MEX
Navolato
Miguel Asua
Juan Aldam
El Dorado
Río Gran
Durango
Fresnillo
Mazatlán
Zacatecas
Guadalupe
Escuinapa
Villanueva
Acaponeta
Aguascalientes
Tuxpan
Jalpa
Tepic
Lagos de More
Yahualica
Guadalajara
Tequila
Puerto Vallarta
Tlaquepaque
Zamora de Hidalg
Ciudad Guzmán
Zapoti
Colima
Tuxpan
Manzanillo
Agui
Tecomán
Lázaro Cárde

Desierto de Altar
Colorado River
Golfo de California
Isla Ángel de la Guarda
Isla Tiburón
Río Bavispe
Río Yaqui
Río Conchos
Sierra Madre Occidental
Bahía Sebastián Vizcaíno
Isla Cedros
Guerrero Negro
San Ignacio
Sierra San Pedro Mártir
Baja California
Sierra de la Giganta
Loreto
Isla Magdalena
Isla Santa Margarita
Bahía de La Paz
La Paz
Tropic of Cancer
Santa Genoveva 2406m
Miraflores

Isla San Juanito
Isla María Madre
Isla María Magdalena
Isla María Cleofas
Islas Marías
Lago Chapa

Isla San Benedicto
Isla Roca Partida
Isla Socorro
Isla Clarión
Islas Revillagigedo (to Mexico)

N

PACIFIC OCEAN

0 km   300

0 miles   300

E   F   G   H

95°   90°   85°

ALABAMA
FLORIDA

MISSISSIPPI

LOUISIANA

Red River

Sabine River

Mississippi River

30°

1

AMERICA

TEXAS

Brazos River

Colorado River

Mississippi River
Delta

ELEVATION

4000 m
13 124 ft

Piedras Negras

Rio Grande

Nuevo Laredo

Padre Island

2000 m
6562 ft

25°

44

2

Sabinas
Hidalgo
Ciudad
Miguel Alemán

G u l f   o f

1000 m
3281 ft

Reynosa
Río
Bravo
Matamoros

85°

500 m
1640 ft

Monterrey

M e x i c o

Tropic of Cancer

Saltillo
Montemorelos
Linares

Laguna Madre

250 m
820 ft

Ciudad Victoria

Yucatan Channel

100 m
328 ft

3

Ciudad
Mante

Rio Lagartos
Cancún

Tizimín

Isla
Cozumel

Sea
Level

Sea
Level

Ciudad Madero

Progreso
Motul

Mérida
Umán
Ticul
Valladolid

-250 m
-820 ft

San Luis
Potosí
Pánuco
Tampico
Ciudad Valles

Peto

20°

Río Verde

Laguna de Tamiahua

Oxkutzcab
Tekax

-500 m
-1640 ft

Dolores
Hidalgo
Tamazunchale
Tuxpán

Bahía de Campeche
Campeche

*Yucatan
Peninsula*

Felipe Carrillo
Puerto

Guanajuato
Poza Rica

Champotón

Chetumal

-1000 m
-3281 ft

Querétaro
Irapuato
Pachuca
Papantla
Tulancingo

*Laguna de
Términos*

Fransisco Escárcega

30

4

Morelia
MÉXICO
(MEXICO CITY)
Teziutlán
Perote
Xalapa

Veracruz

Frontera

Carmen

BELIZE

Toluca
Tlaxcala
Alvarado

Comalcalco

Villahermosa

Cuernavaca
Puebla
Córdoba
Coatzacoalcos

Macuspana

Río Usumacinta

Gulf of Honduras

Zacatepec
Popocatépetl
5452m
Tehuacán
San
Andrés

Teapa

Presa del
Infiernillo
Taxco
Cuautla
Tuxtepec
Tuxtla
Minatitlán

San Cristóbal
de Las Casas

-2000 m
-6562 ft

Balsas
Iguala
*Istmo de
Tehuantepec*
Tuxtla

Chiapa de
Corzo
Comitán

-3000 m
-9843 ft

Sierra
Huajuapan
Ocozocuautla
Matías Romero

Chilpancingo
Oaxaca
Ixtepec
Arriaga

Presa de la
Angostura

Tecpan
Madre del Sur
Tehuantepec
Juchitán
Pijijiapán

-4000 m
-13 124 ft

Tapa
Pinotepa
Nacional
Miahuatlán
Salina Cruz

Escuintla
GUATEMALA
HONDURAS

5

Acapulco
*Golfo de
Tehuantepec*
Huixtla

Puerto
Escondido
Puerto
Angel
Tapachula
Ciudad Hidalgo

EL SALVADOR

100°
95°
90°

131

E   F   G   H

CENTRAL AMERICA

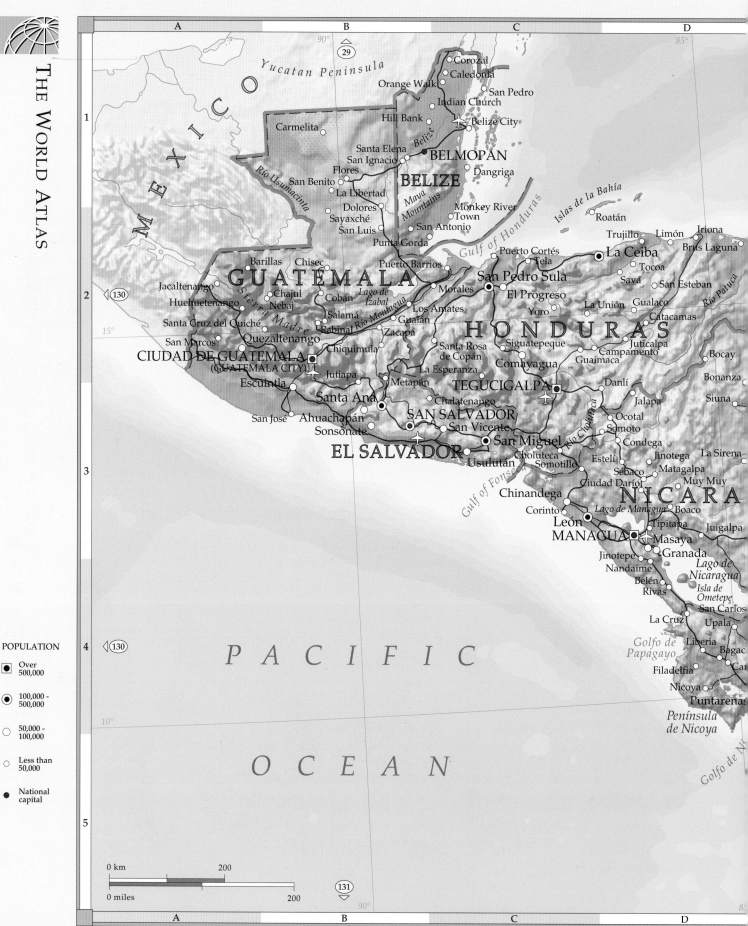

POPULATION

- ◉ Over 500,000
- ◉ 100,000 – 500,000
- ○ 50,000 – 100,000
- ○ Less than 50,000
- ● National capital

MEXICO

Yucatan Peninsula

Carmelita

Hill Bank

Santa Elena
San Ignacio
Flores
San Benito
La Libertad
Dolores
Sayaxché
San Luis

Corozal
Caledonia
Orange Walk
San Pedro
Indian Church
Belize City
BELMOPAN
BELIZE
Dangriga
Maya Mountains
Monkey River Town
San Antonio
Punta Gorda

Barillas
Chisec
GUATEMALA
Sierra Madre
Jacaltenango
Huehuetenango
Chajul
Nebaj
Cobán
Lago de Izabal
Salamá
Río Montagua
Santa Cruz del Quiché
Rabinal
Zacapa
San Marcos
Quezaltenango
Chiquimula
CIUDAD DE GUATEMALA
(GUATEMALA CITY)
Jutiapa
Escuintla
Santa Ana
San José
Ahuachapán
Sonsonate
Metapán
SAN SALVADOR
San Vicente
EL SALVADOR
Usulután

Puerto Barrios
Morales
Los Amates
Gualán
Santa Rosa de Copán
La Esperanza
Chalatenango
San Miguel
Choluteca
Somotillo

Gulf of Honduras
Islas de la Bahía
Roatán
Trujillo
Limón
Iriona
Puerto Cortés
Tela
Brus Laguna
San Pedro Sula
Tocoa
Savá
San Esteban
El Progreso
Yoro
La Unión
Gualaco
Catacamas
HONDURAS
Siguatepeque
Campamento
Bocay
Comayagua
Guaimaca
Bonanza
Juticalpa
Siuna
TEGUCIGALPA
Danlí
Jalapa
Ocotal
Somoto
Condega
Río Choluteca
Estelí
Jinotega
La Sirena
Sébaco
Matagalpa
Ciudad Darío
Muy Muy
Chinandega
NICARA
Corinto
Boaco
León
Lago de Managua
MANAGUA
Tipitapa
Juigalpa
Masaya
Jinotepe
Granada
Lago de Nicaragua
Nandaime
Isla de Ometepe
Belén
Rivas
San Carlos
La Cruz
Upala
Liberia
Golfo de Papagayo
Bagac
Filadelfia
Nicoya
Puntarenas
Península de Nicoya

Río Usumacinta

PACIFIC

OCEAN

15°

10°

0 km   200

0 miles   200

E F G H

N

(32)

ELEVATION

80°

1

4000 m
13 124 ft

2000 m
6562 ft

15°

Bajo Nuevo
(to Colombia)

Cayo de Serranilla
(to Colombia)

s Santanilla
Honduras)

1000 m
3281 ft

na de Caratasca

Puerto Lempira

500 m
1640 ft

Coco

75°

Cayo de Serrana
(to Colombia)

2

(33)

spam

Cayos Miskitos

Tuapi

ablis

Puerto Cabezas

250 m
820 ft

C a r i b b e a n

Isla de Providencia
(to Colombia)

Prinzapolka

100 m
328 ft

Barra de Río Grande

S e a

Mosquito Coast

Isla de San Andrés
(to Colombia)

3

Sea
Level

Sea
Level

A

Laguna de Perlas

Rama

Islas del Maíz

-250 m
-820 ft

Bluefields

Punta Gorda

-500 m
-1640 ft

San Juan del Norte

San Juan
to
ejo

10°

(36)

-1000 m
-3281 ft

4

COSTA RICA

Siquirres

Gulf of

Heredia

Istmo de Panamá

El Porvenir

Darien

Portobelo

Ailigandí

SAN JOSÉ   Limón

Colón

-2000 m
-6562 ft

Cartago

Cristóbal

Cordillera de San Blas

esada

Guabito

rro Chiripó

Almirante

Golfo de los

Panama Canal

Lago Bayano

Puerto Obaldía

Grande
3819m

Cortés

Cordillera de

Mosquitos

Lago Gatún

San Miguelito

Serranía del Darién

-3000 m
-9843 ft

Buenos Aires

Talamanca

Balboa

PANAMÁ

Chimán

os

Penonomé

(PANAMA CITY)

Palmar Sur

Volcán Barú 3475m

Capira

La Palma

Yaviza

-4000 m
-13 124 ft

Bahía

Boquete

Cordillera Central

Aguadulce

Archipiélago

Isla

El Real

Coronado

La Concepción

de las Perlas

del Rey

David

P A N A M A

Garachiné

nsula de Osa

Golfo Dulce

Santiago

Chitré

Golfo

5

Golfo

Guarumal

Ocú

Las Tablas

de Panamá

Jaqué

de Chiriquí

Península de

Azuero

Isla de Coiba

Isla

Cébaco

80°

(131)

E F G H

COLOMBIA

THE CARIBBEAN

Gulf of Mexico

UNITED STATES
OF AMERICA

Grand Bahama
Island

Freeport

Marsh Harbour

Great Abaco

The Everglades

Bimini
Islands

Berry
Islands

Northeast Providence Channel

Nicholls
Town

NASSAU

Eleuthera Island

Florida Keys

Andros Town

New
Providence

Rock Sound

Cat Island

Tropic of Cancer

Straits of Florida

Cay Sal

Andros Island

Exuma
Cays

Exuma
Sound

San Salvador

LA HABANA
(HAVANA)

Anguilla Cays

BAHAMAS

Rum Cay

Guanabacoa

George Town

Long Island

Artemisa

Cárdenas

Great Exuma Island

Matanzas

Sagua la Grande

Archipiélago
de Camagüey

Clarence
Town

Crooked Island

Pinar del Río

Consolación
del Sur

Santa Clara

Crooked Island Passage

Acklins
Island

La Fé

Cienfuegos

Placetas

Mayaguana Passage

Caicos Passage

Nueva Gerona

Isla de
la Juventud

Sancti
Spíritus

Moron

Ciego de Ávila

Ragged Island
Range

Little
Inagua

Cayo Largo

C U B A

Nuevitas

Lake Rosa

Archipiélago de los Canarreos

Camagüey

Holguín

Matthew
Town

Great Inagua

Archipiélago de
los Jardines de la Reina

Las Tunas

Bayamo

Manzanillo

Palma Soriano

Guantánamo

Santiago de Cuba

Guantánamo Bay
(to US)

Cap
Haïtien

Windward Passage

Gonaïves

Little Cayman

Cayman Brac

HAI

GEORGE
TOWN

Grand Cayman

G

NAVASSA
ISLAND
(to US)

Île de la Gonâve

Jérémie

PORT-AU-
PRINCE

CAYMAN ISLANDS
(to UK)

r
e
a
t

Jamaica Channel

Cayes

Jac

Montego Bay

Spanish Town

Portmore

KINGSTON

JAMAICA

Pedro Cays

C
a
r
i
b
b
e
a
n

HONDURAS

NICARAGUA

COSTA
RICA

COLOMBIA

POPULATION

- Over 500,000
- 100,000 – 500,000
- 50,000 – 100,000
- Less than 50,000
- National capital

JAMAICA

Montego Bay

Lucea

Falmouth

Runaway
Bay

St Ann's Bay

Caribbean
Sea

The Cockpit
Country

Ocho Rios

Annotto Bay

Buff Bay

Cambridge

Christiana

Ewarton

Port Antonio

Savanna-
La-Mar

Mandeville

Spanish
Town

Blue Mountain Peak
△ 2258m

Black River

May Pen

KINGSTON

Old Harbour

Portmore

Morant Bay

Portland Bight

Caribbean
Sea

2000m/6562ft
1000m/3281ft
500m/1640ft
200m/656ft
Sea level

0 km   20
0 miles 20

0 km   200
0 miles   200

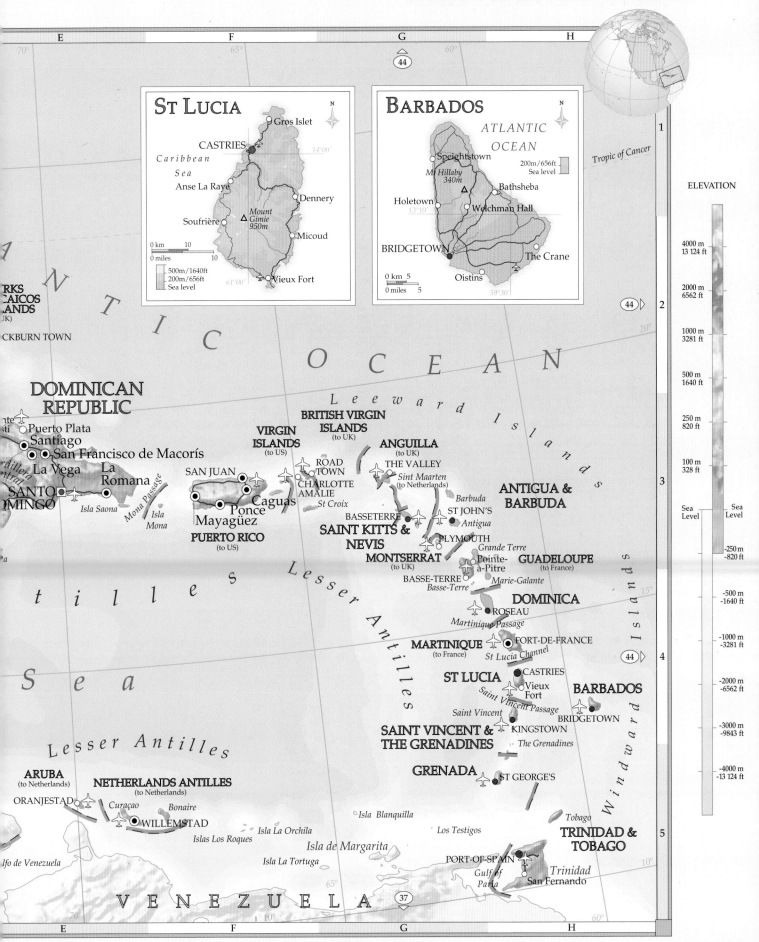

44

ST LUCIA

N

Gros Islet

CASTRIES

Caribbean
Sea

14°00'

Anse La Raye

Dennery

Soufrière

Mount
Gimie
950m

Micoud

0 km   10
0 miles   10

500m/1640ft
200m/656ft
Sea level

61°00'

Vieux Fort

BARBADOS

N

ATLANTIC
OCEAN

Speightstown

200m/656ft
Sea level

Mt Hillaby
340m

Bathsheba

Holetown

Welchman Hall

13°10'

BRIDGETOWN

The Crane

0 km 5
0 miles 5

Oistins

59°30'

44

Tropic of Cancer

ELEVATION

4000 m
13 124 ft

2000 m
6562 ft

1000 m
3281 ft

500 m
1640 ft

250 m
820 ft

100 m
328 ft

Sea
Level

Sea
Level

-250 m
-820 ft

-500 m
-1640 ft

-1000 m
-3281 ft

-2000 m
-6562 ft

-3000 m
-9843 ft

-4000 m
-13 124 ft

1

2

3

4

5

RKS
CAICOS
LANDS
(UK)

CKBURN TOWN

**DOMINICAN
REPUBLIC**

Puerto Plata
Santiago
San Francisco de Macorís
La Vega   La
Romana

SANTO
DMINGO

Isla Saona

Mona Passage

*Isla
Mona*

**VIRGIN
ISLANDS**
(to US)

SAN JUAN

Caguas

Ponce
Mayagüez

PUERTO RICO
(to US)

ROAD
TOWN

CHARLOTTE
AMALIE

St Croix

**BRITISH VIRGIN
ISLANDS**
(to UK)

ANGUILLA
(to UK)

THE VALLEY

Sint Maarten
(to Netherlands)

Barbuda

BASSETERRE

Antigua

ST JOHN'S

**ANTIGUA &
BARBUDA**

**SAINT KITTS &
NEVIS**

PLYMOUTH

MONTSERRAT
(to UK)

Pointe-
à-Pitre

BASSE-TERRE
Basse-Terre

Grande Terre

Marie-Galante

GUADELOUPE
(to France)

DOMINICA

ROSEAU

Martinique Passage

MARTINIQUE
(to France)

FORT-DE-FRANCE

St Lucia Channel

ST LUCIA

CASTRIES

Vieux
Fort

Saint Vincent Passage

Saint Vincent

**SAINT VINCENT &
THE GRENADINES**

KINGSTOWN

The Grenadines

GRENADA

ST GEORGE'S

BARBADOS

BRIDGETOWN

ARUBA
(to Netherlands)

ORANJESTAD

NETHERLANDS ANTILLES
(to Netherlands)

Curaçao

Bonaire

WILLEMSTAD

Islas Los Roques

Isla La Orchila

Isla Blanquilla

Los Testigos

Isla de Margarita

Isla La Tortuga

Tobago

**TRINIDAD &
TOBAGO**

PORT-OF-SPAIN

*Gulf of
Paria*

Trinidad

San Fernando

lfo de Venezuela

V E N E Z U E L A

37

A T L A N T I C   O C E A N

L e e w a r d   I s l a n d s

W i n d w a r d   I s l a n d s

L e s s e r   A n t i l l e s

Lesser Antilles

tilles

Sea

44

SOUTH AMERICA

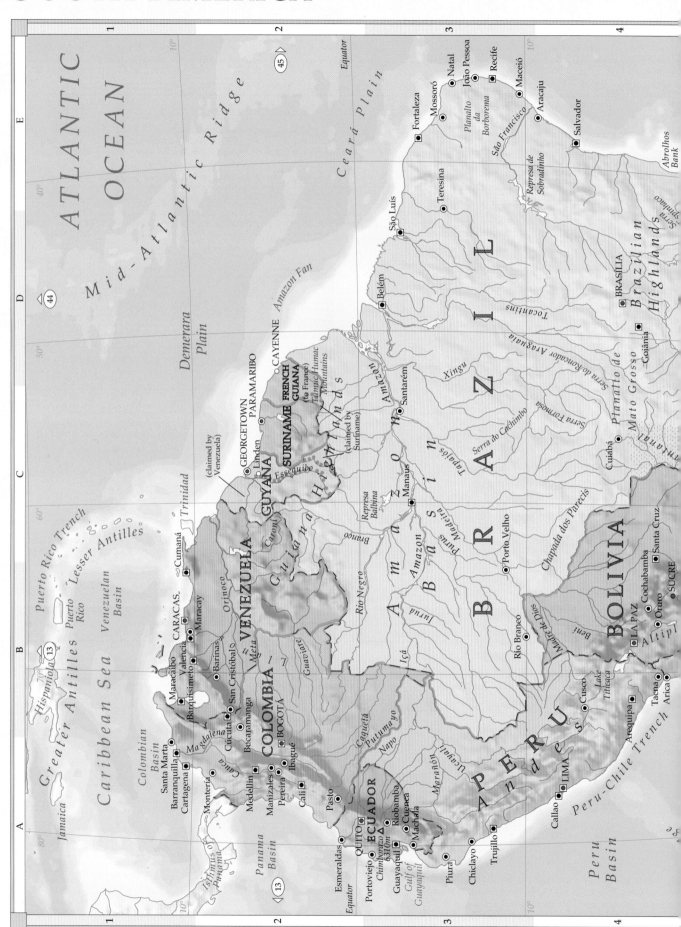

POPULATION

- ▣ Over 500,000
- ◉ 100,000 – 500,000
- ○ 50,000 – 100,000
- ○ Less than 50,000
- ● National capital

ATLANTIC OCEAN

Mid-Atlantic Ridge

Ceará Plain

Equator

Natal
João Pessoa
Recife
Maceió
Aracaju
Salvador

Mossoró
Fortaleza
Planalto da Borborema
São Francisco
Abrolhos Bank

Demerara Plain

Amazon Fan

Teresina
São Luís

Represa de Sobradinho

Serra do Espinhaço

B R A Z I L

Brazilian Highlands

Belém

BRASÍLIA
Goiânia

Tocantins

CAYENNE
PARAMARIBO
FRENCH GUIANA (to France)
SURINAME (claimed by Suriname)

Tumuc-Humac Mountains
Highlands

GEORGETOWN
Linden
GUYANA
(claimed by Venezuela)
Essequibo

Amazon
Santarém

Xingu

Serra do Cachimbo
Tapajós

Serra Formosa
Planalto de Mato Grosso

Cuiabá

Chapada dos Parecis

Pantanal

Trinidad

Caroni

Guiana Highlands

Orinoco

Manaus
Represa Balbina

A m a z o n B a s i n

Porto Velho

Santa Cruz
SUCRE

Cumaná

Lesser Antilles

Puerto Rico Trench

Puerto Rico
Venezuelan Basin

CARACAS
Maracay
Valencia
Barinas

VENEZUELA
Meta

Guaviare

Rio Negro
Branco

Madeira
Purus

Juruá

Rio Branco

BOLIVIA

Cochabamba
LA PAZ
Oruro

Beni

Madre de Dios

Colombian Basin

Maracaibo
Barquisimeto
San Cristóbal

Cúcuta
Bucaramanga

COLOMBIA
BOGOTÁ
Ibagué

Meta

Caquetá
Putumayo
Napo

Ucayali

Altiplano

Cusco
Lake Titicaca

Arequipa
Tacna
Arica

Caribbean Sea

Jamaica
Greater Antilles
Hispaniola

Santa Marta
Barranquilla
Cartagena
Montería
Medellín
Manizales
Pereira
Cali
Pasto

Magdalena
Cauca

ECUADOR
QUITO
Portoviejo
Chimborazo 6310m
Guayaquil

Esmeraldas

Riobamba
Cuenca
Machala

Marañón

P E R U

A n d e s

LIMA
Callao

Peru-Chile Trench

Panama Basin
Isthmus of Panama

Gulf of Guayaquil

Piura
Chiclayo
Trujillo

Peru Basin

Equator

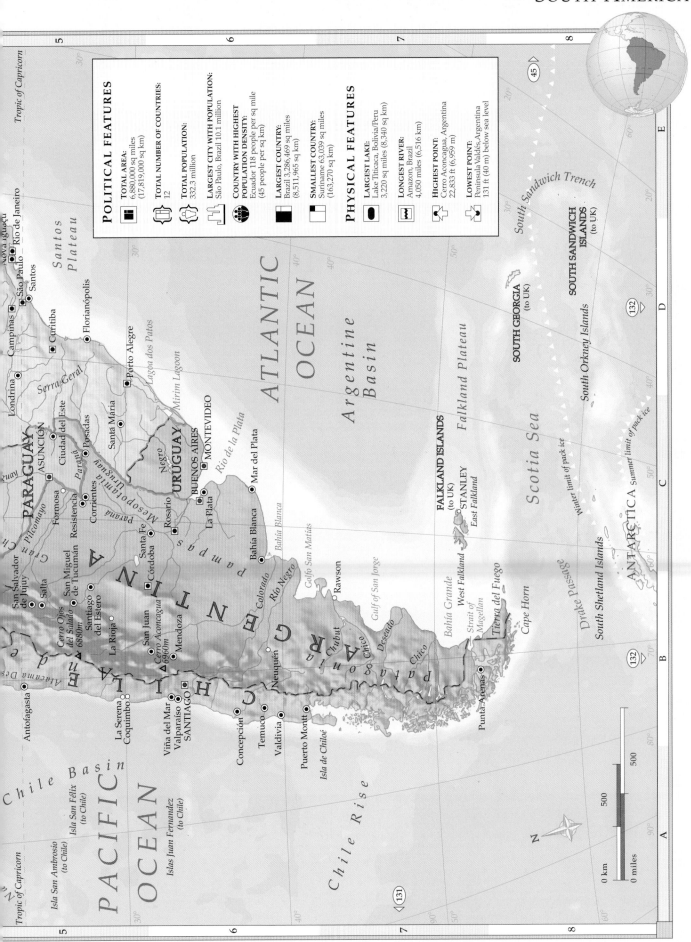

POLITICAL FEATURES

TOTAL AREA:
6,880,000 sq miles
(17,819,000 sq km)

TOTAL NUMBER OF COUNTRIES:
12

TOTAL POPULATION:
332.3 million

LARGEST CITY WITH POPULATION:
São Paulo, Brazil 10.1 million

**COUNTRY WITH HIGHEST
POPULATION DENSITY:**
Ecuador 118 people per sq mile
(45 people per sq km)

LARGEST COUNTRY:
Brazil 3,286,469 sq miles
(8,511,965 sq km)

SMALLEST COUNTRY:
Suriname 63,039 sq miles
(163,270 sq km)

PHYSICAL FEATURES

LARGEST LAKE:
Lake Titicaca, Bolivia/Peru
3,220 sq miles (8,340 sq km)

LONGEST RIVER:
Amazon, Brazil
4,050 miles (6,516 km)

HIGHEST POINT:
Cerro Aconcagua, Argentina
22,833 ft (6,959 m)

LOWEST POINT:
Península Valdés, Argentina
131 ft (40 m) below sea level

Tropic of Capricorn

30°

Nova Iguaçu
Rio de Janeiro
São Paulo
Santos
Santos Plateau
Campinas
Curitiba
Florianópolis
Londrina
Serra Geral
Porto Alegre
Lagoa dos Patos
Mirim Lagoon
Santa Mária
Posadas
Ciudad del Este
PARAGUAY
ASUNCIÓN
Paraná
Mesopotamia
Negro
Rosario
URUGUAY
MONTEVIDEO
Río de la Plata
BUENOS AIRES
La Plata
Mar del Plata
Formosa
Resistencia
Corrientes
Paraná
Santa Fe
Córdoba
Pampas
Bahía Blanca
Bahía Blanca
San Salvador
de Jujuy
Salta
San Miguel
de Tucumán
Santiago
del Estero
Cerro Ojos
del Salado
6880m
La Rioja
San Juan
Cerro Aconcagua
6960m
Mendoza
Colorado
Río Negro
Golfo San Matías
Rawson
Neuquén
Chubut
Chico
Chico
Desado
Gulf of San Jorge

ATLANTIC
OCEAN
Argentine
Basin

40°

50°

FALKLAND ISLANDS
(to UK)
STANLEY
East Falkland
West Falkland
Bahía Grande
Strait of
Magellan
Tierra del Fuego
Cape Horn

Falkland Plateau

SOUTH GEORGIA
(to UK)

Scotia Sea

South Orkney Islands

SOUTH SANDWICH
ISLANDS
(to UK)

South Sandwich Trench

South Shetland Islands
Drake Passage
Winter limit of pack ice
Summer limit of pack ice

ANTÁRCTICA

45

132

132

131

Antofagasta
La Serena
Coquimbo
Viña del Mar
Valparaíso
SANTIAGO
Concepción
Temuco
Valdivia
Puerto Montt
Isla de Chiloé
Punta Arenas

Atacama Desert

Andes

Patagonia

ARGENTINA

CHILE

Chile Basin

Isla San Félix
(to Chile)
Isla San Ambrosio
(to Chile)
Islas Juan Fernández
(to Chile)

PACIFIC
OCEAN

Chile Rise

Tropic of Capricorn

N

0 km   500
0 miles   500

35

NORTHERN SOUTH AMERICA

POPULATION

- ◉ Over 500,000
- ◉ 100,000 – 500,000
- ○ 50,000 – 100,000
- ○ Less than 50,000
- ● National capital

Caribbean Sea

Lesser Ant

ARUBA (to Netherlands)
Curaçao
Bonaire
NETHERLANDS ANTILLES (to Netherlands)
Islas Los Roques
Islas
La O

Península de la Guajira
Puerto López
Punto Fijo
Coro
Puerto Cumarebo
Puerto Cabello
CARAC

Ríohacha
Maicao
Golfo de Venezuela
Sabaneta
San Felipe
Maracay

Santa Marta
Ciénaga
Dabajuro
Maracaibo
Cabimas
San Juan de los Mo

Barranquilla
Soledad
Pico Cristóbal Colón 5775m
La Concepción
Ciudad Ojeda
Carora
Barquisimeto
Valencia
Maracay

Cartagena
Sabanalarga
Valledupar
Machiques
Lago de Maracaibo
Valera
Acarigua

El Carmen de Bolívar
Magangué
San Carlos del Zulia
Mérida
Guanare
Calabozo
Valle de la Pascu

Sincelejo
Cereté
El Vigía
Pico Bolívar 5007m
Barinas
Río Guanare
San Fernan

Montería
Planeta Rica
Aguachica
Ocaña
Cúcuta
San Cristóbal
Río Apure
V E N

Caucasia
Pamplona
Río Arauca
Arauca

Dabeiba
Yarumal
Bucaramanga
Río Meta
Puerto Carre

Barrancabermeja
Arauca
Puerto Ayacu

Bello
Puerto Berrío
Sogamoso
Río Orinoco

Medellín
Itagüí
Tunja
Yopal

Quibdó
Manizales
Zipaquirá
Río Meta

Nuquí
Pereira
BOGOTÁ
Villavicencio

Armenia
Girardot
Río Guaviare
Puerto Inírida

Tuluá
Ibagué
Espinal

Buenaventura
Buga
C O L O M B I A

Palmira
San José del Guaviare

Cali
Neiva

Popayán
Garzón

Tumaco
Pitalito
Río Vaupés
Mitú

Pasto
Mocoa
Florencia

Nevada de Cumbal 4764m
Orito

Ipiales
Río Apaporis

Equator

PANAMA
Panama Canal
Golfo de Panamá

PACIFIC OCEAN

E C U A D O R

Río Putumayo
Río Caquetá

Río Napo

P E R U

Río Icá
Amazon
Río Japurá

Cordillera Occidental
Cordillera Central
Cordillera Oriental
Río Cauca
Río Magdalena
Andes

SAINT VINCENT & THE GRENADINES

BARBADOS

GRENADA

Isla Blanquilla

Isla de Margarita

Islas Los Testigos

Tobago

ortuga

La Asunción

Carúpano

Porlamar

Güiria

maná

Cariaco

Gulf of Paria

TRINIDAD & TOBAGO

Puerto La Cruz

Trinidad

Barcelona

San Mateo

The Serpent's Mouth

Anaco

Maturín

raza

Cantaura

El Tigre

Tucupita

Ciudad Guayana

Río Orinoco

S

Upata

Ciudad Bolívar

Embalse de Guri

Matthews Ridge

Charity

U E L A

El Callao

Spring Garden

Río Paragua

El Dorado

Parika

GEORGETOWN

Aurora

New Amsterdam

Río Caura

Peters Mine

Bartica

Salto Ángel

Rockstone

Nieuw Nickerie

Totness

PARAMARIBO

Nieuw Amsterdam

St-Laurent-du-Maroni

Kamarang

Linden

Kaaimanston

Sinnamary

Río Caroní

Mount Roraima

2810m

GUYANA

Orealla

Apoera

W. J. van Blommesteinmeer

Kourou

CAYENNE

Kurupukari

Ouanary

Pakaraima Mountains

Juliana Top 1230m

Grand-Santi

SURINAME

Montagnes de la Trinité

Montagne Tortue

St-Georges

(Venezuela claims all of Guyana west of Essequibo River)

Lethem

FRENCH GUIANA (to France)

Camopi

G u i a n a

Essequibo River

H i g h l a n d s

Río Orinoco

Courantyne River

Tumuc Humac Mountains

(claimed by Suriname)

Acarai Mountains

(claimed by Suriname)

B R A Z I L

z o n   B a s i n

Amazon

Amazon

Equator

Río Negro

Amazon

Amazon

Río Purus

Río Tapajós

A T L A N T I C

O C E A N

Maroni River

Chiguni River

0 km   200

0 miles   200

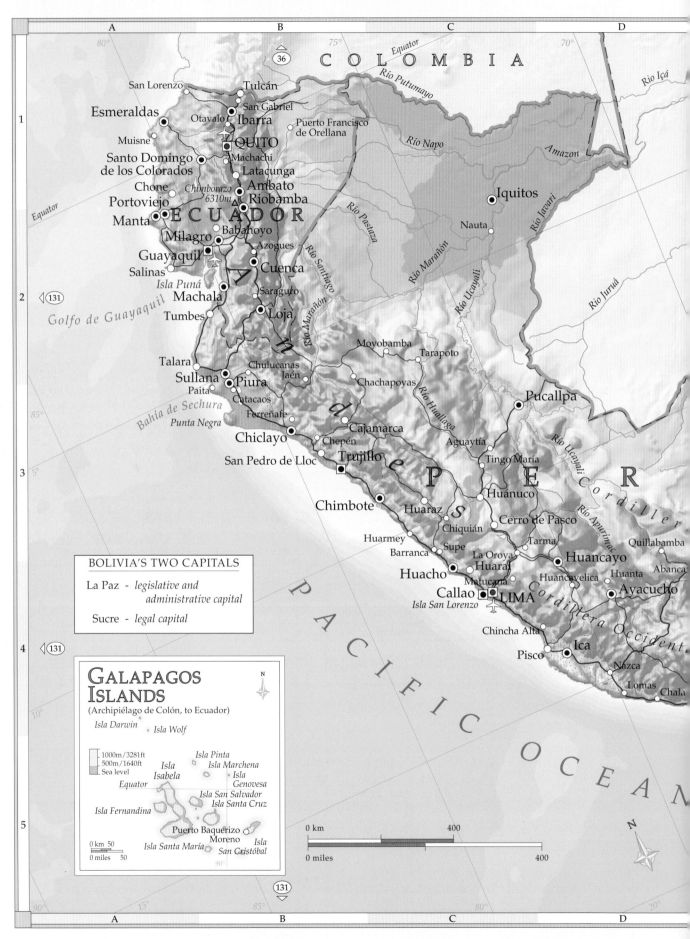

COLOMBIA

San Lorenzo
Tulcán
36
San Gabriel
Esmeraldas
Otavalo · Ibarra
Muisne
QUITO
Machachi
Santo Domingo
de los Colorados
Latacunga
Chone
Ambato
Chimborazo
6310m
Riobamba
Portoviejo
ECUADOR
Manta
Babahoyo
Milagro
Azogues
Guayaquil
Cuenca
Salinas
Isla Puná
Saraguro
Machala
Loja
Tumbes

Golfo de Guayaquil

Puerto Francisco
de Orellana

Río Putumayo
Equator

Río Napo

Amazon
Iquitos
Nauta
Río Pastaza
Río Santiago
Río Marañón
Río Javari
Río Iça
Río Marañón
Río Ucayali
Río Iuruá

Talara
Sullana · Piura
Paita
Catacaos
Ferreñafe
Chulucanas
Jaén
Moyobamba
Tarapoto
Chachapoyas

Río Huallaga

Pucallpa

Río Ucayali

PERÚ

Bahía de Sechura
Punta Negra
Chiclayo
Chepén
Cajamarca
San Pedro de Lloc
Trujillo
Aguaytía
Tingo María
Chimbote
Huaraz
Huánuco
Chiquián
Cerro de Pasco
Tarma
Huarmey
Supe
La Oroya
Quillabamba
Barranca
Huaral
Huancayo
Huacho
Matucana
Huancavelica
Huanta
Callao
LIMA
Ayacucho
Isla San Lorenzo
Chincha Alta
Chinca Alta
Pisco
Ica
Nazca
Lomas
Chala

Río Apurímac
Cordillera
Cordillera Occident.

PACIFIC OCEAN

BOLIVIA'S TWO CAPITALS

La Paz - *legislative and
                administrative capital*

Sucre - *legal capital*

POPULATION

- ◉ Over
    500,000
- ◉ 100,000 -
    500,000
- ○ 50,000 -
    100,000
- ○ Less than
    50,000
- ● National
    capital

GALAPAGOS ISLANDS

(Archipiélago de Colón, to Ecuador)

Isla Darwin   · *Isla Wolf*

	1000m/3281ft
	500m/1640ft
	Sea level

Isla Pinta
Isla Marchena
*Isla
Genovesa*
*Isla
Isabela*
Equator
Isla San Salvador
Isla Santa Cruz
Isla Fernandina
Puerto Baquerizo
Moreno
*Isla
San Cristóbal*
Isla Santa María

0 km 50
0 miles 50

0 km   400

0 miles   400

E   F   G   H

65°   *Amazon*   5°   60°   55°

40

A m a z o n B a s i n

Río Madeira

Serra do Cachimbo

10°

1

Río São Manuel

B   R   A   Z   I   L

Río Purus

41

2

Río Abunã

Fortaleza
Villa Bella

Chapada dos Parecis

15°

Río Juruena

Riberalta

Río Madre de Dios

Río Guaporé

Cobija
Porvenir

Magdalena

Río Beni

55°

Puerto
Maldonado

Santa Ana

Río Mamoré

San Matías

3

Oriental

Reyes

San Ignacio

Trinidad

Río San Miguel

Concepción

Sicuani

B   O   L   I   V   I   A

Nevado Pupuya
△ 5818m

Montero
Warnes

San José

Puerto
Suárez

Pantanal

Ayaviri
Moho
Puerto Acosta

Portachuelo

Juliaca
Lake Titicaca
Achacachi

Buena Vista

Santa Cruz

20°

Puno
Copacabana

Cochabamba

Comarapa

Nevado Ampato
6310m
Ilave   Viacha
Corocoro

LA PAZ

Aiquile

C h a c o

41

Volcán Misti
5822m
△

Oruro
Huanuni
Uncía

SUCRE

Lagunillas

Paraguay

Arequipa
Moquegua

Challapata

Monteagudo

Lago Poopó

Cordillera Oriental

Tacna

Nevado Sajama
6520m

Potosí

P A R A G U A Y

Mollendo
Ilo

Sabaya

La Yarada

Uyuni
Cotagaita

San Lorenzo

Pilcomayo

Tropic of Capricorn

Villa Martín

Tupiza

Tarija

G r a n C h a c o

San Pablo
Villazón

25°

5

Desierto de Atacama

C H I L E

A R G E N T I N A

42

Tropic of Capricorn

70°   65°   25°   60°

E   F   G   H

ELEVATION

4000 m / 13 124 ft
2000 m / 6562 ft
1000 m / 3281 ft
500 m / 1640 ft
250 m / 820 ft
100 m / 328 ft
Sea Level — Sea Level
-250 m / -820 ft
-500 m / -1640 ft
-1000 m / -3281 ft
-2000 m / -6562 ft
-3000 m / -9843 ft
-4000 m / -13 124 ft

BRAZIL

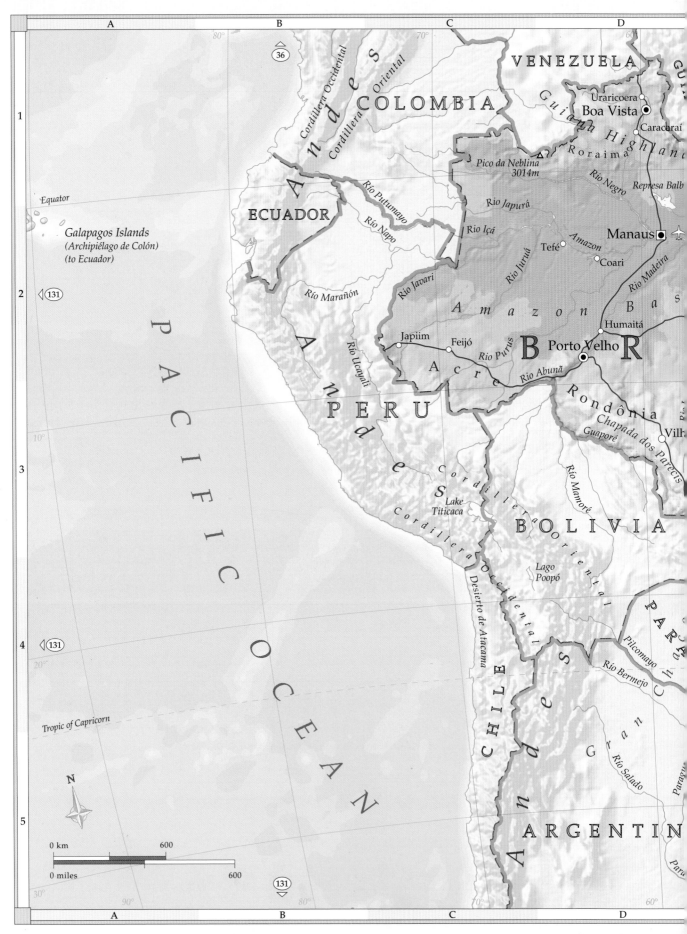

POPULATION

- ⬤ Over 500,000
- ◉ 100,000 - 500,000
- ○ 50,000 - 100,000
- ○ Less than 50,000
- ● National capital

N

0 km   600

0 miles   600

Map labels:

VENEZUELA
COLOMBIA
ECUADOR
PERU
BOLIVIA
CHILE
ARGENTINA
PARAGUAY

Boa Vista
Uraricoera
Caracaraí
Manaus
Tefé
Coari
Humaitá
Porto Velho
Japiim
Feijó
Vilh...

Galapagos Islands
(Archipiélago de Colón)
(to Ecuador)

PACIFIC OCEAN

Equator
Tropic of Capricorn

Pico da Neblina 3014m
Guiana Highlands
Roraima
Río Negro
Represa Balb...
Río Japurá
Río Içá
Amazon
Río Putumayo
Río Napo
Río Marañón
Río Javari
Río Juruá
Río Ucayali
Río Madeira
Amazon Bas...
Acre
Río Purus
Río Abunã
Rondônia
Guaporé
Chapada dos Parecis
Río Mamoré
Río Mamoré
Lake Titicaca
Cordillera Occidental
Cordillera Oriental
Cordillera Occidental
Cordillera Oriental
Desierto de Atacama
Lago Poopó
Pilcomayo
Río Bermejo
Río Salado
Paragu...
Andes
Cordillera Occidental
Cordillera Oriental

36
131

ATLANTIC OCEAN

FRENCH GUIANA (to France)

SURINAME

Tumuc Humac Mountains

Mouths of the Amazon

Amapá

Macapá

Ilha Caviana de Fora

Ilha de Marajó

Baía de Marajó

Baía de São Marco

Belém

São Luís

Parnaíba

Camocim

Equator

Alenquer

Amazon

Santarém

Itaituba

Altamira

Bacabal

Piripiri

Fortaleza

Atol das Rocas

San Fernando de Noronha (to Brazil)

Represa de Tucuruí

Teresina

Marabá

Imperatriz

Maranhão

Ceará

Mossoró

Açu

Cabo de São Roque

Rio Grande do Norte

Natal

Rio Xingu

Carolina

Floriano

Juazeiro do Norte

Paraíba

João Pessoa

Rio Tapajós

Pará

Balsas

Picos

Piauí

Pernambuco

Campina Grande

Serra do Cachimbo

Maraba

Represa de Sobradinho

Juazeiro

Alagoas

Recife

São Manuel

Serra Formosa

Serra dos Gradaús

Rio Tocantins

Rio São Francisco

Chapada Diamantina

Maceió

Rio Araguaia

Tocantins

Aracaju

Estância

Taguatinga

Bahia

Feira de Santana

Salvador

Cuiabá

Goiás

Planalto Central

BRASÍLIA

Janaúba

Itabuna

Baía de Todos os Santos

Mato Grosso

Anápolis

Vitória da Conquista

Canavieiras

Rondonópolis

Jataí

Goiânia

Montes Claros

Araçuaí

Minas Gerais

Mato Grosso do Sul

Araguari

Governador Valadares

Pantanal

Uberlândia

Uberaba

Espírito Santo

Campo Grande

Belo Horizonte

Aquidauana

Ribeirão Preto

Divinópolis

Vitória

Presidente Epitácio

Juiz de Fora

Campos

Marília

Campinas

São Paulo

Nova

Iguaçu

Rio de Janeiro

Londrina

Maringá

São Paulo

Santos

Paraná

Represa de Itaipú

Ponta Grossa

Tropic of Capricorn

Salto do Iguaçu

Rio Iguaçu

Curitiba

Joinville

Paraná

Santa Catarina

Blumenau

Florianópolis

Passo Fundo

Rio Negro

Santa Maria

Canoas

Rio Grande do Sul

Porto Alegre

Bagé

Lagoa dos Patos

ATLANTIC OCEAN

Rio Grande

Mirim Lagoon

URUGUAY

ELEVATION

4000 m	13 124 ft
2000 m	6562 ft
1000 m	3281 ft
500 m	1640 ft
250 m	820 ft
100 m	328 ft
Sea Level	Sea Level
-250 m	-820 ft
-500 m	-1640 ft
-1000 m	-3281 ft
-2000 m	-6562 ft
-3000 m	-9843 ft
-4000 m	-13 124 ft

SOUTHERN SOUTH AMERICA

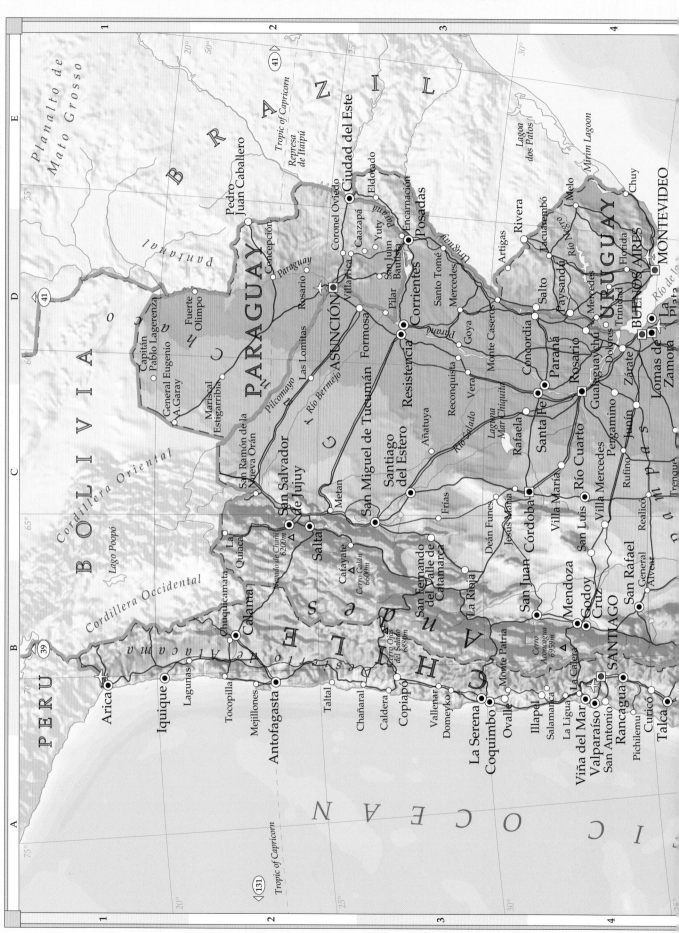

POPULATION

- ⊡ Over 500,000
- ◉ 100,000 – 500,000
- ○ 50,000 – 100,000
- ○ Less than 50,000
- ● National capital

PERU

BOLIVIA

BRAZIL

PARAGUAY

URUGUAY

CHILE

Planalto de Mato Grosso

Pantanal

Cordillera Oriental

Cordillera Occidental

Lago Poopó

Pedro Juan Caballero

Ciudad del Este

Coronel Oviedo

Eldorado

Encarnación

Posadas

Rivera

Tacuarembó

Artigas

MONTEVIDEO

BUENOS AIRES

Concepción

Paraguay

Villarrica

Caazapá

Yuty

San Juan Bautista

Pilar

Corrientes

Santo Tomé

Mercedes

Salto

Paysandú

Mercedes

Florida

Trinidad

Chuy

Lagoa dos Patos

Mirim Lagoon

Capitán Pablo Lagerenza

Fuerte Olimpo

General Eugenio A.Garay

Mariscal Estigarribia

Las Lomitas

ASUNCIÓN

Rosario

Formosa

Resistencia

Goya

Monte Caseros

Concordia

Paraná

Rosario

Gualeguaychú

Dolores

Zárate

La Plata

Lomas de Zamora

Río Bermejo

Pilcomayo

Paraná

Uruguay

San Ramón de la Nueva Orán

Reconquista

Vera

Rafaela

Santa Fe

Pergamino

Junín

Río Salado

Laguna Mar Chiquita

San Salvador de Jujuy

Metán

San Miguel de Tucumán

Santiago del Estero

Añatuya

Frías

Deán Funes

Jesús María

Córdoba

Villa María

Río Cuarto

Villa Mercedes

San Luis

Rufino

Realicó

La Quiaca

La Quiaca

Salta

Cafayate

Nevado de Chañí 6200m

Cerro Galán 6600m

San Fernando del Valle de Catamarca

La Rioja

Chuquicamata

Calama

Antofagasta

Mejillones

Tocopilla

Cerro Ojos del Salado 6888m

San Juan

Mendoza

Godoy Cruz

San Rafael

General Alvear

Cerro Aconcagua 6959m

SANTIAGO

Monte Patria

Arica

Iquique

Lagunas

Taltal

Chañaral

Caldera

Copiapó

Vallenar

Domeyko

La Serena

Coquimbo

Ovalle

Illapel

Salamanca

La Ligua

La Calera

Viña del Mar

Valparaíso

San Antonio

Rancagua

Curicó

Pichilemu

Talca

Atacama

Desierto de Atacama

Tropic of Capricorn

Represa de Itaipú

OCEAN

PACIFIC

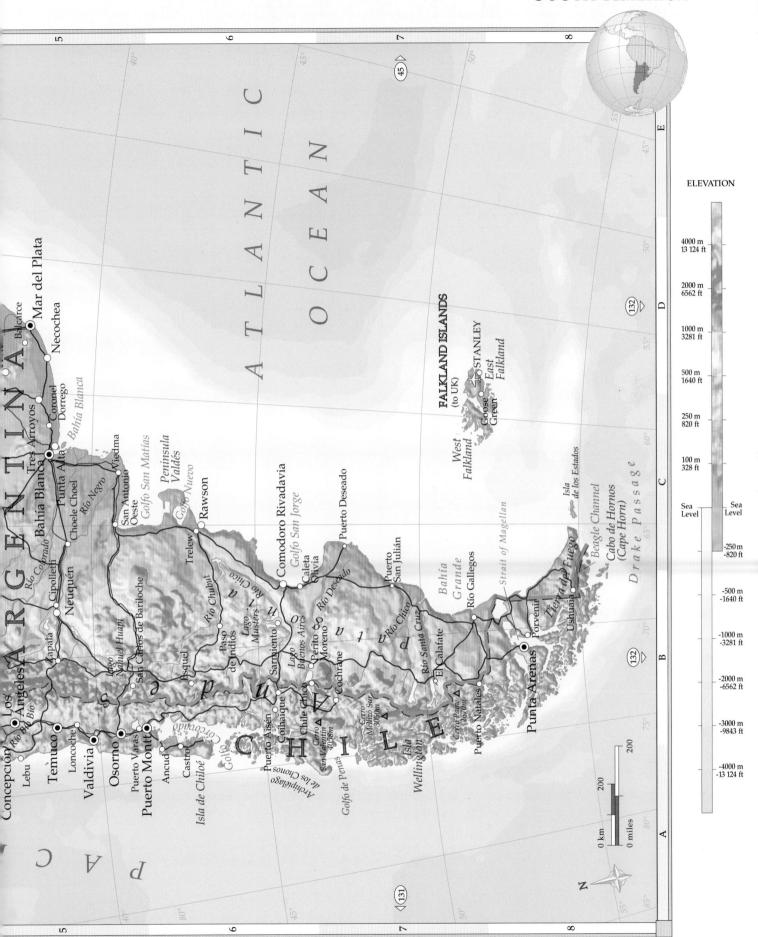

SOUTH AMERICA

ELEVATION

4000 m	13 124 ft
2000 m	6562 ft
1000 m	3281 ft
500 m	1640 ft
250 m	820 ft
100 m	328 ft
Sea Level	Sea Level
-250 m	-820 ft
-500 m	-1640 ft
-1000 m	-3281 ft
-2000 m	-6562 ft
-3000 m	-9843 ft
-4000 m	-13 124 ft

ATLANTIC OCEAN

PACIFIC

ARGENTINA

CHILE

Mar del Plata
Balcarce
Necochea
Coronel
Dorrego
Bahía Blanca
Tres Arroyos
Bahía Blanca
Punta Alta
Viedma
Choele Choel
Cipolletti
San Antonio Oeste
Río Negro
Río Colorado
Golfo San Matías
Península Valdés
Golfo Nuevo
Rawson
Neuquén
Zapala
Trelew
Río Chubut
Esquel
Lago Nahuel Huapi
San Carlos de Bariloche
Paso de Indios
Lago Musters
Sarmiento
Comodoro Rivadavia
Golfo San Jorge
Caleta Olivia
Río Deseado
Puerto Deseado
Lago Buenos Aires
Perito Moreno
Cochrane
Río Chico
Puerto San Julián
Bahía Grande
Río Santa Cruz
El Calafate
Río Gallegos
Puerto Natales
Porvenir
Tierra del Fuego
Ushuaia
Punta Arenas
Strait of Magellan
Beagle Channel
Cabo de Hornos (Cape Horn)
Isla de los Estados
Drake Passage

Concepción
Los Ángeles
Río Bío Bío
Lebu
Temuco
Loncoche
Valdivia
Osorno
Puerto Varas
Puerto Montt
Ancud
Castro
Isla de Chiloé
Corcovado
Golfo Corcovado
Archipiélago de los Chonos
Golfo de Penas
Puerto Aisén
Coihaique
Chile Chico
Cerro San Valentín 4058m
Cerro Melizo Sur 3050m
Isla Wellington
Cerro Paine 3670m

FALKLAND ISLANDS (to UK)
STANLEY
Goose Green
East Falkland
West Falkland

5   6   7   8

45
132
132
131

0 km   200
0 miles   200

N

43

THE ATLANTIC OCEAN

THE WORLD ATLAS

Map labels (selection):

ARCTIC OCEAN

EUROPE

GREENLAND (to Denmark)

NORTH AMERICA

ATLANTIC OCEAN

AFRICA

Sahara

Sahel

Mid-Atlantic Ridge

SVALBARD (to Norway)
JAN MAYEN (to Norway)
ICELAND
FAEROE ISLANDS (to Denmark)
BERMUDA (to UK)
CAPE VERDE

Limit of summer pack ice
Limit of winter pack ice
Arctic Circle
Barents Sea
North Cape
Scandinavia
Norwegian Sea
Norwegian Basin
Greenland Sea
Denmark Strait
Reykjanes Basin
Iceland Basin
Rockall Bank
Baltic Sea
Gulf of Bothnia
Gothenburg
Hamburg
Rotterdam
North Sea
British Isles
Bay of Biscay
Danube
Venice
Adriatic Sea
Alps
Atlas Mountains
Gibraltar
Azores (to Portugal)
East Azores Fracture Zone
Madeira (to Portugal)
Madeira Plain
Canary Islands (to Spain)
Cape Verde Plain
Cape Verde Basin
Great Meteor Tablemount
Mariupol
Odesa
Black Sea
Port Said
Suez
Nile
Red Sea
Caspian Sea
Tropic of Cancer
Mediterranean Sea
Niger
Lagos
Dakar
Freetown
Sierra Leone
Doldrums Fracture Zone
Sierra
Demerara Plain

Lincoln Sea
Ellesmere Island
Baffin Bay
Baffin Island
Davis Strait
Labrador Sea
Labrador Basin
Hudson Bay
Great Lakes
St. Lawrence
Montreal
Halifax
New York
Newfoundland
Grand Banks of Newfoundland
Newfoundland Basin
Northwest Atlantic Mid-Ocean Canyon
Charlie-Gibbs Fracture Zone
Sohm Plain
Bermuda Rise
Hatteras Plain
Sargasso Sea
Kane Fracture Zone
Nares Plain
Puerto Rico Trench
Puerto Rico
La Guaira
Lesser Antilles
Greater Antilles
Caribbean Sea
Colombian Basin
Cristobal
Guatemala Basin
Gulf of Mexico
New Orleans
Mississippi
Appalachian Mountains
Arctic Circle
Tropic of Cancer
Reykjavik

133
90
13

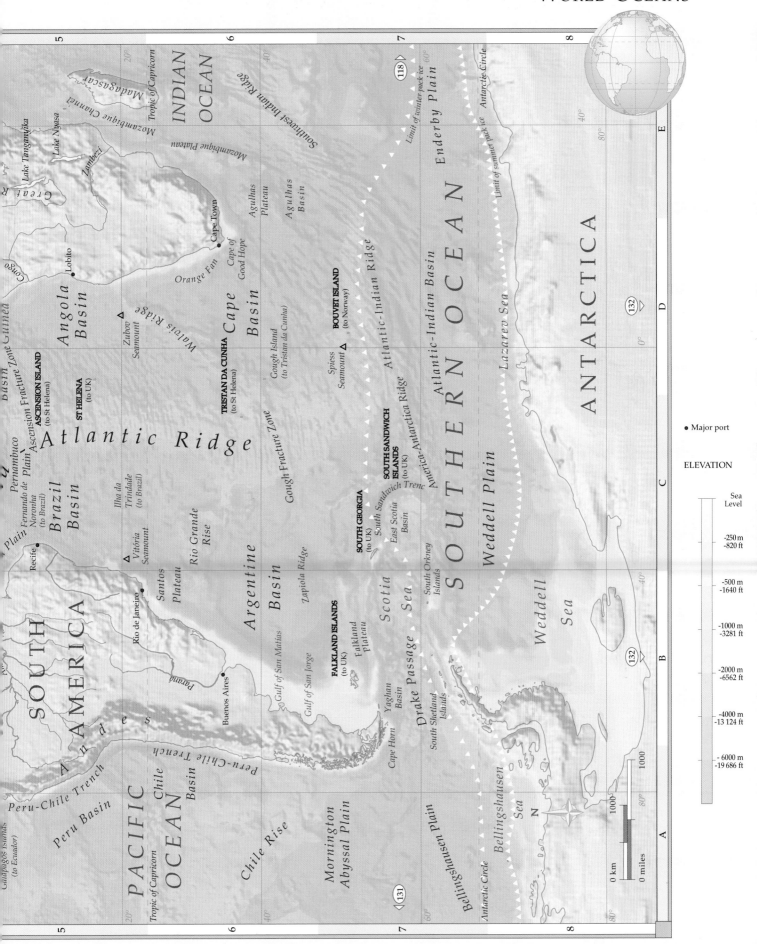

INDIAN OCEAN

Tropic of Capricorn

Madagascar

Mozambique Channel

Lake Tanganyika
Lake Nyasa
Zambezi
Great R

Congo

Guinea Basin
Ascension Fracture Zone
Angola Basin

Mozambique Plateau

Southwest Indian Ridge

Cape Town
Cape of Good Hope
Orange Fan
Lobito

Agulhas Plateau
Agulhas Basin

Cape Basin

Walvis Ridge
Zubov Seamount

ASCENSION ISLAND (to St Helena)
ST HELENA (to UK)

TRISTAN DA CUNHA (to St Helena)

Gough Island (to Tristan da Cunha)

BOUVET ISLAND (to Norway)

Spiess Seamount

Atlantic-Indian Ridge

Atlantic-Indian Basin

Lazarev Sea

Enderby Plain

Limit of winter pack ice
Limit of summer pack ice

Antarctic Circle

SOUTHERN OCEAN

ANTARCTICA

Mid Atlantic Ridge

Pernambuco
Fernando de Noronha (to Brazil)
Recife
Brazil Basin

Ilha da Trindade (to Brazil)

Vitória Seamount

Rio Grande Rise

Santos Plateau

Rio de Janeiro
Paraná
Buenos Aires

SOUTH AMERICA
Andes

Gough Fracture Zone

Argentine Basin

Zapiola Ridge

SOUTH GEORGIA (to UK)
South Sandwich Trench
SOUTH SANDWICH ISLANDS (to UK)
America-Antarctica Ridge

East Scotia Basin

Scotia Sea

South Orkney Islands

Weddell Plain

Weddell Sea

FALKLAND ISLANDS (to UK)
Falkland Plateau
Gulf of San Matias
Gulf of San Jorge

Yaghan Basin
Drake Passage
Cape Horn
South Shetland Islands

Bellingshausen Plain

Bellingshausen Sea

Antarctic Circle

Peru-Chile Trench
Peru Basin
Galápagos Islands (to Ecuador)

PACIFIC OCEAN

Chile Basin

Chile Rise

Mornington Abyssal Plain

Tropic of Capricorn

● Major port

ELEVATION

Sea Level
-250 m
-820 ft
-500 m
-1640 ft
-1000 m
-3281 ft
-2000 m
-6562 ft
-4000 m
-13 124 ft
-6000 m
-19 686 ft

0 km   1000
0 miles   1000

N

⟨118⟩
⟨132⟩
⟨132⟩
⟨131⟩

AFRICA

POPULATION

- ◉ Over 500,000
- ◉ 100,000 – 500,000
- ○ 50,000 – 100,000
- ○ Less than 50,000
- ● National capital

0 km 1000
0 miles 1000

POLITICAL FEATURES

TOTAL AREA:
11,677,250 sq miles
(30,244,050 sq km)

TOTAL NUMBER OF COUNTRIES:
53

TOTAL POPULATION:
776.5 million

LARGEST CITY WITH POPULATION:
Cairo, Egypt 6.4 million

COUNTRY WITH HIGHEST POPULATION DENSITY:
Mauritius 1,671 people per sq mile (645 people per sq km)

LARGEST COUNTRY:
Sudan 967,493 sq miles (2,505,810 sq km)

SMALLEST COUNTRY:
Seychelles 176 sq miles (455 sq km)

PHYSICAL FEATURES

LARGEST LAKE:
Lake Victoria, Uganda, Kenya, Tanzania, 26,828 sq miles (69,484 sq km)

LONGEST RIVER:
Nile, Uganda/Sudan/Egypt 4,160 miles (6,695 km)

HIGHEST POINT:
Kilimanjaro, Tanzania 19,341 ft (5,895 m)

LOWEST POINT:
Lac' Assal, Djibouti 512 ft (156 m) below sea level

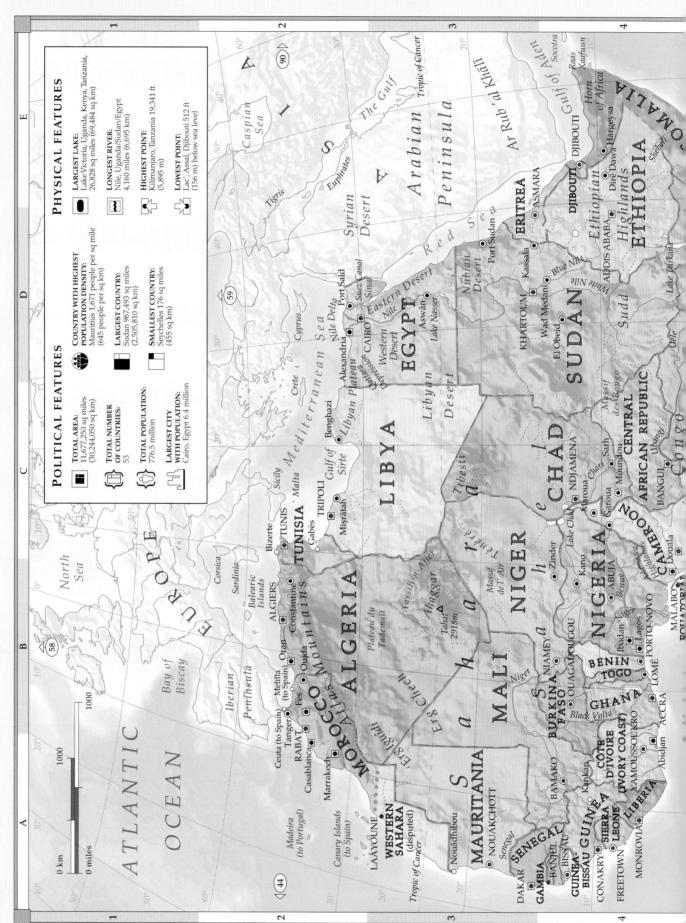

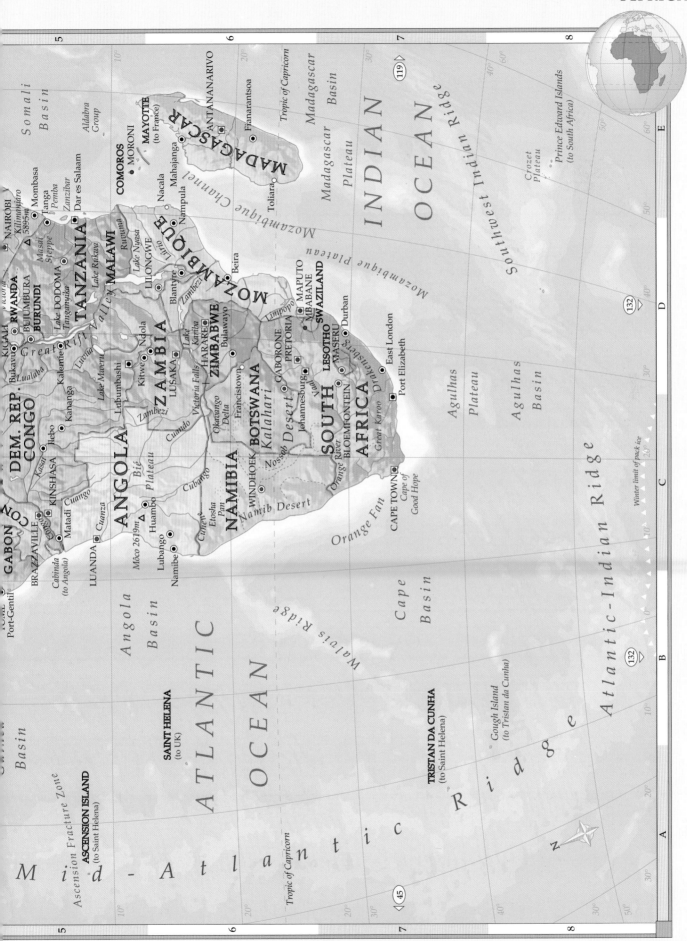

ATLANTIC OCEAN

INDIAN OCEAN

Somali Basin

SOUTH AFRICA

DEM. REP. CONGO

ANGOLA

NAMIBIA

BOTSWANA

ZAMBIA

ZIMBABWE

MOZAMBIQUE

TANZANIA

MALAWI

MADAGASCAR

COMOROS

MAYOTTE (to France)

RWANDA

BURUNDI

GABON

SWAZILAND

LESOTHO

NAIROBI
KIGALI
BUJUMBURA
DODOMA
LILONGWE
LUSAKA
HARARE
GABORONE
PRETORIA
MBABANE
MASERU
MAPUTO
BLOEMFONTEIN
WINDHOEK
LUANDA
KINSHASA
BRAZZAVILLE
MORONI
ANTANANARIVO
CAPE TOWN

Mombasa
Tanga
Zanzibar
Dar es Salaam
Pemba
Kilimanjaro 5895m
Masai Steppe
Lake Victoria
Lake Rukwa
Lake Tanganyika
Lake Nyasa
Lake Mweru
Lake Kariba
Ruvuma
Lufiro
Lake DODOMA
Ruaha
Bukavu
Lualaba
Kalemie
Kananga
Ilebo
Kasai
Matadi
Cabinda (to Angola)
Cuanza
Cuango
Bié Plateau
Móco 2619m
Huambo
Lubango
Namibe
Etosha Pan
Cunene
Cubango
Kalahari
Nossob
Okavango Delta
Francistown
Bulawayo
Victoria Falls
Zambezi
Kitwe
Ndola
Lubumbashi
Kabwe
Luena
Cuando
Namib Desert
Orange River
Great Karoo
Johannesburg
Vaal
Limpopo
Durban
East London
Port Elizabeth
Cape of Good Hope
Drakensberg
Blantyre
Beira
Nacala
Nampula
Mahajanga
Toliara
Fianarantsoa
Aldabra Group
Great Rift Valley

Madagascar Basin
Madagascar Plateau
Mozambique Channel
Mozambique Plateau
Indian Ridge
Southwest Indian Ridge
Prince Edward Islands (to South Africa)
Crozet Plateau
Agulhas Plateau
Agulhas Basin
Cape Basin
Walvis Ridge
Angola Basin
Orange Fan
Mid-Atlantic Ridge
Atlantic-Indian Ridge
Ascension Fracture Zone
Guinea Basin

SAINT HELENA (to UK)
ASCENSION ISLAND (to Saint Helena)
TRISTAN DA CUNHA (to Saint Helena)
Gough Island (to Tristan da Cunha)

Port-Gentil

Tropic of Capricorn

Winter limit of pack ice

N

47

NORTHWEST AFRICA

ATLANTIC

OCEAN

SPAIN

PORTUGAL

Tagus

Ebro

Islas Baleares
(Balearic Islands)

GIBRALTAR
(to UK)

ALGEF
(ALGIERS)

Strait of Gibraltar

Ceuta (to Spain)

Tanger

Chlef

Melilla
(to Spain)

Oran

Tetouan

Ksar-el-Kebir

Mostagan

Chefchaouen

Salé

Sidi Bel Abbè

Kenitra

Oujda

Dj

RABAT

Fès

Tlemcen

Casablanca

Jerada

Chott ech Ch

El-Jadida

Mohammedia

Moyen Atlas

Hauts Plateaux

Khouribga

Lagh

Beni-
Mellal

Atlas Saharien

Safi

Atlas Mountains

Marrakech

Figuig

Essaouira

Haut
Atlas

Er-Rachidia

Béchar

MOROCCO

Ouarzazate

Grand Erg Occiden

El Golé

Agadir

Tiznit

Hamada du Dra

ALGE

Madeira
(to Portugal)

Madeira   *Porto Santo*

Funchal

Ilhas
Desertas

Islas Canarias
(Canary Islands)
(to Spain)

La Palma

Santa Cruz de
Tenerife

Lanzarote

Tan-Tan

Plateau
du Tadem

Adrar

Gomera

Fuerteventura

I-n-Salah

Hierro

Tenerife

Las Palmas
de Gran Canaria

El Mahbas

Tindouf

'Erg Iguidi

Reggane

Gran
Canaria

LAÂYOUNE

Boujdour

Smara

Bou Craa

WESTERN
SAHARA
(disputed territory
under Moroccan occupation)

Galtat-Zemmour

Erg Chech

Tropic of Cancer

Ad Dakhla

Erg

Tanezrouft

S

Ouarâne

Lagouira

a

MAURITANIA

Senegal

M A L I

Azaouâd

Niger

SENEGAL

POPULATION

- ⬛ Over
500,000

- ⊙ 100,000 -
500,000

- ○ 50,000 -
100,000

- ○ Less than
50,000

- ⬤ National
capital

E   F   G   H

Corse
(Corsica)
(to France)

ITALY

ALBANIA   82

GREECE

TURKEY

Sardegna
(Sardinia)
(to Italy)

Tyrrhenian
Sea

Ionian
Sea

Aegean Sea

1

Kritikó Pélagos
(Sea of Crete)

zi

Annaba

Bizerte

TUNIS

Strait of Sicily

Sicilia
(Sicily)

MALTA

Kríti (Crete)

ELEVATION

étif

Constantine

Sousse

Batna

Kairouan

Kasserine

Mahdia

35°

Biskra

Gafsa

Sfax

Golfe de Gabès

M e d i t e r r a n e a n   S e a

Al Baydā'   Darnah

Al Marj   Ţubruq

50   2

4000 m
13 124 ft

Tozeur

Gabès

Île de Jerba

ŢARĀBULUS
(TRIPOLI)

Banghāzī
(Benghazi)

Al Jabal al Akhḍar

2000 m
6562 ft

Touggourt

Médenine

El Oued

TUNISIA

Zuwārah

Az Zāwiyah

Al Khums

Mişrātah

Khalīj Surt
(Gulf of Sirte)

Ajdābiyā

Wādī al Ḥamīm

Al Jaghbūb

30°

1000 m
3281 ft

ardaïa

Ouargla

Nālūt

Gharyān

Yafran

Surt

Marsá al Burayqah

500 m
1640 ft

Marādah

Jālū

EGYPT

250 m
820 ft

Grand Erg Oriental

Waddān

Great Sand Sea

3

100 m
328 ft

A

Bordj Omar Driss

Birāk

L   I   B   Y   A

Sea
Level

Sea
Level

Tiguentourine

Sabhā

25°

-250 m
-820 ft

Awbārī

Zawīlah

Ramlat Rabyānah

Libyan

-500 m
-1640 ft

Tassili-n'Ajjer

Al 'Uwaynāt

Al Khufrah

Tropic of Cancer

-1000 m
-3281 ft

Djanet

Idhān

Desert

50   4

Tahat
2918m

Murzuq

Pic Bette
2286m

20°

-2000 m
-6562 ft

Tamanrasset

a

r

Tibesti

-3000 m
-9843 ft

Ahaggar

Erdi

Erdi Ma

Ennedi

-4000 m
-13 124 ft

Massif
de l'Aïr

Ténéré

SUDAN

5

N   I   G   E   R

C   H   A   D

15°

54

E   F   G   H

5°   10°   15°   20°   25°

NORTHEAST AFRICA

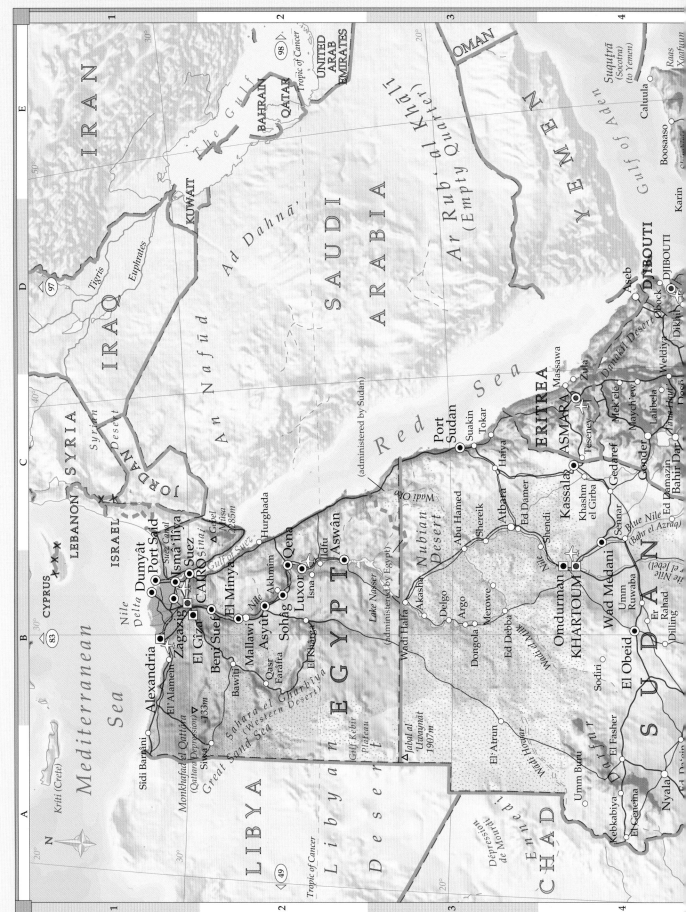

POPULATION

- ● Over 500,000
- ◉ 100,000 – 500,000
- ○ 50,000 – 100,000
- ○ Less than 50,000
- ● National capital

IRAN

IRAQ

SYRIA

LEBANON

ISRAEL

JORDAN

CYPRUS

Kríti (Crete)

Mediterranean Sea

The Gulf

KUWAIT

BAHRAIN

QATAR

UNITED ARAB EMIRATES

OMAN

SAUDI ARABIA

An Nafūd

Ad Dahnā'

Ar Rub' al Khālī (Empty Quarter)

YEMEN

Suquṭrā (Socotra) (to Yemen)

Gulf of Aden

Boosaaso

Raas Xaafuun

Caluula

Karin

Tigris

Euphrates

Syrian Desert

Tropic of Cancer

Red Sea

Port Sudan

Suakin

Tokar

Haiya

ERITREA

Massawa

Zula

ASMARA

Aseb

Dahlak Desert

Obock

DJIBOUTI

Dikhil

Tadjoura

Mek'elē

Maych'ew

Teseney

Gonder

Lalibela

Bahir Dar

Gedaref

Kassala

Khashm el Girba

Ed Damazin

Sennar

Blue Nile (Bahr el Azraq)

Wād Medani

Port Said

Dumyât

Ismā'īliya

Suez

Gulf of Suez

Gebel Mūsa 2285m

Sinai

Hurghada

Qena

Idfu

Aswân

Nubian Desert

Abu Hamed

Shereik

Atbara

Ed Damer

Shendi

Omdurman

KHARTOUM

Umm Ruwaba

Alexandria

El'Alamein

Zagazig

El Gîza

CAIRO

Beni Suef

El Minya

Mallawi

Asyût

Akhmîm

Sohâg

Luxor

Isna

El Kharga

EGYPT

Lake Nasser

(administered by Egypt)

Wadi Halfa

Akasha

Delgo

Argo

Dongola

Ed Debba

Merowe

Sidi Barrâni

Siwa

Monkhafad el Qattâra (Qattara Depression) -133m

Bawîti

Qasr Farâfra

Sahara el Gharbîya (Western Desert)

Great Sand Sea

Libyan Desert

Gilf Kebir Plateau

△ Jabal al 'Uwaynāt 1907m

El'Atrun

Wadi Howar

Wadi el Milk

Sodiri

Umm Badr

SUDAN

El Obeid

Er Rahad

Dilling

Darfur

El Fasher

Kebkabiya

El Geneina

Nyala

Ennedi

Dépression de Mourdi

CHAD

LIBYA

Tropic of Cancer

INDIAN

OCEAN

SEYCHELLES

COMOROS

MAYOTTE
(to France)

MADAGASCAR

ELEVATION

4000 m 13 124 ft	
2000 m 6562 ft	
1000 m 3281 ft	
500 m 1640 ft	
250 m 820 ft	
100 m 328 ft	
Sea Level	Sea Level
-250 m -820 ft	
-500 m -1640 ft	
-1000 m -3281 ft	
-2000 m -6562 ft	
-3000 m -9843 ft	
-4000 m -13 124 ft	

Sinujiif
Garoowe
Gaalkacyo
Hayo Nuqaaleed
Targeysa
Dhuusa Marreeb
Gellinsoor
Shilabo
O g a d ē n
Beledweyne
Buulobarde
Jawhar
MUQDISHO
(MOGADISHU)
Marka
Baraawe
Xuddur
Baydhabo
Doolow
Wanlaweyn
Baardheere
Jilib
Jamaame
Kismaayo
Buur Gaabo

E T H I O P I A

Mīr'eso
Awash
Nazrēt
ADDIS ABABA
(ADĪS ABEBA)
Negēlē
Jima
Agaro
Gore
Yabelo
Ahero Hūyk
Marsabit
Lake Turkana/
Lake Rudolf
Lake Rudolf

K E N Y A

Great Rift Valley

Highlands

Afmadow
Garissa
Garsen
Malindi
Mombasa
Pemba
Tanga
Zanzibar
Dar es Salaam
Mafia
Mohoro
Kilwa Kivinje
Lindi
Mtwara
Newala
Masasi
Tunduru
Songea
Nyamtumbo
Njombe
Sao Hill
Iringa
Morogoro
Kilosa
Dodoma
Singida
Nzega
Tabora
Shinyanga
Mwanza
Bukoba
Musoma
Nakuru
Nyeri
Kisumu
Eldoret
Meru
Moshi
Kilimanjaro
5895m
Kirinyaga
5200m
Arusha
NAIROBI
Masai
Steppe
Kiambu
Mbale
Lodwar
Lokitaung
Kapoeta
Lira
Gulu
Arua
Masindi
Soroti
Jinja
KAMPALA
Entebbe
Masaka
Mbarara
Kabale
Bukaramula
KIGALI
RWANDA
Lake Kivu
BUJUMBURA
BURUNDI

U G A N D A
T A N Z A N I A
M O Z A M B I Q U E
M A L A W I
Z A M B I A
ANGOLA

Lake
Victoria
Lake Albert
Lake Edward
Lake Tanganyika
Lake Rukwa
Lake Nyasa (Lake Malawi)
Lake Mweru
Lake Bangweulu
Lake Mweru Wantipa

Great Rift Valley

Mpanda
Nyakaliro
Nyantakara
Kasulu
Kigoma
Malagarasi
Kipili
Sumbawanga
Mbeya

D E M. R E P. C O N G O

Congo Basin
Lualaba
Sankuru
Kasai
Luvua
Lufira
Lukuga
Lualaba
Luapula
Kafue
Zambezi
Luangwa
Rio Lúrio
Ruaha
Rufiji
Rovuma

C E N T R A L   A F R I C A N   R E P U B L I C

Massif des Bongo
Bahr Aouk
Raga
Wau
Tonj
Rumbek
Tambura
Yambio
Maridi
Amadi
Bor
Juba
Duk Faiwil
Kongor
Kotto
Bomu
Uele
White Nile (Bahr el Jebel)
Sudd
Elemi Triangle
(administered
by Kenya)

Equator

SEYCHELLES

51

WEST AFRICA

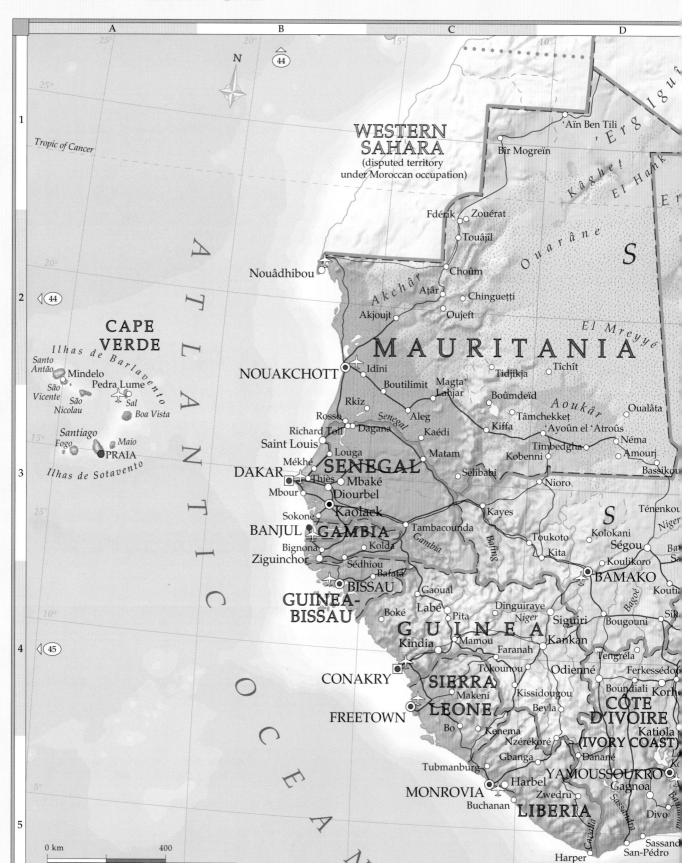

WESTERN SAHARA
(disputed territory
under Moroccan occupation)

Aïn Ben Tili

Bîr Mogreïn

Fdérik • Zouérat

Touâjîl

Choûm

Nouâdhibou

Atâr • Chinguetti

Akjoujt • Oujeft

MAURITANIA

CAPE VERDE

Ilhas de Barlavento

Santo Antão

Mindelo

Pedra Lume

São Vicente

São Nicolau • Sal

Boa Vista

NOUAKCHOTT

Idîni

Boutilimit

Tidjikja • Tîchît

Magta Lahjar

Boûmdeïd • Aoukâr • Oualâta

Rkîz • Aleg • Tâmchekkeṭ

Rosso • *Senegal* • Kaédi • Kiffa • Ayoûn el 'Atroûs • Néma

Richard Toll • Dagana • Amourj

Saint Louis • Matam • Timbedgha • Bassikou

Santiago

Fogo • Maio

Louga • Kobenni

Sélibabi • Nioro

PRAIA

Ilhas de Sotavento

DAKAR

Mékhé • **SENEGAL**

Thiès • Mbaké

Mbour • Diourbel

Kayes • Ténenkou

Sokone • Kaolack • Kolokani • Ségou

BANJUL • **GAMBIA**

Tambacounda • Toukoto • Koulikoro

Bignona • Kolda • Kita • **BAMAKO**

Ziguinchor • *Gambia* • Kouti

Sédhiou • **S**

Balafa

BISSAU • Gaoual • Sik

GUINEA-BISSAU • Labé • Dinguiraye • Siguiri • Bougouni

Boké • Pita • *Niger* • Kankan

GUINEA

Mamou • Tengréla

Kindia • Faranah

CONAKRY • Tokounou • Odienné • Ferkessédo

SIERRA • Kissidougou • Boundiali • Korh

Makeni • Beyla • **CÔTE**

FREETOWN • **LEONE** • **D'IVOIRE**

Bo • Kenema • (**IVORY COAST**)

Nzérékoré • Katiola

Gbanga • Ďanané • Divo

Tubmanburg • **YAMOUSSOUKRO** • Gagnoa

Harbel • Gagnoa

MONROVIA • Zwedru

Buchanan • **LIBERIA** • Divo

Harper • Sassand

San-Pédro

ATLANTIC OCEAN

Tropic of Cancer

POPULATION

● Over
500,000

◉ 100,000 –
500,000

○ 50,000 –
100,000

○ Less than
50,000

● National
capital

0 km — 400

0 miles — 400

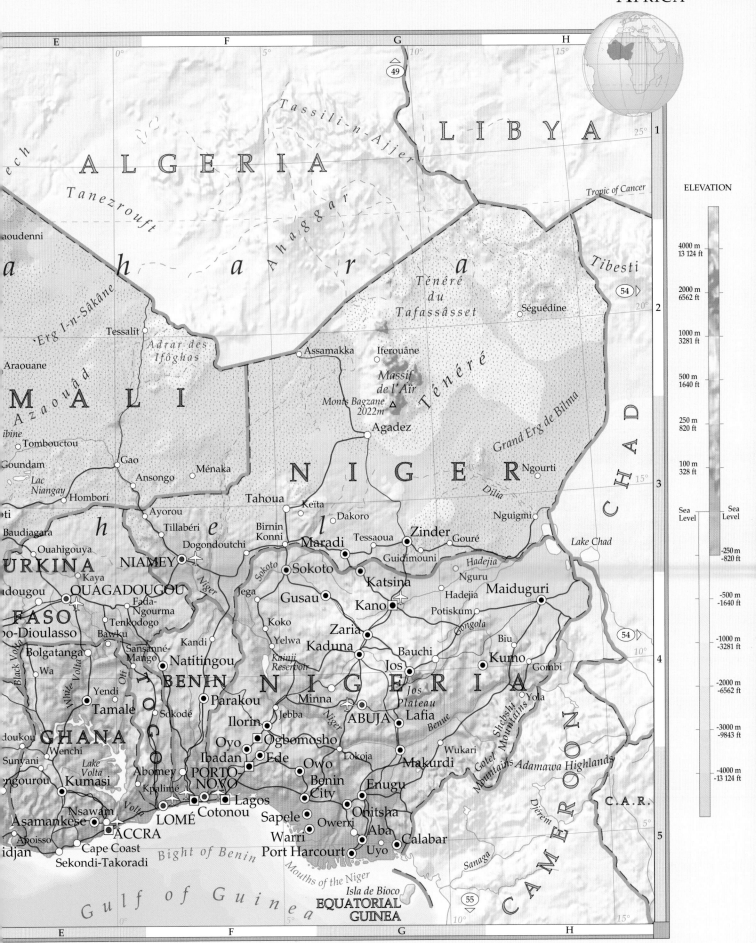

E 0°   F   5°   G   10°   H   15°

49

L I B Y A

A L G E R I A   25° 1

Tassili-n-Ajjer

Tanezrouft

Tropic of Cancer

aoudenni

Tibesti

a   *h*   *A h a g g a r*   *a*   *r*   *a*

*Ténéré
du
Tafassâsset*

54   20° 2

Séguédine

'Erg I-n-Sâkâne

Tessalit

*Adrar des
Ifôghas*

Assamakka   Iferouâne

Araouane

M A L I   *Massif
de l' Aïr*   *Ténéré*

Azaouâd   Monts Bagzane
2022m

ibine   Agadez

Tombouctou   *Grand Erg de Bilma*

Goundam   Gao   *N I G E R*   Ngourti

*Lac
Niangay*   Ansongo   Ménaka   *Dilia*   15° 3

oti   Hombori   Tahoua   Keïta   Dakoro   Nguigmi

Baudiagara   Ayorou   *l*   Tessaoua   Zinder   *Lake Chad*   *C H A D*

Ouahigouya   Tillabéri   *e*   Birnin
Konni   Maradi   Guidimouni   Gouré

URKINA   NIAMEY   *h*   Dogondoutchi   *Hadejia*

dougou   Kaya   *Niger*   Sokoto   Nguru

OUAGADOUGOU   Jega   Katsina   Hadejia   Maiduguri

FASO   Fada-
Ngourma   Koko   Gusau   Kano   Potiskum   10° 4

o-Dioulasso   Tenkodogo   Yelwa   Zaria   *Gongola*   Biu

Bolgatanga   Bawku   Kandi   Kaduna   Bauchi   Kumo

Wa   Sansanné-
Mango   *Kainji
Reservoir*   Jos   Gombi

doukou   *Oti*   *BENIN*   *N I G E R I A*   *Jos
Plateau*   Yola

GHANA   Yendi   Parakou   Minna   *Shebshi
Mountains*   *Adamawa Highlands*

Tamale   Sokodé   Ilorin   Jebba   ABUJA   Lafia   *Benue*

doukou   Wenchi   Oyo   Ogbomosho   *Niger*   Wukari

Sunyani   *Lake
Volta*   Ibadan   Ede   Lokoja   Makurdi   *Mountains*   *Goter*   C. A. R.

ngourou   Kumasi   Abomey   PORTO-
NOVO   Owo   Benin
City   Enugu   5° 5

Nsawam   Kpalimé   Lagos   Onitsha   *Djérem*

Asamankese   LOMÉ   Cotonou   Sapele   Owerri   Aba   *Sanaga*

Apoisso   Cape Coast   Warri   Uyo   Calabar

idjan   Sekondi-Takoradi   *Bight of Benin*   Port Harcourt   *C A M E R O O N*

Gulf of Guinea   *Mouths of the Niger*   55

0°   *Isla de Bioco*
**EQUATORIAL
GUINEA**   5°   10°   15°

E   F   G   H

ELEVATION

4000 m
13 124 ft

2000 m
6562 ft

1000 m
3281 ft

500 m
1640 ft

250 m
820 ft

100 m
328 ft

Sea
Level   Sea
Level

-250 m
-820 ft

-500 m
-1640 ft

-1000 m
-3281 ft

-2000 m
-6562 ft

-3000 m
-9843 ft

-4000 m
-13 124 ft

CENTRAL AFRICA

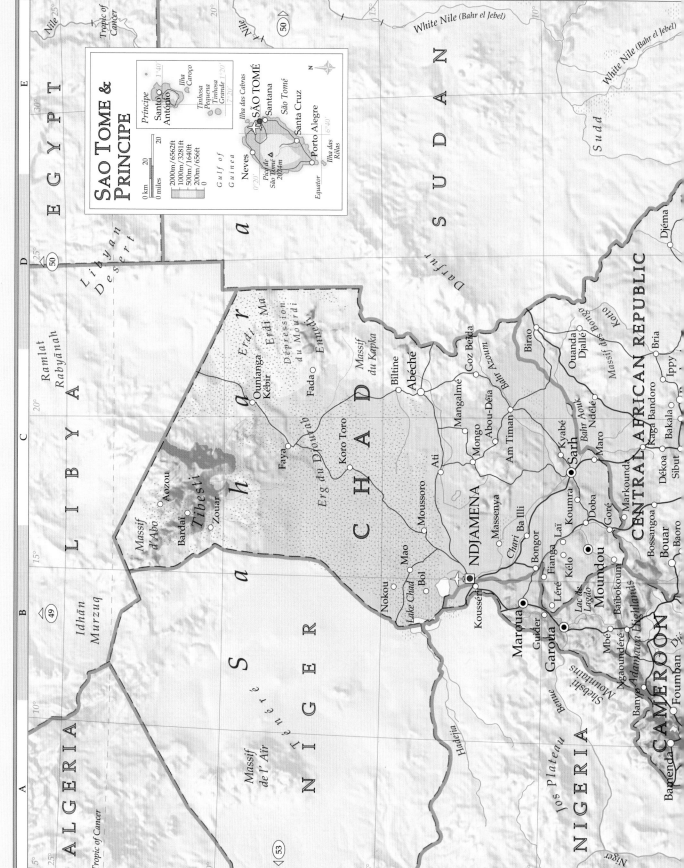

SÃO TOMÉ & PRÍNCIPE

Príncipe
Santo Antônio
Ilha Caroço
Ilha Tinhosa
Tinhosa Pequena
Tinhosa Grande

Ilha das Cabras
SÃO TOMÉ
Santana
São Tomé
Santa Cruz
Neves
Porto Alegre
Pico de São Tomé 2024m
Ilha das Rôlas

Gulf of Guinea

Equator

2000m/6562ft
1000m/3281ft
500m/1640ft
200m/656ft

0 km 20
0 miles 20

POPULATION

- Over 500,000
- 100,000 – 500,000
- 50,000 – 100,000
- Less than 50,000
- National capital

EGYPT

SUDAN

Sudd

Darfur

White Nile (Bahr el Jebel)

Nile

LIBYA

Libyan Desert

Ramlat Rabyānah

Idhān Murzuq

ALGERIA

Tropic of Cancer

NIGER

Ténéré

Massif de l'Aïr

Hadejia

Niger

S a h a r a

CHAD

 Erdi
Erdi Ma
Erdi Ma
Dépression du Mourdi
Ennedi

Ounianga Kébir
Fada
Massif du Kapka
Biltine
Abéché
Goz Beïda
Birao
Ouanda Djallé
Massif des Bongo
Kotto
Djéma

Faya
Koro Toro
Erg du Djourab
Ati
Mangalmé
Mongo
Abou-Déïa
Am Timan
Bahr Azoum
Kyabé
Bahr Aouk
Ndélé
Raga
Bandoro
Bria
Ippy
Bakala

Tibesti
Aozou
Azou
Bardaï
Zouar
Massif d'Abo

Moussoro
Massenya
Maro
Sarh
Markounda
Bossangoa
Dékoa
Sibut
Baoro

Mao
Nokou
Bol
Lake Chad
NDJAMENA
Chari Ba Illi
Bongor
Fianga
Laï
Koumra
Doba
Goré
Moundou
Bouar
Kousséri
Massenya

CENTRAL AFRICAN REPUBLIC

CAMEROON

Maroua
Guider
Garoua
Mbé
Ngaoundéré
Shebshi Mountains
Bénue
Adamawa Highlands
Léré
Kélo
Baïbokoum
Lac de Léré
Lac de Lagdo
Mbéré
Banyo
Tibati
Foumban
Bamenda

NIGERIA

Jos Plateau

Tropic of Cancer

Gulf of Guinea

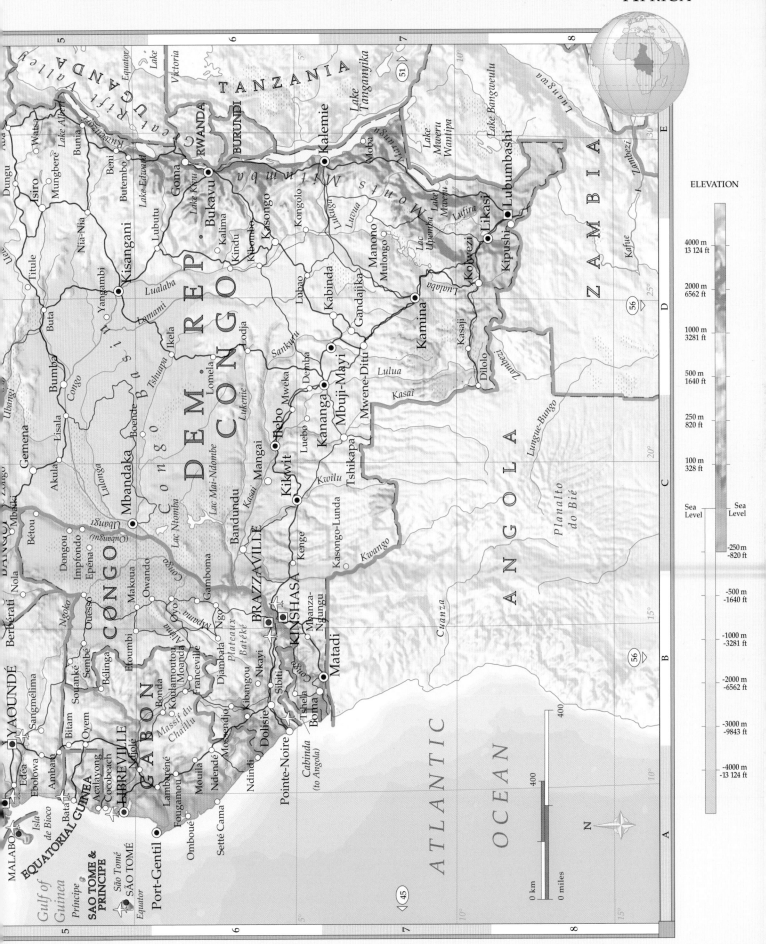

ELEVATION

4000 m
13 124 ft

2000 m
6562 ft

1000 m
3281 ft

500 m
1640 ft

250 m
820 ft

100 m
328 ft

Sea Level — Sea Level

−250 m
−820 ft

−500 m
−1640 ft

−1000 m
−3281 ft

−2000 m
−6562 ft

−3000 m
−9843 ft

−4000 m
−13 124 ft

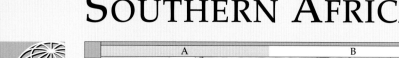

THE WORLD ATLAS

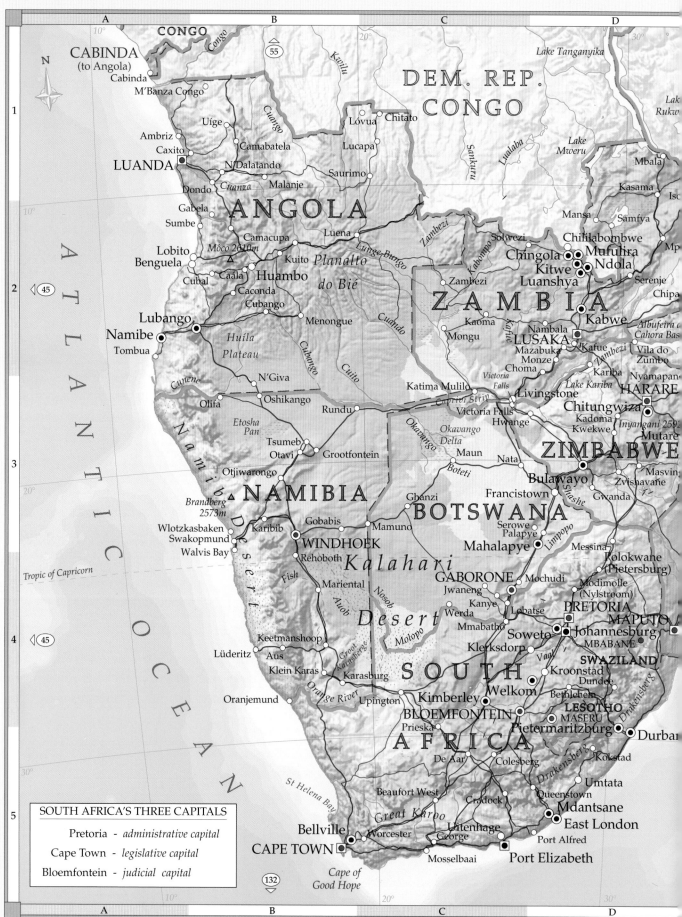

CONGO

CABINDA
(to Angola)
Cabinda
M'Banza Congo
Uíge
Ambriz
Caxito
LUANDA
Dondo
Cuanza
Gabela
Sumbe
Camacupa
Lobito
Benguela
Môco 2610m
Kuito
Caála Huambo
Cubal
Caconda
Cubango
Lubango
Namibe
Tombua
Menongue

DEM. REP. CONGO

Lóvua   Chitato
Lucapa
Camabatela
N'Dalatando   Saurimo
Malanje

ANGOLA

Luena   *Lunge-Bungo*
Zambezi
Planalto do Bié
Cuando

Lake Tanganyika

Mbala
Kasama
Mansa   Samfya
Chililabombwe
Chingola   Mufulira
Kitwe   Ndola
Luanshya   Serenje
Solwezi
Zambezi

ZAMBIA

Kaoma   Nambala   Kabwe
Mongu   *Kafue*   *Albufeira da Cahora Bassa*
LUSAKA   Kafue   Vila do Zumbo
Mazabuka   *Zambezi*
Monze   Kariba
Choma   Nyangani
Victoria Falls   Lake Kariba
Katima Mulilo   Livingstone   HARARE
Caprivi Strip   Victoria Falls   Chitungwiza
Rundu   Hwange   Kadoma   *Inyangani 2592*
Oshikango   Kwekwe   Mutare
Okavango   Maun   ZIMBABWE
Okavango Delta   Nata   Bulawayo   Masvingo
Boteti   Zvishavane
Ghanzi   Francistown   Gwanda
Serowe
BOTSWANA   Palapye   Messina
Mahalapye   *Limpopo*   Polokwane (Pietersburg)
GABORONE   Mochudi   Modimolle (Nylstroom)
Jwaneng   Kanye   PRETORIA   MAPUTO
Werda   Lobatse   Soweto   Johannesburg
Mmabatho   MBABANE
Klerksdorp   SWAZILAND
Kroonstad   Dundee
Welkom   Bethlehem
Kimberley   *Vaal*   LESOTHO
BLOEMFONTEIN   MASERU
Pieteritzburg   Durban
Kokstad
Umtata
Queenstown
Mdantsane
East London
Port Alfred

Lake Mweru

Serenje
Chipa

Cuango
Congo
Kasai
Sankuru
Lualaba

ATLANTIC OCEAN

Huíla Plateau
N'Giva
Olifa
Cunene
Etosha Pan
Tsumeb
Otavi   Grootfontein
Otjiwarongo
Brandberg 2573m
NAMIBIA
Wlotzkasbaken
Swakopmund   Karibib   Gobabis
Walvis Bay
Rehoboth   WINDHOEK   Mamuno
Kalahari
Mariental   *Desert*
Fish   *Nosob*
Auob
Keetmanshoop   *Molopo*
Lüderitz   Aus
Klein Karas
Karasburg
Oranjemund   Upington
Orange River   Kimberley
Prieska
De Aar
Colesberg
SOUTH

Tropic of Capricorn

Namib Desert

SOUTH AFRICA

St Helena Bay
Beaufort West
Cradock
Great Karoo
Bellville   Worcester   Uitenhage
CAPE TOWN   George   Port Elizabeth
Mosselbaai
Cape of Good Hope

SOUTH AFRICA'S THREE CAPITALS

Pretoria - *administrative capital*

Cape Town - *legislative capital*

Bloemfontein - *judicial capital*

E   F   G   H

118

ANZANIA

MALAWI

Great Ruaha

Mzuzu

Lake Nyasa

Negomane   *Rio Rovuma*   Mocímboa da Praia

LONGWE   *Rio Lugenda*   Mucojo

Rio Messalo

Salima   Pemba

Monkey Bay   *Rio Lúrio*   Lúrio

Zomba   Nacala

Blantyre   Lumbo

Milange   Nampula

Mocuba

anje   Quelimane

Beira

Machanga

Inhambane

Quissico

ai

SEYCHELLES

Amirante Islands   VICTORIA
Mahé
Inner Islands

Outer Islands

Aldabra Group

Farquhar Group

COMOROS

MORONI   *Grande Comore*
Anjouan

Mohéli   MAMOUDZOU

MAYOTTE
(to France)

Tanjona Bobaomby

Antsirañana

Ambanja   *Maromokotro*
2376m
Analalava   Sambava
Antsohihy
Antalaha
Mahajanga   Maroantsetra

Bemaraha

Fenoarivo

Toamasina

ANTANANARIVO

Morondava   Betafo

Makay   Ambositra

Mananjary

Mangoky   Fianarantsoa

Ihosy   Manakara

Toliara   Farafangana

Vangaindrano

Tanjona Vohimena   Amboasary

MAURITIUS

PORT LOUIS

ST-DENIS
RÉUNION
(to France)

Mascarene Islands

Tropic of Capricorn

MADAGASCAR

Mozambique Channel

I N D I A N

O C E A N

119

119

132

ELEVATION

4000 m	13 124 ft
2000 m	6562 ft
1000 m	3281 ft
500 m	1640 ft
250 m	820 ft
100 m	328 ft
Sea Level	Sea Level
-250 m	-820 ft
-500 m	-1640 ft
-1000 m	-3281 ft
-2000 m	-6562 ft
-3000 m	-9843 ft
-4000 m	-13 124 ft

0 km   400

0 miles   400

E   F   G   H

POLITICAL FEATURES

TOTAL AREA:
4,809,200 sq miles
(12,456,000 sq km)

TOTAL NUMBER OF COUNTRIES:
43

TOTAL POPULATION:
582.5

LARGEST CITY WITH POPULATION:
Moscow, European Russia 9 million

COUNTRY WITH HIGHEST POPULATION DENSITY:
Monaco 42,104 people per sq mile
(16,256 people per sq km)

LARGEST COUNTRY:
European Russia 1,527,341 sq miles
(3,955,818 sq km)

SMALLEST COUNTRY:
Vatican City, Italy 0.17 sq miles
(0.44 sq km)

PHYSICAL FEATURES

LARGEST LAKE:
Lagoda, European Russia
7,100 sq miles (18,390 sq km)

LONGEST RIVER:
Volga, European Russia
2,290 miles (3,688 km)

HIGHEST POINT:
El'brus, Caucasus Mts, European Russia
18,510ft (5,642 m)

LOWEST POINT:
Volga Delta, Caspian Sea, European
Russia 92 ft (28m) below sea level

POPULATION

▪ Over 500,000

◉ 100,000 – 500,000

○ 50,000 – 100,000

○ Less than 50,000

● National capital

ATLANTIC OCEAN

Reykjanes Ridge

REYKJAVÍK
ICELAND
Vatnajökull

Limit of winter pack ice

Arctic Circle

Iceland Basin

Faeroe-Iceland Ridge

Norwegian Basin

Norwegian Sea

FAEROE ISLANDS (to Denmark)

Faeroe-Shetland Trough

Trondheim

Hatton Ridge

Shetland Islands

Bergen

Rockall Bank

Outer Hebrides

Orkney Islands

Stavanger

OSLO

Rockall Trough

British Isles

Glasgow
Edinburgh

Ireland

Belfast

North Sea

Gothenburg

Ålborg

Jönkö

REPUBLIC OF IRELAND

ISLE OF MAN (to UK)
DUBLIN

UNITED KINGDOM

DENMARK
Odense

COPENH

Maln

Porcupine Plain

Liverpool
Manchester

Britain

Celtic Sea

Birmingham

Cardiff

LONDON

NETHERLANDS
THE HAGUE
AMSTERDAM
Rotterdam

Hamburg

Hannover

BERLIN

Elbe

N

Celtic Shelf

English Channel

CHANNEL IS. (to UK)

BELGIUM
BRUSSELS

le Havre

Liège
Bonn

GERMANY

Wrocła

Biscay Plain

Rennes

LUXEMBOURG
LUXEMBOURG

Frankfurt am Main

PRA

Seine

PARIS

Nantes

Loire

Orleans

Rhine

Stuttgart

CZECH REPUBI

A Coruña

Bay of Biscay

FRANCE

Strasbourg

Munich

Galicia Bank

Bordeaux

Bilbao

Cordillera Cantábrica

Massif Central

Mont Blanc 4807m

Zürich

BERN

SWITZERLAND

Innsbruck

LIECH.
VIENNA

Salzburg
AUSTRIA

Azores-Biscay Rise

Charcot Seamounts

Iberian Plain

Porto

Duero

Pyrenees

Lyon

Garonne

Toulouse

Rhône

Milan

Po

Turin

Venice

SLOVENIA
LJUBLJ

Trieste

CRO

Iberian Plain

PORTUGAL

Iberian Peninsula

Zaragoza

Ebro

ANDORRA

Marseille

Nice

MONACO

Pisa

Bologna

SAN MARINO

BO

Tagus Plain

Horseshoe Seamounts

LISBON

Tagus

MADRID

SPAIN

Guadalquivir

Barcelona

Valencia

Corsica

ITALY

VATICAN CITY
ROME

Apennines

Adriatic Se

SAR

Most

Madeira (to Portugal)

Seville

Málaga

Palma

Balearic Islands

Sardinia

Naples

Bari

Algerian Basin

Tyrrhenian Sea

GIBRALTAR (to UK)

Strait of Gibraltar

Ceuta (to Spain)

Cagliari

Cosenza

Canary Islands (to Spain)

Melilla (to Spain)

Mediterranea

Palermo

Sicily

Mount Etna 3340m

Catania

Io

Ba

Atlas Mountains

AFRICA

MALTA
VALLETTA

0 km   500

0 miles   500

Barents Sea

North Cape

Ostrov Kolguyev

Arctic Circle

Ob'

Ural Mountains

133

Irtysh

Murmansk

Kola
Peninsula

White
Sea

Archangel

Northern Dvina

R U S S I A N

80°

1

FINLAND

Gulf of Bothnia

Lake Onega

Perm'

F E D E R A T I O N

90

70°

2

50°

Tampere

Lake Ladoga

Vologda

Saint Petersburg

Ufa

Aland
asala

Turku   HELSINKI

Yaroslavl'

Kazan'

OCKHOLM   TALLINN

Nizhniy
Novgorod

ESTONIA

MOSCOW

Ul'yanovsk

Orenburg

LATVIA

Samara

RĪGA

Ural

LITHUANIA

Volga Uplands

Volga

3

LININGRAD
(to Russ.Fed.)

Central
Russian
Upland

Syr Darya

ngrad

Kaunas

Vitsyebsk

VILNIUS

MINSK

Aral Sea

goszcz

Babruysk

Voronezh

Ural

WARSAW

BELARUS

Homyel'

Amu Darya

Brest

Pripet
Marshes

Dnieper Lowlands

Don

LAND

Bug

KIEV

Kharkiv

Volgograd

Kraków

L'viv

Dnieper

Astrakhan'

Carpathian Mountains

Dniester

UKRAINE

Dnipropetrovs'k

VAKIA

Chernivtsi

Donets'k

Rostov-na-Donu

APEST

MOLDOVA

Caspian Sea

40°

GARY   Cluj-Napoca

CHIŞINĂU

Sea of
Azov

Stavropol'

90

60°

4

ROMANIA

Odesa

Crimea

Braşov

Simferopol'

Caucasus

El'brus 5642m

BELGRADE

BUCHAREST

Black Sea

SERB.
& MON.
(YUGO.)

Constanţa

BULGARIA

Varna

Danube

Balkan Mountains

SKOPJE   SOFIA

Burgas

MACED.

TURKEY

RANA

ANIA

Aegean
Sea

Anatolia

A S I A

Pindus Mountains

GREECE   ATHENS

30°

5

Piraeus

Peloponnese

Zagros Mountains

Tigris

e a

Cyprus

Euphrates

50°

Irákleio

96

Crete

THE NORTH ATLANTIC

Arctic Circle

Gulf of Boothia

Devon Island

Ellesmere Island

Nares Strait

NUNAVUT

Hudson Bay

Southampton Island

Foxe Basin

CANADA

Baffin Island

Baffin Bay

Qaanaaq

Knud Rasmussen L.

Innaanganeq

Savissivik

Qimusseriarsuaq

Kullorsuaq

Upernavik

Péninsule d'Ungava

QUEBEC

Hudson Strait

Arnaud

Cumberland Sound

Frobisher Bay

Baffin Island

Davis Strait

Limit of summer pack ice

Uummannaq

Qeqertarsuaq

Qeqertarsuaq

Qeqertarsuup Tunua

Qasigiannguit

Sisimiut

Kong Frederik IX Land

GREENLAND

(to Denmark)

Ungava Bay

George

Maniitsoq

NUUK

Kong Christian IX Land

Gunnbjørn F

Mont Forel 3360m

Ammassalik

Denmar

Paamiut

Ivittuut

Labrador Sea

Kong Frederik VI Kyst

Qaqortoq

Nanortalik

Nunap Isua (Kap Farvel)

Limit of winter pack ice

Reykjanes Basin

ATLANTIC OCEAN

NEWFOUNDLAND & LABRADOR

POPULATION

- ● Over 500,000
- ◉ 100,000 – 500,000
- ○ 50,000 – 100,000
- ○ Less than 50,000
- ● National capital

0 km   400

0 miles   400

ARCTIC
OCEAN

*Lincoln
Sea*

Kap Morris Jesup

*Wandel
Sea*

Independence Fjord

Nord

SVALBARD
(to Norway)

*Zemlya
Frantsa-Iosifa*

Kvitøya

Nordaustlandet

*Novaya
Zemlya*

Kong Karls Land

Spitsbergen

Barentsøya

*Barents
Sea*

LONGYEARBYEN

Barentsberg

Edgeøya

Storfjorden

*Greenland
Sea*

Limit of winter pack ice

Bjørnøya
(to Norway)

Nordkapp
(North Cape)

Daneborg

Limit of summer pack ice

△ Petermann Bjerg
2940m

*King Christian X
Land*

Kong Frederik VIII Land

Kong Oscar Fjord

Mohns Ridge

F I N L A N D

Ittoqqortoormiit

Kangertittivaq

Kangikajik

JAN MAYEN
(to Norway)

*Norwegian
Sea*

Vestfjorden

Arctic Circle

trait

ICELAND

Norwegian Basin

**S
W
E
D
E
N**

Bolungarvík

Siglufjördhur

Raufarhöfn

fjördhur

Húsavík

Akureyri

Seydhisfjördhur

Stykkishólmur

Neskaupstadhur

REYKJAVÍK

Vatnajökull

Selfoss

Djúpivogur

flói

*Gulf
of
Bothnia*

orlákshöfn

Hvannadalshnúkur
2119m

Surtsey

Vestmannaeyjar

FAEROE ISLANDS
(to Denmark)

N O R W A Y

N

TÓRSHAVN

*Shetland
Islands*

ELEVATION

4000 m 13 124 ft	
2000 m 6562 ft	
1000 m 3281 ft	
500 m 1640 ft	
250 m 820 ft	
100 m 328 ft	
Sea Level	Sea Level
-250 m -820 ft	
-500 m -1640 ft	
-1000 m -3281 ft	
-2000 m -6562 ft	
-3000 m -9843 ft	
-4000 m -13 124 ft	

SCANDINAVIA & FINLAND

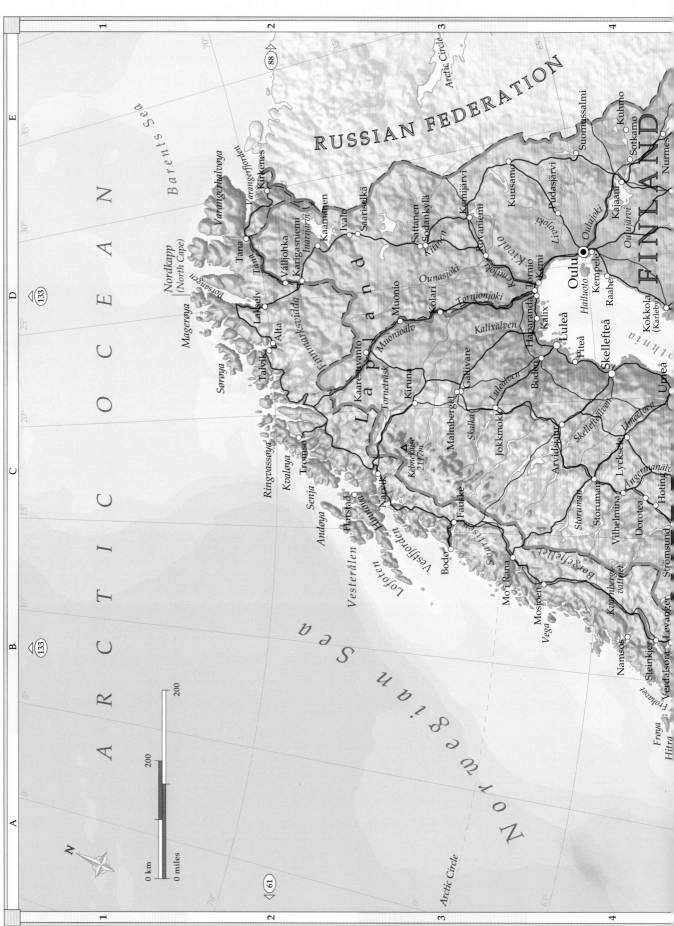

POPULATION

- ■ Over 500,000
- ◉ 100,000 – 500,000
- ○ 50,000 – 100,000
- ○ Less than 50,000
- ● National capital

N

RUSSIAN FEDERATION

FINLAND

Barents Sea

ARCTIC OCEAN

Nordkapp (North Cape)
Varangerhalvøya
Varangerfjorden
Kirkenes
Tana
Vardø
Vadsø
Vålljohka
Karigasniemi
Inarijärvi
Kaamanen
Ivalo
Saariselkä
Mageroya
Soroya
Porsangen
Lakselv
Alta
Talvik
Finnmarksvidda
Muonio
Sattanen
Sodankylä
Kittilä
Kemijärvi
Kuusamo
Pudasjärvi
Suomussalmi
Sotkamo
Kuhmo
Nurmes
Kajaani
Oulujärvi
Oulujoki
Oulu
Kempele
Hailuoto
Raahe
Kokkola (Karleby)
Kovaniemi
Ounasjoki
Rovaniemi
Kemijoki
Kentjoki
Kivalo
Kolari
Tornionjoki
Tornio
Haparanda
Kemi
Kalix
Luleå
Piteå
Skellefteå
Umeå
Kaaresuvanto
Torneträsk
Kiruna
Kalixälven
Muonioälv
Muonioälv
Kebnekaise 2117m
Malmberget
Gällivare
Skaite
Jokkmokk
Luleälven
Boden
Bodø
Fauske
Saltfjorden
Arvidsjaur
Skellefteälven
Lycksele
Ångermanälv
Hoting
Storuman
Vilhelmina
Dorotea
Strömsund
Mo-Rana
Mosjøen
Vega
Namsos
Steinkjer
Levanger
Verdalsøra
Froan
Frøya
Hitra
Ringvassøya
Kvaløya
Senja
Tromsø
Andøya
Harstad
Hinnøya
Narvik
Vesterålen
Lofoten
Vestfjorden
Borgefjellet
Kvarnbergs-vattnet

Norwegian Sea

Arctic Circle

Lapland

Gulf of Bothnia

62

RUSS. FED.

BELARUS

LATVIA

LITHUANIA

ESTONIA

POLAND

GERMANY

DENMARK

NORWAY

ELEVATION

4 000 m
13 124 ft

2000 m
6562 ft

1000 m
3281 ft

500 m
1640 ft

250 m
820 ft

100 m
328 ft

Sea Level

Sea Level

-50 m
-164 ft

-100 m
-328 ft

-250 m
-820 ft

-500 m
-1640 ft

-1000 m
-3281 ft

-2000 m
-6562 ft

KALININGRAD
(to Russian Federation)

Ladozhskoye Ozero

Varkaus
Haukivesi
Saimaa
Imatra
Outseno
Äänekoski
Nadavesi
Jyväskylä
Keuru
Seinäjoki
Lapua
Näsijärvi
Kankaanpää
Närpes (Närpiö)
Pori
Rauma
Nokia
Tampere
Hämeenlinna
Riihimäki
Hyvinkää
Vantaa
HELSINKI
Espoo
Porvoo
Kouvola
Kotka
Lappeenranta
Lahti
Salo
Turku (Åbo)
Hanko (Hangö)

Gulf of Finland

Lake Peipus

Hiiumaa
Saaremaa
Gulf of Riga

Gulf of Bothnia

Åland
Ålands hav

Härnösand
Sundsvall
Hudiksvall
Söderhamn
Gävle
Kramfors
Timrå
Ange
Ljusdal
Bollnäs
Leksand
Rättvik
Mora
Malung
Sveg
Idre
Svenstavik
Ratan
Klarälven
Borlänge
Ludvika
Falun
Avesta
Sala
Sandviken
Tierp
Uppsala
Norrtälje
Täby
STOCKHOLM
Södertälje
Mälaren
Västerås
Enköping
Örebro
Sollentuna
Nyköping
Flen
Katrineholm
Norrköping
Linköping
Hjälmaren
Askersund
Mariestad
Vättern
Motala
Vänern
Jönköping
Borås
Mölndal
Kungsbacka
Varberg
Ljungby
Lahom
Göteborg (Gothenburg)
Halmstad
Helsingborg
Lund
Malmö
Kristianstad
Karlskrona
Karlshamn
Växjö
Oskarshamn
Borgholm
Kalmar
Öland
Visby
Gotland

Baltic Sea

Ronne
Bornholm

Oder

Courland Lagoon
Gulf of Danzig
Wisla
Neman
Western Dvina

Røros
Dombås
Andalsnes
Ringebu
Hamar
Lillehammer
Gjøvik
Mjøsa
Lillestrøm
OSLO
Ski
Moss
Drammen
Sandvika
Horten
Kongsberg
Sarpsborg
Halden
Fredrikstad
Strömstad
Mellerud
Uddevalla
Trollhättan
Åmål
Säffle
Lidköping
Grums
Karlstad
Filipstad

Gol
Geilo
Eidfjord
Hardangervidda
Setesdal
Haugesund
Stavanger
Sandnes
Moi
Evje
Kristiansand
Bergen
Leirvik
Sognefjorden
Hardanger
Boknafjorden

North Sea

Skagerrak

Hjørring
Ålborg
Hobro
Randers
Århus
Holstebro
Viborg
Silkeborg
Jylland
KØBENHAVN (Copenhagen)
Slagelse
Sjælland
Møn
Falster
Lolland
Nyköbing
Odense
Fyn
Kolding
Varde
Esbjerg
Ringkøbing Fjord
Storebælt
Kattegat

Hanöbukten

Elbe
Weser
Ems

89
76
72
67

△ Glittertind 2464 m
Jotunheimen

THE LOW COUNTRIES

THE WORLD ATLAS

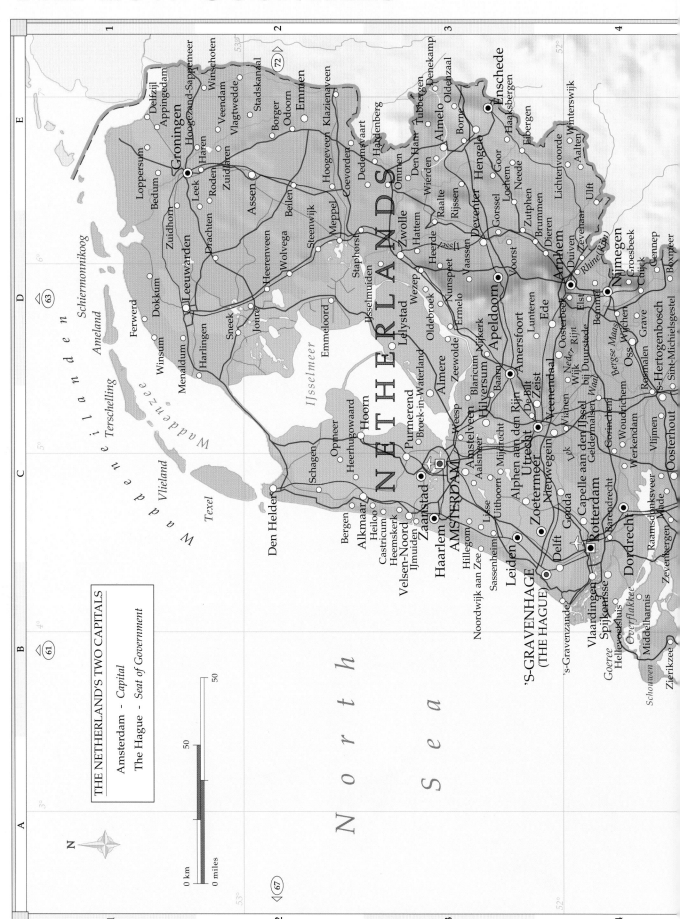

POPULATION

- ⊡ Over 500,000
- ◉ 100,000 - 500,000
- ○ 50,000 - 100,000
- ○ Less than 50,000
- ● National capital

THE NETHERLAND'S TWO CAPITALS

Amsterdam - *Capital*
The Hague - *Seat of Government*

50

50

0 km
0 miles

N

North Sea

Waddenzee

Waddeneilanden

Schiermonnikoog
Ameland
Terschelling
Vlieland
Texel

IJsselmeer

NETHERLANDS

Groningen
Delfzijl
Appingedam
Hoogezand-Sappemeer
Winschoten
Veendam
Vlagtwedde
Stadskanaal
Loppersum
Bedum
Zuidhorn
Haren
Leek
Roden
Zuidlaren
Borger
Odoorn
Emmen
Klazienaveen
Hoogeveen
Coevorden
Dedemsvaart
Hardenberg
Den Ham
Tubbergen
Denekamp
Enschede
Oldenzaal
Haaksbergen
Eibergen
Winterswijk
Aalten
Ulft
Lichtenvoorde
Ommen
Wierden
Almelo
Borne
Hengelo
Goor
Lochem
Neede
Rijssen
Raalte
Deventer
Gorssel
Zutphen
Brummen
Dieren
Vaassen
Voorst
Apeldoorn
Epe
Heerde
Hattem
Zwolle
Staphorst
Meppel
Steenwijk
Wolvega
Heerenveen
IJsselmuiden
Lelystad
Emmeloord
Oldebroek
Kunspeet
Ermelo
Wezep
Nijkerk
Baarn
Hilversum
Blaricum
Weesp
Zeewolde
Almere
Broek-in-Waterland
Purmerend
Hoorn
Heerhugowaard
Opmeer
Schagen
Bergen
Alkmaar
Heiloo
Castricum
Heemskerk
Velsen-Noord
IJmuiden
Den Helder
AMSTERDAM
Zaanstad
Haarlem
Aalsmeer
Amstelveen
Uithoorn
Mijdrecht
Amersfoort
Lunteren
Ede
Oosterbeek
Wijk bij Duurstede
De Bilt
Utrecht
Zeist
Veenendaal
Vianen
Apeldoorn
Arnhem
Elst
Bennekom
Nijmegen
Groesbeek
Gennep
Cuijk
Boxmeer
Sint-Michielsgestel
's-Hertogenbosch
Grave
Wijchen
Oss
Ravenstein
Woudrichem
Vlijmen
Oosterhout
Made
Raamsdonksveer
Zevenbergen
Middelharnis
Zierikzee
Schouwen
Overflakkee
Goeree
Hellevoetsluis
'S-GRAVENHAGE (THE HAGUE)
's-Gravenzande
Vlaardingen
Spijkenisse
Rotterdam
Dordrecht
Barendrecht
Werkendam
Gorinchem
Capelle aan den IJssel
Geldermalsen
Gouda
Lek
Nieuwegein
Zoetermeer
Delft
Leiden
Sassenheim
Hillegom
Lisse
Noordwijk aan Zee
Zoetermeer
Alphen aan den Rijn
Nieder Rijn
Lek
Waal
Bergse Maas
Rhine (Rijn)
Duiven
Zevenaar

Ferwerd
Dokkum
Winsum
Menaldum
Harlingen
Leeuwarden
Drachten
Sneek
Joure
Staphorst

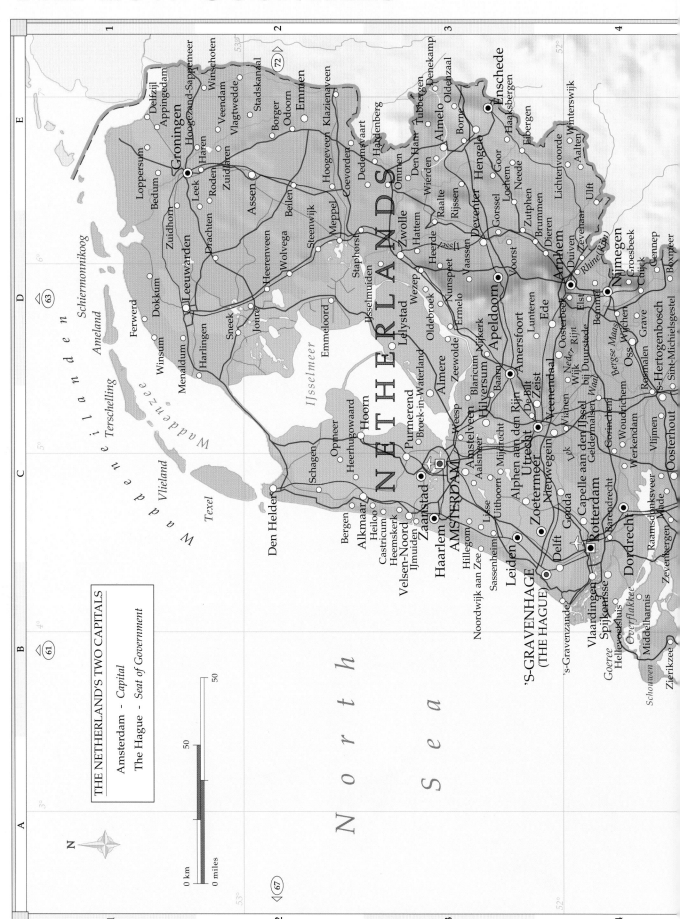

64

5 6 7 8

GERMANY

Rhine (Rhein)

Mosel

(72)

50°

51°

Venlo
Baarle-Hertog (Veldhoven)
Eindhoven
Someren
Nederweert
Reuver
Beesel
Roermond
Posterholt
Weert
Echt
Susteren
Sittard
Geleen
Heerlen
Kerkrade
Simpelveld
Vaals
Maastricht
Eijsden
Visé
Herstal
Liège
Seraing
Verviers
Eupen
Malmédy
Weiswampach
Hosingen
Diekirch
Ettelbrück
Grevenmacher
LUXEMBOURG
LUXEMBOURG
Alzette
Pétange
Differdange
Dudelange
Esch-sur-Alzette
Arlon
Aubange
Étalle
Virton

4000 m
13 124 ft

2000 m
6562 ft

1000 m
3281 ft

6°

(68)

Essen
Kalmthout
Brecht
Kapellen
Schoten
Schelde
Wijnik
Antwerpen (Antwerp)
Schaerbeek
BRUSSEL/BRUXELLES (BRUSSELS)
Halle
Tubize
Braine-le-Comte
Enghien
Ath
Leuze-en-Hainaut
Péruwelz
Tournai
Mouscron
Kortrijk

B E L G I U M

Nijlen
Duffel
Mechelen
Lier
Zemst
Vilvoorde
Tervuren
Overijse
Wavre
Louvain-la-Neuve
Ottignies
Gembloux
Éghezée
Namur
Charleroi
Châtelet
Gerpinnes
Binche
Anderlues
Morlanwelz
La Louvière
Mons
Jemappes

Leuven
Tienen
Landen
Waremme
Amay
Huy
Andenne
Ciney
Dinant
Rochefort
Recogne
Bastogne
Neufchâteau
Marche-en-Famenne
Couvin
Walcourt

Hasselt
Genk
Tongeren
Bilzen
Riemst
Oupeye
Meersen
Bree
Maaseik
Kinrooi
Peer
Bergijk
Beringen
Diepenbeek
Herk-de-Stad
Zonhoven

Ourthe
Semois
Meuse
Lesse
A r d e n n e
F a g n e
F a m e n n e
Hautes Fagnes
Botrange 694m
Vesdre
Our
Süre
Mosselle
Alzette

F R A N C E

L o r r a i n e

Somme
Oise
Sambre
Dender
Schelde

500 m
1640 ft

250 m
820 ft

100 m
328 ft

5°

Sea Level

Vissingen
Zuid-Beveland
Westerschelde
Knokke-Heist
Zeebrugge
Blankenberge
Oostende (Ostend)
Middelkerke
Koksijde
Veurne
Nieuwpoort
Poperinge
Ieper
Roeselare
Torhout
Brugge (Bruges)
Eeklo
Aalter
Beernem
Deinze
Gent (Ghent)
Zelzate
Assenede
Oostakker
Willebroek
Sint-Niklaas
Beveren
Hulst
Terneuzen
Axel
Stabroek

F l a n d e r s
IJzer
Leie

4°

(68)

3°

A
B
C
D
E

ELEVATION

Sea Level
-10 m -33 ft
-25 m -82 ft
-50 m -164 ft
-100 m -328 ft
-250 m -820 ft
-500 m -1640 ft

THE BRITISH ISLES

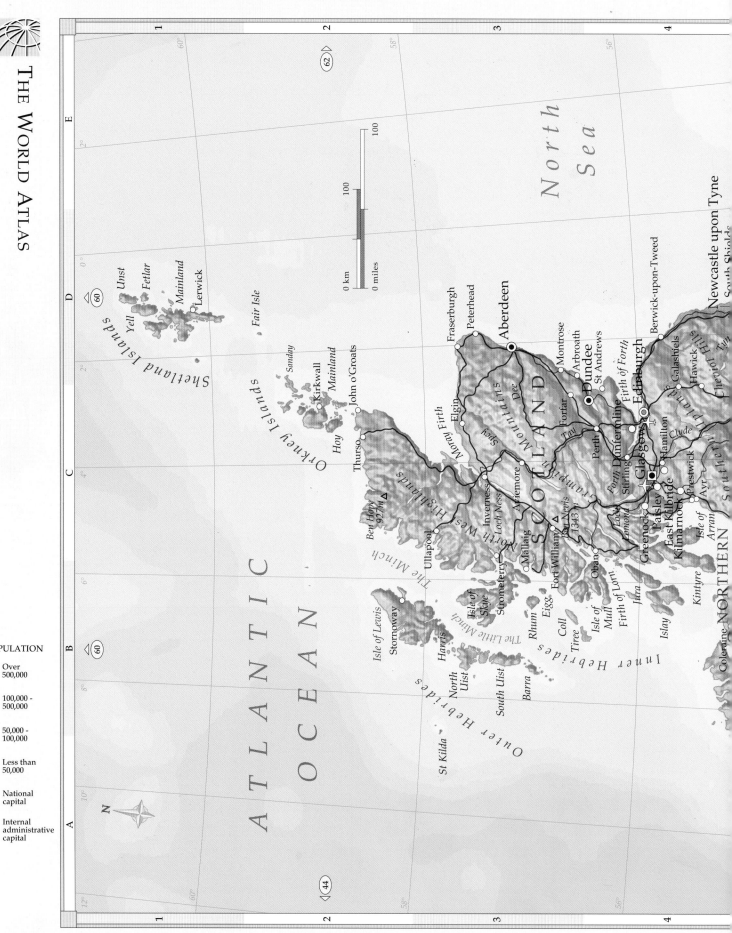

POPULATION

- Over 500,000
- 100,000 – 500,000
- 50,000 – 100,000
- Less than 50,000
- National capital
- Internal administrative capital

ATLANTIC OCEAN

North Sea

SCOTLAND

Shetland Islands

Unst
Fetlar
Yell
Mainland
Lerwick

Fair Isle

Orkney Islands

Sanday
Kirkwall
Mainland
Hoy
John o'Groats

Thurso

Ben Hope 927m

North West Highlands

The Minch

Ullapool

Stornoway
Isle of Lewis
Harris
North Uist
South Uist
Barra
St Kilda

Outer Hebrides

The Little Minch

Isle of Skye
Stromeferry
Rhum
Eigg
Coll
Tiree
Isle of Mull
Firth of Lorn
Jura
Islay

Inner Hebrides

Mallaig
Fort William
Ben Nevis 1343m
Oban
Kintyre
Isle of Arran

Inverness
Aviemore
Loch Ness
Spey
Grampian Mountains
Dee
Elgin
Moray Firth

Fraserburgh
Peterhead
Aberdeen
Montrose
Arbroath
Forfar
Dundee
St Andrews
Perth
Tay
Firth of Forth
Dunfermline
Loch Lomond
Forth
Stirling
Clyde
Greenock
Glasgow
Paisley
Hamilton
East Kilbride
Kilmarnock
Prestwick
Ayr

Edinburgh
Galashiels
Hawick
Cheviot Hills
Southern
Berwick-upon-Tweed
Newcastle upon Tyne
South Shields

Coleraine
NORTHERN

0 km 100
0 miles 100

N

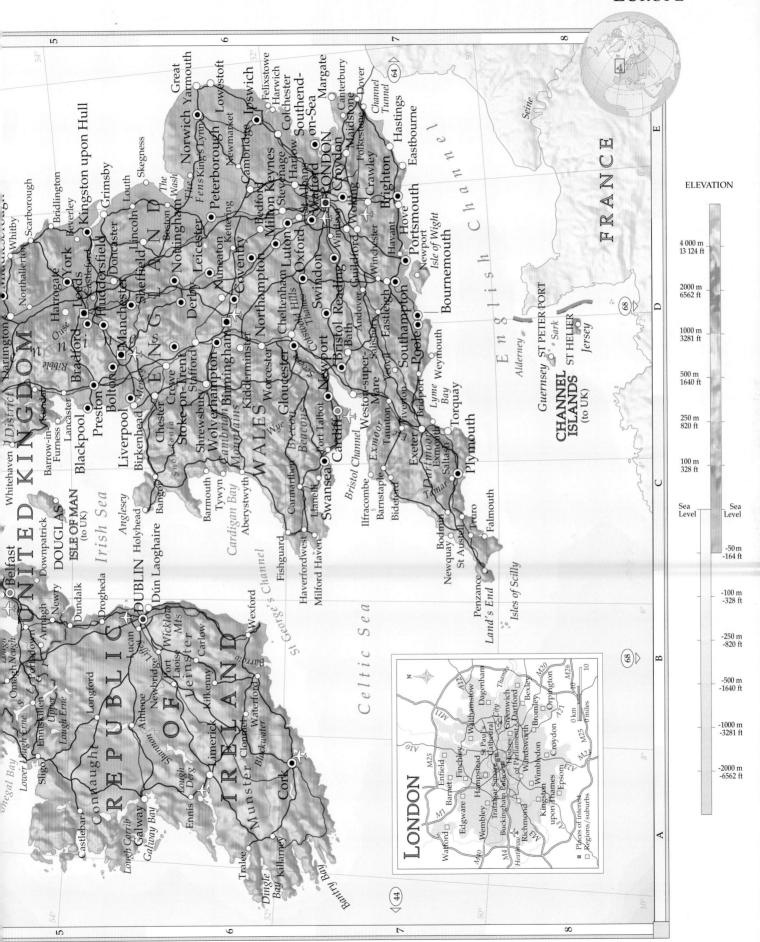

ELEVATION

4 000 m
13 124 ft

2000 m
6562 ft

1000 m
3281 ft

500 m
1640 ft

250 m
820 ft

100 m
328 ft

Sea Level — Sea Level

-50 m
-164 ft

-100 m
-328 ft

-250 m
-820 ft

-500 m
-1640 ft

-1000 m
-3281 ft

-2000 m
-6562 ft

FRANCE, ANDORRA & MONACO

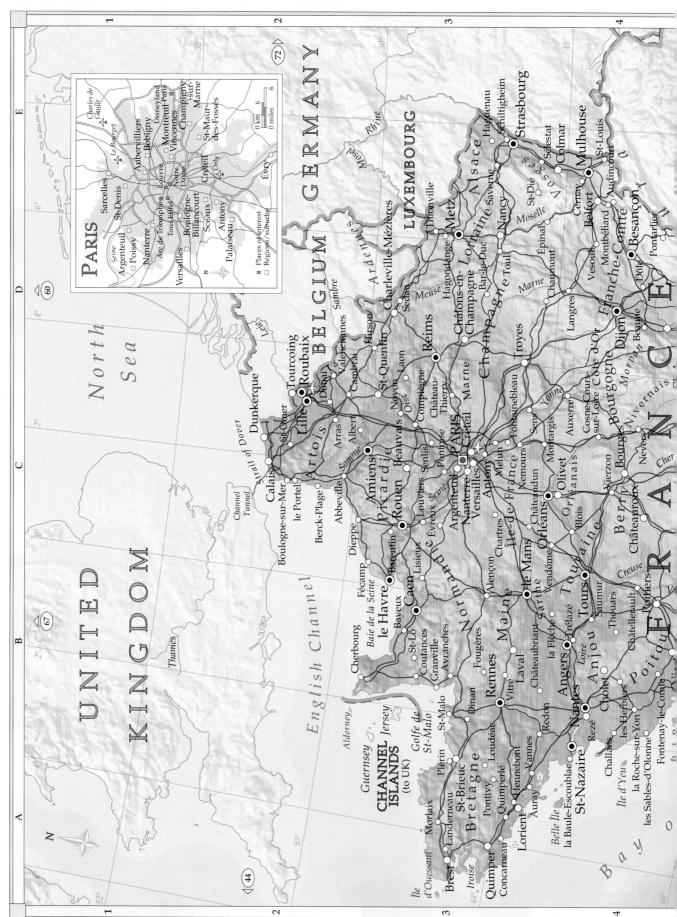

POPULATION

- Over 500,000
- 100,000 – 500,000
- 50,000 – 100,000
- Less than 50,000
- National capital

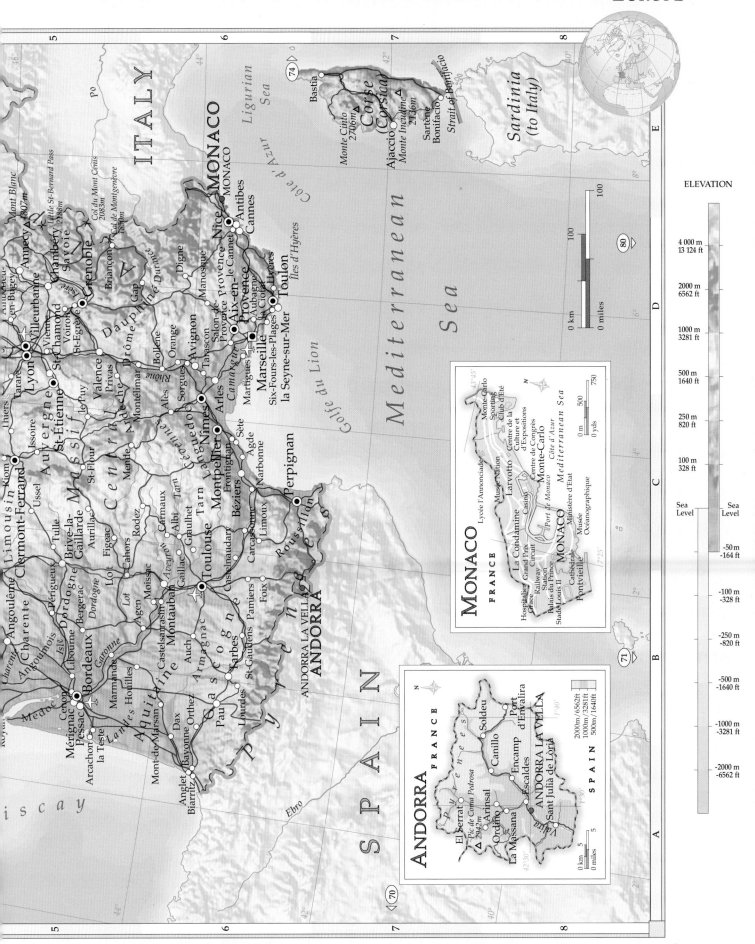

SPAIN & PORTUGAL

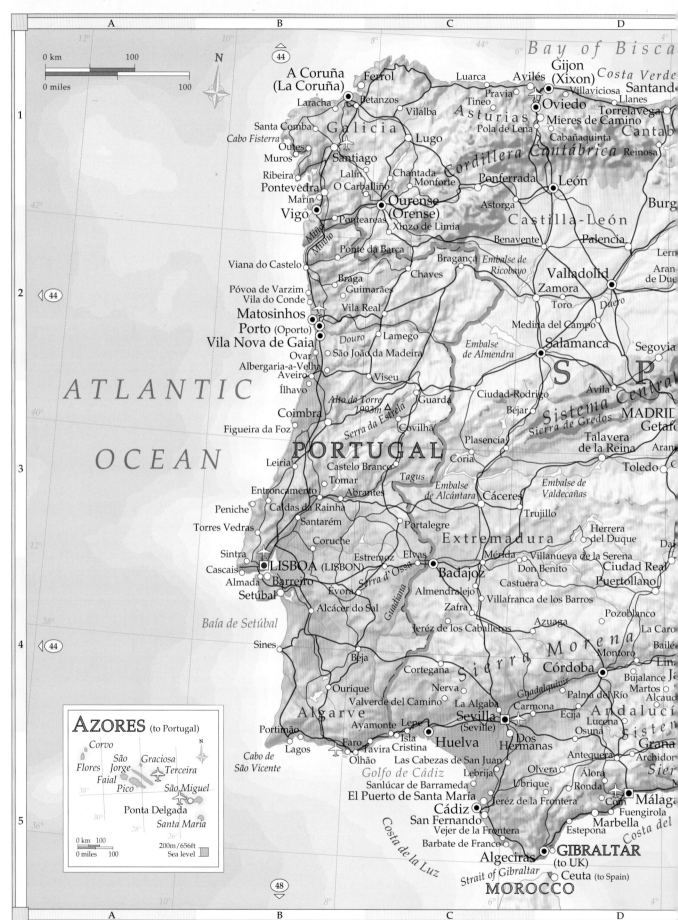

A Coruña (La Coruña)
Ferrol
Betanzos
Laracha
Santa Comba
Cabo Fisterra
Outes
Muros
Ribeira
Pontevedra
Marín
Vigo
Santiago
Lalín
O Carballiño
Ourense (Orense)
Ponteareas
Xinzo de Limia
Viana do Castelo
Póvoa de Varzim
Vila do Conde
Matosinhos
Porto (Oporto)
Vila Nova de Gaia
Ovar
Albergaria-a-Velha
Aveiro
Ílhavo
Coimbra
Figueira da Foz
Leiria
Entroncamento
Peniche
Caldas da Rainha
Torres Vedras
Santarém
Sintra
Cascais
LISBOA (LISBON)
Almada
Barreiro
Setúbal
Sines
Beja
Ourique
Portimão
Lagos
Faro
Olhão
Tavira
Cabo de São Vicente

Luarca
Avilés
Gijon (Xixon)
Costa Verde
Santand
Pravia
Tineo
Oviedo
Villaviciosa
Llanes
Torrelavega
Mieres de Camino
Reinosa
Pola de Lena
Cabañaquinta
Cantáb
Lugo
Vilalba
Cordillera Cantábrica
Ponferrada
León
Astorga
Burg
Castilla-León
Benavente
Palencia
Aran de Due
Bragança
Embalse de Ricobayo
Valladolid
Zamora
Lern
Chaves
Braga
Guimarães
Vila Real
Toro
Duero
Medina del Campo
Lamego
São João da Madeira
Embalse de Almendra
Salamanca
Douro
Viseu
Segovia
Alto da Torre 1993m
Guarda
Ciudad-Rodrigo
Ávila
S
P
Serra da Estrela
Covilhã
Béjar
Sistema Central
MADRID
Getafe
Castelo Branco
Tagus
Plasencia
Sierra de Gredos
Talavera de la Reina
Aran
Tomar
Coria
Toledo
Abrantes
Cáceres
Embalse de Valdecañas
Embalse de Alcántara
Trujillo
Portalegre
Extremadura
Herrera del Duque
Coruche
Estremoz
Elvas
Mérida
Villanueva de la Serena
Dai
Sierra d' Ossa
Badajoz
Don Benito
Ciudad Real
Évora
Almendralejo
Castuera
Puertollano
Guadiana
Villafranca de los Barros
Alcácer do Sal
Zafra
Pozoblanco
Baía de Setúbal
Jerez de los Caballeros
Azuaga
La Caro
Cortegana
Sierra Morena
Montoro
Bailé
Nerva
Córdoba
Lin
Guadalquivir
Bujalance Ja
Valverde del Camino
La Algaba
Palma del Río
Martos
Alcau
Algarve
Carmona
Ecija
Andalucí
Ayamonte
Lepe
Sevilla (Seville)
Lucena
Sistem
Isla Cristina
Dos Hermanas
Osuna
Gran
Huelva
Antequera
Archidon
Las Cabezas de San Juan
Sier
Golfo de Cádiz
Lebrija
Olvera
Álora
Sanlúcar de Barrameda
Ubrique
Ronda
Córd
Málaga
El Puerto de Santa María
Jerez de la Frontera
Fuengirola
Cádiz
Marbella
Estepona
San Fernando
Costa de
Vejer de la Frontera
GIBRALTAR (to UK)
Barbate de Franco
Algeciras
Ceuta (to Spain)
Costa de la Luz
Strait of Gibraltar
MOROCCO

Bay of Bisca

ATLANTIC

OCEAN

PORTUGAL

POPULATION

- Over 500,000
- 100,000 – 500,000
- 50,000 – 100,000
- Less than 50,000
- National capital

AZORES (to Portugal)

Corvo
Flores
São Jorge
Graciosa
Faial
Terceira
Pico
São Miguel
Ponta Delgada
Santa Maria

0 km 100
0 miles 100
200m/656ft
Sea level

0 km 100
0 miles 100

N

44
44
44
48

F R A N C E

Golfe du Lion

ELEVATION

4000 m
13 124 ft

2000 m
6562 ft

1000 m
3281 ft

500 m
1640 ft

250 m
820 ft

100 m
328 ft

Sea
Level

Sea
Level

-250 m
-820 ft

-500 m
-1640 ft

-1000 m
-3281 ft

-2000 m
-6562 ft

-3000 m
-9843 ft

-4000 m
-13 124 ft

Bermeo
Zarautz
Eibar
Donostia-San Sebastián
Irún
Tolosa
Bergara
País Vasco
Pamplona
(Iruña)
itoria-Gasteiz
Miranda
de Ebro
Estella-Lizarra
ogroño
Navarra
Jaca
Monte Perdido
3348m
La Rioja
Arnedo
Calahorra
Ejea de
los Caballeros
Huesca
ANDORRA
La See d'Urgel
Figueres
Berga
Ripoll
Girona
Banyoles
(Gerona)
Manlleu
Palafrugell
Tudela
Barbastro
Cataluña
Vic
Palamós
Tarazona
Soria
Monzón
Balaguer
Blanes
Burgo
Osma
Zaragoza
Lleida
Cervera
Sabadell
Arenys de Mar
Calatayud
(Lérida)
Terrassa
Mataró
Medinaceli
Daroca
Tarrega
Barcelona
Aragón
Fraga
Vilafranca del Penedès
L'Hospitalet de Llobregat
I
N
Alcañiz
Valls
Sitges
Guadalajara
Reus
El Vendrell
lcalá de Henares
Tortosa
Tarragona
rejón de Ardoz
Costa Brava
Amposta
Teruel
Javalambre
2020m
Sant Carles de la Ràpita
Cuenca
Onda
Vinaròs
Tarancón
Menorca
Ciutadella de Menorca
(Minorca)
Castelló de la Plana
Mahón
astilla-La Mancha
Burriana
Pollença
Sa Pobla
Mota del Cuervo
Vall d' Uxó
Golfo de
Palma
Manacor
Campo de Criptana
Burjassot
Sagunto
Valencia
Llucmajor
Felanitx
Socuéllamos
Torrente
Catarroja
Mallorca
La Roda
Júcar
Sueca
(Majorca)
Tomelloso
Algemesí
Cullera
Cabrera
Xàtiva
Gandía
Islas Baleares
nzanares
Albacete
Oliva
(Balearic Islands)
epeñas
Almansa
Denia
Villanueva de los Infantes
Onthayent
Alcoy
Eivissa
Villena
(Ibiza)
Beas de Segura
Hellín
Jumilla
Elda
Benidorm
Eivissa
Moratalla
Segura
Monóvar
Villajoyosa
Villacarrillo
Cieza
San Juan de Alicante
Formentera
eda
Mula
Elche
Alicante
Cazorla
Murcia
Callosa de Segura
Béticos
Huéscar
Orihuela
Murcia
Costa Blanca
Lorca
La Unión
Baza
Cartagena
Guadix
ulhacén
Aguilas
481m
Mediterranean Sea
evada
Berja
Mojácar
Almería
Adra

A L G E R I A

68

74

75

49

GIBRALTAR (to UK)

N

5° 21'
SPAIN

Gibraltar
Airport

North Mole

Gibraltar
Harbour

Catalan Bay

Catalan
Bay

Rosia

The Rock

Sandy
Bay

36° 8'

Rosia
Bay

Summit
426m

Bay of Gibraltar

Buena Vista

Little
Bay

200m/656ft
Sea level

Europa Point

0 km   1

0 mile   1

Strait of Gibraltar

36°

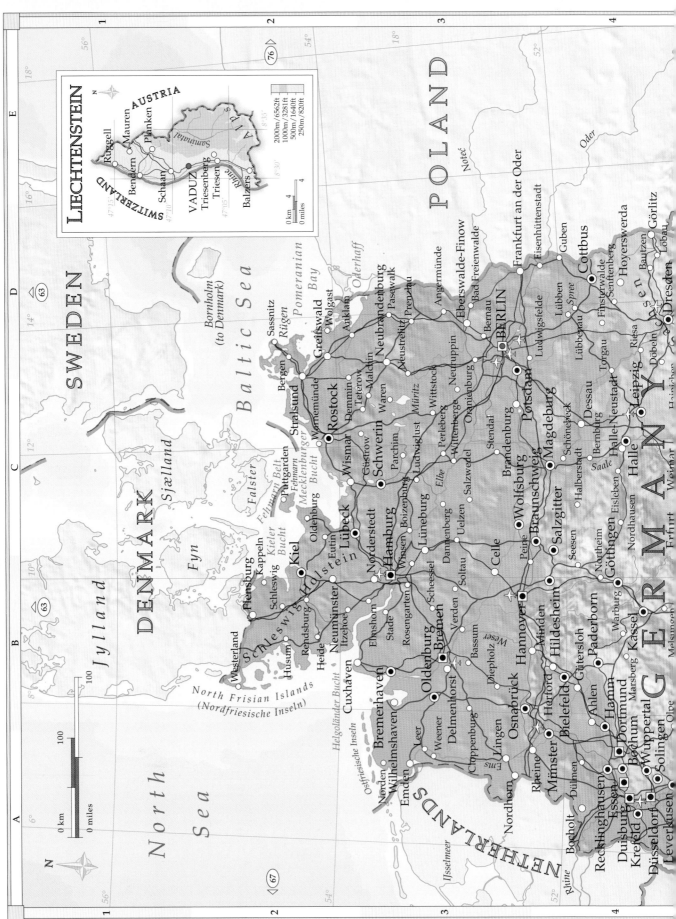

POPULATION

- ▣ Over 500,000
- ◉ 100,000 – 500,000
- ○ 50,000 – 100,000
- ○ Less than 50,000
- ● National capital

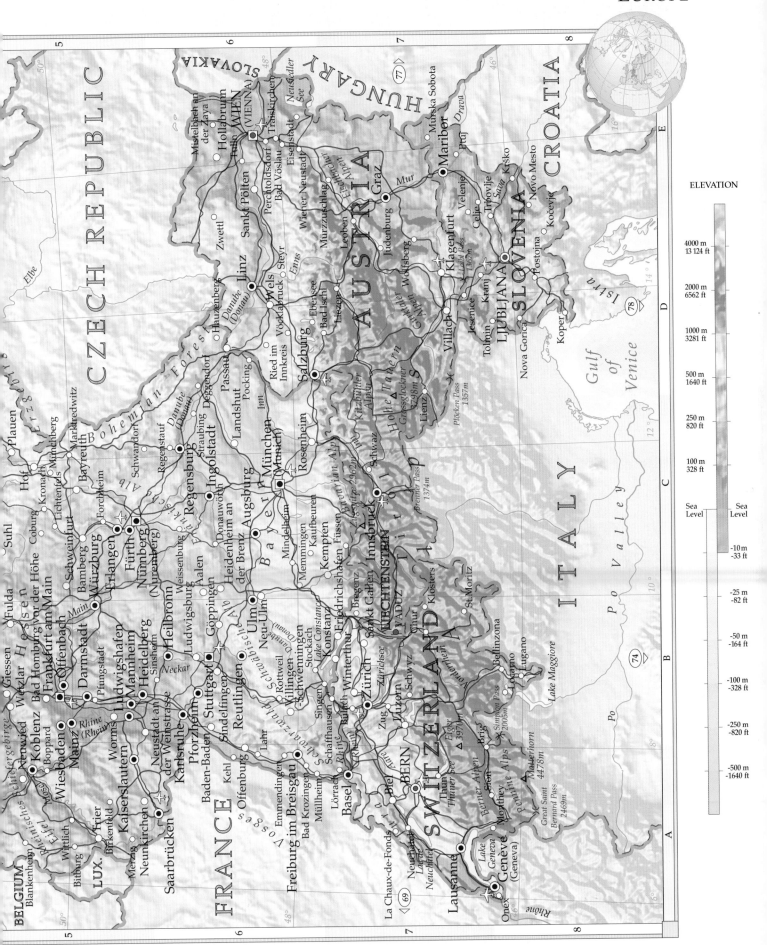

ELEVATION

4000 m 13 124 ft	
2000 m 6562 ft	
1000 m 3281 ft	
500 m 1640 ft	
250 m 820 ft	
100 m 328 ft	
Sea Level	Sea Level
	-10 m -33 ft
	-25 m -82 ft
	-50 m -164 ft
	-100 m -328 ft
	-250 m -820 ft
	-500 m -1640 ft

ITALY

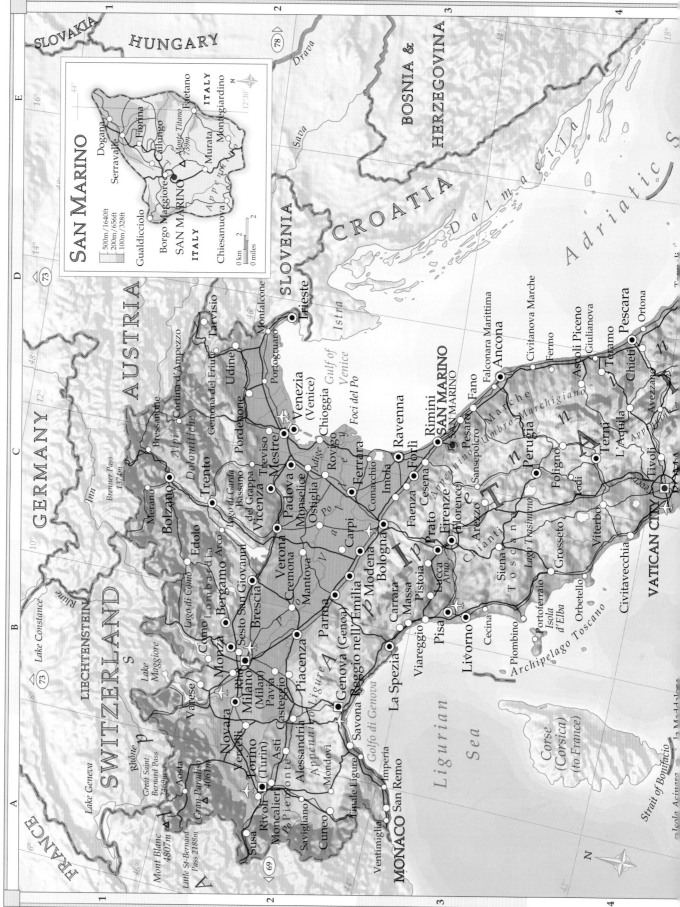

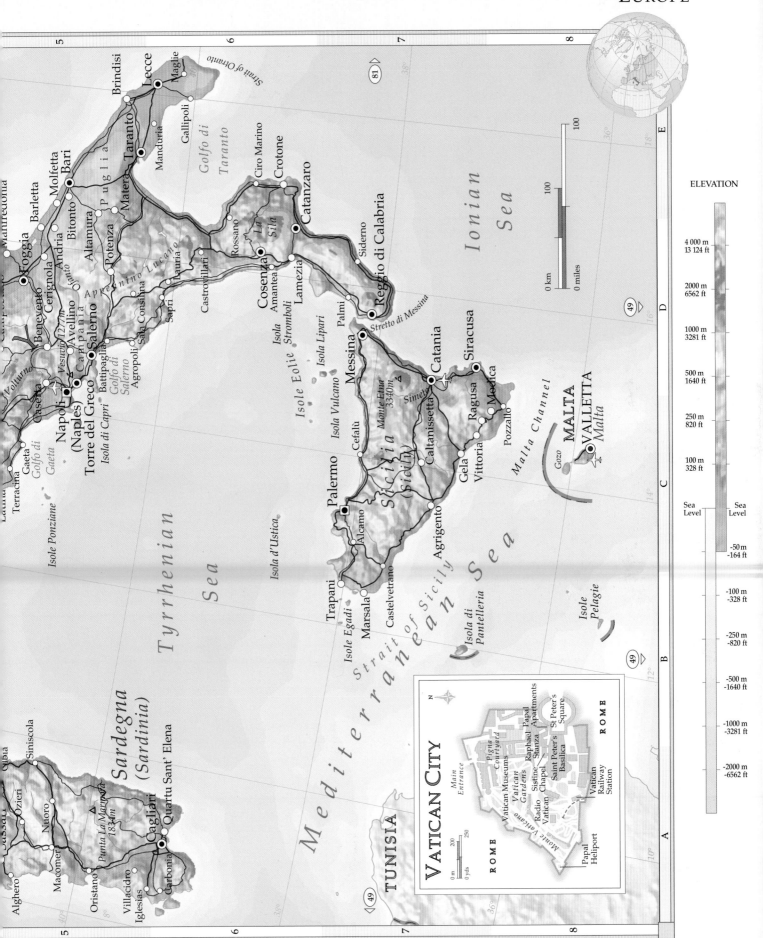

5 6 7 8

81

38°

36°

18°

E

ELEVATION

100

100

0 km

0 miles

D

49

4 000 m
13 124 ft

2000 m
6562 ft

1000 m
3281 ft

500 m
1640 ft

250 m
820 ft

100 m
328 ft

Sea
Level

Sea
Level

-50 m
-164 ft

-100 m
-328 ft

-250 m
-820 ft

-500 m
-1640 ft

-1000 m
-3281 ft

-2000 m
-6562 ft

Brindisi
Lecce
Maglie
Strait of Otranto
Taranto
Manduria
Gallipoli
Golfo di
Taranto
Molfetta
Bari
Bitonto
Matera
Andria
Altamura
Barletta
Puglia
Potenza
Ciro Marino
Crotone
Manfredonia
Cerignola
Foggia
Benevento
Avellino
Quanto
Rossano
La Sila
Catanzaro
Siderno
Appennino Lucano
Sapri
Castrovillari
Cosenza
Amantea
Lamezia
Reggio di Calabria
Vesuvio 1277m
Campania
Salerno
Agropoli
San Consilina
Lauria
Stromboli
Isola
Palmi
Stretto di Messina
Napoli
(Naples)
Torre del Greco
Battipaglia
Golfo di
Salerno
Isola di Capri
Isola Lipari
Messina
Catania
Siracusa
Caserta
Volturno
Isole Eolie
Isola Vulcano
Monte Etna
3340m
Simeto
Medica
Gaeta
Golfo di
Gaeta
Cefalù
Palermo
Caltanissetta
Ragusa
Pozzallo
Terracina
Isole Ponziane
Sicilia
(Sicily)
Gela
Vittoria
Alcamo
Agrigento
Trapani
Marsala
Castelvetrano
Isola d'Ustica
Isole Egadi
Strait of Sicily
Isola di
Pantelleria

Ionian
Sea

Tyrrhenian
Sea

Mediterranean Sea

Malta Channel
Gozo
MALTA
VALLETTA
Malta

Isole
Pelagie

C

14°

B

12°

49

TUNISIA

49

Sardegna
(Sardinia)
Olbia
Siniscola
Siniscola
Ozieri
Nuoro
Punta La Marmora
1834m
Macomer
Cagliari
Quartu Sant' Elena
Alghero
Oristano
Villacidro
Iglesias
Carbonia

A

10°

38°

8°

5 6 7

VATICAN CITY

N

Main
Entrance
Vatican Museums
Vatican
Gardens
Radio
Vatican
Pigna
Courtyard
Raphael
Stanza
Sistine
Chapel
Papal
Apartments
St Peter's
Square
Saint Peter's
Basilica
Vatican
Railway
Station
Monte Vaticano
Papal
Heliport
ROME
ROME
R O M E
0 m 200 250
0 yds

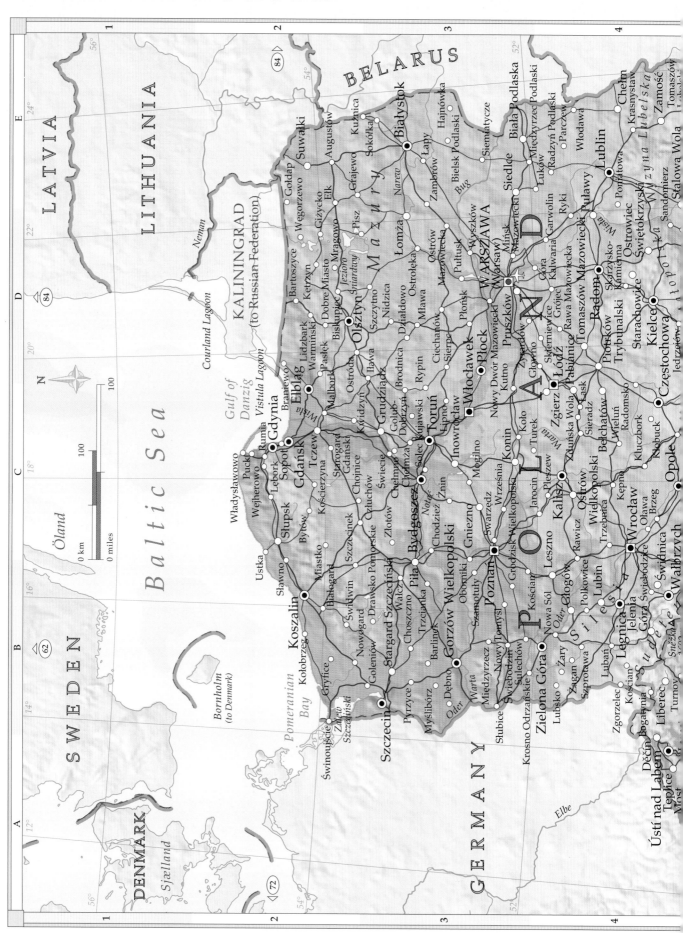

POPULATION

- ◉ Over 500,000
- ◉ 100,000 – 500,000
- ○ 50,000 – 100,000
- ○ Less than 50,000
- ● National capital

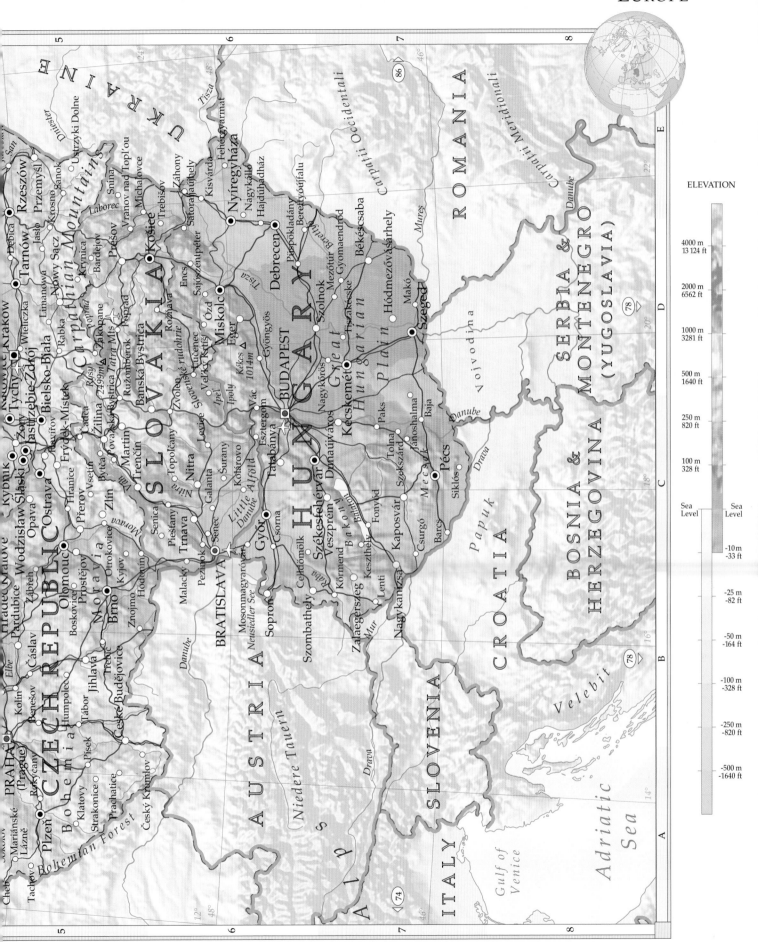

ELEVATION

| 4000 m
13 124 ft |
| 2000 m
6562 ft |
| 1000 m
3281 ft |
| 500 m
1640 ft |
| 250 m
820 ft |
| 100 m
328 ft |
| Sea Level — Sea Level |
| -10 m
-33 ft |
| -25 m
-82 ft |
| -50 m
-164 ft |
| -100 m
-328 ft |
| -250 m
-820 ft |
| -500 m
-1640 ft |

UKRAINE

ROMANIA

Carpaţii Occidentali

Carpaţii Meridionali

SERBIA & MONTENEGRO (YUGOSLAVIA)

BOSNIA & HERZEGOVINA

CROATIA

SLOVENIA

ITALY

AUSTRIA

SLOVAKIA

HUNGARY

CZECH REPUBLIC

Bohemia

Moravia

Carpathian Mountains

Great Hungarian Plain

Little Alföld

Bakony

Mecsek

Papuk

Vojvodina

Velebit

Niedere Tauern

Bohemian Forest

Alps

Adriatic Sea

Gulf of Venice

Neusiedler See

PRAHA (Prague)

BRATISLAVA

BUDAPEST

Debrecen

Miskolc

Szeged

Pécs

Košice

Brno

Ostrava

Nyíregyháza

Kecskemét

Szolnok

Békéscsaba

Hódmezővásárhely

Dunaújváros

Székesfehérvár

Győr

Praha

Mariánské Lázně

Plzeň

Cheb

Tachov

Klatovy

Strakonice

Prachatice

Český Krumlov

České Budějovice

Tábor

Jihlava

Třebíč

Znojmo

Pelhřimov

Písek

Benešov

Čáslav

Kolín

Rokycany

Pardubice

Hradec Králové

Zábřeh

Boskovice

Prostějov

Olomouc

Přerov

Zlín

Kroměříž

Kyjov

Hodonín

Břeclav

Otrokovice

Frýdek-Místek

Ostrava

Opava

Wodzisław Śląski

Jastrzębie-Zdrój

Žory

Tychy

Rybnik

Racibórz

Kraków

Wieliczka

Nowy Sącz

Limanowa

Rabka

Bielsko-Biała

Třinec

Čadca

Žilina

Martin

Trenčín

Púchov

Považská Bystrica

Ružomberok

Poprad

Banská Bystrica

Zvolen

Prešov

Bardejov

Krynica

Sanok

Krosno

Jasło

Debica

Tarnów

Rzeszów

Przemyśl

Ustrzyki Dolne

Snina

Michalovce

Vranov nad Topľou

Trebišov

Humenné

Strážske

Giraltovce

Levoča

Kežmarok

Zakopane

Nitra

Levice

Šurany

Galanta

Senec

Trnava

Piešťany

Topoľčany

Senica

Malacky

Pezinok

Komárno

Mosonmagyaróvár

Sopron

Szombathely

Zalaegerszeg

Nagykanizsa

Lenti

Keszthely

Kaposvár

Csurgó

Barcs

Siklós

Baja

Jánoshalma

Kiskunhalas

Szekszárd

Tolna

Paks

Fonyód

Körmend

Celldömölk

Veszprém

Tatabánya

Esztergom

Vác

Gyöngyös

Eger

Ózd

Sajószentpéter

Encs

Sátoraljaújhely

Sárospatak

Kisvárda

Záhony

Nagykálló

Hajdúnánás

Hajdúhadház

Püspökladány

Berettyóújfalu

Mezőtúr

Tiszakécske

Gyomaendrőd

Makó

Nagykőrös

Cegléd

Szentendre

Fehérgyarmat

Nyírbátror

San

Dniester

Tisza

Tisza

Danube

Danube

Danube

Drava

Drava

Mur

Mures

Berettyó

Laborec

Morava

Elbe

Ipoly

Ipel'

Hron

Nitra

Váh

Rába

Zala

Bükk

Velká Fatra

Nízke Tatry Mts

Vysoké Tatry Mts

Slovenské rudohorie

Gerlachovský štít 2655m

Rysy 2499m

Králov holá 1514m

Kékes 1014m

86

78

78

74

5 6 7 8

E

D

C

B

A

22°

20°

18°

16°

14°

12°

46°

48°

SOUTHEAST EUROPE

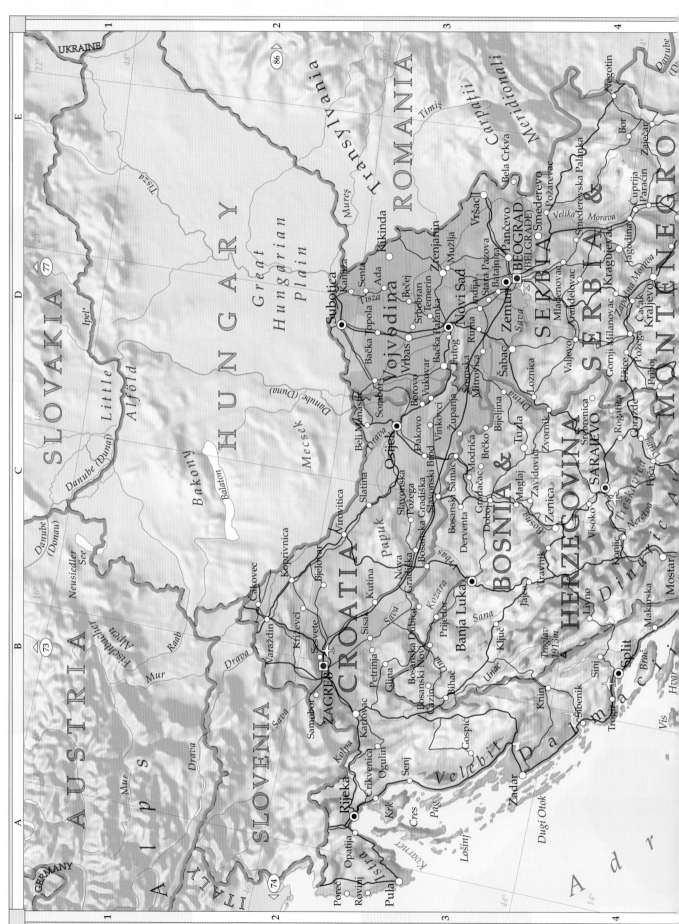

POPULATION

- ◉ Over 500,000
- ◉ 100,000 – 500,000
- ○ 50,000 – 100,000
- ○ Less than 50,000
- ● National capital

UKRAINE

ROMANIA

Transylvania

Carpaţii Meridionali

Timiş

Mureş

SLOVAKIA

AUSTRIA

GERMANY

Ipel'

Danube (Dunaj)

Danube (Donau)

Neusiedler See

Fischbacher Alpen

Little Alföld

Bakony

Balaton

Mecsek

H U N G A R Y

Great Hungarian Plain

Tisza

Tisza

Raab

Mur

Drava

Danube (Duna)

Subotica

Kanjiža

Senta

Ada

Bačka Topola

Bečej

Kikinda

Zrenjanin

Temerin

Srbobran

Vrbas

Bačka Palanka

Muzlja

Vršac

Bela Crkva

Pančevo

BEOGRAD (BELGRADE)

Smederevo

Velika Morava

Smederevska Palanka

Požarevac

Negotin

Bor

Zaječar

VOJVODINA

Novi Sad

Zemun

Batajnica

Stara Pazova

Ruma

Inđija

Šabac

SERBIA

Mladenovac

Aranđelovac

Jagodina

Ćuprija

Paraćin

SERBIA

Gornji Milanovac

Kragujevac

Kraljevo

Zapadna Morava

Čačak

Požega

Užice

Priboj

MONTENEGRO

ITALY

SLOVENIA

A L p s

Mur

Drava

Sava

Kolpa

Čakovec

Varaždin

Koprivnica

Križevci

Sesvete

ZAGREB

Samobor

Karlovac

Petrinja

Glina

Sisak

Kutina

Bjelovar

Virovitica

Slatina

Nova Gradiška

Požega

Slavonski Brod

Slavonska Požega

Osijek

Beli Manastir

Sombor

Apatin

Đakovo

Borovo

Vukovar

Vinkovci

Županja

Srijemska Mitrovica

C R O A T I A

Papuk

Sava

Spreča

Kozara

Una

Sana

Vrbas

Bosna

Drina

Bosanska Dubica

Bosanski Novi

Bosanska Gradiška

Prijedor

Bosanski Šamac

Derventa

Modriča

Gradačac

Doboj

Brčko

Bijeljina

Tuzla

Zvornik

Srebrenica

BOSNIA & HERZEGOVINA

Banja Luka

Ključ

Jajce

Zenica

Zavidovići

Maglaj

Visoko

SARAJEVO

Rogatica

Goražde

Foča

Treskavica

Neretva

Travnik

Konjic

Livno

Troglav 1913 m

Dinarica Alpi

Unac

Knin

Sinj

Mostar

Makarska

Split

Brač

Hvar

Vis

Šibenik

Trogir

Velebit

Kvarner

Rijeka

Opatija

Crikvenica

Ogulin

Senj

Gospić

Zadar

Dugi Otok

Krk

Cres

Pag

Lošinj

Istra

Poreč

Rovinj

Pula

A d r

5   6   7   8

Balkan Mountains

Piroi

Vlasotince

Surdulica

B U L G A R I A

Leskovac

Južna Morava

Vranje

Bujanovac

Radoviš

Strumica

Štip

Bregalnica

Kočani

Strymónas

Strymónas

Podujevo

Gnjilane

Preševo

Kumanovo

Vardar

Vardar

Kavadari

Gevgelija

Thermaïkós
Kólpos

A e g e a n   S e a

Évvoia
(Euboea)

Priština

KOSOVO

SKOPJE

Veles

Prilep

Crna Reka

Bitola

Lake
Prespa

Pinčiós

Kosovska
Mitrovica

Vučitrn

Kosovo Polje

Orahovac

Uroševac

Gostivar

Kičevo

M A C E D O N I A

P i n d o s

(Pindus Mountains)

Peč

Dečani

Djakovica

Prizren

Tetovo

Debar

Struga

Ohrid

Pogradec

Korçë

G R E E C E

Berane

North
Albanian
Alps

Drava

2658m

Kukës

Peshkopi

Black Drim

Lake
Ohrid

Lumi i Devollit

i Drinit

Burrel

Elbasan

Lumi i Osumit

Bajram Curri

Lumi i Drinit

Ilezhe

Burrel

A L B A N I A

Lumi i Vjosës

Lumi Shkumbin

Podgorica

Lumi i

Shkodër

Lezhë

Lac

Krujë

TIRANË
(TIRANA)

Kavajë

Lushnjë

Kuçovë

Berat

Tepelenë

Gjirokastër

Sarandë

Kónispol

Lefkáda

Kérkyra
(Corfu)

I ó n i o i   N í s o i

(Ionian Islands)

MONTENEGRO

Cetinje

Lake Scutari

Bar

Durrës

Fier

Vlorë

Trebinje

Nikšić

Dubrovnik

Mljet

Palagruža

A d r i a t i c   S e a

S t r a i t   o f   O t r a n t o

I o n i a n

S e a

Kefallinía

I T A L Y

Golfo di
Taranto

Appennino Lucano

ELEVATION

4 000 m / 13 124 ft	
2000 m / 6562 ft	
1000 m / 3281 ft	
500 m / 1640 ft	
250 m / 820 ft	
100 m / 328 ft	
Sea Level	Sea Level
-50 m / -164 ft	
-100 m / -328 ft	
-250 m / -820 ft	
-500 m / -1640 ft	
-1000 m / -3281 ft	
-2000 m / -6562 ft	

100 km / 100 miles

0 km / 0 miles

BOSNIA & HERZEGOVINA

S E R B I A (YUGO.)

Drina

M O N T E N E G R O

MONTENEGRO

SERB. & MON. (YUGO.)

C R O A T I A

Sava

Banja Luka

Bihać

Brčko

Tuzla

Vrbas

Bosna

Sarajevo

Goražde

Mostar

Split

Dubrovnik

C R O A T I A

A d r i a t i c   S e a

Territorial extent
Republika Srpska
Federacija Bosna
i Hercegovina

0   50 km
0   50 miles

THE MEDITERRANEAN

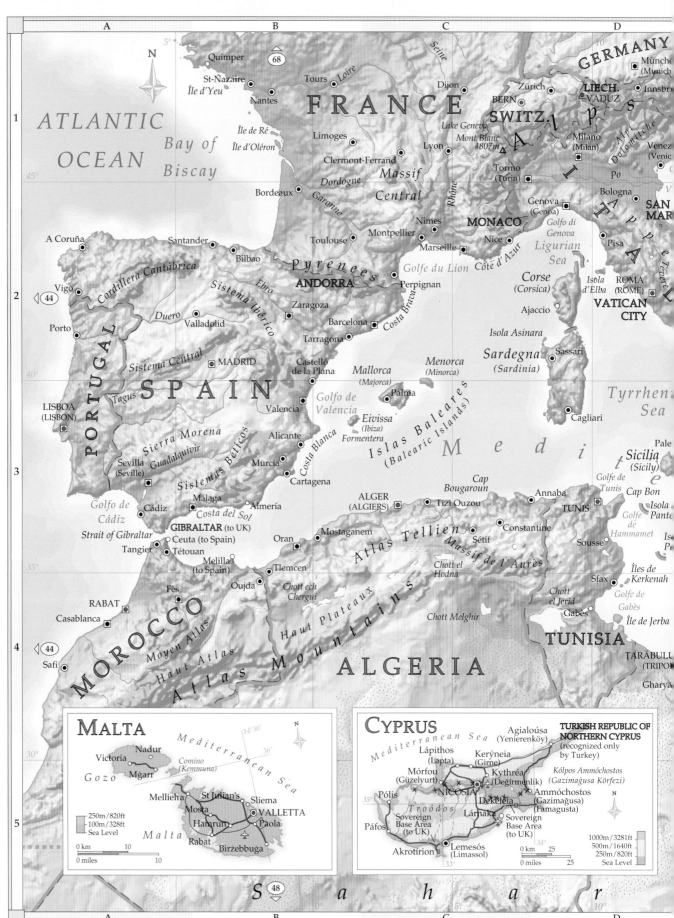

A   B   C   D

GERMANY
München
(Munich)
Innsbr
Seine
Quimper
68
N
Tours   Loire
F R A N C E
Dijon
Zürich
LIECH.
VADUZ
St-Nazaire
Nantes
BERN
SWITZ.
Milano
(Milan)
Alpi Dolomitiche
Venez
(Venic)
Île d'Yeu
ATLANTIC
Bay of
Biscay
Limoges
Lyon
Lake Geneva
Mont Blanc
4807m
Torino
(Turin)
Po
OCEAN
Clermont-Ferrand
Massif
Central
Bologna
SAN MAR
45°
Bordeaux
Dordogne
Garonne
Genova
(Genoa)
Rhône
Toulouse
Nîmes
MONACO
Golfo di
Genova
A Coruña
Santander
Bilbao
Montpellier
Nice
Pisa
Marseille
Côte d'Azur
Ligurian
Sea
Pyrenees
ANDORRA
Golfe du Lion
Corse
(Corsica)
Isola
d'Elba
ROMA
(ROME)
e Tevere
Vigo
44
Cordillera Cantábrica
Sistema Ibérico
Perpignan
Ebro
Zaragoza
**VATICAN
CITY**
Porto
Duero
Valladolid
Barcelona
Costa Brava
Ajaccio
Isola Asinara
Sardegna
(Sardinia)
Sassari
Tyrrhen
Sea
Tarragona
Sistema Central
MADRID
Castelló
de la Plana
Mallorca
(Majorca)
Menorca
(Minorca)
Tagus
P O R T U G A L
S P A I N
Valencia
Golfo de
Valencia
Palma
M   e   d   i
Cagliari
Pale
LISBOA
(LISBON)
Sierra Morena
Guadalquivir
Alicante
Costa Blanca
Eivissa
(Ibiza)
Formentera
Islas Baleares
(Balearic Islands)
Sicilia
(Sicily)
Golfe de
Tunis
Sevilla
(Seville)
Sistemas Béticos
Murcia
Cap
Bougaroun
Annaba
Cap Bon
Isola
Pante
40°
Cartagena
Golfo de
Cádiz
Málaga
Almería
ALGER
(ALGIERS)
Tizi Ouzou
TUNIS
Golfe
de
Hammamet
Ise
P
Cádiz
Costa del Sol
GIBRALTAR (to UK)
Oran
Mostaganem
Constantine
Sétif
Sousse
Strait of Gibraltar
Ceuta (to Spain)
Massif de l'Aurès
35°
Tangier
Tétouan
Atlas Tellien
Chott el
Hodna
Sfax
Îles de
Kerkenah
Melilla
(to Spain)
Tlemcen
M O R O C C O
Fès
Oujda
Chott ech
Chergui
Chott
el Jerid
Golfe de
Gabès
RABAT
Chott Melghir
Gabès
Île de Jerba
Casablanca
Moyen Atlas
Haut Plateaux
TUNISIA
Safi
44
Haut Atlas
Atlas Mountains
A L G E R I A
ṬARĀBULU
(TRIPO
Gharyā

POPULATION
■● Over
500,000
◉ 100,000 -
500,000
○ 50,000 -
100,000
○ Less than
50,000
● National
capital

MALTA
Mediterranean Sea
14°30'
N
36°
Victoria
Nadur
Comino
(Kemmuna)
Gozo
Mġarr
Mellieħa
St Julian's
Sliema
Mosta
VALLETTA
Mosta
Hamrun
Paola
Rabat
Birżebbuġa
Malta
250m/820ft
100m/328ft
Sea Level
0 km   10
0 miles   10

CYPRUS
Mediterranean Sea
Agialoúsa
(Yenierenköy)
**TURKISH REPUBLIC OF
NORTHERN CYPRUS**
(recognized only
by Turkey)
Lápithos
(Lapta)
Kerýneia
(Girne)
Mórfou
(Güzelyurt)
Kythréa
(Değirmenlik)
Kólpos Ammóchostos
(Gazimağusa Körfezi)
35°
Pólis
NICOSIA
Dekéleia
Ammóchostos
(Gazimağusa)
(Famagusta)
N
Troódos
Lárnaka
Páfos
Sovereign
Base Area
(to UK)
Sovereign
Base Area
(to UK)
33°
1000m/3281ft
500m/1640ft
250m/820ft
Sea Level
Akrotírion
Lemesós
(Limassol)
34°
0 km   25
0 miles   25

S   48   a   h   a   r

A   B   C   D

SLOVAKIA

WIEN
(VIENNA)

Danube

BUDAPEST

HUNGARY

Great
Hungarian
Plain

Tisza

Carpathian Mountains

Satu Mare

Târgu Mures

ROMANIA

Carpații Meridonali

Bâlti

86

MOLD.

CHIȘINĂU

Nistru

UKRAINE

Kakhovs'ka
Vodoskhovyshche

Dnieper

Odesa

Berdyans'k

Sea of Azov

Kerch

Kryms'kyy
Pivostrov

RUSS.
FED.

Sevastopol'

Novorossiysk

UBLJANA

ZAGREB

N

CROATIA

Sava

BOSNIA
& HERZ.

Novi Sad

BEOGRAD
(BELGRADE)

Galați

BUCUREŞTI
(BUCHAREST)

Danube

Constanța

Black Sea

ELEVATION

4000 m
13 124 ft

2000 m
6562 ft

SARAJEVO

ka

Dalmatia

Adriatic Sea

SERBIA &
MONTENEGRO
(YUGOSLAVIA)

Priština

SKOPJE

BULGARIA

Balkan Mountains

SOFIYA
(SOFIA)

Varna

Burgas

İstanbul
Boğazı
(Bosporus)

Zonguldak

95

Küre Dağları

Samsun

Ordu

1000 m
3281 ft

a

TIRANË
(TIRANA)

MACED.

Rhodope
Mountains

Edirne

İstanbul

Kızıl Irmak

500 m
1640 ft

Bari

oli (Naples)

Vesuvio 1277m

Lecce

Golfo di
Taranto

ALBANIA

Strait of Otranto

Pindos (Pindus) Mts

Kérkyra
(Corfu)

Thessaloníki
(Salonica)

Límnos

Lárisa

Marmara
Denizi

Balıkesir

Bursa

ANKARA

TURKEY

Tuz
Gölü

Kayseri

250 m
820 ft

100 m
328 ft

Cosenza

Catanzaro

Ionian
Sea

Kefallinía

Zákynthos

GREECE

Aegean
Sea

ATHÍNA
(ATHENS)

Chíos

Sámos

İzmir

Sea Level

Sea Level

Monte Etna
3340m

Catania

Siracusa

Mirtóo
Pelagos

Kykládes
(Cyclades)

Sámos

Dodekánisos
(Dodecanese)

Gaziantep

-250 m
-820 ft

VALLETTA

ALTA

a

Kýthira

Kritikó Pélagos
(Sea of Crete)

Ródos
(Rhodes)

Kárpathos

Antalya

Toros Dağları

Antalya
Körfezi

Adana

İskenderun Körfezi

Halab
(Aleppo)

Euphrates

SYRIA

-500 m
-1640 ft

n

Irakleio

Kríti
(Crete)

NICOSIA

CYPRUS

Lemesós
(Limassol)

Lárnaka

LEBANON

BEYROUTH
(BEIRUT)

-1000 m
-3281 ft

e

a

Mişrātah

Darnah

Banghāzī
(Benghazi)

Khalīj Surt
(Gulf of Sirte)

S

Ţubruq

e

a

Libyan
Plateau

Darnah

Alexandria

Nile
Delta

Port Said

DIMASHQ
(DAMASCUS)

Hefa

ISRAEL

Tel Aviv-Yafo

JERUSALEM

Gaza

Dead Sea

Suez
Canal

97

'AMMĀN

JORDAN

-2000 m
-6562 ft

-3000 m
-9843 ft

Surt

Ajdābiyā

Great Sand Sea

Monkhafad al Qattâra
(Qattâra Depression)

CAIRO

Suez

Elat

Al 'Aqabah

-4000 m
-13 124 ft

Waddān

LIBYA

0 km   400

0 miles   400

Libyan

Desert

EGYPT

El Gîza

Nile

Sahara el Sharqīya
(Eastern Desert)

Gulf of Suez

Sinai

Red
Sea

50

SAUDI
ARABIA

1

2

3

4

5

E   F   G   H

Bulgaria & Greece

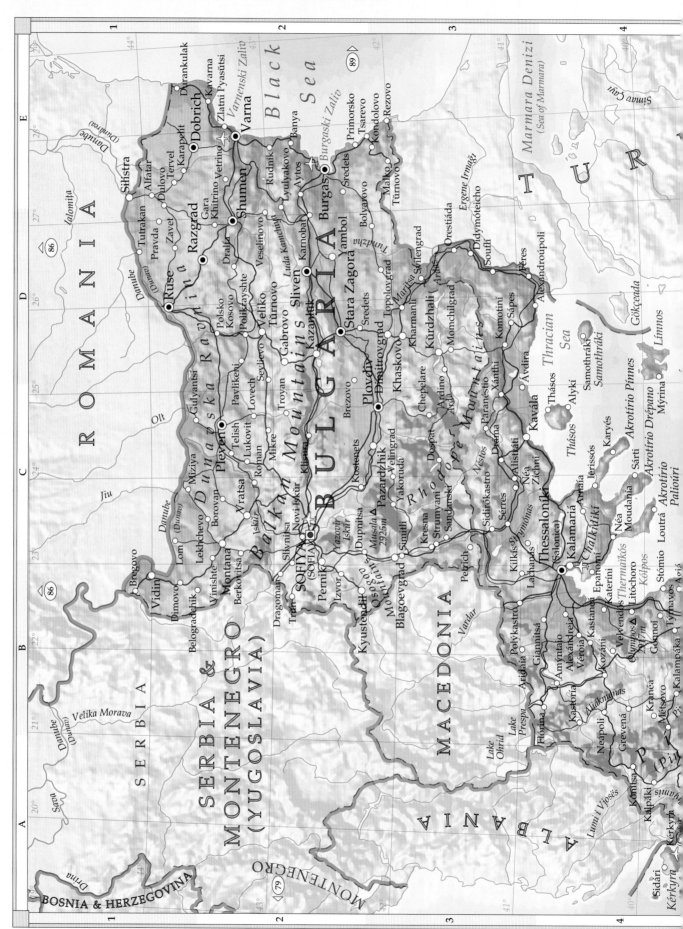

POPULATION

- ■ Over 500,000
- ◉ 100,000 – 500,000
- ○ 50,000 – 100,000
- ∘ Less than 50,000
- ● National capital

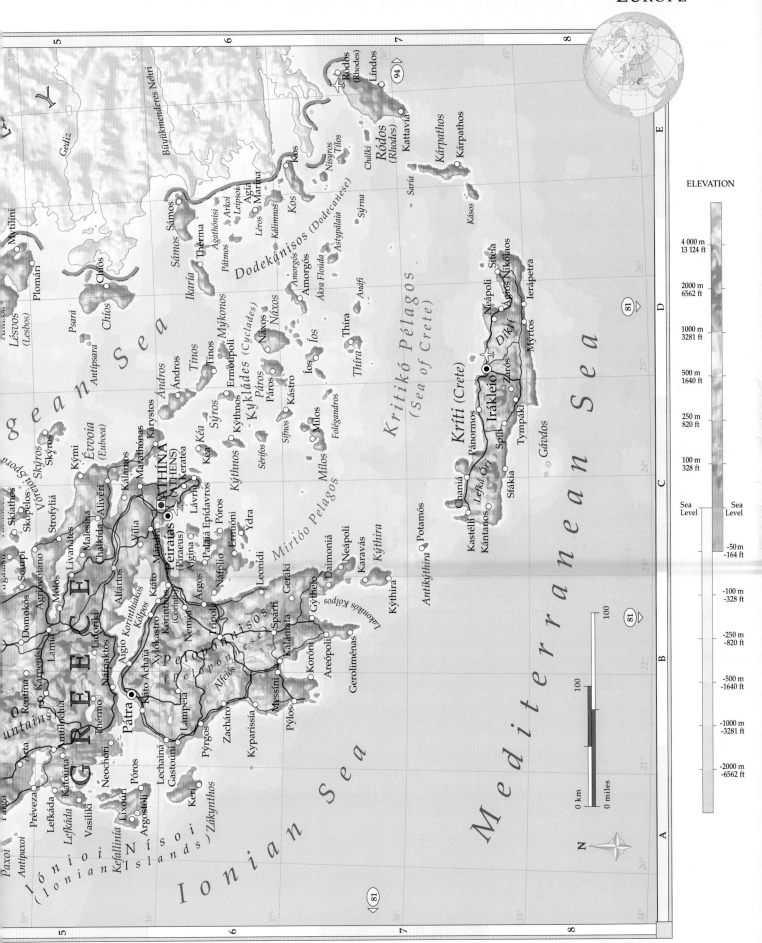

THE WORLD ATLAS

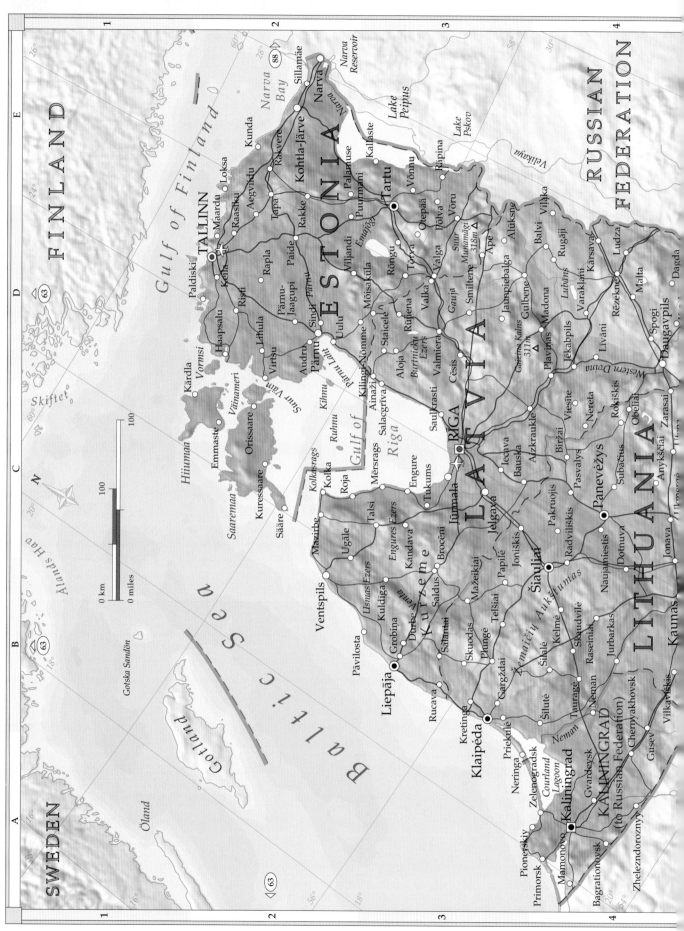

POPULATION

- ◉ Over 500,000
- ◉ 100,000 – 500,000
- ○ 50,000 – 100,000
- ○ Less than 50,000
- ● National capital

ELEVATION

4000 m
13 124 ft

2000 m
6562 ft

1000 m
3281 ft

500 m
1640 ft

250 m
820 ft

100 m
328 ft

Sea Level — Sea Level

-10 m
-33 ft

-25 m
-82 ft

-50 m
-164 ft

-100 m
-328 ft

-250 m
-820 ft

-500 m
-1640 ft

RUSSIAN FEDERATION

UKRAINE

POLAND

B E L A R U S

VILNIUS

Dnieper Lowland

Mazury

Wyżyna Lubelska

Pripet Marshes

Minskaya Wzvyshsha

Byelaruskaya Hrada

Byerezino

Viliya

Neman

Bug

Pripet

Dnieper

Horyn'

Styr

Yasyel'da

Pisich

Ptsich

Kyyivs'ke Vodoskhovyshche

Western Dvina

Cities and towns:

Yezyaryshcha, Haradok, Surazh, Vitsyebsk, Lyozna, Bahushewsk, Dnieper, Sava, Khodasy, Knyahaw, Klimavichy, Kastsyukovichy, Baron'ki, Tsyerakhowka, Dobrush, Kastsyukowka, Bal'shavik, Uvaravichy, Buda-Kashalyova, Myerkulavichy, Homyel, Loyew, Khoyniki, Byval'ki, Loyew, Narowlya, Milashavichy, Yel'sk, Dabryn', Tonyezh, Luminyets, Pinsk, Mazyr, Rechytsa, Kalinkavichy, Sbychy, Pyetrykaw, Kaptsevichy, Simanichy, Lyel'chytsy, Tonyezh, Ivanava, Lyusina, Hantsavichy, Lyakhavichy, Ivatsevichy, Drahichyn, Kobryn, Haradzyets, Zhabinka, Pruzhany, Ruzhany, Novy Dvor, Makrany, Damachava, Brest, Bug, Hrandzichy, Hrodna, Vawkavysk, Masty, Shchuchyn, Skidal', Zel'va, Slonim, Navahrudak, Orlya, Abrova, Baranavichy, Nyasvizh, Kapyl', Syemyezhava, Bastyn', Starobyn, Salihorsk, Staryya Darohi, Lyuban, Tal'ka, Asipovichy, Shyshchytsy, Slutsk, Stowbtsy, Rudzyensk, Mar''ina Horka, Pukhavichy, Byerezino, Shcheadryn, Aktsyabrski, Svyetlahorsk, Brozha, Babruysk, Kirawsk, Chachevichy, Yalizava, Dashkawka, Byalynichy, Talachyn, Krupki, Barysaw, Zhodzina, Krasnaye, Maladzyechna, Vilyeyka, Smarhon, Ashmyany, Valozhyn, Lida, Varena, Votanava, Salčininkai, Šalčininkai, Trakai, Rūdiškės, Merkinė, Druskininkai, Veisiejai, Alytus, Parechcha, Vasilishki, Orlya, Skidal', Pastavy, Myadzyel, Byahoml', Plyeshchanitsy, Lyepyel', Byahoml', Hlybokaye, Harany, Obal', Bacheykava, Shumilina, Chashniki, Navapolatsk, Polatsk, Vyetryna, Sarochyna, Chashniki, Orsha, Shklow, Horki, Kruhlaye, Dubrowna, Mahilyow, Chavusy, Harbavichy, Cherykaw, Slawharad, Rahachow, Zhlobin, Buda-Kashalyova, Abidavichy, Chachersk, Vyetka, Dobrush, Starobyn

Minsk, Vilnius, Polatsk, Navapolatsk, Vitsyebsk, Orsha, Mahilyow, Babruysk, Homyel, Mazyr, Brest, Hrodna, Barysaw

76, 86, 87, 89

50°, 52°, 54°, 56°, 30°, 32°, 28°, 24°, 26°, 22°

POPULATION

- Over 500,000
- 100,000 - 500,000
- 50,000 - 100,000
- Less than 50,000
- National capital

ELEVATION

4 000 m
13 124 ft

2000 m
6562 ft

1000 m
3281 ft

500 m
1640 ft

250 m
820 ft

100 m
328 ft

Sea
Level

Sea
Level

-50 m
-164 ft

-100 m
-328 ft

-250 m
-820 ft

-500 m
-1640 ft

-1000 m
-3281 ft

-2000 m
-6562 ft

THE WORLD ATLAS

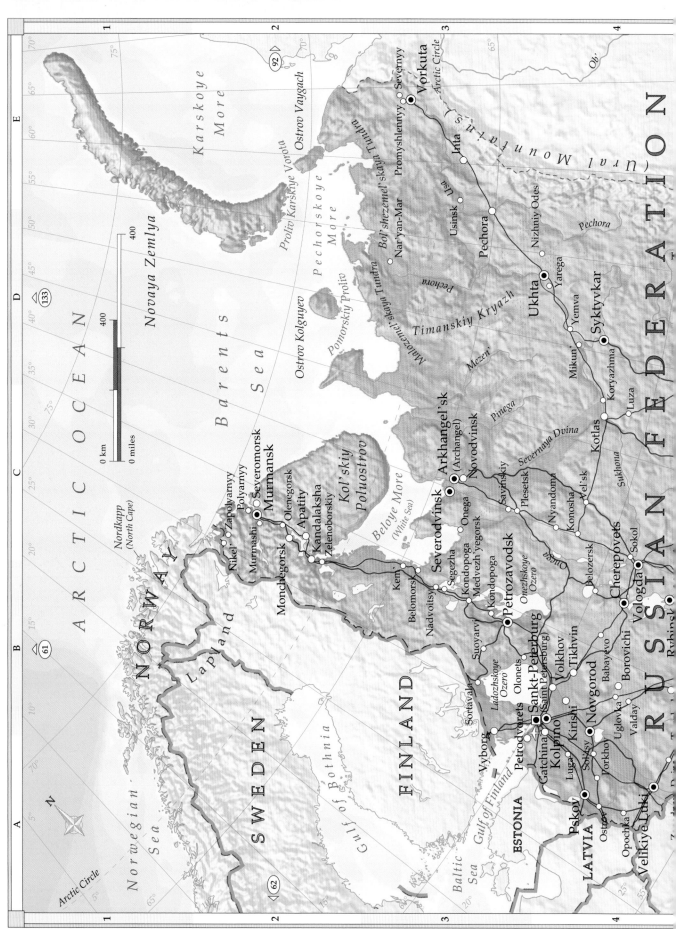

POPULATION

- ▣ Over 500,000
- ◉ 100,000 – 500,000
- ○ 50,000 – 100,000
- ○ Less than 50,000
- ● National capital

Map labels

ARCTIC OCEAN

Karskoye More

Novaya Zemlya

Barents Sea

Pechorskoye More

Ostrov Vaygach

Proliv Karskiye Vorota

Pomorskiy Proliv

Ostrov Kolguyev

Nordkapp (North Cape)

NORWAY

SWEDEN

Norwegian Sea

Lapland

Gulf of Bothnia

Baltic Sea

FINLAND

ESTONIA

LATVIA

RUSSIAN FEDERATION

Ural Mountains

Arctic Circle

Ob'

Vorkuta

Severnyy

Promyshlennyy

Ikhta

Usa

Bol'shezemel'skaya Tundra

Nar'yan-Mar

Usinsk

Pechora

Nizhniy Odes

Pechora

Malozemel'skaya Tundra

Timanskiy Kryazh

Yarega

Ukhta

Syktyvkar

Pechora

Mezen'

Yemva

Mikun'

Koryazhma

Luza

Pinega

Kotlas

Yel'sk

Severnaya Dvina

Sukhona

Arkhangel'sk (Archangel)

Novodvinsk

Severodvinsk

Beloye More (White Sea)

Onega

Savinskiy

Plesetsk

Nyandoma

Konosha

Belozersk

Cherepovets

Sokol

Vologda

Rybinsk

Kol'skiy Poluostrov

Zapolyarnyy

Polyarnyy

Severomorsk

Murmansk

Nikel'

Murmashi

Olenegorsk

Apatity

Monchegorsk

Kandalaksha

Zelenoborskiy

Kem'

Belomorsk

Nadvoitsy

Segezha

Kondopoga

Medvezh'yegorsk

Kondopoga

Onezhskoye Ozero

Petrozavodsk

Onega

Suoyarvi

Olonets

Ladozhskoye Ozero

Sortavala

Vyborg

Petrodvorets

Sankt-Peterburg (Saint Petersburg)

Gatchina

Kolpino

Kirishi

Volkhov

Tikhvin

Babayevo

Borovichi

Novgorod

Luga

Sol'tsy

Uglovka

Valday

Pskov

Ostrov

Opochka

Velikiye Luki

Yorkho

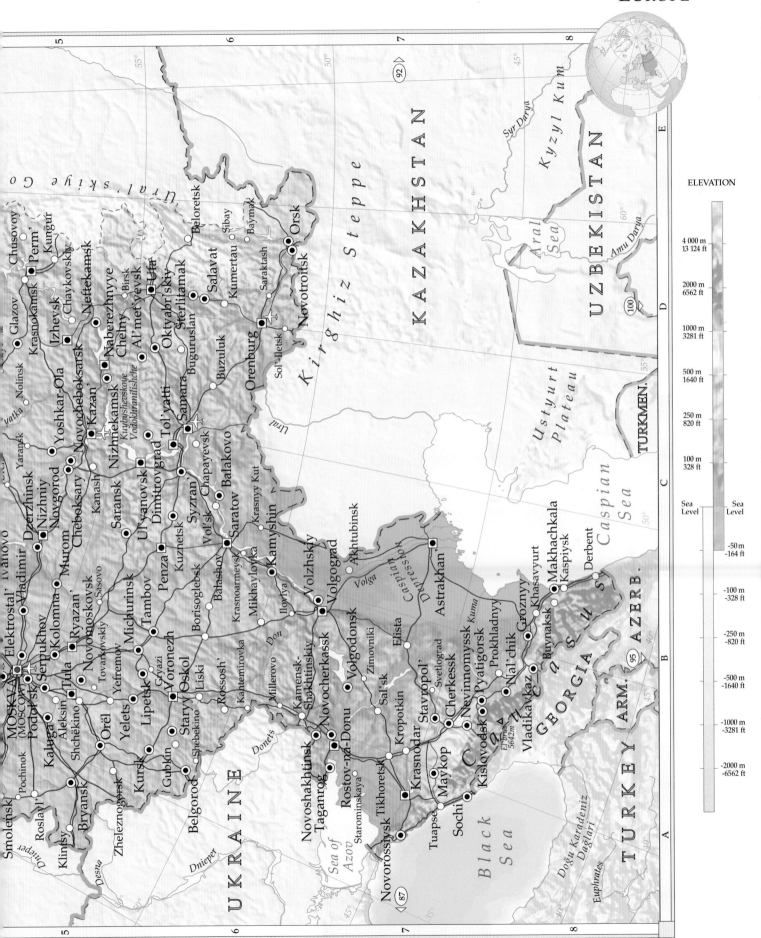

ELEVATION

4 000 m	13 124 ft
2000 m	6562 ft
1000 m	3281 ft
500 m	1640 ft
250 m	820 ft
100 m	328 ft
Sea Level	Sea Level
-50 m	-164 ft
-100 m	-328 ft
-250 m	-820 ft
-500 m	-1640 ft
-1000 m	-3281 ft
-2000 m	-6562 ft

NORTH & WEST ASIA

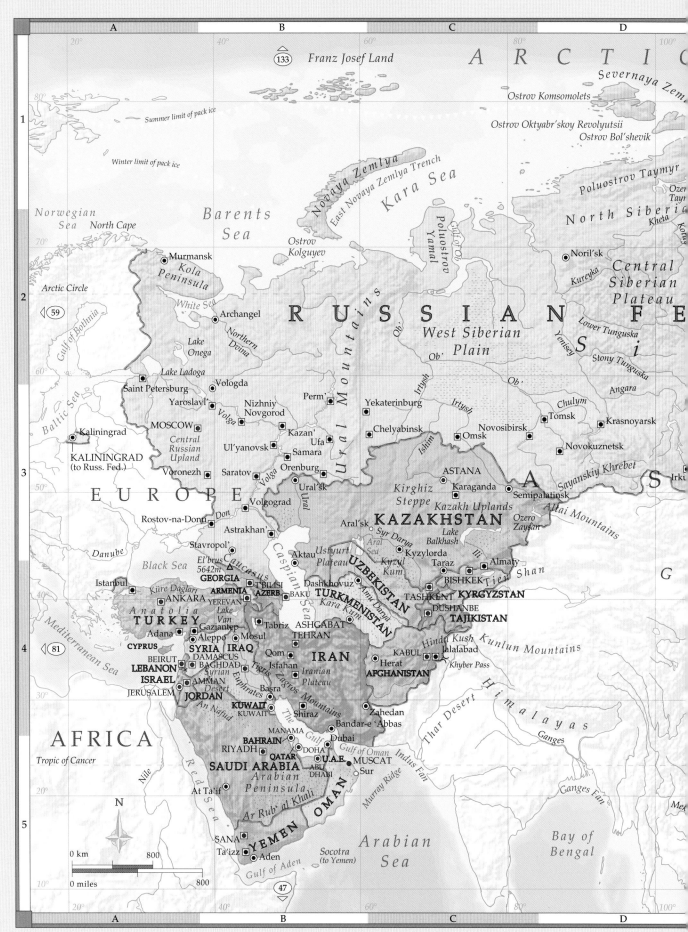

A C T I C

Franz Josef Land

Severnaya Zem

Ostrov Komsomolets

Ostrov Oktyabr'skoy Revolyutsii
Ostrov Bol'shevik

Summer limit of pack ice

Winter limit of pack ice

Poluostrov Taymyr

Ozer
Tayn
Kheta

North Siberia

Norwegian
Sea   North Cape

Barents
Sea

Novaya Zemlya

East Novaya Zemlya Trench

Kara Sea

Poluostrov
Yamal

Gulf of Ob

Noril'sk

Kureyka

Central
Siberian
Plateau

Kola
Peninsula

Murmansk

Ostrov
Kolguyev

Arctic Circle

White Sea

R U S S I A N   F E

Lower Tunguska

Yenisey

Stony Tunguska

Angara

Irki

Gulf of Bothnia

Archangel

Northern
Dvina

West Siberian
Plain

Ob'

Ob'

Chulym

Saint Petersburg

Lake
Onega

Vologda

Perm'

Yekaterinburg

Irtysh

Novosibirsk

Tomsk

Krasnoyarsk

Baltic Sea

Lake Ladoga

Yaroslavl'

Nizhniy
Novgorod

Kazan'

Ufa

Chelyabinsk

Irtysh

Omsk

Novokuznetsk

Kaliningrad

MOSCOW

Volga

Ul'yanovsk

Samara

Orenburg

ASTANA

Sayanskiy Khrebet

A

S

KALININGRAD
(to Russ. Fed.)

Central
Russian
Upland

Saratov

Voronezh

Ural'sk

Kirghiz
Steppe

Karaganda

Semipalatinsk

E U R O P E

Volgograd

Volga

Ural

Kazakh Uplands

Altai Mountains

Rostov-na-Donu

Don

Astrakhan'

KAZAKHSTAN

Ozero
Zaysan

Danube

Stavropol'

Black Sea

El'brus
5642m

Caucasus

Caspian Sea

Aktau

Aral'sk

Aral
Sea

Ustyurt
Plateau

Kyzyl
Kum

Syr Darya

Lake
Balkhash

Ili

Tien Shan

Taraz

Almaty

G

Istanbul

Küre Daglari

GEORGIA

TBILISI

ARMENIA AZERB.

BAKU

Dashkhovuz

Kara Kum

Amu Darya

UZBEKISTAN

Kyzylorda

BISHKEK

KYRGYZSTAN

ANKARA

YEREVAN
Lake
Van

TURKMENISTAN

TASHKENT

Anatolia

TURKEY

Gaziantep

Tabriz

ASHGABAT

TEHRAN

DUSHANBE

TAJIKISTAN

Adana

Aleppo

Mosul

Qom

Hindu Kush

Kunlun Mountains

CYPRUS

SYRIA IRAQ

DAMASCUS

BAGHDAD

Isfahan

IRAN

KABUL

Jalalabad

Khyber Pass

Mediterranean Sea

BEIRUT

LEBANON

Syrian
Desert

Tigris

Zagros Mountains

Iranian
Plateau

AFGHANISTAN

Herat

H
i
m
a
l
a
y
a
s

ISRAEL

AMMAN

Euphrates

Basra

Thar Desert

Ganges

JERUSALEM

JORDAN

An Nafud

KUWAIT

KUWAIT

The Gulf

Shiraz

Zahedan

Bandar-e 'Abbas

Indus Fan

AFRICA

Nile

Tropic of Cancer

MANAMA

BAHRAIN

RIYADH

QATAR

DOHA

Dubai

Gulf of Oman

MUSCAT

Ganges Fan

Mei

SAUDI ARABIA

Arabian
Peninsula

U.A.E.

ABU
DHABI

Sur

Murray Ridge

Red Sea

Ar Rub' al Khali

OMAN

At Ta'if

N

Arabian
Sea

Bay of
Bengal

SANA

YEMEN

Ta'izz Aden

Socotra
(to Yemen)

Gulf of Aden

POPULATION

- ◉ Over
  500,000

- ◉ 100,000 –
  500,000

- ○ 50,000 –
  100,000

- ○ Less than
  50,000

- ● National
  capital

0 km   800

0 miles   800

90

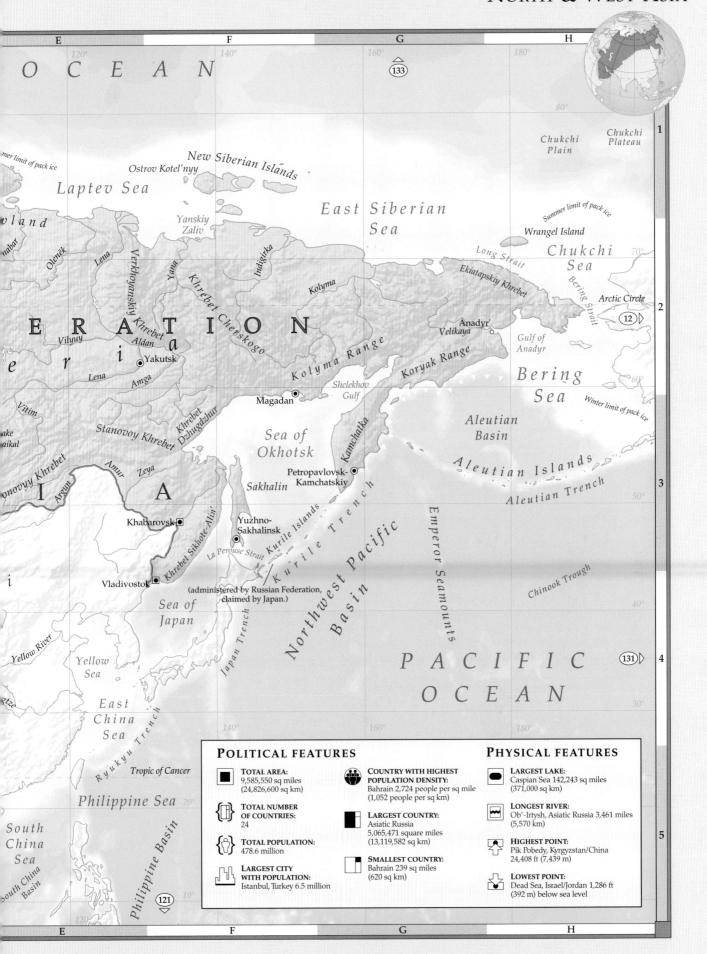

E   F   G   H

120°   140°   160°   180°

80°

133

1

OCEAN

Chukchi
Plain

Chukchi
Plateau

mer limit of pack ice

New Siberian Islands

Ostrov Kotel'nyy

Laptev Sea

*East Siberian
Sea*

Summer limit of pack ice

Wrangel Island

*Chukchi
Sea*

70°

Long Strait

Yanskiy
Zaliv.

Olenëk

Lena

Indigirka

Kolyma

Ekiatapskiy Khrebet

Bering Strait

Arctic Circle

Arctic Circle

2

12

island

Verkhoyanskiy Khrebet

Khrebet Cherskogo

ERATION

Vilyuy

Aldan

Anadyr'

Velikaya

Gulf of
Anadyr

Yakutsk

Kolyma Range

Koryak Range

*Bering
Sea*

60°

Lena

Amga

Vitim

Shelekhov
Gulf

Winter limit of pack ice

ake
aikal

Stanovoy Khrebet

Khrebet
Dzhugdzhur

Magadan

*Aleutian
Basin*

onovyy Khrebet

Amur

Zeya

*Sea of
Okhotsk*

Kamchatka

Aleutian Islands

3

50°

Petropavlovsk-
Kamchatskiy

Aleutian Trench

I A

Sakhalin

Khabarovsk

Yuzhno-
Sakhalinsk

Kurile Islands

Kurile Trench

Emperor Seamounts

i

Khrebet Sikhote-Alin'

La Perouse Strait

*Northwest Pacific
Basin*

Chinook Trough

40°

Vladivostok

(administered by Russian Federation,
claimed by Japan.)

*Sea of
Japan*

Japan Trench

4

131

Yellow River

*Yellow
Sea*

PACIFIC

OCEAN

30°

*East
China
Sea*

Ryukyu Trench

Tropic of Cancer

140°   160°   180°

Philippine Sea

20°

*South
China
Sea*

Philippine Basin

5

*South China
Basin*

121

10°

120°   E   F   G   H

POLITICAL FEATURES

TOTAL AREA:
9,585,550 sq miles
(24,826,600 sq km)

**TOTAL NUMBER
OF COUNTRIES:**
24

TOTAL POPULATION:
478.6 million

**LARGEST CITY
WITH POPULATION:**
Istanbul, Turkey 6.5 million

**COUNTRY WITH HIGHEST
POPULATION DENSITY:**
Bahrain 2,724 people per sq mile
(1,052 people per sq km)

LARGEST COUNTRY:
Asiatic Russia
5,065,471 square miles
(13,119,582 sq km)

SMALLEST COUNTRY:
Bahrain 239 sq miles
(620 sq km)

PHYSICAL FEATURES

LARGEST LAKE:
Caspian Sea 142,243 sq miles
(371,000 sq km)

LONGEST RIVER:
Ob'-Irtysh, Asiatic Russia 3,461 miles
(5,570 km)

HIGHEST POINT:
Pik Pobedy, Kyrgyzstan/China
24,408 ft (7,439 m)

LOWEST POINT:
Dead Sea, Israel/Jordan 1,286 ft
(392 m) below sea level

RUSSIA & KAZAKHSTAN

POPULATION

- ■ Over 500,000
- ◉ 100,000 – 500,000
- ○ 50,000 – 100,000
- ○ Less than 50,000
- ● National capital

ALASKA
(to US)

*Chukchi
Sea*

Bering Strait

Arctic Circle

14

ELEVATION

Ostrov Vrangelya

Proliv Longa

*Vostochno-Sibirskoye
More*

Pevek

Ekiatapskiy Khrebet

Anadyr'

*Anadyrskiy
Zaliv*

Anadyr'

180°

*Bering
Sea*

Ostrov
Komsomolets

OCEAN

Novosibirskiye
Ostrova

Ostrov
Novaya Sibir'

Ambarchik
Cherskiy

Koryakskoye Nagor'ye

170°

Ostrov Oktyabr'skoy Revolyutsii
*Severnaya
Zemlya*

-shevik

Ostrov Kotel'nyy

Ostrov Bol'shoy
Lyakhovskiy

Alazeya

Indigirka

Kolyma

Ossora

Ostrov Karaginskiy

130

4000 m
13 124 ft

2

*More
Laptevykh*

-o-Sibirskaya Nizmennost'

Kheta

Ust'-Olenëk

Tiksi

Kazach'ye

Yana

Khrebet Cherskogo

Adycha

Susuman

*Zaliv
Shelikhova*

Ust'-Kamchatsk
Vulkan Klyucheyskaya
△ *Sopka*
4750m

160°

2000 m
6562 ft

1000 m
3281 ft

500 m
1640 ft

Ostrov Taymyr

Ozero
Taymyr

Anabar

Olenëk

Verkhoyanskiy Khrebet

Atka
Magadan

Atlasovo

Mil'kovo

*Poluostrov
Kamchatka*

250 m
820 ft

50°

100°

120°

140°

160°

80°

180°

170°

70°

Kotuy

-rana

Olenëk

Lena

Aldan

Okhotsk

**Petropavlovsk-
Kamchatskiy**

100 m
328 ft

*Srednesibirskoye
Ploskogor'ye*

Nyurba

Vilyuy

Yakutsk

Lena

Anga

Aldan

Khrebet Dzhugdzhur

*Okhotskoye
More*

Pervyy Kuril'skiy Proliv
Ostrov
Paramushir

Sea
Level

Sea
Level

3

-aya Tunguska

SIBIR'
(SIBERIA)

Chunya

Mirnyy

Suntar

Olëkminsk

Lena

Olëkma

*Shantarskiye
Ostrova*

-250 m
-820 ft

Angara

FEDERATION

Bodaybo

Neryungri

Vitim

Yablonovyy Khrebet

Tynda
Skovorodino

**Komsomol'sk-
na-Amure**

Amur

Ostrov Sakhalin

Ostrov Urup

Kuril'skiye Ostrova
(Kurile Islands)

-500 m
-1640 ft

-1000 m
-3281 ft

Ust'-Ilimsk

Ust'-Kut

-nsk

Bratsk

Tulun

*Ozero
Baykal*

Shilka

Amur

Svobodnyy

Khrebet Sikhote-Alin'

Ostrov Iturup

Kuril'sk

130

4

Usol'ye-Sibirskoye

Angarsk

Irkutsk

-n Sayan

Ulan-Ude

Chita

Olovyannaya

Blagoveshchensk

Khabarovsk
Birobidzhan

Khor

*La Perouse
Strait*

Yuzhno-Sakhalinsk

40°

(administered by
Russian Federation,
claimed by Japan)

-2000 m
-6562 ft

-3000 m
-9843 ft

Kyakhta

Krasnokamensk

Zabaykal'sk

Bikin

150°

CHINA

Ussuriysk

JAPAN

-4000 m
-13 124 ft

MONGOLIA

N

110°

120°

40°

Vladivostok

Nakhodka

*Sea of
Japan*

130°

5

Gobi

100°

**NORTH
KOREA**

106

140°

ROMANIA

UKRAINE

Krymś'kyy Pivostriv

Danube

BULGARIA

Black Sea

Varnenski Zaliv

Burgaski Zaliv

Maritsa

Kırklareli

Edirne

Cide

İnebolu

Sinop

Gerze

Küre Dağları

Bartın

Zonguldak

Bafra

Kastamonu

Samsun

Ergene Nehri

Çorlu

Devrek

Karabük

Kargı

Ünye

Ord

Tekirdag

İstanbul

İzmit

Adapazarı

Çerkeş

Merzifon

Çanik Dağları

Marmara Denizi (Sea of Marmara)

Yalova

İznik Gölü

Bolu

Gerede

Çankırı

Kızıl Irmak

Çorum

Bandırma

Çanakkale

Bursa

Bilecik

ANKARA

Kalecik

Alaca

Tokat

Yıldızeli

Çanakkale Boğazı (Dardanelles)

Balıkesir

Bozüyük

Eskişehir

Kırıkkale

Sorgun

Sivas

Edremit

Ayvalık

Kütahya

T

Polatlı

U

R

Hirfanlı Barajı

Şarkışla

Boğazlıyan

K

Lésvos

Simav

Gediz

Kulu

Akhisar

Tuz Gölü

Bünyan

Heki

Chíos

Manisa

Uşak

Afyon

Cihanbeyli

Nevşehir

İncesu

Gürün

İzmir

Alaşehir

Akşehir

Aksaray

Kayseri

G

ü

Sámos

Ödemiş

Dinar

A

n

a

t

o

l

i

a

Göksun

Aydın

Nazilli

Denizli

Beyşehir Gölü

Konya

Niğde

Söke

Büyükmenderes Nehri

Burdur

Isparta

Kahramanmar

Milas

Tavas

Burdur Gölü

T

o

r

Suğla Gölü

Ereğli

Muğla

o

s

Karaman

Ceyhan

Gazıar

Bodrum

D

a

ğ

l

a

r

Tarsus

Osmaniye

Marmaris

Dalaman

Antalya

Manavgat

Mut

Mersin

Adana

Kilis

Dodekánisos (Dodecánese)

Fethiye

Alanya

İskenderun

Kırıkhan

Ródos (Rhodes)

Kaş

Finike

Antalya Körfezi

Silifke

Antakya

Anamur

Kárpathos

Orantes

TURKISH REPUBLIC OF NORTHERN CYPRUS (recognised only by Turkey)

CYPRUS

Mediterranean Sea

LEBANON

GREECE

POPULATION

⬤ Over 500,000

◉ 100,000 - 500,000

○ 50,000 - 100,000

· Less than 50,000

🔴 National capital

0 km ———— 200

0 miles ———— 200

E   40°   45°   F   45°   G   50°   H

RUSSIAN

FEDERATION

89

Caspian

C a u c a s u s

Sea

Gagra
Gudaut'a
Sokhumi
Och'amch'ire

Abkhazia
Mestia
Enguri
Kazbek
5047m

South
Ossetia

Kut'aisi
Samtredia
P'ot'i
K'obulet'i
Bat'umi
Hopa

GEORGIA

Gori
Tsalka
Akhalts'ikhe

T'BILISI
Rust'avi

Zaqatala
Xaçmaz
Quba
Siyäzän

Greater Caucasus

Şäki
Mingäçevir
Şamaxı

Sumqayıt

ELEVATION

Ajaria
Artvin

Trabzon
Rize
Of
Giresun

Pazar

Lasser Cau

Vanadzor

Gäncä
Yevlax

Kura

BAKI
(BAKU)

4 000 m
13 124 ft

2000 m
6562 ft

1000 m
3281 ft

Doğu Karadeniz Dağları
Çoruh Nehri

Gyumri
Kars
Artik
Sevan

ARMENIA

AZERBAIJAN

Nagornyy
Karabakh

Qazimämmäd
Äli Bayramı

500 m
1640 ft

müşhane

İspir
Sarıkamış

YEREVAN
Sevana Lich

Artashat

İmişli

Kura

250 m
820 ft

Pasinler
Horasan

Aras
Büyükağrı Dağı
(Mount Ararat)
5137m

Xankändi

Biläsuvar

Aşkale
Erzincan
Tercan

Ağrı
Erzurum

Doğubayazıt

AZERBAIJAN

Goris

Aras

100 m
328 ft

Kemah
Bingöl
Elâzığ

Patnos
Erciş

Naxçıvan

Länkäran

Muradiye

Sea
Level

Sea
Level

Euphrates
(t Nehri)

Keban
Barajı

Muş
Tatvan
Bitlis

Van
Gölü

Van

Gevaş

Daryācheh-ye
Orūmīyeh

-50 m
-164 ft

alatya

Toros

Silvan
Siirt

Reshteh-ye Kūhhā - ye Alborz
(Elburz Mountains)

-100 m
-328 ft

ıyaman
Diyarbakır
Silverek

Batman

Dağları

Tigris

-250 m
-820 ft

Atatürk
Barajı
Viranşehir

Mardin
Şırnak

I R A N

98

-500 m
-1640 ft

Şanlıurfa
Ceylanpınar

Nusaybin

K u r d i s t a n

-1000 m
-3281 ft

ayrat
Asad

Al Jazīrah

-2000 m
-6562 ft

Euphrates

Jabal Bishrī

I R A Q

Kūhhā-ye Zāgros
(Zagros Mountains)

RIA

Buḥayrat
ath
Tharthār

98

E   40°   F   45°   G   H

95

THE NEAR EAST

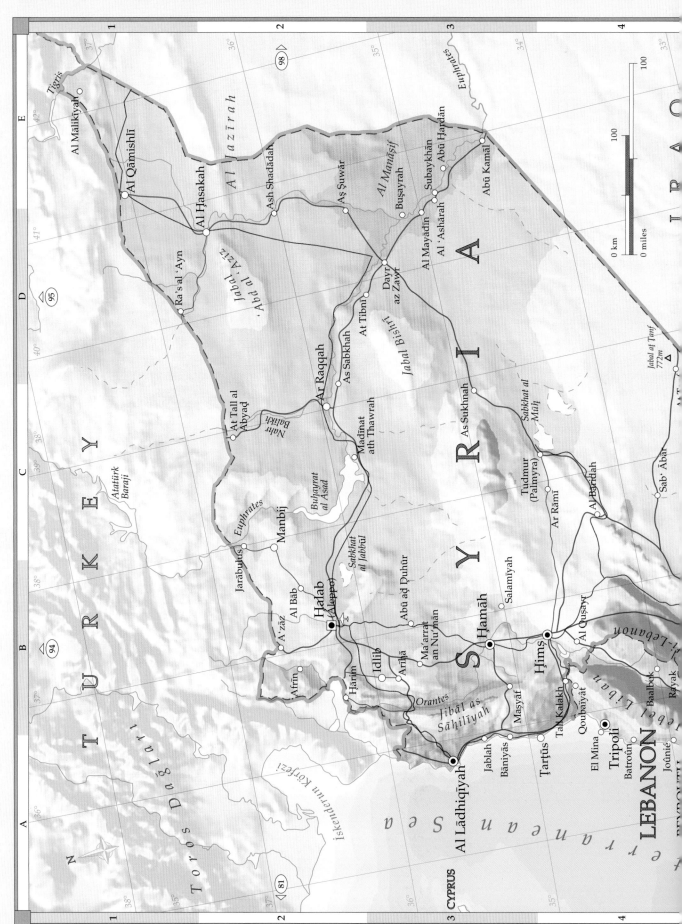

POPULATION

- ■ Over 500,000
- ◉ 100,000 - 500,000
- ○ 50,000 - 100,000
- ○ Less than 50,000
- ● National capital

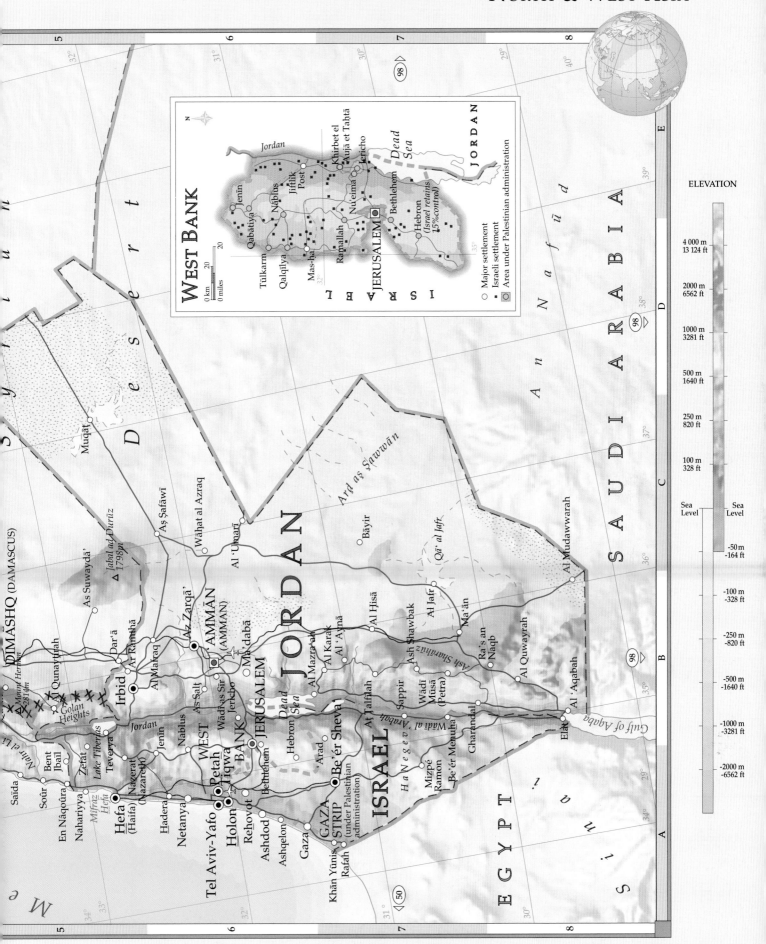

THE MIDDLE EAST

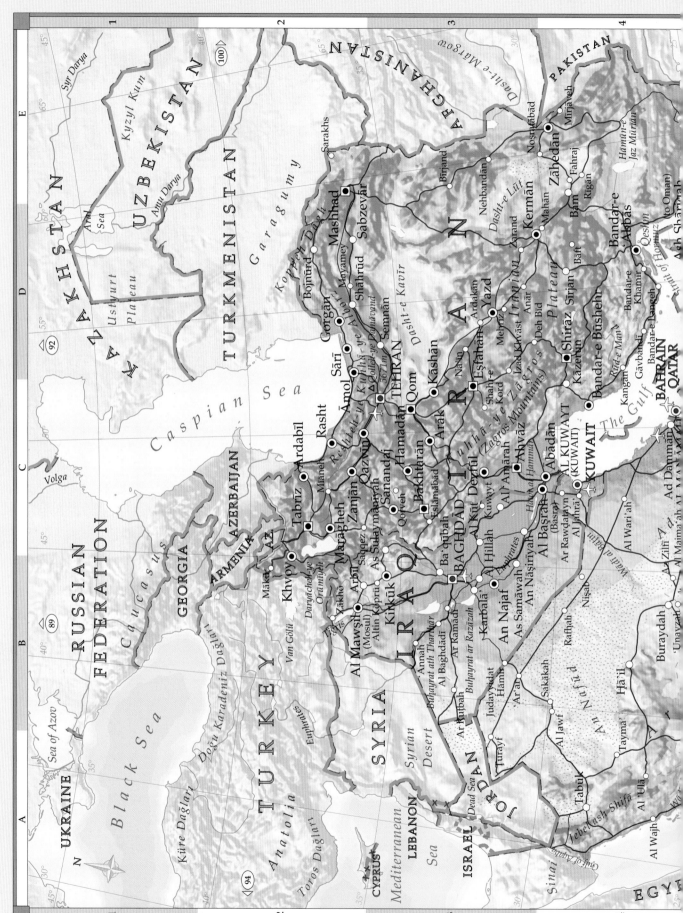

THE WORLD ATLAS

POPULATION

- ■ Over 500,000
- ◉ 100,000 – 500,000
- ○ 50,000 – 100,000
- ○ Less than 50,000
- ● National capital

(MUSCAT)
Ṣūr
Ar Rustāq
Ramlat
Al Ghābah
Hadd al Ghabī
Al Ghābah
Ramlat
Al Wāhibah
Jazīrat Maṣīrah
Khalīj Maṣīrah
Duqm

O M A N

Şawqirah

A r a b i a n   S e a

Thamarīt
Şalālah
Damqawt
Sayḥūt
Juzur al Ḥalānīyāt

UNITED ARAB EMIRATES
(ABU DHABI)

SAUDI ARABIA

Ar Rub' al Khālī
(Empty Quarter)

Sanāw

Al Mahrah
Tarīm
Say'ūn

Ḥaḍramawt

Ash Shiḥr
Al Mukallā

Wydayʻah

Y E M E N

P e n i n s u l a

(RIYADH)

Jabal Tuwayq

Laylā
As Sulayyil

Ramlat as Sab'atayn
ṢAN'Ā'
(SANA)

Shuqrah

Adan
(Aden)

Suquṭrā
(Socotra)
(to Yemen)

Raas Xaafuun

G u l f   o f   A d e n

I N D I A N

O C E A N

S O M A L I A

Ogaden

Tathlīth
Khamīs Mushayṭ
Najrān
Ramlat Dahm
Şa'dah

Ta'izz

Bab el-Mandeb

Qal'at Bīshah

Zalim
Turabah
Aṭ Ṭā'if

(Medina)
Ḥarrat Rahaṭ

Makkah
(Mecca)
Al Līth
Jiddah
(Jedda)

Al Bāḥah
Abhā
Şabyā
Jīzān

Jazā'ir Farasān

Al Hudaydah
(Hodeida)
Zabīd

DJIBOUTI

Danakil Desert

R e d   S e a

Nubian
Desert

SUDAN

ERITREA

E T H I O P I A

Ethiopian Highlands

Great Rift Valley

ELEVATION

4000 m
13 124 ft

2000 m
6562 ft

1000 m
3281 ft

500 m
1640 ft

250 m
820 ft

100 m
328 ft

Sea Level | Sea Level

-250 m
-820 ft

-500 m
-1640 ft

-1000 m
-3281 ft

-2000 m
-6562 ft

-3000 m
-9843 ft

-4000 m
-13 124 ft

400 km
0 km

400 miles
0 miles

Central Asia

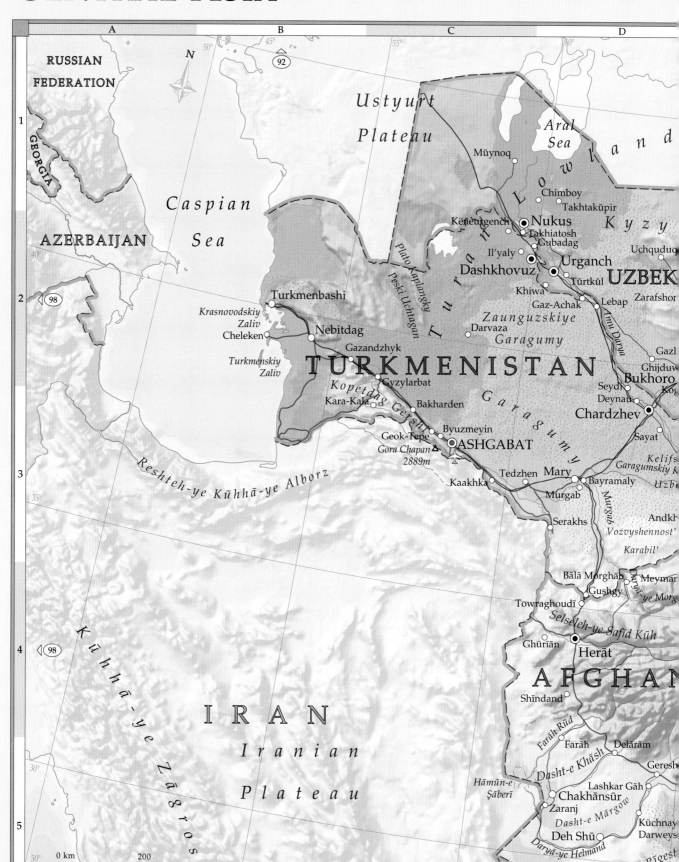

RUSSIAN
FEDERATION

GEORGIA

AZERBAIJAN

*Caspian
Sea*

*Ustyurt
Plateau*

*Aral
Sea*

Můynoq

Chimboy
Takhtakůpir

Kěneutgench ● Nukus
Takhiatosh
Il'yaly ● Gubadag
Dashkhovuz ● Urganch
Tůrtkůl UZBEK
Khiwa
Gaz-Achak Lebap Zarafshor

Turkmenbashi
*Krasnovodskiy
Zaliv*
Cheleken
Nebitdag
Gazandzhyk
*Turkmenskiy
Zaliv*
Gyzylarbat
Kara-Kala
Bakharden
Byuzmeyin
Geok-Tepe ● ASHGABAT
Gora Chapan
2889m
Kaakhka

Darvaza
*Zaunguzskiye
Garagumy*

Uchquduq

Plato Kaplangky
Peski Uchtagan

Turan

TURKMENISTAN

Garagumy

Gazli
Ghijduw
Seydi Bukhoro
Deynau Kog
Chardzhev
Sayat
Kelifs
Garagumskiy K
Uzbe

Kyzy
Lowland

Tedzhen Mary
Murgab ● Bayramaly

Kopetdag Gershi

Reshteh-ye Kůhhā-ye Alborz

Serakhs
Murgab

Andkh
Vozvyshennost'
Karabil'

Bālā Morghāb
Gushgy
Towraghoudī
Selseleh-ye Safīd Kūh
Ghūriān ● Herāt

AFGHAN

Darya-ye Mor
Meymar

Kůhhā-ye Zāgros

I R A N

*Iranian
Plateau*

Shīndand

Farāh Rūd
Farāh Delārām
Geresh
Dasht-e Khāsh
Lashkar Gāh
*Hāmūn-e
Şāberī* Chakhānsūr
Zaranj
Dasht-e Mārgow
Deh Shū Kůchnay
Darweys
Daryā-ye Helmand
Rigest
Chāgai Hills

POPULATION

- ■ Over 500,000
- ◉ 100,000 – 500,000
- ○ 50,000 – 100,000
- ∘ Less than 50,000
- ● National capital

0 km _____ 200
0 miles _____ 200

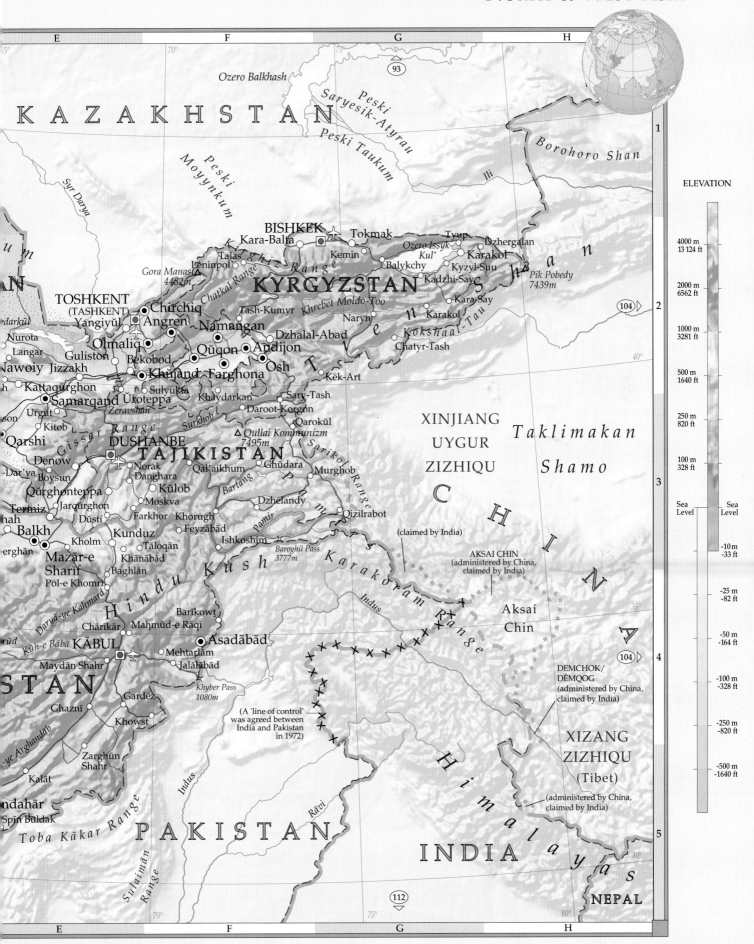

KAZAKHSTAN

Ozero Balkhash

Peski Saryesik-Atyrau

Peski Taukum

Peski Moyynkum

Syr Darya

Borohoro Shan

BISHKEK
Kara-Balta
Tokmak
Tyup
Kirghiz Range
Talas
Kemin
Ozero Issyk-Kul'
Dzhergalan
Lenimpol
Balykchy
Karakol
Gora Manas 4482m
Chatkal Range
Kyzyl-Suu
Kadzhi-Say
Pik Pobedy 7439m

KYRGYZSTAN
TOSHKENT
(TASHKENT)
Chirchiq
Tash-Kumyr
Khrebet Moldo-Too
Kara-Say
Yangiyŭl
Angren
Namangan
Naryn
Karakol
Kokshaal-Tau
Olmaliq
Qŭqon
Dzhalal-Abad
Chatyr-Tash
Bekobod
Andijon
Osh
Jizzakh
Khŭjand
Farghona
Nawoiy
Kattaqŭrghon
Sulyukta
Kĕk-Art
Kitob
Samarqand
Ŭroteppa
Khaydarkan
Sary-Tash
Zeravshan
Daroot-Korgon
Urgut
Gissar Range
Qarokŭl
Qarshi
Surkhob
Denow
DUSHANBE
Qullai Kommunizm 7495m
Murghob
Boysun
Norak
Qal'aikhum
Ghŭdara
Qŭrghonteppa
Danghara
Bartang
Jarqŭrghon
Kŭlob
Dzhelandy
Termiz
Moskva
Farkhor
Khorugh
Qizilrabot
Dŭstí
Kunduz
Feyzābād
Ishkoshim
Sarikol Range
Kholm
Tāloqān
Baroghil Pass 3777m
Balkh
Khānābād
Mazār-e Sharif
Baghlān
Indus
Pol-e Khomrí

Hindu Kush
Karakoram Range

XINJIANG
UYGUR
ZIZHIQU

Taklimakan
Shamo

C H I N A

(claimed by India)

AKSAI CHIN
(administered by China,
claimed by India)

Aksai
Chin

Barīkowt
Charīkār
Mahmūd-e Rāqí
Asadābād
KĀBUL
Mehtarlām
Jalālābād
Maydān Shahr
Khyber Pass 1080m
Gardēz
Ghaznī
Khowst

(A 'line of control' was agreed between India and Pakistan in 1972)

DEMCHOK/
DÊMQOG
(administered by China,
claimed by India)

XIZANG
ZIZHIQU
(Tibet)
(administered by China,
claimed by India)

Zarghūn
Shahr
Kalāt
Indus
Rāvi

Spin Buldak

Toba Kākar Range
P A K I S T A N
Sulaimān Range

H i m a l a y a s

I N D I A

NEPAL

SOUTH & EAST ASIA

THE WORLD ATLAS

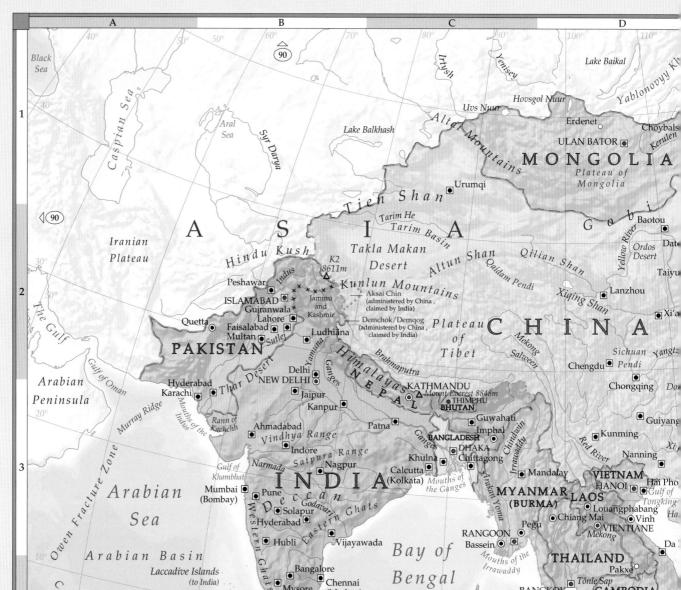

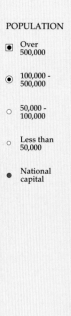

POPULATION

- Over 500,000
- 100,000 – 500,000
- 50,000 – 100,000
- Less than 50,000
- National capital

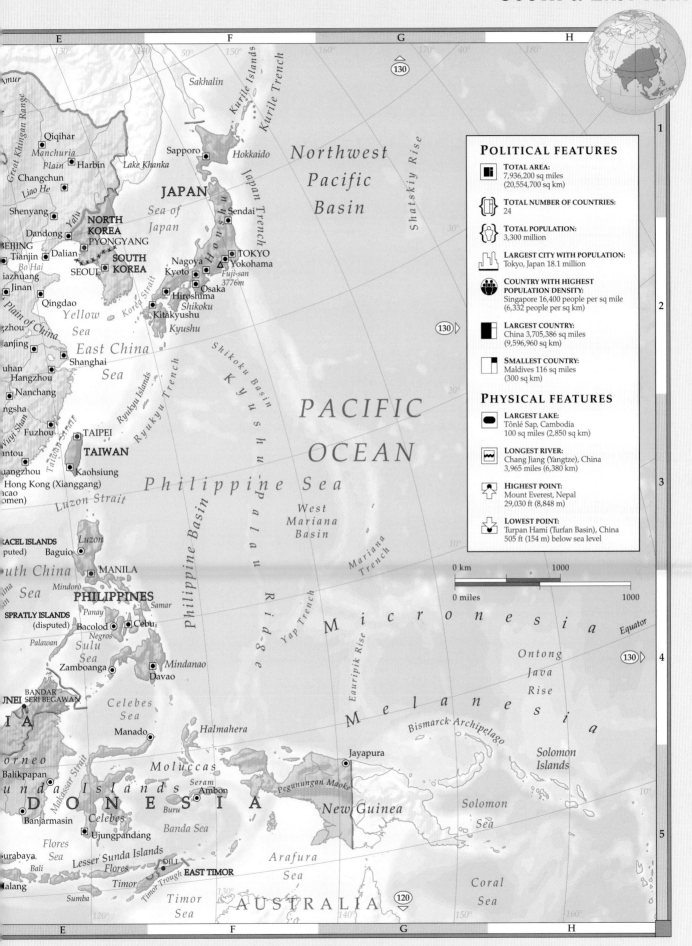

E   F   G   H

130°   140°   50°   150°   160°   40°   170°   180°

130

Great Khingan Range

Amur

Qiqihar

Manchuria
Plain   Harbin   *Lake Khanka*

Sakhalin

Changchun

Liao He

Shenyang

Sapporo

Hokkaido

Kurile Islands

Kurile Trench

Northwest
Pacific
Basin

Shatskiy Rise

1

JAPAN

Sea of
Japan

Sendai

Japan Trench

NORTH
KOREA

Yalu

Dandong   **PYONGYANG**

Honshu

BEIJING

Tianjin   Dalian

SOUTH
SEOUL   **KOREA**

Bo Hai

TOKYO
Nagoya   Yokohama
Kyoto   *Fuji-san*
3776m

△

POLITICAL FEATURES

TOTAL AREA:
7,936,200 sq miles
(20,554,700 sq km)

TOTAL NUMBER OF COUNTRIES:
24

TOTAL POPULATION:
3,300 million

LARGEST CITY WITH POPULATION:
Tokyo, Japan 18.1 million

COUNTRY WITH HIGHEST
POPULATION DENSITY:
Singapore 16,400 people per sq mile
(6,332 people per sq km)

LARGEST COUNTRY:
China 3,705,386 sq miles
(9,596,960 sq km)

SMALLEST COUNTRY:
Maldives 116 sq miles
(300 sq km)

PHYSICAL FEATURES

LARGEST LAKE:
Tônlé Sap, Cambodia
100 sq miles (2,850 sq km)

LONGEST RIVER:
Chang Jiang (Yangtze), China
3,965 miles (6,380 km)

HIGHEST POINT:
Mount Everest, Nepal
29,030 ft (8,848 m)

LOWEST POINT:
Turpan Hami (Turfan Basin), China
505 ft (154 m) below sea level

2

iazhuang   Jinan

Osaka
Hiroshima

Shikoku

Qingdao

Kitakyushu

Kyushu

30°

130

nanjing

Yellow
Sea

Korea Strait

uhan

East China
Shanghai   *Sea*

Hangzhou

Nanchang

Shikoku Basin

ngsha

K   y   u   s   h   u

PACIFIC

20°

Wuyi Shan

Fuzhou

TAIPEI

Ryukyu Islands

Ryukyu Trench

antou

TAIWAN

OCEAN

uangzhou
Kaohsiung

Taiwan Strait

Hong Kong (Xianggang)
acao   men)

Luzon Strait

Philippine Sea

3

West
Mariana
Basin

RACEL ISLANDS
puted)   *Luzon*

Baguio

Philippine Basin

Mariana Trench

uth China

MANILA

Mindoro

Sea

PHILIPPINES   *Samar*

Palau Ridge

Yap Trench

SPRATLY ISLANDS   *Panay*
(disputed)   Bacolod   Cebu

0 km   1000

Palawan   *Negros*

0 miles   1000

Sulu
Sea

M   i   c   r   o   n   e   s   i   a

Equator

Zamboanga

Mindanao
Davao

130

4

BANDAR
JNEI   SERI BEGAWAN

Celebes
Sea

Eauripik Rise

M   e   l   a   n   e   s   i   a

Ontong
Java
Rise

IA

orneo

Manado

Halmahera

Bismarck Archipelago

Solomon
Islands

Balikpapan

Moluccas

Jayapura

Solomon
Sea

10°

unda   *Islands*   **DONESIA**

Seram
Ambon

Pegunungan Maoke

5

Banjarmasin   *Celebes*

Buru

Banda Sea

New Guinea

Flores
Sea
urabaya

Ujungpandang

Lesser Sunda Islands

Arafura
Sea

Bali   *Flores*

Timor Trough   DILI   **EAST TIMOR**

Coral
Sea

alang   *Sumba*   *Timor*

Timor
Sea

AUSTRALIA

120°   130°   140°   120   150°   160°

E   F   G   H

WESTERN CHINA & MONGOLIA

POPULATION

- ◉ Over 500,000
- ◉ 100,000 – 500,000
- ○ 50,000 – 100,000
- ○ Less than 50,000
- ● National capital
- ● Internal administrative capital

0 km — 400
0 miles — 400

N

RUSSIAN FED

KAZAKHSTAN

Kazakhskiy Melkosopochnik

Kulunda Steppe

Zapadnyy Sayan

Yenisey

Hövsgöl Nuur

Uvs Nuur

Ulaangom

Ölgiy

Charus Nuur

Hyargas Nuur

Har Nuur

Hovd

Mörö

Tsetserleg

M O N

Altay

Bayanhongor

Ozero Zaysan

Altay

Hangayn Nuruu

Altai Mountains

Ozero Balkhash

Ulungur Hu

Karamay

Gurbantünggüt Shamo

Kuytun

Shihezi

Fukang

Jimsar

Aj Bogd Uul 3802m

Atas Bogd 2702m

G

Ozero Issyk-Kul'

Yining

Ürümqi

Qitai

KYRGYZSTAN

Tien Shan

Turpan

Turpan Pendi

Hami

Xingxingxia

Ejin Qi

Bohoro Shan

Pik Pobedy 7439m

Korla

Bosten Hu

Lop Nur

GANSU

Kuruktag

Qilian Shan

Kashi

Tarim He

Tarim Basin

XINJIANG UYGUR

TAJIKISTAN

Yengisar

Shache

ZIZHIQU

Ruoqiang

Altun Shan

Danghe Nanshan

Qinghai Hu

AFGH.

Yecheng
(claimed by India)

Pishan

Moyu

Taklimakan Shamo

Qaidam Pendi

Karakoram Range

K2 8611m

Hotan

Qira

Kunlun Shan

Golmud

Burhan Budai Shan

Dulan

PAKISTAN

Kashmir

AKSAI CHIN

AKSAI CHIN
(administered by China, claimed by India)

Anyêmaqên S

C

QINGHAI

H

JAMMU AND KASHMIR

Indus

Rutog

Qingzang Gaoyuan
(Plateau of Tibet)

Tongtian He

Bayan Har Sha

Yushu

Mekong

DEMCHOK/DÊMQOG
(administered by China, claimed by India)

Gar

Zanda

XIZANG

ZIZHIQU

Tanggula Shan

Nyima

Amdo

Qamdo

Tangra Yumco

Gyaring Co

Nam Co

Nagqu

Saliween

Jinsha Jiang

(Tibet)

Ngangzê Co

Damxung

Nyainqêntanglha Shan

Siling Co

Yamuna

Ganges

Brahmaputra

Lhazê

Xigazê

Maizhokunggar

Lhasa

ARUNÁCHAL PRADESH
(claimed by China)

Hengduan Shan

NEPAL

Gonggar

Gyangzê

Mount Everest 8848m

Himalayas

INDIA

BHUTAN

INDIA

MYANMAR (BURMA)

104

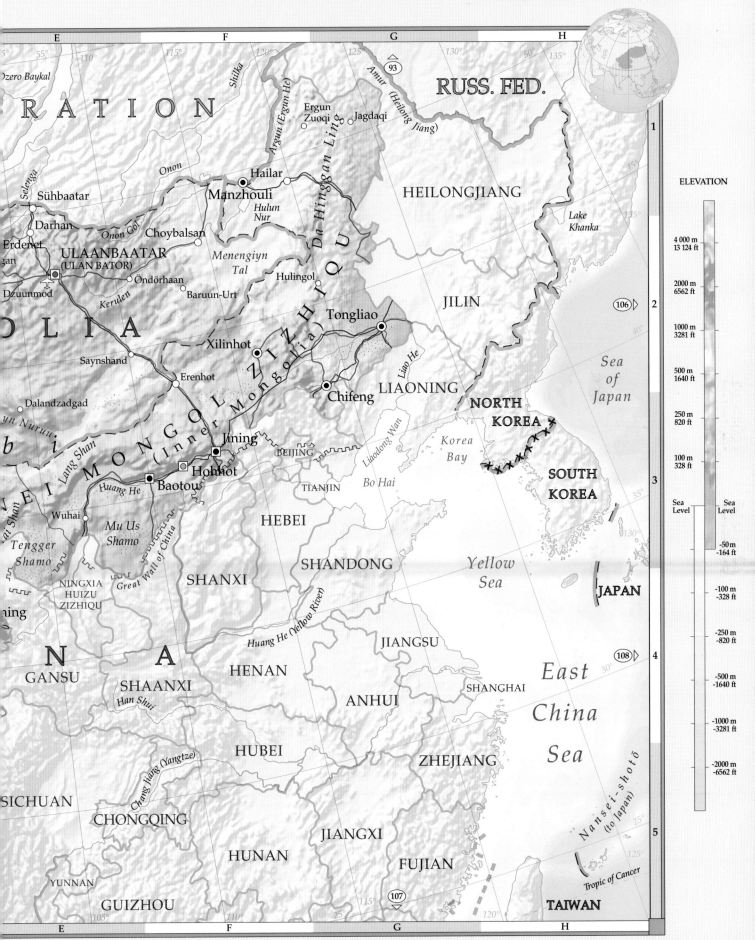

Ozero Baykal

R A T I O N

RUSS. FED.

93

Amur (Heilong Jiang)

HEILONGJIANG

Shilka

Argun (Ergun He)

Ergun Zuoqi

Jagdaqi

Hailar

Manzhouli

Hulun Nur

Da Hinggan Ling

Lake Khanka

Selenga

Sühbaatar

Onon

Darhan

Onon Gol

Choybalsan

Erdenet

ULAANBAATAR
(ULAN BATOR)

Dzuunmod

Kerulen

Öndörhaan

Baruun-Urt

Menengiyn Tal

Hulingol

JILIN

Tongliao

Sea
of
Japan

O L I A

Xilinhot

Saynshand

Erenhot

Chifeng

NEI MONGOL ZIZHIQU
(Inner Mongolia)

Liao He

LIAONING

Liaodong Wan

NORTH
KOREA

106

Dalandzadgad

yn Nuruu

b i

Jining

Hohhot

Baotou

Huang He

Wuhai

Lang Shan

BEIJING

TIANJIN

Korea Bay

Bo Hai

SOUTH
KOREA

JAPAN

Tengger Shamo

Mu Us Shamo

Great Wall of China

HEBEI

Yellow
Sea

NINGXIA
HUIZU
ZIZHIQU

ning

N   A

GANSU

SHANXI

SHANDONG

SHAANXI

Han Shui

HENAN

Huang He (Yellow River)

JIANGSU

SHANGHAI

East

108

ANHUI

China

SICHUAN

Chang Jiang (Yangtze)

HUBEI

ZHEJIANG

Sea

Nansei-shotō (to Japan)

CHONGQING

JIANGXI

HUNAN

FUJIAN

Tropic of Cancer

YUNNAN

GUIZHOU

107

TAIWAN

ELEVATION

4 000 m
13 124 ft

2000 m
6562 ft

1000 m
3281 ft

500 m
1640 ft

250 m
820 ft

100 m
328 ft

Sea
Level

Sea
Level

-50 m
-164 ft

-100 m
-328 ft

-250 m
-820 ft

-500 m
-1640 ft

-1000 m
-3281 ft

-2000 m
-6562 ft

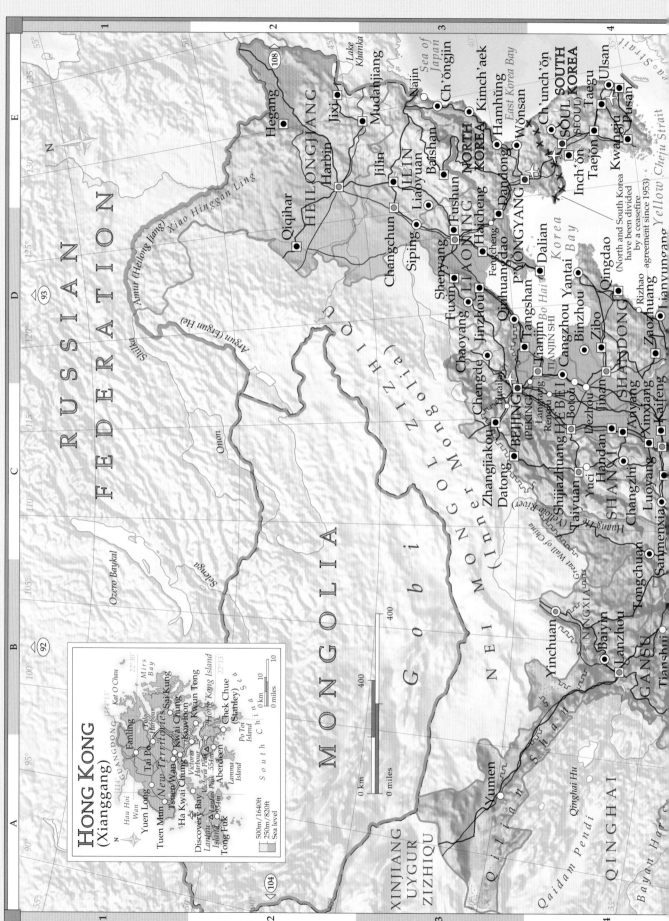

POPULATION

- Over 500,000
- 100,000 – 500,000
- 50,000 – 100,000
- Less than 50,000
- National capital
- Internal administrative capital

RUSSIAN FEDERATION

MONGOLIA

Nei Mongol Zizhiqu (Inner Mongolia)

Gobi

108

93

92

104

HONG KONG (Xianggang)

GUANGDONG
Hau Hoi Wan
Mirs Bay
Kat O Chau
Yuen Long
Fanling
Tolo Harbour
Sai Kung
Tuen Mun
New Territories
Tai Po
Tsuen Wan
Kwai Chung
Kwun Tong
Hong Kong Island
Ha Kwai Chung
Kowloon
Victoria Harbour
Victoria Peak 554m
Lantau Island
Lantau Park 934m
Discovery Bay
Aberdeen
Chek Chue (Stanley)
Tong Fuk
Lamma Island
Po Toi Island
South China Sea

500m/1640ft
250m/820ft
Sea level

Heilongjiang
Amur (Heilong Jiang)
Shilka
Argun (Ergun He)
Onon
Xiao Hinggan Ling
Hegang
Harbin
Jixi
Mudanjiang
Qiqihar
HEILONGJIANG
Changchun
Jilin
JILIN
Liaoyuan
Siping
Baishan
Najin
Ch'ŏngjin
Kimch'aek
Sea of Japan
Lake Khanka
Fushun
Shenyang
LIAONING
Haicheng
Fengcheng
Dandong
Liaoyang
Fuxin
Chaoyang
Jinzhou
P'YONGYANG
NORTH KOREA
Hamhŭng
Wŏnsan
East Korea Bay
Ch'unch'ŏn
SOUTH KOREA
SOUL (SEOUL)
Inch'ŏn
Taejŏn
Taegu
Kwangju
Ulsan
Pusan
Yellow Sea / Cheju Strait
(North and South Korea have been divided by a ceasefire agreement since 1953)
Qinhuangdao
Dalian
Korea Bay
Yantai
Cangzhou
Qingdao
SHANDONG
Zibo
Jinan
Binzhou
Dezhou
Botou
Zaozhuang
Rizhao
Lianyungang
Chengde
Zhangjiakou
Datong
BEIJING (PEKING)
Langfang
Rengqiu
HEBEI
TIANJIN SHI
Tianjin
Tangshan
Bo Hai
Shijiazhuang
Handan
Anyang
Xinxiang
Kaifeng
Yuci
Taiyuan
SHANXI
Changzhi
Luoyang
Tongchuan
Sanmenxia
Huang He (Yellow River)
Great Wall of China
Qilian Shan
Yumen
Yinchuan
NINGXIA
Baiyin
Lanzhou
GANSU
Tianshui
QINGHAI
Qinghai Hu
Qaidam Pendi
Bayan Har
Ozero Baykal
Selenga
Bayin
South China Sea

400
400
0 km
0 miles
10
0 km 10
0 miles

JAPAN

East China Sea

Okinawa

Nansei-shotō
(part of Japan)

Tropic of Cancer

Taiwan Strait

Chilung
TAIPEI
T'aichung
Chiai
TAIWAN
T'ainan
Kaohsiung

PACIFIC OCEAN

Luzon Strait

PHILIPPINES

(China and Taiwan claim
all of each other's territory)

(130)

(117)

Shanghai
Suzhou
Wuxi
Jiaxing
Nanjing
Hefei
Wuhu
Anqing
Ningbo
Wenzhou
Hangzhou
ZHEJIANG
Jinhua
Shangrao
ANHUI
Jingdezhen
Lichuan
Nanping
Fuzhou
Yong'an
Quanzhou
Xiamen
Shantou
Shangzhou
Hong Kong (Xianggang)
Macao (Aomen)
Maoming
Haikou
Zhanjiang
Hainan Dao

JIANGXI FUJIAN

Nanchang
Xiangtan
Ganzhou
Longyan
Shaoguan
GUANGDONG
Guangzhou
Dongguan
Jiangmen
Zhaoqing
Yulin

HUNAN

Changsha
Loudi
Hengyang
Chenzhou

South China Sea

PARACEL ISLANDS
(disputed by China,
Taiwan and Vietnam)
Amphitrite Group
Crescent Group
Triton Island

SPRATLY ISLANDS
(disputed by China,
Malaysia, Philippines,
Taiwan and Vietnam)
Flat Island
Nanshan Island
Thitu Island
Loaita Island
Namyit Island
Len Dao
Spratly Island

Thithu Island

XIZANG ZIZHIQU (Tibet)

SICHUAN
Sichuan Pendi
Chengdu
Leshan
Zigong
Neijiang
Chongqing
CHONGQING
GUIZHOU
Zunyi
Guiyang
Anshun

HUBEI
Xinyang
Yichang
Wuhan
Huangshi
Jiujiang

Nanyang
Guangyuan
Mianyang
Ya'an
Litang
Xichang

Huaihua
Lengshuitan
Quanzhou
Liuzhou
GUANGXI
ZHUANGZU
ZIZHIQU
Nanning
Qinzhou
Beihai
Xuwen
Danzhou
Dongfang
HAINAN

Gulf of Tongking

VIETNAM

LAOS

Red River

Gejiu
Kunming
YUNNAN
Wuliang Shan
Dali
Baoshan
Jinghong
Mekong

THAILAND

CAMBODIA

Gulf of Thailand

(114)

(114)

INDIA

Hengduan Shan

Salween

MYANMAR (BURMA)

Tropic of Cancer

Jinsha Jiang

Chang Jiang (Yangtze)

Zhengzhou

ELEVATION

4 000 m	13 124 ft
2000 m	6562 ft
1000 m	3281 ft
500 m	1640 ft
250 m	820 ft
100 m	328 ft
Sea Level	Sea Level
-50 m	-164 ft
-100 m	-328 ft
-250 m	-820 ft
-500 m	-1640 ft
-1000 m	-3281 ft
-2000 m	-6562 ft

JAPAN

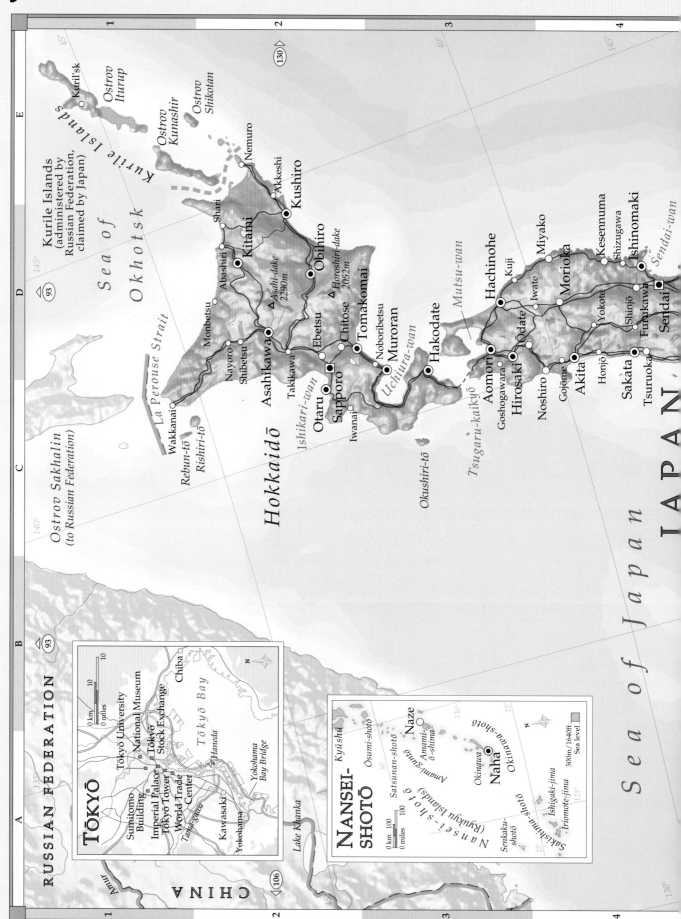

POPULATION

- ● Over 500,000
- ◉ 100,000 – 500,000
- ○ 50,000 – 100,000
- ∘ Less than 50,000
- ● National capital

RUSSIAN FEDERATION 93

Ostrov Sakhalin (to Russian Federation)

Amur

CHINA

Lake Khanka

106

Kurile Islands (administered by Russian Federation, claimed by Japan)

Kurile Islands

93

Sea of Okhotsk

Kuril'sk
Ostrov Iturup
Ostrov Kunashir
Ostrov Shikotan

Nemuro
Akkeshi
Kushiro
Shari
Kitami
Abashiri
Monbetsu
△ Asahi-dake 2290m
Obihiro
△ Horoshiri-dake 2052m
Tomakomai
Noboribetsu
Muroran
Uchiura-wan
Hakodate
Nayoro
Shibetsu
Asahikawō
Takikawa
Ebetsu
Chitose
Ishikari-wan
Otaru
Sapporo
Iwanai

La Perouse Strait
Wakkanai
Rebun-tō
Rishiri-tō

Hokkaidō

Okushiri-tō

Tsugaru-kaikyō
Mutsu-wan

Aomori
Goshogawara
Hirosaki
Noshiro
Gojōme
Akita
Honjō
Sakata
Tsuruoka

Hachinohe
Kuji
Iwate
Odate
Miyako
Morioka
Yokote
Shinjō
Furukawa

Kesennuma
Shizugawa
Ishinomaki
Sendai
Sendai-wan

JAPAN

Sea of Japan

TŌKYŌ

Chiba
Tōkyō Bay
Tōkyō University
National Museum
Tōkyō Stock Exchange
Sumitomo Building
Imperial Palace
Tōkyō Tower
World Trade Center
Haneda
Yokohama Bay Bridge
Kawasaki
Yokohama
Tama-gawa

130

NANSEI-SHOTŌ

Kyūshū
Ōsumi-shotō
Satsunan-shotō
Naze
Amami-ō-shima
Amami-shotō
Okinawa-shotō
Naha
Okinawa
Nansei-shotō (Ryūkyū Islands)
Senkaku-shotō
Sakishima-shotō
Ishigaki-jima
Iriomote-jima

500m/1640ft
Sea level

Honshū

Iwaki
Hitachi
Sukagawa
Utsunomiya
Mito
Ōyama
Chōshi
Maebashi
Kawagoe
Chiba
Yokohama
TOKYO
Kawasaki
Nagaoka
Matsumoto
Jōetsu
Nagano
Toyama
Kōfu
Fuji
Shizuoka
Hamamatsu
Fujisan 3776m △
Takaoka
Kanazawa
Toyota
Okazaki
Ise
Komatsu
Gifu
Ōgaki
Nagoya
Ōtsu
Tsu
Owase
Fukui
Nakatsugawa
Tsuruga
Kyōto
Ōsaka
Wakayama
Shingū
Tsu
Gobō
Tanabe
Tottori
Himeji
Kōbe
Awaji-shima
Yonago
Matsue
Okayama
Kurashiki
Kure
Niihama
Matsuyama
Kōchi
Nakamura
Sukumo
Gōtsu
Hamada
Masuda
Hiroshima
Iwakuni
Hōfu
Ube
Ōita
Nobeoka
Miyazaki
Miyakonojō
Nagato
Yamaguchi
Kurume
Ōmuta
Natsushiro
Shimonoseki
Kitakyūshū
Fukuoka
Kumamoto
Sendai
Kagoshima
Sasebo
Kumamoto
Nagasaki

Boso-hanto
Sagami-nada
Ō-shima
Nii-jima
Miyake-jima
Mikura-jima
Izu-shotō
Hachijō-jima
Izu-hantō
Suruga-wan
Kōzu-shima

Shinano-gawa
Mikuni-samnyaku
Itoigawa
Hida-sanmyaku
Toyama-wan
Wakasa-wan
Biwa-ko
Ise-wan

PACIFIC OCEAN

Shikoku
Tosa-wan
Kii-suidō
Harima-nada

Chūgoku-sanchi

Oki-shotō
Dōgo
Dōzen

Liancourt Rocks
(claimed by Japan
& South Korea)

SOUTH
KOREA

Korea Strait
Tsushima
Iki
Kō-saki

Kyūshū
Bungo-suidō
Iyo-nada
Ōita
Natsushiro

Amakusa-nada
Koshikijima-rettō
Goto-rettō

Shibushi-wan
Ōsumi-shotō
Tanega-shima
Yaku-shima
Kagoshima-wan

East
China Sea

N

ELEVATION

4000 m
13 124 ft

2000 m
6562 ft

1000 m
3281 ft

500 m
1640 ft

250 m
820 ft

100 m
328 ft

Sea
Level

Sea
Level

-250 m
-820 ft

-500 m
-1640 ft

-1000 m
-3281 ft

-2000 m
-6562 ft

-3000 m
-9843 ft

-4000 m
-13 124 ft

0 km   200
0 miles   200

POPULATION

- Over 500,000
- 100,000 – 500,000
- 50,000 – 100,000
- Less than 50,000
- National capital

Arabian Sea

Kalyān
Mumbai (Bombay)
Pune
Ahmadnagar
Bārāmati
Nizāmābād
Nānded
Jagdalpur
Andhra Pradesh
Karīmnagar
Vizianagaram
Visākhapatnam
Solāpur
Sāngli
Secunderābād
Rājahmund
Kolhāpur
Gulbarga
Hyderābād
Kākinā
Belgaum
Rāichūr
Krishna
Vijayawāda
Pānji
Gadag
Kurnool
Chīrāla
Machilīpatnam
Hubli
Nandyāl
Ongole
Dāvangere
Tādpatri
Kāvali
Anantapur
Nellore
Shimoga
Cuddapah
Bhadrāvati
Udupi
Tumkūr
Chennai (Madras)
Mangalore
Bangalore
Vellore
Kānchīpuram
Kāsargod
Mandya
Krishnagiri
Tiruppattur
Cannanore
Mysore
Salem
Pondicherry
Calicut
Erode
Neyveli
Coimbatore
Tamil Nādu
Trichūr
Tiruchchirāppalli
Ernākulam
Dindigul
Cochin
Madurai
Alleppey
Rājapālaiyam
Jaffna
Quilon
SRI LANKA
Tuticorin
Mannar
Trivandrum
Vavuniya
Trincomalee
Nāgercoil
Puttalam
Anuradhapura
Gulf of Mannar
Matale
Batticaloa
Negombo
Kandy
COLOMBO
Sri Jayawardanapura
Kalutara
Ratnapura
Galle
Matara

West... Ghats
Godāvari
Karnātaka
Deccan
Tungabhadra Reservoir
Malabār Coast
Kerala
Palk Strait
Coromandel Coast

Amīndīvi Islands

Lakshadweep (Laccadive Islands) (to India)

Kavaratti Island

Kalpeni Island

Nine Degree Channel

Minicoy Island

Eight Degree Channel

Ihavandippolhu Atoll

MALDIVES

Faadhippolhu Atoll

Horsburgh Atoll

Ari Atoll

Male'Atoll
MALE'

Felidhu Atoll

Mulaku Atoll

Kolhumadulu Atoll

Hadhdhunmathi Atoll

North Huvadhu Atoll

Equator

South Huvadhu Atoll

Gan 118

Addu Atoll

INDIAN

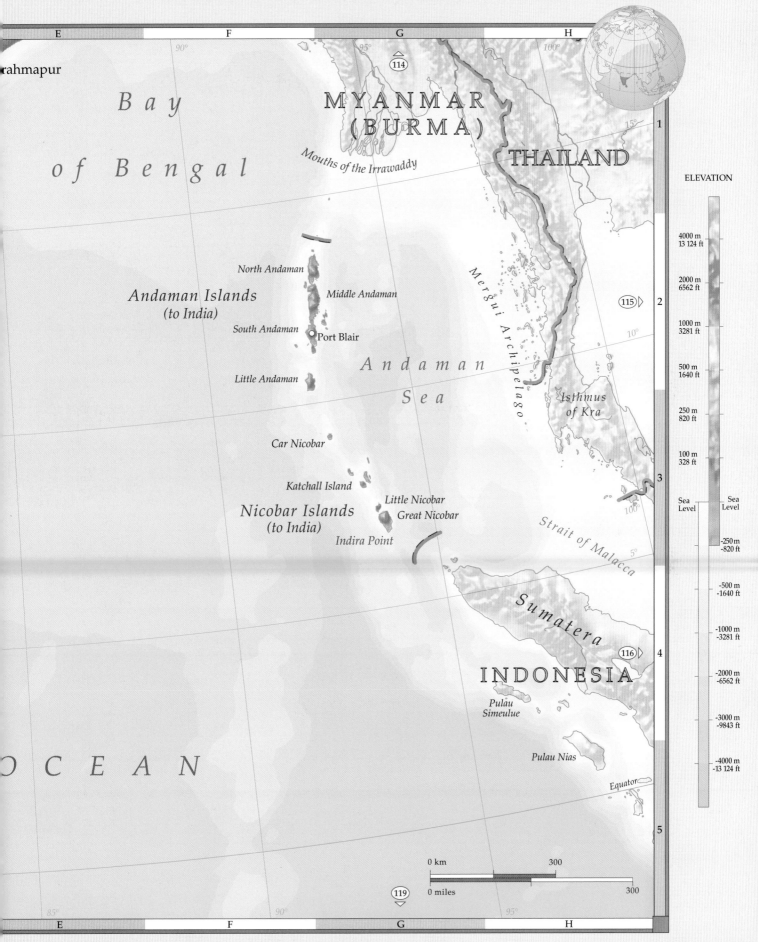

Bay

of Bengal

MYANMAR
(BURMA)

THAILAND

Mouths of the Irrawaddy

North Andaman

Middle Andaman

Andaman Islands
(to India)

South Andaman   ○ Port Blair

Little Andaman

Andaman

Sea

Mergui Archipelago

*Isthmus
of Kra*

Car Nicobar

Katchall Island

Nicobar Islands
(to India)

Little Nicobar
Great Nicobar

Indira Point

Strait of Malacca

Sumatera

INDONESIA

*Pulau
Simeulue*

O C E A N

Pulau Nias

Equator

rahmapur

ELEVATION

4000 m
13 124 ft

2000 m
6562 ft

1000 m
3281 ft

500 m
1640 ft

250 m
820 ft

100 m
328 ft

Sea   Sea
Level   Level

-250 m
-820 ft

-500 m
-1640 ft

-1000 m
-3281 ft

-2000 m
-6562 ft

-3000 m
-9843 ft

-4000 m
-13 124 ft

0 km   300

0 miles   300

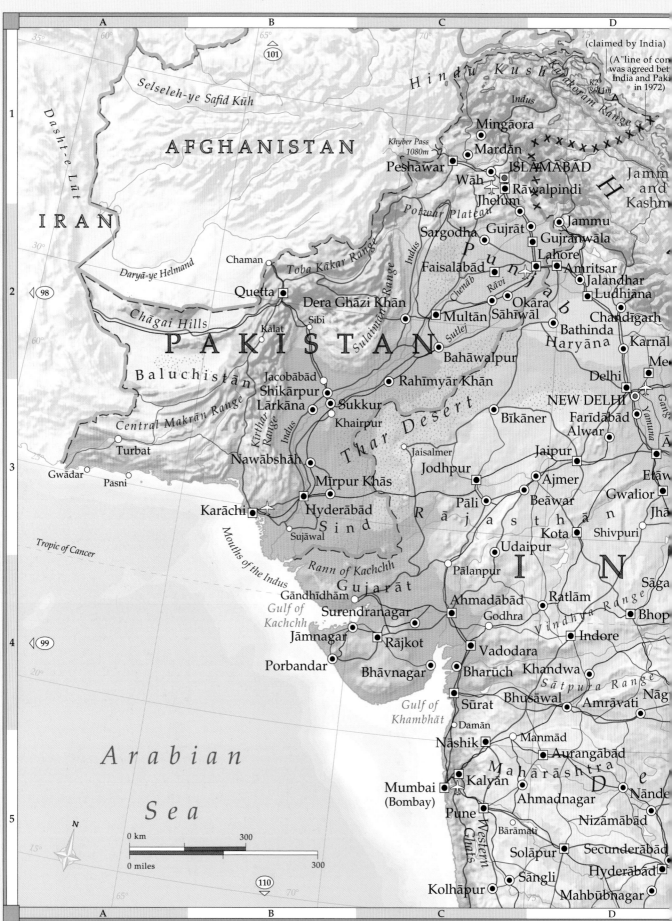

(claimed by India)

(A "line of con
was agreed bet
India and Paki
in 1972)

POPULATION

- ◉ Over 500,000
- ◎ 100,000 – 500,000
- ○ 50,000 – 100,000
- ∘ Less than 50,000
- ● National capital

Tropic of Cancer

Arabian Sea

0 km   300

0 miles   300

110

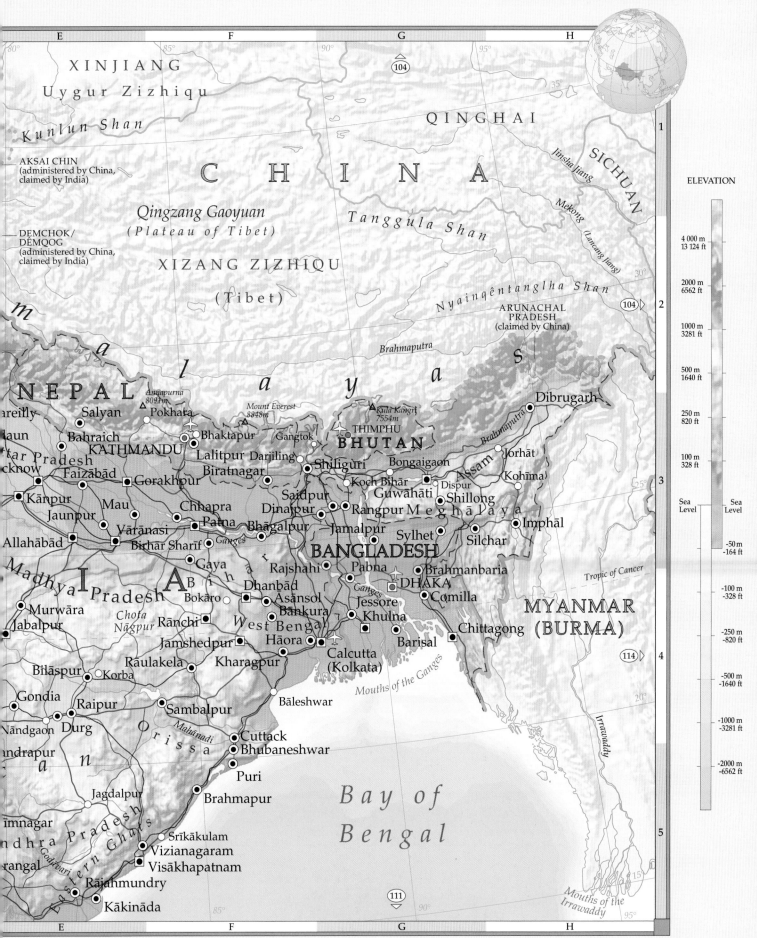

XINJIANG

Uygur Zizhiqu

Kunlun Shan

QINGHAI

SICHUAN

C H I N A

AKSAI CHIN
(administered by China,
claimed by India)

Jinsha Jiang

Qingzang Gaoyuan
(Plateau of Tibet)

Tanggula Shan

Mekong (Lancang Jiang)

DEMCHOK/
DÊMQOG
(administered by China,
claimed by India)

XIZANG ZIZHIQU

(Tibet)

Nyainqêntanglha Shan

ARUNACHAL
PRADESH
(claimed by China)

Brahmaputra

m   a   l   a   y   a   s

NEPAL

Annapurna
8091m
Pokhara

Mount Everest
8848m

Kula Kangri
7554m

Dibrugarh

Brahmaputra

reilly   Salyan

THIMPHU

Bahraich

Bhaktapur

Gangtok

BHUTAN

Jorhāt

aun

KATHMANDU

Lalitpur Darjiling

Shiliguri

Bongaigaon

Assam

Kohīma

tar Pradesh   Faizābād

Biratnagar

Koch Bihār

Dispur

cknow

Gorakhpur

Saidpur

Guwāhāti

Shillong

Kānpur   Mau

Chhapra

Dinajpur

Rangpur

Me g h ā l a y a

Imphāl

Jaunpur   Vārānasi

Patna

Bhāgalpur

Jamalpur

Silchar

Allahābād   Bihār Sharif   Ganges

Sylhet

Gaya

BANGLADESH

Madhya

I   A

Rajshahi

Pabna

Brahmanbaria

Murwāra

Dhanbād

DHAKA

Comilla

Jabalpur

Pradesh

Bokāro   Asānsol

Jessore

MYANMAR
(BURMA)

Chota
Nāgpur   Rānchi

Bankura

Khulna

Bilāspur   Korba

Jamshedpur

West Bengal

Chittagong

Gondia   Raipur

Rāulakela

Kharagpur

Hāora

Barisal

Sambalpur

Bāleshwar

Calcutta
(Kolkata)

Nāndgaon   Durg

Mahānadi

Mouths of the Ganges

ndrapur   Orissa   Cuttack

Jagdalpur

Bhubaneshwar

Bay of

imnagar   Pradesh   Puri   Brahmapur

Bengal

rangal   Srīkākulam

Godāvari

Eastern Ghats

Vizianagaram

Visākhapatnam

Rājahmundry

Kākināda

Mouths of the
Irrawaddy

ELEVATION

4 000 m
13 124 ft

2000 m
6562 ft

1000 m
3281 ft

500 m
1640 ft

250 m
820 ft

100 m
328 ft

Sea
Level

Sea
Level

-50 m
-164 ft

-100 m
-328 ft

-250 m
-820 ft

-500 m
-1640 ft

-1000 m
-3281 ft

-2000 m
-6562 ft

Tropic of Cancer

Irrawaddy

MAINLAND SOUTHEAST ASIA

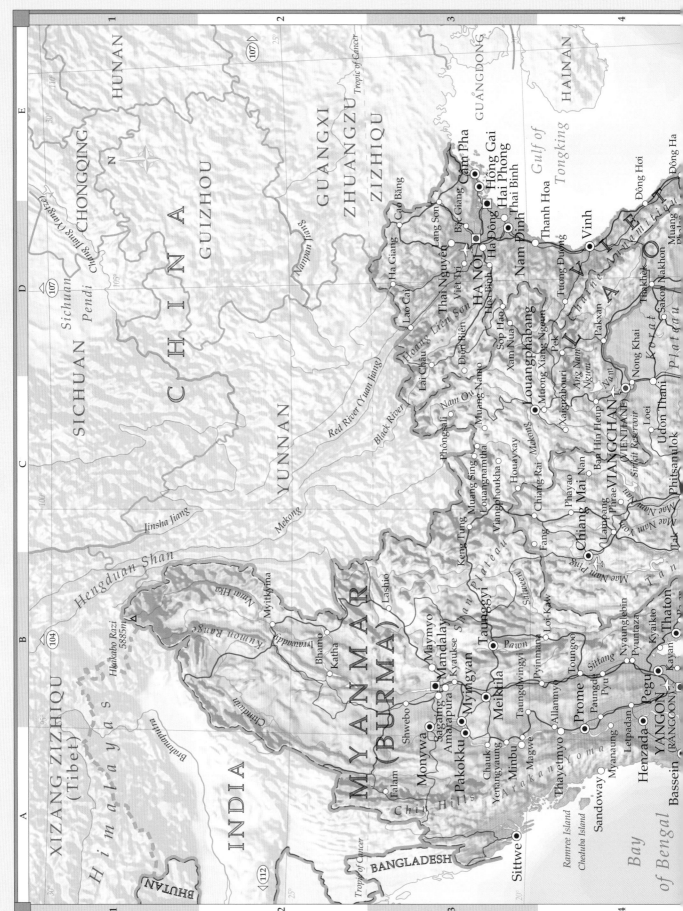

POPULATION

- ▣ Over 500,000
- ◉ 100,000 – 500,000
- ○ 50,000 – 100,000
- ○ Less than 50,000
- ● National capital

Quảng Ngãi
Quy Nhơn
Pléy Cu
Tuy Hòa
Nha Trang
Đà Lạt
Cam Ranh
Phan Rang-Tháp Chàm
Phan Thiết
Biên Hòa
Mỹ Tho
Hồ Chí Minh
Vũng Tàu
Trà Vinh
Sóc Trăng
Bạc Liêu
Di Linh
Kâmpong Chàm
Svay Riêng
Long Xuyên
Cần Thơ
Châu Đốc
Rạch Gia
Ca Mau
Cà Mau
Vĩnh Rạch Gia
Mouths of the Mekong
Côn Đảo

South China Sea

Kepulauan Natuna
(to Indonesia)

Khöngxedôn
Pakxé
Champasak
Samakhixai
Virôchey
Lôm
Tônlé Sab
Kâmpong Tráběk
Stoeng Trèng
Krâchéh
Kâmpong Chhnang
Suông
Kâmpong Cham

M

CAMBODIA

KRUNG THEP

Ubon Ratchathani
Surin
Buriram
Nakhon Ratchasima
Nakhon Sawan
Lop Buri
Sara Buri
Samut Prakan
Chon Buri
Pattaya
Rayong

Muang Khōng
Stoeng Sěn
Moung Roessei
Kampong
Pôtîpisăt
Bătdâmbâng
Reăng Kesei
Chanthaburi

Phnum Dângrèk
Krâ'lanh
Chuŏr Phnum Krâvanh
Kâ'âmh Odông
Kâmpong Spœ
Kâmpông Saôm

PHNUM PENH

Mekong

Ko Chang

Gulf of Thailand

Nakhon Pathom
Ratchaburi
Phetchaburi
Ayutthaya
Ao Krung Thep
Ban Hua Hin

Srinagarind Reservoir

Chatthaburi

Bilauktaung Range

Ye
Tavoy

Mali Kyun
Kadan Kyun
Mergui
Daung Kyun
Letsôk-aw Kyun
Lambi Kyun

Zadetkyi Kyun

Tenasserim

Isthmus of Kra

Ranong

Phang-Nga
Ko Phra Thong
Ko Phuket
Phuket

Chumphon
Lang Suan

Surat Thani
Sichon

Ko Phangan
Ko Samui

Nakhon Si Thammarat

Pak Phanang
Thung Song
Thale Luang
Phatthalung
Songkhla
Hat Yai
Yala
Pattani
Narathiwat

Trang
Ko Lanta
Ko Ta Ru Tao
Pulau Langkawi
Pulau Pinang

MALAYSIA

Malay Peninsula

Strait of Malacca

Mergui Archipelago

Andaman Sea

North Andaman
Middle Andaman
South Andaman
Little Andaman

Andaman Islands
(to India)

Katchall Island
Great Nicobar
Little Nicobar

Nicobar Islands
(to India)

Car Nicobar

INDIAN OCEAN

Pulau Simeulue

INDONESIA

Sumatera
(Sumatra)

the Irrawaddy

117
116
116
111

200
200
0 km
0 miles

ELEVATION

4 000 m
13 124 ft

2000 m
6562 ft

1000 m
3281 ft

500 m
1640 ft

250 m
820 ft

100 m
328 ft

Sea Level — Sea Level

-50 m
-164 ft

-100 m
-328 ft

-250 m
-820 ft

-500 m
-1640 ft

-1000 m
-3281 ft

-2000 m
-6562 ft

SINGAPORE

0 km   10
0 miles   10

MALAYSIA

Johore Strait

Causeway

Pulau Ubin

Pulau Tekong

Lim Chu Kang

Hougang New Town

Changi

Bukit Panjang

Choa Chu Kang

△ *Bukit Timah* 176m

Queenstown

Bedok New Town

Jurong Industrial Estate

City

Telok Blangah

Sentosa

Selat Pandan

Pulau Sudong

Pulau Pawai

Urban areas
Open areas
Nature reserves

Strait of Singapore

MYANMAR (BURMA)

LAOS

VIETNAM

THAILAND

CAMBODIA

Mekong

Gulf of Tongking

Hainan Dao (to China)

PARACEL ISLANDS
(disputed by China, Taiwan and Vietnam)

South China Sea

Gulf of Thailand

Mouths of the Mekong

SPRATLY ISLANDS
(disputed by China, Malaysia, Philippines, Taiwan and Vietnam)

Andaman Sea

Nicobar Islands (to India)

Isthmus of Kra

Bandaaceh   Sigli

Meulaboh   Langsa

Pulau Simeulue

Medan
Tebingtinggi

Pematangsiantar

Kepulauan Banyak

Sibolga

Pulau Nias

George Town

Butterworth

Pulau Pinang

Taiping

Ipoh

Klang

Seremban

Danau Toba

Melaka

Muar

Batu Pahat

Kota Bharu

Kuala Terengganu

Dungun

Cukai

Kuantan

KUALA LUMPUR

Keluang

Johor Bahru

SINGAPORE

Kepulauan Natuna

MALAYSIA

Kuching

Singkawang

Selat Serasan

Bintulu

Sibu

Batang Raja

Sri Aman

Sarawak

BRUNEI

Miri

Kota Kinabalu

BANDAR SERI BEGAWAN

Gunung Kinab... 410...

Banjaran Tama...

Sungai Kaya...

Batang Hari

Pekanbaru

Solok   Rengat

Kualatungkal

Kepulauan Lingga

Pontianak

Sungai Kapuas

Sidas

Pegunungan Muller

Borneo

Samarinda

Balikpapan

Sungai Mahaka...

Padang

Sungaipenuh

Kepulauan Mentawai

Pulau Siberut

Jambi

Pangkalpinang

Bangka

Palembang

Lahat

Kalimantan

Selat Karimata

Sampit

Pulau Belitung

Sungai Barito

Amuntai
Kandang

Banjarmasin

Pulau Laut

Bengkulu

Kotabumi

Java Sea

Pulau Mak...

Sumatera (Sumatra)

Bandarlampung

Serang

JAKARTA

Bogor

Sukabumi

Bandung

Tasikmalaya

Cirebon

Tegal

Pekalongan

Semarang

Kudus

Pulau Madura

Surabaya

Probolinggo

Malang

Jember   Mata...

Selat Sunda

Jawa (Java)

Cilacap

Magelang

Yogyakarta

Surakarta

Kediri

Madiun

Denpasar

Bali

Pulau Lombok

INDIAN OCEAN

Equator

0 km   400
0 miles   400

POPULATION

■ Over 500,000

● 100,000 - 500,000

○ 50,000 - 100,000

○ Less than 50,000

● National capital

ELEVATION

4000 m	13 124 ft
2000 m	6562 ft
1000 m	3281 ft
500 m	1640 ft
250 m	820 ft
100 m	328 ft
Sea Level	Sea Level
-250 m	-820 ft
-500 m	-1640 ft
-1000 m	-3281 ft
-2000 m	-6562 ft
-3000 m	-9843 ft
-4000 m	-13 124 ft

Labels on map:

Luzon Strait
120°
Babuyan Channel
Babuyan Island
Tuguegarao
Ilagan
Cordillera Central
Luzon
guio
guio
Dagupan
eles
Cabanatuan
NILA
Lucena
PHILIPPINES
tangas
Naga
Mindoro
Legaspi
Mindoro Strait
Sibuyan Sea
Calbayog
Samar
Roxas City
Cadiz
Tacloban
Panay Island
Leyte
Iloilo
Palawan
Bacolod City
Cebu
uerto ncesa
Negros
Bohol Sea
Butuan
Sulu Sea
Iligan
Cagayan de Oro
Bislig
Zamboanga
Moro Gulf
Mindanao
Davao
Basilan
Sulu Archipelago
Lebak
Davao Gulf
akan
General Santos

130°
Philippine Sea

109

NORTHERN MARIANA ISLANDS (to US)

GUAM (to US)

P A C I F I C
10°
Yap
MICRONESIA
122
O C E A N
Babeldaob
P A L A U

140°

1

2

3

Equator

Kepulauan Talaud
Celebes Sea
Kepulauan Sangir
Manado
Bitung
Gorontalo
Molucca Sea
Gulf of Tomini
lu
Kepulauan Banggai
Sulawesi (Celebes)
Kepulauan Sula
Danau Towuti
N
Kendari
E
Kolaka
Pulau Buton
Teluk Bone
epare
kang
Watampone
Ujungpandang
Bulukumba

Pulau Morotai
Pulau Halmahera
Halmahera Sea
Maluku (Moluccas)
Ceram Sea
Waflia
Tifu
Pulau Buru
Ambon
S
Pulau Seram
Wahai
Banda Sea
Kepulauan Kai

Pulau Waigeo
Sorong
Selat Dampier
Jazirah Doberai
Pulau Misool
Teluk Berau
I
Kepulauan Aru

Pulau Biak
Pulau Yapen
Teluk Cenderawasih
Puncak Jaya 5030m
Pegunungan Maoke
A
Papua (Irian Jaya)
Sungai Mamberamo
Jayapura
122
PAPUA
NEW
New Guinea
GUINEA
Sungai Digul

4

res
Tenggara
Flores
Savu Sea
Sumba
Kepulauan Alor
Pulau Wetar
DILI
Timor
EAST TIMOR
Nikiniki
Kupang
Kepulauan Leti
Kepulauan Tanimbar
Pulau Yamdena

A r a f u r a   S e a
Torres Strait
10°

5

Timor Sea
126
A U S T R A L I A

120°
130°
140°

E
F
G
H

THE INDIAN OCEAN

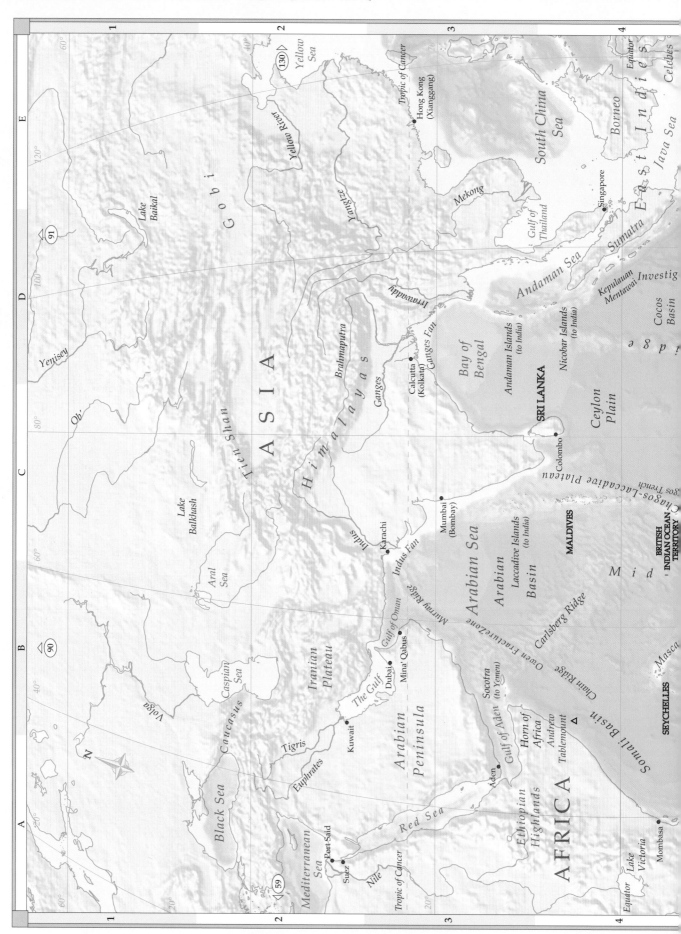

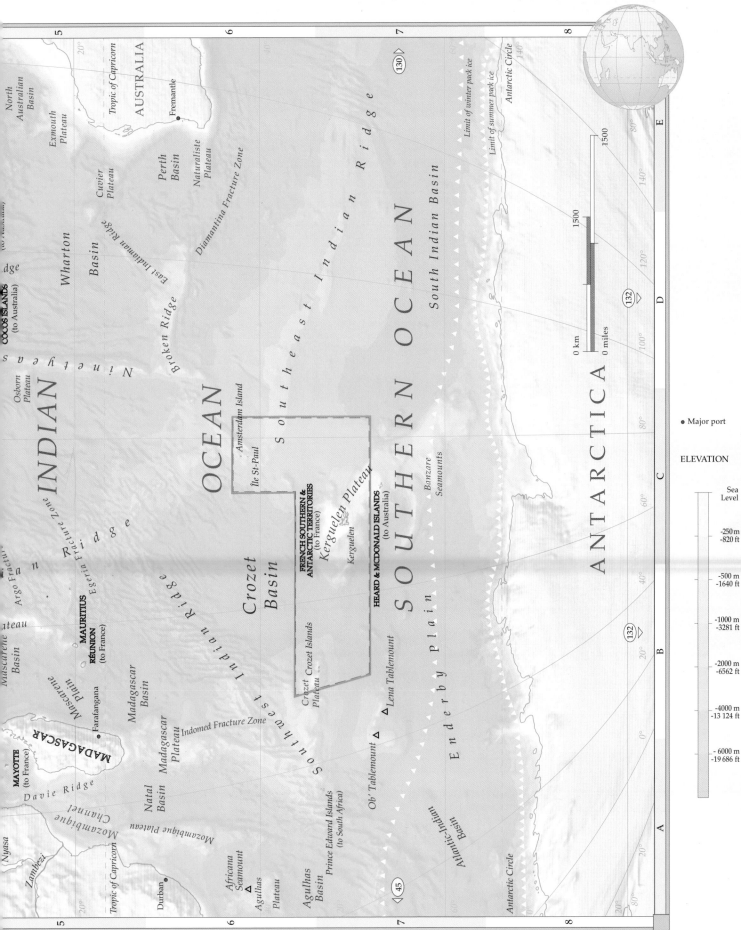

WORLD OCEANS

INDIAN OCEAN

SOUTHERN OCEAN

ANTARCTICA

AUSTRALIA

MADAGASCAR

North Australian Basin

Exmouth Plateau

Cuvier Plateau

Perth Basin

Naturaliste Plateau

Diamantina Fracture Zone

East Indiaman Ridge

Broken Ridge

Wharton Basin

COCOS ISLANDS (to Australia)

Osborn Plateau

Ninetyeast Ridge

Southeast Indian Ridge

South Indian Basin

Tropic of Capricorn

Fremantle

Amsterdam Island

Île St-Paul

Kerguelen Plateau

FRENCH SOUTHERN & ANTARCTIC TERRITORIES (to France)

Kerguelen

HEARD & McDONALD ISLANDS (to Australia)

Banzare Seamounts

Crozet Basin

Crozet Islands

Crozet Plateau

Lena Tablemount

Ob' Tablemount

Enderby Plain

Atlantic-Indian Basin

Prince Edward Islands (to South Africa)

Indomed Fracture Zone

Southwest Indian Ridge

Egeria Fracture Zone

Indian Ridge

Argo Fracture Zone

Madagascar Basin

Madagascar Plateau

Natal Basin

Mozambique Plateau

Mozambique Channel

Davie Ridge

Zambezi

Nyasa

Tropic of Capricorn

Durban

Farafangana

MAURITIUS

RÉUNION (to France)

MAYOTTE (to France)

Mascarene Basin

Mascarene Plateau

Muscarene Basin

Africana Seamount

Agulhas Plateau

Agulhas Basin

Antarctic Circle

Antarctic Circle

Limit of winter pack ice

Limit of summer pack ice

● Major port

ELEVATION

Sea Level

-250 m / -820 ft

-500 m / -1640 ft

-1000 m / -3281 ft

-2000 m / -6562 ft

-4000 m / -13 124 ft

-6000 m / -19 686 ft

0 km   1500

0 miles   1500

AUSTRALASIA & OCEANIA

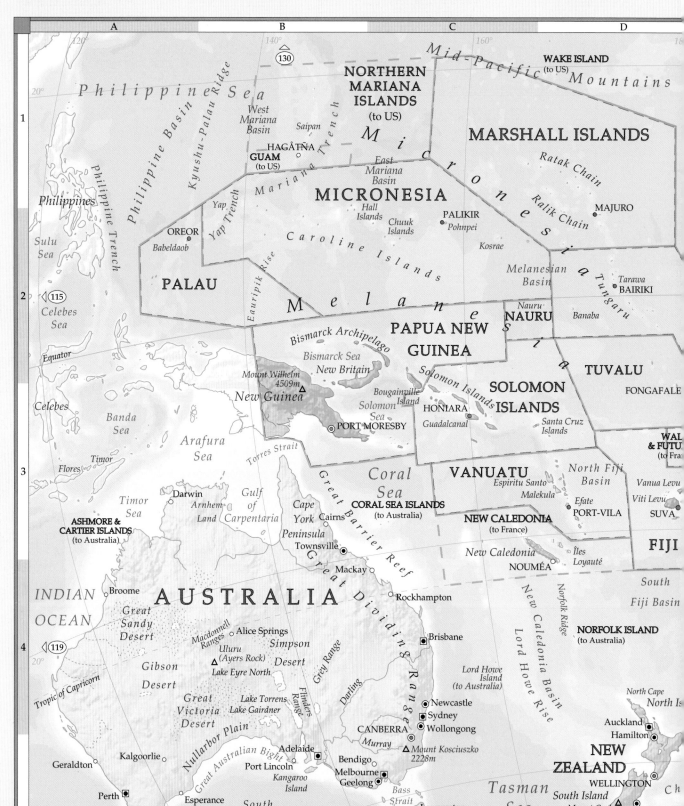

A B C D

130

Philippine Sea

Mid-Pacific Mountains

WAKE ISLAND
(to US)

NORTHERN
MARIANA
ISLANDS
(to US)

West
Mariana
Basin

Saipan

MARSHALL ISLANDS

1

Philippine Basin

Kyushu-Palau Ridge

HAGÅTÑA

GUAM
(to US)

East
Mariana
Basin

M
i
c
r
o
n
e
s
i
a

Ratak Chain

Philippine Trench

MICRONESIA

MAJURO

Ralik Chain

Philippines

Yap

Hall
Islands

Chuuk
Islands

PALIKIR

Pohnpei

Sulu
Sea

OREOR

Yap Trench

Caroline Islands

Kosrae

Melanesian
Basin

Tarawa

2

115

Babeldaob

PALAU

Eauripik Rise

M e l a n

e

Nauru
NAURU

Banaba

BAIRIKI

Tungaru

Celebes
Sea

Bismarck Archipelago

PAPUA NEW
GUINEA

s

i

a

TUVALU

Equator

Bismarck Sea
New Britain

Mount Wilhelm
4509m

New Guinea

Solomon Islands

FONGAFALE

Celebes

Banda
Sea

Bougainville
Island

SOLOMON
ISLANDS

Flores

Timor

Arafura
Sea

Solomon
Sea

HONIARA

Santa Cruz
Islands

WAL
& FUTU
(to Fra

PORT MORESBY

Guadalcanal

3

Timor

Torres Strait

Coral
Sea

VANUATU

North Fiji
Basin

Vanua Levu

Timor
Sea

Darwin

Gulf
of
Carpentaria

Cape
York

CORAL SEA ISLANDS
(to Australia)

Espiritu Santo
Malekula

Efate

Viti Levu

ASHMORE &
CARTIER ISLANDS
(to Australia)

Arnhem
Land

Great Barrier Reef

Cairns

Peninsula

NEW CALEDONIA
(to France)

PORT-VILA

SUVA

FIJI

Townsville

New Caledonia

Îles
Loyauté

Mackay

NOUMÉA

INDIAN
OCEAN

Broome

Great Dividing

Rockhampton

South
Fiji Basin

AUSTRALIA

New Caledonia Ridge

Norfolk Ridge

NORFOLK ISLAND
(to Australia)

Great
Sandy
Desert

Macdonnell
Ranges

Alice Springs

Simpson

Brisbane

Lord Howe
Island
(to Australia)

North Cape

North Is

4

119

Uluru
(Ayers Rock)

Desert

Range

Lord Howe Rise

Auckland

Gibson
Desert

Lake Eyre North

Grey Range

Newcastle

Hamilton

Tropic of Capricorn

Great
Victoria
Desert

Lake Torrens
Lake Gairdner

Flinders Range

Darling

Sydney
Wollongong

**NEW
ZEALAND**

Kalgoorlie

CANBERRA

WELLINGTON

Geraldton

Adelaide

Murray

Mount Kosciuszko
2228m

South Island

Mount Cook
3744m

Ch

POPULATION

- ▣ Over
  500,000
- ◉ 100,000 -
  500,000
- ○ 50,000 -
  100,000
- ○ Less than
  50,000
- ● National
  capital

Nullarbor Plain

Great Australian Bight

Port Lincoln

Kangaroo
Island

Bendigo

Melbourne
Geelong

Bass
Strait

*Tasman
Sea*

Dunedin

Bounty Isla

Perth

Esperance

South
Australian
Basin

Launceston

Tasman Basin

Antipodes Isla

5

Cape Leeuwin

Albany

Hobart

Stewart Island

Campbell
Plateau

Tasmania

Auckland Islands
(to New Zealand)

Campbell Island
(to New Zealand)

Tasman
Plateau

132

A B C D

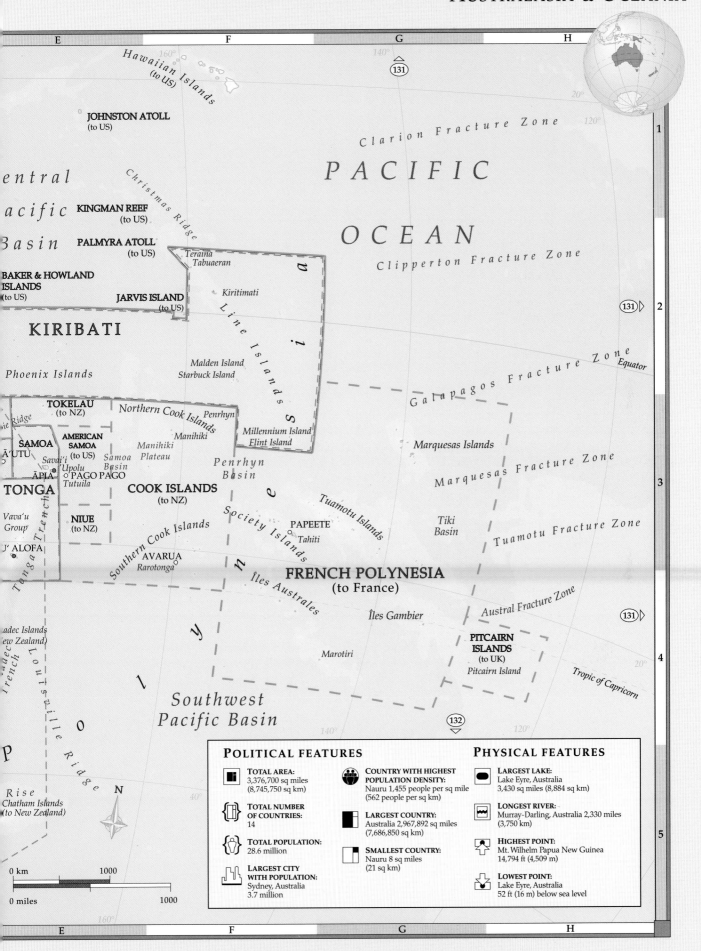

E   F   G   H

Hawaiian Islands
(to US)

JOHNSTON ATOLL
(to US)

Clarion Fracture Zone

PACIFIC

entral

acific

KINGMAN REEF
(to US)

Christmas Ridge

OCEAN

Clipperton Fracture Zone

Basin

PALMYRA ATOLL
(to US)

Teraina
Tabuaeran

**BAKER & HOWLAND
ISLANDS**
(to US)

JARVIS ISLAND
(to US)

Kiritimati

KIRIBATI

Line Islands

Galapagos Fracture Zone

Equator

Phoenix Islands

Malden Island
Starbuck Island

TOKELAU
(to NZ)

Northern Cook Islands

Penrhyn

Millennium Island
Flint Island

Marquesas Islands

Marquesas Fracture Zone

Ridge

**AMERICAN
SAMOA**
(to US)

Manihiki

*Manihiki
Plateau*

SAMOA

Ā'UTU

Savai'i
Upolu

*Samoa
Basin*

*Penrhyn
Basin*

*Tiki
Basin*

ĀPIA

○ PAGO PAGO

Tutuila

COOK ISLANDS
(to NZ)

Tuamotu Islands

Tuamotu Fracture Zone

TONGA

*Vava'u
Group*

NIUE
(to NZ)

Southern Cook Islands

Society Islands

PAPEETE

○ Tahiti

J' ALOFA

AVARUA

Rarotonga

FRENCH POLYNESIA
(to France)

Îles Australes

Austral Fracture Zone

*adec Islands
ew Zealand)*

Îles Gambier

**PITCAIRN
ISLANDS**
(to UK)

Pitcairn Island

Tropic of Capricorn

Marotiri

Southwest
Pacific Basin

Rise

*Chatham Islands
(to New Zealand)*

N

Louisville Ridge

0 km	1000	
0 miles	1000	

POLITICAL FEATURES

TOTAL AREA:
3,376,700 sq miles
(8,745,750 sq km)

**TOTAL NUMBER
OF COUNTRIES:**
14

TOTAL POPULATION:
28.6 million

**LARGEST CITY
WITH POPULATION:**
Sydney, Australia
3.7 million

**COUNTRY WITH HIGHEST
POPULATION DENSITY:**
Nauru 1,455 people per sq mile
(562 people per sq km)

LARGEST COUNTRY:
Australia 2,967,892 sq miles
(7,686,850 sq km)

SMALLEST COUNTRY:
Nauru 8 sq miles
(21 sq km)

PHYSICAL FEATURES

LARGEST LAKE:
Lake Eyre, Australia
3,430 sq miles (8,884 sq km)

LONGEST RIVER:
Murray-Darling, Australia 2,330 miles
(3,750 km)

HIGHEST POINT:
Mt. Wilhelm Papua New Guinea
14,794 ft (4,509 m)

LOWEST POINT:
Lake Eyre, Australia
52 ft (16 m) below sea level

THE SOUTHWEST PACIFIC

A	B	C	D

NORTHERN MARIANA ISLANDS (to US)

140°

150°

160°

170°

130

Tinian · Saipan · Rota

GUAM (to US)

✈ HAGÁTÑA

MARSHALL ISLANDS

10°

Micronesia

MICRONESIA

Enewetak Atoll · Bikini Atoll · Rongelap Atoll

Yap

Ujelang Atoll · Kwajalein Atoll · Namu Atoll · Ailinglaplap Atoll · Jaluit Atoll

Ailuk Atoll · Wotje Atoll · Maloela · Majuro

Babeldaob

OREOR ✈

PALAU

117

Caroline Islands

Chuuk Islands

PALIKIR ✈ · Pohnpei

Kosrae

Ebon Atoll

Mak

Tara

BAIRIK

Equator

NAURU

Abem

Non

Banaba

Admiralty Islands

St.Matthias Group

New Guinea

Bismarck Archipelago

Bismarck Sea

New Ireland

PAPUA NEW GUINEA

INDONESIA

Madang

△ Mount Wilhelm 4509m

Central Range

Lae

Queen Stanley Range

Bougainville Island

New Britain

Solomon Sea

Choiseul

Santa Isabel

Solomon Islands

SOLOMON ISLANDS

New Georgia Islands

Malaita

Arafura Sea

Gulf of Papua

PORT MORESBY ✈

Torres Strait

D'Entrecasteaux Islands

HONIARA ✈

Guadalcanal

San Cristobal

Rennell

Santa Cruz Islands

Louisiade Archipelago

Coral Sea

VANUATU

Banks Islands

10°

Melanesia

Arnhem Land

Groote Eylandt

Gulf of Carpentaria

Cape York Peninsula

Great Barrier Reef

CORAL SEA ISLANDS (to Australia)

Espiritu Santo

Maéwo · Pentecost

Malekula · Ambrym · Epi

124

Barkly Tableland

Great Dividing Range

Efate ✈ PORT-VILA

Erromango

Tanna

NEW CALEDONIA (to France)

Ouvéa · Aneityum

20°

NORTHERN

New Caledonia

Lifou · Maré

Iles Loyauté

TERRITORY

Tropic of Capricorn

Macdonnell

QUEENSLAND

✈

NOUMÉA

Ranges

AUSTRALIA

127

140°

150°

160°

170°

A	B	C	D

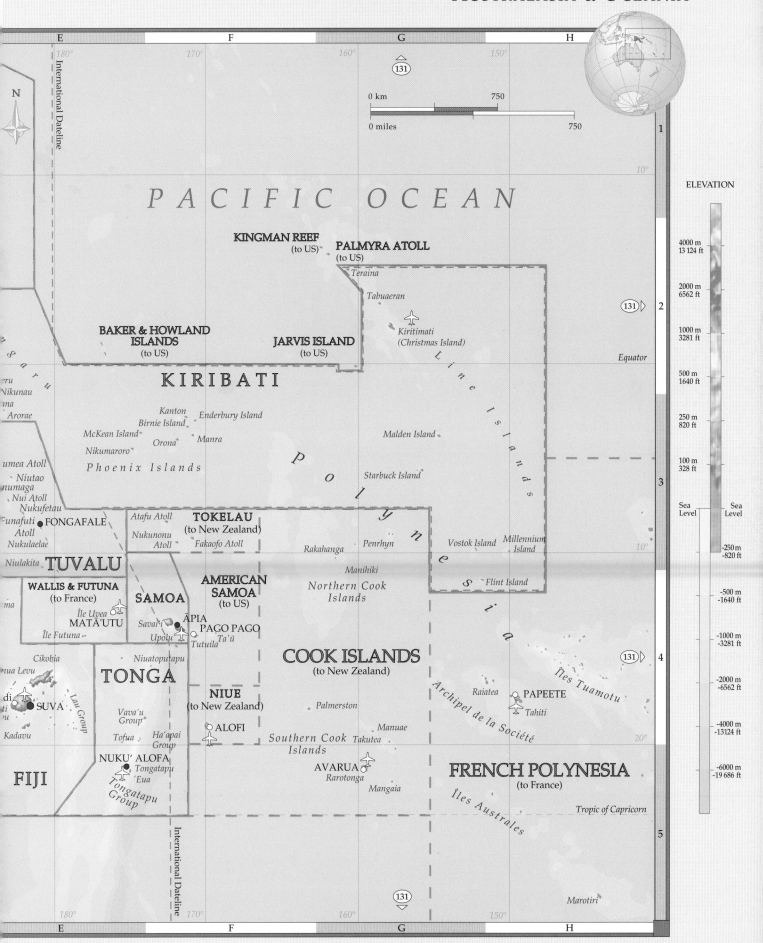

E F G H

131

0 km 750
0 miles 750

N

International Dateline

PACIFIC OCEAN

10°

ELEVATION

KINGMAN REEF
(to US)

PALMYRA ATOLL
(to US)

Teraina

Tabuaeran

131

**BAKER & HOWLAND
ISLANDS**
(to US)

JARVIS ISLAND
(to US)

Kiritimati
(Christmas Island)

Equator

K I R I B A T I

Kanton
Enderbury Island
Birnie Island
McKean Island
Orona
Manra
Malden Island
Nikumaroro

Phoenix Islands

Starbuck Island

Line Islands

P o l y

umea Atoll
Niutao
numaga
Nui Atoll
Nukufetau
Atafu Atoll
TOKELAU
(to New Zealand)
unafuti
Atoll
FONGAFALE
Nukunonu
Atoll
Fakaofo Atoll
Rakahanga
Penrhyn
Vostok Island
Millennium
Island
Nukulaelae

Niulakita

TUVALU

n

e

s

Manihiki

Flint Island

WALLIS & FUTUNA
(to France)
Île Uvea
MATĀ'UTU
Île Futuna

SAMOA
Savai'i
ĀPIA
Upolu
Tutuila
Ta'ū

**AMERICAN
SAMOA**
(to US)
PAGO PAGO

*Northern Cook
Islands*

i

a

Cikobia
ua Levu
di
i
u
SUVA
Kadavu

Lau Group

Niuatoputapu

TONGA

Vava'u
Group
Tofua
Ha'apai
Group
NUKU' ALOFA
Tongatapu
'Eua
Tongatapu
Group

COOK ISLANDS
(to New Zealand)

NIUE
(to New Zealand)
ALOFI

Palmerston

Manuae
Takutea

AVARUA
Rarotonga
Mangaia

*Southern Cook
Islands*

Raiatea
PAPEETE
Tahiti

Archipel de la Société

Îles Tuamotu

131

FRENCH POLYNESIA
(to France)

Îles Australes

Tropic of Capricorn

FIJI

International Dateline

131

Marotiri

180° 170° 160° 150°

E F G H

4000 m	13 124 ft
2000 m	6562 ft
1000 m	3281 ft
500 m	1640 ft
250 m	820 ft
100 m	328 ft
Sea Level	Sea Level
-250 m	-820 ft
-500 m	-1640 ft
-1000 m	-3281 ft
-2000 m	-6562 ft
-4000 m	-13124 ft
-6000 m	-19 686 ft

1
2
3
4
5

WESTERN AUSTRALIA

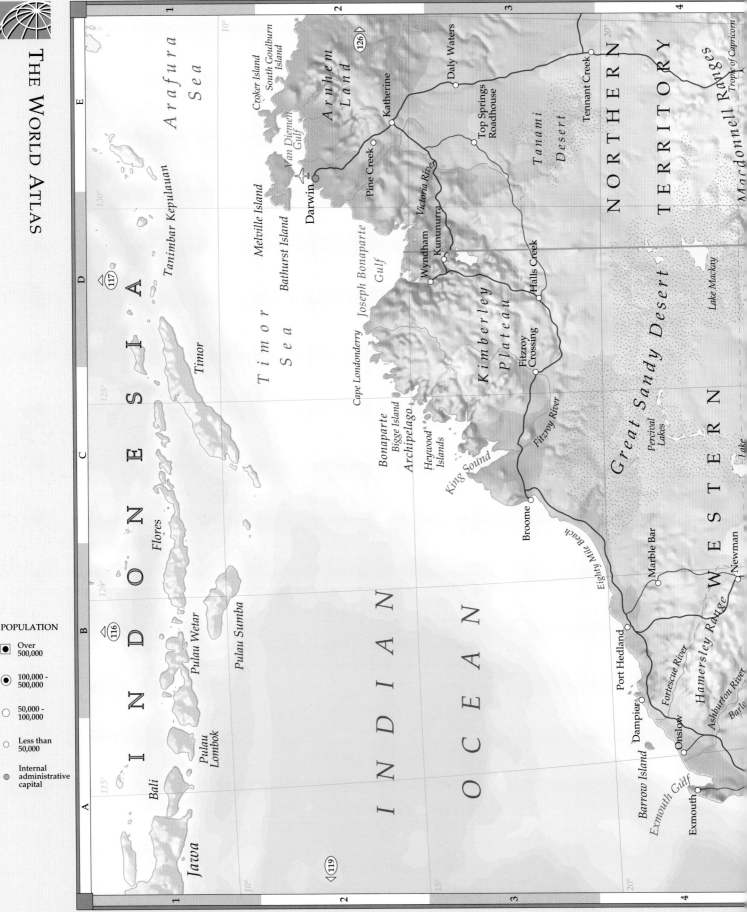

POPULATION

- ⦿ Over 500,000
- ◉ 100,000 – 500,000
- ○ 50,000 – 100,000
- ○ Less than 50,000
- ● Internal administrative capital

AUSTRALIA

SOUTH AUSTRALIA

Musgrave Ranges

Uluru (Ayers Rock) 862m △

Great Victoria Desert

Coober Pedy

Tarcoola
Lake Everard
Lake Gairdner
Penong
Ceduna
Elliston
Port Lincoln

Nullarbor Plain

Eucla

Reid

Great Australian Bight

AUSTRALIA

Lake Carnegie
Lake Wells

Robinson Range

Meekatharra

Murchison River
Gascoyne River

Carnarvon
Bernier Island
Dorre Island
Shark Bay
Dirk Hartog Island

Denham

Kalbarri

Geraldton

Moora

Gingin
Perth
Fremantle
Rockingham
Mandurah
Bunbury
Busselton
Augusta

Mount Magnet

Lake Moore

Lake Barlee

Lake Rebecca
Lake Carey

Lake Cowan

Zanthus
Kalgoorlie
Coolgardie
Norseman
Balladonia

Esperance

Southern Cross
Merredin
Northam
Brookton
Narrogin
Collie
Wagin
Katanning
Manjimup

Albany

INDIAN OCEAN

N

ELEVATION

4000 m
13 124 ft

2000 m
6562 ft

1000 m
3281 ft

500 m
1640 ft

250 m
820 ft

100 m
328 ft

Sea Level | Sea Level

-250 m
-820 ft

-500 m
-1640 ft

-1000 m
-3281 ft

-2000 m
-6562 ft

-3000 m
-9843 ft

-4000 m
-13 124 ft

0 km
0 miles
400
400

EASTERN AUSTRALIA

THE WORLD ATLAS

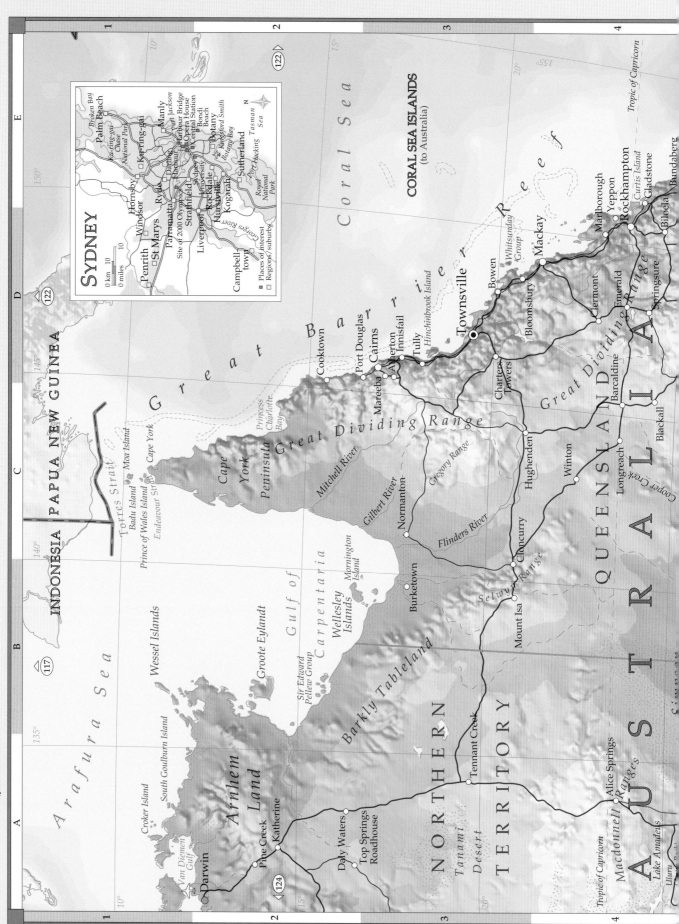

POPULATION

- Over 500,000
- 100,000 – 500,000
- 50,000 – 100,000
- Less than 50,000
- National capital
- Internal administrative capital

SYDNEY

Broken Bay
Palm Beach
Ku-ring-gai Chase National Park
Ku-ring-gai
Manly
Port Jackson
Harbour Bridge
Opera House
Central Station
Bondi Beach
Botany
Kingsford Smith
Tasman Sea
Hornsby
Windsor
Darling Harbour
Sydney
University
Ryde
Strathfield
Site of 2000 Olympics
Rockdale
Hurstville
Sutherland
Penrith
St Marys
Parramatta
Liverpool
Kogarah
Port Hacking
Royal National Park
Campbell-town
Georges River
Botany Bay

0 km 10
0 miles 10

- Places of interest
- Regions/suburbs

Map labels

Coral Sea

CORAL SEA ISLANDS
(to Australia)

Tropic of Capricorn

Great Barrier Reef

INDONESIA
PAPUA NEW GUINEA

Arafura Sea
Van Diemen Gulf
Croker Island
South Goulburn Island
Wessel Islands
Arnhem Land
Darwin
Pine Creek
Katherine

Torres Strait
Moa Island
Badu Island
Prince of Wales Island
Endeavour Strait
Cape York
Cape York Peninsula
Princess Charlotte Bay

Groote Eylandt
Sir Edward Pellew Group
Gulf of Carpentaria
Wellesley Islands
Mornington Island

Great Dividing Range
Mitchell River
Gilbert River
Normanton
Flinders River
Burketown

NORTHERN TERRITORY
Barkly Tableland
Tanami Desert
Tennant Creek
Daly Waters
Top Springs Roadhouse
Tropic of Capricorn
Alice Springs
Macdonnell Ranges
Lake Amadeus
Uluru

Cooktown
Port Douglas
Cairns
Mareeba
Atherton
Innisfail
Tully
Hinchinbrook Island
Townsville
Bowen
Whitsunday Group
Mackay
Bloomsbury
Charters Towers
Clermont
Emerald
Marlborough
Yeppon
Rockhampton
Curtis Island
Gladstone
Springsure
Biloela
Bundaberg

Gregory Range
Gregory Range
Hughenden
Winton
Longreach
Barcaldine
Blackall
Cooper Creek
Mount Isa
Cloncurry
Selwyn Range

QUEENSLAND
AUSTRALIA
Great Dividing Range

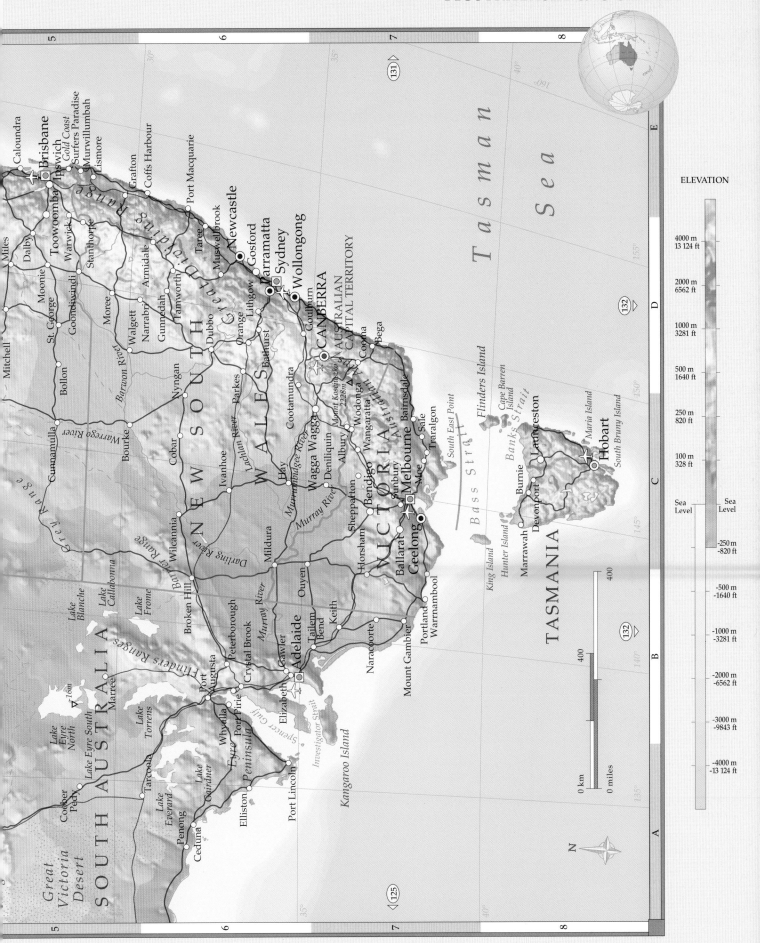

ELEVATION

4000 m
13 124 ft

2000 m
6562 ft

1000 m
3281 ft

500 m
1640 ft

250 m
820 ft

100 m
328 ft

Sea Level

-250 m
-820 ft

Sea Level

-500 m
-1640 ft

-1000 m
-3281 ft

-2000 m
-6562 ft

-3000 m
-9843 ft

-4000 m
-13 124 ft

T a s m a n   S e a

Tasman Sea

TASMANIA

Hobart
Launceston
Burnie
Devonport
Marrawah

Maria Island
South Bruny Island
Flinders Island
Cape Barren Island
Banks Strait
Bass Strait
King Island
Hunter Island

Brisbane
Ipswich
Toowoomba
Warwick
Stanthorpe
Caloundra
Gold Coast
Surfers Paradise
Murwillumbah
Lismore
Grafton
Coffs Harbour
Port Macquarie
Taree
Newcastle
Gosford
Sydney
Parramatta
Wollongong
Goulburn
CANBERRA
AUSTRALIAN CAPITAL TERRITORY
Bega
Cooma
Wodonga
Wangaratta
Wagga Wagga
Albury
Deniliquin
Bendigo
Shepparton
Sunbury
Bairnsdale
Sale
Traralgon
Moe
Melbourne
Geelong
Ballarat
Horsham
Warrnambool
Portland
Mount Gambier
Naracoorte
Keith
Tailem Bend
Bordertown

VICTORIA
South Australia

NEW SOUTH WALES

Great Dividing Range

Mount Kosciuszko 2228m

Miles
Dalby
Moonie
St. George
Goondiwindi
Mitchell
Bollon
Cunnamulla
Moree
Narrabri
Gunnedah
Tamworth
Armidale
Muswellbrook
Walgett
Nyngan
Cobar
Bourke
Dubbo
Parkes
Orange
Bathurst
Lithgow
Cootamundra
Hay
Ivanhoe
Mildura
Ouyen

Warrego River
Barwon River
Darling River
Lachlan River
Murrumbidgee River
Murray River

SOUTH AUSTRALIA

Great Victoria Desert
Flinders Ranges
Grey Range
Barrier Range

Lake Eyre North
Lake Eyre South
Lake Blanche
Lake Callabonna
Lake Frome
Lake Torrens
Lake Gairdner
Lake Everard

Marree
Tarcoola
Coober Pedy
Penong
Ceduna
Elliston
Port Lincoln
Kangaroo Island
Whyalla
Port Augusta
Port Pirie
Peterborough
Broken Hill
Wilcannia
Crystal Brook
Gawler
Elizabeth
Adelaide

Eyre Peninsula
Spencer Gulf
Investigator Strait

South East Point
Bass Strait

-16m

N

NEW ZEALAND

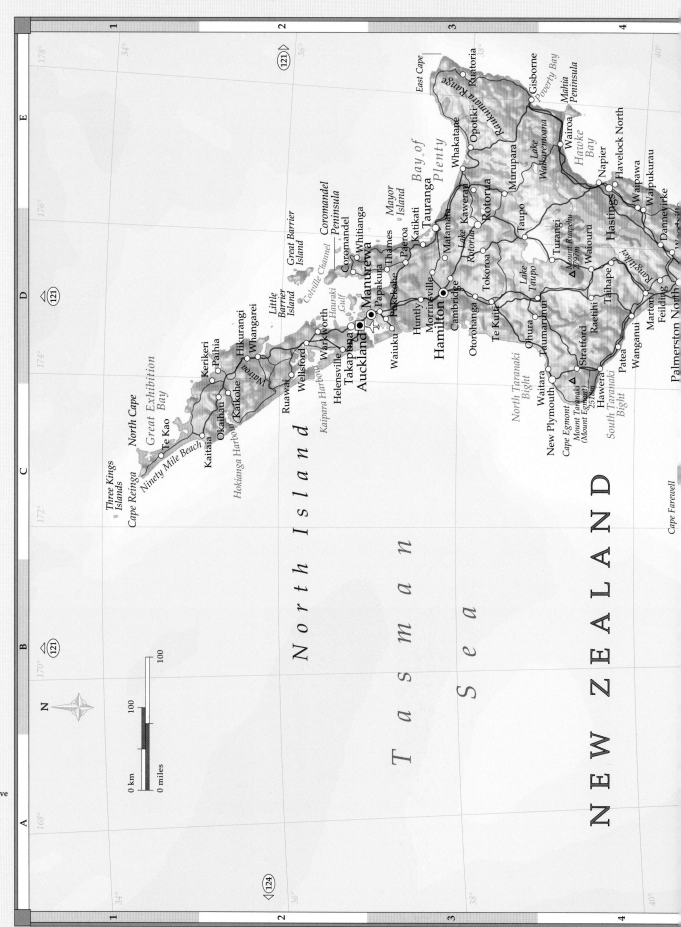

POPULATION

- ◉ Over 500,000
- ◉ 100,000 – 500,000
- ○ 50,000 – 100,000
- ○ Less than 50,000
- ● National capital
- ● Internal administrative capital

N

100

100

100

0 km

0 miles

Tasman Sea

North Island

NEW ZEALAND

Three Kings Islands

Cape Reinga

North Cape

Great Exhibition Bay

Te Kao

Ninety Mile Beach

Kaitaia

Okaihau

Kaikohe

Kerikeri

Paihia

Hikurangi

Whangarei

Hokianga Harbour

Wairoa

Ruawai

Wellsford

Warkworth

Helensville

Kaipara Harbour

Takapuna

Auckland

Waiuku

Manurewa

Papakura

Pukekohe

Little Barrier Island

Great Barrier Island

Coromandel Peninsula

Coromandel

Whitianga

Thames

Paeroa

Colville Channel

Hauraki Gulf

Mayor Island

Katikati

Tauranga

Bay of Plenty

Whakatane

Opotiki

Rakumara Range

East Cape

Ruatoria

Gisborne

Poverty Bay

Mahia Peninsula

Huntly

Morrinsville

Cambridge

Hamilton

Matamata

Lake Karapiro

Rotorua

Lake Rotorua

Murupara

Lake Waikaremoana

Wairoa

Hawke Bay

Napier

Havelock North

Waipawa

Waipukurau

Danneyirke

Otorohanga

Te Kuiti

Tokoroa

Taupo

Lake Taupo

Turangi

Mount Ruapehu 2797m

Waiouru

Taihape

Hastings

Ohura

Taumarunui

Raetihi

Marton

Feilding

Palmerston North

Rangitikei

North Taranaki Bight

Waitara

New Plymouth

Cape Egmont

Mount Taranaki (Mount Egmont) 2518m

Stratford

Hawera

South Taranaki Bight

Patea

Wanganui

Cape Farewell

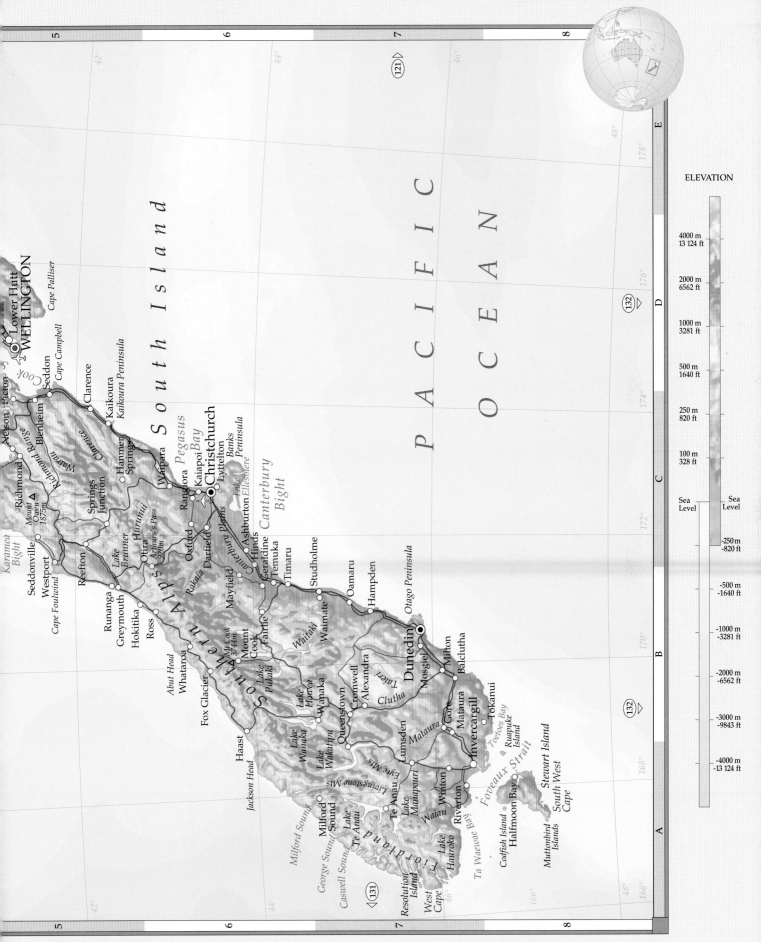

ELEVATION

4000 m	13 124 ft
2000 m	6562 ft
1000 m	3281 ft
500 m	1640 ft
250 m	820 ft
100 m	328 ft
Sea Level	Sea Level
-250 m	-820 ft
-500 m	-1640 ft
-1000 m	-3281 ft
-2000 m	-6562 ft
-3000 m	-9843 ft
-4000 m	-13 124 ft

South Island

PACIFIC OCEAN

Lower Hutt
WELLINGTON
Cape Palliser
Cape Campbell
Seddon
Clarence
Kaikoura
Kaikoura Peninsula
Nelson
Picton
Blenheim
Richmond
Mount Owen 1875m
Wairau
Richmond Range
Clarence
Hanmer Springs
Springs Junction
Waipara
Rangiora
Pegasus Bay
Kaiapoi
Christchurch
Lyttelton
Banks Peninsula
Lake Ellesmere
Canterbury Bight
Hurunui
Otira
Arthur's Pass 920m
Oxford
Darfield
Canterbury Plains
Ashburton
Hinds
Geraldine
Temuka
Timaru
Studholme
Waimate
Oamaru
Hampden
Otago Peninsula
Reefton
Runanga
Greymouth
Hokitika
Ross
Lake Brunner
Rakaia
Mayfield
Fairlie
Waitaki
Seddonville
Westport
Cape Foulwind
Karamea Bight
Abut Head
Whataroa
Fox Glacier
Southern Alps
Mt Cook 3744m
Mount Cook
Lake Pukaki
Lake Hawea
Wanaka
Waimate
Haast
Jackson Head
Lake Wanaka
Lake Wakatipu
Queenstown
Cromwell
Alexandra
Clutha
Taieri
Dunedin
Mosgiel
Milton
Balclutha
Lumsden
Mataura
Gore
Mataura
Tokanui
Invercargill
Toetoes Bay
Ruapuke Island
Eyre Mts
Livingstone Mts
Lake Te Anau
Lake Manapouri
Waiau
Winton
Riverton
Te Waewae Bay
Foveaux Strait
Stewart Island
South West Cape
Fiordland
Milford Sound
Milford
Lake Te Anau
Lake Hauroka
Codfish Island
Halfmoon Bay
Muttonbird Islands
George Sound
Caswell Sound
Resolution Island
West Cape

THE PACIFIC OCEAN

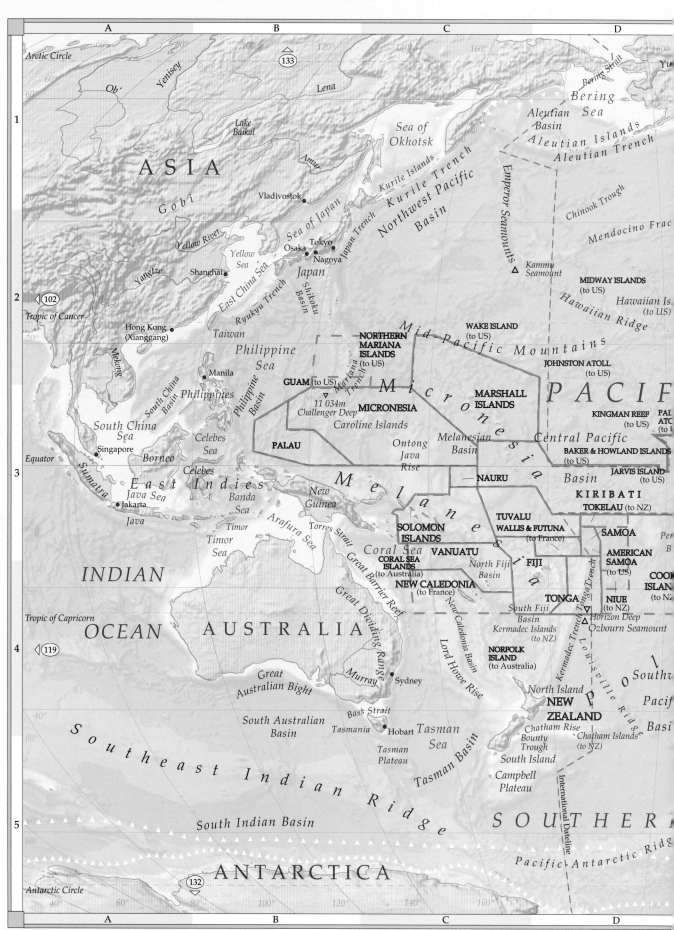

Arctic Circle

ASIA

Ob'

Yenisey

Lena

Lake Baikal

Amur

Sea of Okhotsk

Gobi

Vladivostok

Kurile Islands

Kurile Trench

Northwest Pacific Basin

Bering Sea

Aleutian Basin

Aleutian Islands

Aleutian Islands

Aleutian Trench

Emperor Seamounts

Chinook Trough

Bering Strait

Yu

Mendocino Frac

Yellow River

Yangtze

Sea of Japan

Shanghai

Yellow Sea

Osaka Tokyo

Nagoya

Japan

East China Sea

Japan Trench

Kammu Seamount

MIDWAY ISLANDS
(to US)

Hawaiian Is.
(to US)

Tropic of Cancer

Hong Kong
(Xianggang)

Taiwan

Shikoku Basin

Ryukyu Trench

Mekong

Philippine Sea

South China Basin

Manila

Philippines

Philippine Basin

Mariana Trench

Mid Pacific Mountains

NORTHERN MARIANA ISLANDS
(to US)

GUAM (to US)

11 034m
Challenger Deep

MICRONESIA

Caroline Islands

Micronesia

WAKE ISLAND
(to US)

JOHNSTON ATOLL
(to US)

PACIFI

MARSHALL ISLANDS

KINGMAN REEF
(to US)

PAL
ATC
(to

Hawaiian Ridge

South China Sea

Singapore

Celebes Sea

Borneo

PALAU

Melanesian Basin

Central Pacific

BAKER & HOWLAND ISLANDS
(to US)

Equator

Java Sea

Jakarta

Java

East Indies

Celebes

Banda Sea

New Guinea

Ontong Java Rise

Melanesia

Basin

JARVIS ISLAND
(to US)

NAURU

KIRIBATI

TOKELAU (to NZ)

Sumatra

Timor

Timor Sea

Arafura Sea

Torres Strait

Great Barrier Reef

Coral Sea

SOLOMON ISLANDS

TUVALU

WALLIS & FUTUNA
(to France)

VANUATU

North Fiji Basin

FIJI

SAMOA

AMERICAN SAMOA
(to US)

Per

COO
ISLAN
(to N

INDIAN

CORAL SEA ISLANDS
(to Australia)

NEW CALEDONIA
(to France)

New Caledonia Basin

South Fiji Basin

TONGA
(to NZ)

NIUE
(to NZ)

Horizon Deep

Ozbourn Seamount

Tropic of Capricorn

OCEAN

AUSTRALIA

Great Dividing Range

Murray

Sydney

Lord Howe Rise

NORFOLK ISLAND
(to Australia)

Kermadec Islands
(to NZ)

Kermadec Trench

Tonga Trench

Louisville Ridge

Southu

Pacif

Basi

Great Australian Bight

South Australian Basin

Bass Strait

Tasmania Hobart

Tasman Plateau

Tasman Sea

Tasman Basin

North Island

NEW ZEALAND

Chatham Rise

Bounty Trough

South Island

Chatham Islands
(to NZ)

Campbell Plateau

International Dateline

Southeast Indian Ridge

SOUTHERN

South Indian Basin

ANTARCTICA

Pacific Antarctic Ridge

Antarctic Circle

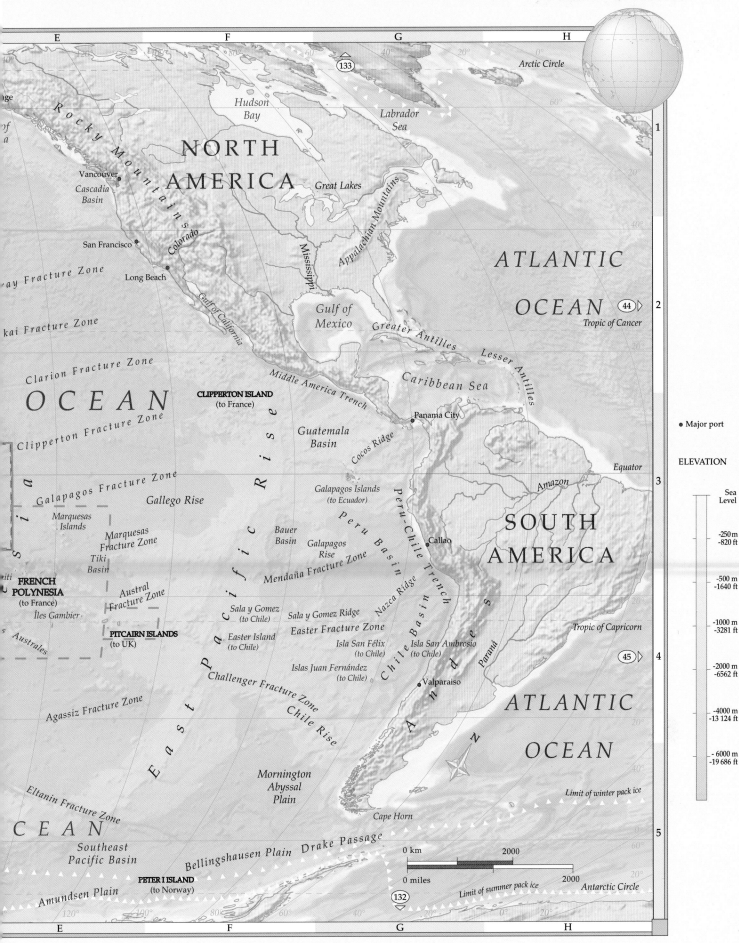

Arctic Circle

Hudson Bay

Labrador Sea

NORTH AMERICA

Vancouver

Cascadia Basin

Great Lakes

ATLANTIC

San Francisco

Rocky Mountains

Colorado

OCEAN

ay Fracture Zone

Long Beach

Mississippi

Appalachian Mountains

Tropic of Cancer

kai Fracture Zone

Gulf of California

Gulf of Mexico

Greater Antilles

Clarion Fracture Zone

CLIPPERTON ISLAND
(to France)

Middle America Trench

Caribbean Sea

Lesser Antilles

OCEAN

Clipperton Fracture Zone

Guatemala Basin

Panama City

Major port

Cocos Ridge

ELEVATION

Galapagos Fracture Zone

Gallego Rise

Galapagos Islands
(to Ecuador)

Amazon

Equator

Sea Level

Marquesas Islands

Bauer Basin

Peru Basin

SOUTH AMERICA

-250 m
-820 ft

Marquesas Fracture Zone

Galapagos Rise

Callao

Tiki Basin

Mendaña Fracture Zone

Nazca Ridge

-500 m
-1640 ft

iti

FRENCH POLYNESIA
(to France)

Sala y Gomez
(to Chile)

Sala y Gomez Ridge

Easter Fracture Zone

Peru–Chile Trench

Andes

-1000 m
-3281 ft

Îles Gambier

Austral Fracture Zone

Chile Basin

Tropic of Capricorn

s Australes

PITCAIRN ISLANDS
(to UK)

Easter Island
(to Chile)

Isla San Félix
(to Chile)

Isla San Ambrosio
(to Chile)

Paraná

-2000 m
-6562 ft

Islas Juan Fernández
(to Chile)

Valparaiso

Challenger Fracture Zone

Chile Rise

-4000 m
-13 124 ft

Agassiz Fracture Zone

East Pacific Rise

ATLANTIC

Eltanin Fracture Zone

Mornington Abyssal Plain

N

OCEAN

- 6000 m
-19 686 ft

OCEAN

Limit of winter pack ice

Southeast Pacific Basin

Bellingshausen Plain

Drake Passage

Cape Horn

Amundsen Plain

PETER I ISLAND
(to Norway)

Limit of summer pack ice

Antarctic Circle

0 km   2000

0 miles   2000

ANTARCTICA

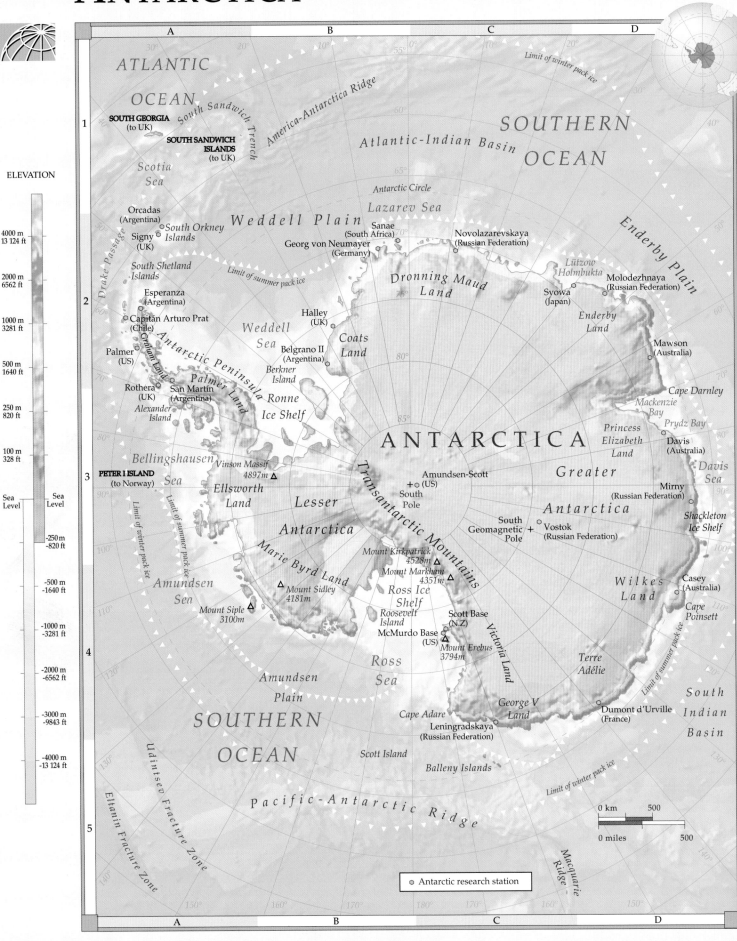

ATLANTIC

OCEAN

SOUTH GEORGIA
(to UK)

**SOUTH SANDWICH
ISLANDS**
(to UK)

*Scotia
Sea*

South Sandwich Trench

America-Antarctica Ridge

SOUTHERN

OCEAN

Atlantic-Indian Basin

Antarctic Circle

Lazarev Sea

*Enderby
Plain*

ELEVATION

4000 m
13 124 ft

2000 m
6562 ft

1000 m
3281 ft

500 m
1640 ft

250 m
820 ft

100 m
328 ft

Sea
Level

Sea
Level

-250 m
-820 ft

-500 m
-1640 ft

-1000 m
-3281 ft

-2000 m
-6562 ft

-3000 m
-9843 ft

-4000 m
-13 124 ft

Orcadas
(Argentina)

South Orkney
Islands

Signy
(UK)

Weddell Plain

South Shetland
Islands

Esperanza
(Argentina)

Capitán Arturo Prat
(Chile)

Palmer
(US)

Rothera
(UK)

San Martin
(Argentina)

*Alexander
Island*

PETER I ISLAND
(to Norway)

*Bellingshausen
Sea*

Vinson Massif
4897m △

*Ellsworth
Land*

*Lesser

Antarctica*

Marie Byrd Land

△ Mount Sidley
4181m

Mount Siple
3100m △

*Amundsen
Sea*

*Amundsen

Plain*

SOUTHERN

OCEAN

Sanae
(South Africa)

Georg von Neumayer
(Germany)

Novolazarevskaya
(Russian Federation)

*Dronning Maud
Land*

*Lützow
Holmbukta*

Syowa
(Japan)

Molodezhnaya
(Russian Federation)

*Enderby
Land*

Mawson
(Australia)

Cape Darnley

*Mackenzie
Bay*

Prydz Bay

Halley
(UK)

*Weddell
Sea*

*Coats
Land*

Belgrano II
(Argentina)

*Berkner
Island*

*Ronne
Ice Shelf*

Graham Land

Antarctic Peninsula

Palmer Land

ANTARCTICA

*Princess
Elizabeth
Land*

Davis
(Australia)

*Davis
Sea*

Amundsen-Scott
+ ◌ (US)
◌ South
Pole

*Greater

Antarctica*

Mirny
(Russian Federation)

South
Geomagnetic +
Pole

◌ Vostok
(Russian Federation)

*Shackleton
Ice Shelf*

Transantarctic Mountains

Mount Kirkpatrick
4528m △

Mount Markham
4351m △

*Ross Ice

Shelf*

*Roosevelt
Island*

Scott Base
(N.Z)

McMurdo Base
(US)

△ Mount Erebus
3794m

*Ross

Sea*

Victoria Land

*Wilkes

Land*

Casey
(Australia)

*Cape
Poinsett*

*Terre
Adélie*

Cape Adare

*George V
Land*

Leningradskaya
(Russian Federation)

Dumont d'Urville
(France)

*South

Indian

Basin*

Scott Island

Balleny Islands

Pacific-Antarctic Ridge

Udintsev Fracture Zone

Eltanin Fracture Zone

*Macquarie
Ridge*

Limit of winter pack ice

Limit of summer pack ice

Limit of winter pack ice

Limit of summer pack ice

Limit of winter pack ice

Drake Passage

0 km   500

0 miles   500

◌ Antarctic research station

132

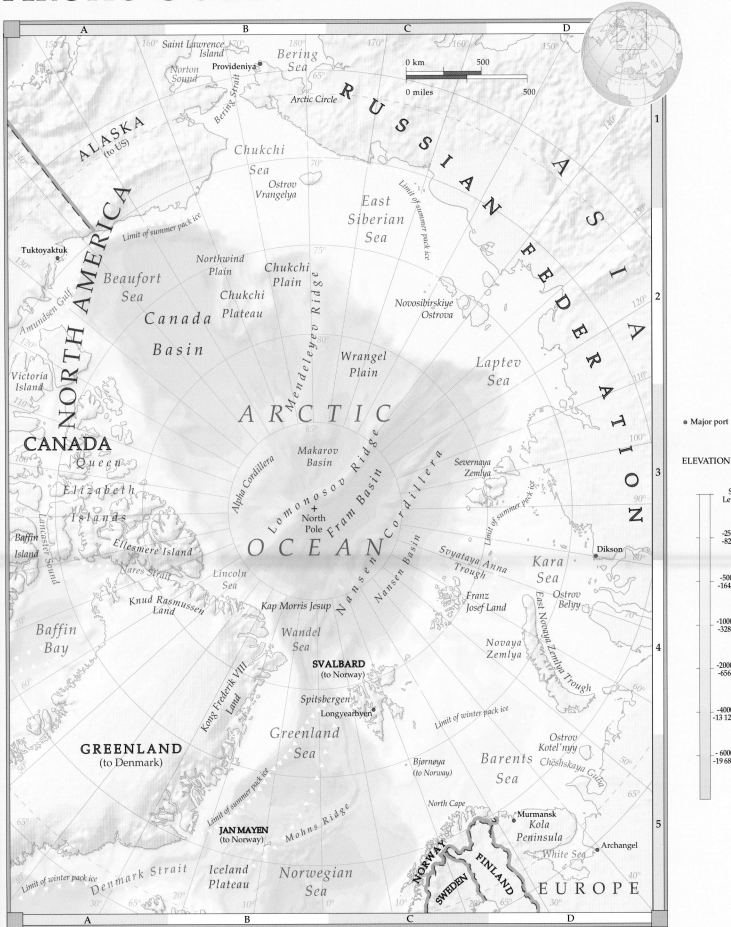

A B C D

RUSSIAN FEDERATION

Saint Lawrence Island

Bering Sea

Providepiya

Norton Sound

Bering Strait

Arctic Circle

1

ALASKA (to US)

Chukchi Sea

Ostrov Vrangelya

East Siberian Sea

Limit of summer pack ice

NORTH AMERICA

Tuktoyaktuk

Limit of summer pack ice

Northwind Plain

Chukchi Plain

Chukchi Plateau

Mendeleyev Ridge

Novosibirskiye Ostrova

2

Beaufort Sea

Canada Basin

Wrangel Plain

Laptev Sea

● Major port

CANADA

Victoria Island

ARCTIC

Makarov Basin

Severnaya Zemlya

ELEVATION

Queen

Alpha Cordillera

Lomonosov Ridge

Nansen Cordillera

3

Elizabeth

Islands

Baffin Island

+ North Pole

Fram Basin

Svyataya Anna Trough

Sea Level

Lancaster Sound

Ellesmere Island

OCEAN

Franz Josef Land

Kara Sea

Dikson

-250 m -820 ft

Nares Strait

Lincoln Sea

Nansen Basin

East Novaya Zemlya Trough

Ostrov Belyy

-500 m -1640 ft

Knud Rasmussen Land

Kap Morris Jesup

Novaya Zemlya

-1000 m -3281 ft

Baffin Bay

Wandel Sea

-2000 m -6562 ft

Kong Frederik VIII Land

SVALBARD (to Norway)

4

Spitsbergen

Longyearbyen

Limit of winter pack ice

Ostrov Kotel'nyy

-4000 m -13 124 ft

GREENLAND (to Denmark)

Greenland Sea

Bjørnøya (to Norway)

Barents Sea

Chëshskaya Guba

- 6000 m -19 686 ft

Limit of summer pack ice

North Cape

Murmansk

Mohns Ridge

JAN MAYEN (to Norway)

Kola Peninsula

Archangel

5

NORWAY

White Sea

Limit of winter pack ice

Denmark Strait

Iceland Plateau

Norwegian Sea

SWEDEN

FINLAND

EUROPE

A B C D

Overseas Territories and Dependencies

DESPITE THE RAPID PROCESS of decolonization since the end of the Second World War, around 10 million people in more than 50 territories around the world continue to live under the protection of France, Australia, the Netherlands, Denmark, Norway, New Zealand, the United Kingdom or the USA. These remnants of former colonial empires may have persisted for economic, strategic or political reasons, and are administered in a variety of ways.

AUSTRALIA

ASHMORE & CARTIER ISLANDS
Indian Ocean
Status External territory
Claimed 1978
Capital *not applicable*
Population None
Area 2 sq miles (5.2 sq km)

 CHRISTMAS ISLAND
Indian Ocean
Status External territory
Claimed 1958
Capital Flying Fish Cove
Population 1,275
Area 52 sq miles (134.6 sq km)

COCOS ISLANDS
Indian Ocean
Status External territory
Claimed 1955
Capital No official capital
Population 670
Area 5.5 sq miles (14.24 sq km)

CORAL SEA ISLANDS
South Pacific
Status External territory
Claimed 1969
Capital None
Population 8 (meteorologists)
Area Less than 1.16 sq miles (3 sq km)

HEARD & MCDONALD ISLANDS
Indian Ocean
Status External territory
Claimed 1947
Capital *not applicable*
Population None
Area 161 sq miles (417 sq km)z

 NORFOLK ISLAND
South Pacific
Status External territory
Claimed 1774
Capital Kingston
Population 2,181
Area 13.3 sq miles (34.4 sq km)

DENMARK

 FAEROE ISLANDS
North Atlantic
Status External territory
Claimed 1380
Capital Tórshavn
Population 43,382
Area 540 sq miles (1,399 sq km)

 **GREENLAND**
North Atlantic
Status External territory
Claimed 1380
Capital Nuuk
Population 56,076
Area 840,000 sq miles (2,175,516 sq km)

FRANCE

CLIPPERTON ISLAND
East Pacific
Status Dependency of French Polynesia
Claimed 1930
Capital *not applicable*
Population None
Area 2.7 sq miles (7 sq km)

FRENCH GUIANA South America
Status Overseas department
Claimed 1817
Capital Cayenne
Population 152,300
Area 35,135 sq miles (90,996 sq km)

 FRENCH POLYNESIA
South Pacific
Status Overseas territory
Claimed 1843
Capital Papeete
Population 219,521
Area 1,608 sq miles (4,165 sq km)

GUADELOUPE West Indies
Status Overseas department
Claimed 1635
Capital Basse-Terre
Population 419,500
Area 687 sq miles (1,780 sq km)

MARTINIQUE West Indies
Status Overseas department
Claimed 1635
Capital Fort-de-France
Population 381,200
Area 425 sq miles (1,100 sq km)

MAYOTTE Indian Ocean
Status Territorial collectivity
Claimed 1843
Capital Mamoudzou
Population 131,320
Area 144 sq miles (374 sq km)

NEW CALEDONIA South Pacific
Status Overseas territory
Claimed 1853
Capital Nouméa
Population 196,836
Area 7,374 sq miles (19,103 sq km)

RÉUNION Indian Ocean
Status Overseas department
Claimed 1638
Capital Saint-Denis
Population 697,000
Area 970 sq miles (2,512 sq km)

ST. PIERRE & MIQUELON
North America
Status Territorial collectivity
Claimed 1604
Capital Saint-Pierre
Population 6,600
Area 93.4 sq miles (242 sq km)

WALLIS & FUTUNA
South Pacific
Status Overseas territory
Claimed 1842
Capital Matā'Utu
Population 15,000
Area 106 sq miles (274 sq km)

NETHERLANDS

 ARUBA
West Indies
Status Autonomous part of the Netherlands
Claimed 1643
Capital Oranjestad
Population 88,000
Area 75 sq miles (194 sq km)

 NETHERLANDS ANTILLES
West Indies
Status Autonomous part of the Netherlands
Claimed 1816
Capital Willemstad
Population 207,175
Area 308 sq miles (800 sq km)

NEW ZEALAND

 COOK ISLANDS
South Pacific
Status Associated territory
Claimed 1901
Capital Avarua
Population 20,200
Area 113 sq miles (293 sq km)

 NIUE
South Pacific
Status Associated territory
Claimed 1901
Capital Alofi
Population 2,080
Area 102 sq miles (264 sq km)

TOKELAU
South Pacific
Status Dependent territory
Claimed 1926
Capital *not applicable*
Population 1,577
Area 4 sq miles (10.4 sq km)

NORWAY

BOUVET ISLAND
South Atlantic
Status Dependency
Claimed 1928
Capital *not applicable*
Population None
Area 22 sq miles (58 sq km)JAN

MAYEN
North Atlantic
Status Dependency
Claimed 1929
Capital *not applicable*
Population None
Area 147 sq miles (381 sq km)

PETER I ISLAND
Southern Ocean
Status Dependency
Claimed 1931
Capital *not applicable*
Population None
Area 69 sq miles (180 sq km)

SVALBARD Arctic Ocean
Status Dependency
Claimed 1920
Capital Longyearbyen
Population 3,231
Area 24,289 sq miles (62,906 sq km)

UNITED KINGDOM

 ANGUILLA
West Indies
Status Dependent territory
Claimed 1650
Capital The Valley
Population 10,300
Area 37 sq miles (96 sq km)

ASCENSION ISLAND
South Atlantic
Status Dependency of St. Helena
Claimed 1673
Capital Georgetown
Population 1,099
Area 34 sq miles (88 sq km)

 **BERMUDA**
North Atlantic
Status Crown colony
Claimed 1612
Capital Hamilton
Population 60,144
Area 20.5 sq miles (53 sq km)

BRITISH INDIAN OCEAN TERRITORY Indian Ocean
Status Dependent territory
Claimed 1814
Capital Diego Garcia
Population 930
Area 23 sq miles (60 sq km)

BRITISH VIRGIN ISLANDS West Indies
Status Dependent territory
Claimed 1672
Capital Road Town
Population 17,896
Area 59 sq miles (153 sq km)

CAYMAN ISLANDS West Indies
Status Dependent territory
Claimed 1670
Capital George Town
Population 35,000
Area 100 sq miles (259 sq km)

FALKLAND ISLANDS South Atlantic
Status Dependent territory
Claimed 1832
Capital Stanley
Population 2,564
Area 4,699 sq miles (12,173 sq km)

GIBRALTAR Southwest Europe
Status Crown colony
Claimed 1713
Capital Gibraltar
Population 27,086
Area 2.5 sq miles (6.5 sq km)

GUERNSEY Channel Islands
Status Crown dependency
Claimed 1066
Capital St Peter Port
Population 56,681
Area 25 sq miles (65 sq km)

ISLE OF MAN British Isles
Status Crown dependency
Claimed 1765
Capital Douglas
Population 71,714
Area 221 sq miles (572 sq km)

JERSEY Channel Islands
Status Crown dependency
Claimed 1066
Capital St. Helier
Population 85,150
Area 45 sq miles (116 sq km)

MONTSERRAT West Indies
Status Dependent territory
Claimed 1632
Capital Plymouth (uninhabited)
Population 2,850
Area 40 sq miles (102 sq km)

PITCAIRN ISLANDS South Pacific
Status Dependent territory
Claimed 1887
Capital Adamstown
Population 55
Area 1.35 sq miles (3.5 sq km)

ST. HELENA South Atlantic
Status Dependent territory
Claimed 1673
Capital Jamestown
Population 6,472
Area 47 sq miles (122 sq km)

SOUTH GEORGIA &

THE SOUTH SANDWICH ISLANDS South Atlantic
Status Dependent territory
Capital *not applicable*
Claimed 1775
Population No permanent residents
Area 1,387 sq miles (3,592 sq km)

TRISTAN DA CUNHA South Atlantic
Status Dependency of St. Helena
Claimed 1612
Capital Edinburgh
Population 297
Area 38 sq miles (98 sq km)

TURKS & CAICOS ISLANDS West Indies
Status Dependent territory
Claimed 1766
Capital Cockburn Town
Population 13,800
Area 166 sq miles (430 sq km)

UNITED STATES OF AMERICA

AMERICAN SAMOA South Pacific
Status Unincorporated territory
Claimed 1900
Capital Pago Pago
Population 60,000
Area 75 sq miles (195 sq km)

BAKER & HOWLAND ISLANDS South Pacific
Status Unincorporated territory
Claimed 1856
Capital *not applicable*
Population None
Area 0.54 sq miles (1.4 sq km)

GUAM West Pacific
Status Unincorporated territory
Claimed 1898
Capital Hagåtña
Population 149,249
Area 212 sq miles (549 sq km)

JARVIS ISLAND South Pacific
Status Unincorporated territory
Claimed 1856
Capital *not applicabl*
Population None
Area 1.7 sq miles (4.5 sq km)

NORTHERN MARIANA ISLANDS West Pacific
Status Commonwealth territory
Claimed 1947
Capital Saipan
Population 58,846
Area 177 sq miles (457 sq km)

PALMYRA ATOLL Central Pacific
Status Unincorporated territory
Claimed 1898
Capital *not applicable*
Population None
Area 5 sq miles (12 sq km)

PUERTO RICO West Indies
Status Commonwealth territory
Claimed 1898
Capital San Juan
Population 3.8 million
Area 3,458 sq miles (8,959 sq km)

VIRGIN ISLANDS West Indies
Status Unincorporated territory
Claimed 1917
Capital Charlotte Amalie
Population 101,809
Area 137 sq miles (355 sq km)

WAKE ISLAND Central Pacific
Status Unincorporated territory
Claimed 1898
Capital *not applicable*
Population 302
Area 2.5 sq miles (6.5 sq km)

COUNTRY PROFILES

THIS FACTFILE IS INTENDED as a guide to a world that is continually changing as political fashions and personalities come and go. Nevertheless, all the material in these factfiles has been researched from the most up-to-date and authoritative sources to give an incisive portrait of the geographical, political, and social characteristics that make each country so unique.

There are currently 193 independent countries in the world - more than at any previous time - and 59 dependencies. Antarctica is the only land area on Earth that is not officially part of, and does not belong to, any single country.

AFGHANISTAN

Page 100 D4

In 2001, following a US-led offensive, the hard-line Muslim taliban militia was replaced by a new interim government under Hamid Karazi

Official name Islamic State of Afghanistan
Formation 1919
Capital Kabul
Population 22.5 million / 90 people per sq mile (35 people per sq km)
Total area 250,000 sq miles (647,500 sq km)
Languages Pashtu, Tajik, Dari, Farsi
Religions Sunni Muslim 84%, Shi'a Muslim 15%, other 1%
Ethnic mix Pashtun 38%, Tajik 25%, Hazara 19%, other 18%
Government Transitional regime
Currency Afghani = 100 puls
Literacy rate 37.3%
Calorie consumption 1,539 kilocalories

135

ALBANIA

Page 79 C6

Lying at the southeastern end of the Adriatic Sea, Albania held its first multiparty elections in 1991, after nearly five decades of communism.

Official name Republic of Albania
Formation 1912
Capital Tiranë
Population 3.1 million/
279 people per sq mile (108 people per sq km)
Total area 11,100 sq miles
(28,748 sq km) sq miles
Languages Albanian, Greek
Religions Sunni Muslim 70%,
Orthodox Christian 20%, Roman Catholic 10%
Ethnic mix Albanian 86%,
Greek 12%, other 2%
Government Multiparty republic
Currency Lek = 100 qindars
Literacy rate 84.7%
Calorie consumption 2,864 kilocalories

ALGERIA

Page 48 C3

Algeria achieved independence from France in 1962. Today, its military-dominated government faces a severe challenge from Islamic extremists.

Official name People's Democratic Republic of Algeria
Formation 1962
Capital Algiers
Population 30.8 million / 33 people per sq mile (13 people per sq km)
Total area 919,590 sq miles
(2,381,740 sq km)
Languages Arabic, Tamazight, French
Religions Sunni Muslim 99%, other 1%
Ethnic mix Arab 75%, Berber 24%, European 1%
Government Multiparty republic
Currency Algerian dinar =
100 centimes
Literacy rate 67.8%
Calorie consumption 2,944 kilocalories

ANDORRA

Page 69 B6

A tiny landlocked principality, Andorra lies high in the eastern Pyrenees between France and Spain. It held its first full elections in 1993.

Official name Principality of Andorra
Formation 1278
Capital Andorra la Vella
Population 66,800 / 370 people per sq mile (143 people per sq km)
Total area 181 sq miles (468 sq km)
Languages Catalan, Spanish, French, Portuguese
Religions Roman Catholic 94%, other 6%
Ethnic mix Spanish 46%, Andorrian 28%, other 18%, French 8%
Government Parliamentary democracy
Currency Euro (French franc and Spanish peseta until 2002)
Literacy rate 99%
Calorie consumption not available

ANGOLA

Page 56 B2

Located in southwest Africa, Angola has been in a state of civil war following its independence from Portugal, except for a brief period from 1994–98.

Official name Republic of Angola
Formation 1975
Capital Luanda
Population 13.5 million /28 people per sq mile (11 people per sq km)
Total area 481,351 sq miles
(1,246,700 sq km)
Languages Portuguese, Umbundu, Kimbundu, Kikongo
Religions Roman Catholic 50%, other 30%, Protestant 20%
Ethnic mix Ovimbundu 37%, other 25%, Kimbundu 25%, Bakongo 13%
Government Presidential regime
Currency Readjusted kwanza =
100 lwei
Literacy rate 40%
Calorie consumption 1,903 kilocalories

ANTIGUA & BARBUDA

Page 33 H3

Lying on the Atlantic edge of the Leeward Islands, Antigua and Barbuda's area includes the uninhabited islet of Redonda.

Official name Antigua and Barbuda
Formation 1981
Capital St. John's
Population 66,400 /
389 people per sq mile (150 people per sq km)
Total area 171 sq miles (442 sq km)
Languages English, English patois
Religions Anglican 45%,
other Protestant 42%, Roman Catholic 10%, Rastafarian 1%, other 2%
Ethnic mix Black African 95%, other 5%
Government Parliamentary democracy
Currency Eastern Caribbean dollar = 100 cents
Literacy rate 95%
Calorie consumption 2,396 kilocalories

ARGENTINA

Page 43 B5

Most of the southern half of South America is occupied by Argentina. The country returned to civilian rule in 1983 after a series of military coups.

Official name Republic of Argentina
Formation 1816
Capital Buenos Aires
Population 37.5 million / 35 people per sq mile (14 people per sq km)
Total area 1,068,296 sq miles
(2,766,890 sq km)
Languages Spanish, Italian, Amerindian languages
Religions Roman Catholic 90%, Jewish 2%, Protestant 2%, other 6%
Ethnic mix Indo European 85%, Mestizo 14%, Amerindian 1%
Government Presidential democracy
Currency Peso = 100 centavos
Literacy rate 96.8%
Calorie consumption 3,181 kilocalories

ARMENIA

Page 95 F3

Smallest of the former USSR's republics, Armenia lies in the Lesser Caucasus mountains. Territorial war with Azerbaijan ended in a 1994 ceasefire.

Official name Republic of Armenia
Formation 1991
Capital Yerevan
Population 3.8 million/
330 people per sq mile (128 people per sq km)
Total area 11,506 sq miles
(29,800 sq km)
Languages Armenian, Russian
Religions The Armenian Apostolic Church 94%, other 6%
Ethnic mix Armenian 93%,
Azeri 3%, Russian 2%, other 2%
Government Multiparty republic
Currency Dram = 100 louma
Literacy rate 98.4%
Calorie consumption 1,944 kilocalories

AUSTRALIA

Page 120 A4

An island continent located between the Indian and Pacific oceans, Australia was settled by Europeans 200 years ago, but now has many Asian immigrants.

Official name Commonwealth of Australia
Formation 1901
Capital Canberra
Population 19.3 million / 7 people per sq mile (3 people per sq km)
Total area 2,967,893 sq miles
(7,686,893 sq km)
Languages English, Vietnamese, Greek, Arabic, Italian, Aboriginal languages
Religions Christian 64%, other 34%
Ethnic mix European 95%, Asian 4%, Aboriginal and other 1%
Government Parliamentary democracy
Currency Australian dollar = 100 cents
Literacy rate 99%
Calorie consumption 3,176 kilocalories

AUSTRIA

Page 73 D7

Bordering eight countries in the heart of Europe, Austria was created in 1920 after the collapse of the Austro-Hungarian Empire the previous year.

Official name Republic of Austria
Formation 1918
Capital Vienna
Population 8.1 million / 250 people per sq mile (97 people per sq km)
Total area 32,378 sq miles (83,858 sq km)
Languages German, Croatian, Slovenian
Religions Roman Catholic 78%, non-religious 9%, Protestant 5%, other (including Muslim and Jewish) 8%
Ethnic mix German 93%, Croat, Slovene, Hungarian 6%, other 1%
Government Parliamentary democracy
Currency Euro (Austrian schilling until 2002)
Literacy rate 99%
Calorie consumption 3,757 kilocalories

AZERBAIJAN

Page 95 G2

Situated on the western coast of the Caspian Sea, Azerbaijan was the first Soviet republic to declare independence from Moscow in 1991.

Official name Republic of Azerbaijan
Formation 1991
Capital Baku
Population 8.1 million / 242 people per sq mile (94 people per sq km)
Total area 33,436 sq miles
(86,600 sq km)
Languages Azeri, Russian
Religions Shi'a ithna Muslims 61%, Sunni Muslims 26%, Armenian and Russian Orthodox 11%, other 2%
Ethnic mix Azeri 90%, Russian 3%, Daghestani 3%, Armenian 2%, other 2%
Government Multiparty republic
Currency Manat = 100 gopik
Literacy rate 96%
Calorie consumption 2,468 kilocalories

BAHAMAS

Page 32 C1

Located in the western Atlantic, off the Florida coast, the Bahamas comprise some 700 islands and 2,400 cays, only 30 of which are inhabited.

Official name Commonwealth of the Bahamas
Formation 1973
Capital Nassau
Population 308,000 / 57 people per sq mile (22 people per sq km)
Total area 5,382 sq miles
(13,940 sq km)
Languages English, English Creole, French Creole
Religions Baptist 32%, Anglican 20%, Roman Catholic 19%, Church of God 6%, Methodist 6%, other 17%
Ethnic mix Black African 85%, Other 15%
Government Parliamentary democracy
Currency Bahamian dollar = 100 cents
Literacy rate 95.7%
Calorie consumption 2,443 kilocalories

BAHRAIN

Page 98 C4

Bahrain is an archipelago of 33 islands between the Qatar peninsula and the Saudi Arabian mainland. Only three of these islands are inhabited.

Official name State of Bahrain
Formation 1971
Capital Manama
Population 652,000 /
2,724 people per sq mile (1,052 people per sq km)
Total area 239 sq miles (620 sq km)
Languages Arabic
Religions Muslim (mainly Shi'a) 99%, other 1%
Ethnic mix Bahraini 70%, Iranian, Indian, Pakistani 24%, other Arab 4%, European 2%
Government Constitutional monarchy
Currency Bahraini dinar = 1,000 fils
Literacy rate 87.6%
Calorie consumption not available

BANGLADESH

Page 113 G3

Bangladesh lies at the north of the Bay of Bengal. It seceded from Pakistan in 1971 and, after much political instability, returned to democracy in 1991.

Official name People's Republic of Bangladesh
Formation 1971
Capital Dhaka
Population 140.4 million /2,525 people per sq mile (975 people per sq km)
Total area 55,598 sq miles (144,000 sq km)
Languages Bengali, Urdu, Chakma, Marma (Magh), Garo, Khasi, Santhali, Tripuri, Mro
Religions Muslim (mainly Sunni) 87%, Hindu 12%, other 1%
Ethnic mix Bengali 98%, other 2%
Government Parliamentary democracy
Currency Taka = 100 paisa
Literacy rate 41.4%
Calorie consumption 2,103 kilocalories

BELGIUM

Page 65 B6

Located in northwestern Europe, Belgium's history has been marked by the division between its Flemish- and French-speaking communities.

Official name Kingdom of Belgium
Formation 1830
Capital Brussels
Population 10.3 million / 874 people per sq mile (338 people per sq km)
Total area 11,780 sq miles 30,510 sq km)
Languages Dutch, French, German
Religions Roman Catholic 88%, Muslim 2%, other 10%
Ethnic mix Fleming 58%, Walloon 33%, Italian 2%, Moroccan 1%, other 6%
Government Parliamentary democracy
Currency Euro (Belgian franc until 2002)
Literacy rate 99%
Calorie consumption 3,701 kilocalories

BHUTAN

Page 113 G3

The landlocked Buddhist kingdom of Bhutan is perched in the eastern Himalayas between India and China. Gradual reforms protect its cultural identity.

Official name Kingdom of Bhutan
Formation 1656
Capital Thimpu
Population 2.1 million / 116 people per sq mile (45 people per sq km)
Total area 18,147 sq miles (47,000 sq km)
Languages Dzongkha, Nepali, Assamese
Religions Mahayana Buddhist 70%, Hindu 24%, other 6%
Ethnic mix Bhote 50%, Nepalese 25%, other 25%
Government Monarchy
Currency Ngultrum = 100 chetrum
Literacy rate 47.3%
Calorie consumption not available

BOTSWANA

Page 56 C3

Once the British protectorate of Bechuanaland, Botswana lies landlocked in southern Africa. Diamonds provide it with a prosperous economy.

Official name Republic of Botswana
Formation 1966
Capital Gaborone
Population 1.6 million / 7 people per sq mile (3 people per sq km)
Total area 231,803 sq miles (600,370 sq km)
Languages English, Tswana, Shona, San, Khoikhoi, Ndebele
Religions Traditional beliefs 50%, Christian (mainly Protestant) 30%, other (including Muslim) 20%
Ethnic mix Tswana 98% other 2%
Government Presidential democracy
Currency Pula = 100 thebe
Literacy rate 77.2%
Calorie consumption 2,255 kilocalories

BARBADOS

Page 33 H4

Barbados is the most easterly of the Caribbean Windward Islands. Under British rule for 339 years, it became fully independent in 1966.

Official name Barbados
Formation 1966
Capital Bridgetown
Population 268,000 /1,614 people per sq mile (623 people per sq km)
Total area 166 sq miles (430 sq km)
Languages English, Bajan (Barbadian English)
Religions Anglican 40%, other 24%, non-religious 17%, Pentecostal 8%, Methodist 7%, Roman Catholic 4%
Ethnic mix Black African 90%, other 10%
Government Parliamentary democracy
Currency Barbados dollar = 100 cents
Literacy rate 98%
Calorie consumption 3,022 kilocalories

BELIZE

Page 30 B1

The last Central American country to gain independence, this former British colony lies on the eastern shore of the Yucatan Peninsula.

Official name Belize
Formation 1981
Capital Belmopan
Population 200,000 /23 people per sq mile (9 people per sq km)
Total area 8,867 sq miles (22,966 sq km)
Languages English, English Creole, Spanish, Mayan, Garifuna (Carib)
Religions Roman Catholic 62%, Anglican 12%, Mennonite 4%, Methodist 6%, other 16%
Ethnic mix Mestizo 44%, Creole 30%, Maya 11%, Garifuna 7%, Asian Indian 4%, other 4%
Government Parliamentary democracy
Currency Belizean dollar = 100 cents
Literacy rate 93.2%
Calorie consumption 2,888 kilocalories

BOLIVIA

Page 39 F3

Bolivia lies landlocked high in central South America. Mineral riches once made it the region's wealthiest state. Today, it is the poorest.

Official name Republic of Bolivia
Formation 1825
Capital Sucre (judicial)/La Paz (administrative)
Population 8.5 million / 20 people per sq mile (8 people per sq km)
Total area 424,162 sq miles (1,098,580 sq km)
Languages Spanish, Aymara, Quechua
Religions Roman Catholic 93%, other 7%
Ethnic mix Quechua 37%, Aymara 32%, mixed 13%, European 10%, other 8%
Government Presidential democracy
Currency Boliviano = 100 centavos
Literacy rate 85.6%
Calorie consumption 2,218 kilocalories

BRAZIL

Page 40 C2

Brazil covers more than half of South America and is the site of the world's largest rain forest. The country has immense natural resources.

Official name Federative Republic of Brazil
Formation 1822
Capital Brasilia
Population 172.6 million / 53 people per sq mile (20 people per sq km)
Total area 3,286,470 sq miles (8,511,965 sq km)
Languages Portuguese, German, Italian, Spanish, Polish, Japanese
Religions Roman Catholic 74%, Protestant 15%, Atheist 7%, other 4%
Ethnic mix Black 53%, Mixed 40%, White 6%, other 1%
Government Presidential democracy
Currency Real = 100 centavos
Literacy rate 85.2%
Calorie consumption 2,985 kilocalories

BELARUS

Page 85 B6

Formerly known as White Russia, Belarus lies landlocked in eastern Europe. The country reluctantly became independent of the USSR in 1991.

Official name Republic of Belarus
Formation 1991
Capital Minsk
Population 10.1 million / 126 people per sq mile (49 people per sq km)
Total area 80,154 sq miles (207,600 sq km)
Languages Belorussian, Russian
Religions Russian Orthodox 60%, other (including Muslim, Jews and Protestant) 32% Roman Catholic 8%
Ethnic mix Belorussian 78%, Russian 13%, Polish 4%, Ukrainian 3%, other 2%
Government Presidential regime
Currency Belorussian rouble = 100 kopeks
Literacy rate 99%
Calorie consumption 2,902 kilocalories

BENIN

Page 53 F4

Stretching north from the West African coast, Benin became one of the pioneers of African democratization in 1990, ending years of military rule.

Official name Republic of Benin
Formation 1960
Capital Porto-Novo
Population 6.4 million / 147 people per sq mile (57 people per sq km)
Total area 43,483 sq miles (112,620 sq km)
Languages French, Fon, Bariba, Yoruba, Adja, Houeda, Somba
Religions Indigenous beliefs 70%, Muslim 15%, Christian 15%
Ethnic mix Fon 47%, Baraba 10%, Adja 12%, other 31%
Government Presidential democracy
Currency CFA franc = 100 centimes
Literacy rate 40.3%
Calorie consumption 2,558 kilocalories

BOSNIA & HERZEGOVINA

Page 78 B3

At the heart of the western Balkans, Bosnia and Herzegovina was the focus of the bitter conflict surrounding the breakup of former Yugoslavia.

Official name Bosnia and Herzegovina
Formation 1992
Capital Sarajevo
Population 4.1 million /208 people per sq mile (80 people per sq km)
Total area 19,741 sq miles (51,129 sq km)
Languages Serbo-Croat
Religions Muslim (mainly Sunni) 40%, Serbian Orthodox 31%, Roman Catholic 15%, Protestant 4%, other 10%
Ethnic mix Bosniak 44%, Serb 31%, Croat 17%, other 8%
Government Multiparty republic
Currency Marka = 100 pfenniga
Literacy rate 93%
Calorie consumption 2,661 kilocalories

BRUNEI

Page 116 D3

Lying on the northwestern coast of the island of Borneo, Brunei is surrounded and divided in two by the Malaysian state of Sarawak.

Official name Sultanate of Brunei
Formation 1984
Capital Bandar Seri Begawan
Population 335,000 / 150 people per sq mile (58 people per sq km)
Total area 2,228 sq miles (5,770 sq km)
Languages Malay, English, Chinese
Religions Muslim 66%, Buddhist 14%, Christian 10%, other 10%
Ethnic mix Malay 67%, Chinese 16%, Indigenous 6%, other 11%
Government Monarchy
Currency Brunei dollar = 100 cents
Literacy rate 91.5%
Calorie consumption 2,832 kilocalories

BULGARIA

Page 82 C2

Located in southeastern Europe, Bulgaria has made slow progress toward democracy since the fall of its communist regime in 1990.

Official name Republic of Bulgaria
Formation 1908
Capital Sofia
Population 7.9 million / 184 people per sq mile (71 people per sq km)
Total area 42,822 sq miles (110,910 sq km)
Languages Bulgarian, Turkish, Macedonian, Romany
Religions Bulgarian Orthodox 84%, Muslim 13%, Jewish 1%, Roman Catholic 1%, other 1%
Ethnic mix Bulgarian 85%, Turkish 9%, Macedonian 3%, Romany 3%
Government Multiparty republic
Currency Lev = 100 stoninki
Literacy rate 98.4%
Calorie consumption 2,467 kilocalories

BURKINA FASO

Page 53 E4

Known as Upper Volta until 1984, the West African state of Burkina Faso has been under military rule for most of its post-independence history.

Official name Burkina Faso
Formation 1960
Capital Ouagadougou
Population 11.9 million / 112 people per sq mile (43 people per sq km)
Total area 105,869 sq miles (274,200 sq km)
Languages French, Mossi, Fulani, Tuareg, Dyula, Songhai
Religions Traditional beliefs 55%, Muslim 35%, Roman Catholic 9%, other Christian 1%
Ethnic mix Mossi 50%, other 50%
Government Multiparty republic
Currency CFA franc = 100 centimes
Literacy rate 23.9%
Calorie consumption 2,293 kilocalories

BURUNDI

Page 51 B7

Small, landlocked Burundi lies just south of the Equator, on the Nile-Congo watershed in Central Africa. Since 1993 it has been marked by violent ethnic conflict.

Official name Republic of Burundi
Formation 1962
Capital Bujumbura
Population 6.5 million / 605 people per sq mile (234 people per sq km)
Total area 10,745 sq miles (27,830 sq km)
Languages Kirundi, French, Kiswahili
Religions Christian 60%, Traditional beliefs 39%, Muslim 1%
Ethnic mix Hutu 85%, Tutsi 14%, Twa 1%
Government Transitional regime
Currency Burundi franc = 100 centimes
Literacy rate 48.3%
Calorie consumption 1,605 kilocalories

CAMBODIA

Page 115 D5

Located in mainland Southeast Asia, Cambodia has emerged from two decades of civil war and invasion from Vietnam.

Official name Kingdom of Cambodia
Formation 1953
Capital Phnom Penh
Population 13.4 million / 192 people per sq mile (74 people per sq km)
Total area 69,900 sq miles (181,040 sq km)
Languages Khmer, French, Chinese, Vietnamese, Cham
Religions Buddhist 93%, Muslim 6%, Christian 1%
Ethnic mix Khmer 90%, Vietnamese 4%, Chinese 1%, other 5%
Government Constitutional monarchy
Currency Riel = 100 sen
Literacy rate 37.4%
Calorie consumption 2,070 kilocalories

CAMEROON

Page 54 A4

Situated on the central West African coast, Cameroon was effectively a one-party state for 30 years. Multiparty elections were held in 1992.

Official name Republic of Cameroon
Formation 1960
Capital Yaoundé
Population 15.2 million / 83 people per sq mile (32 people per sq km)
Total area 183,567 sq miles (475,440 sq km)
Languages English, French, Bamileke, Fang, Fulani
Religions Traditional beliefs 25%, Christian 53%, Muslim 22%
Ethnic mix Cameroon highlanders 31%, Bantu 19%, Kirdi 11%, other 39%
Government Presidential democracy
Currency CFA franc = 100 centimes
Literacy rate 75.9%
Calorie consumption 2,255 kilocalories

CANADA

Page 15 E4

Canada extends from its US border norh to the Arctic Ocean. In recent years, French-speaking Quebec has sought independence from the rest of the country.

Official name Canada
Formation 1867
Capital Ottawa
Population 31.4 million /8 people per sq mile (3 people per sq km)
Total area 3,851,788 sq miles (9,976,140 sq km)
Languages English, French, Chinese, Italian, German, Ukranian, Inuktitut
Religions Roman Catholic 43%, Protestant 29%, non-religious 16%, other 12%
Ethnic mix British origin 44%, French origin 25%, Other European 20%, other 11%
Government Parlimentary democracy
Currency Canadian dollar = 100 cents
Literacy rate 99%
Calorie consumption 3,174 kilocalories

CAPE VERDE

Page 52 A2

Off the west coast of Africa, in the Atlantic Ocean, lies the group of islands that make up Cape Verde, a Portuguese colony until 1975.

Official name Republic of Cape Verde
Formation 1975
Capital Praia
Population 437,000/ 281 people per sq mile (108 people per sq km)
Total area 1,557 sq miles (4,033 sq km)
Languages Portuguese Creole, Portuguese
Religions Roman Catholic 97%, Protestant (Church of Nazarene) 1%, other 2%
Ethnic mix Mestico 60%, African 30%, other 10%
Government Multiparty republic
Currency Cape Verde escudo = 100 centavos
Literacy rate 74.2%
Calorie consumption 3,278 kilocalories

CENTRAL AFRICAN REPUBLIC

Page 54 C4

This landlocked country lies between the basins of the Chad and Congo rivers. Its arid north sustains less than 2% of the population.

Official name Central African Republic
Formation 1960
Capital Bangui
Population 3.8 million / 16 people per sq mile (6 people per sq km)
Total area 240,534 sq miles (622,984 sq km)
Languages French, Sango, Banda, Gbaya
Religions Traditional beliefs 60%, Christian 35%, Muslim 5%
Ethnic mix Baya 34%, Banda 27%, Mandjia 21%, Sara 10%, other 8%
Government Multiparty republic
Currency CFA franc = 100 centimes
Literacy rate 46.7%
Calorie consumption 1,946 kilocalories

CHAD

Page 54 C3

Landlocked in north central Africa, Chad has been torn by intermittent periods of civil war since it gained independence from France in 1960.

Official name Republic of Chad
Formation 1960
Capital N'Djamena
Population 8.1 million / 16 people per sq mile (6 people per sq km)
Total area 495,752 sq miles (1,284,000 sq km)
Languages French, Arabic, Sara, Maba
Religions Muslim 50%, Traditional beliefs 43%, Christian 7%
Ethnic mix Nomads (Tuareg and Toubou) 38%, Sara 30, Arab 15%, other 17%
Government Presidential democracy
Currency CFA franc = 100 centimes
Literacy rate 42.6%
Calorie consumption 2,046 kilocalories

CHILE

Page 42 B3

Chile extends in a ribbon down the west coast of South America. It returned to democracy in 1989 after a referendum rejected its military dictator.

Official name Republic of Chile
Formation 1818
Capital Santiago
Population 15.4 million / 53 people per sq mile (20 people per sq km)
Total area 292,258 sq miles (756,950 sq km)
Languages Spanish, Amerindian languages
Religions Roman Catholic 80%, other and non-religious 20%
Ethnic mix Mixed and European 90%, Amerindian 10%
Government Multiparty republic
Currency Chilean peso = 100 centavos
Literacy rate 95.7%
Calorie consumption 2,882 kilocalories

CHINA

Page 104 C4

This vast East Asian country was dominated by Mao Zedong, who founded the Communist republic, and Deng Xiaoping, his successor (1976–1997).

Official name People's Republic of China
Formation 960
Capital Beijing
Population 1.29 billion / 348 people per sq mile (134 people per sq km)
Total area 3,705,386 sq miles (9,596,960 sq km)
Languages Mandarin, Wu, Cantonese, Hsiang, Min, Hakka, Kan
Religions Non-religious 59%, Traditional beliefs 20%, other 21%
Ethnic mix Han 93%, other 7%
Government One-party state
Currency Yuan (Renminbi) = 10 jiao
Literacy rate 84.2%
Calorie consumption 3,029 kilocalories

COLOMBIA

Page 36 B3

Lying in northwest South America, Colombia is one of the world's most violent countries, with powerful drugs cartels and guerrilla activity.

Official name Republic of Columbia
Formation 1819
Capital Bogotá
Population 42.8 million /97 people per sq mile (38 people per sq km)
Total area 439,733 sq miles (1,138,910 sq km)
Languages Spanish, Amerindian languages, English Creole
Religions Roman Catholic 95%, other 5%
Ethnic mix Mestizo 58%, White 20%, other 22%
Government Presidential democracy
Currency Colombian peso = 100 centavos
Literacy rate 91.8%
Calorie consumption 2,597 kilocalories

COMOROS

In the Indian Ocean, between Mozambique and Madagascar, lie the Comoros, comprising three main islands, and a number of smaller islets.

Official name Federal Islamic Republic of the Comoros
Formation 1975
Capital Moroni
Population 727,000 / 868 people per sq mile (335 people per sq km)
Total area 838 sq miles (2,170 sq km)
Languages Arabic, French, Comoran
Religions Muslim (mainly Sunni) 98%, Roman Catholic 1%, other 1%
Ethnic mix Comorian 97%, other 3%
Government Presidential democracy
Currency Comoros franc = 100 centimes
Literacy rate 59.6%
Calorie consumption 1,753 kilocalories

COSTA RICA

Costa Rica is the most stable country in Central America. Its neutrality in foreign affairs is long-standing, but it has very strong ties with the US.

Official name Republic of Costa Rica
Formation 1838
Capital San José
Population 4.1 million / 208 people per sq mile (80 people per sq km)
Total area 19,730 sq miles (51,100 sq km)
Languages Spanish, English Creole, Bribri, Cabecar
Religions Roman Catholic 76%, other (including Protestant) 24%
Ethnic mix Mesitzo and European 96%, Black 2%, Indian 1%, Chinese 1%
Government Presidential democracy
Currency Costa Rican colón = 100 centimes
Literacy rate 95.6%
Calorie consumption 2,783 kilocalories

CUBA

Cuba is the largest island in the Caribbean and the only Communist country in the Americas. It has been led by Fidel Castro since 1959.

Official name Republic of Cuba
Formation 1902
Capital Havana
Population 11.2 million / 262 people per sq mile (101 people per sq km)
Total area 42,803 sq miles (110,860 sq km)
Languages Spanish
Religions Non-religious 49%, Roman Catholic 40%, Atheist 6%, Protestant 1%, other 4%
Ethnic mix White 66%, European-African 22%, Black 12%
Government One-party state
Currency Cuban peso = 100 centavos
Literacy rate 96.7%
Calorie consumption 2,564 kilocalories

DENMARK

The country occupies the Jutland peninsula and over 400 islands in Scandinavia. Greenland and the Faeroe Islands are self-governing associated territories.

Official name Kingdom of Denmark
Formation AD 950
Capital Copenhagen (Koebenhavn)
Population 5.3 million / 319 people per sq mile (123 people per sq km)
Total area 16,639 sq miles (43,094 sq km)
Languages Danish
Religions Evangelical Lutheran 89%, Roman Catholic 1%, other 10%
Ethnic mix Danish 96%, Faeroe and Inuit 1%, other (including Scandinavian) 3%
Government Parliamentary democracy
Currency Danish krone = 100 ore
Literacy rate 99%
Calorie consumption 3,396 kilocalories

CONGO

Astride the Equator in west central Africa, this former French colony emerged from 26 years of Marxist-Leninist rule in 1990.

Official name Republic of the Congo
Formation 1960
Capital Brazzaville
Population 3.1 million / 23 people per sq mile (9 people per sq km)
Total area 132,046 sq miles (342,000 sq km)
Languages French, Kongo, Teke, Lingala
Religions Traditional beliefs 50%, Christian 48%, Muslim 2%
Ethnic mix Bakongo 48%, Sangha 20%, Teke 17%, Mbochi 12%, other 3%
Government Presidential democracy
Currency CFA franc = 100 centimes
Literacy rate 80.7%
Calorie consumption 2,223 kilocalories

CÔTE D'IVOIRE

One of the larger nations along the coast of West Africa, Côte d'Ivoire remains under the influence of its former colonial ruler, France.

Official name Republic of Côte d'Ivoire
Formation 1960
Capital Yamoussoukro
Population 16.3 million / 131 people per sq mile (51 people per sq km)
Total area 124,502 sq miles (322,460 sq km)
Languages French, Akan, Kru, Voltaic
Religions Traditional beliefs 23%, Muslim 25%, Roman Catholic 23%, Protestant 6%, other 23%
Ethnic mix Baoule 23%, Bete 18%, Senufo 15% Agni-Ashanti 14%, Mandinka 11%, other 19%
Government Multiparty republic
Currency CFA franc = 100 centimes
Literacy rate 47.1%
Calorie consumption 2,590 kilocalories

CYPRUS

Cyprus lies in the eastern Mediterranean. Since 1974, it has been partitioned between the Turkish-occupied north and the Greek south.

Official name Republic of Cyprus
Formation 1960
Capital Nicosia
Population 790,000 / 221 people per sq mile (85 people per sq km)
Total area 3,571 sq miles (9,250 sq km)
Languages Greek, Turkish, English
Religions Greek Orthodox 73%, Muslim 23%, other 4%
Ethnic mix Greek 77%, Turkish 18%, other (mainly British) 5%
Government Presidential democracy
Currency Cyprus pound/Turkish lira
Literacy rate 97.1%
Calorie consumption 3,259 kilocalories

DJIBOUTI

A city state with a desert hinterland, Djibouti lies in northeast Africa. Once known as French Somaliland, its economy relies on its port.

Official name Republic of Djibouti
Formation 1977
Capital Djibouti
Population 644,000 / 76 people per sq mile (29 people per sq km)
Total area 8,490 sq miles (22,000 sq km)
Languages French, Arabic, Somali, Afar
Religions Muslim 94%, Christian 6%
Ethnic mix Issa 60%, Afar 35%, other 5%
Government Presidential democracy
Currency Djibouti franc = 100 centimes
Literacy rate 64.6%
Calorie consumption 2,050 kilocalories

CONGO, DEM. REP.

Straddling the Equator in east central Africa, Dem. Rep. Congo is one of Africa's largest countries. It achieved independence from Belgium in 1960.

Official name Democratic Republic of the Congo
Formation 1960
Capital Kinshasa
Population 52.5 million / 58 people per sq mile (22 people per sq km)
Total area 905,563 sq miles (2,345,410 sq km)
Languages French, Kiswahili, Tshiluba
Religions Traditional beliefs 50%, Roman Catholic 37%, Protestant 13%
Ethnic mix Bantu and Hamitic 45%, other 55%
Government Military-based regime
Currency franc = 100 centimes
Literacy rate 61.4%
Calorie consumption 1,514 kilocalories

CROATIA

Post-independence fighting in this former Yugoslav republic, thwarted its plans to capitalize on its prime location along the east Adriatic coast.

Official name Republic of Croatia
Formation 1991
Capital Zagreb
Population 4.7 million / 215 people per sq mile (83 people per sq km)
Total area 21,831 sq miles (56,542 sq km)
Languages Croatian
Religions Roman Catholic 76%, Orthodox 11%, Muslim 1%, other 12%
Ethnic mix Croat 78%, Serb 12%, Yugoslav 2%, other 8%
Government Parliamentary democracy
Currency Kuna = 100 lipa
Literacy rate 98.3%
Calorie consumption 2,843 kilocalories

CZECH REPUBLIC

Once part of Czechoslovakia in eastern Europe, it became independent in 1993, after peacefully dissolving its federal union with Slovakia.

Official name Czech Republic
Formation 1993
Capital Prague
Population 10.3 million / 338 people per sq mile (131 people per sq km)
Total area 30,450 sq miles (78,866 sq km)
Languages Czech, Slovak, Hungarian
Religions Atheist 38%, Roman Catholic 39%, Protestant 3%, Hussites 2%, other 18%
Ethnic mix Czech 81%, Moravian 13%, Slovak 6%
Government Parliamentary democracy
Currency Czech koruna = 100 halura
Literacy rate 99%
Calorie consumption 3,104 kilocalories

DOMINICA

The Caribbean island Dominica resisted European colonization until the 18th century, when it first came under the French, and then, the British.

Official name Commonwealth of Dominica
Formation 1978
Capital Roseau
Population 73,000 / 251 people per sq mile (97 people per sq km)
Total area 291 sq miles (754 sq km)
Languages English, French Creole
Religions Roman Catholic 77%, Protestant 15%, other 8%
Ethnic mix Black 91%, Mixed 6%, Indian 2%, other 1%
Government Parliamentary democracy
Currency East Caribbean dollar = 100 cents
Literacy rate 94%
Calorie consumption 2,994 kilocalories

DOMINICAN REPUBLIC

Page 33 E2

The republic occupies the eastern two-thirds of the island of Hispaniola in the Caribbean. Frequent coups and a strong US influence mark its recent past.

Official name Dominican Republic
Formation 1865
Capital Santo Domingo
Population 8.5 million / 452 people per sq mile (174 people per sq km)
Total area 18,815 sq miles (48,730 sq km)
Languages Spanish, French Creole
Religions Roman Catholic 92%, other and non-religious 8%
Ethnic mix Mixed 75%, White 15%, Black 10%
Government Presidential democracy
Currency Dominican Republic peso = 100 centavos
Literacy rate 83.6%
Calorie consumption 2,325 kilocalories

EAST TIMOR

Page 116 F5

This new nation occupies the eastern half of the island of Timor. Invaded by Indonesia in 1975, it declared independence in 1999.

Official name East Timor
Formation 2002
Capital Dili
Population 737,811 /196 people per sq mile (49 per sq km)
Total area 3,756 sq miles (14, 874 sq km)
Languages Tetum (Portuguese/Austronesian), Bahasa Indonesia, Portuguese
Religions Roman Catholic 93%, other 7%
Ethnic mix Various Papuan groups; 2% Chinese. In the 1990's Indonesian settlers became numerous, accounting for 20% of the population by 1999.
Government Multiparty republic
Currency US dollar
Literacy rate 41 %
Calorie consumption not available

ECUADOR

Page 38 A2

Ecuador sits high on South America's western coast. Once part of the Inca heartland, its territory includes the Galapagos Islands, to the west.

Official name Republic of Ecuador
Formation 1830
Capital Quito
Population 12.9 million / 118 people per sq mile (45 people per sq km)
Total area 109,483 sq miles (283,560 sq km)
Languages Spanish, Quechua, other Amerindian languages
Religions Roman Catholic 93%, Protestant, Jewish and other 7%
Ethnic mix Mestizo 55%, Indian 25%, Black 10%, White 10%
Government Presidential democracy
Currency US dollar
Literacy rate 91.3%
Calorie consumption 2,693 kilocalories

EGYPT

Page 50 B2

Egypt occupies the northeast corner of Africa. Its essentially pro-Western, military-backed regime is being challenged by Islamic fundamentalists.

Official name Arab Republic of Egypt
Formation 1936
Capital Cairo
Population 69.1 million / 179 people per sq mile (69 people per sq km)
Total area 386,660 sq miles (1,001,450 sq km)
Languages Arabic, French, English, Berber
Religions Muslim (mainly Sunni) 94%, Coptic Christian and other 6%
Ethnic mix Eastern Hamitic 90%, other (Nubian, Armenian, Greek) 10%
Government Presidential democracy
Currency Egyptian pound = 100 piastres
Literacy rate 55.4%
Calorie consumption 3,346 kilocalories

EL SALVADOR

Page 30 B3

El Salvador is Central America's smallest state. A 12-year war between US-backed government troops and left-wing guerrillas ended in 1992.

Official name Republic of El Salvador
Formation 1841
Capital San Salvador
Population 6.4 million / 788 people per sq mile (304 people per sq km)
Total area 8,124 sq miles (21,040 sq km)
Languages Spanish
Religions Roman Catholic 80%, Evangelical 18%, other 2%
Ethnic mix Mestizo 94%, Indian 5%, White 1%
Government Presidential democracy
Currency Salvadorean colón = 100 centavos
Literacy rate 78.8%
Calorie consumption 2,503 kilocalories

EQUATORIAL GUINEA

Page 55 A5

The country comprises the Rio Muni mainland and five islands on the west coast of central Africa. Free elections were first held in 1988.

Official name Republic of Equatorial Guinea
Formation 1968
Capital Malabo
Population 470,000 / 43 people per sq mile (17 people per sq km)
Total area 10,830 sq miles (28,051 sq km)
Languages Spanish, Fang, Bubi
Religions Roman Catholic 90%, other 10%
Ethnic mix Fang 85%, Bubi 4%, other 11%
Government Presidential regime
Currency CFA franc = 100 centimes
Literacy rate 83.2%
Calorie consumption not available

ERITREA

Page 50 C3

Lying on the shores of the Red Sea, Eritrea effectively seceded from Ethiopia in 1993, following a 30-year war for independence.

Official name State of Eritrea
Formation 1993
Capital Asmara
Population 3.8 million / 81 people per sq mile (31 people per sq km)
Total area 46,842 sq miles (121,320 sq km)
Languages Tigrinya, English, Tigre, Afar, Arabic, Bilen, Kunama, Nara, Saho, Hadareb
Religions Christian 45%, Muslim 45%, other 10%
Ethnic mix Tigray and Kunama 40%, Tigray 50%, Afar 4%, Saho 3%, other 4%
Government Transitional regime
Currency Nafka = 100 cents
Literacy rate 55.7%
Calorie consumption 1,665 kilocalories

ESTONIA

Page 84 D2

Estonia is the smallest and most developed of the three Baltic states. It has the highest standard of living of any of the former Soviet republics.

Official name Republic of Estonia
Formation 1991
Capital Tallinn
Population 1.4 million / 80 people per sq mile (31 people per sq km)
Total area 17,462 sq miles (45,226 sq km)
Languages Estonian, Russian
Religions Evangelical Lutheran 56%, Russian Orthodox 25%, Other 19%
Ethnic mix Estonian 62%, Russian 30%, other 8%
Government Parliamentary democracy
Currency Kroon = 100 cents
Literacy rate 99%
Calorie consumption 3 376 kilocalories

ETHIOPIA

Page 51 C5

Located in northeast Africa, Ethiopia was a Marxist regime from 1974–91. It has suffered a series of economic, civil, and natural crises.

Official name Federal Democratic Republic of Ethiopia
Formation 1896
Capital Addis Ababa
Population 64.5 million / 148 people per sq mile (57 people per sq km)
Total area 435,184 sq miles (1,127,127 sq km)
Languages Amharic, Tigrinya, Galla
Religions Muslim 40%, Ethiopian Orthodox 40%, other 20%
Ethnic mix Oromo 40%, Amhara 25%, Sidamo 9%, Somali 6%, Berta 6%, other 14%
Government Multiparty republic
Currency Ethiopian birr = 100 cents
Literacy rate 38.4%
Calorie consumption 2,023 kilocalories

FIJI

Page 123 E5

A volcanic archipelago, Fiji comprises 882 islands in the southern Pacific Ocean. Ethnic Fijians and Indo-Fijians have been in conflict since 1987.

Official name Republic of the Fiji Islands
Formation 1970
Capital Suva
Population 823,000 / 117 people per sq mile (45 people per sq km)
Total area 7,054 sq miles (18,270 sq km)
Languages Fijian, English, Hindi, Urdu, Tamil, Telegu
Religions Hindu 38%, Methodist 37%, Roman Catholic 9%, other 16%
Ethnic mix Melanesian 48%, Indian 46%, other 6%
Government Multiparty republic
Currency Fiji dollar = 100 cents
Literacy rate 92.9%
Calorie consumption 2,861 kilocalories

FINLAND

Page 62 D4

Finland's distinctive language and national identity have been influenced by both its Scandinavian and its Russian neighbors.

Official name Republic of Finland
Formation 1917
Capital Helsinki
Population 5.2 million / 40 people per sq mile (15 people per sq km)
Total area 130,127 sq miles (337,030 sq km)
Languages Finnish, Swedish, Sami
Religions Evangelical Lutheran 89%, Finnish Orthodox 1%, Roman Catholic 1%, other 9%
Ethnic mix Finnish 93%, other (including Sami) 7%
Government Paliamentary democracy
Currency Euro (Markka until 2002)
Literacy rate 99%
Calorie consumption 3,227 kilocalories

FRANCE

Page 68 B4

Straddling Western Europe from the English Channel to the Mediterranean Sea, France is one of the world's leading industrial powers.

Official name French Republic
Formation 987
Capital Paris
Population 59.5 million / 282 people per sq mile (109 people per sq km)
Total area 211,208 sq miles (547,030 sq km)
Languages French, Provenial, German, Breton, Catalan, Basque
Religions Roman Catholic 88%, Muslim 8%, Protestant 2%, other 2%
Ethnic mix French 90%, North African 6%, German 2%, other 2%
Government Multiparty republic
Currency Euro (French franc until 2002)
Literacy rate 99%
Calorie consumption 3,591 kilocalories

GABON

Page 55 A5

A former French colony straddling the Equator on Africa's west coast, it returned to multiparty politics in 1990, after 22 years of one-party rule.

Official name Gabonese Republic
Formation 1960
Capital Libreville
Population 1.3 million / 13 people per sq mile (5 people per sq km)
Total area 103,346 sq miles (267,667 sq km)
Languages French, Fang, Punu, Sira, Nzebi, Mpongwe
Religions Christian 55%, Traditional beliefs 40%, Muslim 1%, other 4%
Ethnic mix Fang 35%, other Bantu 29%, Eshira 25%, other 11%
Government Multiparty republic
Currency CFA franc = 100 centimes
Literacy rate 70.8%
Calorie consumption 2,564 kilocalories

GERMANY

Page 72 B4

Europe's strongest economic power, Germany's democratic west and Communist east were re-unified in 1990, after the fall of the east's regime.

Official name Federal Republic of Germany
Formation 1871
Capital Berlin
Population 82 million / 595 people per sq mile (230 people per sq km)
Total area 137,846 sq miles (357,021 sq km)
Languages German, Turkish
Religions Protestant 34%, Roman Catholic 33%, Muslim 3%, other 30%
Ethnic mix German 92%, other 8%
Government Parliamentary democracy
Currency Euro (Deutsche Mark until 2002)
Literacy rate 99%
Calorie consumption 3,451 kilocalories

GRENADA

Page 33 G5

The Windward island of Grenada became a focus of attention in 1983, when the US mounted an invasion to sever its growing links with Cuba.

Official name Grenada
Formation 1974
Capital St. George's
Population 98,000 / 747 people per sq mile (288 people per sq km)
Total area 131 sq miles (340 sq km)
Languages English, English Creole
Religions Roman Catholic 68%, Anglican 17%, other 15%
Ethnic mix Black 82%, Mulatto 13%, Indian 3%, other 2%
Government Parliamentary democracy
Currency East Caribbean dollar = 100 cents
Literacy rate 96%
Calorie consumption 2,764 kilocalorie

GUINEA-BISSAU

Page 52 B4

Known as Portuguese Guinea during its days as a colony, Guinea-Bissau is situated on Africa's west coast, bordered by Senegal and Guinea.

Official name Republic of Guinea-Bissau
Formation 1974
Capital Bissau
Population 1.2 million / 86 people per sq mile (33 people per sq km)
Total area 13,946 sq miles (36,120 sq km)
Languages Portuguese Creole, Fulani Balante, Malinke, Portuguese
Religions Indigenous beliefs 52%, Muslim 40%, Christian 8%
Ethnic mix Balante 25%, Madinka 12%, Fila 20%, Mandyako 11%, other 32%
Government Presidential democracy
Currency CFA franc = 100 centimes
Literacy rate 38.8%
Calorie consumption 2,333 kilocalories

GAMBIA

Page 52 B3

A narrow state on the west coast of Africa, The Gambia was renowned for its stability until its government was overthrown in a coup in 1994.

Official name Republic of The Gambia
Formation 1965
Capital Banjul
Population 1.34 million / 307 people per sq mile (119 people per sq km)
Total area 4,363 sq miles (11,300 sq km)
Languages English, Mandinka, Fulani, Wolof, Jola, Soninke
Religions Sunni Muslim 90%, Christian 9%, Indigenous beliefs 1%
Ethnic mix Mandinka 42%, Fulani 18%, Wolof 16%, Jola 10%, Serahuli 9%, other 5%
Government Multiparty republic
Currency Dalasi = 100 butut
Literacy rate 36.6%
Calorie consumption 2,474 kilocalories

GHANA

Page 53 E5

Once known as the Gold Coast, Ghana in West Africa has experienced intermittent periods of military rule since independence in 1957.

Official name Republic of Ghana
Formation 1957
Capital Accra
Population 19.7 million / 214 people per sq mile (83 people per sq km)
Total area 92,100 sq miles (238,540 sq km)
Languages English, Twi, Fanti, Ewe, Ga, Adangbe, Gurma, Dagomba
Religions Christian 43%, Traditional beliefs 38%, Muslim 11%, other 8%
Ethnic mix Ashanti and Fanti 52%, Moshi-Dagomba 16%, Ewe 12%, Ga 8%, Yoruba 1%, other 11%
Government Presidential democracy
Currency Cedi = 100 pesewas
Literacy rate 71.5%
Calorie consumption 2,699 kilocalories

GUATEMALA

Page 30 A2

The largest state on the Central American isthmus, Guatemala returned to civilian rule in 1986, after 32 years of repressive military rule.

Official name Republic of Guatemala
Formation 1838
Capital Guatemala City
Population 11.7 million / 278 people per sq mile (107 people per sq km)
Total area 42,042 sq miles (108,890 sq km)
Languages Spanish, Quiché, Mam, Cakchiquel, Kekchí
Religions Roman Catholic 65%, Protestant 33%, other 2%
Ethnic mix Amerindian 60%, Mestizo 30%, other 10%
Government Presidential democracy
Currency Quetzal = 100 centavos
Literacy rate 68.8%
Calorie consumption 2,171 kilocalories

GUYANA

Page 37 F3

The only English-speaking country in South America, Guyana gained independence from Britain in 1966, and became a republic in 1970.

Official name Cooperative Republic of Guyana
Formation 1966
Capital Georgetown
Population 763,000 / 9 people per sq mile (4 people per sq km)
Total area 83,000 sq miles (214,970 sq km)
Languages English, English Creole, Hindi, Tamil, Amerindian languages
Religions Christian 57%, Hindu 33%, Muslim 9%, other 1%
Ethnic mix East Indian 52%, Black African 38%, other 10%
Government Presidential democracy
Currency Guyana dollar = 100 cents
Literacy rate 98.5%
Calorie consumption 2,582 kilocalories

GEORGIA

Page 95 F2

Located on the eastern shore of the Black Sea, Georgia's northern provinces have been torn by civil war since independence from the USSR in 1991.

Official name Georgia
Formation 1991
Capital Tbilisi
Population 5.2 million /193 people per sq mile (75 people per sq km)
Total area 26,911 sq miles (69,700 sq km)
Languages Georgian, Russian
Religions Georgian Orthodox 65%, Muslim 11%, Russian Orthodox 10%, Amenian Orthodox 8%, Unknown 6%
Ethnic mix Georgian 70%, Armenian 8%, Russian 6%, Azeri 6%, Ossetian 3%, other 7%
Government Presidential democracy
Currency Lari = 100 tetri
Literacy rate 99%
Calorie consumption 2,412 kilocalories

GREECE

Page 83 A5

Greece is the southernmost Balkan nation. Surrounded by the Mediterranean, Aegean, and Ionian Seas, it has a strong seafaring tradition.

Official name Hellenic Republic
Formation 1829
Capital Athens
Population 10.6 million / 208 people per sq mile (80 people per sq km)
Total area 50,942 sq miles (131,940 sq km)
Languages Greek, Turkish, Macedonian, Albanian
Religions Greek Orthodox 98%, Muslim 1%, other 1%
Ethnic mix Greek 98%, other 2%
Government Presidential democracy
Currency Euro (Drachma until 2002)
Literacy rate 97.3%
Calorie consumption 3,705 kilocalories

GUINEA

Page 52 C4

Facing the Atlantic Ocean, on the west coast of Africa, Guinea became the first French colony in Africa to gain independence, in 1958.

Official name Republic of Guinea
Formation 1958
Capital Conakry
Population 8.3 million / 87 people per sq mile (34 people per sq km)
Total area 94,925 sq miles (245,857 sq km)
Languages French, Fulani, Malinke, Soussou
Religions Muslim 65%, Traditional beliefs 33%, Christian 2%
Ethnic mix Fila (Fulani) 30%, Malinke 30%, Soussou 15%, Kissi 10%, other tribes 10%, other 25%
Government Multiparty republic
Currency Guinea franc = 100 centimes
Literacy rate 41.1%
Calorie consumption 2,353 kilocalories

HAITI

Page 32 D3

Haiti shares the Caribbean island of Hispaniola with the Dominican Republic. At independence, in 1804, it became the world's first Black republic.

Official name Republic of Haiti
Formation 1804
Capital Port-au-Prince
Population 8.3 million / 775 people per sq mile (299 people per sq km)
Total area 10,714 sq miles (27,750 sq km)
Languages English, French Creole
Religions Roman Catholic 80%, Protestant 16%, non-religious 1%, other 3%
Ethnic mix Black African 95%, Mulatto and European 5%
Government Multiparty republic
Currency Gourde = 100 centimes
Literacy rate 49.8%
Calorie consumption 2,056 kilocalories

HONDURAS

Page 30 C2

Honduras straddles the Central American isthmus. The country returned to full democratic civilian rule in 1984, after a succession of military regimes.

Official name Republic of Honduras
Formation 1838
Capital Tegucigalpa
Population 6.6 million / 153 people per sq mile (59 people per sq km)
Total area 43,278 sq miles (112,090 sq km)
Languages Spanish, Black Carib, English Creole
Religions Roman Catholic 97%, Protestant minority 3%
Ethnic mix Mestizo 90%, Black African 5%, Amerindian 4%, White 1%
Government Presidential democracy
Currency Lempira = 100 centavos
Literacy rate 74.6%
Calorie consumption 2,395 kilocalories

INDIA

Page 112 D4

Separated from the rest of Asia by the Himalayan mountain ranges, India forms a subcontinent. It is the world's second most populous country.

Official name Republic of India
Formation 1947
Capital New Delhi
Population 1.03 billion / 790 people per sq mile (305 people per sq km)
Total area 1,269,339 sq miles (3,287,590 sq km)
Languages Hindi, English, and 16 regional languages
Religions Hindu 83%, Muslim 11%, Christian 2%, Sikh 2%, other 2%
Ethnic mix Indo-Aryan 72%, Dravidian 25%, Mongoloid and other 3%
Government Parliamentary democracy
Currency Indian rupee = 100 paisa
Literacy rate 57.2%
Calorie consumption 2,428 kilocalories

IRAQ

Page 98 B3

Oil-rich Iraq is situated in the central Middle East. Since the removal of the monarchy in 1958, it has experienced considerable political turmoil.

Official name Republic of Iraq
Formation 1932
Capital Baghdad
Population 23.6 million / 140 people per sq mile (54 people per sq km)
Total area 168,753 sq miles (437,072 sq km)
Languages Arabic, Kurdish, Armenian, Assyrian, Turkic languages
Religions Shi'a ithna Muslim 62%, Sunni Muslim 33%, other 5%
Ethnic mix Arab 79%, Kurdish 16%, Persian 3%, Turkman 2%
Government One-party republic
Currency Iraqi dinar = 1,000 fils
Literacy rate 55.9%
Calorie consumption 2,197 kilocalories

ITALY

Page 74 B3

Projecting into the Mediterranean Sea in Southern Europe, Italy is an ancient land, but also one of the continent's newest unified states.

Official name Italian Republic
Formation 1861
Capital Rome
Population 57.5 million / 494 people per sq mile (191 people per sq km)
Total area 116,305 sq miles (301,230 sq km)
Languages Italian, German, French, Rhaeto-Romanic, Sardinian
Religions Roman Catholic 83%, other and non-religious 17%
Ethnic mix Italian 94%, Sardinian 2%, other 4%
Government Parliamentary democracy
Currency Euro (Italian lira until 2002)
Literacy rate 98.4%
Calorie consumption 3,661 kilocalories

HUNGARY

Page 77 C6

Hungary is bordered by seven states in Central Europe. It has changed its economic and political policies to develop closer ties with the EU.

Official name Republic of Hungary
Formation 1918
Capital Budapest
Population 9.9 million / 276 people per sq mile (106 people per sq km)
Total area 35,919 sq miles (93,030 sq km)
Languages Hungarian
Religions Roman Catholic 64%, Calvinist 20%, non-religious 7%, Lutheran 4%, other 5%
Ethnic mix Magyar 90%, German 2%, Romany 1%, Slovak 1%, other 6%
Government Parliamentary democracy
Currency Forint = 100 filler
Literacy rate 99%
Calorie consumption 3,458 kilocalories

INDONESIA

Page 116 C4

Formerly the Dutch East Indies, Indonesia, the world's largest archipelago, stretches over 5,000 km (3,100 miles), from the Indian Ocean to the Pacific Ocean.

Official name Republic of Indonesia
Formation 1949
Capital Jakarta
Population 214 million / 289 people per sq mile (111 people per sq km)
Total area 741,096 sq miles (1,919,440 sq km)
Languages Bahasa Indonesia, Javanese, Madurese, Sundanese, Dutch
Religions Muslim 87%, Protestant 6%, Roman Catholic 3%, other 4%
Ethnic mix Javanese 45%, Sundanese 14%, Coastal Malays 8%, Madurese 8%, other 25%
Government Multiparty republic
Currency Rupiah = 100 sen
Literacy rate 86.9%
Calorie consumption 2,902 kilocalories

IRELAND

Page 67 A6

The Republic of Ireland occupies about 85% of the island of Ireland, with the remainder (Northern Ireland) being part of the United Kingdom.

Official name Ireland
Formation 1922
Capital Dublin
Population 3.8 million / 140 people per sq mile (54 people per sq km)
Total area 27,135 sq miles (70,280 sq km)
Languages English, Irish Gaelic
Religions Roman Catholic 88%, Anglican 3%, other and non-religious 9%
Ethnic mix Irish 95%, other 5%
Government Parliamentary democracy
Currency Euro (Punt until 2002)
Literacy rate 99%
Calorie consumption 3,613 kilocalories

JAMAICA

Page 32 C3

First colonized by the Spanish and then, from 1655, by the English, Jamaica was the first of the Caribbean island nations to achieve independence, in 1962.

Official name Jamaica
Formation 1962
Capital Kingston
Population 2.6 million / 613 people per sq mile (237 people per sq km)
Total area 4,243 sq miles (10,990 sq km)
Languages English, English Creole
Religions Christian (Church of God, Baptist, Anglican, other Protestant) 55%, other and non-religious 45%
Ethnic mix Black African 75%, Mulatto 13%, European and Chinese 11%, Indian 1%
Government Parliamentary democracy
Currency Jamaican dollar = 100 cents
Literacy rate 86.8%
Calorie consumption 2,693 kilocalories

ICELAND

Page 61 E4

Europe's westernmost country, Iceland lies in the North Atlantic, straddling the mid-Atlantic ridge. Its spectacular, volcanic landscape is largely uninhabited.

Official name Republic of Iceland
Formation 1944
Capital Reykjavik
Population 281,000 / 7 people per sq mile (3 people per sq km)
Total area 39,768 sq miles (103,000 sq km)
Languages Icelandic
Religions Evangelical Lutheran 93%, non-religious 6%, other Christian 1%
Ethnic mix Icelandic 94%, Danish 1%, other 5%
Government Parliamentary democracy
Currency Icelandic króna = 100 aurar
Literacy rate 99%
Calorie consumption 3,342 kilocalories

IRAN

Page 98 B3

Since the 1979 revolution led by Ayatollah Khomeini, which sent Iran's Shah into exile, this Middle Eastern country has become the world's largest theocracy.

Official name Islamic Republic of Iran
Formation 1502
Capital Tehran
Population 71.4 million / 112 people per sq mile (43 people per sq km)
Total area 636,406 sq miles (1,648,293 sq km)
Languages Farsi, Azeri, Gilaki, Baluchi, Mazanderani, Kurdish, Arabic
Religions Shi'a Muslim 95%, Sunni Muslim 4%, other 1%
Ethnic mix Persian 50%, Azeri 24%, Lur and Bakhtiari 8%, Kurd 8%, other 10%
Government Islamic theocracy
Currency Iranian rial = 100 dinars
Literacy rate 76.8%
Calorie consumption 2,913 kilocalories

ISRAEL

Page 97 A7

Israel was created as a new state in 1948 on the east coast of the Mediterranean. Following wars with its Arab neighbors, it has extended its boundaries.

Official name State of Israel
Formation 1948
Capital Jerusalem
Population 6.2 million / 773 people per sq mile (305 people per sq km)
Total area 8,019 sq miles (20,770 sq km)
Languages Hebrew, Arabic, Yiddish, German, Russian, Polish, Romanian, Persian
Religions Jewish 82%, Muslim (mainly Sunni) 14%, other (including Druze) 4%
Ethnic mix Jewish 82%, other (mostly Arab) 18%
Government Parliamentary democracy
Currency Shekel = 100 agorot
Literacy rate 96%
Calorie consumption 3,562 kilocalories

JAPAN

Page 108 C4

Japan comprises four principal islands and over 3,000 smaller ones. With the emperor as constitutional head, it is now the world's most powerful economy.

Official name Japan
Formation 1590
Capital Tokyo
Population 127.3 million / 873 people per sq mile (337 people per sq km)
Total area 145,882 sq miles (377,835 sq km)
Languages Japanese, Korean, Chinese
Religions Shinto and Buddhist 76%, Buddhist 16%, other (including Christian) 8%
Ethnic mix Japanese 99%, other (mainly Korean) 1%
Government Parliamentary democracy
Currency Yen = 100 sen
Literacy rate 99%
Calorie consumption 2,762 kilocalories

JORDAN

Page 97 B6

The kingdom of Jordan lies east of Israel. In 1993, King Hussein responded to calls for greater democracy by agreeing to multiparty elections.

Official name Hashemite Kingdom of Jordan
Formation 1946
Capital Amman
Population 5.1 million / 143 people per sq mile (55 people per sq km)
Total area 35,637 sq miles (92,300 sq km)
Languages Arabic
Religions Muslim (mainly Sunni) 92%, other (mostly Christian) 8%
Ethnic mix Arab 98% (Palestinian 40%), Armenian 1%, Circassian 1%
Government Constitutional monarchy
Currency Jordanian dinar = 1,000 fils
Literacy rate 89.2%
Calorie consumption 2,749 kilocalories

KAZAKHSTAN

Page 92 B4

Second largest of the former Soviet republics, mineral-rich Kazakhstan has the potential to become the major Central Asian economic power.

Official name Republic of Kazakhstan
Formation 1991
Capital Astana
Population 16.1 million / 15 people per sq mile (6 people per sq km)
Total area 1,049,150 sq miles (2,717,300 sq km)
Languages Kazakh, Russian, German, Uighur, Korean
Religions Muslim (mainly Sunni) 50%, Russian Orthodox 13%, other 37%
Ethnic mix Kazakh 53%, Russian 30%, Ukrainan 4%, German 2%, Tartar 2%, other 9%
Government Presidential democracy
Currency Tenge = 100 tein
Literacy rate 99%
Calorie consumption 2,991 kilocalories

KENYA

Page 51 C6

Kenya straddles the Equator on Africa's east coast. It became a multiparty democracy in 1992 and has been led by President Moi since 1978.

Official name Republic of Kenya
Formation 1963
Capital Nairobi
Population 31.3 million / 139 people per sq mile (54 people per sq km)
Total area 224,961 sq miles (582,650 sq km)
Languages Kiswahili, English, Kikuyu, Luo, Kamba
Religions Christian 60%, Traditional beliefs 25%, Muslim 6%, other 9%
Ethnic mix Kikuyu 21%, Luhya 14%, Luo 13%, Kamba 11%, Kalenjin 11%, other 30%
Government Presidential democracy
Currency Kenya shilling = 100 cents
Literacy rate 82.4%
Calorie consumption 1,965 kilocalories

KIRIBATI

Page 123 F3

Part of the British colony of the Gilbert and Ellice Islands until independence in 1979, Kiribati comprises 33 islands in the mid-Pacific Ocean.

Official name Republic of Kiribati
Formation 1979
Capital Bairiki (Tarawa Atoll)
Population 92,000 / 332 people per sq mile (128 people per sq km)
Total area 277 sq miles (717 sq km)
Languages English, Micronesian dialect
Religions Roman Catholic 53%, Kiribati Protestant Church 39%, other 8%
Ethnic mix Micronesian 96%, other 4%
Government Non-party democracy
Currency Australian dollar = 100 cents
Literacy rate 98%
Calorie consumption 2,957 kilocalories

KUWAIT

Page 98 C4

Kuwait lies on the northwest extreme of the Persian Gulf. The state was a British protectorate from 1914 until 1961, when full independence was granted.

Official name State of Kuwait
Formation 1961
Capital Kuwait City
Population 2 million / 291 people per sq mile (112 people per sq km)
Total area 6880 sq miles (17,820 sq km)
Languages Arabic, English
Religions Muslim (mainly Sunni) 85%, Christian, Hindu and other 15%
Ethnic mix Kuwaiti 45%, other Arab 35%, South Asian 9%, Iranian 4%, other 7%
Government Constitutional monarchy
Currency Kuwaiti dinar = 1,000 fils
Literacy rate 82.6%
Calorie consumption 3,132 kilocalories

KYRGYZSTAN

Page 101 F2

A mountainous, landlocked state in Central Asia. The most rural of the ex-Soviet republics, it only gradually developed its own cultural nationalism.

Official name Kyrgyz Republic
Formation 1991
Capital Bishkek
Population 5 million / 65 people per sq mile (25 people per sq km)
Total area 76,641 sq miles (198,500 sq km)
Languages Kyrgyz, Russian
Religions Muslim (mainly Sunni) 70%, Russian Orthodox 30%
Ethnic mix Kyrgyz 57%, Russian 19%, Uzbek 13%, Tartar 2%, Ukrainian 2%, other 7%
Government Presidential democracy
Currency Som = 100 teen
Literacy rate 97%
Calorie consumption 2,871 kilocalories

LAOS

Page 114 D4

A former French colony, independent in 1953, Laos lies landlocked in Southeast Asia. It has been under communist rule since 1975.

Official name Lao People's Democratic Republic
Formation 1953
Capital Vientiane
Population 5.4 million / 59 people per sq mile (23 people per sq km)
Total area 91,428 sq miles (236,800 sq km)
Languages Lao, Mon-Khmer, Chinese, Yao, Vietnamese, French
Religions Buddhist 85%, other (including Animist) 15%
Ethnic mix Lao Loum 66%, Lao Theung 30%, Lao Soung 2%, other 2%
Government One-party republic
Currency New kip = 100 cents
Literacy rate 48.7%
Calorie consumption 2,266 kilocalories

LATVIA

Page 84 C3

Situated on the east coast of the Baltic Sea, Lativa, like its Baltic neighbors, became independent in 1991. It retains a large Russian population.

Official name Republic of Latvia
Formation 1991
Capital Riga
Population 2.4 million / 96 people per sq mile (37 people per sq km)
Total area 24,938 sq miles (64,589 sq km)
Languages Latvian, Russian
Religions Lutheran 55%, Roman Catholic 24%, Russian Orthodox 9%, other 12%
Ethnic mix Latvian 57%, Russian 32%, Belarussian 4%, Ukrainan 3%, Polish 2%, other 2%
Government Presidential democracy
Currency Lat = 100 santimi
Literacy rate 99%
Calorie consumption 2,855 kilocalories

LEBANON

Page 96 A4

Lebanon is dwarfed by its two powerful neighbors, Syria and Israel. The state started rebuilding in 1989, after 14 years of intense civil war.

Official name Republic of Lebanon
Formation 1941
Capital Beirut
Population 3.6 million / 897 people per sq mile (346 people per sq km)
Total area 4,015 sq miles (10,400 sq km)
Languages Arabic, French, Armenian, Assyrian
Religions Muslim 70%, Christian 30%
Ethnic mix Arab 94%, Armenian 4%, other 2%
Government Multiparty republic
Currency Lebanese pound = 100 piastres
Literacy rate 86%
Calorie consumption 3,155 kilocalories

LESOTHO

Page 56 D4

The landlocked kingdom of Lesotho is entirely surrounded by South Africa, which provides all its land transportation links with the outside world.

Official name Kingdom of Lesotho
Formation 1966
Capital Maseru
Population 2.1 million / 179 people per sq mile (69 people per sq km)
Total area 11,720 sq miles (30,355 sq km)
Languages English, Sesotho, Zulu
Religions Traditional beliefs 10% Christian 90%,
Ethnic mix Sotho 97%, European and Asian 3%
Government Constitutional monarchy
Currency Loti = 100 lisente
Literacy rate 83.3%
Calorie consumption 2,300 kilocalories

LIBERIA

Page 52 C5

Liberia faces the Atlantic Ocean in equatorial West Africa. Africa's oldest republic, it was established in 1847. Today, it is torn by civil war.

Official name Republic of Liberia
Formation 1847
Capital Monrovia
Population 3.1 million / 72 people per sq mile (28 people per sq km)
Total area 43,000 sq miles (111,370 sq km)
Languages English, Kpelle, Vai, Bassa, Kru, Grebo, Kissi, Gola, Loma
Religions Christian 68%, Traditional beliefs 18%, Muslim 14%
Ethnic mix Indigenous tribes (16 main groups) 95%, Americo-Liberians 5%
Government Multiparty republic
Currency Liberian dollar = 100 cents
Literacy rate 54%
Calorie consumption 2,076 kilocalories

LIBYA

Page 49 F3

Situated on the Mediterranean coast of North Africa, Libya is a Muslim dictatorship, politically marginalized by the West for its terrorist links.

Official name Great Socialist People's Libyan Arab Jamahariyah
Formation 1951
Capital Tripoli
Population 5.4 million / 8 people per sq mile (3 people per sq km)
Total area 679,358 sq miles (1,759,540 sq km)
Languages Arabic, Tuareg
Religions Muslim (mainly Sunni) 97%, other 3%
Ethnic mix Arab and Berber 95%, other 5%
Government One-party state
Currency Libyan dinar = 1,000 dirhams
Literacy rate 80.1%
Calorie consumption 3,305 kilocalories

LIECHTENSTEIN

Page 73 B7

Tucked in the Alps between Switzerland and Austria, Liechtenstein became an independent principality of the Holy Roman Empire in 1719.

Official name Principality of Liechtenstein
Formation 1719
Capital Vaduz
Population 32,200/ 521 people per sq mile (201 people per sq km)
Total area 62 sq miles (160 sq km)
Languages German, Alemannish dialect, Italian
Religions Roman Catholic 81%, Protestant 7%, other 12%
Ethnic mix Liechtensteiner 63%, Foreign residents 37%
Government Parliamentary democracy
Currency Swiss franc = 100 centimes
Literacy rate 99%
Calorie consumption not available

LITHUANIA

Page 84 B4

The largest, most powerful and stable of the Baltic states, Lithuania was the first Baltic country to declare independence from Moscow, in 1991.

Official name Republic of Lithuania
Formation 1991
Capital Vilnius
Population 3.7 million / 147 people per sq mile (57 people per sq km)
Total area 25,174 sq miles (65,200 sq km)
Languages Lithuanian, Russian
Religions Roman Catholic 83%, Protestant 5%, other 12%
Ethnic mix Lithuanian 80%, Russian 9%, Polish 7%, Belarussian 2%, other 2%
Government Parliamentary democracy
Currency Litas = 100 centas
Literacy rate 99%
Calorie consumption 3,040 kilocalories

LUXEMBOURG

Page 65 D8

Making up part of the plateau of the Ardennes in Western Europe, Luxembourg is Europe's last independent duchy and one of its richest states.

Official name Grand Duchy of Luxembourg
Formation 1867
Capital Luxembourg
Population 442,000/ 433 people per sq mile (171 people per sq km)
Total area 998 sq miles (2,586 sq km)
Languages French, German, Luxembourgish
Religions Roman Catholic 97%, other 3%
Ethnic mix Luxembourger 73%, Foreign residents 27%
Government Parliamentary democracy
Currency Euro (Luxembourg and Belgian Franc until 2002)
Literacy rate 99%
Calorie consumption 3,701 kilocalories

MACEDONIA

Page 79 D6

Landlocked in the southern Balkans, Macedonia has been affected by sanctions imposed on its northern trading partners and by Greek antagonism.

Official name Former Yugoslav Republic of Macedonia
Formation 1991
Capital Skopje
Population 2 million / 204 people per sq mile (79 people per sq km)
Total area 9,781 sq miles (25,333 sq km)
Languages Macedonian, Albania, Serbo-Croat
Religions Christian 74%, Muslim 26%
Ethnic mix Macedonian 67%, Albanian 23%, Turkish 4%, other 6%
Government Multiparty republic
Currency Macedonian denar = 100 deni
Literacy rate 94%
Calorie consumption 3,006 kilocalories

MADAGASCAR

Page 57 F4

Lying in the Indian Ocean, Madagascar is the world's fourth largest island. Free elections in 1993 ended 18 years of radical socialist government.

Official name Republic of Madagascar
Formation 1960
Capital Antananarivo
Population 16.4 million / 72 people per sq mile (28 people per sq km)
Total area 226,656 sq miles (587,040 sq km)
Languages French, Malagasy
Religions Traditional beliefs 52%, Christian 41%, Muslim 7%
Ethnic mix Merina 26%, Betsilio 12%, Betsimisaraka 15%, other 47%
Government Presidential democracy
Currency Malagasy franc = 100 centimes
Literacy rate 66.5%
Calorie consumption 2,007 kilocalories

MALAWI

Page 57 E1

A former British colony, Malawi lies landlocked in southeast Africa. Its name means "the land where the sun is reflected in the water like fire."

Official name Republic of Malawi
Formation 1964
Capital Lilongwe
Population 11.6 million / 254 people per sq mile (98 people per sq km)
Total area 45,745 sq miles (118,480 sq km)
Languages English, Chewa, Lomwe, Yao, Ngoni
Religions Protestant 55%, Roman Catholic 20%, Muslim 20%, other 5%
Ethnic mix Bantu 99%, other 1%
Government Presidential democracy
Currency Malawi kwacha = 100 tambala
Literacy rate 60.1%
Calorie consumption 2,181 kilocalories

MALAYSIA

Page 116 B3

Malaysia's three separate territories include Malaya, Sarawak, and Sabah. A financial crisis in 1997 ended a decade of spectacular financial growth.

Official name Federation of Malaysia
Formation 1963
Capital Kuala Lumpur
Population 22.6 million / 178 people per sq mile (69 people per sq km)
Total area 127,316 sq miles (329,750 sq km)
Languages English, Bahasa Malaysia, Malay, Chinese, Tamil
Religions Muslim 53%, Buddhist 19%, Chinese faiths 12%, other 16%
Ethnic mix Malay 48%, Chinese 29%, Indigenous tribes 12%, other 11%
Government Presidential democracy
Currency Ringgit = 100 cents
Literacy rate 87.5%
Calorie consumption 2,919 kilocalories

MALDIVES

Page 110 A4

Only 200 of the more than 1,000 Maldivian small coral islands in the Indian Ocean, are inhabited. Government rests in the hands of a few influential families.

Official name Republic of Maldives
Formation 1965
Capital Malé
Population 300,000 / 2,590 people per sq mile (1000 people per sq km)
Total area 116 sq miles (300 sq km)
Languages Dhivehi (Maldivian),
Religions Sunni Muslim 100%
Ethnic mix Mixed Arab, Sinhalese, Malay 100%
Government Non-party democracy
Currency Rufiyaa (Maldivian rupee) = 100 laari
Literacy rate 96.4%
Calorie consumption 2,592 kilocalories

MALI

Page 53 E2

Landlocked in the heart of West Africa, Mali held its first free elections in 1992, more than 30 years after it gained independence from France.

Official name Republic of Mali
Formation 1960
Capital Bamako
Population 11.7 million / 24 people per sq mile (9 people per sq km)
Total area 478,764 sq miles (1,240,000 sq km)
Languages French, Bambara, Fulani, Senufo, Soninké
Religions Muslim (mainly Sunni) 80%, Traditional beliefs 18%, other 2%
Ethnic mix Bambara 32%, Fula 14%, Senufu 12%, Soninka 9%, other 33%
Government Multiparty republic
Currency CFA franc = 100 centimes
Literacy rate 41.4%
Calorie consumption 2,403 kilocalories

MALTA

Page 80 A5

The Maltese archipelago lies off southern Sicily, midway between Europe and North Africa. The only inhabited islands are Malta, Gozo, and Kemmuna.

Official name Republic of Malta
Formation 1964
Capital Valletta
Population 392,000 / 3,213 people per sq mile (1,241 people per sq km)
Total area 122 sq miles (316 sq km)
Languages Maltese, English
Religions Roman Catholic 98%, other and non-religious 2%
Ethnic mix Maltese (mixed Arab, Sicilian, Norman, Spanish, Italian, English) 96%, other 4%
Government Parliamentary democracy
Currency Maltese lira = 100 cents
Literacy rate 92.1%
Calorie consumption 3,543 kilocalories

MARSHALL ISLANDS

Page 122 D1

A group of 34 atolls, the Marshall Islands were under US rule as part of the UN Trust Territory of the Pacific Islands until 1986. The economy depends on US aid.

Official name Republic of the Marshall Islands
Formation 1986
Capital Majuro
Population 68,100 / 973 people per sq mile (376 people per sq km)
Total area 70 sq miles (181 sq km)
Languages Marshallese, English, Japanese, German
Religions Protestant 90%, Roman Catholic 8%, other 2%
Ethnic mix Micronesian 97%, other 3%
Government Parliamentary democracy
Currency US dollar = 100 cents
Literacy rate 91%
Calorie consumption not available

MAURITANIA

Page 52 C2

Situated in northwest Africa, two-thirds of Mauritania's territory is desert. A former French colony, it achieved independence in 1960.

Official name Islamic Republic of Mauritania
Formation 1960
Capital Nouakchott
Population 2.7 million / 7 people per sq mile (3 people per sq km)
Total area 397,953 sq miles (1,030,700 sq km)
Languages Hassaniyah Arabic, French, Wolof
Religions Muslim (Sunni) 100%
Ethnic mix Maure 81%, Wolof 7%, Tukolor 5%, Soninka 3%, other 4%
Government Multiparty republic
Currency Ouguiya = 5 khoums
Literacy rate 42.3%
Calorie consumption 2,638 kilocalories

MAURITIUS

Page 57 H3

Located to the east of Madagascar in the Indian Ocean, Mauritius became a republic 25 years after it gained independence. Tourism is a mainstay of its economy.

Official name Mauritius
Formation 1968
Capital Port Louis
Population 1.2 million / 1,671 people per sq mile (645 people per sq km)
Total area 718 sq miles (1,860 sq km)
Languages English, French, French Creole, Hindi, Urdu, Tamil, Chinese
Religions Hindu 52%, Muslim 17%, Roman Catholic 26%, other 5%
Ethnic mix Indo-Mauritian 68%, Creole 27%, Sino Mauritian 3%, Franco-Mauritian 2%
Government Parliamentary democracy
Currency Mauritian rupee = 100 cents
Literacy rate 84.6%
Calorie consumption 2,985 kilocalories

MOLDOVA

Page 86 D3

The smallest and most densely populated of the ex-Soviet republics, Moldova has strong linguistic and cultural links with Romania to the west.

Official name Republic of Moldova
Formation 1991
Capital Chisinau
Population 4.3 million / 329 people per sq mile (127 people per sq km)
Total area 13,067 sq miles (33,843 sq km)
Languages Romanian, Moldovan, Russian
Religions Eastern Orthodox 98%, Jewish 2%
Ethnic mix Moldovan 65%, Ukranian 14%, Russian 13%, Gagauzi 4%, other 4%
Government Parliamentary democracy
Currency Moldovan leu = 100 bani
Literacy rate 99%
Calorie consumption 2,764 kilocalories

MOROCCO

Page 48 C2

A former French colony in northwest Africa, independent in 1956, Morocco has occupied the disputed territory of Western Sahara since 1975.

Official name Kingdom of Morocco
Formation 1956
Capital Rabat
Population 30.4 million / 176 people per sq mile (68 people per sq km)
Total area 172,316 sq miles (446,300 sq km)
Languages Arabic, Berber (Shluh, Tamazight, Riffian), French, Spanish
Religions Muslim 99%, other 1%
Ethnic mix Arab 70%, Berber 29%, European 1%
Government Constititional monarchy
Currency Moroccan dirham = 100 centimes
Literacy rate 48.9%
Calorie consumption 2,964 kilocalories

NAMIBIA

Page 56 B3

Located in southwestern Africa, Namibia became free of South African control in 1990, after years of uncertainty and guerrilla activity.

Official name Republic of Namibia
Formation 1990
Capital Windhoek
Population 1.8 million / 6 people per sq mile (2 people per sq km)
Total area 318,694 sq miles (825,418 sq km)
Languages English, Ovambo, Kavango, Bergdama, German, Afrikaans
Religions Christian 90%, other 10%
Ethnic mix Ovambo 50%, other tribes 16%, Kavango 9%, Herero 8%, Damara 8%, other 9%
Government Parliamentary democracy
Currency Namibian dollar = 100 cents
Literacy rate 82%
Calorie consumption 2,649 kilocalories

MEXICO

Page 28 D3

Located between the United States of America and the Central American states, Mexico was a Spanish colony for 300 years until 1836.

Official name United States of Mexico
Formation 1836
Capital Mexico City
Population 100.4 million / 132 people per sq mile (51 people per sq km)
Total area 761,602 sq miles (1,972,550 sq km)
Languages Spanish, Nahuatl, Mayan, Zapotec, Mixtec, Otomi, Totonac, Tzotzil, Tzeltal
Religions Roman Catholic 95%, Protestant 1%, other 4%
Ethnic mix Mestizo 55%, Amerindian 20%, European 16%, other 9%
Government Presidential democracy
Currency Mexican peso = 100 centavos
Literacy rate 91.3%
Calorie consumption 3,165 kilocalories

MONACO

Page 69 E6

A jet-set image and a thriving service sector define the modern identity of this tiny enclave on the Côte d'Azur in southeastern France.

Official name Principality of Monaco
Formation 1861
Capital Monaco
Population 31,700 / 42,104 people per sq mile (16,256 people per sq km)
Total area 0.75 sq miles (1.95 sq km)
Languages French, Italian, Monégasque, English
Religions Roman Catholic, 89%, Protestant 6%, other 5%
Ethnic mix French 47%, Monégasque 17%, Italian 16%, other 20%
Government Constitutional monarchy
Currency Euro (French franc until 2002)
Literacy rate 99%
Calorie consumption not available

MOZAMBIQUE

Page 57 E3

Mozambique lies on the southeast African coast. It was torn by a civil war between the Marxist government and a rebel group from 1977–1992.

Official name Republic of Mozambique
Formation 1975
Capital Maputo
Population 18.6 million / 60 people per sq mile (23 people per sq km)
Total area 309,494 sq miles (801,590 sq km)
Languages Portuguese, Makua, Tsonga, Sena, Lomwe
Religions Traditional beliefs 60%, Christian 30%, Muslim 10%
Ethnic mix Makua Lomwe 47%, Tsonga 23%, Malawi 12%, Shona 11%, Yao 4%, other 3%
Government Multiparty republic
Currency Metical = 100 centavos
Literacy rate 44%
Calorie consumption 1,927 kilocalories

NAURU

Page 122 D3

Nauru lies in the Pacific, 4,000 km (2,480 miles) northeast of Australia. Phosphate deposits have made its citizens among the richest in the world.

Official name Republic of Nauru
Formation 1968
Capital No official capital
Population 11,800 / 1,455 people per sq mile (562 people per sq km)
Total area 8 sq miles (21 sq km)
Languages Nauruan, English, Kiribati, Chinese, Tuvaluan
Religions Nauruan Congregational Church 60%, Roman Catholic 35, other 5%
Ethnic mix Nauruan 62%, other Pacific islanders 25%, Chinese and Vietnamese 8%, European 5%
Government Non-party democracy
Currency Australian dollar = 100 cents
Literacy rate 99%
Calorie consumption not available

MICRONESIA

Page 122 B1

The Federated States of Micronesia, situated in the western Pacific, comprise 607 islands and atolls grouped into four main island states.

Official name Federated States of Micronesia
Formation 1986
Capital Palikir (Pohnpei island)
Population 133,000 / 490 people per sq mile (189 people per sq km)
Total area 271 sq miles (702 sq km)
Languages English, Trukese, Pohnpeian, Mortlockese, Losrean
Religions Roman Catholic 50%, Protestant 48%, other 2%
Ethnic mix Micronesian 100%
Government Non-party democracy
Currency US dollar = 100 cents
Literacy rate 89%
Calorie consumption not available

MONGOLIA

Page 104 D2

Lying between Russia and China, Mongolia is a vast and isolated country with a small population. Over two-thirds of the country is desert.

Official name Mongolia
Formation 1924
Capital Ulan Bator
Population 2.6 million / 4 people per sq mile (2 people per sq km)
Total area 604,247 sq miles (1,565,000 sq km)
Languages Khalkha Mongolian, Kazakh, Chinese, Russian
Religions Tibetan Buddhist 96%, Muslim 4%
Ethnic mix Mongol 90%, Kazakh 4%, Chinese 2%, Russian 2%, other 2%
Government Multiparty republic
Currency Tugrik (togrog) = 100 möngös
Literacy rate 99%
Calorie consumption 1,981 kilocalories

MYANMAR (BURMA)

Page 114 A3

Myanmar forms the eastern shores of the Bay of Bengal and the Andaman Sea in Southeast Asia. Since 1988 it has been ruled by a repressive military regime.

Official name Union of Myanmar
Formation 1948
Capital Rangoon (Yangoon)
Population 48.4 million / 185 people per sq mile (71 people per sq km)
Total area 261,969 sq miles (678,500 sq km)
Languages Burmese, Karen, Shan, Chin, Kachin, Mon, Palaung, Wa
Religions Buddhist 87%, Christian 6%, Muslim 4%, Hindu 1%, other 2%
Ethnic mix Burman (Bamah) 68%, Shan 9%, Karen 6%, Rakhine 4%, other 13%
Government Military-based regime
Currency Kyat = 100 pyas
Literacy rate 84.7%
Calorie consumption 2,842 kilocalories

NEPAL

Page 113 E3

Nepal lies between India and China, on the shoulder of the southern Himalayas. The elections of 1991 ended a period of absolute monarchy.

Official name Kingdom of Nepal
Formation 1769
Capital Kathmandu
Population 23.6 million / 434 people per sq mile (168 people per sq km)
Total area 54,363 sq miles (140,800 sq km)
Languages Nepali, Maithili, Bhojpuri
Religions Hindu 90%, Buddhist 5%, Muslim 3%, other 2%
Ethnic mix Nepalese 52%, Maithili 11%, Tibeto-Burmese 10%, Bhojpuri 8%, other 19%
Government Constitutional monarchy
Currency Nepalese rupee = 100 paisa
Literacy rate 41.5%
Calorie consumption 2,436 kilocalories

NETHERLANDS

Page 64 C3

Astride the delta of five major rivers in northwest Europe, the Netherlands has a long trading tradition. Rotterdam is the world's largest port.

Official name Kingdom of the Netherlands
Formation 1648
Capital Amsterdam, The Hague
Population 16.2 million / 1,010 people per sq mile (390 people per sq km)
Total area 16,033 sq miles (41,526 sq km)
Languages Dutch, Frisian
Religions Roman Catholic 36%, Protestant 27%, Muslim 3%, other 34%
Ethnic mix Dutch 82%, other 18%
Government Parliamentary democracy
Currency Euro (Netherlands guilder until 2002)
Literacy rate 99%
Calorie consumption 3,294 kilocalories

NEW ZEALAND

Page 128 A4

One of the Pacific Rim countries, New Zealand lies southeast of Australia, and comprises the North and South Islands, separated by the Cook Strait.

Official name Dominion of New Zealand
Formation 1947
Capital Wellington
Population 3.8 million /37 people per sq mile (14 people per sq km)
Total area 103,737 sq miles (268,680 sqkm)
Languages English, Maori
Religions Methodist 24%, Presbyterian 18%, non-religious 16%, Roman Catholic 15%, Methodist 5%, other 22%
Ethnic mix European 77%, Maori 12%, Pacific Islanders 5%, other 6%
Government Parliamentary democracy
Currency New Zealand dollar = 100 cents
Literacy rate 99%

NICARAGUA

Page 30 D3

Nicaragua lies at the heart of Central America. An 11-year war between left-wing Sandinistas and right-wing US-backed Contras ended in 1989.

Official name Republic of Nicaragua
Formation 1838
Capital Managua
Population 5.2 million /104 people per sq mile (40 people per sq km)
Total area 49,998 sq miles (129,494 sq km)
Languages Spanish, English Creole, Miskito
Religions Protestant Evangelicals 17%, Roman Catholic 80%, Zambos 3%
Ethnic mix Mestizo 69%, White 14%, Black 8%, Amerindian 5%, Zambos 4%
Government Presidential democracy
Currency Córdoba oro = 100 pence
Literacy rate 68.6%
Calorie consumption 2,227 kilocalories

NIGER

Page 53 F3

Niger lies landlocked in West Africa, but it is linked to the sea by the River Niger. Since 1973 it has suffered civil unrest and two major droughts.

Official name Republic of Niger
Formation 1960
Capital Niamey
Population 11.2 million / 23 people per sq mile (9 people per sq km)
Total area 489,189 sq miles (1,267,000 sq km)
Languages French, Hausa, Djerma
Religions Muslim 85%, Traditional beliefs 14%, other 1%
Ethnic mix Hausa 54%, Djerma and Songhai 21%, Fulani 10%, Tuareg 9%, other 6%
Government Multiparty republic
Currency CFA franc = 100 centimes
Literacy rate 15.9%
Calorie consumption 2,089 kilocalories

NIGERIA

Page 53 F4

Africa's most populous state Nigeria, in West Africa, is a federation of 30 states. It adopted civilian rule in 1999 after 33 years of military government.

Official name Federal Republic of Nigeria
Formation 1960
Capital Abuja
Population 116.9 million / 328 people per sq mile (127 people per sq km)
Total area 356,667 sq miles (923,768 sq km)
Languages English, Hausa, Yoruba, Ibo
Religions Muslim 50%, Christian 40%, Traditional beliefs 10%
Ethnic mix Hausa 21%, Yoruba 21%, Ibo 18%, Fulani 11%, other 29%
Government Multiparty republic
Currency Naira = 100 kobo
Literacy rate 63.9%
Calorie consumption 2,850 kilocalories

NORTH KOREA

Page 106 E3

North Korea comprises the northern half of the Korean peninsula. A communist state since 1948, it is largely isolated from the outside world.

Official name Democratic People's Republic of Korea
Formation 1948
Capital Pyongyang
Population 22.4 million / 481 people per sq mile (186 people per sq km)
Total area 46,540 sq miles (120,540 sq km)
Languages Korean, Chinese
Religions Atheist 100%
Ethnic mix Korean 100%
Government One-party republic
Currency N Korean won = 100 chon
Literacy rate 95%
Calorie consumption 2,185 kilocalories

NORWAY

Page 63 A5

The Kingdom of Norway traces the rugged western coast of Scandinavia. Settlements are largely restricted to southern and coastal areas.

Official name Kingdom of Norway
Formation 1905
Capital Oslo
Population 4.5 million / 36 people per sq mile (14 people per sq km)
Total area 125,181 sq miles (324,220 sq km)
Languages Norwegian, Sami
Religions Evangelical Lutheran 89%, Roman Catholic 1%, other and non-religious 10%
Ethnic mix Norwegian 93%, Sami 1%, other 6%
Government Parliamentary democracy
Currency Norwegian krone = 100 ore
Literacy rate 99%
Calorie consumption 3,414 kilocalories

OMAN

Page 99 D6

Situated on the eastern coast of the Arabian Peninsula, Oman is the least developed of the Gulf states, despite modest oil exports.

Official name Sultanate of Oman
Formation 1951
Capital Muscat
Population 2.6 million / 32 people per sq mile (12 people per sq km)
Total area 82,031 sq miles (212,460 sq km)
Languages Arabic, Baluchi
Religions Ibadi Muslim 75%, other Muslim and Hindu 25%
Ethnic mix Arab 88%, Baluch 4%, Persian 3%, Indian and Pakistani 3%, African 2%
Government Monarchy
Currency Omani rial = 1,000 baizas
Literacy rate 71.8%
Calorie consumption not available

PAKISTAN

Page 112 B2

Once a part of British India, Pakistan was created in 1947 as an independent Muslim state. Today, the country is divided into four provinces.

Official name Islamic Republic of Pakistan
Formation 1947
Capital Islamabad
Population 145 million / 467 people per sq mile (180 people per sq km)
Total area 310,401 sq miles (803,940 sq km)
Languages Urdu, Punjabi, Sindhi
Religions Sunni Muslim 77%, Shi'a Muslim 20%, Hindu 2%, Christian 1%
Ethnic mix Punjabi 50%, Sindhi 15%, Pashto 15%, Mohajir 8%, other 12%
Government Military-based regime
Currency Pakistani rupee = 100 paisa
Literacy rate 46.1%
Calorie consumption 2,452 kilocalories

PALAU

Page 122 A2

The Palau archipelago, a group of over 200 islands, lies in the western Pacific Ocean. In 1994, it became the world's newest independent state.

Official name Republic of Palau
Formation 1994
Capital Koror
Population 19,100 / 108 people per sq mile (42 people per sq km)
Total area 177 sq miles (458 sq km)
Languages Palauan, English, Japanese, Angaur, Tobi, Sonsorolese
Religions Christian 66%, Modekngei 34%
Ethnic mix Micronesian 87%, Filipino 8%, Chinese 5%
Government Non-party democracy
Currency US dollar = 100 cents
Literacy rate 92%
Calorie consumption not available

PANAMA

Page 31 F5

Southernmost of the Central American countries. The Panama Canal (returned to Panama from US control in 2000) links the Pacific and Atlantic oceans.

Official name Republic of Panama
Formation 1903
Capital Panama City
Population 2.9 million / 96 people per sq mile (37 people per sq km)
Total area 30,193 sq miles (78,200 sq km)
Languages Spanish, English Creole, Amerindian languages, Chibchan
Religions Roman Catholic 86%, Protestant 6%, other 8%
Ethnic mix Mestizo 60%, White 14%, Black 12%, Amerindian 8%, Asian 4%, other 2%
Government Presidential democracy
Currency Balboa = 100 centesimos
Literacy rate 91.9%
Calorie consumption 2,488 kilocalories

PAPUA NEW GUINEA

Page 122 B3

Achieving independence from Australia in 1975, PNG occupies the eastern section of the island of New Guinea and several other island groups.

Official name Independent State of Papua New Guinea
Formation 1975
Capital Port Moresby
Population 5.2 million / 29 people per sq mile (11 people per sq km)
Total area 178,703 sq miles (462,840 sq km)
Languages English, Pidgin English, Papuan, Motu, c.750 native languages
Religions Protestant 60%, Roman Catholic 37%, other 3%
Ethnic mix Melanesian and mixed 100%
Government Multiparty republic
Currency Kina = 100 toea
Literacy rate 63.9%
Calorie consumption 2,175 kilocalories

PARAGUAY

Page 42 D2

Landlocked in central South America. Its post-independence history has included periods of military rule. Free elections were held in 1993.

Official name Republic of Paraguay
Formation 1811
Capital Asunción
Population 5.6 million /
36 people per sq mile (14 people per sq km)
Total area 157,046 sq miles
(406,750 sq km)
Languages Spanish, Guaraní
Religions Roman Catholic 96%,
Protestant (including Mennonite) 4%
Ethnic mix Mestizo 90%,
Amerindian 2%, other 8%
Government Presidential democracy
Currency Guaraní =
100 centimos
Literacy rate 93.3%
Calorie consumption 2,533 kilocalories

POLAND

Page 76 B3

With its seven international borders and strategic location in the heart of Europe, Poland has always played an important role in European affairs.

Official name Republic of Poland
Formation 1918
Capital Warsaw
Population 38.6 million /
320 people per sq mile (123 people per sq km)
Total area 120,728 sq miles
(312,685 sq km)
Languages Polish
Religions Roman Catholic 93%,
Eastern Orthodox 2%, other
and non-religious 5%
Ethnic mix Polish 98%, German 1%,
other 1%
Government Parliamentary democracy
Currency Zloty = 100 groszy
Literacy rate 99%
Calorie consumption 3,376 kilocalories

ROMANIA

Page 86 B4

Romania lies on the Black Sea coast. Since the overthrow of its communist regime in 1989, it has been slowly converting to a free-market economy.

Official name Romania
Formation 1878
Capital Bucharest
Population 21.7 million /
237 people per sq mile (91 people per sq km)
Total area 91,699 sq miles
(237,500 sq km)
Languages Romanian, Hungarian,
German, Romany
Religions Romanian Orthodox 87%,
Roman Catholic 5%, other 8%
Ethnic mix Romanian 89%, Magyar 9%,
Romany 1%, other 1%
Government Multiparty republic
Currency Romanian Leu = 100 bani
Literacy rate 98.1%
Calorie consumption 3,274 kilocalories

SAINT KITTS & NEVIS

Page 33 G3

Separated by a channel, the two islands of Saint Kitts and Nevis are part of the Leeward Islands chain in the Caribbean. Nevis is the less developed of the two.

Official name Federation of Saint Christopher and Nevis
Formation 1983
Capital Basseterre
Population 41,000 / 407 people per sq mile (157 people per sq km)
Total area 101 sq miles (261 sq km)
Languages English, English Creole
Religions Anglican 33%,
Methodist 29%, Moravian 9%,
Roman Catholic 7%, other 22%
Ethnic mix Black 94%, Mixed 3%, Other and Amerindian 2%, other 1%
Government Parliamentary democracy
Currency Eastern Caribbean dollar =
100 cents
Literacy rate 90%
Calorie consumption 2,685 kilocalories

PERU

Page 38 C3

Once the heart of the Inca empire, before the Spanish conquest in the 16th century, Peru lies on the Pacific coast of South America.

Official name Republic of Peru
Formation 1824
Capital Lima
Population 26.1 million /
53 people per sq mile (20 people per sq km)
Total area 496,223 sq miles
(1,285,220 sq km)
Languages Spanish, Quechua,
Aymará
Religions Roman Catholic 95%,
other 5%
Ethnic mix Amerindian 54%,
Mestizo 32%, White 12%, other 2%
Government Presidential democracy
Currency New sol = 100 centimos
Literacy rate 89.9%
Calorie consumption 2,624 kilocalories

PORTUGAL

Page 70 B3

Facing the Atlantic on the western side of the Iberian Peninsula, Portugal is the most westerly country on the European mainland.

Official name Republic of Portugal
Formation 1139
Capital Lisbon
Population 10 million /
280 people per sq mile (108 people per sq km)
Total area 35,672 sq miles
(92,391 sq km)
Languages Portuguese
Religions Roman Catholic 97%,
Protestant 1%, other 2%
Ethnic mix Portuguese 98%,
African and other 2%
Government Parliamentary democracy
Currency Euro (Portuguese escudo until 2002)
Literacy rate 92.3%
Calorie consumption 3,716 kilocalories

RUSSIAN FEDERATION

Page 92 D4

Still the world's largest state, despite the breakup of the USSR in 1991, the Russian Federation is struggling to capitalize on its diversity.

Official name Russian Federation
Formation 1991
Capital Moscow
Population 144.7 million /
22 people per sq mile (8 people per sq km)
Total area 6,592,735 sq miles
(17,075,200 sq km)
Languages Russian
Religions Russian Orthodox 75%,
other 25%
Ethnic mix Russian 82%, Tatar 4%,
Ukranian 3%, Chavash 1%,
other 10%
Government Presidential democracy
Currency Rouble = 100 kopeks
Literacy rate 99%
Calorie consumption 2,917 kilocalories

SAINT LUCIA

Page 33 G4

Among the most beautiful of the Caribbean Windward Islands, Saint Lucia retains both French and British influences from its colonial history.

Official name Saint Lucia
Formation 1979
Capital Castries
Population 156,300 /
653 people per sq mile (252 people per sq km)
Total area 239 sq miles
(620 sq km)
Languages English, French Creole
Religions Roman Catholic 90%,
other 10%
Ethnic mix Black 90%, Mulatto 6%,
Asian 3%, White 1%
Government Parliamentary democracy
Currency Eastern Caribbean dollar
= 100 cents
Literacy rate 82%
Calorie consumption 2,838 kilocalories

PHILIPPINES

Page 117 E1

An archipelago of 7,107 islands between the South China Sea and the Pacific. After 21 years of dictatorship, democracy was restored in 1986.

Official name Republic of the Philippines
Formation 1946
Capital Manila
Population 77.1 million / 666 people per sq mile (257 people per sq km)
Total area 115,830 sq miles
(300,000 sq km)
Languages Filipino, English,
Cebuano
Religions Roman Catholic 83%,
Protestant 9%, Muslim 5%, other 3%
Ethnic mix Filipino 50%, Indonesian and Polynesian 30%, other 20%
Government Presidential democracy
Currency Peso = 100 centavos
Literacy rate 95.3%
Calorie consumption 2,379 kilocalories

QATAR

Page 98 C4

Projecting north from the Arabian Peninsula into the Persian Gulf, Qatar's reserves of oil and gas make it one of the region's wealthiest states.

Official name State of Qatar
Formation 1971
Capital Doha
Population 575,000 /
130 people per sq mile (50 people per sq km)
Total area 4,416 sq miles
(11,437 sq km)
Languages Arabic
Religions Muslim (mainly Sunni) 95%,
other 5%
Ethnic mix Arab 40%, Pakistani 18%,
Indian 18%, Iranian 10%,
other 14%
Government Monarchy
Currency Qatar riyal = 100 dirhams
Literacy rate 81.2%
Calorie consumption not available

RWANDA

Page 51 B6

Rwanda lies just south of the Equator in east central Africa. Since independence from France in 1962, ethnic tensions have dominated politics.

Official name Republic of Rwanda
Formation 1962
Capital Kigali
Population 7.9 million / 777 people per sq mile (300 people per sq km)
Total area 10,169 sq miles
(26,338 sq km)
Languages French, Kinyarwanda,
Kiswahili, English
Religions Roman Catholic 65%,
Traditional beliefs 25%, Protestant 9%,
Muslim 1%
Ethnic mix Hutu 90%, Tutsi 9%, other
(including Twa) 1%
Government Transitional regime
Currency Rwanda franc = 100 centimes
Literacy rate 66.8%
Calorie consumption 2,2077 kilocalories

SAINT VINCENT & THE GRENADINES

Page 33 G4

Formerly ruled by Britain, these volcanic islands form part of the Caribbean Windward Islands.

Official name Saint Vincent and the Grenadines
Formation 1979
Capital Kingston
Population 115,500 / 769 people per sq mile (297 people per sq km)
Total area 150 sq miles (389 sq km)
Languages English, English Creole
Religions Anglican 42%,
Methodist 20%, Roman Catholic 19%,
other 19%
Ethnic mix Black 66%, Mulatto 19%,
Asian 6%, White 4%, other 5%
Government Parliamentary democracy
Currency Eastern Caribbean dollar =
100 cents
Literacy rate 82%
Calorie consumption 2,579 kilocalories

SAMOA

Page 123 F4

The southern Pacific islands of Samoa gained independence from New Zealand in 1962. Four of the nine islands are inhabited.

Official name Independent State of Samoa
Formation 1962
Capital Apia
Population 159,000/ 144 people per sq mile (56 people per sq km)
Total area 1,104 sq miles (2,860 sq km)
Languages Samoan, English
Religions Christian 99%, other 1%
Ethnic mix Polynesian 90%, Euronesian 9%, other 1%
Government Parliamentary democracy
Currency Tala = 100 sene
Literacy rate 80.2%
Calorie consumption not available

SAN MARINO

Page 74 C3

Perched on the slopes of Monte Titano in the Italian Appennino, San Marino has maintained its independence since the 4th century AD.

Official name Republic of San Marino
Formation 1631
Capital San Marino
Population 26,900 / 1,138 people per sq mile (440 people per sq km)
Total area 24 sq miles (61 sq km)
Languages Italian
Religions Roman Catholic 93%, other and non-religious 7%
Ethnic mix Sammarinese 80%, Italian 19%, other 1%
Government Parliamentary democracy
Currency Euro (Lira until 2002)
Literacy rate 99%
Calorie consumption not available

SAO TOME & PRINCIPE

Page 55 A5

A former Portuguese colony off Africa's west coast, comprising two main islands and smaller islets. The 1991 elections ended 15 years of Marxism.

Official name Democratic Republic of São Tomé and Príncipe
Formation 1975
Capital São Tomé
Population 159,900 / 414 people per sq mile (160 people per sq km)
Total area 386 sq miles (1,001 sq km)
Languages Portuguese, Portuguese Creole
Religions Roman Catholic 84%, other Christian 16%
Ethnic mix Black 90%, Portuguese and Creole 10%
Government Multiparty republic
Currency Dobra = 100 centimos
Literacy rate 75%
Calorie consumption 2,390 kilocalories

SAUDI ARABIA

Page 99 B5

Occupying most of the Arabian Peninsula, the desert kingdom of Saudi Arabia, rich in oil and gas, covers an area the size of Western Europe.

Official name Kingdom of Saudi Arabia
Formation 1932
Capital Riyadh
Population 21 million / 28 people per sq mile (11 people per sq km)
Total area 756,981 sq miles (1,960,582 sq km)
Languages Arabic
Religions Sunni Muslim 85%, Shi'a Muslim 15%
Ethnic mix Arab 90%, Afro-Asian 10%
Government Monarchy
Currency Saudi riyal = 100 malalah
Literacy rate 77%
Calorie consumption 2,875 kilocalories

SENEGAL

Page 52 B3

A former French colony, Senegal achieved independence in 1960. Its capital, Dakar, stands on the westernmost cape of Africa.

Official name Republic of Senegal
Formation 1960
Capital Dakar
Population 9.7 million / 128 people per sq mile (49 people per sq km)
Total area 75,749 sq miles (196,190 sq km)
Languages French, Wolof, Fulani, Serer, Diola, Malinke, Soninke, Arabic
Religions Sunni Muslim 90%, Christian (mainly Roman Catholic) 5%, Traditional beliefs 5%
Ethnic mix Wolof 44%, Serer 15%, Fula 12%, Diola 5%, Malinke 4%, other 20%
Government Presidential democracy
Currency CFA franc = 100 centimes
Literacy rate 37.4%
Calorie consumption 2,257 kilocalories

SERBIA & MONTENEGRO (YUGOSLAVIA)

Page 78 D4

Serbia and Montenegro is the successor state to the former Yugoslavia.

Official name Serbia and Montenegro
Formation 1992
Capital Belgrade
Population 10.5 million / 266 people per sq mile (103 people per sq km)
Total area 39,449 sq miles (102,173 sq km)
Languages Serbo-Croat, Albanian, Hungarian
Religions Eastern Orthodox 65, Muslim 19%, Roman Catholic 4%, other 12%
Ethnic mix Serb 62%, Albanian 17%, Montenegrin 5%, other 16%
Government Multiparty republic
Currency Dinar (Euro widely used in Montenegro)
Literacy rate 93.3%
Calorie consumption 2,570 kilocalories

SEYCHELLES

Page 57 G1

A former British colony comprising 115 islands in the Indian Ocean. Under one-party rule for 16 years, it became a multiparty democracy in 1993.

Official name Republic of the Seychelles
Formation 1976
Capital Victoria
Population 79,300/ 451 people per sq mile (174 people per sq km)
Total area 176 sq miles (455 sq km)
Languages French Creole (Seselwa), English, French
Religions Roman Catholic 90%, Anglican 8%, other 2%
Ethnic mix Creole 89%, Indian 5%, Chinese 2%, other 4%
Government Multiparty republic
Currency Seychelles rupee = 100 cents
Literacy rate 84%
Calorie consumption 2,432 kilocalories

SIERRA LEONE

Page 52 C4

The West African state of Sierra Leone achieved independence from the British in 1961. Today, it is one of the world's poorest nations.

Official name Republic of Sierra Leone
Formation 1961
Capital Freetown
Population 4.6 million / 166 people per sq mile (64 people per sq km)
Total area 27,699 sq miles (71,740 sq km)
Languages English, Mende, Temne, Krio
Religions Traditional beliefs 30%, Muslim 30%, Christian 10%, other 30%
Ethnic mix Mende 35%, Temne 32%, Limba 8%, Kuranko 4%, other 21%
Government Multiparty republic
Currency Leone = 100 cents
Literacy rate 36.3%
Calorie consumption 1,863 kilocalories

SINGAPORE

Page 116 A1

A city state linked to the southernmost tip of the Malay Peninsula by a causeway, Singapore is one of Asia's most important commercial centers.

Official name Republic of Singapore
Formation 1965
Capital Singapore
Population 4.1 million / 16,400 people per sq mile (6,332 people per sq km)
Total area 250 sq miles (648 sq km)
Languages Malay, English, Mandarin, Tamil
Religions Buddhist 55%, Taoism 22%, Muslim 16%, Hindu, Christian, Sikh 7%
Ethnic mix Chinese 77%, Malay 14%, Indian 8%, other 1%
Government Parliamentary democracy
Currency Singapore dollar = 100 cents
Literacy rate 92.4%
Calorie consumption not available

SLOVAKIA

Page 77 C6

Landlocked in Central Europe, Slovakia has been independent since 1993. It is the less developed half of the former Czechoslovakia.

Official name Slovak Republic
Formation 1993
Capital Bratislava
Population 5.4 million / 286 people per sq mile (111 people per sq km)
Total area 18,859 sq miles (48,845 sq km)
Languages Slovak, Hungarian, Czech
Religions Roman Catholic 60%, Atheist 10%, Protestant 8%, Orthodox 4%, other 18%
Ethnic mix Slovak 85%, Magyar 11%, Romany 1%, Czech 1%, other 2%
Government Parliamentary democracy
Currency Koruna = 100 halierov
Literacy rate 99%
Calorie consumption 3,133 kilocalories

SLOVENIA

Page 73 D8

Northernmost of the former Yugoslav republics, Slovenia has the closest links with Western Europe. In 1991, it gained independence with little violence.

Official name Republic of Slovenia
Formation 1991
Capital Ljubljana
Population 2 million / 256 people per sq mile (99 people per sq km)
Total area 7820 sq miles (20,253 sq km)
Languages Slovene, Serbo-Croat
Religions Roman Catholic 96%, Muslim 1%, other 3%
Ethnic mix Slovene 88%, Croat 3%, Serb 2%, Muslim 1%, other 6%
Government Parliamentary democracy
Currency Tolar = 100 stotins
Literacy rate 99%
Calorie consumption 3,168 kilocalories

SOLOMON ISLANDS

Page 122 C3

The Solomon archipelago comprises several hundred islands scattered in the southwestern Pacific. Independence from Britain came in 1978.

Official name Solomon Islands
Formation 1978
Capital Honiara
Population 463,000 / 42 people per sq mile (16 people per sq km)
Total area 10,985 sq miles (28,450 sq km)
Languages English, Pidgin English, Melanesian Pidgin
Religions Anglican 34%, Roman Catholic 19%, South Seas Evangelical Church 17%, Methodist 11%, other 19%
Ethnic mix Melanesian 94%, other 6%
Government Parliamentary democracy
Currency Solomon Islands dollar = 100 cents
Literacy rate 62%
Calorie consumption 2,277 kilocalories

SOMALIA

Page 51 E5

Italian and British Somaliland were united in 1960 to create this semiarid state occupying the horn of Africa. It has suffered years of civil war.

Official name Somali
Formation 1960
Capital Mogadishu
Population 9.2 million / 37 people per sq mile (14 people per sq km)
Total area 246,199 sq miles (637,657 sq km)
Languages Arabic, Somali, English, Italian
Religions Sunni Muslim 98%, other 2%
Ethnic mix Somali 85%, other 15%
Government Transitional regime
Currency Somali shilling = 100 cents
Literacy rate 24.1%
Calorie consumption 1,628 kilocalories

SPAIN

Page 70 D2

Lodged between mainland Europe and Africa, the Atlantic and the Mediterranean, Spain has occupied a pivotal position since it was united in 1492.

Official name Kingdom of Spain
Formation 1492
Capital Madrid
Population 39.9 million / 205 people per sq mile (79 people per sq km)
Total area 194,896 sq miles (504,782 sq km)
Languages Spanish, Catalan, Galician, Basque
Religions Roman Catholic 96%, other 4%
Ethnic mix Castilian Spanish 72%, Catalan 17%, Galician 6%, other 5%
Government Parliamentary democracy
Currency Euro (pesata until 2002)
Literacy rate 97.7%
Calorie consumption 3,352 kilocalories

SURINAME

Page 37 G3

Suriname is a former Dutch colony on the north coast of South America. Democracy was restored in 1991, after almost 11 years of military rule.

Official name Republic of Suriname
Formation 1975
Capital Paramaribo
Population 419,000 / 7 people per sq mile (3 people per sq km)
Total area 63,039 sq miles (163,270 sq km)
Languages Dutch, Sranan, Saramaccan, Javanese, Sarnami Hindi, Chinese
Religions Christian 48%, Hindu 27%, Muslim 20%, other 5%
Ethnic mix South Asian 34%, Creole 34%, Javanese 18%, Black 9%, other 5%
Government Parliamentary democracy
Currency Suriname guilder = 100 cents
Literacy rate 94.2%
Calorie consumption 2,652 kilocalories

SWITZERLAND

Page 73 A7

One of the world's most prosperous countries, with a long tradition of neutrality in foreign affairs, it lies at the center of Western Europe.

Official name Swiss Confederation
Formation 1291
Capital Bern
Population 7.2 million / 469 people per sq mile (174 people per sq km)
Total area 15,942 sq miles (41,290 sq km)
Languages German, French, Italian, Swiss German, Romansch
Religions Roman Catholic 46%, Protestant 40%, other 14%
Ethnic mix German 65%, French 18%, Italian 10%, Romansh 1%, other 6%
Government Parliamentary democracy
Currency Swiss franc = 100 centimes
Literacy rate 99%
Calorie consumption 3,293 kilocalories

SOUTH AFRICA

Page 56 C4

South Africa is the most southerly nation on the African continent. The multiracial elections of 1994 overturned 80 years of white minority rule.

Official name Republic of South Africa
Formation 1934
Capital Pretoria (administrative)
Population 43.8 million / 93 people per sq mile (36 people per sq km)
Total area 471,008 sq miles (1,219,912 sq km)
Languages Afrikaans, English, 9 other African languages
Religions Black Independent 17%, Duthc reformed 11%, Roman Catholic 8%, Methodist 6%, other 58%
Ethnic mix Zulu 23%, other Black 38%, White 16%, Mixed 10%, other 13%
Government Parliamentary democracy
Currency Rand = 100 cents
Literacy rate 85.3%
Calorie consumption 2,886 kilocalories

SRI LANKA

Page 110 D3

The island republic of Sri Lanka is separated from India by the narrow Palk Strait. Since 1983, the Sinhalese and Tamil population have been in conflict.

Official name Democratic Socialist Republic of Sri Lanka
Formation 1948
Capital Colombo
Population 19.1 million / 754 people per sq mile (291 people per sq km)
Total area 25,332 sq miles (65,610 sq km)
Languages Sinhalese, Tamil, English
Religions Buddhist 69%, Hindu 15%, Christian 8%, Muslim 8%
Ethnic mix Sinhalese 74%, Tamil 18%, Moor 7%, other 1%
Government Presidential democracy
Currency Sri Lanka rupee = 100 cents
Literacy rate 91.7%
Calorie consumption 2,405 kilocalories

SWAZILAND

Page 56 D4

The tiny southern African kingdom of Swaziland gained independence from Britain in 1968. It is economically dependent on South Africa.

Official name Kingdom of Swaziland
Formation 1968
Capital Mbabane
Population 938,000 / 140 people per sq mile (54 people per sq km)
Total area 6,704 sq miles (17,363 sq km)
Languages Siswati, English, Zulu, Tsonga
Religions Christian 60%, Traditional beliefs 40%
Ethnic mix Swazi 97%, other 3%
Government Constitutional monarchy
Currency Lilangeni = 100 cents
Literacy rate 79.6%
Calorie consumption 2,620 kilocalories

SYRIA

Page 96 B3

Stretching from the eastern Mediterranean to the River Tigris, Syria's borders were created on its independence from France in 1946.

Official name Syrian Arab Republic
Formation 1941
Capital Damascus
Population 16.6 million / 232 people per sq mile (90 people per sq km)
Total area 71,498 sq miles (185,180 sq km)
Languages Arabic, French, Kurdish
Religions Sunni Muslim 74%, other Muslim 16%, Christian 10%
Ethnic mix Arab 89%, Kurdish 6%, Armenian, Turkmen, Circassian 2%, other 3%
Government One-party republic
Currency Syrian pound = 100 piastres
Literacy rate 74.5%
Calorie consumption 3,038 kilocalories

SOUTH KOREA

Page 106 E4

South Korea occupies the southern half of the Korean peninsula. It was separated from the communist North in 1948.

Official name Republic of Korea
Formation 1948
Capital Seoul
Population 47.1 million / 1,239 people per sq mile (478 people per sq km)
Total area 38,023 sq miles (98,480 sq km)
Languages Korean, Chinese
Religions Mahayana Buddhist 47%, Protestant 38%, Roman Catholic 11%, Confucian 3%, other 1%
Ethnic mix Korean 100%
Government Presidential democracy
Currency Korean won = 100 chon
Literacy rate 97.8%
Calorie consumption 3,093 kilocalories

SUDAN

Page 50 B4

The largest country in Africa, part of Sudan borders the Red Sea. In 1989, an army coup installed a military Islamic fundamentalist regime.

Official name Republic of the Sudan
Formation 1956
Capital Khartoum
Population 31.8 million / 33 people per sq mile (13 people per sq km)
Total area 967,493 sq miles (2,505,810 sq km)
Languages Arabic, Dinka, Nuer, Zande, Nubian, Beja, Bari, Fur, Shilluk, Lotuko
Religions Muslim (mainly Sunni) 70%, Traditional beliefs 20%, other 10%
Ethnic mix Arab 40%, Tribal 30%, Dinka and Beja 7%, other 23%
Government Presidential regime
Currency Sudanese pound or dinar = 100 piastres
Literacy rate 58%
Calorie consumption 2,348 kilocalories

SWEDEN

Page 62 B4

The largest Scandinavian country in both population and area, Sweden's strong industrial base helps to fund its extensive welfare system.

Official name Kingdom of Sweden
Formation 1523
Capital Stockholm
Population 8.8 million / 51 people per sq mile (20 people per sq km)
Total area 173,731 sq miles (449,964 sq km)
Languages Swedish, Finnish, Sami
Religions Evangelical Lutheran 89%, Roman Catholic 2%, other 9%
Ethnic mix Swedish 91%, Finnish and Sami 3%, other European 6%
Government Parliamentary democracy
Currency Swedish krona = 100 ore
Literacy rate 99%
Calorie consumption 3,109 kilocalories

TAIWAN

Page 107 D6

The island republic of Taiwan lies 130 km (80 miles) off the southeast coast of mainland China. China considers it to be one of its provinces.

Official name Republic of China (Taiwan)
Formation 1949
Capital Taipei
Population 22.2 million / 1,598 people per sq mile (617 people per sq km)
Total area 13,892 sq miles (35,980 sq km)
Languages Mandarin Chinese, Amoy Chinese, Hakka Chinese
Religions Buddhist, Confucian, Taoist 93%, Christian 5%, other 2%
Ethnic mix Indigenous Chinese 84%, Mainland Chinese 14%, Aborigine 2%
Government Multiparty republic
Currency Taiwan dollar = 100 cents
Literacy rate 94%
Calorie consumption not available

TAJIKISTAN

Page 101 F3

Tajikistan lies landlocked on the western slopes of the Pamirs in Central Asia. The Tajiks' language and traditions are similar to those of Iran.

Official name Republic of Tajikistan
Formation 1991
Capital Dushanbe
Population 6.1 million / 110 people per sq mile (43 people per sq km)
Total area 55,251 sq miles (143,100 sq km)
Languages Tajik, Russian
Religions Sunni Muslim 80%, Shi'a Muslim 5%, other 15%
Ethnic mix Tajik 62%, Uzbek 24%, Russian 8%, Tatar 1%, Kyrgyz 1%, other 4%
Government Multiparty republic
Currency Somoni
Literacy rate 99%
Calorie consumption 1720 kilocalories

TANZANIA

Page 51 B7

The East African state of Tanzania was formed in 1964 by the union of Tanganyika and Zanzibar. A third of its area is game reserve or national park.

Official name United Republic of Tanzania
Formation 1961
Capital Dodoma
Population 36 million / 99 people per sq mile (38 people per sq km)
Total area 364,898 sq miles (945,087 sq km)
Languages English, Kiswahili, Sukuma
Religions Muslim 33%, Christian 33%, Traditional beliefs 30%, other 4%
Ethnic mix Native African (over 120 tribes) 99%, European and Asian 1%
Government Presidential democracy
Currency Tanzanian shilling = 100 cents
Literacy rate 75.8%
Calorie consumption 1,906 kilocalories

THAILAND

Page 115 C5

Thailand lies at the heart of mainland Southeast Asia. Continuing rapid industrialization has resulted in massive congestion in the capital.

Official name Kingdom of Thailand
Formation 1238
Capital Bangkok
Population 63.6 million / 322 people per sq mile (124 people per sq km)
Total area 197,254 sq miles (510,890 sq km)
Languages Thai, Chinese, Malay, Khmer, Mon, Karen, Miao
Religions Buddhist 95%, Muslim 3%, Christian 1%, other 1%
Ethnic mix Thai 83%, Chinese 12%, Malay 3%, Khmer and other 2%
Government Parliamentary democracy
Currency Baht = 100 stangs
Literacy rate 95.5%
Calorie consumption 2,506 kilocalories

TOGO

Page 53 F4

Togo lies sandwiched between Ghana and Benin in West Africa. The 1993–94 presidential elections were the first since its independence in 1960.

Official name Republic of Togo
Formation 1960
Capital Lomé
Population 4.7 million / 214 people per sq mile (83 people per sq km)
Total area 21,925 sq miles (56,785 sq km)
Languages French, Ewe, Kabye, Gurma
Religions Traditional beliefs 50%, Christian 35%, Muslim 15%
Ethnic mix Ewe 46%, other African 53%, European 1%
Government Presidential regime
Currency CFA franc = 100 centimes
Literacy rate 57.3%
Calorie consumption 2,329 kilocalories

TONGA

Page 123 E4

Northeast of New Zealand, in the South Pacific, Tonga is an archipelago of 170 islands, 45 of which are inhabited. Politics is effectively controlled by the king.

Official name Kingdom of Tonga
Formation 1970
Capital Nuku'alofa
Population 102,200 / 354 people per sq mile (137 people per sq km)
Total area 289 sq miles (748 sq km)
Languages Tongan, English
Religions Free Wesleyan 64%, Roman Catholic 15%, Other 21%
Ethnic mix Polynesian 99%, other Pacific groups and European 1%
Government Monarchy
Currency Pa'anga (Tongan dollar) = 100 seniti
Literacy rate 98.5%
Calorie consumption not available

TRINIDAD & TOBAGO

Page 33 H5

The former British colony of Trinidad and Tobago is the most southerly of the West Indies, lying just 15 km (9 miles) off the coast of Venezuela.

Official name Republic of Trinidad and Tobago
Formation 1962
Capital Port-of-Spain
Population 1.3 million / 657 people per sq mile (254 people per sq km)
Total area 1980 sq miles (5,128 sq km)
Languages English, English Creole, Hindi. French, Spanish
Religions Christian 61%, Hindu 24%, other and non-religious 15%
Ethnic mix Asian 40%, Black 40%, Mixed 19%, White and Chinese 1%
Government Parliamentary democracy
Currency Trinidad and Tobago dollar = 100 cents
Literacy rate 93.8%
Calorie consumption 2,777 kilocalories

TUNISIA

Page 49 E2

Tunisia, in North Africa, has traditionally been one of the more liberal Arab states, but is now facing a challenge from Islamic fundamentalists.

Official name Republic of Tunisia
Formation 1956
Capital Tunis
Population 9.6 million / 152 people per sq mile (59 people per sq km)
Total area 63,170 sq miles (163,610 sq km)
Languages Arabic, French
Religions Muslim (mainly Sunni) 98%, Christian 1%, Jewish 1%
Ethnic mix Arab and Berber 98%, European 1%, other 1%
Government Presidential democracy
Currency Tunisian dinar = 1,000 millimes
Literacy rate 71%
Calorie consumption 3,299 kilocalories

TONGA

Page 123 E4

TURKEY

Page 94 B3

Lying partly in Europe, but mostly in Asia, Turkey's position gives it significant influence in the Mediterranean, Black Sea, and Middle East.

Official name Republic of Turkey
Formation 1923
Capital Ankara
Population 67.6 million / 224 people per sq mile (87 people per sq km)
Total area 301,382 sq miles (780,580 sq km)
Languages Turkish, Kurdish, Arabic, Circassian, Armenian, Greek, Georgian
Religions Muslim (mainly Sunni) 99%, other 1%
Ethnic mix Turkish 70%, Kurdish 20%, Arab 2%, other 8%
Government Parliamentary democracy
Currency Turkish lira = 100 krural
Literacy rate 85.1%
Calorie consumption 3,416 kilocalories

TURKMENISTAN

Page 100 B2

Stretching from the Caspian Sea into the deserts of Central Asia, the ex-Soviet state of Turkmenistan has adjusted better than most to independence.

Official name Turkmenistan
Formation 1991
Capital Ashgabat
Population 4.8 million / 25 people per sq mile (10 people per sq km)
Total area 188,455 sq miles (488,100 sq km)
Languages Turkmen, Uzbek, Russian
Religions Sunni Muslim 87%, Eastern Orthodox 11%, other 2%
Ethnic mix Turkmen 73%, Russian 10%, Uzbek 9%, Kazakh 2%, Tatar 1%, other 5%
Government One-party state
Currency Manat = 100 tenge
Literacy rate 98%
Calorie consumption 2,675 kilocalories

TUVALU

Page 123 E3

The former Ellice Islands, linked to the Gilbert Islands as a British colony until 1978, Tuvalu is an isolated chain of nine atolls in the Central Pacific.

Official name Tuvalu
Formation 1978
Capital Fongafale, on Funafuti Atoll
Population 10,800 / 1,076 people per sq mile (415 people per sq km)
Total area 10 sq miles (26 sq km)
Languages English, Tuvaluan, Kiribati
Religions Church of Tuvalu 97%, Seventh-day Adventist 1%, Baha'i 1%, other 1%
Ethnic mix Polynesian 96%, other 4%
Government Non-party democracy
Currency Australian dollar and Tuvaluan dollar = 100 cents
Literacy rate 95%
Calorie consumption not available

UGANDA

Page 51 B6

Uganda lies landlocked in East Africa. It was ruled by one of Africa's more eccentric leaders, the dictator Idi Amin Dada, from 1971–1980.

Official name Republic of Uganda
Formation 1962
Capital Kampala
Population 24 million / 263 people per sq mile (102 people per sq km)
Total area 91,135 sq miles (236,040 sq km)
Languages English, Nkole, Luganda
Religions Roman Catholic 38%, Protestant 33%, Traditional beliefs 13%, Muslim (mainly Sunni) 5%, other 11%
Ethnic mix Bantu Tribes 50%, other 50%
Government Non-party democracy
Currency New Uganda shilling = 100 cents
Literacy rate 67.1%
Calorie consumption 2,359 kilocalories

UKRAINE

Page 86 C2

Bordered by seven states, the former "breadbasket of the Soviet Union" balances assertive nationalism with concerns over its relations with Russia.

Official name Ukraine
Formation 1991
Capital Kiev
Population 48.4 million / 208 people per sq mile (80 people per sq km)
Total area 223,089 sq miles (603,700 sq km)
Languages Ukrainian, Russian, Tartar
Religions Christian (mainly Ukrainian Orthodox) 95%, Jewish 1%, other 4%
Ethnic mix Ukrainian 73%, Russian 22%, Jewish 1%, other 4%
Government Presidential democracy
Currency Hryvnia = 100 kopiykas
Literacy rate 99%
Calorie consumption 2,871 kilocalories

United Arab Emirates

Page 99 D5

Bordering the Persian Gulf on the northern coast of the Arabian Peninsula, is the United Arab Emirates, a working federation of seven states.

Official name United Arab Emirates
Formation 1971
Capital Abu Dhabi
Population 2.7 million /
84 people per sq mile (33 people per sq km)
Total area 32,000 sq miles
(82,880 sq km)
Languages Arabic, Farsi, English, Indian and Pakistani languages
Religions Muslim (mainly Sunni) 96%, Christian, Hindu and other 4%
Ethnic mix Asian 60%, Emirian 25%, other Arab 12%, European 3%
Government Monarchy
Currency UAE dirham = 100 fils
Literacy rate 75.6%
Calorie consumption 3,192 kilocalories

Uruguay

Page 42 D4

Uruguay is situated in southeastern South America. It returned to civilian government in 1985, after 12 years of military dictatorship.

Official name Eastern Republic of Uruguay
Formation 1828
Capital Montevideo
Population 3.4 million /50 people per sq mile (19 people per sq km)
Total area 68,039 sq miles
(176,220 sqkm)
Languages Spanish
Religions Roman Catholic 66%, non-religious 30%, Jewish 2%, Protestant 2%
Ethnic mix White 90%, other 10%
Government Presidential democracy
Currency Uruguayan peso = 100 centimes
Literacy rate 97.8%
Calorie consumption 2,879 kilocalories

Vatican City

Page 75 A8

The Vatican City, seat of the Roman Catholic Church, is a walled enclave in the city of Rome. It is the world's smallest fully independent state.

Official name State of the Vatican City
Formation 1929
Capital Vatican City
Population 524 /3,082 people per mile (1,191 people per sq km)
Total area 0.17 sq miles (0.44 sq km)
Languages Italian, Latin
Religions Roman Catholic 100%
Ethnic mix The current pope is Polish, ending nearly 500 years of Italian popes. Cardinals are from many nationalities, but Italians form the largest group. Most of the resident lay persons are Italian.
Government Papal state
Currency Euro (Lira until 2002)
Literacy rate 99%
Calorie consumption not available

Yemen

Page 99 C7

Located in southern Arabia, Yemen was formerly two countries – a socialist regime in the south, and a republic in the north. Both united in 1990.

Official name Republic of Yemen
Formation 1990
Capital Sana
Population 19.1 million /
94 people per sq mile (36 people per sq km)
Total area 203,849 sq miles
(527,970 sq km)
Languages Arabic
Religions Shi'a Muslim 42%, Sunni Muslim 55%, Christian, Hindu and Jewish 3%
Ethnic mix Arab 95%, Afro-Arab 3%, Indian, Somali and European 2%
Government Multiparty republic
Currency Yemeni Rial
Literacy rate 46.3%
Calorie consumption 2,038 kilocalories

United Kingdom

Page 67 B5

Separated from continental Europe by the North Sea and the English Channel, the UK comprises England, Wales, Scotland, and Northern Ireland.

Official name United Kingdom of Great Britain and Northern Ireland
Formation 1707
Capital London
Population 59.5 million / 629 people per sq mile (243 people per sq km)
Total area 94,525 sq miles
(244,820 sq km)
Languages English, Welsh, Scottish
Religions Anglican 47%, Presbyterian 4%, Roman Catholic 9% , other 40%
Ethnic mix English 80%, Scottish 9%, Northern Irish 3%, Welsh 3%, other 5%
Government Parliamentary democracy
Currency Pound sterling = 100 pence
Literacy rate 99%
Calorie consumption 3,334 kilocalories

Uzbekistan

Page 100 D2

Sharing the Aral Sea coastline with its northern neighbor, Kazakhstan, Uzbekistan lies on the ancient Silk Road between Asia and Europe.

Official name Republic of Uzbekistan
Formation 1991
Capital Tashkent
Population 25.3 million /
146 people per sq mile (57 people per sq km)
Total area 172,741 sq miles
(447,400 sq km)
Languages Uzbek, Russian
Religions Sunni Muslim 88%, Eastern Orthodox 9%, other 3%
Ethnic mix Uzbek 71%, Russian 8%, Tajik 5%, Kazakh 4%, other 12%
Government Presidential democracy
Currency Som = 100 teen
Literacy rate 88.9%
Calorie consumption 2,317 kilocalories

Venezuela

Page 36 D2

Located on the north coast of South America, Venezuela has the continent's most urbanized society. Most people live in the northern cities.

Official name Bolivarian Republic of Venezuela
Formation 1830
Capital Caracas
Population 24.6 million /70 people per sq mile (27 people per sq km)
Total area 352,143 sq miles
(912,050 sq km)
Languages Spanish, Amerindian languages
Religions Roman Catholic 89%, Protestant and other 11%
Ethnic mix Mestizo 69%, White 20%, Black 9%, Amerindian 2%
Government Presidential democracy
Currency Bolivar = 100 centimos
Literacy rate 92.6%
Calorie consumption 2,256 kilocalories

Zambia

Page 56 C2

Zambia lies landlocked at the heart of southern Africa. In 1991, it made a peaceful transition from single-party rule to multiparty democracy.

Official name Republic of Zambia
Formation 1964
Capital Lusaka
Population 10.6 million /
36 people per sq mile (14 people per sq km)
Total area 290,584 sq miles
(752,612 sq km)
Languages English, Bemba, Nyanja, Tonga, Kaonde, Lunda, Luvale, Lozi
Religions Christian 63%, Indigenous beliefs 36%, other 1%
Ethnic mix Bemba 34%, European 1%, other African 65%
Government Presidential democracy
Currency Zambian kwacha = 100 ngwee
Literacy rate 78.1%
Calorie consumption 1,912 kilocalories

United States of America

Page 13 B5

Stretching across the most temperate part of North America, and with many natural resources, the USA is the sole truly global superpower.

Official name United States of America
Formation 1776
Capital Washington DC
Population 281.4 million /76 people per sq mile (29 people per sq km)
Total area 3,717,792 sq miles
(9,629,091 sq km)
Languages English, Spanish, Italian, German, French, Polish, Chinese, Greek
Religions Protestant 61%, Roman Catholic 25%, Jewish 2%, other 12%
Ethnic mix White (including Hispanic) 81%, Native American 2%, Asia 4%, Black American/African 13%
Government Presidential democracy
Currency US dollar = 100 cents
Literacy rate 99%
Calorie consumption 3,772 kilocalories

Vanuatu

Page 122 D4

An archipelago of 82 islands and islets in the Pacific Ocean, it was ruled jointly by Britain and France from 1906 until independence in 1980.

Official name Republic of Vanuatu
Formation 1980
Capital Port Vila
Population 200,000 / 42 people per sq mile (16 people per sq km)
Total area 4,710 sq miles
(12,200 sq km)
Languages Bislama, English, French
Religions Presbyterian 37%, Anglican 15%, Roman Catholic 15%, Indigenous beliefs 8%, Seventh-day Adventist 6%, other 19%
Ethnic mix Melanesian 94%, Polynesian 3%, other 3%
Government Parliamentary democracy
Currency Vatu = 100 centimes
Literacy rate 64%
Calorie consumption 2,587 kilocalories

Vietnam

Page 114 D4

Situated in the far east of mainland Southeast Asia, the country is still rebuilding after the devastating 1962–1975 Vietnam War.

Official name Socialist Republic of Vietnam
Formation 1976
Capital Hanoi
Population 79.2 million / 622 people per sq mile (240 people per sq km)
Total area 127,243 sq miles
(329,560 sq km)
Languages Vietnamese, Chinese, Thai, Khmer, Muong, Nung, Miao, Yao
Religions Buddhist 55%, Christian 7%, other and non-religious 38%
Ethnic mix Vietnamese 88%, Chinese 4%, Thai 2%, other 6%
Government One-party republic
Currency Dông = 10 hao = 100 xu
Literacy rate 93.4%
Calorie consumption 2,583 kilocalories

Zimbabwe

Page 56 D3

The former British colony of Southern Rhodesia became fully independent as Zimbabwe in 1980, after 15 years of troubled white minority rule.

Official name Republic of Zimbabwe
Formation 1980
Capital Harare
Population 12.9 million / 86 people per sq mile (33 people per sq km)
Total area 150,803 sq miles
(390,580 sq km)
Languages English, Shona, Ndebele
Religions Syncretic (Christian and traditional beliefs) 50%, Christian 25%, Traditional beliefs 24%, other 1%
Ethnic mix Shona 71%, Ndebele 16%, other African 11%, Asian 1%, White 1%
Government Presidential regime
Currency Zimbabwe dollar = 100 cents
Literacy rate 88.7%
Calorie consumption 2,117 kilocalories

GEOGRAPHICAL COMPARISONS

LARGEST COUNTRIES

Russ. Fed.	6,592,735 sq miles	(17,075,200 sq km)
Canada	3,851,788 sq miles	(9,976,140 sq km)
USA	3,717,792 sq miles	(9,629,091 sq km)
China	3,705,386 sq miles	(9,596,960 sq km)
Brazil	3,286,470 sq miles	(8,511,965 sq km)
Australia	2,967,893 sq miles	(7,686,893 sq km)
India	1,269,339 sq miles	(3,287,590 sq km)
Argentina	1,068,296 sq miles	(2,766,890 sq km)
Kazakhstan	1,049,150 sq miles	(2,717,300 sq km)
Sudan	967,493 sq miles	(2,505,810 sq km)

SMALLEST COUNTRIES

Vatican City	0.17 sq miles	(0.44 sq km)
Monaco	0.75 sq miles	(1.95 sq km)
Nauru	.8 sq miles	(21 sq km)
Tuvalu	10 sq miles	(26 sq km)
San Marino	24 sq miles	(61 sq km)
Liechtenstein	62 sq miles	(160 sq km)
Marshall Islands	70 sq miles	(181 sq km)
St. Kitts & Nevis	101 sq miles	(261 sq km)
Maldives	116 sq miles	(300 sq km)
Malta	122 sq miles	(316 sq km)

LARGEST ISLANDS

(TO THE NEAREST 1,000 - OR 100,000 FOR THE LARGEST)

Greenland	849,400 sq miles	(2,200,000 sq km)
New Guinea	312,000 sq miles	(808,000 sq km)
Borneo	292,222 sq miles	(757,050 sq km)
Madagascar	229,300 sq miles	(594,000 sq km)
Sumatra	202,300 sq miles	(524,000 sq km)
Baffin Island	183,800 sq miles	(476,000 sq km)
Honshu	88,800 sq miles	(230,000 sq km)
Britain	88,700 sq miles	(229,800 sq km)

RICHEST COUNTRIES

(GNP PER CAPITA, IN US$)

Luxembourg	42,930
Liechtenstein	40,000
Switzerland	38,380
Norway	33,470
Denmark	32,050
Japan	32,030
USA	31,910
Germany	25,620
Austria	25,430
Singapore	24,150

POOREST COUNTRIES

(GNP PER CAPITA, IN US$)

Somalia	100
Ethiopia	100
Congo, Dem. Rep.	110
Sierra Leone	130
Malawi	180
Niger	190
Mozambique	220
Burundi	240
Rwanda	250
Tanzania	260

MOST POPULOUS COUNTRIES

China	1,290,000,000
India	1,030,000,000
USA	281,400,000
Indonesia	214,000,000
Brazil	172,600,000
Pakistan	145,000,000
Russian Federation	144,700,000

MOST POPULOUS COUNTRIES continued

Bangladesh	140,400,000
Nigeria	116,900,000
Japan	127,300,000

LEAST POPULOUS COUNTRIES

Vatican City	524
Tuvalu	10,800
Nauru	11,800
Palau	19,100
San Marino	26,900
Liechtenstein	32,200
Monaco	31,700
St. Kitts & Nevis	41,000
Andorra	66,800
Marshall Islands	68,100

MOST DENSELY POPULATED COUNTRIES

Monaco	42,104 people per sq mile	(16,256 per sq km)
Singapore	16,400 people per sq mile	(6,332 per sq km)
Malta	3,213 people per sq mile	(1,241 per sq km)
Vatican City	3,084 people per sq mile	(1,191 per sq km)
Bahrain	2,724 people per sq mile	(1,052 per sq km)
Maldives	2,590 people per sq mile	(1,000 per sq km)
Bangladesh	2,525 people per sq mile	(975 per sq km)
Mauritius	1,671 people per sq mile	(645 per sq km)
Barbados	1,614 people per sq mile	(623 per sq km)
Taiwan	1,598 people per sq mile	(617 per sq km)

MOST SPARSELY POPULATED COUNTRIES

Mongolia	.4 people per sq mile	(2 per sq km)
Namibia	.6 people per sq mile	(2 per sq km)
Australia	.7 people per sq mile	(3 per sq km)
Suriname	.7 people per sq mile	(3 per sq km)
Mauritania	.7 people per sq mile	(3 per sq km)
Botswana	.7 people per sq mile	(3 per sq km)
Iceland	.7 people per sq mile	(3 per sq km)
Libya	.8 people per sq mile	(3 per sq km)
Canada	.8 people per sq mile	(3 per sq km)
Guyana	.9 people per sq mile	(4 per sq km)

MOST WIDELY SPOKEN LANGUAGES

1. Chinese (Mandarin)	6. Arabic
2. English	7. Bengali
3. Hindi	8. Portuguese
4. Spanish	9. Malay-Indonesian
5. Russian	10. French

COUNTRIES WITH THE MOST LAND BORDERS

14: China (*Afghanistan, Bhutan, Myanmar, India, Kazakhstan, Kyrgyzstan, Laos, Mongolia, Nepal, North Korea, Pakistan, Russian Federation, Tajikistan, Vietnam*)

14: Russ. Fed. (*Azerbaijan, Belarus, China, Estonia, Finland, Georgia, Kazakhstan, Latvia, Lithuania, Mongolia, North Korea, Norway, Poland, Ukraine*)

10: Brazil (*Argentina, Bolivia, Colombia, French Guiana, Guyana, Paraguay, Peru, Suriname, Uruguay, Venezuela*)

9: Congo, Dem. Rep. (*Angola, Burundi, Central African Republic, Congo, Rwanda, Sudan, Tanzania, Uganda, Zambia*)

9: Germany (*Austria, Belgium, Czech Republic, Denmark, France, Luxembourg, Netherlands, Poland, Switzerland*)

9: Sudan (*Central African Republic, Chad, Congo, Dem. Rep., Egypt, Eritrea, Ethiopia, Kenya, Libya, Uganda*)

8: Austria (*Czech Republic, Germany, Hungary, Italy, Liechtenstein, Slovakia, Slovenia, Switzerland*)

8: France (*Andorra, Belgium, Germany, Italy, Luxembourg, Monaco, Spain, Switzerland*)

8: Tanzania (*Burundi, Congo, Dem. Rep., Kenya, Malawi, Mozambique, Rwanda, Uganda, Zambia*)

8: Turkey (*Armenia, Azerbaijan, Bulgaria, Georgia, Greece, Iran, Iraq, Syria*)

LONGEST RIVERS

Nile (NE Africa)	.4,160 miles	(6,695 km)
Amazon (South America)	.4,049 miles	(6,516 km)
Yangtze (China)	.3,915 miles	(6,299 km)
Mississippi/Missouri (US)	.3,710 miles	(5,969 km)
Ob'-Irtysh (Russ. Fed.)	.3,461 miles	(5,570 km)
Yellow River (China)	.3,395 miles	(5,464 km)
Congo (Central Africa)	.2,900 miles	(4,667 km)
Mekong (Southeast Asia)	.2,749 miles	(4,425 km)
Lena (Russian Federation)	.2,734 miles	(4,400 km)
Mackenzie (Canada)	.2,640 miles	(4,250 km)

HIGHEST MOUNTAINS
(HEIGHT ABOVE SEA LEVEL)

Everest	.29,030 ft	(8,848 m)
K2	.28,253 ft	(8,611 m)
Kanchenjunga I	.28,210 ft	(8,598 m)
Makalu I	.27,767 ft	(8,463 m)
Cho Oyu	.26,907 ft	(8,201 m)
Dhaulagiri I	.26,796 ft	(8,167 m)
Manaslu I	.26,783 ft	(8,163 m)
Nanga Parbat I	.26,661 ft	(8,126 m)
Annapurna I	.26,547 ft	(8,091 m)
Gasherbrum I	.26,471 ft	(8,068 m)

LARGEST BODIES OF INLAND WATER
(WITH AREA AND DEPTH)

Caspian Sea	.143,243 sq miles (371,000 sq km)	.3,215 ft (980 m)
Lake Superior	.32,150 sq miles (83,270 sq km)	.1,289 ft (393 m)
Lake Victoria	.26,828 sq miles (69,484 sq km)	.328 ft (100 m)
Lake Huron	.23,436 sq miles (60,700 sq km)	.751 ft (229 m)
Lake Michigan	.22,402 sq miles (58,020 sq km)	.922 ft (281 m)
Lake Tanganyika	.12,703 sq miles (32,900 sq km)	.4,700 ft (1,435 m)
Great Bear Lake	.12,274 sq miles (31,790 sq km)	.1,047 ft (319 m)
Lake Baikal	.11,776 sq miles (30,500 sq km)	.5,712 ft (1,741 m)
Great Slave Lake	.10,981 sq miles (28,440 sq km)	.459 ft (140 m)
Lake Erie	.9,915 sq miles (25,680 sq km)	.197 ft (60 m)

DEEPEST OCEAN FEATURES

Challenger Deep, Marianas Trench (Pacific)	.36,201 ft	(11,034 m)
Vityaz III Depth, Tonga Trench (Pacific)	.35,704 ft	(10,882 m)
Vityaz Depth, Kurile-Kamchatka Trench (Pacific)	.34,588 ft	(10,542 m)
Cape Johnson Deep, Philippine Trench (Pacific)	.34,441 ft	(10,497 m)
Kermadec Trench (Pacific)	.32,964 ft	(10,047 m)
Ramapo Deep, Japan Trench (Pacific)	.32,758 ft	(9,984 m)
Milwaukee Deep, Puerto Rico Trench (Atlantic)	.30,185 ft	(9,200 m)
Argo Deep, Torres Trench (Pacific)	.30,070 ft	(9,165 m)
Meteor Depth, South Sandwich Trench (Atlantic)	.30,000 ft	(9,144 m)
Planet Deep, New Britain Trench (Pacific)	.29,988 ft	(9,140 m)

GREATEST WATERFALLS
(MEAN FLOW OF WATER)

Boyoma (Congo, Dem. Rep.)	600,400 cu. ft/sec	(17,000 cu.m/sec)
Khône (Laos/Cambodia)	.410,000 cu. ft/sec	(11,600 cu.m/sec)
Niagara (USA/Canada)	.195,000 cu. ft/sec	(5,500 cu.m/sec)
Grande (Uruguay)	.160,000 cu. ft/sec	(4,500 cu.m/sec)
Paulo Afonso (Brazil)	.100,000 cu. ft/sec	(2,800 cu.m/sec)
Urubupunga (Brazil)	.97,000 cu. ft/sec	(2,750 cu.m/sec)
Iguaçu (Argentina/Brazil)	.62,000 cu. ft/sec	(1,700 cu.m/sec)
Maribondo (Brazil)	.53,000 cu. ft/sec	(1,500 cu.m/sec)
Victoria (Zimbabwe)	.39,000 cu. ft/sec	(1,100 cu.m/sec)
Kabalega (Uganda)	.42,000 cu. ft/sec	(1,200 cu.m/sec)

HIGHEST WATERFALLS

Angel (Venezuela)	.3,212 ft	(979 m)
Tugela (South Africa)	.3,110 ft	(948 m)
Utigard (Norway)	.2,625 ft	(800 m)
Mongefossen (Norway)	.2,539 ft	(774 m)
Mtarazi (Zimbabwe)	.2,500 ft	(762 m)
Yosemite (USA)	.2,425 ft	(739 m)
Ostre Mardola Foss (Norway)	.2,156 ft	(657 m)
Tyssestrengane (Norway)	.2,119 ft	(646 m)
*Cuquenan (Venezuela)	.2,001 ft	(610 m)
Sutherland (New Zealand)	.1,903 ft	(580 m)

indicates that the total height is a single leap

LARGEST DESERTS

Sahara	.3,450,000 sq miles	(9,065,000 sq km)
Gobi	.500,000 sq miles	(1,295,000 sq km)
Ar Rub al Khali	.289,600 sq miles	(750,000 sq km)
Great Victorian	.249,800 sq miles	(647,000 sq km)
Sonoran	.120,000 sq miles	(311,000 sq km)
Kalahari	.120,000 sq miles	(310,800 sq km)
Kara Kum	.115,800 sq miles	(300,000 sq km)
Takla Makan	.100,400 sq miles	(260,000 sq km)
Namib	.52,100 sq miles	(135,000 sq km)
Thar	.33,670 sq miles	(130,000 sq km)

NB – Most of Antarctica is a polar desert, with only 50 mm of precipitation annually

HOTTEST INHABITED PLACES

Djibouti (Djibouti)	.86° F	(30 °C)
Timbouctou (Mali)	.84.7° F	(29.3 °C)
Tirunelveli (India)		
Tuticorin (India)		
Nellore (India)	.84.5° F	(29.2 °C)
Santa Marta (Colombia)		
Aden (Yemen)	.84° F	(28.9 °C)
Madurai (India)		
Niamey (Niger)		
Hodeida (Yemen)	.83.8° F	(28.8 °C)

DRIEST INHABITED PLACES

Aswân (Egypt)	.0.02 in	(0.5 mm)
Luxor (Egypt)	.0.03 in	(0.7 mm)
Arica (Chile)	.0.04 in	(1.1 mm)
Ica (Peru)	.0.1 in	(2.3 mm)
Antofagasta (Chile)	.0.2 in	(4.9 mm)
El Minya (Egypt)	.0.2 in	(5.1 mm)
Asyût (Egypt)	.0.2 in	(5.2 mm)
Callao (Peru)	.0.5 in	(12.0 mm)
Trujillo (Peru)	.0.55 in	(14.0 mm)
El Faiyûm (Egypt)	.0.8 in	(19.0 mm)

WETTEST INHABITED PLACES

Buenaventura (Colombia)	.265 in	(6,743 mm)
Monrovia (Liberia)	.202 in	(5,131 mm)
Pago Pago (American Samoa)	.196 in	(4,990 mm)
Moulmein (Myanmar)	.191 in	(4,852 mm)
Lae (Papua New Guinea)	.183 in	(4,645 mm)
Baguio (Luzon Island, Philippines)	180 in	(4,573 mm)
Sylhet (Bangladesh)	.176 in	(4,457 mm)
Padang (Sumatra, Indonesia)	.166 in	(4,225 mm)
Bogor (Java, Indonesia)	.166 in	(4,225 mm)
Conakry (Guinea)	.171 in	(4,341 mm)

Aachen – Alexandria

GLOSSARY OF ABBREVIATIONS
This Glossary provides a comprehensive guide to the abbreviations used in this Atlas, and in the Index.

A **abbrev.** abbreviated
Afr. Afrikaans
Alb. Albanian
Amh. Amharic
anc. ancient
Ar. Arabic
Arm. Armenian
Az. Azerbaijani
B **Basq.** Basque
Bel. Belorussian
Ben. Bengali
Bibl. Biblical
Bret. Breton
Bul. Bulgarian
Bur. Burmese
C **Cam.** Cambodian
Cant. Cantonese
Cast. Castilian
Cat. Catalan
Chin. Chinese
Cro. Croat
Cz. Czech
D **Dan.** Danish
Dut. Dutch
E **Eng.** English
Est. Estonian
est. estimated
F **Faer.** Faeroese
Fij. Fijian
Fin. Finnish
Flem. Flemish
Fr. French
Fris. Frisian
G **Geor.** Georgian
Ger. German
Gk. Greek
Guj. Gujarati
H **Haw.** Hawaiian
Heb. Hebrew
Hind. Hindi
hist. historical
Hung. Hungarian
I **Icel.** Icelandic
Ind. Indonesian
Ir. Irish
It. Italian
J **Jap.** Japanese
K **Kaz.** Kazakh
Kir. Kirghiz
Kor. Korean
Kurd. Kurdish
L **Lao.** Laotian
Lapp. Lappish
Lat. Latin
Latv. Latvian
Lith. Lithanian
Lus. Lusatian
M **Mac.** Macedonian
Mal. Malay
Malg. Malagasy
Malt. Maltese
Mong. Mongolian
N **Nepali.** Nepali
Nor. Norwegian
O **off.** officially
P **Pash.** Pashtu
Per. Persian
Pol. Polish
Port. Portuguese
prev. previously
R **Rmsch.** Romansch
Roman. Romanian
Rus. Russian
S **SCr.** Serbo-Croatian
Serb. Serbian
Slvk. Slovak
Slvn. Slovene
Som. Somali
Sp. Spanish
Swa. Swahili
Swe. Swedish
T **Taj.** Tajik
Th. Thai
Tib. Tibetan
Turk. Turkish
Turkm. Turkmenistan
U **Uigh.** Uighur
Ukr. Ukrainian
Uzb. Uzbek
V **var.** variant
Vtn. Vietnamese
W **Wel.** Welsh
X **Xh.** Xhosa
Y **Yugo.** Yugoslavia

INDEX

INDEX

A

Aachen 72 A4 *Dut.* Aken, *Fr.*Aix-la-Chapelle; *anc.* Aquae Grani, Aquisgranum. Nordrhein-Westfalen, W Germany
Aaiún *see* Laâyoune
Aalborg *see* Ålborg
Aalen 73 B6 Baden-Württemberg, S Germany
Aalsmeer 64 C3 Noord-Holland, C Netherlands
Aalst 65 B6 *Fr.* Alost. Oost-Vlaanderen, C Belgium
Aalten 64 E4 Gelderland, E Netherlands
Aalter 65 B5 Oost-Vlaanderen, NW Belgium
Äänekoski 63 D5 Länsi-Suomi, W Finland
Aar *see* Aare
Aare 73 A7 *var.* Aar. *River* W Switzerland
Aarhus *see* Århus
Aat *see* Ath
Aba 53 G5 Abia, S Nigeria
Aba 55 E5 Orientale, NE Dem. Rep. Congo
Abā as Su'ūd *see* Najrān
Abaco Island *see* Great Abaco
Ābādān 98 C4 Khūzestān, SW Iran
Abai *see* Blue Nile
Abakan 92 D4 Respublika Khakasiya, S Russian Federation
Abancay 38 D4 Apurímac, SE Peru
Abariringa *see* Kanton
Abashiri 108 D2 *var.* Abasiri. Hokkaidō, NE Japan
Abasiri *see* Abashiri
Ābaya Hāyk' 51 C5 *Eng.* Lake Margherita, *It.* Abbaia. *Lake* SW Ethiopia
Ābay Wenz *see* Blue Nile
Abbeville 68 C2 *anc.* Abbatis Villa. Somme, N France
'Abd al 'Azīz, Jabal 96 D2 *mountain range* NE Syria
Abéché 54 C3 *var.* Abécher, Abeshr. Ouaddaï, SE Chad
Abécher *see* Abéché
Abela *see* Ávila
Abemama 122 D2 *var.* Apamama; *prev.* Roger Simpson Island. *Atoll* Tungaru, W Kiribati
Abengourou 53 E5 E Côte d'Ivoire
Aberdeen 66 D3 *anc.* Devana. NE Scotland, UK
Aberdeen 23 E2 South Dakota, N USA
Aberdeen 24 B2 Washington, NW USA
Abergwaun *see* Fishguard
Abertawe *see* Swansea
Aberystwyth 67 C6 W Wales, UK
Abeshr *see* Abéché
Abhā 99 B6 'Asīr, SW Saudi Arabia
Abidavichy 85 D7 *Rus.* Obidovichi. Mahilyowskaya Voblasts', E Belarus
Abidjan 53 E5 S Côte d'Ivoire
Abilene 27 F3 Texas, SW USA
Abingdon *see* Pinta, Isla
Abkhazia 95 E1 *autonomous republic* NW Georgia
Åbo 63 D6 Länsi-Suomi, W Finland
Aboisso 53 E5 SE Côte d'Ivoire
Abo, Massif d' 54 B1 *mountain range* NW Chad
Abomey 53 F5 S Benin
Abou-Déïa 54 C3 Salamat, SE Chad
Abrantes 70 B3 *var.* Abrántes. Santarém, C Portugal
Abrolhos Bank 34 E4 *undersea feature* W Atlantic Ocean
Abrova 85 B6 *Rus.* Obrovo. Brestskaya Voblasts', SW Belarus
Abrud 86 B4 *Ger.* Gross-Schlatten, *Hung.* Abrudbánya. Alba, SW Romania
Abruzzese, Appennino 74 C4 *mountain range* C Italy
Absaroka Range 22 B2 *mountain range* Montana/Wyoming, NW USA
Abū aḍ Ḍuhūr 96 B3 *Fr.* Aboudouhour. Idlib, NW Syria
Abu Dhabi *see* Abū Ẓaby
Abu Hamed 50 C3 River Nile, N Sudan
Abū Ḩardān 96 E3 *var.* Hajîne. Dayr az Zawr, E Syria
Abuja 53 G4 *country capital* (Nigeria) Federal Capital District, C Nigeria
Abū Kamāl 96 E3 *Fr.* Abou Kémal. Dayr az Zawr, E Syria
Abula *see* Ávila
Abunã, Rio 40 C2 *var.* Río Abuná. *River* Bolivia/Brazil
Abut Head 129 B6 *headland* South Island, NZ
Ābuyē Mēda 50 D4 *mountain* C Ethiopia
Abū Ẓabī *see* Abū Ẓaby
Abū Ẓaby 99 C5 *var.* Abū Ẓabī, *Eng.* Abu Dhabi. *Country capital* (UAE) Abū Ẓaby, C UAE
Abyla *see* Ávila
Acalayong 55 A5 SW Equatorial Guinea
Acaponeta 28 D4 Nayarit, C Mexico
Acapulco 29 E5 *var.* Acapulco de Juárez. Guerrero, S Mexico
Acapulco de Juárez *see* Acapulco
Acarai Mountains 37 F4 *Sp.* Serra Acaraí. *Mountain range* Brazil/Guyana
Acarigua 36 D2 Portuguesa, N Venezuela
Accra 53 E5 *country capital* (Ghana) SE Ghana
Achacachi 39 E4 La Paz, W Bolivia
Acklins Island 32 C2 *island* SE Bahamas
Aconcagua, Cerro 42 B4 *mountain* W Argentina
Açores *see* Azores
A Coruña 70 B1 *Cast.* La Coruña, *Eng.* Corunna; *anc.* Caronium. Galicia, NW Spain
Acre 40 C2 *off.* Estado do Acre. *State* W Brazil
Açu 41 G2 *var.* Assu. Rio Grande do Norte, E Brazil
Ada 27 G2 Oklahoma, C USA
Ada 78 D3 Serbia, N Serbia and Montenegro (Yugo.)
Adalia, Gulf of *see* Antalya Körfezi
Adama *see* Nazrēt
Adamawa Highlands 54 B4 *plateau* NW Cameroon
'Adan 99 B7 *Eng.* Aden. SW Yemen
Adana 94 D4 *var.* Seyhan. Adana, S Turkey
Adapazarı 94 B2 *prev.* Ada Bazar. Sakarya, NW Turkey
Adare, Cape 132 B4 *headland* Antarctica
Ad Dahnā' 98 C4 *desert* E Saudi Arabia
Ad Dakhla 48 A4 *var.* Dakhla. SW Western Sahara
Ad Dalanj *see* Dilling
Ad Damar *see* Ed Damer
Ad Damazīn *see* Ed Damazin
Ad Dāmir *see* Ed Damer
Ad Dammān 98 C4 *var.* Dammām. Ash Sharqīyah, NE Saudi Arabia
Ad Dāmūr *see* Damoûr
Ad Dawḩah 98 C4 *Eng.* Doha. *Country capital* (Qatar) C Qatar
Aḍ Ḍiffah *see* Libyan Plateau
Addis Ababa *see* Ādīs Ābeba
Addu Atoll 110 A5 *atoll* S Maldives
Adelaide 127 B6 *state capital* South Australia
Aden *see* 'Adan
Aden, Gulf of 99 C7 *gulf* SW Arabian Sea
Adige 74 C2 *Ger.* Etsch. *River* N Italy
Adirondack Mountains 19 F2 *mountain range* New York, NE USA
Ādīs Ābeba 51 C5 *Eng.* Addis Ababa. *Country capital* (Ethiopia) C Ethiopia
Adıyaman 95 E4 Adıyaman, SE Turkey
Adjud 86 C4 Vrancea, E Romania
Admiralty Islands 122 B3 *island group* N PNG
Adra 71 E5 Andalucía, S Spain
Adrar 48 D3 C Algeria
Adrar des Iforas *see* Ifôghas, Adrar des
Adrian 18 C3 Michigan, N USA
Adriatic Sea 81 E2 *Alb.* Deti Adriatik, *It.* Mare Adriatico, *SCr.* Jadransko More, *Slvn.* Jadransko Morje. *Sea* N Mediterranean Sea
Adycha 93 F2 *river* NE Russian Federation
Aegean Sea 83 C5 *Gk.* Aigaíon Pélagos, Aigaío Pélagos, *Turk.* Ege Denizi. *Sea* NE Mediterranean Sea
Aegviidu 84 D2 *Ger.* Charlottenhof. Harjumaa, NW Estonia
Aelana *see* Al 'Aqabah
Aelok *see* Ailuk Atoll
Aelōnlaplap *see* Ailinglaplap Atoll
Aeolian Islands *see* Eolie, Isole
Afar Depression *see* Danakil Desert
Afghanistan 100 C4 *off.* Islamic State of Afghanistan, *Per.* Dowlat-e Eslāmī-ye Afghānestān; *prev.* Republic of Afghanistan. *Country* C Asia
Afmadow 51 D6 Jubbada Hoose, S Somalia
Africa 46 *continent*
Africa, Horn of 46 E4 *physical region* Ethiopia/Somalia
Africana Seamount 119 A6 *undersea feature* SW Indian Ocean
'Afrīn 96 B2 Ḩalab, N Syria
Afyon 94 B3 *prev.* Afyonkarahisar. Afyon, W Turkey
Agadez 53 G3 *prev.* Agadès. Agadez, C Niger
Agadir 48 B3 SW Morocco
Agana/Agaña *see* Hagåtña
Āgaro 51 C5 C Ethiopia
Agassiz Fracture Zone 121 G5 *tectonic feature* S Pacific Ocean
Agathónisi 83 D6 *island* Dodekánisos, Greece, Aegean Sea
Agde 69 C6 *anc.* Agatha. Hérault, S France
Agedabia *see* Ajdābiyā
Agen 69 B5 *anc.* Aginnum. Lot-et-Garonne, SW France
Aghri Dagh *see* Büyükağrı Dağı
Agiá 82 B4 *var.* Ayiá. Thessalía, C Greece
Agialoúsa 80 D4 *var.* Yenierenköy. NE Cyprus
Agía Marína 83 E6 Léros, Dodekánisos, Greece, Aegean Sea
Ágios Nikólaos 83 D8 *var.* Áyios Nikólaos. Kríti, Greece, E Mediterranean Sea
Āgra 112 D3 Uttar Pradesh, N India
Agram *see* Zagreb
Ağrı 95 F3 *var.* Karaköse; *prev.* Karakılısse. Ağrı, NE Turkey
Agri Dagi *see* Büyükağrı Dağı
Agrigento 75 C7 *Gk.* Akragas; *prev.* Girgenti. Sicilia, Italy, C Mediterranean Sea
Agriovótano 83 C5 Évvoia, C Greece
Agropoli 75 D5 Campania, S Italy
Aguachica 36 B2 Cesar, N Colombia
Aguadulce 31 F5 Coclé, S Panama
Agua Prieta 28 B1 Sonora, NW Mexico
Aguascalientes 28 D4 Aguascalientes, C Mexico
Aguaytía 38 C3 Ucayali, C Peru
Aguilas 71 E4 Murcia, SE Spain
Aguililla 28 D4 Michoacán de Ocampo, SW Mexico
Agulhas Basin 47 D8 *undersea feature* SW Indian Ocean
Agulhas Plateau 45 D6 *undersea feature* SW Indian Ocean
Ahaggar 53 F2 *high plateau region* SE Algeria
Ahlen 72 B4 Nordrhein-Westfalen, W Germany
Ahmadābād 112 C4 *var.* Ahmedabad. Gujarāt, W India
Ahmadnagar 112 C5 *var.* Ahmednagar. Mahārāshtra, W India
Ahmedabad *see* Ahmadābād
Ahmednagar *see* Ahmadnagar
Ahuachapán 30 B3 Ahuachapán, W El Salvador
Ahvāz 98 C3 *var.* Ahwāz; *prev.* Nāsiri. Khūzestān, SW Iran
Ahvenanmaa *see* Åland
Ahwāz *see* Ahvāz
Aïdin *see* Aydın
Aígina 83 C6 *var.* Aíyina, Egina. Aígina, C Greece
Aígio 83 B5 *var.* Egio; *prev.* Aíyion. Dytikí Ellás, S Greece
Aiken 21 E2 South Carolina, SE USA
Ailigandí 31 G4 San Blas, NE Panama
Ailinglaplap Atoll 122 D2 *var.* Aelōnlaplap. *Atoll* Ralik Chain, S Marshall Islands
Ailuk Atoll 122 D1 *var.* Aelok. *Atoll* Ratak Chain, NE Marshall Islands
Ainaži 84 D3 *Est.* Heinaste, *Ger.* Hainasch. Limbaži, N Latvia
'Aïn Ben Tili 52 D1 Tiris Zemmour, N Mauritania
Aintab *see* Gaziantep
Aïoun el Atrous *see* 'Ayoûn el 'Atroûs
Aïoun el Atroûss *see* 'Ayoûn el 'Atroûs
Aiquile 39 F4 Cochabamba, C Bolivia
Aïr *see* Aïr, Massif de l'
Air du Azbine *see* Aïr, Massif de l'
Aïr, Massif de l' 53 G2 *var.* Aïr, Air du Azbine, Asben. *Mountain range* NC Niger
Aiud 86 B4 *Ger.* Strassburg, *Hung.* Nagyenyed; *prev.* Engeten. Alba, SW Romania
Aix *see* Aix-en-Provence
Aix-en-Provence 69 D6 *var.* Aix; *anc.* Aquae Sextiae. Bouches-du-Rhône, SE France
Aíyina *see* Aígina
Aíyion *see* Aígio
Aizkraukle 84 C4 Aizkraukle, S Latvia
Ajaccio 69 E7 Corse, France, C Mediterranean Sea
Ajaria 95 F2 *autonomous republic* SW Georgia
Aj Bogd Uul 104 D2 *mountain* SW Mongolia
Ajdābiyā 49 G2 *var.* Agedabia, Ajdābiyah. NE Libya
Ajdābiyah *see* Ajdābiyā
Ajjinena *see* El Geneina
Ajmer 112 D3 *var.* Ajmere. Rājasthān, N India
Ajmere *see* Ajmer
Ajo 26 A3 Arizona, SW USA
Akaba *see* Al 'Aqabah
Akamagaseki *see* Shimonoseki
Akasha 50 B3 Northern, N Sudan
Akchâr 52 C2 *desert* W Mauritania
Akhalts'ikhe 95 F2 SW Georgia
Akhisar 94 A3 Manisa, W Turkey
Akhmīm 50 B2 *anc.* Panopolis. C Egypt
Akhtubinsk 89 C7 Astrakhanskaya Oblast', SW Russian Federation
Akimiski Island 16 C3 *island* Northwest Territories, C Canada
Akinovka 87 F4 Zaporiz'ka Oblast', S Ukraine
Akita 108 D4 Akita, Honshū, C Japan
Akjoujt 52 C2 *prev.* Fort-Repoux. Inchiri, W Mauritania
Akkeshi 108 E2 Hokkaidō, NE Japan
Aklavik 14 D3 Northwest Territories, NW Canada
Akmola *see* Astana
Akpatok Island 17 E1 *island* Northwest Territories, E Canada
Akra Dhrepanon *see* Drépano, Akrotírio
Akra Kanestron *see* Palioúri, Akrotírio
Akron 18 D4 Ohio, N USA
Akrotiri *see* Akrotírion
Akrotírion 80 C5 *var.* Akrotiri. *UK air base* S Cyprus
Aksai Chin 102 B2 *Chin.* Aksayqin. *Disputed region* China/India
Aksaray 94 C4 Aksaray, C Turkey
Akşehir 94 B4 Konya, W Turkey
Aktau 92 A4 *Kaz.* Aqtaū; *prev.* Shevchenko. Mangistau, W Kazakhstan
Aktobe 92 B4 *Kaz.* Aqtöbe. *prev.* Aktyubinsk. Aktyubinsk, NW Kazakhstan
Aktsyabrski 85 C7 *Rus.* Oktyabr'skiy; *prev.* Karpilovka. Homyel'skaya Voblasts', SE Belarus
Aktyubinsk *see* Aktobe
Akula 55 C5 Equateur, NW Dem. Rep. Congo
Akureyri 61 E4 Nordhurland Eystra, N Iceland
Akyab *see* Sittwe
Alabama 29 G1 *off.* State of Alabama; also known as Camellia State, Heart of Dixie, The Cotton State, Yellowhammer State. *State* S USA
Alabama River 20 C3 *river* Alabama, S USA
Alaca 94 C3 Çorum, N Turkey
Alagoas 41 G2 *off.* Estado de Alagoas. *State* E Brazil
Alajuela 31 E4 Alajuela, C Costa Rica
Alakanuk 14 C2 Alaska, USA
Al 'Alamayn *see* El 'Alamein
Al 'Amārah 98 C3 *var.* Amara. E Iraq
Alamo 25 D6 Nevada, W USA
Alamogordo 26 D3 New Mexico, SW USA
Alamosa 22 C5 Colorado, C USA
Åland 63 C6 *var.* Aland Islands, *Fin.* Ahvenanmaa. *Island group* SW Finland
Aland Islands *see* Åland
Aland Sea *see* Ålands Hav
Ålands Hav 63 C6 *var.* Aland Sea. *Strait* Baltic Sea/Gulf of Bothnia
Alanya 94 C4 Antalya, S Turkey
Alappuzha *see* Alleppey
Al 'Aqabah 97 B8 *var.* Akaba, Aqaba, 'Aqaba; *anc.* Aelana, Elath. Ma'ān, SW Jordan
Alasca, Golfo de *see* Alaska, Gulf of
Alaşehir 94 A4 Manisa, W Turkey
Al 'Ashārah 96 E3 *var.* Ashara. Dayr az Zawr, E Syria
Alaska 14 C3 *off.* State of Alaska; also known as Land of the Midnight Sun, The Last Frontier, Seward's Folly; *prev.* Russian America. *State* NW USA
Alaska, Gulf of 14 C4 *var.* Golfo de Alasca. *Gulf* Canada/USA
Alaska Peninsula 14 C3 *peninsula* Alaska, USA
Alaska Range 12 B2 *mountain range* Alaska, USA
Al-Asnam *see* Chlef
Al Awaynāt *see* Al 'Uwaynāt
Al 'Aynā 97 B7 Al Karak, W Jordan
Alazeya 93 G2 *river* NE Russian Federation
Al Bāb 96 B2 Ḩalab, N Syria
Albacete 71 E3 Castilla-La Mancha, C Spain
Al Baghdādī 98 B3 *var.* Khān al Baghdādī. SW Iraq
Al Bāha *see* Al Bāḩah
Al Bāḩah 99 B5 *var.* Al Bāha. Al Bāḩah, SW Saudi Arabia
Al Baḩr al Mayyit *see* Dead Sea
Alba Iulia 86 B4 *Ger.* Weissenburg, *Hung.* Gyulafehérvár; *prev.* Bălgrad, Karlsburg, Károly-Fehérvár. Alba, W Romania
Albania 79 C7 *off.* Republic of Albania, *Alb.* Republika e Shqipërisë, Shqipëria; *prev.* People's Socialist Republic of Albania. *Country* SE Europe
Albany 16 C3 *river* Ontario, S Canada
Albany 19 F3 *state capital* New York, NE USA
Albany 20 D3 Georgia, SE USA
Albany 24 B3 Oregon, NW USA
Albany 125 B7 Western Australia
Al Bāridah 96 C4 *var.* Bāridah. Ḩimş, C Syria
Al Başrah 98 C3 *Eng.* Basra; *hist.* Busra, Bussora. SE Iraq
Al Batrūn *see* Batroûn
Al Bayḑā' 49 G2 *var.* Beida. NE Libya
Albemarle Island *see* Isabela, Isla
Albemarle Sound 21 G1 *inlet* W Atlantic Ocean
Albergaria-a-Velha 70 B2 Aveiro, N Portugal
Albert 68 C3 Somme, N France
Alberta 15 E4 *province* SW Canada
Albert Edward Nyanza *see* Edward, Lake
Albert, Lake 51 B6 *var.* Albert Nyanza, Lac Mobutu Sese Seko. *Lake* Uganda/Dem. Rep. Congo
Albert Lea 23 F3 Minnesota, N USA
Albert Nyanza *see* Albert, Lake
Albi 69 C6 *anc.* Albiga. Tarn, S France
Ålborg 58 D3 *var.* Aalborg, Ålborg-Nørresundby; *anc.* Alburgum. Nordjylland, N Denmark
Ålborg-Nørresundby *see* Ålborg
Alborz, Reshteh-ye Kūhhā-ye 98 C2 *Eng.* Elburz Mountains. *Mountain range* N Iran
Albuquerque 26 D2 New Mexico, SW USA
Al Burayqah *see* Marsá al Burayqah
Alburgum *see* Ålborg
Albury 127 C7 New South Wales, SE Australia
Alcácer do Sal 70 B4 Setúbal, W Portugal
Alcalá de Henares 71 E3 *Ar.* Alkal'a; *anc.* Complutum. Madrid, C Spain
Alcamo 75 C7 Sicilia, Italy, C Mediterranean Sea
Alcañiz 71 F2 Aragón, NE Spain
Alcántara, Embalse de 70 C3 *reservoir* W Spain
Alcaudete 70 D4 Andalucía, S Spain
Alcázar *see* Ksar-el-Kebir
Alcoi *see* Alcoy
Alcoy 71 F4 *var.* Alcoi. País Valenciano, E Spain
Aldabra Group 57 G2 *island group* SW Seychelles
Aldan 93 F3 *river* NE Russian Federation
al Dar al Baida *see* Rabat
Alderney 68 A2 *island* Channel Islands
Aleg 52 C3 Brakna, SW Mauritania
Aleksandropol' *see* Gyumri
Aleksin 89 B5 Tul'skaya Oblast', W Russian Federation
Aleksinac 78 E4 Serbia, SE Serbia and Montenegro (Yugo.)
Alençon 68 B3 Orne, N France
Alenquer 41 E2 Pará, NE Brazil
Aleppo *see* Ḩalab
Alert 15 F1 Ellesmere Island, Nunavut, N Canada
Alès 69 C6 *prev.* Alais. Gard, S France
Aleşd 86 B3 *Hung.* Élesd. Bihor, SW Romania
Alessandria 74 B2 *Fr.* Alexandrie. Piemonte, N Italy
Ålesund 63 A5 Møre og Romsdal, S Norway
Aleutian Basin 91 G3 *undersea feature* Bering Sea
Aleutian Islands 14 A3 *island group* Alaska, USA
Aleutian Range 12 A2 *mountain range* Alaska, USA
Aleutian Trench 91 H3 *undersea feature* S Bering Sea
Alexander Archipelago 14 D4 *island group* Alaska, USA
Alexander City 20 D2 Alabama, S USA
Alexander Island 132 A3 *island* Antarctica
Alexandra 129 B7 Otago, South Island, NZ
Alexándreia 82 B4 *var.* Alexándria. Kentrikí Makedonía, N Greece
Alexandria 50 B1 *Ar.* Al Iskandarīyah. N Egypt

Bahama Islands – Bemidji

ahama Islands see Bahamas
ahamas 32 C2 off. Commonwealth of the Bahamas. Country N West Indies
ahamas 13 D6 var. Bahama Islands. Island group N West Indies
ahāwalpur 112 C2 Punjab, E Pakistan
ahía 41 F3 off. Estado da Bahia. State E Brazil
ahía Blanca 43 C5 Buenos Aires, E Argentina
ahía, Islas de la 30 C1 Eng. Bay Islands. Island group N Honduras
ahir Dar 50 C4 var. Bahr Dar, Bahrdar Giyorgis. NW Ethiopia
ahraich 113 E3 Uttar Pradesh, N India
ahrain 98 C4 off. State of Bahrain, Dawlat al Bahrayn, Ar. Al Baḥrayn; prev. Bahrein, anc. Tylos or Tyros. Country SW Asia
ahr al Milḥ see Razāzah, Buḥayrat ar
ahrat Lūt see Dead Sea
ahrat Tabariya see Tiberias, Lake
ahr Dar see Bahir Dar
ahrdar Giyorgis see Bahir Dar
ahr el Azraq see Blue Nile
ahr el Jebel see White Nile
ahret Lut see Dead Sea
ahr Tabariya, Sea of see Tiberias, Lake
ahushewsk 85 E6 Rus. Bogushëvsk. Vitsyebskaya Voblasts', NE Belarus
aia Mare 86 B3 Ger. Frauenbach, Hung. Nagybánya; prev. Neustadt. Maramureș, NW Romania
aia Sprie 86 B3 Ger. Mittelstadt, Hung. Felsőbánya. Maramureș, NW Romania
aïbokoum 54 B4 Logone-Oriental, SW Chad
aidoa see Baydhabo
aie-Comeau 17 E3 Quebec, SE Canada
aikal, Lake see Baykal, Ozero
aile Átha Luain see Athlone
ailén 70 D4 Andalucía, S Spain
ailé na Mainistreach see Newtownabbey
ăilești 86 B5 Dolj, SW Romania
a Illi 54 B3 Chari-Baguirmi, SW Chad
ainbridge 20 D3 Georgia, SE USA
'ir see Bāyir
aireuth see Bayreuth
airiki 122 D2 country capital (Kiribati) Tarawa, NW Kiribati
airnsdale 127 C7 Victoria, SE Australia
aishan 107 E3 prev. Hunjiang. Jilin, NE China
aiyin 106 B4 Gansu, C China
aja 77 C7 Bács-Kiskun, S Hungary
aja California 26 A4 Eng. Lower California. Peninsula NW Mexico
aja California 28 B2 state NW Mexico
ajo Boquete see Boquete
ajram Curri 79 D5 Kukës, N Albania
akala 54 C4 Ouaka, C Central African Republic
akan see Shimonoseki
aker 24 C3 Oregon, NW USA
aker and Howland Islands 123 E2 US unincorporated territory W Polynesia
aker Lake 15 F3 Nunavut, N Canada
akersfield 25 C7 California, W USA
akharden 100 C3 Turkm. Bäherden; prev. Bakherden. Akhalskiy Velayat, C Turkmenistan
akhchysaray 87 F5 Rus. Bakhchisaray. Respublika Krym, S Ukraine
akhmach 87 F1 Chernihivs'ka Oblast', N Ukraine
ākhtarān 98 C3 prev. Kermānshāh, Qahremānshahr. Kermānshāh. W Iran
akı 95 H2 Eng. Baku. Country capital (Azerbaijan) E Azerbaijan
akony 77 C7 Eng. Bakony Mountains, Ger. Bakonywald. Mountain range W Hungary
aku see Bakı
alabac Island 107 C8 island W Philippines
alabac Strait 116 D2 var. Selat Balabac. Strait Malaysia/Philippines
a'labakk see Baalbek
alaguer 71 F2 Cataluña, NE Spain
alakovo 89 C6 Saratovskaya Oblast', W Russian Federation
ālā Morghāb 100 D4 Laghmān, NW Afghanistan
alashov 89 B6 Saratovskaya Oblast', W Russian Federation
alaton C7 var. Lake Balaton, Ger. Plattensee. Lake W Hungary
alaton, Lake see Balaton
albina, Represa 40 D1 reservoir NW Brazil
alboa 31 G4 Panamá, C Panama
alcarce 43 D5 Buenos Aires, E Argentina
alclutha 129 B7 Otago, South Island, NZ
aldy Mountain 22 C1 mountain Montana, NW USA
âle see Basel
aleares, Islas 71 G3 Eng. Balearic Islands. Island group Spain, W Mediterranean Sea
alearic Islands see Baleares, Islas
alearic Plain see Algerian Basin
aleine, Rivière à la 17 E2 river Quebec, E Canada
alen 65 C5 Antwerpen, N Belgium
aleshwar 113 F4 prev. Balasore. Orissa, E India
ali 116 D5 island C Indonesia
alıkesir 94 A3 Balıkesir, W Turkey
alīkh, Nahr 96 C2 river N Syria
alikpapan 116 D4 Borneo, C Indonesia
alkan Mountains 82 C2 Bul./SCr. Stara Planina. Mountain range Bulgaria/Serbia and Montenegro (Yugo.)
alkh 101 E3 anc. Bactra. Balkh, N Afghanistan
alkhash 92 C5 Kaz. Balqash. Karaganda, SE Kazakhstan
alkhash, Lake see Balkhash, Ozero
alkhash, Ozero 92 C5 Eng. Lake Balkhash, Kaz. Balqash. Lake SE Kazakhstan
alladonia 125 C6 Western Australia
allarat 127 C7 Victoria, SE Australia
alleny Islands 132 B5 island group Antarctica
Ballinger 27 F3 Texas, SW USA
Balochistān see Baluchistān
Balș 86 B5 Olt, S Romania
Balsas 41 F2 Maranhão, E Brazil
Balsas, Río 29 E5 var. Río Mexcala. River S Mexico
Bal'shavik 85 D7 Rus. Bol'shevik. Homyel'skaya Voblasts', SE Belarus
Balta 86 D3 Odes'ka Oblast', SW Ukraine
Bălți 86 D3 Rus. Bel'tsy. N Moldova
Baltic Sea 63 C7 Ger. Ostee, Rus. Baltiskoye More. Sea N Europe
Baltimore 19 F4 Maryland, NE USA
Baltkrievija see Belarus
Baluchistān 112 B3 var. Balochistān, Beluchistan. Admin. region province SW Pakistan
Balvi 84 D4 Balvi, NE Latvia
Balykchy 101 G2 Kir. Ysyk-Köl; prev. Issyk-Kul', Rybach'ye. Issyk-Kul'skaya Oblast', NE Kyrgyzstan
Balzers 72 E2 S Liechtenstein
Bam 98 E4 Kermān, SE Iran
Bamako 52 D4 country capital (Mali) Capital District, SW Mali
Bambari 54 C4 Ouaka, C Central African Republic
Bamberg 73 C5 Bayern, SE Germany
Bamenda 54 A4 Nord-Ouest, W Cameroon
Banaba 122 D2 var. Ocean Island. Island Tungaru, W Kiribati
Bandaaceh 116 A3 var. Banda Atjeh; prev. Koetaradja, Kutaradja, Kutaraja. Sumatera, W Indonesia
Banda Atjeh see Bandaaceh
Bandama 52 D5 var. Bandama Fleuve. River S Côte d'Ivoire
Bandama Fleuve see Bandama
Bandar 'Abbās see Bandar-e 'Abbās
Bandarbeyla 51 E5 var. Bender Beila, Bender Beyla. Bari, NE Somalia
Bandar-e 'Abbās 98 D4 var. Bandar 'Abbās; prev. Gombroon. Hormozgān, S Iran
Bandar-e Būshehr 98 C4 var. Būshehr, Eng. Bushire. Būshehr, S Iran
Bandar-e Khamīr 98 D4 Hormozgān, S Iran
Bandar-e Langeh 98 D4 var. Bandar-e Lengeh, Lingeh. Hormozgān, S Iran
Bandar-e Lengeh see Bandar-e Langeh
Bandar Kassim see Boosaaso
Bandarlampung 116 C4 prev. Tanjungkarang, Teloekbetoeng, Telukbetung. Sumatera, W Indonesia
Bandar Maharani see Muar
Bandar Masulipatnam see Machilīpatnam
Bandar Seri Begawan 116 D3 prev. Brunei Town. Country capital (Brunei) N Brunei
Bandar Sri Aman see Sri Aman
Banda Sea 117 F5 var. Laut Banda. Sea E Indonesia
Bandiagara 53 E3 Mopti, C Mali
Bandırma 94 A3 var. Penderma. Balıkesir, NW Turkey
Bandundu 55 C6 prev. Banningville. Bandundu, W Dem. Rep. Congo
Bandung 116 C5 prev. Bandoeng. Jawa, C Indonesia
Bangalore 110 C2 Karnātaka, S India
Bangassou 54 D4 Mbomou, SE Central African Republic
Banggai, Kepulauan 117 E4 island group C Indonesia
Banghāzī 49 G2 Eng. Bengazi, Benghazi, It. Bengasi. NE Libya
Bangka, Pulau 116 C4 island W Indonesia
Bangkok see Krung Thep
Bangkok, Bight of see Krung Thep, Ao
Bangladesh 113 G3 off. People's Republic of Bangladesh; prev. East Pakistan. Country S Asia
Bangor 67 B5 Ir. Beannchar. E Northern Ireland, UK
Bangor 19 G2 Maine, NE USA
Bangor 67 C6 NW Wales, UK
Bangui 55 B5 country capital (Central African Republic) Ombella-Mpoko, SW Central African Republic
Bangweulu, Lake 51 B8 var. Lake Bengweulu. Lake N Zambia
Ban Hat Yai see Hat Yai
Ban Hin Heup 114 C4 Viangchan, C Laos
Ban Houayxay see Houayxay
Ban Houei Sai see Houayxay
Ban Hua Hin 115 C6 var. Hua Hin. Prachuap Khiri Khan, SW Thailand
Bani 52 D3 river S Mali
Banias see Bāniyās
Banī Suwayf see Beni Suef
Bāniyās 96 B3 var. Banias, Baniyas, Paneas. Tarṭūs, W Syria
Baniyas see Bāniyās
Banja Luka 78 B3 Republika Srpska, NW Bosnia and Herzegovina
Banjarmasin 116 D4 prev. Bandjarmasin. Borneo, C Indonesia
Banjul 52 B3 prev. Bathurst. Country capital (Gambia) W Gambia
Banks Island 15 E2 island Banks Island, Northwest Territories, NW Canada
Banks Islands 122 D4 Fr. Îles Banks. Island group N Vanuatu
Banks Lake 24 B1 reservoir Washington, NW USA
Banks Peninsula 129 C6 peninsula South Island, NZ
Banks Strait 127 C8 strait SW Tasman Sea
Bānkura 113 F4 West Bengal, NE India
Ban Mak Khaeng see Udon Thani
Banmo see Bhamo
Bañolas see Banyoles
Ban Pak Phanang see Pak Phanang
Ban Sichon see Sichon
Banská Bystrica 77 C6 Ger. Neusohl, Hung. Besztercebánya. Banskobystrický Kraj, C Slovakia
Bantry Bay 67 A7 Ir. Bá Bheanntraí. Bay SW Ireland
Banya 82 E2 Burgas, E Bulgaria
Banyak, Kepulauan 116 A3 prev. Kepulauan Banjak. Island group NW Indonesia
Banyo 54 B4 Adamaoua, NW Cameroon
Banyoles 71 G2 var. Bañolas. Cataluña, NE Spain
Banzare Seamounts 119 C7 undersea feature S Indian Ocean
Baoji 106 B4 var. Pao-chi, Paoki. Shaanxi, C China
Baoro 54 B4 Nana-Mambéré, W Central African Republic
Baoshan 106 A6 var. Pao-shan. Yunnan, SW China
Baotou 105 F3 var. Pao-t'ou, Paotow. Nei Mongol Zizhiqu, N China
Ba'qūbah 98 B3 var. Qubba. C Iraq
Baquerizo Moreno see Puerto Baquerizo Moreno
Bar 79 C5 It. Antivari. Montenegro, SW Serbia and Montenegro (Yugo.)
Baraawe 51 D6 It. Brava. Shabeellaha Hoose, S Somalia
Baraji, Hirfanli 94 C3 lake C Turkey
Bārāmati 112 C5 Mahārāshtra, W India
Baranavichy 85 B6 Pol. Baranowicze, Rus. Baranovichi. Brestskaya Voblasts', SW Belarus
Barbados 33 G1 country SE West Indies
Barbastro 71 F2 Aragón, NE Spain
Barbate de Franco 70 C5 Andalucía, S Spain
Barbuda 33 G3 island N Antigua and Barbuda
Barcaldine 126 C4 Queensland, E Australia
Barce see Al Marj
Barcelona 71 G2 anc. Barcino, Barcinona. Cataluña, E Spain
Barcelona 37 E2 Anzoátegui, NE Venezuela
Barcoo see Cooper Creek
Barcs 77 C7 Somogy, SW Hungary
Bardaï 54 C1 Borkou-Ennedi-Tibesti, N Chad
Bardejov 77 D5 Ger. Bartfeld, Hung. Bártfa. Prešovský Kraj, E Slovakia
Bardera see Baardheere
Bardere see Baardheere
Bareilly 113 E3 var. Bareli. Uttar Pradesh, N India
Bareli see Bareilly
Barendrecht 64 C4 Zuid-Holland, SW Netherlands
Barentin 68 C3 Seine-Maritime, N France
Barentsberg 61 G2 Spitsbergen, W Svalbard
Barentsøya 61 G2 island E Svalbard
Barents Sea 88 C2 Nor. Barents Havet, Rus. Barentsevo More. Sea Arctic Ocean
Barents Trough 59 E1 undersea feature SW Barents Sea
Bar Harbor 19 H2 Mount Desert Island, Maine, NE USA
Bari 75 E5 var. Bari delle Puglie; anc. Barium. Puglia, SE Italy
Bāridah see Al Bāridah
Bari delle Puglie see Bari
Barikot see Barīkowṭ
Barīkowṭ 101 F4 var. Barikot. Kunar, NE Afghanistan
Barillas 30 A2 var. Santa Cruz Barillas. Huehuetenango, NW Guatemala
Barinas 36 C2 Barinas, W Venezuela
Barisal 113 G4 Khulna, S Bangladesh
Barisan, Pegunungan 116 B4 mountain range Sumatera, W Indonesia
Barito, Sungai 116 D4 river Borneo, C Indonesia
Barium see Bari
Barka see Al Marj
Barkly Tableland 126 B3 plateau Northern Territory/Queensland, N Australia
Bârlad 86 D4 prev. Bîrlad. Vaslui, E Romania
Barlavento, Ilhas de 52 A2 var. Windward Islands. Island group N Cape Verde
Bar-le-Duc 68 D3 var. Bar-sur-Ornain. Meuse, NE France
Barlee, Lake 125 B6 lake Western Australia
Barlee Range 124 A4 mountain range Western Australia
Barletta 75 D5 anc. Barduli. Puglia, SE Italy
Barlinek 76 B3 Ger. Berlinchen. Zachodniopomorskie, NW Poland
Barmouth 67 C6 NW Wales, UK
Barnaul 92 D4 Altayskiy Kray, C Russian Federation
Barnet 67 A7 SE England, UK
Barnstaple 67 C7 SW England, UK
Baroghil Pass 101 F3 var. Kowtal-e Barowghīl. Pass Afghanistan/Pakistan
Baron'ki 85 E7 Rus. Boron'ki. Mahilyowskaya Voblasts', E Belarus
Barquisimeto 36 C2 Lara, NW Venezuela
Barra 66 B3 island NW Scotland, UK
Barra de Río Grande 31 E3 Región Autónoma Atlántico Sur, E Nicaragua
Barragem de Sobradinho see Sobradinho, Represa de
Barranca 38 C3 Lima, W Peru
Barrancabermeja 36 B2 Santander, N Colombia
Barranquilla 36 B1 Atlántico, N Colombia
Barreiro 70 B4 Setúbal, W Portugal
Barrier Range 127 C6 hill range New South Wales, SE Australia
Barrow 67 B6 Ir. An Bhearú. River SE Ireland
Barrow 14 D2 Alaska, USA
Barrow-in-Furness 67 C5 NW England, UK
Barrow Island 124 A4 island Western Australia
Barstow 25 C7 California, W USA
Bar-sur-Ornain see Bar-le-Duc
Bartang 101 F3 river SE Tajikistan
Bartica 37 F3 N Guyana
Bartın 94 C2 Bartın NW Turkey
Bartlesville 27 G1 Oklahoma, C USA
Bartoszyce 76 D2 Ger. Bartenstein. Warmińsko-Mazurskie, NE Poland
Baruun-Urt 105 F2 Sühbaatar, E Mongolia
Barú, Volcán 31 E5 var. Volcán de Chiriquí. Volcano W Panama
Barwon River 127 D5 river New South Wales, SE Australia
Barysaw 85 D6 Rus. Borisov. Minskaya Voblasts', NE Belarus
Basarabeasca 86 D4 Rus. Bessarabka. SE Moldova
Basel 73 A7 Eng. Basle, Fr. Bâle. Basel-Stadt, NW Switzerland
Basilan 117 E3 island SW Philippines
Basle see Basel
Basra see Al Baṣrah
Bassano del Grappa 74 C2 Veneto, NE Italy
Bassein 114 A4 var. Pathein. Irrawaddy, SW Myanmar
Basse-Terre 33 G4 dependent territory capital (Guadeloupe) Basse Terre, SW Guadeloupe
Basse Terre 33 G4 island W Guadeloupe
Basseterre 33 G3 country capital (Saint Kitts and Nevis) Saint Kitts, Saint Kitts and Nevis
Bassikounou 52 D3 Hodh ech Chargui, SE Mauritania
Bass Strait 127 C7 strait SE Australia
Bassum 72 B3 Niedersachsen, NW Germany
Bastia 69 E7 Corse, France, C Mediterranean Sea
Bastogne 65 D7 Luxembourg, SE Belgium
Bastrop 20 B2 Louisiana, S USA
Bastyn' 85 B7 Rus. Bostyn'. Brestskaya Voblasts', SW Belarus
Basuo see Dongfang
Bata 55 A5 NW Equatorial Guinea
Batabanó, Golfo de 32 A2 gulf W Cuba
Batajnica 78 D3 Serbia, N Serbia and Montenegro (Yugo.)
Batangas 117 E2 off. Batangas City. Luzon, N Philippines
Bătdâmbâng 115 C5 prev. Battambang. Bătdâmbâng, NW Cambodia
Batéké, Plateaux 55 B6 plateau S Congo
Bath 67 D7 hist. Akermanceaster, anc. Aquae Calidae, Aquae Solis. SW England, UK
Bathinda 112 D2 Punjab, NW India
Bathsheba 33 G1 E Barbados
Bathurst 17 F4 New Brunswick, SE Canada
Bathurst 127 D6 New South Wales, SE Australia
Bathurst Island 124 D2 island Northern Territory, N Australia
Bathurst Island 15 F2 island Parry Islands, Nunavut, N Canada
Bāṭin, Wādī al 136 C4 dry watercourse SW Asia
Batman 95 E4 var. Iluh. Batman, SE Turkey
Batna 49 E2 NE Algeria
Baton Rouge 20 B3 state capital Louisiana, S USA
Batroûn 96 A4 var. Al Batrūn. N Lebanon
Batticaloa 110 D3 Eastern Province, E Sri Lanka
Battipaglia 75 D5 Campania, S Italy
Bat'umi 95 F2 W Georgia
Batu Pahat 116 B3 prev. Bandar Penggaram. Johor, Peninsular Malaysia
Bauchi 53 G4 Bauchi, NE Nigeria
Bauer Basin 131 F3 undersea feature E Pacific Ocean
Bauska 84 C3 Ger. Bauske. Bauska, S Latvia
Bautzen 72 D4 Lus. Budyšin. Sachsen, E Germany
Bavarian Alps 73 C7 Ger. Bayrische Alpen. Mountain range Austria/Germany
Bavispe, Río 28 C2 river NW Mexico
Bawīṭi 50 B2 N Egypt
Bawku 53 E4 N Ghana
Bayamo 32 C3 Granma, E Cuba
Bayan Har Shan 104 D4 var. Bayan Khar. Mountain range C China
Bayanhongor 104 D2 Bayanhongor, C Mongolia
Bayan Khar see Bayan Har Shan
Bayano, Lago 31 G4 lake E Panama
Bay City 18 C3 Michigan, N USA
Bay City 27 G4 Texas, SW USA
Baydhabo 51 D6 var. Baydhowa, Isha Baydhabo, It. Baidoa. Bay, SW Somalia
Baydhowa see Baydhabo
Bayern 73 C6 cultural region SE Germany
Bayeux 68 B3 anc. Augustodurum. Calvados, N France
Bāyir 97 C7 var. Bā'ir. Ma'ān, S Jordan
Baykal, Ozero 93 E4 Eng. Lake Baikal. Lake S Russian Federation
Baymak 89 D6 Respublika Bashkortostan, W Russian Federation
Bayonne 69 A6 anc. Lapurdum. Pyrénées-Atlantiques, SW France
Bayramaly 100 D3 prev. Bayram-Ali. Maryyskiy Velayat, S Turkmenistan
Bayreuth 73 C5 var. Baireuth. Bayern, SE Germany
Bayrūt see Beyrouth
Baytown 27 H4 Texas, SW USA
Baza 71 E4 Andalucía, S Spain
Beagle Channel 43 C8 channel Argentina/Chile
Béal Feirste see Belfast
Beannchar see Bangor
Bear Lake 24 E4 lake Idaho/Utah, NW USA
Beas de Segura 71 E4 Andalucía, S Spain
Beata, Isla 33 E3 island SW Dominican Republic
Beatrice 23 F4 Nebraska, C USA
Beaufort Sea 14 D2 sea Arctic Ocean
Beaufort West 56 C5 Afr. Beaufort-Wes. Western Cape, SW South Africa
Beaumont 27 H3 Texas, SW USA
Beaune 68 D4 Côte d'Or, C France
Beauvais 68 C3 anc. Bellovacum, Caesaromagus. Oise, N France
Beaver Island 18 C2 island Michigan, N USA
Beaver Lake 27 H1 reservoir Arkansas, C USA
Beaver River 27 F1 river Oklahoma, C USA
Beāwar 112 C3 Rājasthān, N India
Bečej 78 D3 Ger. Altbetsche, Hung. Óbecse, Rácz-Becse; prev. Magyar-Becse, Stari Bečej. Serbia, N Serbia and Montenegro (Yugo.)
Béchar 48 D2 prev. Colomb-Béchar. W Algeria
Beckley 18 D5 West Virginia, NE USA
Bedford 67 D6 E England, UK
Bedum 64 E1 Groningen, NE Netherlands
Be'ér Menuḥa 97 B7 var Be'er Menukha. Southern, S Israel
Be'er Menukha see Be'ér Menuḥa
Beernem 65 A5 West-Vlaanderen, NW Belgium
Beersheba see Be'ér Sheva'
Be'ér Sheva' 97 A7 var. Beersheba, Ar. Bir es Saba. Southern, S Israel
Beesel 65 D5 Limburg, SE Netherlands
Beeville 27 G4 Texas, SW USA
Bega 127 D7 New South Wales, SE Australia
Beida see Al Bayḍā'
Beihai 106 B6 Guangxi Zhuangzu Zizhiqu, S China
Beijing 106 C3 var. Pei-ching, Eng. Peking; prev. Pei-p'ing. Country/municipality capital (China) Beijing Shi, E China
Beilen 64 E2 Drenthe, NE Netherlands
Beira 57 E3 Sofala, C Mozambique
Beirut see Beyrouth
Beit Leḥm see Bethlehem
Beiuș 86 B3 Hung. Belényes. Bihor, NW Romania
Beja 70 B4 anc. Pax Julia. Beja, SE Portugal
Béjar 70 C3 Castilla-León, N Spain
Bejraburi see Phetchaburi
Békéscsaba 77 D7 Rom. Bichiș-Ciaba. Békés, SE Hungary
Bekobod 101 E2 Rus. Bekabad; prev. Begovat. Toshkent Wiloyati, E Uzbekistan
Bela Crkva 78 E3 Ger. Weisskirchen, Hung. Fehértemplom. Serbia, W Serbia and Montenegro (Yugo.)
Belarus 85 B6 off. Republic of Belarus, var. Belorussia, Latv. Baltkrievija; prev. Belorussian SSR, Rus. Belorusskaya SSR. Country E Europe
Belau see Palau
Belchatow see Bełchatów
Bełchatów 76 C4 var. Belchatow. Łódzkie, C Poland
Belcher Islands 16 C2 Fr. Îles Belcher. Island group Northwest Territories, SE Canada
Beledweyne 51 D5 var. Belet Huen, It. Belet Uen. Hiiraan, C Somalia
Belém 41 F1 var. Pará. State capital Pará, N Brazil
Belen 26 D2 New Mexico, SW USA
Belén 30 D4 Rivas, SW Nicaragua
Belet Huen see Beledweyne
Belet Uen see Beledweyne
Belfast 67 B5 Ir. Béal Feirste. Admin capital E Northern Ireland, UK
Belfield 22 D2 North Dakota, N USA
Belfort 68 E4 Territoire-de-Belfort, E France
Belgaum 110 B1 Karnātaka, W India
Belgium 65 B6 off. Kingdom of Belgium, Dut. België, Fr. Belgique. Country NW Europe
Belgorod 89 A6 Belgorodskaya Oblast', W Russian Federation
Belgrade see Beograd
Belgrano II 132 B2 Argentinian research station Antarctica
Belice see Belize City
Beligrad see Berat
Beli Manastir 78 C3 Hung. Pélmonostor; prev. Monostor. Osijek-Baranja, NE Croatia
Bélinga 55 B5 Ogooué-Ivindo, NE Gabon
Belitung, Pulau 116 C4 island W Indonesia
Belize 30 B1 Sp. Belice; prev. British Honduras, Colony of Belize. Country Central America
Belize 30 B1 river Belize/Guatemala
Belize see Belize City
Belize City 30 C1 var. Belize, Sp. Belice. Belize, NE Belize
Belkofski 14 B3 Alaska, USA
Belle Île 68 A4 island NW France
Belle Isle, Strait of 17 G3 strait Newfoundland and Labrador, E Canada
Belleville 18 B4 Illinois, N USA
Bellevue 23 F4 Iowa, C USA
Bellevue 24 B2 Washington, NW USA
Bellingham 24 B1 Washington, NW USA
Belling Hausen Mulde see Southeast Pacific Basin
Bellingshausen Abyssal Plain see Bellingshausen Plain
Bellingshausen Plain 131 F5 var. Bellingshausen Abyssal Plain. Undersea feature SE Pacific Ocean
Bellingshausen Sea 132 A3 sea Antarctica
Bellinzona 73 B8 Ger. Bellenz. Ticino, S Switzerland
Bello 36 B2 Antioquia, W Colombia
Bellville 56 B5 Western Cape, SW South Africa
Belmopan 30 C1 country capital (Belize) Cayo, C Belize
Belogradchik 82 B1 Vidin, NW Bulgaria
Belo Horizonte 41 F4 prev. Bello Horizonte. State capital Minas Gerais, SE Brazil
Belomorsk 88 B3 Respublika Kareliya, NW Russian Federation
Beloretsk 89 D6 Respublika Bashkortostan, W Russian Federation
Belorussia/Belorussian SSR see Belarus
Belorusskaya SSR see Belarus
Beloye More 88 C3 Eng. White Sea. Sea NW Russian Federation
Belozersk 88 B4 Vologodskaya Oblast', NW Russian Federation
Belton 27 G3 Texas, SW USA
Beluchistan see Baluchistān
Belukha, Gora 92 D5 mountain Kazakhstan/Russian Federation
Belyy, Ostrov 92 D2 island N Russian Federation
Bemaraha 57 F3 var. Plateau du Bemaraha. Mountain range W Madagascar
Bemidji 23 F1 Minnesota, N USA

Botrange – Canoas

Botrange 65 D6 mountain E Belgium
Botswana 56 C3 off. Republic of Botswana. Country S Africa
Bouar 54 B4 Nana-Mambéré, W Central African Republic
Bou Craa 48 B3 var. Bu Craa. NW Western Sahara
Bougainville Island 120 B3 island NE PNG
Bougaroun, Cap 80 C3 headland NE Algeria
Bougouni 52 D4 Sikasso, SW Mali
Boujdour 48 A3 var. Bojador. W Western Sahara
Boulder 22 C4 Colorado, C USA
Boulder 22 B2 Montana, NW USA
Boulogne see Boulogne-sur-Mer
Boulogne-Billancourt 68 D1 prev. Boulogne-sur-Seine. Hauts-de-Seine, N France
Boulogne-sur-Mer 68 C2 var. Boulogne; anc. Bononia, Gesoriacum, Gessoriacum. Pas-de-Calais, N France
Boûmdeïd 52 C3 var. Boumdeït. Assaba, S Mauritania
Boumdeït see Boûmdeïd
Boundiali 52 D4 N Côte d'Ivoire
Bountiful 22 B4 Utah, W USA
Bounty Basin see Bounty Trough
Bounty Islands 120 D5 island group S NZ
Bounty Trough 130 C5 var. Bounty Basin. Undersea feature S Pacific Ocean
Bourbonnais 68 C4 Illinois, N USA
Bourg see Bourg-en-Bresse
Bourgas see Burgas
Bourge-en-Bresse see Bourg-en-Bresse
Bourg-en-Bresse 69 D5 var. Bourg, Bourge-en-Bresse. Ain, E France
Bourges 68 C4 anc. Avaricum. Cher, C France
Bourgogne 68 C4 Eng. Burgundy. Cultural region E France
Bourke 127 C5 New South Wales, SE Australia
Bournemouth 67 D7 S England, UK
Boutilimit 52 C3 Trarza, SW Mauritania
Bouvet Island 45 D7 Norwegian dependency S Atlantic Ocean
Bowen 126 D3 Queensland, NE Australia
Bowling Green 18 B5 Kentucky, S USA
Bowling Green 18 C3 Ohio, N USA
Boxmeer 64 D4 Noord-Brabant, SE Netherlands
Boyarka 87 E2 Kyyivs'ka Oblast', N Ukraine
Boysun 101 E3 Rus. Baysun. Surkhondaryo Wiloyati, S Uzbekistan
Bozeman 22 B2 Montana, NW USA
Bozüyük 94 B3 Bilecik, NW Turkey
Brač 78 B4 var. Brach, It. Brazza; anc. Brattia. Island S Croatia
Brach see Brač
Bradford 67 D5 N England, UK
Brady 27 F3 Texas, SW USA
Braga 70 B2 anc. Bracara Augusta. Braga, NW Portugal
Bragança 70 C2 Eng. Braganza; anc. Julio Briga. Bragança, NE Portugal
Brahmanbaria 113 G4 Chittagong, E Bangladesh
Brahmapur 113 F5 Orissa, E India
Brahmaputra 113 H3 var. Padma, Tsangpo, Ben. Jamuna, Chin. Yarlung Zangbo Jiang, Ind. Bramaputra, Dihang, Siang. River S Asia
Brăila 86 D4 Brăila, E Romania
Braine-le-Comte 65 B6 Hainaut, SW Belgium
Brainerd 23 F2 Minnesota, N USA
Brak see Birāk
Bramaputra see Brahmaputra
Brampton 16 D5 Ontario, S Canada
Branco, Rio 34 C3 river N Brazil
Brandberg 56 A3 mountain NW Namibia
Brandenburg 72 C3 var. Brandenburg an der Havel. Brandenburg, NE Germany
Brandenburg an der Havel see Brandenburg
Brandon 15 F5 Manitoba, S Canada
Braniewo 76 D2 Ger. Braunsberg. Warmińsko-Mazurskie, NE Poland
Brasília 41 F3 country capital (Brazil) Distrito Federal, C Brazil
Braşov 86 C4 Ger. Kronstadt, Hung. Brassó; prev. Oraşul Stalin. Braşov, C Romania
Bratislava 77 C6 Ger. Pressburg, Hung. Pozsony. Country capital (Slovakia) Bratislavský Kraj, SW Slovakia
Bratsk 93 E4 Irkutskaya Oblast', C Russian Federation
Brattia see Brač
Braunschweig 72 C4 Eng./Fr. Brunswick. Niedersachsen, N Germany
Brava, Costa 71 H2 coastal region NE Spain
Bravo del Norte, Río see Grande, Rio
Bravo del Norte, Río see Bravo, Río
Bravo del Norte, Río see Bravo, Río
Bravo del Norte, Río see Grande, Rio
Bravo, Río 28 C1 var. Río Bravo del Norte, Rio Grande. River Mexico/USA
Bravo, Río see Grande, Rio
Brawley 25 D8 California, W USA
Brazil 40 C2 off. Federative Republic of Brazil, Port. República Federativa do Brasil, Sp. Brasil; prev. United States of Brazil. Country South America
Brazil Basin 45 C5 var. Brazilian Basin, Brazil'skaya Kotlovina. Undersea feature W Atlantic Ocean
Brazilian Basin see Brazil Basin
Brazilian Highlands see Central, Planalto
Brazil'skaya Kotlovina see Brazil Basin
Brazos River 27 G3 river Texas, SW USA
Brazza see Brač
Brazzaville 55 B6 country capital (Congo) Capital District, S Congo
Brčko 78 C3 Republika Srpska, NE Bosnia and Herzegovina
Brecht 65 C5 Antwerpen, N Belgium
Brecon Beacons 67 C6 mountain range S Wales, UK
Breda 64 C4 Noord-Brabant, S Netherlands
Bree 65 D5 Limburg, NE Belgium
Bregalnica 79 E6 river E FYR Macedonia
Bregenze 35 B7 anc. Brigantium. Vorarlberg, W Austria
Bregovo 82 B1 Vidin, NW Bulgaria
Bremen 72 B3 Fr. Brême. Bremen, NW Germany
Bremerhaven 72 B3 Bremen, NW Germany
Bremerton 24 B2 Washington, NW USA
Brenham 27 G3 Texas, SW USA
Brenner Pass 74 C1 var. Brenner Sattel, Fr. Col du Brenner, Ger. Brennerpass, It. Passo del Brennero. Pass Austria/Italy
Brennerpass see Brenner Pass
Brenner Sattel see Brenner Pass
Brescia 74 B2 anc. Brixia. Lombardia, N Italy
Bressanone 74 C1 Ger. Brixen. Trentino-Alto Adige, N Italy
Brest 85 A6 Pol. Brześć nad Bugiem, Rus. Brest-Litovsk; prev. Brześć Litewski. Brestskaya Voblasts', SW Belarus
Brest 68 A3 Finistère, NW France
Bretagne 68 A3 Eng. Brittany; Lat. Britannia Minor. Cultural region NW France
Brewton 20 C3 Alabama, S USA
Brezovo 82 D2 prev. Abrashlare. Plovdiv, C Bulgaria
Bria 54 D4 Haute-Kotto, C Central African Republic
Briançon 69 D5 anc. Brigantio. Hautes-Alpes, SE France
Bridgeport 19 F3 Connecticut, NE USA
Bridgetown 33 G2 country capital (Barbados) SW Barbados
Bridlington 67 D5 E England, UK
Bridport 67 D7 S England, UK
Brig 73 A7 Fr. Brigue, It. Briga. Valais, SW Switzerland
Brigham City 22 B3 Utah, W USA
Brighton 22 D4 Colorado, C USA
Brighton 67 E7 SE England, UK
Brindisi 75 E5 anc. Brundisium, Brundusium. Puglia, SE Italy
Brisbane 127 E5 state capital Queensland, E Australia
Bristol 67 D7 anc. Bricgstow. SW England, UK
Bristol 19 F3 Connecticut, NE USA
Bristol 18 D5 Virginia, NE USA
Bristol Bay 14 B3 bay Alaska, USA
Bristol Channel 67 C7 inlet England/Wales, UK
Britain 58 C3 var. Great Britain. Island UK
British Columbia 14 D4 Fr. Colombie-Britannique. Province SW Canada
British Indian Ocean Territory 119 B5 UK dependent territory C Indian Ocean
British Isles 67 island group NW Europe
British Virgin Islands 33 F3 var. Virgin Islands. UK dependent territory E West Indies
Brive-la-Gaillarde 69 C5 prev. Brive, anc. Briva Curretia. Corrèze, C France
Brno 77 B5 Ger. Brünn. Brněnský Kraj, SE Czech Republic
Broćeni 84 B3 Saldus, SW Latvia
Brodeur Peninsula 15 F2 peninsula Baffin Island, Nunavut, NE Canada
Brodnica 76 C3 Ger. Buddenbrock. Kujawski-pomorskie, C Poland
Broek-in-Waterland 64 C3 Noord-Holland, C Netherlands
Broken Arrow 27 G1 Oklahoma, C USA
Broken Bay 126 E1 bay New South Wales, SE Australia
Broken Hill 127 B6 New South Wales, SE Australia
Broken Ridge 119 D6 undersea feature S Indian Ocean
Bromley 67 B8 SE England, UK
Brookhaven 20 B3 Mississippi, S USA
Brookings 23 F3 South Dakota, N USA
Brooks Range 14 D2 mountain range Alaska, USA
Brookton 125 B6 Western Australia
Broome 124 B3 Western Australia
Broomfield 22 D4 Colorado, C USA
Broucsella see Brussel
Brovary 87 E2 Kyyivs'ka Oblast', N Ukraine
Brownfield 27 E2 Texas, SW USA
Brownville 27 G5 Texas, SW USA
Brownwood 27 F3 Texas, SW USA
Brozha 85 D7 Mahilyowskaya Voblasts', E Belarus
Brugge 65 A5 Fr. Bruges. West-Vlaanderen, NW Belgium
Brummen 64 D3 Gelderland, E Netherlands
Brunei 116 D3 off. Sultanate of Brunei, Mal. Negara Brunei Darussalam. Country SE Asia
Brunner, Lake 129 C5 lake South Island, NZ
Brunswick 21 E3 Georgia, SE USA
Brusa see Bursa
Brus Laguna 30 D2 Gracias a Dios, E Honduras
Brussa see Bursa
Brussel var. Brussels, Fr. Bruxelles, Ger. Brüssel; anc. Broucsella. Country capital (Belgium) Brussels, C Belgium see also Bruxelles
Brüssel see Brussel
Brussels see Brussel
Bruxelles see Brussels
Bryan 27 G3 Texas, SW USA
Bryansk 89 A5 Bryanskaya Oblast', W Russian Federation
Brzeg 76 C4 Ger. Brieg; anc. Civitas Altae Ripae. Opolskie, S Poland
Bucaramanga 36 B2 Santander, N Colombia
Buchanan 52 C5 prev. Grand Bassa. SW Liberia
Buchanan, Lake 27 F3 reservoir Texas, SW USA
Bucharest see București
Bu Craa see Bou Craa
București 86 C5 Eng. Bucharest, Ger. Bukarest; prev. Altenburg, anc. Cetatea Damboviței. Country capital (Romania) București, S Romania
Buda-Kashalyova 85 D7 Rus. Buda-Koshelëvo. Homyel'skaya Voblasts', SE Belarus
Budapest 77 C6 off. Budapest Főváros, SCr. Budimpešta. Country capital (Hungary) Pest, N Hungary
Budaun 112 D3 Uttar Pradesh, N India
Buena Park 24 E2 California, W USA
Buenaventura 36 A3 Valle del Cauca, W Colombia
Buena Vista 71 H5 S Gibraltar
Buena Vista 39 G4 Santa Cruz, C Bolivia
Buenos Aires 42 D4 hist. Santa Maria del Buen Aire. Country capital (Argentina) Buenos Aires, E Argentina
Buenos Aires 31 E5 Puntarenas, SE Costa Rica
Buenos Aires, Lago 43 B6 var. Lago General Carrera. Lake Argentina/Chile
Buffalo 19 E3 New York, NE USA
Buffalo Narrows 15 F4 Saskatchewan, C Canada
Buff Bay 32 B5 E Jamaica
Buftea 86 C5 București, S Romania
Bug 59 E3 Bel. Zakhodni Buh, Eng. Western Bug, Rus. Zapadnyy Bug, Ukr. Zakhidnyy Buh. River E Europe
Buga 36 B3 Valle del Cauca, W Colombia
Bughotu see Santa Isabel
Buguruslan 89 D6 Orenburgskaya Oblast', W Russian Federation
Buḥayrat Nāṣir see Nasser, Lake
Buḥeiret Nâṣir see Nasser, Lake
Bujalance 70 D4 Andalucía, S Spain
Bujanovac 79 E5 Serbia, SE Serbia and Montenegro (Yugo.)
Bujnurd see Bojnūrd
Bujumbura 51 B7 prev. Usumbura. Country capital (Burundi) W Burundi
Bukavu 55 E6 prev. Costermansville. Sud Kivu, E Dem. Rep. Congo
Bukhara see Bukhoro
Bukhoro 100 D2 var. Bokhara, Rus. Bukhara. Bukhoro Wiloyati, C Uzbekistan
Bukoba 51 B6 Kagera, NW Tanzania
Bülach 73 B7 Zürich, NW Switzerland
Bulawayo 56 D3 var. Buluwayo. Matabeleland North, SW Zimbabwe
Buldur see Burdur
Bulgan 105 E2 Bulgan, N Mongolia
Bulgaria 82 C2 off. Republic of Bulgaria, Bul. Bŭlgariya; prev. People's Republic of Bulgaria. Country SE Europe
Bull Shoals Lake 20 B1 reservoir Arkansas/Missouri, C USA
Bulukumba 117 E4 prev. Boeloekoemba. Sulawesi, C Indonesia
Buluwayo see Bulawayo
Bumba 55 D5 Equateur, N Dem. Rep. Congo
Bunbury 125 A7 Western Australia
Bundaberg 126 E4 Queensland, E Australia
Bungo-suidō 109 B7 strait SW Japan
Bunia 55 E5 Orientale, NE Dem. Rep. Congo
Bünyan 94 D3 Kayseri, C Turkey
Buraida see Buraydah
Buraydah 98 B4 var. Buraida. Al Qaşīm, N Saudi Arabia
Burdur 94 B4 var. Buldur. Burdur, SW Turkey
Burdur Gölü 94 B4 salt lake SW Turkey
Burē 50 C4 C Ethiopia
Burgas 82 E2 var. Bourgas. Burgas, E Bulgaria
Burgaski Zaliv 82 E2 gulf E Bulgaria
Burgos 70 D2 Castilla-León, N Spain
Burhan Budai Shan 104 D4 mountain range C China
Buri Ram see Buriram
Buriram 115 D5 var. Buri Ram, Puriramya. Buri Ram, E Thailand
Burjassot 71 F3 País Valenciano, E Spain
Burkburnett 27 F2 Texas, SW USA
Burketown 126 B3 Queensland, NE Australia
Burkina see Burkina Faso
Burkina Faso 53 E4 off. Burkina Faso, var. Burkina; prev. Upper Volta. Country W Africa
Burley 24 D4 Idaho, NW USA
Burlington 23 G4 Iowa, C USA
Burlington 19 F2 Vermont, NE USA
Burma see Myanmar
Burnie 127 C8 Tasmania, SE Australia
Burns 24 C3 Oregon, NW USA
Burnside 15 F3 river Nunavut, NW Canada
Burnsville 23 F2 Minnesota, N USA
Burrel 79 D6 var. Burreli. Dibër, C Albania
Burreli see Burrel
Burriana 71 F3 País Valenciano, E Spain
Bursa 94 B3 var. Brussa; prev. Brusa, anc. Prusa. Bursa, NW Turkey
Burtnieks see Burtnieku Ezers
Burtnieku Ezers 84 C3 var. Burtnieks. Lake N Latvia
Burundi 51 B7 off. Republic of Burundi; prev. Kingdom of Burundi, Urundi. Country C Africa
Buru, Pulau 117 F4 prev. Boeroe. Island E Indonesia
Buşayrah 96 D3 Dayr az Zawr, E Syria
Büshehr see Bandar-e Büshehr
Bushire see Bandar-e Büshehr
Busselton 125 A7 Western Australia
Buta 55 D5 Orientale, N Dem. Rep. Congo
Butembo 55 E5 Nord Kivu, NE Dem. Rep. Congo
Butler 19 E4 Pennsylvania, NE USA
Buton, Pulau 117 E4 var. Pulau Butung; prev. Boetoeng. Island C Indonesia
Butte 22 B2 Montana, NW USA
Butterworth 116 B3 Pinang, Peninsular Malaysia
Button Islands 17 E1 island group Northwest Territories, NE Canada
Butuan 117 F2 off. Butuan City. Mindanao, S Philippines
Buulobarde 51 D5 var. Buulo Berde. Hiiraan, C Somalia Africa
Buulo Berde see Buulobarde
Buur Gaabo 51 D6 Jubbada Hoose, S Somalia
Buynaksk 89 B8 Respublika Dagestan, SW Russian Federation
Büyükağrı Dağı 95 F3 var. Aghri Dagh, Agri Dagi, Koh I Noh, Masis, Eng. Great Ararat, Mount Ararat. Mountain E Turkey
Büyükmenderes Nehri 94 A4 river SW Turkey
Buzău 86 C4 Buzău, SE Romania
Buzuluk 89 D6 Akmola, C Kazakhstan
Byahoml' 85 D5 Rus. Begoml'. Vitsyebskaya Voblasts', N Belarus
Byalynichy 85 D6 Rus. Belynichi. Mahilyowskaya Voblasts', E Belarus
Bydgoszcz 76 C3 Ger. Bromberg. Kujawskie-pomorskie, C Poland
Byelaruskaya Hrada 85 B6 Rus. Belorusskaya Gryada. Ridge N Belarus
Byerezino 85 D6 Rus. Berezina. River C Belarus
Byron Island see Nikunau
Bytom 77 C5 Ger. Beuthen. Śląskie, S Poland
Bytča 77 C5 Žilinský Kraj, N Slovakia
Bytów 76 C2 Ger. Bütow. Pomorskie, N Poland
Byuzmeyin 100 C3 Turkm. Büzmeyin; prev. Bezmein. Akhalskiy Velayat, C Turkmenistan
Byval'ki 85 D8 Homyel'skaya Voblasts', SE Belarus
Byzantium see İstanbul

C

Caála 56 B2 var. Kaala, Robert Williams, Port. Vila Robert Williams. Huambo, C Angola
Caazapá 42 D3 Caazapá, S Paraguay
Caballo Reservoir 26 C3 reservoir New Mexico, SW USA
Cabañaquinta 70 D1 Asturias, N Spain
Cabanatuan 117 E1 off. Cabanatuan City. Luzon, N Philippines
Cabimas 36 C1 Zulia, NW Venezuela
Cabinda 56 A1 var. Kabinda. Cabinda, NW Angola
Cabinda 56 A1 var. Kabinda. Admin. region province NW Angola
Cabora Bassa, Lake see Cahora Bassa, Albufeira de
Caborca 28 B1 Sonora, NW Mexico
Cabot Strait 17 G4 strait E Canada
Cabras, Ilha das 54 E2 island S Sao Tome and Principe
Cabrera 71 G3 anc. Capraria. Island Islas Baleares, Spain, W Mediterranean Sea
Cáceres 70 C3 Ar. Qazris. Extremadura, W Spain
Cachimbo, Serra do 41 E2 mountain range C Brazil
Caconda 56 B2 Huíla, C Angola
Čadca 77 C5 Hung. Csaca. Žilinský Kraj, N Slovakia
Cadillac 18 C2 Michigan, N USA
Cadiz 117 E2 off. Cadiz City. Negros, C Philippines
Cádiz 70 C5 anc. Gades, Gadier, Gadir, Gadire. Andalucía, SW Spain
Cádiz, Golfo de 70 B5 Eng. Gulf of Cadiz. Gulf Portugal/Spain
Cadiz, Gulf of see Cádiz, Golfo de
Caen 68 B3 Calvados, N France
Caene see Qena
Caenepolis see Qena
Caerdydd see Cardiff
Caer Gybi see Holyhead
Caesarea Mazaca see Kayseri
Cafayate 42 C2 Salta, N Argentina
Cagayan de Oro 117 E2 off. Cagayan de Oro City. Mindanao, S Philippines
Cagliari 75 A6 anc. Caralis. Sardegna, Italy, C Mediterranean Sea
Caguas 33 F3 E Puerto Rico
Cahora Bassa, Albufeira de 56 D2 var. Lake Cabora Bassa. Reservoir NW Mozambique
Cahors 69 C5 anc. Cadurcum. Lot, S France
Cahul 86 D4 Rus. Kagul. S Moldova
Caicos Passage 32 D2 strait Bahamas/Turks and Caicos Islands
Caiffa see Ḥefa
Cailungo 74 E1 N San Marino
Caiphas see Ḥefa
Cairns 126 D3 Queensland, NE Australia
Cairo 50 B2 Ar. Al Qāhirah, var. El Qâhira. Country capital (Egypt) N Egypt
Caisleán an Bharraigh see Castlebar
Cajamarca 38 B3 prev. Caxamarca. Cajamarca, NW Peru
Čakovec 78 B2 Ger. Csakathurn, Hung. Csáktornya; prev. Ger. Tschakathurn. Medimurje, N Croatia
Calabar 53 G5 Cross River, S Nigeria
Calabozo 36 D2 Guárico, C Venezuela
Calafat 86 B5 Dolj, SW Romania
Calafate see El Calafate
Calahorra 71 E2 La Rioja, N Spain
Calais 19 H2 Maine, NE USA
Calais 68 C2 Pas-de-Calais, N France
Calama 42 B2 Antofagasta, N Chile
Calamianes see Calamian Group
Calamian Group 107 C7 var. Calamianes. Island group W Philippines
Călăras see Călăraşi
Călăraşi 86 D3 var. Călăras, Rus. Kalarash. C Moldova
Călăraşi 86 C5 Călăraşi, SE Romania
Calatayud 71 E2 Aragón, NE Spain
Calbayog 117 E2 off. Calbayog City. Samar, C Philippines
Calcutta 113 G4 var. Kolkata West Bengal, NE India
Caldas da Rainha 70 B3 Leiria, W Portugal
Caldera 42 B3 Atacama, N Chile
Caldwell 24 C3 Idaho, NW USA
Caledonia 30 C1 Corozal, N Belize
Caleta see Catalan Bay
Caleta Olivia 43 B6 Santa Cruz, SE Argentina
Calgary 15 E5 Alberta, SW Canada
Cali 36 B3 Valle del Cauca, W Colombia
Calicut 110 C2 var. Kozhikode. Kerala, SW India
California 25 B7 off. State of California; also known as El Dorado, The Golden State. State W USA
California, Golfo de 28 B2 Eng. Gulf of California; prev. Sea of Cortez. Gulf W Mexico
California, Gulf of see California, Golfo de
Călimăneşti 86 B4 Vâlcea, SW Romania
Callabonna, Lake 127 B5 lake South Australia
Callao 38 C4 Callao, W Peru
Callosa de Segura 71 F4 País Valenciano, E Spain
Calmar see Kalmar
Caloundra 127 E5 Queensland, E Australia
Caltanissetta 75 C7 Sicilia, Italy, C Mediterranean Sea
Caluula 50 E4 Bari, NE Somalia
Camabatela 56 B1 Cuanza Norte, NW Angola
Camacupa 56 B2 var. General Machado, Port. Vila General Machado. Bié, C Angola
Camagüey 32 C2 prev. Puerto Príncipe. Camagüey, C Cuba
Camagüey, Archipiélago de 32 C2 island group C Cuba
Camaná 39 E4 Arequipa, SW Peru
Camargue 69 D6 physical region SE France
Ca Mau 115 D6 prev. Quan Long. Minh Hai, S Vietnam
Cambodia 115 D5 off. Kingdom of Cambodia, var. Democratic Kampuchea, Roat Kampuchea, Cam. Kampuchea; prev. People's Democratic Republic of Kampuchea. Country SE Asia
Cambrai 68 C2 Flem. Kambryk; prev. Cambray, anc. Cameracum. Nord, N France
Cambrian Mountains 67 C6 mountain range C Wales, UK
Cambridge 67 E6 Lat. Cantabrigia. E England, UK
Cambridge 19 F4 Maryland, NE USA
Cambridge 18 D4 Ohio, NE USA
Cambridge 32 A4 W Jamaica
Cambridge 128 D3 Waikato, North Island, NZ
Cambridge Bay 15 F3 district capital Victoria Island, Nunavut, NW Canada
Camden 20 B2 Arkansas, C USA
Cameroon 54 A4 off. Republic of Cameroon, Fr. Cameroun. Country W Africa
Camocim 41 F2 Ceará, E Brazil
Camopi 37 H3 E French Guiana
Campamento 30 C2 Olancho, C Honduras
Campania 75 D5 cultural region SE Italy
Campbell, Cape 129 D5 headland South Island, NZ
Campbell Island 120 D5 island S NZ
Campbell Plateau 120 D5 undersea feature SW Pacific Ocean
Campbell River 14 D5 Vancouver Island, British Columbia, SW Canada
Campeche 29 G4 Campeche, SE Mexico
Campeche, Bahía de 29 F4 Eng. Bay of Campeche. Bay E Mexico
Câm Pha 114 E3 Quang Ninh, N Vietnam
Câmpina 86 C4 prev. Cîmpina. Prahova, SE Romania
Campina Grande 41 G2 Paraíba, E Brazil
Campinas 41 F4 São Paulo, S Brazil
Campobasso 75 D5 Molise, C Italy
Campo Criptana see Campo de Criptana
Campo de Criptana 71 E3 var. Campo Criptana. Castilla-La Mancha, C Spain
Campo dos Goitacazes see Campos
Campo Grande 41 E4 state capital Mato Grosso do Sul, SW Brazil
Campos 41 F4 var. Campo dos Goitacazes. Rio de Janeiro, SE Brazil
Câmpulung 86 B4 prev. Câmpulung-Muşcel, Cîmpulung. Argeş, S Romania
Campus Stellae see Santiago
Cam Ranh 115 E6 Khanh Hoa, S Vietnam
Canada 12 B4 country N North America
Canada Basin 12 C2 undersea feature Arctic Ocean
Canadian River 27 E2 river SW USA
Çanakkale 94 A3 var. Dardanelli; prev. Chanak, Kale Sultanie. Çanakkale, W Turkey
Çanakkale Boğazı 94 A2 Eng. Dardanelles. Strait NW Turkey
Cananea 28 B1 Sonora, NW Mexico
Canarias, Islas 48 A2 Eng. Canary Islands. Island group Spain, NE Atlantic Ocean
Canarreos, Archipiélago de los 32 B2 island group W Cuba
Canary Islands see Canarias, Islas
Cañas 30 D4 Guanacaste, NW Costa Rica
Canaveral, Cape 21 E4 headland Florida, SE USA
Canavieiras 41 G3 Bahia, E Brazil
Canberra 120 C4 country capital (Australia) Australian Capital Territory, SE Australia
Cancún 29 H3 Quintana Roo, SE Mexico
Candia see Irákleio
Canea see Chaniá
Cangzhou 106 D4 Hebei, E China
Caniapiscau 17 E2 river Quebec, E Canada
Caniapiscau, Réservoir de 16 D3 reservoir Quebec, C Canada
Canik Dağları 94 D2 mountain range N Turkey
Canillo 69 A7 C Andorra
Çankırı 94 C3 var. Chankiri; anc. Gangra, Germanicopolis. Çankın, N Turkey
Cannanore 110 B2 var. Kananur, Kannur. Kerala, SW India
Cannes 69 D6 Alpes-Maritimes, SE France
Canoas 41 E5 Rio Grande do Sul, S Brazil

D

Fontainebleau – Gljøvik

Fontainebleau *68 C3* Seine-et-Marne, N France
Fontenay-le-Comte *68 B4* Vendée, NW France
Fontvieille *69 B8* SW Monaco
Fonyód *77 C7* Somogy, W Hungary
Foochow *see* Fuzhou
Forchheim *73 C5* Bayern, SE Germany
Forel, Mont *60 D4 mountain* SE Greenland
Forfar *66 C3* E Scotland, UK
Forge du Sud *see* Dudelange
Forlì *74 C3 anc.* Forum Livii. Emilia-Romagna, N Italy
Formentera *71 G4 anc.* Ophiusa, *Lat.* Frumentum. *Island* Islas Baleares, Spain, W Mediterranean Sea
Formosa *42 D2* Formosa, NE Argentina
Formosa, Serra *41 E3 mountain range* C Brazil
Formosa Strait *see* Taiwan Strait
Forrest City *20 B1* Arkansas, C USA
Fort Albany *16 C3* Ontario, C Canada
Fortaleza *41 G2 prev.* Ceará. *State capital* Ceará, NE Brazil
Fortaleza *39 F2* Pando, N Bolivia
Fort-Bayard *see* Zhanjiang
Fort-Cappolani *see* Tidjikja
Fort Collins *22 D4* Colorado, C USA
Fort Davis *27 E3* Texas, SW USA
Fort-de-France *33 H4 prev.* Fort-Royal. *Dependent territory capital* (Martinique) W Martinique
Fort Dodge *23 F3* Iowa, C USA
Fortescue River *124 A4 river* Western Australia
Fort Frances *16 B4* Ontario, S Canada
Fort Good Hope *15 E3 var.* Good Hope. Northwest Territories, NW Canada
Fort Gouraud *see* Fdérik
Forth *66 C4 river* C Scotland, UK
Forth, Firth of *66 C4 estuary* E Scotland, UK
Fort-Lamy *see* Ndjamena
Fort Lauderdale *21 F5* Florida, SE USA
Fort Liard *15 E4 var.* Liard. Northwest Territories, W Canada
Fort Madison *23 G4* Iowa, C USA
Fort McMurray *15 E4* Alberta, C Canada
Fort McPherson *14 D3 var.* McPherson. Northwest Territories, NW Canada
Fort Morgan *22 D4* Colorado, C USA
Fort Myers *21 E5* Florida, SE USA
Fort Nelson *15 E4* British Columbia, W Canada
Fort Peck Lake *22 C1 reservoir* Montana, NW USA
Fort Pierce *21 F4* Florida, SE USA
Fort Providence *15 E4 var.* Providence. Northwest Territories, W Canada
Fort St.John *15 E4* British Columbia, W Canada
Fort Scott *23 F5* Kansas, C USA
Fort Severn *16 C2* Ontario, C Canada
Fort-Shevchenko *92 A4* Mangistau, W Kazakhstan
Fort Simpson *15 E4 var.* Simpson. Northwest Territories, W Canada
Fort Smith *15 E4 district capital* Northwest Territories, W Canada
Fort Smith *20 B1* Arkansas, C USA
Fort Stockton *27 E3* Texas, SW USA
Fort-Trinquet *see* Bîr Mogreïn
Fort Vermilion *15 E4* Alberta, W Canada
Fort Walton Beach *20 C3* Florida, SE USA
Fort Wayne *18 C4* Indiana, N USA
Fort William *66 C3* N Scotland, UK
Fort Worth *27 G2* Texas, SW USA
Fort Yukon *14 D3* Alaska, USA
Fougamou *55 A6* Ngounié, C Gabon
Fougères *68 B3* Ille-et-Vilaine, NW France
Fou-hsin *see* Fuxin
Foulwind, Cape *129 B5 headland* South Island, NZ
Foumban *54 A4* Ouest, NW Cameroon
Fou-shan *see* Fushun
Foveaux Strait *129 A8 strait* S NZ
Foxe Basin *15 G3 sea* Nunavut, N Canada
Fox Glacier *129 B6* West Coast, South Island, NZ
Fox Mine *15 F4* Manitoba, C Canada
Fraga *71 F2* Aragón, NE Spain
Fram Basin *133 C3 var.* Amundsen Basin. *Undersea feature* Arctic Ocean
France *68 B4 off.* French Republic, *It./Sp.* Francia; *prev.* Gaul, Gaule, *Lat.* Gallia. *Country* W Europe
Franceville *55 B6 var.* Massoukou, Masuku. Haut-Ogooué, E Gabon
Francfort prev *see* Frankfurt am Main
Franche-Comté *68 D4 cultural region* E France
Francis Case, Lake *23 E3 reservoir* South Dakota, N USA
Francisco Escárcega *29 G4* Campeche, SE Mexico
Francistown *56 D3* North East, NE Botswana
Franconian Jura *see* Fränkische Alb
Frankenalb *see* Fränkische Alb
Frankenstein *see* Ząbkowice Śląskie
Frankenstein in Schlesien *see* Ząbkowice Śląskie
Frankfort *18 C5 state capital* Kentucky, S USA
Frankfort on the Main *see* Frankfurt am Main
Frankfurt *see* Frankfurt am Main
Frankfurt am Main *73 B5 var.* Frankfurt, *Fr.* Francfort; prev. *Eng.* Frankfort on the Main. Hessen, SW Germany
Frankfurt an der Oder *72 D3* Brandenburg, E Germany
Fränkische Alb *73 C6 var.* Frankenalb, *Eng.* Franconian Jura. *Mountain range* S Germany
Franklin *20 C1* Tennessee, S USA
Franklin D.Roosevelt Lake *24 C1 reservoir* Washington, NW USA
Frantsa-Iosifa, Zemlya *92 D1 Eng.* Franz Josef Land. *Island group* N Russian Federation
Franz Josef Land *see* Frantsa-Iosifa, Zemlya
Fraserburgh *66 D3* NE Scotland, UK
Fraser Island *126 E4 var.* Great Sandy Island. *Island* Queensland, E Australia
Fredericksburg *19 E5* Virginia, NE USA
Fredericton *17 F4* New Brunswick, SE Canada
Frederikshåb *see* Paamiut
Fredrikstad *63 B6* Østfold, S Norway
Freeport *32 C1* Grand Bahama Island, N Bahamas
Freeport *27 H4* Texas, SW USA
Freetown *52 C4 country capital* (Sierra Leone) W Sierra Leone
Freiburg *see* Freiburg im Breisgau
Freiburg im Breisgau *73 A6 var.* Freiburg, *Fr.* Fribourg-en-Brisgau. Baden-Württemberg, SW Germany
Fremantle *125 A6* Western Australia
Fremont *23 F4* Nebraska, C USA
French Guiana *37 H3 var.* Guiana, Guyane. *French overseas department* N South America
French Polynesia *121 F4 French overseas territory* C Polynesia
French Southern and Antarctic Territories *119 B7 Fr.* Terres Australes et Antarctiques Françaises. *French overseas territory* S Indian Ocean
Fresnillo *28 D3 var.* Fresnillo de González Echeverría. Zacatecas, C Mexico
Fresnillo de González Echeverría *see* Fresnillo
Fresno *25 C6* California, W USA
Frías *42 C3* Catamarca, N Argentina
Fribourg-en-Brisgau *see* Freiburg im Breisgau
Friedrichshafen *73 B7* Baden-Württemberg, S Germany
Frobisher Bay *60 B3 inlet* Baffin Island, Northwest Territories, NE Canada
Frohavet *62 B4 sound* C Norway
Frome, Lake *127 B6 salt lake* South Australia
Frontera *29 G4* Tabasco, SE Mexico
Frontignan *69 C6* Hérault, S France
Frostviken *see* Kvarnbergsvattnet
Frøya *62 A4 island* W Norway
Frunze *see* Bishkek
Frýdek-Místek *77 C5 Ger.* Friedek-Mistek. Ostravský Kraj, E Czech Republic
Fu-chien *see* Fujian
Fu-chou *see* Fuzhou
Fuengirola *70 D5* Andalucía, S Spain
Fuerte Olimpo *42 D2 var.* Olimpo. Alto Paraguay, NE Paraguay
Fuerte, Río *26 C5 river* C Mexico
Fuerteventura *48 B3 island* Islas Canarias, Spain, NE Atlantic Ocean
Fuhkien *see* Fujian
Fu-hsin *see* Fuxin
Fuji *109 D6 var.* Huzi. Shizuoka, Honshū, S Japan
Fujian *106 D6 var.* Fu-chien, Fuhkien, Fujian Sheng, Fukien, Min. Admin. region *province* SE China
Fujian Sheng *see* Fujian
Fuji-san *109 C6 var.* Fujiyama, *Eng.* Mount Fuji. *Mountain* Honshū, SE Japan
Fujiyama *see* Fuji-san
Fukang *104 C2* Xinjiang Uygur Zizhiqu, W China
Fukien *see* Fujian
Fukui *109 C6 var.* Hukui. Fukui, Honshū, SW Japan
Fukuoka *109 A7 var.* Hukuoka; *hist.* Najima. Fukuoka, Kyūshū, SW Japan
Fukushima *108 D4 var.* Hukusima. Fukushima, Honshū, C Japan
Fulda *73 B5* Hessen, C Germany
Funafuti *see* Fongafale
Funafuti Atoll *123 E3 atoll* C Tuvalu
Funchal *48 A2* Madeira, Portugal, NE Atlantic Ocean
Fundy, Bay of *17 F5 bay* Canada/USA
Furnes *see* Veurne
Fürth *73 C5* Bayern, S Germany
Furukawa *108 D4 var.* Hurukawa. Miyagi, Honshū, C Japan
Fushun *106 D3 var.* Fou-shan, Fu-shun. Liaoning, NE China
Fu-shun *see* Fushun
Fusin *see* Fuxin
Füssen *73 C7* Bayern, S Germany
Futog *78 D3* Serbia, NW Serbia and Montenegro (Yugo.)
Futuna, Île *123 E4 island* S Wallis and Futuna
Fuxin *106 D3 var.* Fou-hsin, Fu-hsin, Fusin. Liaoning, NE China
Fuzhou *106 D6 var.* Foochow, Fu-chou. Fujian, SE China
Fuzhou *see* Linchuan
Fyn *63 B8 Ger.* Fünen. *Island* C Denmark
Fyzabad *see* Feyzābād

G

Gaafu Alifu Atoll *see* North Huvadhu Atoll
Gaafu Dhaalu Atoll *see* South Huvadhu Atoll
Gaalkacyo *51 E5 var.* Galka'yo, *It.* Galcaio. Mudug, C Somalia
Gabela *56 B2* Cuanza Sul, W Angola
Gabès *49 E2 var.* Qābis. E Tunisia
Gabès, Golfe de *49 F2 Ar.* Khalīj Qābis. *Gulf* E Tunisia
Gabon *55 B6 off.* Gabonese Republic. *Country* C Africa
Gaborone *56 C4 prev.* Gaberones. *Country capital* (Botswana) South East, SE Botswana
Gabrovo *82 D2* Gabrovo, N Bulgaria
Gadag *110 C1* Karnātaka, W India
Gadsden *20 D2* Alabama, S USA
Gaeta *75 C5* Lazio, C Italy
Gaeta, Golfo di *75 C5 var.* Gulf of Gaeta. *Gulf* C Italy
Gaeta, Gulf of *see* Gaeta, Golfo di
Gäfle *see* Gävle
Gafsa *49 E2 var.* Qafşah. W Tunisia
Gagnoa *52 D5* C Côte d'Ivoire
Gagra *95 E1* NW Georgia
Gaillac *69 C6 var.* Gaillac-sur-Tarn. Tarn, S France
Gaillac-sur-Tarn *see* Gaillac
Gaillimh *see* Galway
Gainesville *21 E3* Florida, SE USA
Gainesville *20 D2* Georgia, SE USA
Gainesville *27 G2* Texas, SW USA
Gairdner, Lake *127 A6 salt lake* South Australia
Gaiziņ *see* Gaizina Kalns
Gaizina Kalns *84 C3 var.* Gaiziņ. *Mountain* E Latvia
Galán, Cerro *42 B3 mountain* NW Argentina
Galanta *77 C6 Hung.* Galánta. Trnavský Kraj, W Slovakia
Galapagos Fracture Zone *131 E3 tectonic feature* E Pacific Ocean
Galapagos Islands *131 F3 var.* Islas de los Galápagos,*Tortoise Islands. Island group* Ecuador, E Pacific Ocean
Galapagos Rise *131 F3 undersea feature* E Pacific Ocean
Galashiels *66 C4* SE Scotland, UK
Galați *86 D4 Ger.* Galatz. Galați, E Romania
Galcaio *see* Gaalkacyo
Galesburg *18 B3* Illinois, N USA
Galicia *70 B1 cultural region* NW Spain
Galicia Bank *58 B4 undersea feature* E Atlantic Ocean
Galilee, Sea of *see* Tiberias, Lake
Galka'yo *see* Gaalkacyo
Galle *110 D4 prev.* Point de Galle. Southern Province, SW Sri Lanka
Gallego Rise *131 F3 undersea feature* E Pacific Ocean
Gallegos *see* Río Gallegos
Gallipoli *75 E6* Puglia, SE Italy
Gällivare *62 C3* Norrbotten, N Sweden
Gallup *26 C1* New Mexico, SW USA
Galtat-Zemmour *48 B3* C Western Sahara
Galveston *27 H4* Texas, SW USA
Galway *67 A5 Ir.* Gaillimh. W Ireland
Galway Bay *67 A6 Ir.* Cuan na Gaillimhe. *Bay* W Ireland
Gambell *14 C2* Saint Lawrence Island, Alaska, USA
Gambia *52 C3 Fr.* Gambie. *River* W Africa
Gambia *52 B3 off.* Republic of The Gambia, The Gambia. *Country* W Africa
Gambier, Îles *121 G4 island group* E French Polynesia
Gamboma *55 B6* Plateaux, E Congo
Gan *see* Gansu
Gan *see* Jiangxi
Gan *110 B5* Addu Atoll, C Maldives
Gäncä *95 G2 Rus.* Gyandzha; *prev.* Kirovabad, Yelisavetpol. W Azerbaijan
Gandajika *55 D7* Kasai Oriental, S Dem. Rep. Congo
Gander *17 G3* Newfoundland, Newfoundland and Labrador, SE Canada
Gāndhīdhām *112 C4* Gujarāt, W India
Gandía *71 F3* País Valenciano, E Spain
Ganges *113 F3 Ben.* Padma. *River* Bangladesh/India *see also* Padma
Ganges Cone *see* Ganges Fan
Ganges Fan *118 D3 var.* Ganges Cone. *Undersea feature* N Bay of Bengal
Ganges, Mouths of the *113 G4 delta* Bangladesh/India
Gangra *see* Çankiri
Gangtok *113 F3* Sikkim, N India
Gansu *106 B4 var.* Gan, Gansu Sheng, Kansu. Admin. region *province* N China
Gansu Sheng *see* Gansu
Ganzhou *106 D6* Jiangxi, S China
Gao *53 E3* Gao, E Mali
Gaoual *52 C4* Moyenne-Guinée, N Guinea
Gaoxiong *see* Kaohsiung
Gap *69 D5 anc.* Vapincum. Hautes-Alpes, SE France
Gar *104 A4 var.* Gar Xincun. Xizang Zizhiqu, W China
Garachiné *31 G5* Darién, SE Panama
Garagum *see* Garagumy
Garagum Kanaly *see* Garagumskiy Kanal
Garagumskiy Kanal *100 D3 var.* Kara Kum Canal, Karakumskiy Kanal, *Turkm.* Garagum Kanaly. *Canal* C Turkmenistan
Garagumy *100 C3 var.* Qara Qum, *Eng.* Black Sand Desert, Kara Kum, *Turkm.* Garagum; *prev.* Peski Karakumy. *Desert* C Turkmenistan
Gara Khitrino *82 D2* Shumen, NE Bulgaria
Garda, Lago di *C2 var.* Benaco, *Eng.* Lake Garda, *Ger.* Gardasee. *Lake* NE Italy
Garda, Lake *see* Garda, Lago di
Gardasee *see* Garda, Lago di
Garden City *23 E5* Kansas, C USA
Gardeyz *see* Gardēz
Gardēz *101 E4 var.* Gardeyz, Gordiaz. Paktīā, E Afghanistan
Gargždai *84 B3* Gargždai, W Lithuania
Garissa *51 D6* Coast, E Kenya
Garland *27 G2* Texas, SW USA
Garman, Loch *see* Wexford
Garoe *see* Garoowe
Garonne *69 B5 anc.* Garumna. *River* S France
Garoowe *51 E5 var.* Garoe. Nugaal, N Somalia
Garoua *54 B4 var.* Garua. Nord, N Cameroon
Garrygala *see* Kara-Kala
Garry Lake *15 F3 lake* Nunavut, N Canada
Garsen *51 D6* Coast, S Kenya
Garua *see* Garoua
Garwolin *76 D4* Mazowieckie, C Poland
Gar Xincun *see* Gar
Gary *18 B3* Indiana, N USA
Garzón *36 B4* Huila, S Colombia
Gascogne *69 B6 Eng.* Gascony. *Cultural region* S France
Gascoyne River *125 A5 river* Western Australia
Gaspé *17 F3* Quebec, SE Canada
Gaspé, Péninsule de *17 E4 var.* Péninsule de la Gaspésie. *Peninsula* Quebec, SE Canada
Gastonia *21 E1* North Carolina, SE USA
Gastoúni *83 B6* Dytikí Ellás, S Greece
Gatchina *88 B4* Leningradskaya Oblast', NW Russian Federation
Gatineau *16 D4* Quebec, SE Canada
Gatún, Lago *31 F4 reservoir* C Panama
Gauja *84 D3 Ger.* Aa. *River* Estonia/Latvia
Gauteng *see* Johannesburg
Gāvbandī *98 D4* Hormozgān, S Iran
Gávdos *83 C8 island* SE Greece
Gavere *65 B6* Oost-Vlaanderen, NW Belgium
Gävle *63 C6 var.* Gäfle; *prev.* Gefle. Gävleborg, C Sweden
Gawler *127 B6* South Australia
Gaya *113 F3* Bihār, N India
Gayndah *127 E5* Queensland, E Australia
Gaza *97 A6 Ar.* Ghazzah, *Heb.* 'Azza. NE Gaza Strip
Gaz-Achak *100 D2 Turkm.* Gazojak. Lebapskiy Velayat, NE Turkmenistan
Gazandzhyk *100 B2 Turkm.* Gazanjyk; *prev.* Kazandzhik. Balkanskiy Velayat, W Turkmenistan
Gaza Strip *97 A7 Ar.* Qiṭā' Ghazzah. *Disputed region* SW Asia
Gazi Antep *see* Gaziantep
Gaziantep *94 D4 var.* Gazi Antep; *prev.* Aintab, Antep. Gaziantep, S Turkey
Gazimağusa *see* Ammóchostos
Gazimağusa Körfezi *see* Kólpos Ammóchostos
Gazli *100 D2* Bukhoro Wiloyati, C Uzbekistan
Gbanga *52 D5 var.* Gbarnga. N Liberia
Gbarnga *see* Gbanga
Gdańsk *76 C2 Fr.* Dantzig, *Ger.* Danzig. Pomorskie, N Poland
Gdan'skaya Bukhta *see* Danzig, Gulf of
Pomorskie, Gulf of *see* Danzig, Gulf of
Gdynia *76 C2 Ger.* Gdingen. Pomorskie, N Poland
Gedaref *50 C4 var.* Al Qaḍārif, El Gedaref. Gedaref, E Sudan
Gediz *94 B3* Kütahya, W Turkey
Gediz Nehri *94 A3 river* W Turkey
Geel *65 C5 var.* Gheel. Antwerpen, N Belgium
Geelong *127 C7* Victoria, SE Australia
Ge'e'mu *see* Golmud
Gefle *see* Gävle
Geilo *63 A5* Buskerud, S Norway
Gejiu *106 B6 var.* Kochiu. Yunnan, S China
Gëkdepe *see* Geok-Tepe
Gela *75 C7 prev.* Terranova di Sicilia. Sicilia, Italy, C Mediterranean Sea
Geldermalsen *64 C4* Gelderland, C Netherlands
Geleen *65 D6* Limburg, SE Netherlands
Gelinsoor *see* Gellinsoor
Gellinsoor *51 E5 var.* Gelinsoor. Mudug, NE Somalia
Gembloux *65 C6* Namur, Belgium
Gemena *55 C5* Equateur, NW Dem. Rep. Congo
Gemona del Friuli *74 D2* Friuli-Venezia Giulia, NE Italy
Genck *see* Genk
General Alvear *42 B4* Mendoza, W Argentina
General Eugenio A.Garay *42 C1* Guairá, S Paraguay
General Machado *see* Camacupa
General Santos *117 F3 off.* General Santos City. Mindanao, S Philippines
Geneva *see* Genève
Geneva, Lake *A7 Fr.* Lac de Genève, Lac Léman, le Léman, *Ger.* Genfer See. *Lake* France/Switzerland
Genève *73 A7 Eng.* Geneva, *Ger.* Genf, *It.* Ginevra. Genève, SW Switzerland
Genf *see* Genève
Genk *65 D6 var.* Genck. Limburg, NE Belgium
Gennep *64 D4* Limburg, SE Netherlands
Genoa *see* Genova
Genova *80 D1 Eng.* Genoa, *Fr.* Gênes; *anc.* Genua. Liguria, NW Italy
Genova, Golfo di *74 A3 Eng.* Gulf of Genoa. *Gulf* NW Italy
Genovesa, Isla *38 B5 var.* Tower Island. *Island* Galapagos Islands, Ecuador, E Pacific Ocean
Gent *65 B5 Eng.* Ghent, *Fr.* Gand. Oost-Vlaanderen, NW Belgium
Geok-Tepe *100 C3 var.* Gëkdepe, *Turkm.* Gökdepe. Akhalskiy Velayat, C Turkmenistan
George *60 A4 river* Newfoundland and Labrador/Quebec, E Canada
George *56 C5* Western Cape, S South Africa
George, Lake *21 E3 lake* Florida, SE USA
Georges Bank *13 D5 undersea feature* W Atlantic Ocean
George Sound *129 A7 sound* South Island, NZ
Georges River *126 D2 river* New South Wales, SE Australia
George Town *32 B3 var.* Georgetown. *Dependent territory capital* (Cayman Islands) Grand Cayman, SW Cayman Islands
George Town *116 B3 var.* Penang, Pinang. Pinang, Peninsular Malaysia
George Town *32 C2* Great Exuma Island, C Bahamas
Georgetown *37 F2 country capital* (Guyana) N Guyana
Georgetown *21 F2* South Carolina, SE USA
George V Land *132 C4 physical region* Antarctica
Georgia *95 F2 off.* Republic of Georgia, *Geor.* Sak'art'velo, *Rus.* Gruzinskaya SSR, Gruziya; *prev.* Georgian SSR. *Country* SW Asia
Georgia *20 D2 off.* State of Georgia; also known as Empire State of the South, Peach State. *State* SE USA
Georgian Bay *18 D2 lake bay* Ontario, S Canada
Georgia, Strait of *24 A1 strait* British Columbia, W Canada
Georg von Neumayer *132 A2 German research station* Antarctica
Gera *72 C4* Thüringen, E Germany
Geráki *83 B6* Pelopónnisos, S Greece
Geraldine *129 B6* Canterbury, South Island, NZ
Geraldton *125 A6* Western Australia
Geral, Serra *35 D5 mountain range* S Brazil
Gerede *94 C2* Bolu, N Turkey
Gereshk *100 D5* Helmand, SW Afghanistan
Gering *22 D3* Nebraska, C USA
Germanicopolis *see* Çankiri
Germany *72 B4 off.* Federal Republic of Germany, *Ger.* Bundesrepublik Deutschland, Deutschland. *Country* N Europe
Geroliménas *83 B7* Pelopónnisos, S Greece
Gerona *see* Girona
Gerpinnes *65 C7* Hainaut, S Belgium
Gerunda *see* Girona
Gerze *94 D2* Sinop, N Turkey
Gesoriacum *see* Boulogne-sur-Mer
Gessoriacum *see* Boulogne-sur-Mer
Getafe *70 D3* Madrid, C Spain
Gevaş *95 F3* Van, SE Turkey
Gevgeli *see* Gevgelija
Gevgelija *79 E6 var.* Đevđelija, Djevdjelija, *Turk.* Gevgeli. SE FYR Macedonia
Ghaba *see* Al Ghābah
Ghana *53 E5 off.* Republic of Ghana. *Country* W Africa
Ghanzi *56 C3 var.* Khanzi. Ghanzi, W Botswana
Gharandal *97 B7* Ma'ān, SW Jordan
Ghardaïa *48 D2* N Algeria
Gharvān *see* Gharyān
Gharyān *49 F2 var.* Gharvān. NW Libya
Ghaznī *101 E4 var.* Ghazni. Ghaznī, E Afghanistan
Ghazni *see* Ghaznī
Gheel *see* Geel
Gheorgheni *86 C4 prev.* Gheorghieni, Sînt-Miclăuş, *Ger.* Niklasmarkt, *Hung.* Gyergyószentmiklós. Harghita, C Romania
Ghijduwon *100 D2 Rus.* Gizhduvan. Bukhoro Wiloyati, C Uzbekistan
Ghŭdara *101 F3 var.* Gudara, *Rus.* Kudara. SE Tajikistan
Ghurdaqah *see* Hurghada
Ghūrīān *100 D4* Herāt, W Afghanistan
Giannitsá *82 B4 var.* Yiannitsá. Kentrikí Makedonía, N Greece
Gibraltar *71 G4 UK dependent territory* SW Europe
Gibraltar, Bay of *71 G5 bay* Gibraltar/Spain
Gibraltar, Strait of *70 C5 Fr.* Détroit de Gibraltar, *Sp.* Estrecho de Gibraltar. *Strait* Atlantic Ocean/Mediterranean Sea
Gibson Desert *125 B5 desert* Western Australia
Giedraičiai *85 C5* Molėtai, E Lithuania
Giessen *73 B5* Hessen, W Germany
Gifu *109 C6 var.* Gihu. Gifu, Honshū, SW Japan
Giganta, Sierra de la *28 B3 mountain range* W Mexico
Gihu *see* Gifu
Gijón *70 D1 var.* Xixón. Asturias, NW Spain
Gilani *see* Gnjilane
Gila River *26 A2 river* Arizona, SW USA
Gilbert River *126 C3 river* Queensland, NE Australia
Gilf Kebir Plateau *50 A2 Ar.* Haḍabat al Jilf al Kabīr. *Plateau* SW Egypt
Gillette *22 D3* Wyoming, C USA
Gilroy *25 B6* California, W USA
Gimie, Mount *33 F1 mountain* C Saint Lucia
Gimma *see* Jīma
Ginevra *see* Genève
Gingin *125 A6* Western Australia
Giohar *see* Jawhar
Girardot *36 B3* Cundinamarca, C Colombia
Giresun *95 E2 var.* Kerasunt; *anc.* Cerasus, Pharnacia. Giresun, NE Turkey
Girin *see* Jilin
Girne *see* Kerýneia
Girona *71 G2 var.* Gerona; *anc.* Gerunda. Cataluña, NE Spain
Gisborne *128 E3* Gisborne, North Island, NZ
Gissar Range *101 E3 Rus.* Gissarskiy Khrebet. *Mountain range* Tajikistan/Uzbekistan
Githio *see* Gýtheio
Giulianova *74 D4* Abruzzo, C Italy
Giumri *see* Gyumri
Giurgiu *86 C5* Giurgiu, S Romania
Gîza *see* El Gîza
Gizeh *see* El Gîza
Giżyeko *76 D2* Warmiúsko-Mazurskie, NE Poland
Gjakovë *see* Đakovica
Gjilan *see* Gnjilane
Gjinokastër *see* Gjirokastër
Gjirokastër *79 C7 var.* Gjirokastra; *prev.* Gjinokastër, *Gk.* Argyrokastron, *It.* Argirocastro. Gjirokastër, S Albania
Gjirokastra *see* Gjirokastër
Gjoa Haven *15 F3* King William Island, Nunavut, NW Canada
Gjøvik *63 B5* Oppland, S Norway

H

Haguenau – Hsining

Haguenau 68 E3 Bas-Rhin, NE France
Haicheng 106 D3 Liaoning, NE China
Haidarabad *see* Hyderābād
Haifa *see* Ḥefa
Haifong *see* Hai Phong
Haikou 106 C7 *var.* Hai-k'ou, Hoihow, *Fr.* Hoï-Hao. Hainan, S China
Hai-k'ou *see* Haikou
Ḩā'il 98 B4 *off.* Minṭaqah Ḩā'il. *Province* N Saudi Arabia
Hai-la-erh *see* Hailar
Hailar 105 F1 *var.* Hai-la-erh; *prev.* Hulun. Nei Mongol Zizhiqu, N China
Hailuoto 62 D4 *Swe.* Karlö. *Island* W Finland
Hainan 106 B7 *var.* Hainan Sheng, Qiong. Admin. region *province* S China
Hainan Dao 106 C7 *island* S China
Hainan Sheng *see* Hainan
Haines 14 D4 Alaska, USA
Hainichen 72 D4 Sachsen, E Germany
Hai Phong 114 D3 *var.* Haifong, Haiphong. N Vietnam
Haiphong *see* Hai Phong
Haiti 32 D3 *off.* Republic of Haiti. *Country* C West Indies
Haiya 50 C3 Red Sea, NE Sudan
Hajdúhadház 77 D6 Hajdú-Bihar, E Hungary
Hajîne *see* Abū Ḩardān
Hajnówka 76 E3 *Ger.* Hermhausen. Podlaskie, NE Poland
Hakodate 108 D3 Hokkaidō, NE Japan
Ḩalab 96 B2 *Eng.* Aleppo, *Fr.* Alep; *anc.* Beroea. Ḩalab, NW Syria
Ḩalāniyāt, Juzur al 137 D6 *var.* Jazā'ir Bin Ghalfān, *Eng.* Kuria Muria Islands. *Island group* S Oman
Halberstadt 72 C4 Sachsen-Anhalt, C Germany
Halden 63 B6 *prev.* Fredrikshald. Østfold, S Norway
Halfmoon Bay 129 A8 *var.* Oban. Stewart Island, Southland, NZ
Halifax 17 F4 Nova Scotia, SE Canada
Halkida *see* Chalkída
Halle 65 B6 *Fr.* Hal. Vlaams Brabant, C Belgium
Halle 72 C4 *var.* Halle an der Saale. Sachsen-Anhalt, C Germany
Halle an der Saale *see* Halle
Halle-Neustadt 72 C4 Sachsen-Anhalt, C Germany
Halley 132 B2 *UK research station* Antarctica
Hall Islands 120 B2 *island group* C Micronesia
Halls Creek 124 C3 Western Australia
Halmahera, Pulau 117 F3 *prev.* Djailolo, Gilolo, Jailolo. *Island* E Indonesia
Halmahera Sea 117 F4 *Ind.* Laut Halmahera. *Sea* E Indonesia
Halmstad 63 B7 Halland, S Sweden
Hama *see* Ḩamāh
Hamada 109 B6 Shimane, Honshū, SW Japan
Hamadān 98 C3 *anc.* Ecbatana. Hamadān, W Iran
Ḩamāh 96 B3 *var.* Hama; *anc.* Epiphania, *Bibl.* Hamath. Ḩamāh, W Syria
Hamamatsu 109 D6 *var.* Hamamatu. Shizuoka, Honshū, S Japan
Hamamatu *see* Hamamatsu
Hamar 63 B5 *prev.* Storhammer. Hedmark, S Norway
Hamath *see* Ḩamāh
Hamburg 72 B3 Hamburg, N Germany
Ḩamḑ, Wādī al 136 A4 *dry watercourse* W Saudi Arabia
Hämeenlinna 63 D5 *Swe.* Tavastehus. Etelä-Suomi, S Finland
Hamersley Range 124 A4 *mountain range* Western Australia
Hamhŭng 107 E3 C North Korea
Hami 104 C3 *var.* Ha-mi, *Uigh.* Kumul, Qomul. Xinjiang Uygur Zizhiqu, NW China
Ha-mi *see* Hami
Hamilton 20 C2 Alabama, S USA
Hamilton 16 D5 Ontario, S Canada
Hamilton 66 C4 S Scotland, UK
Hamilton 128 D3 Waikato, North Island, NZ
Ḩamīm, Wādī al 87 G2 *river* NE Libya
Hamïs Musait *see* Khamīs Mushayt
Hamiton 20 A5 *dependent territory capital* (Bermuda) C Bermuda
Hamm 72 B4 *var.* Hamm in Westfalen. Nordrhein-Westfalen, W Germany
Hammada du Drâa *see* Dra, Hamada du
Hammamet, Golfe de 80 D3 *Ar.* Khalīj al Ḩammāmāt. *Gulf* NE Tunisia
Ḩammār, Hawr al 136 C3 *lake* SE Iraq
Hamm in Westfalen *see* Hamm
Hampden 129 B7 Otago, South Island, NZ
Hampstead 67 A7 SE England, UK
Hamrun 80 B5 C Malta
Hânceşti *see* Hînceşti
Handan 106 C4 *var.* Han-tan. Hebei, E China
Haneda 108 A2 *international airport* (Tōkyō) Tōkyō, Honshū, S Japan
HaNegev 97 A7 *Eng.* Negev. *Desert* S Israel
Hanford 25 C6 California, W USA
Hangayn Nuruu 104 D2 *mountain range* C Mongolia
Hang-chou *see* Hangzhou
Hangchow *see* Hangzhou
Hangö *see* Hanko
Hangzhou 106 D5 *var.* Hang-chou, Hangchow. Zhejiang, SE China
Hania *see* Chaniá
Hanka, Lake *see* Khanka, Lake
Hanko 63 D6 *Swe.* Hangö. Etelä-Suomi, SW Finland
Han-k'ou *see* Wuhan
Hankow *see* Wuhan
Hanmer Springs 129 C5 Canterbury, South Island, NZ
Hannibal 23 G4 Missouri, C USA
Hannover 72 B3 *Eng.* Hanover. Niedersachsen, NW Germany
Hanöbukten 63 B7 *bay* S Sweden
Ha Nôi 114 D3 *Eng.* Hanoi, *Fr.* Ha noï. *Country capital* (Vietnam) N Vietnam
Hanoi *see* Ha Nôi
Han Shui 105 E4 *river* C China
Han-tan *see* Handan
Hantsavichy 85 B6 *Pol.* Hancewicze, *Rus.* Gantsevichi. Brestskaya Voblasts', SW Belarus
Hanyang *see* Wuhan
Hanzhong 106 B5 Shaanxi, C China
Hāora 113 F4 *prev.* Howrah. West Bengal, NE India
Haparanda 62 D4 Norrbotten, N Sweden
Haradok 85 E5 *Rus.* Gorodok. Vitsyebskaya Voblasts', N Belarus
Haradzyets 85 B6 *Rus.* Gorodets. Brestskaya Voblasts', SW Belarus
Haramachi 108 D4 Fukushima, Honshū, E Japan
Harany 85 D5 *Rus.* Gorany. Vitsyebskaya Voblasts', N Belarus
Harare 56 D3 *prev.* Salisbury. *Country capital* (Zimbabwe) Mashonaland East, NE Zimbabwe
Harbavichy 85 E6 *Rus.* Gorbovichi. Mahilyowskaya Voblasts', E Belarus
Harbel 52 C5 W Liberia
Harbin 107 E2 *var.* Haerbin, Ha-erh-pin, Kharbin; *prev.* Haerhpin, Pingkiang, Pinkiang. Heilongjiang, NE China
Hardangerfjorden 63 A6 *fjord* S Norway
Hardangervidda 63 A6 *plateau* S Norway
Hardenberg 64 E3 Overijssel, E Netherlands
Harelbeke 65 A6 *var.* Harlebeke. West-Vlaanderen, W Belgium
Harem *see* Ḩārim
Haren 64 E2 Groningen, NE Netherlands
Hārer 51 D5 E Ethiopia
Hargeisa *see* Hargeysa
Hargeysa 51 D5 *var.* Hargeisa. Woqooyi Galbeed, NW Somalia
Hariana *see* Haryāna
Hari, Batang 116 B4 *prev.* Djambi. *River* Sumatera, W Indonesia
Ḩārim 96 B2 *var.* Harem. Idlib, W Syria
Harima-nada 109 B6 *sea* S Japan
Harīrūd *var.* Tedzhen, *Turkm.* Tejen. *River* Afghanistan/Iran *see also* Tedzhen
Harlan 23 F3 Iowa, C USA
Harlebeke *see* Harelbeke
Harlingen 64 D2 *Fris.* Harns. Friesland, N Netherlands
Harlingen 27 G5 Texas, SW USA
Harlow 67 E6 E England, UK
Harney Basin 24 B4 *basin* Oregon, NW USA
Härnösand 63 C5 *var.* Hernösand. Västernorrland, C Sweden
Har Nuur 104 C2 *lake* NW Mongolia
Harper 52 D5 *var.* Cape Palmas. NE Liberia
Harricana 16 D3 *river* Quebec, SE Canada
Harris 66 B3 *physical region* NW Scotland, UK
Harrisburg 19 E4 *state capital* Pennsylvania, NE USA
Harrisonburg 19 E4 Virginia, NE USA
Harrison, Cape 17 F2 *headland* Newfoundland and Labrador, E Canada
Harris Ridge *see* Lomonosov Ridge
Harrogate 67 D5 N England, UK
Hârşova 86 D5 *prev.* Hîrşova. Constanţa, SE Romania
Harstad 62 C2 Troms, N Norway
Hartford 19 G3 *state capital* Connecticut, NE USA
Hartlepool 67 D5 N England, UK
Harunabad *see* Eslāmābād
Harwich 67 E6 E England, UK
Haryāna 112 D2 *var.* Hariana. Admin. region *state* N India
Hasselt 65 C6 Limburg, NE Belgium
Hassetché *see* Al Ḩasakah
Hastings 128 E4 Hawke's Bay, North Island, NZ
Hastings 23 E4 Nebraska, C USA
Hastings 67 E7 SE England, UK
Haţeg 86 B4 *Ger.* Wallenthal, *Hung.* Hátszeg; *prev.* Hatzeg, Hötzing. Hunedoara, SW Romania
Hatizyô Zima *see* Hachijō-jima
Hattem 64 D3 Gelderland, E Netherlands
Hatteras, Cape 21 G1 *headland* North Carolina, SE USA
Hatteras Plain 13 D6 *undersea feature* W Atlantic Ocean
Hattiesburg 20 C3 Mississippi, S USA
Hatton Bank *see* Hatton Ridge
Hatton Ridge 58 B2 *var.* Hatton Bank. *Undersea feature* N Atlantic Ocean
Hat Yai 115 C7 *var.* Ban Hat Yai. Songkhla, SW Thailand
Haugesund 63 A6 Rogaland, S Norway
Haukeligrend 63 A6 Telemark, S Norway
Haukivesi 63 E5 *lake* SE Finland
Hauraki Gulf 128 D2 *gulf* North Island, NZ
Hauroko, Lake 129 A7 *lake* South Island, NZ
Haut Atlas 48 B3 *Eng.* High Atlas. *Mountain range* C Morocco
Hautes Fagnes 65 D6 *Ger.* Hohes Venn. *Mountain range* E Belgium
Haut Plateau du Dra *see* Dra, Hamada du
Hauts Plateaux 48 D2 *plateau* Algeria/Morocco
Hauzenberg 73 D6 Bayern, SE Germany
Havana *see* La Habana
Havana 13 D6 Illinois, N USA
Havant 67 D7 S England, UK
Havelock 21 F1 North Carolina, SE USA
Havelock North 128 E4 Hawke's Bay, North Island, NZ
Haverfordwest 67 C6 SW Wales, UK
Havířov 77 C5 Ostravský Kraj, E Czech Republic
Havre 22 C1 Montana, NW USA
Havre-St-Pierre 17 F3 Quebec, E Canada
Hawaii 25 B8 *Haw.* Hawai'i. *Island* Hawaiian Islands, USA, C Pacific Ocean
Hawaii 25 A8 *off.* State of Hawaii; also known as Aloha State, Paradise of the Pacific. *State* USA, C Pacific Ocean
Hawaiian Islands 130 D2 *prev.* Sandwich Islands. *Island group* Hawaii, USA, C Pacific Ocean
Hawaiian Ridge 91 H4 *undersea feature* N Pacific Ocean
Hawash *see* Āwash
Hawea, Lake 129 B6 *lake* South Island, NZ
Hawera 128 D4 Taranaki, North Island, NZ
Hawick 66 C4 SE Scotland, UK
Hawke Bay 128 E4 *bay* North Island, NZ
Hawlēr *see* Arbīl
Hawthorne 25 C6 Nevada, W USA
Hay 127 C6 New South Wales, SE Australia
Hayes 16 B2 *river* Manitoba, C Canada
Hay River 15 E4 Northwest Territories, W Canada
Hays 23 E5 Kansas, C USA
Haysyn 86 D3 *Rus.* Gaysin. Vinnyts'ka Oblast', C Ukraine
Heard and McDonald Islands 119 B7 *Australian external territory* S Indian Ocean
Hearst 16 C4 Ontario, S Canada
Heathrow 67 A8 *international airport* (London)SE England, UK
Hebei 106 C4 *var.* Hebei Sheng, Hopeh, Hopei, Ji; *prev.* Chihli. Admin. region *province* E China
Hebei Sheng *see* Hebei
Hebron 97 A6 *var.* Al Khalīl, El Khalil, *Heb.* Ḥevron; *anc.* Kiriath-Arba. S West Bank
Hebrus *see* Maritsa
Heemskerk 64 C3 Noord-Holland, W Netherlands
Heerde 64 D3 Gelderland, E Netherlands
Heerenveen 64 D2 *Fris.* It Hearrenfean. Friesland, N Netherlands
Heerhugowaard 64 C2 Noord-Holland, NW Netherlands
Heerlen 65 D6 Limburg, SE Netherlands
Heerwegen *see* Polkowice
Ḥefa 97 A5 *var.* Haifa; *hist.* Caiffa, Caiphas, *anc.* Sycaminum. Haifa, N Israel
Ḥefa, Mifraz 97 A5 *Eng.* Bay of Haifa. *Bay* N Israel
Hefei 106 D5 *var.* Hofei; *hist.* Luchow. Anhui, E China
Hegang 107 E2 Heilongjiang, NE China
Hei *see* Heilongjiang
Heide 72 B2 Schleswig-Holstein, N Germany
Heidelberg 73 B5 Baden-Württemberg, SW Germany
Heidenheim *see* Heidenheim an der Brenz
Heidenheim an der Brenz 73 B6 *var.* Heidenheim. Baden-Württemberg, S Germany
Heilbronn 73 B6 Baden-Württemberg, SW Germany
Heilongjiang 106 D2 *var.* Hei, Heilongjiang Sheng, Hei-lung-chiang, Heilungkiang. Admin. region *province* NE China
Heilongjiang Sheng *see* Heilongjiang
Heiloo 64 C3 Noord-Holland, NW Netherlands
Hei-lung-chiang *see* Heilongjiang
Heilungkiang *see* Heilongjiang
Heimdal 63 B5 Sør-Trøndelag, S Norway
Hekimhan 94 D3 Malatya, C Turkey
Helena 22 B2 *state capital* Montana, NW USA
Helensville 128 D2 Auckland, North Island, NZ
Helgoland Bay *see* Helgoländer Bucht
Helgoländer Bucht 72 A2 *var.* Helgoland Bay, Heligoland Bight. *Bay* NW Germany
Heligoland Bight *see* Helgoländer Bucht
Heliopolis *see* Baalbek
Hellevoetsluis 64 B4 Zuid-Holland, SW Netherlands
Hellín 71 E4 Castilla-La Mancha, C Spain
Helmand, Daryā-ye *var.* Rūd-e Hīrmand. *River* Afghanistan/Iran *see also* Hīrmand, Rūd-e
Helmond 65 D5 Noord-Brabant, S Netherlands
Helsingborg 63 B7 *prev.* Hälsingborg. Skåne, S Sweden
Helsinki 63 D6 *Swe.* Helsingfors. *Country capital* (Finland) Etelä-Suomi, S Finland
Henan 106 C5 *var.* Henan Sheng, Honan, Yu. Admin. region *province* C China
Henan Sheng *see* Henan
Henderson 18 B5 Kentucky, S USA
Henderson 25 D7 Nevada, W USA
Henderson 27 H3 Texas, SW USA
Hengchow *see* Hengyang
Hengduan Shan 106 A5 *mountain range* SW China
Hengelo 64 E3 Overijssel, E Netherlands
Hengnan *see* Hengyang
Hengyang 106 C6 *var.* Hengnan, Heng-yang; *prev.* Hengchow. Hunan, S China
Heng-yang *see* Hengyang
Heniches'k 87 F4 *Rus.* Genichesk. Khersons'ka Oblast', S Ukraine
Hennebont 68 A3 Morbihan, NW France
Henzada 114 B4 Irrawaddy, SW Myanmar
Herakleion *see* Irákleio
Herāt 100 D4 *var.* Herat; *anc.* Aria. Herāt, W Afghanistan
Herat *see* Herāt
Heredia 31 E4 Heredia, C Costa Rica
Hereford 27 E2 Texas, SW USA
Herford 72 B4 Nordrhein-Westfalen, NW Germany
Herk-de-Stad 65 C6 Limburg, NE Belgium
Hermansverk 63 A5 Sogn Og Fjordane, S Norway
Hermhausen *see* Hajnówka
Hermiston 24 C2 Oregon, NW USA
Hermon, Mount 97 B5 *Ar.* Jabal ash Shaykh. *Mountain* S Syria
Hermosillo 28 B2 Sonora, NW Mexico
Hermoupolis *see* Ermoúpoli
Hernösand *see* Härnösand
Herrera del Duque 70 D3 Extremadura, W Spain
Herselt 65 C5 Antwerpen, C Belgium
Herstal 65 D6 *Fr.* Héristal. Liège, E Belgium
Hessen 73 B5 *cultural region* C Germany
Ḥevron *see* Hebron
Heydebrech *see* Kędzierzyn-Kole
Heywood Islands 124 C3 *island group* Western Australia
Hibbing 23 F1 Minnesota, N USA
Hidalgo del Parral 28 C2 *var.* Parral. Chihuahua, N Mexico
Hida-sanmyaku 109 C5 *mountain range* Honshū, S Japan
Hierro 48 A3 *var.* Ferro. *Island* Islas Canarias, Spain, NE Atlantic Ocean
High Plains *see* Great Plains
High Point 21 E1 North Carolina, SE USA
High Veld *see* Great Karoo
Hiiumaa 84 C2 *Ger.* Dagden, *Swe.* Dagö. *Island* W Estonia
Hikurangi 128 D2 Northland, North Island, NZ
Hildesheim 72 B4 Niedersachsen, N Germany
Hilla *see* Al Ḩillah
Hillaby, Mount 33 G1 *mountain* N Barbados
Hill Bank 30 C1 Orange Walk, N Belize
Hillegom 64 C3 Zuid-Holland, W Netherlands
Hilo 25 B8 Hawaii, USA, C Pacific Ocean
Hilton Head Island 21 E2 South Carolina, SE USA
Hilversum 64 C3 Noord-Holland, C Netherlands
Himalaya *see* Himalayas
Himalayas 113 E2 *var.* Himalaya, *Chin.* Himalaya Shan. *Mountain range* S Asia
Himalaya Shan *see* Himalayas
Himeji 109 C6 *var.* Himezi. Hyōgo, Honshū, SW Japan
Himezi *see* Himeji
Ḩimş 96 B4 *var.* Homs; *anc.* Emesa. Ḩimş, C Syria
Hînceşti 86 D4 *var.* Hânceşti; *prev.* Kotovsk. C Moldova
Hinchinbrook Island 126 D3 *island* Queensland, NE Australia
Hinds 129 C6 Canterbury, South Island, NZ
Hindu Kush 101 F4 *Per.* Hendū Kosh. *Mountain range* Afghanistan/Pakistan
Hinesville 21 E3 Georgia, SE USA
Hinnøya 62 C3 *island* C Norway
Hinson Bay 20 A5 *bay* W Bermuda
Hios *see* Chíos
Hirosaki 108 D3 Aomori, Honshū, C Japan
Hiroshima 109 B6 *var.* Hirosima. Hiroshima, Honshū, SW Japan
Hirosima *see* Hiroshima
Hirson 68 D3 Aisne, N France
Hispaniola 34 B1 *island* Dominion Republic/Haiti
Hitachi 109 D5 *var.* Hitati. Ibaraki, Honshū, S Japan
Hitati *see* Hitachi
Hitra 62 A4 *prev.* Hitteren. *Island* S Norway
Hjälmaren 63 C6 *Eng.* Lake Hjalmar. *Lake* C Sweden
Hjørring 63 B7 Nordjylland, N Denmark
Hkakabo Razi 114 B1 *mountain* Myanmar/China
Hlobyne 87 F2 *Rus.* Globino. Poltavs'ka Oblast', NE Ukraine
Hlukhiv 87 F1 *Rus.* Glukhov. Sums'ka Oblast', NE Ukraine
Hlybokaye 85 D5 *Rus.* Glubokoye. Vitsyebskaya Voblasts', N Belarus
Hoa Binh 114 D3 Hoa Binh, N Vietnam
Hoang Liên Son 114 D3 *mountain range* N Vietnam
Hobart 127 C8 *prev.* Hobarton, Hobart Town. *State capital* Tasmania, SE Australia
Hobbs 27 E3 New Mexico, SW USA
Hobro 63 A7 Nordjylland, N Denmark
Hô Chi Minh 115 E6 *var.* Ho Chi Minh City; *prev.* Saigon. S Vietnam
Ho Chi Minh City *see* Hô Chi Minh
Hódmezővásárhely 77 D7 Csongrád, SE Hungary
Hodna, Chott El 118 C4 *var.* Chott el-Hodna, *Ar.* Shatt al-Hodna. *Salt lake* N Algeria
Hodonín 77 C5 *Ger.* Göding. Brněnský Kraj, SE Czech Republic
Hoë Karoo *see* Great Karoo
Hof 73 C5 Bayern, SE Germany
Hofei *see* Hefei
Hōfu 109 B7 Yamaguchi, Honshū, SW Japan
Hofuf *see* Al Hufūf
Hogoley Islands *see* Chuuk Islands
Hohe Tauern 73 C7 *mountain range* W Austria
Hohhot 105 F3 *var.* Huhehot, Huhuohaote, *Mong.* Kukukhoto; *prev.* Kweisui, Kwesui. Nei Mongol Zizhiqu, N China
Hôi An 115 E5 *prev.* Faifo. Quang Nam-Đa Nāng, C Vietnam
Hoï-Hao *see* Haikou
Hoihow *see* Haikou
Hokianga Harbour 128 C2 *inlet* SE Tasman Sea
Hokitika 129 B5 West Coast, South Island, NZ
Hokkaidō 108 C2 *prev.* Ezo, Yeso, Yezo. *Island* NE Japan
Hola Prystan' 87 E4 *Rus.* Golaya Pristan. Khersons'ka Oblast', S Ukraine
Holbrook 26 B2 Arizona, SW USA
Holetown 33 G1 *prev.* Jamestown. W Barbados
Holguín 32 C2 Holguín, SE Cuba
Hollabrunn 73 E6 Niederösterreich, NE Austria
Hollandia *see* Jayapura
Holly Springs 20 C1 Mississippi, S USA
Holman 15 E3 Victoria Island, Northwest Territories, N Canada
Holmsund 62 D4 Västerbotten, N Sweden
Ḥolon 97 A6 *var.* Kholon. Tel Aviv, C Israel
Holovanivs'k 87 E3 *Rus.* Golovanevsk. Kirovohrads'ka Oblast', C Ukraine
Holstebro 63 A7 Ringkøbing, W Denmark
Holsteinborg *see* Sisimiut
Holsteinsborg *see* Sisimiut
Holstenborg *see* Sisimiut
Holstensborg *see* Sisimiut
Holyhead 67 C5 *Wel.* Caer Gybi. NW Wales, UK
Hombori 53 E3 Mopti, S Mali
Homs *see* Al Khums
Homs *see* Ḩimş
Homyel' 85 D7 *Rus.* Gomel'. Homyel'skaya Voblasts', SE Belarus
Honan *see* Henan
Honan *see* Luoyang
Hondo *see* Honshū
Hondo 27 F4 Texas, SW USA
Honduras 30 C2 *off.* Republic of Honduras. *Country* Central America
Honduras, Gulf of 30 C2 *Sp.* Golfo de Honduras. *Gulf* W Caribbean Sea
Hønefoss 63 B6 Buskerud, S Norway
Honey Lake 25 B5 *lake* California, W USA
Hon Gai *see* Hông Gai
Hongay *see* Hông Gai
Hông Gai 114 E3 *var.* Hon Gai, Hongay. Quang Ninh, N Vietnam
Hong Kong 106 A1 *Chin.* Xianggang. S China
Hong Kong Island 106 B2 *Chin.* Xianggang. *Island* S China
Honiara 122 C3 *country capital* (Solomon Islands) Guadalcanal, C Solomon Islands
Honjō 108 D4 *var.* Honzyô. Akita, Honshū, C Japan
Honolulu 25 A8 *admin capital* Oahu, Hawaii, USA, C Pacific Ocean
Honshū 109 E5 *var.* Hondo, Honsyû. *Island* SW Japan
Honsyû *see* Honshū
Honzyô *see* Honjō
Hoogeveen 64 E2 Drenthe, NE Netherlands
Hoogezand-Sappemeer 64 E2 Groningen, NE Netherlands
Hoorn 64 C2 Noord-Holland, NW Netherlands
Hopa 95 E2 Artvin, NE Turkey
Hope 14 C3 British Columbia, SW Canada
Hopedale 17 F2 Newfoundland and Labrador, NE Canada
Hopeh *see* Hebei
Hopei *see* Hebei
Hopkinsville 18 B5 Kentucky, S USA
Horasan 95 F3 Erzurum, NE Turkey
Horizon Deep 130 D4 *undersea feature* W Pacific Ocean
Horki 85 E6 *Rus.* Gorki. Mahilyowskaya Voblasts', E Belarus
Horlivka 87 G3 *Rom.* Adâncata, *Rus.* Gorlovka. Donets'ka Oblast', E Ukraine
Hormuz, Strait of 98 D4 *var.* Strait of Ormuz, *Per.* Tangeh-ye Hormoz. *Strait* Iran/Oman
Hornos, Cabo de 43 C8 *Eng.* Cape Horn. *Headland* S Chile
Hornsby 126 E1 New South Wales, SE Australia
Horodnya 87 E1 *Rus.* Gorodnya. Chernihivs'ka Oblast', NE Ukraine
Horodyshche 87 E2 *Rus.* Gorodishche. Cherkas'ka Oblast', C Ukraine
Horokok 86 B2 *Pol.* Gródek Jagielloński, *Rus.* Gorodok, Gorodok Yagellonski. L'vivs'ka Oblast', NW Ukraine
Horoshiri-dake 108 D2 *var.* Horosiri Dake. *Mountain* Hokkaidō, N Japan
Horosiri Dake *see* Horoshiri-dake
Horsburgh Atoll 110 A4 *atoll* N Maldives
Horseshoe Bay 20 A5 *bay* W Bermuda
Horseshoe Seamounts 58 A4 *undersea feature* E Atlantic Ocean
Horsham 127 B7 Victoria, SE Australia
Horst 65 D5 Limburg, SE Netherlands
Horten 63 B6 Vestfold, S Norway
Horyn' 85 B7 *Rus.* Goryn. *River* NW Ukraine
Hosingen 65 D7 Diekirch, NE Luxembourg
Hospitalet *see* L'Hospitalet de Llobregat
Hotan 104 B4 *var.* Khotan, *Chin.* Ho-t'ien. Xinjiang Uygur Zizhiqu, NW China
Ho-t'ien *see* Hotan
Hoting 62 C4 Jämtland, C Sweden
Hot Springs 20 B1 Arkansas, C USA
Houayxay 114 C3 *var.* Ban Houayxay, Ban Houei Sai. Bokèo, N Laos
Houghton 18 B1 Michigan, N USA
Houilles 69 B5 Yvelines, N France
Houlton 19 H1 Maine, NE USA
Houma 20 B3 Louisiana, S USA
Houston 27 H4 Texas, SW USA
Hovd 104 C2 *var.* Khovd. Hovd, W Mongolia
Hove 67 E7 SE England, UK
Hoverla, Hora 86 C3 *Rus.* Gora Goverla. *Mountain* W Ukraine
Hovsgol, Lake *see* Hövsgöl Nuur
Hövsgöl Nuur 104 D1 *var.* Lake Hovsgol. *Lake* N Mongolia
Howar, Wādi 50 A3 *var.* Ouadi Howa. *River* Chad/Sudan *see also* Howa, Ouadi
Hoy 66 C2 *island* N Scotland, UK
Hoyerswerda 72 D4 Sachsen, E Germany
Hradec Králové 77 B5 *Ger.* Königgrätz. Hradecký Kraj, N Czech Republic
Hrandzichy 85 B5 *Rus.* Grandichi. Hrodzyenskaya Voblasts', W Belarus
Hranice 77 C5 *Ger.* Mährisch-Weisskirchen. Olomoucký Kraj, E Czech Republic
Hrebinka 87 E2 *Rus.* Grebenka. Poltavs'ka Oblast', NE Ukraine
Hrodna 85 B5 *Pol.* Grodno. Hrodzyenskaya Voblasts', W Belarus
Hsia-men *see* Xiamen
Hsiang-t'an *see* Xiangtan
Hsi Chiang *see* Xi Jiang
Hsing-k'ai Hu *see* Khanka, Lake
Hsining *see* Xining

Jaffna – Karaginskiy, Ostrov

Jaffna 110 D3 Northern Province, N Sri Lanka
Jagannath *see* Puri
Jagdalpur 113 E5 Madhya Pradesh, C India
Jagdaqi 105 G1 Nei Mongol Zizhiqu, N China
Jagodina 78 D4 *prev.* Svetozarevo. Serbia, C Serbia and Montenegro (Yugo.)
Jahra *see* Al Jahrā'
Jaipur 112 D3 *prev.* Jeypore. Rājasthān, N India
Jaisalmer 112 C3 Rājasthān, NW India
Jajce 78 B3 Federacija Bosna I Hercegovina, W Bosnia and Herzegovina
Jakarta 116 C5 *prev.* Djakarta, *Dut.* Batavia. *Country capital* (Indonesia) Jawa, C Indonesia
Jakobstad 62 D4 *Fin.* Pietarsaari. Länsi-Suomi, W Finland
Jalālābād 101 F4 *var.* Jalalabad, Jelalabad. Nangarhār, E Afghanistan
Jalandhar 112 D2 *prev.* Jullundur. Punjab, N India
Jalapa *see* Xalapa
Jalapa 30 D3 Nueva Segovia, NW Nicaragua
Jalapa Enríquez *see* Xalapa
Jalpa 28 D4 Zacatecas, C Mexico
Jālū 49 G3 *var.* Jūlā. NE Libya
Jaluit Atoll 122 D2 *var.* Jālwōj. *Atoll* Ralik Chain, S Marshall Islands
Jālwōj *see* Jaluit Atoll
Jamaame 51 D6 *It.* Giamame; *prev.* Margherita. Jubbada Hoose, S Somalia
Jamaica 32 A4 *country* W West Indies
Jamaica 34 A1 *island* W West Indies
Jamaica Channel 32 D3 *channel* Haiti/Jamaica
Jamālpur 113 F3 Bihār, NE India
Jambi 116 B4 *var.* Telanaipura; *prev.* Djambi. Sumatera, W Indonesia
James Bay 16 C3 *bay* Ontario/Quebec, E Canada
James River 23 E2 *river* North Dakota/South Dakota, N USA
James River 19 E5 *river* Virginia, NE USA
Jamestown 19 E3 New York, NE USA
Jamestown 23 E2 North Dakota, N USA
Jammu 112 D2 *prev.* Jummoo. Jammu and Kashmir, NW India
Jammu and Kashmīr 112 D1 *disputed region* India/Pakistan
Jāmnagar 112 C4 *prev.* Navanagar. Gujarāt, W India
Jamshedpur 113 F4 Bihār, NE India
Jamuna *see* Brahmaputra
Janaúba 41 F3 Minas Gerais, SE Brazil
Janesville 18 B3 Wisconsin, N USA
Janīn *see* Jenīn
Janina *see* Ioánnina
Jan Mayen 61 F4 *Norwegian dependency* N Atlantic Ocean
Jánoshalma 77 C7 *SCr.* Jankovac. Bács-Kiskun, S Hungary
Japan 108 C4 *var.* Nippon, *Jap.* Nihon. *Country* E Asia
Japan, Sea of 108 A4 *var.* East Sea, *Rus.* Yapanskoye More. *Sea* NW Pacific Ocean
Japan Trench 103 F1 *undersea feature* NW Pacific Ocean
Japiim 40 C2 *var.* Máncio Lima. Acre, W Brazil
Japurá, Rio 40 C2 *var.* Río Caquetá, Yapurá. *River* Brazil/Colombia *see also* Caquetá, Río
Jaqué 31 G5 Darién, SE Panama
Jaquemel *see* Jacmel
Jarablos *see* Jarābulus
Jarābulus 96 C2 *var.* Jarablos, Jerablus, *Fr.* Djérablous. Ḩalab, N Syria
Jardines de la Reina, Archipiélago de los 32 B2 *island group* C Cuba
Jarocin 76 C4 Wielkopolskie, C Poland
Jarosław 77 E5 *Ger.* Jaroslau, *Rus.* Yaroslav. Podkarpackie, SE Poland
Jarqŭrghon 101 E3 *Rus.* Dzharkurgan. Surkhondaryo Wiloyati, S Uzbekistan
Jarvis Island 123 G2 *US unincorporated territory* C Pacific Ocean
Jasło 77 D5 Podkarpackie, SE Poland
Jastrzębie-Zdrój 77 C5 Śląskie, S Poland
Jataí 41 E3 Goiás, C Brazil
Jativa *see* Xátiva
Jauf *see* Al Jawf
Jaunpiebalga 84 D3 Gulbene, NE Latvia
Jaunpur 113 E3 Uttar Pradesh, N India
Java 130 A3 *prev.* Djawa. *Island* C Indonesia
Javalambre 71 E3 *mountain* E Spain
Javari, Rio 40 C2 *var.* Yavarí. *River* Brazil/Peru
Java Sea 116 D4 *Ind.* Laut Jawa. *Sea* W Indonesia
Java Trench 102 D5 *var.* Sunda Trench. *Undersea feature* E Indian Ocean
Jawhar 51 D6 *var.* Jowhar, *It.* Giohar. Shabeellaha Dhexe, S Somalia
Jaya, Puncak 117 G4 *prev.* Puntjak Carstensz, Puntjak Sukarno. *Mountain* Irian Jaya, E Indonesia
Jayapura 117 H4 *var.* Djajapura, *Dut.* Hollandia; *prev.* Kotabaru, Sukarnapura. Irian Jaya, E Indonesia
Jaza'ir Bin Ghalfān *see* Ḩalāniyāt, Juzur al
Jazīrat Jarbah *see* Jerba, Île de
Jazīreh-ye Qeshm *see* Qeshm
Jaz Mūrīān, Hāmūn-e 98 E4 *lake* SE Iran
Jebba 53 F4 Kwara, W Nigeria
Jebel esh Sharqi *see* Anti-Lebanon
Jebel Uweinat *see* 'Uwaynāt, Jabal al
Jeble *see* Jablah
Jędrzejów 76 D4 *Ger.* Endersdorf. Świętokrzyskie, C Poland
Jefferson City 23 G5 *state capital* Missouri, C USA
Jega 53 F4 Kebbi, NW Nigeria
Jehol *see* Chengde
Jēkabpils 84 D4 *Ger.* Jakobstadt. Jēkabpils, S Latvia
Jelalabad *see* Jalālābād
Jelenia Góra 76 B4 *Ger.* Hirschberg, Hirschberg im Riesengebirge, Hirschberg in Riesengebirge, Hirschberg in Schlesien. Dolnośląskie, SW Poland
Jelgava 84 C3 *Ger.* Mitau. Jelgava, C Latvia
Jemappes 65 B6 Hainaut, S Belgium
Jember 116 D5 *prev.* Djember. Jawa, C Indonesia
Jena 72 C4 Thüringen, C Germany
Jenīn 97 A6 *var.* Janīn, Jinīn; *anc.* Engannim. N West Bank
Jerablus *see* Jarābulus
Jerada 48 D2 NE Morocco
Jerba, Île de 49 F2 *var.* Djerba, Jazīrat Jarbah. *Island* E Tunisia
Jérémie 32 D3 SW Haiti
Jerez *see* Jeréz de la Frontera
Jeréz de la Frontera 70 C5 *var.* Jerez; *prev.* Xeres. Andalucía, SW Spain
Jeréz de los Caballeros 70 C4 Extremadura, W Spain
Jericho 97 B6 *Ar.* Arīḩā, *Heb.* Yeriḥo. E West Bank
Jerid, Chott el 87 E2 *var.* Shaṭṭ al Jarīd. *Salt lake* SW Tunisia
Jersey 67 D8 *UK dependent territory* NW Europe
Jerusalem 97 H4 *Ar.* El Quds, *Heb.* Yerushalayim; *anc.* Hierosolyma. *Country capital* (Israel) Jerusalem, NE Israel
Jerusalem 90 A4 Admin. region *district* E Israel
Jesenice 73 D7 *Ger.* Assling. NW Slovenia
Jessore 113 G4 Khulna, W Bangladesh
Jesús María 42 C3 Córdoba, C Argentina
Jhānsi 112 D3 Uttar Pradesh, N India
Jhelum 112 C2 Punjab, NE Pakistan
Ji *see* Hebei
Ji *see* Jilin
Jiangmen 106 C6 Guangdong, S China
Jiangsu 106 D4 *var.* Chiang-su, Jiangsu Sheng, Kiangsu, Su. Admin. region *province* E China
Jiangsu Sheng *see* Jiangsu
Jiangxi 106 C6 *var.* Chiang-hsi, Gan, Jiangxi Sheng, Kiangsi. Admin. region *province* S China
Jiangxi Sheng *see* Jiangxi
Jiaxing 106 D5 Zhejiang, SE China
Jiayi *see* Chiai
Jibuti *see* Djibouti
Jiddah 99 A5 *Eng.* Jedda. Makkah, W Saudi Arabia
Jih-k'a-tse *see* Xigazê
Jihlava 77 B5 *Ger.* Iglau, *Pol.* Igława. Jihlavský Kraj, C Czech Republic
Jilib 51 D6 *It.* Gelib. Jubbada Dhexe, S Somalia
Jilin 106 D3 *var.* Chi-lin, Girin, Ji, Jilin Sheng, Kirin. Admin. region *province* NE China
Jilin 107 E3 *var.* Chi-lin, Girin, Kirin; *prev.* Yungki, Yunki. Jilin, NE China
Jilin Sheng *see* Jilin
Jīma 51 C5 *var.* Jimma, *It.* Gimma. C Ethiopia
Jimbolia 86 A4 *Ger.* Hatzfeld, *Hung.* Zsombolya. Timiş, W Romania
Jiménez 28 D2 Chihuahua, N Mexico
Jimma *see* Jīma
Jimsar 104 C3 Xinjiang Uygur Zizhiqu, NW China
Jin *see* Shanxi
Jin *see* Tianjin Shi
Jinan 106 C4 *var.* Chinan, Chi-nan, Tsinan. Shandong, E China
Jingdezhen 106 C5 Jiangxi, S China
Jinghong 106 A6 *var.* Yunjinghong. Yunnan, SW China
Jinhua 106 D5 Zhejiang, SE China
Jinīn *see* Jenīn
Jining 105 F3 Shandong, E China
Jinja 51 C6 S Uganda
Jinotega 30 D3 Jinotega, NW Nicaragua
Jinotepe 30 D3 Carazo, SW Nicaragua
Jinsha Jiang 106 A5 *river* SW China
Jinzhou 106 D3 *var.* Chin-chou, Chinchow; *prev.* Chinhsien. Liaoning, NE China
Jisr ash Shadadi *see* Ash Shadādah
Jiu 86 B5 *Ger.* Schil, Schyl, *Hung.* Zsil, Zsily. *River* S Romania
Jiujiang 106 C5 Jiangxi, S China
Jixi 107 E2 Heilongjiang, NE China
Jīzān 99 B6 *var.* Qīzān. Jīzān, SW Saudi Arabia
Jizzakh 101 E2 *Rus.* Dzhizak. Jizzakh Wiloyati, C Uzbekistan
João Pessoa 41 G2 *prev.* Paraíba. *State capital* Paraíba, E Brazil
Jo'burg *see* Johannesburg
Jo-ch'iang *see* Ruoqiang
Jodhpur 112 C3 Rājasthān, NW India
Joensuu 63 E5 Itä-Suomi, E Finland
Jōetsu 109 C5 *var.* Zyôetu. Niigata, Honshū, C Japan
Johanna Island *see* Anjouan
Johannesburg 56 D4 *var.* Egoli, Erautini, Gauteng, *abbrev.* Jo'burg. Gauteng, NE South Africa
John Day River 24 C3 *river* Oregon, NW USA
John o'Groats 66 C2 N Scotland, UK
Johnston Atoll 121 E1 *US unincorporated territory* C Pacific Ocean
Johor Baharu *see* Johor Bahru
Johor Bahru 116 B3 *var.* Johor Baharu, Johore Bahru. Johor, Peninsular Malaysia
Johore Bahru *see* Johor Bahru
Johore Strait 116 A1 *Mal.* Selat Johor. *Strait* Malaysia/Singapore
Joinvile *see* Joinville
Joinville 41 E4 *var.* Joinvile. Santa Catarina, S Brazil
Jokkmokk 62 C3 Norrbotten, N Sweden
Joliet 18 B3 Illinois, N USA
Jonava 84 B4 *Ger.* Janow, *Pol.* Janów. Jonava, C Lithuania
Jonesboro 20 B1 Arkansas, C USA
Joniškis 84 C3 *Ger.* Janischken. Joniškis, N Lithuania
Jönköping 63 B7 Jönköping, S Sweden
Jonquière 17 E4 Quebec, SE Canada
Joplin 23 F5 Missouri, C USA
Jordan 97 B5 *Ar.* Urdunn, *Heb.* HaYarden. *River* SW Asia
Jordan 97 B6 *off.* Hashemite Kingdom of Jordan, *Ar.* Al Mamlakah al Urdunīyah al Hāshimīyah, Al Urdunn; *prev.* Transjordan. *Country* SW Asia
Jorhāt 113 H3 Assam, NE India
Jos 53 G4 Plateau, C Nigeria
Joseph Bonaparte Gulf 124 D2 *gulf* N Australia
Jos Plateau 53 G4 *plateau* C Nigeria
Jotunheimen 63 A5 *mountain range* S Norway
Joûnié 96 A4 *var.* Junīyah. W Lebanon
Joure 64 D2 *Fris.* De Jouwer. Friesland, N Netherlands
Joutseno 63 E5 Etelä-Suomi, S Finland
Jowhar *see* Jawhar
JStorm Thurmond Reservoir *see* Clark Hill Lake
Juan Aldama 28 D3 Zacatecas, C Mexico
Juan de Fuca, Strait of 24 A1 *strait* Canada/USA
Juan Fernández, Islas 35 A6 *Eng.* Juan Fernandez Islands. *Island group* W Chile
Juazeiro 41 G2 *prev.* Joazeiro. Bahia, E Brazil
Juazeiro do Norte 41 G2 Ceará, E Brazil
Juba 51 D6 *Amh.* Genalē Wenz, *It.* Guiba, *Som.* Ganaane, Webi Jubba. *River* Ethiopia/Somalia
Juba 51 B5 *var.* Jūbā. Bahr el Gabel, S Sudan
Júcar 71 E3 *var.* Jucar. *River* C Spain
Juchitán 29 F5 *var.* Juchitán de Zaragosa. Oaxaca, SE Mexico
Juchitán de Zaragosa *see* Juchitán
Judayyidat Hāmir 98 B3 S Iraq
Judenburg 73 D7 Steiermark, C Austria
Juigalpa 30 D3 Chontales, S Nicaragua
Juiz de Fora 41 F4 Minas Gerais, SE Brazil
Jujuy *see* San Salvador de Jujuy
Jūlā *see* Jālū
Juliaca 39 E4 Puno, SE Peru
Juliana Top 37 G3 *mountain* C Suriname
Jumilla 71 E4 Murcia, SE Spain
Jumporn *see* Chumphon
Junction City 23 F4 Kansas, C USA
Juneau 14 D4 *state capital* Alaska, USA
Junín 42 C4 Buenos Aires, E Argentina
Junīyah *see* Joûnié
Junkseylon *see* Phuket
Jur 51 B5 *river* C Sudan
Jura 66 B4 *island* SW Scotland, UK
Jura 73 A7 *canton* NW Switzerland
Jura 68 D4 *department* E France
Jurbarkas 84 B4 *Ger.* Georgenburg, Jurburg. Jurbarkas, W Lithuania
Jūrmala 84 C3 Rīga, C Latvia
Juruá, Rio 40 C2 *var.* Río Yuruá. *River* Brazil/Peru
Juruena, Rio 40 D3 *river* W Brazil
Jutiapa 30 B2 Jutiapa, S Guatemala
Juticalpa 30 D2 Olancho, C Honduras
Juventud, Isla de la 32 A2 *var.* Isla de Pinos, *Eng.* Isle of Youth; *prev.* The Isle of the Pines. *Island* W Cuba
Južna Morava 79 E5 *Ger.* Südliche Morava. *River* SE Serbia and Montenegro (Yugo.)
Juzur Qarqannah *see* Kerkenah, Îles de
Jwaneng 56 C4 Southern, SE Botswana
Jylland 63 A7 *Eng.* Jutland. *Peninsula* W Denmark
Jyväskylä 63 D5 Länsi-Suomi, W Finland

K

K2 104 A4 *Chin.* Qogir Feng, *Eng.* Mount Godwin Austen. *Mountain* China/Pakistan
Kaafu Atoll *see* Male' Atoll
Kaaimanston 37 G3 Sipaliwini, N Suriname
Kaakhka 100 C3 *var.* Kaka. Akhalskiy Velayat, S Turkmenistan
Kaala *see* Caála
Kaamanen 62 D2 *Lapp.* Gámas. Lappi, N Finland
Kaapstad *see* Cape Town
Kaaresuvanto 62 C3 *Lapp.* Gárassavon. Lappi, N Finland
Kabale 51 B6 SW Uganda
Kabinda *see* Cabinda
Kabinda 55 D7 Kasai Oriental, SE Dem. Rep. Congo
Kābol *see* Kābul
Kabompo 56 C2 *river* W Zambia
Kābul 101 E4 *var.* Kabul, *Per.* Kābol. *Country capital* (Afghanistan) Kābul, E Afghanistan
Kabul *see* Kābul
Kabwe 56 D2 Central, C Zambia
Kachchh, Gulf of 112 B4 *var.* Gulf of Cutch, Gulf of Kutch. *Gulf* W India
Kachchh, Rann of 112 B4 *var.* Rann of Kachh, Rann of Kutch. *Salt marsh* India/Pakistan
Kachh, Rann of *see* Kachchh, Rann of
Kadan Kyun 115 B5 *prev.* King Island. *Island* Mergui Archipelago, S Myanmar
Kadavu 123 E4 *prev.* Kandavu. *Island* S Fiji
Kadoma 56 D3 *prev.* Gatooma. Mashonaland West, C Zimbabwe
Kadugli 50 B4 Southern Kordofan, S Sudan
Kaduna 53 G4 Kaduna, C Nigeria
Kadzhi-Say 101 G2 *Kir.* Kajisay. Issyk-Kul'skaya Oblast', NE Kyrgyzstan
Kaédi 52 C3 Gorgol, S Mauritania
Kaffa *see* Feodosiya
Kafue 56 C2 *river* C Zambia
Kafue 56 D2 Lusaka, SE Zambia
Kaga Bandoro 54 C4 *prev.* Fort-Crampel. Nana-Grébizi, C Central African Republic
Kâghet 52 D1 *var.* Karet. *Physical region* N Mauritania
Kagi *see* Chiai
Kagoshima 109 B8 *var.* Kagosima. Kagoshima, Kyūshū, SW Japan
Kagoshima-wan 109 A8 *bay* SW Japan
Kagosima *see* Kagoshima
Kahmard, Daryā-ye 101 E4 *prev.* Darya-i-Surkhab. *River* NE Afghanistan
Kahraman Maraş *see* Kahramanmaraş
Kahramanmaraş 94 D4 *var.* Kahraman Maraş, Maraş, Marash. Kahramanmaraş, S Turkey
Kaiapoi 129 C6 Canterbury, South Island, NZ
Kaifeng 106 C4 Henan, C China
Kai, Kepulauan 117 F4 *prev.* Kei Islands. *Island group* Maluku, SE Indonesia
Kaikohe 128 C2 Northland, North Island, NZ
Kaikoura 129 C5 Canterbury, South Island, NZ
Kaikoura Peninsula 129 C5 *peninsula* South Island, NZ
Kainji Lake *see* Kainji Reservoir
Kainji Reservoir 53 F4 *var.* Kainji Lake. *Reservoir* W Nigeria
Kaipara Harbour 128 C2 *harbour* North Island, NZ
Kairouan 49 E2 *var.* Al Qayrawān. E Tunisia
Kaisaria *see* Kayseri
Kaiserslautern 73 A5 Rheinland-Pfalz, SW Germany
Kaišiadorys 85 B5 Kaišiadorys, S Lithuania
Kaitaia 128 C2 Northland, North Island, NZ
Kajaani 62 E4 *Swe.* Kajana. Oulu, C Finland
Kaka *see* Kaakhka
Kake 14 D4 Kupreanof Island, Alaska, USA
Kakhovka 87 F4 Khersons'ka Oblast', S Ukraine
Kakhovs'ka Vodoskhovyshche 87 F4 *Rus.* Kakhovskoye Vodokhranilishche. *Reservoir* SE Ukraine
Kākināda 110 D1 *prev.* Cocanada. Andhra Pradesh, E India
Kaktovik 14 D2 Alaska, USA
Kalahari Desert 56 B4 *desert* Southern Africa
Kalamariá 82 B4 Kentrikí Makedonía, N Greece
Kalámata 83 B6 *prev.* Kalámai. Pelopónnisos, S Greece
Kalamazoo 18 C3 Michigan, N USA
Kalambaka *see* Kalampáka
Kálamos 83 C5 Attikí, C Greece
Kalampáka 82 B4 *var.* Kalambaka. Thessalía, C Greece
Kalanchak 87 F4 Khersons'ka Oblast', S Ukraine
Kalarash *see* Călăraşi
Kalasin 114 D4 *var.* Muang Kalasin. Kalasin, E Thailand
Kalāt 101 E5 *Per.* Qalāt. Zābul, S Afghanistan
Kālat 112 B2 *var.* Kelat, Khelat. Baluchistān, SW Pakistan
Kalbarri 125 A5 Western Australia
Kalecik 94 C3 Ankara, N Turkey
Kalemie 55 E6 *prev.* Albertville. Shaba, SE Dem. Rep. Congo
Kale Sultanie *see* Çanakkale
Kalgan *see* Zhangjiakou
Kalgoorlie 125 B6 Western Australia
Kalima 55 D6 Maniema, E Dem. Rep. Congo
Kalimantan 116 D4 *Eng.* Indonesian Borneo. *Geopolitical region* Borneo, C Indonesia
Kálimnos *see* Kálymnos
Kaliningrad *see* Kaliningradskaya Oblast'
Kaliningrad 84 A4 Kaliningradskaya Oblast', W Russian Federation
Kaliningradskaya Oblast' 84 B4 *var.* Kaliningrad. Admin. region *province and enclave* W Russian Federation
Kalinkavichy 85 C7 *Rus.* Kalinkovichi. Homyel'skaya Voblasts', SE Belarus
Kalispell 22 B1 Montana, NW USA
Kalisz 76 C4 *Ger.* Kalisch, *Rus.* Kalish; *anc.* Calisia. Wielkopolskie, C Poland
Kalix 62 D4 Norrbotten, N Sweden
Kalixälven 62 D3 *river* N Sweden
Kallaste 84 E3 *Ger.* Krasnogor. Tartumaa, SE Estonia
Kallavesi 63 E5 *lake* SE Finland
Kalloní 83 D5 Lésvos, E Greece
Kalmar 63 C7 *var.* Calmar. Kalmar, S Sweden
Kalmthout 65 C5 Antwerpen, N Belgium
Kalpáki 82 A4 Ípeiros, W Greece
Kalpeni Island 110 B3 *island* Lakshadweep, India, N Indian Ocean
Kaluga 89 B5 Kaluzhskaya Oblast', W Russian Federation
Kalush 86 C2 *Pol.* Kałusz. Ivano-Frankivs'ka Oblast', W Ukraine
Kalutara 110 D4 Western Province, SW Sri Lanka
Kalvarija 85 B5 *Pol.* Kalwaria. Marijampolė, S Lithuania
Kalyān 112 C5 Mahārāshtra, W India
Kálymnos 83 D6 *var.* Kálimnos. *Island* Dodekánisos, Greece, Aegean Sea
Kama 88 D4 *river* NW Russian Federation
Kamarang 37 F3 W Guyana
Kamchatka *see* Kamchatka, Poluostrov
Kamchatka, Poluostrov 93 G3 *Eng.* Kamchatka. *Peninsula* E Russian Federation
Kamensk-Shakhtinskiy 89 B6 Rostovskaya Oblast', SW Russian Federation
Kamina 55 D7 Shaba, S Dem. Rep. Congo
Kamishli *see* Al Qāmishlī
Kamloops 15 E5 British Columbia, SW Canada
Kammu Seamount 130 C2 *undersea feature* N Pacific Ocean
Kampala 51 B6 *country capital* (Uganda) S Uganda
Kâmpóng Cham 115 D6 *prev.* Kompong Cham. Kâmpóng Cham, C Cambodia
Kâmpóng Chhnăng 115 D6 *prev.* Kompong. Kâmpóng Chhnăng, C Cambodia
Kâmpóng Saôm 115 D6 *prev.* Kompong Som, Sihanoukville. Kâmpóng Saôm, SW Cambodia
Kâmpóng Spoe 115 D6 *prev.* Kompong Speu. Kâmpóng Spœ, S Cambodia
Kâmpôt 115 D6 Kâmpôt, SW Cambodia
Kam"yanets'-Podil's'kyy 86 C3 *Rus.* Kamenets-Podol'skiy. Khmel'nyts'ka Oblast', W Ukraine
Kam"yanka-Dniprovs'ka 87 F3 *Rus.* Kamenka Dneprovskaya. Zaporiz'ka Oblast', SE Ukraine
Kamyshin 89 B6 Volgogradskaya Oblast', SW Russian Federation
Kanaky *see* New Caledonia
Kananga 55 D6 *prev.* Luluabourg. Kasai Occidental, S Dem. Rep. Congo
Kananur *see* Cannanore
Kanara *see* Karnātaka
Kanash 89 C5 Chuvashskaya Respublika, W Russian Federation
Kanazawa 109 C5 Ishikawa, Honshū, SW Japan
Kanbe 114 B4 Yangon, SW Myanmar
Kānchīpuram 110 C2 *prev.* Conjeeveram. Tamil Nādu, SE India
Kandahār 101 E5 *Per.* Qandahār. Kandahār, S Afghanistan
Kandalakša *see* Kandalaksha
Kandalaksha 88 B2 *var.* Kandalakša, *Fin.* Kantalahti. Murmanskaya Oblast', NW Russian Federation
Kandangan 116 D4 Borneo, C Indonesia
Kandava 84 C3 *Ger.* Kandau. Tukums, W Latvia
Kandi 53 F4 N Benin
Kandy 110 D3 Central Province, C Sri Lanka
Kane Fracture Zone 44 B4 *tectonic feature* NW Atlantic Ocean
Kaneohe 25 A8 *Haw.* Kāne'ohe. Oahu, Hawaii, USA, C Pacific Ocean
Kangān 98 D4 Būshehr, S Iran
Kangaroo Island 127 A7 *island* South Australia
Kangertittivaq 61 E4 *Dan.* Scoresby Sund. *Fjord* E Greenland
Kangikajik 61 E4 *var.* Kap Brewster. *Headland* E Greenland
Kaniv 87 E2 *Rus.* Kanëv. Cherkas'ka Oblast', C Ukraine
Kanivs'ke Vodoskhovyshche 87 E2 *Rus.* Kanevskoye Vodokhranilishche. *Reservoir* C Ukraine
Kanjiža 78 D2 *Ger.* Altkanischa, *Hung.* Magyarkanizsa, Ókanizsa; *prev.* Stara Kanjiža. Serbia, N Serbia and Montenegro (Yugo.)
Kankaanpää 63 D5 Länsi-Suomi, W Finland
Kankakee 18 B3 Illinois, N USA
Kankan 52 D4 Haute-Guinée, E Guinea
Kannur *see* Cannanore
Kano 53 G4 Kano, N Nigeria
Kānpur 113 E3 *Eng.* Cawnpore. Uttar Pradesh, N India
Kansas 27 F1 *off.* State of Kansas; *also known as* Jayhawker State, Sunflower State. *State* C USA
Kansas 23 F5 Kansas, C USA
Kansas City 23 F4 Kansas, C USA
Kansas City 23 F4 Missouri, C USA
Kansas River 23 F5 *river* Kansas, C USA
Kansk 93 E4 Krasnoyarskiy Kray, S Russian Federation
Kansu *see* Gansu
Kantalahti *see* Kandalaksha
Kántanos 83 C7 Kríti, Greece, E Mediterranean Sea
Kantemirovka 89 B6 Voronezhskaya Oblast', W Russian Federation
Kanton 123 F3 *var.* Abariringa, Canton Island; *prev.* Mary Island. *Atoll* Phoenix Islands, C Kiribati
Kanye 56 C4 Southern, SE Botswana
Kaohsiung 106 D6 *var.* Gaoxiong, *Jap.* Takao, Takow. S Taiwan
Kaolack 52 B3 *var.* Kaolak. W Senegal
Kaolak *see* Kaolack
Kaolan *see* Lanzhou
Kaoma 56 C2 Western, W Zambia
Kap Brewster *see* Kangikajik
Kapelle 65 B5 Zeeland, SW Netherlands
Kapellen 65 C5 Antwerpen, N Belgium
Kap Farvel *see* Uummannarsuaq
Kapka, Massif du 54 C2 *mountain range* E Chad
Kaplangky, Plato 100 C2 *ridge* Turkmenistan/Uzbekistan
Kapoeta 51 C5 Eastern Equatoria, SE Sudan
Kaposvár 77 C7 Somogy, SW Hungary
Kappeln 72 B2 Schleswig-Holstein, N Germany
Kapstad *see* Cape Town
Kaptsevichy 85 C7 *Rus.* Koptsevichi. Homyel'skaya Voblasts', SE Belarus
Kapuas, Sungai 116 C4 *prev.* Kapoeas. *River* Borneo, C Indonesia
Kapuskasing 16 C4 Ontario, S Canada
Kapyl' 85 C6 *Rus.* Kopyl'. Minskaya Voblasts', C Belarus
Kap York *see* Innaanganeq
Kara-Balta 101 F2 Chuyskaya Oblast', N Kyrgyzstan
Karabil', Vozvyshennost' 100 D3 *mountain range* S Turkmenistan
Karabük 94 C2 Karabük NW Turkey
Karāchi 112 B3 Sind, SE Pakistan
Karadeniz *see* Black Sea
Karadeniz Boğazı *see* İstanbul Boğazı
Karaferiye *see* Véroia
Karaganda 92 C4 *Kaz.* Qaraghandy. Karaganda, C Kazakhstan
Karaginskiy, Ostrov 93 H2 *island* E Russian Federation

Kitchener – Kurile Trench

Kitchener 16 C5 Ontario, S Canada
Kíthira see Kýthira
Kíthnos see Kýthnos
Kitimat 14 D4 British Columbia, SW Canada
Kitinen 62 D3 river N Finland
Kitob 101 E3 Rus. Kitab. Qashqadaryo Wiloyati, S Uzbekistan
Kitwe 56 D2 var. Kitwe-Nkana. Copperbelt, C Zambia
Kitwe-Nkana see Kitwe
Kitzbühler Alpen 73 C7 mountain range W Austria
Kivalina 14 C2 Alaska, USA
Kivalo 62 D3 ridge C Finland
Kivertsi 86 C1 Pol. Kiwerce, Rus. Kivertsy. Volyns'ka Oblast', NW Ukraine
Kivu, Lake 55 E6 Fr. Lac Kivu. Lake Rwanda/Dem. Rep. Congo
Kızıl Irmak 94 C3 river C Turkey
Kizil Kum see Kyzyl Kum
Kladno 77 A5 Středočesky Kraj, NW Czech Republic
Klagenfurt 73 D7 Slvn. Celovec. Kärnten, S Austria
Klaipėda 84 B3 Ger. Memel. Klaipėda, NW Lithuania
Klamath Falls 24 B4 Oregon, NW USA
Klamath Mountains 24 A4 mountain range California/Oregon, W USA
Klang 116 B3 var. Kelang; prev. Port Swettenham. Selangor, Peninsular Malaysia
Klarälven 63 B6 river Norway/Sweden
Klatovy 77 A5 Ger. Klattau. Plzeňský Kraj, W Czech Republic
Klazienaveen 64 E2 Drenthe, NE Netherlands
Klein Karas 56 B4 Karas, S Namibia
Kleisoúra 83 A5 Ípeiros, W Greece
Klerksdorp 56 D4 North-West, N South Africa
Klimavichy 85 E7 Rus. Klimovichi. Mahilyowskaya Voblasts', E Belarus
Klintsy 89 A5 Bryanskaya Oblast', W Russian Federation
Klisura 82 C2 Plovdiv, C Bulgaria
Ključ 78 B3 Federacija Bosna I Hercegovina, NW Bosnia and Herzegovina
Kłobuck 76 C4 Śląskie, S Poland
Klosters 73 B7 Graubünden, SE Switzerland
Kluang see Keluang
Kluczbork 76 C4 Ger. Kreuzburg, Kreuzburg in Oberschlesien. Opolskie, S Poland
Klyuchevskaya Sopka, Vulkan 93 H3 volcano E Russian Federation
Knin 78 B4 Šibenik-Knin, S Croatia
Knjaževac 78 E4 Serbia, E Serbia and Montenegro (Yugo.)
Knokke-Heist 65 A5 West-Vlaanderen, NW Belgium
Knoxville 20 D1 Tennessee, S USA
Knud Rasmussen Land 60 D1 physical region N Greenland
Kōbe 109 C6 Hyōgo, Honshū, SW Japan
København 63 B7 Eng. Copenhagen; anc. Hafnia. Country capital (Denmark) Sjælland, København, E Denmark
Kobenni 52 D3 Hodh el Gharbi, S Mauritania
Koblenz 73 A5 prev. Coblenz, Fr. Coblence, anc. Confluentes. Rheinland-Pfalz, W Germany
Kobryn 85 A6 Pol. Kobryn, Rus. Kobrin. Brestskaya Voblasts', SW Belarus
K'obulet'i 95 F2 W Georgia
Kočani 79 E6 NE FYR Macedonia
Kočevje 73 D8 Ger. Gottschee. S Slovenia
Koch Bihār 113 G3 West Bengal, NE India
Kōchi 109 B7 var. Kôti. Kōchi, Shikoku, SW Japan
Kochi see Cochin
Kochiu see Gejiu
Kodiak 14 C3 Kodiak Island, Alaska, USA
Kodiak Island 14 C3 island Alaska, USA
Koeln see Köln
Ko-erh-mu see Golmud
Koetai see Mahakam, Sungai
Koetaradja see Bandaaceh
Kōfu 109 D5 var. Kôhu. Yamanashi, Honshū, S Japan
Kogarah 126 E2 New South Wales, SE Australia
Kogon 100 D2 Rus. Kagan. Bukhoro Wiloyati, C Uzbekistan
Kohīma 113 H3 Nāgāland, E India
Koh I Noh see Büyükağrı Dağı
Kohtla-Järve 84 E2 Ida-Virumaa, NE Estonia
Kôhu see Kōfu
Kokand see Qŭqon
Kokkola 62 D4 Swe. Karleby; prev. Swe. Gamlakarleby. Länsi-Suomi, W Finland
Koko see Qinghai Hu
Koko 53 F4 Kebbi, W Nigeria
Kokomo 18 C4 Indiana, N USA
Koko Nor see Qinghai
Kokrines 14 C2 Alaska, USA
Kokshaal-Tau 101 G2 Rus. Khrebet Kakshaal-Too. Mountain range China/Kyrgyzstan
Kokshetau 92 C4 Kaz. Kökshetaū; prev. Kokchetav. Severnyy Kazakhstan, N Kazakhstan
Koksijde 65 A5 West-Vlaanderen, W Belgium
Koksoak 16 D2 river Quebec, E Canada
Kokstad 56 D5 KwaZulu/Natal, E South Africa
Kola see Kol'skiy Poluostrov
Kolaka 117 E4 Sulawesi, C Indonesia
Kolam see Quilon
K'o-la-ma-i see Karamay
Kola Peninsula see Kol'skiy Poluostrov
Kolari 62 D3 Lappi, NW Finland
Kolárovo 77 C6 Ger. Gutta; prev. Guta, Hung. Gúta. Nitriansky Kraj, SW Slovakia
Kolda 52 C3 S Senegal
Kolding 63 A7 Vejle, C Denmark
Kölen 59 E1 Nor. Kjølen. Mountain range Norway/Sweden
Kolguyev, Ostrov 88 C2 island NW Russian Federation
Kolhāpur 110 B1 Mahārāshtra, SW India
Kolhumadulu Atoll 110 A5 var. Kolumadulu Atoll, Thaa Atoll. Atoll S Maldives
Kolín 77 B5 Ger. Kolin. Středočesky Kraj, C Czech Republic
Kolka 84 C2 Talsi, NW Latvia
Kolkasrags 84 C2 prev. Eng. Cape Domesnes. Headland NW Latvia
Kolkata see Calcutta
Kollam see Quilon
Köln 72 A4 var. Koeln, Eng./Fr. Cologne; prev. Cöln, anc. Colonia Agrippina, Oppidum Ubiorum. Nordrhein-Westfalen, W Germany
Koło 76 C3 Wielkopolskie, C Poland
Kołobrzeg 76 B2 Ger. Kolberg. Zachodniopomorskie, NW Poland
Kolokani 52 D3 Koulikoro, W Mali
Kolomna 89 B5 Moskovskaya Oblast', W Russian Federation
Kolomyya 86 C3 Ger. Kolomea. Ivano-Frankivs'ka Oblast', W Ukraine
Kolpa 78 A2 Ger. Kulpa, SCr. Kupa. River Croatia/Slovenia
Kolpino 88 B4 Leningradskaya Oblast', NW Russian Federation
Kólpos Ammóchostos 80 C5 var. Famagusta Bay, bay E Cyprus
Kol'skiy Poluostrov 88 C2 Eng. Kola Peninsula. Peninsula NW Russian Federation
Kolumadulu Atoll see Kolhumadulu Atoll
Kolwezi 55 D7 Shaba, S Dem. Rep. Congo
Kolyma 93 G2 river NE Russian Federation
Kolyma Range 91 G2 var. Khrebet Kolymskiy, Eng. Kolyma Range. Mountain range E Russian Federation
Komatsu 109 C5 var. Komatu. Ishikawa, Honshū, SW Japan
Komatu see Komatsu
Kommunizm Pik see Kommunizm, Qullai
Kommunizm, Qullai 101 F3 var. Qullai Garmo, Eng. Communism Peak, Rus. Kommunizma Pik; prev. Stalin Peak. Mountain E Tajikistan
Komoé 53 E4 var. Komoé Fleuve. River E Côte d'Ivoire
Komoé Fleuve see Komoé
Komotiní 82 D3 var. Gümüljina, Turk. Gümülcine. Anatolikí Makedonía kai Thráki, NE Greece
Komsomolets, Ostrov 93 E1 island Severnaya Zemlya, N Russian Federation
Komsomol'sk-na-Amure 93 G4 Khabarovskiy Kray, SE Russian Federation
Kondolovo 82 E3 Burgas, E Bulgaria
Kondopoga 88 B3 Respublika Kareliya, NW Russian Federation
Kondoz see Kunduz
Kondūz see Kunduz
Kong Christian IX Land 60 D4 Eng. King Christian IX Land. Physical region SE Greenland
Kong Frederik IX Land 60 C3 Eng. King Frederik IX Land. Physical region SW Greenland
Kong Frederik VIII Land 61 E2 Eng. King Frederik VIII Land. Physical region NE Greenland
Kong Frederik VI Kyst 60 C4 Eng. King Frederik VI Coast. Physical region SE Greenland
Kong Karls Land 61 G2 Eng. King Charles Islands. Island group SE Svalbard
Kongo see Congo
Kongolo 55 D6 Shaba, E Dem. Rep. Congo
Kongor 51 B5 Jonglei, SE Sudan
Kong Oscar Fjord 61 E3 fjord E Greenland
Kongsberg 63 B6 Buskerud, S Norway
Kông, Tônle 115 E5 Lao. Xê Kong. River Cambodia/Laos
Konia see Konya
Konieh see Konya
Konin 76 C3 Ger. Kuhnau. Wielkopolskie, C Poland
Konispol 79 C7 var. Konispoli. Vlorë, S Albania
Konispoli see Konispol
Kónitsa 82 A4 Ípeiros, W Greece
Konitz see Chojnice
Konjic 78 C4 Federacija Bosna I Hercegovina, S Bosnia and Herzegovina
Konosha 88 C4 Arkhangel'skaya Oblast', NW Russian Federation
Konotop 87 F1 Sums'ka Oblast', NE Ukraine
Konstanz 73 B7 var. Constanz, Eng. Constance; hist. Kostnitz, anc. Constantia. Baden-Württemberg, S Germany
Konstanza see Constanța
Konya 94 C4 var. Konieh; prev. Konia, anc. Iconium. Konya, C Turkey
Kopaonik 79 D5 mountain range S Serbia and Montenegro (Yugo.)
Koper 73 D8 It. Capodistria; prev. Kopar. SW Slovenia
Kopetdag Gershi 100 C3 mountain range Iran/Turkmenistan
Koppeh Dāgh 98 D2 var. Khrebet Kopetdag. Mountain range Iran/Turkmenistan
Koprivnica 78 B2 Ger. Kopreinitz, Hung. Kaproncza. Koprivnica-Križevci, N Croatia
Korat see Nakhon Ratchasima
Korat Plateau 114 D4 plateau E Thailand
Korba 113 E4 Madhya Pradesh, C India
Korça see Korçë
Korçë 79 D6 var. Korça, Gk. Korytsa, It. Corriza; prev. Koritsa. Korçë, SE Albania
Korčula 78 B4 It. Curzola; anc. Corcyra Nigra. Island S Croatia
Korea Bay 105 G3 bay China/North Korea
Korea Strait 109 A7 Jap. Chōsen-kaikyō, Kor. Taehan-haehyŏp. Channel Japan/South Korea
Korhogo 52 D4 N Côte d'Ivoire
Korinthiakós Kólpos 83 B5 Eng. Gulf of Corinth; anc. Corinthiacus Sinus. Gulf C Greece
Kórinthos 83 B6 Eng. Corinth; anc. Corinthus. Pelopónnisos, S Greece
Koritsa see Korçë
Kōriyama 109 D5 Fukushima, Honshū, C Japan
Korla 104 C3 Chin. K'u-erh-lo. Xinjiang Uygur Zizhiqu, NW China
Körmend 77 B7 Vas, W Hungary
Koróni 83 B6 Pelopónnisos, S Greece
Koror see Oreor
Korosten' 86 D1 Zhytomyrs'ka Oblast', NW Ukraine
Koro Toro 54 C2 Borkou-Ennedi-Tibesti, N Chad
Kortrijk 65 A6 Fr. Courtrai. West-Vlaanderen, W Belgium
Koryak Range see Koryakskoye Nagor'ye
Koryakskiy Khrebet see Koryakskoye Nagor'ye
Koryakskoye Nagor'ye 93 H2 var. Koryakskiy Khrebet, Eng. Koryak Range. Mountain range NE Russian Federation
Koryazhma 88 C4 Arkhangel'skaya Oblast', NW Russian Federation
Korytsa see Korçë
Kos 83 E6 It. Coo; anc. Cos. Island Dodekánisos, Greece, Aegean Sea
Kos 83 E6 Kos, Dodekánisos, Greece, Aegean Sea
Kō-saki 109 A7 headland Nagasaki, Tsushima, SW Japan
Kościan 76 B4 Ger. Kosten. Wielkopolskie, C Poland
Koscian see Luban
Kościerzyna 76 C2 Pomorskie, NW Poland
Kosciusko, Mount see Kosciuszko, Mount
Kosciuszko, Mount 127 C7 prev. Mount Kosciusko. Mountain New South Wales, SE Australia
Koshikijima-rettō 109 A8 var. Kosikizima Rettô. Island group SW Japan
Košice 77 D6 Ger. Kaschau, Hung. Kassa. Košický Kraj, E Slovakia
Kosikizima Rettô see Koshikijima-rettō
Koson 101 E3 Rus. Kasan. Qashqadaryo Wiloyati, S Uzbekistan
Kosovo 79 D5 prev. Autonomous Province of Kosovo and Metohija. Region S Serbia and Montenegro (Yugo.)
Kosovo Polje 79 D5 Serbia, S Serbia and Montenegro (Yugo.)
Kosovska Mitrovica 79 D5 Alb. Mitrovicë; prev. Mitrovica, Titova Mitrovica. Serbia, S Serbia and Montenegro (Yugo.)
Kosrae 122 C2 prev. Kusaie. Island Caroline Islands, E Micronesia
Kossou, Lac de 52 D5 lake C Côte d'Ivoire
Kostanay 130 C4 var. Kustanay, Kaz. Qostanay. Kostanay, N Kazakhstan
Kosten see Lubań
Kostenets 82 C2 prev. Georgi Dimitrov. Sofiya, W Bulgaria
Kostnitz see Konstanz
Kostroma 88 B4 Kostromskaya Oblast', NW Russian Federation
Kostyantynivka 87 G3 Rus. Konstantinovka. Donets'ka Oblast', SE Ukraine
Koszalin 76 B2 Ger. Köslin. Zachodniopomorskie, NW Poland
Kota 112 D3 prev. Kotah. Rājasthān, N India
Kota Baharu see Kota Bharu
Kota Bahru see Kota Bharu
Kotabaru see Jayapura
Kota Bharu 116 B3 var. Kota Baharu, Kota Bahru. Kelantan, Peninsular Malaysia
Kotabumi 116 B4 prev. Kotaboemi. Sumatera, W Indonesia
Kota Kinabalu 116 D3 prev. Jesselton. Sabah, East Malaysia
Kotel'nyy, Ostrov 93 E2 island Novosibirskiye Ostrova, N Russian Federation
Kôti see Kōchi
Kotka 63 E5 Kymi, S Finland
Kotlas 88 C4 Arkhangel'skaya Oblast', NW Russian Federation
Kotonu see Cotonou
Kotor 79 C5 It. Cattaro. Montenegro, SW Serbia and Montenegro (Yugo.)
Kotovs'k 86 D3 Rus. Kotovsk. Odes'ka Oblast', SW Ukraine
Kotovsk see Hînceşti
Kotte see Sri Jayawardanapura
Kotto 54 D4 river Central African Republic/Dem. Rep. Congo
Kotuy 93 E2 river N Russian Federation
Koudougou 53 E4 C Burkina faso
Koulamoutou 55 B6 Ogooué-Lolo, C Gabon
Koulikoro 52 D3 Koulikoro, SW Mali
Koumra 54 C4 Moyen-Chari, S Chad
Kourou 37 H3 N French Guiana
Kousseir see Al Quşayr
Kousséri 54 B3 prev. Fort-Foureau. Extrême-Nord, NE Cameroon
Koutiala 52 D4 Sikasso, S Mali
Kouvola 63 E5 Kymi, S Finland
Kovel' 86 C1 Pol. Kowel. Volyns'ka Oblast', NW Ukraine
Kowloon 106 A2 Chin. Jiulong. Hong Kong, S China
Kowtal-e Barowghīl see Baroghil Pass
Kowtal-e Khaybar see Khyber Pass
Kozáni 82 B4 Dytikí Makedonía, N Greece
Kozara 78 B3 mountain range NW Bosnia and Herzegovina
Kozarska Dubica see Bosanska Dubica
Kozhikode see Calicut
Kōzu-shima 109 D6 island E Japan
Kozyatyn 86 D2 Rus. Kazatin. Vinnyts'ka Oblast', C Ukraine
Kpalimé 53 E5 var. Palimé. SW Togo
Krâchéh 115 D6 prev. Kratie. Krâchéh, E Cambodia
Kragujevac 78 D4 Serbia, C Serbia and Montenegro (Yugo.)
Kra, Isthmus of 115 B6 isthmus Malaysia/Thailand
Kraków 77 D5 Eng. Cracow, Ger. Krakau; anc. Cracovia. Małopolskie, S Poland
Krâlănh 115 D5 Siĕmréab, NW Cambodia
Kraljevo 78 D4 prev. Rankovićevo. Serbia, C Serbia and Montenegro (Yugo.)
Kramators'k 87 G3 Rus. Kramatorsk. Donets'ka Oblast', SE Ukraine
Kramfors 63 C5 Västernorrland, C Sweden
Kranéa 82 B4 Dytikí Makedonía, N Greece
Kranj 73 D7 Ger. Krainburg. NW Slovenia
Krāslava 84 D4 Krāslava, SE Latvia
Krasnaye 85 C5 Rus. Krasnoye. Minskaya Voblasts', C Belarus
Krasnoarmeysk 89 C6 Saratovskaya Oblast', W Russian Federation
Krasnodar 89 A7 prev. Ekaterinodar, Yekaterinodar. Krasnodarskiy Kray, SW Russian Federation
Krasnodon 87 H3 Luhans'ka Oblast', E Ukraine
Krasnohvardiys'ke 87 F4 Rus. Krasnogvardeyskoye. Respublika Krym, S Ukraine
Krasnokamensk 93 F4 Chitinskaya Oblast', S Russian Federation
Krasnokamsk 89 D5 Permskaya Oblast', W Russian Federation
Krasnoperekops'k 87 F4 Rus. Krasnoperekopsk. Respublika Krym, S Ukraine
Krasnovodskiy Zaliv 100 A2 Turkm. Krasnowodsk Aylagy. Lake gulf W Turkmenistan
Krasnoyarsk 92 D4 Krasnoyarskiy Kray, S Russian Federation
Krasnystaw 76 E4 Rus. Krasnostav. Lubelskie, E Poland
Krasnyy Kut 89 C6 Saratovskaya Oblast', W Russian Federation
Krasnyy Luch 87 H3 prev. Krindachevka. Luhans'ka Oblast', E Ukraine
Krâvanh, Chuŏr Phnum 115 C6 Eng. Cardamom Mountains, Fr. Chaîne des Cardamomes. Mountain range W Cambodia
Krefeld 72 A4 Nordrhein-Westfalen, W Germany
Kremenchuk 87 F2 Rus. Kremenchug. Poltavs'ka Oblast', NE Ukraine
Kremenchuts'ke Vodoskhovyshche 87 F2 Eng. Kremenchuk Reservoir, Rus. Kremenchugskoye Vodokhranilishche. Reservoir C Ukraine
Kremenets' 86 C2 Pol. Krzemieniec, Rus. Kremenets. Ternopil's'ka Oblast', W Ukraine
Kreminna 87 G2 Rus. Kremennaya. Luhans'ka Oblast', E Ukraine
Kresena see Kresna
Kresna 82 C3 var. Kresena. Blagoevgrad, SW Bulgaria
Kretikon Delagos see Kritikó Pélagos
Kretinga 84 B3 Ger. Krottingen. Kretinga, NW Lithuania
Krishna 110 C1 prev. Kistna. River C India
Krishnagiri 110 C2 Tamil Nādu, SE India
Kristiansand 63 A6 var. Christiansand. Vest-Agder, S Norway
Kristianstad 63 B7 Skåne, S Sweden
Kristiansund 62 A4 var. Christiansund. Møre og Romsdal, S Norway
Kríti 83 C7 Eng. Crete. Island Greece, Aegean Sea
Kritikó Pélagos 83 D7 var. Kretikon Delagos, Eng. Sea of Crete; anc. Mare Creticum. Sea Greece, Aegean Sea
Križevci 78 B2 Ger. Kreuz, Hung. Kőrös. Varaždin, NE Croatia
Krk 78 A3 It. Veglia; anc. Curieta. Island NW Croatia
Krolevets' 87 F1 Rus. Krolevets. Sums'ka Oblast', NE Ukraine
Kronach 73 C5 Bayern, E Germany
Kroonstad 56 D4 Free State, C South Africa
Kropotkin 89 A7 Krasnodarskiy Kray, SW Russian Federation
Krosno 77 D5 Ger. Krossen. Podkarpackie, SE Poland
Krosno Odrzańskie 76 B3 Ger. Crossen, Kreisstadt. Lubuskie, W Poland
Krško 73 E8 Ger. Gurkfeld; prev. Videm-Krško. E Slovenia
Kruhlaye 85 D6 Rus. Krugloye. Mahilyowskaya Voblasts', E Belarus
Kruja see Krujë
Krujë 79 C6 var. Kruja, It. Croia. Durrës, C Albania
Krummau see Český Krumlov
Krung Thep 115 C5 var. Krung Thep Mahanakhon, Eng. Bangkok. Country capital (Thailand) Bangkok, C Thailand
Krung Thep, Ao 115 C5 var. Bight of Bangkok. Bay S Thailand
Krung Thep Mahanakhon see Krung Thep
Krupki 85 D6 Rus. Krupki. Minskaya Voblasts', C Belarus
Krychaw 85 E7 Rus. Krichëv. Mahilyowskaya Voblasts', E Belarus
Krym see Crimea
Krymskaya Oblast' see Crimea
Kryms'ki Hory 87 F5 mountain range S Ukraine
Kryms'kyy Pivostriv 87 F5 peninsula S Ukraine
Krynica 77 D5 Ger. Tannenhof. Małopolskie, S Poland
Kryve Ozero 87 E3 Odes'ka Oblast', SW Ukraine
Kryvyy Rih 87 F3 Rus. Krivoy Rog. Dnipropetrovs'ka Oblast', SE Ukraine
Ksar al Kabir see Ksar-el-Kebir
Ksar al Soule see Er-Rachidia
Ksar-el-Kebir 48 C2 var. Alcázar, Ksar al Kabir, Ksar-el-Kébir, Ar. Al-Kasr al-Kebir, Al-Qsar al-Kbir, Sp. Alcazarquivir. NW Morocco
Ksar-el-Kébir see Ksar-el-Kebir
Kuala Dungun see Dungun
Kuala Lumpur 116 B3 country capital (Malaysia) Kuala Lumpur, Peninsular Malaysia
Kuala Terengganu 116 B3 var. Kuala Trengganu. Terengganu, Peninsular Malaysia
Kuala Trengganu see Kuala Terengganu
Kualatungkal 116 B4 Sumatera, W Indonesia
Kuang-chou see Guangzhou
Kuang-hsi see Guangxi Zhuangzu Zizhiqu
Kuang-tung see Guangdong
Kuang-yuan see Guangyuan
Kuantan 116 B3 Pahang, Peninsular Malaysia
Kuban' 87 G5 var. Hypanis. River SW Russian Federation
Kubango see Cubango
Kuching 116 C3 prev. Sarawak. Sarawak, East Malaysia
Kūchnay Darweyshān 100 D5 Helmand, S Afghanistan
Kuçova see Kuçovë
Kuçovë 79 C6 var. Kuçova; prev. Qyteti Stalin. Berat, C Albania
Kudara see Ghŭdara
Kudus 116 C5 prev. Koedoes. Jawa, C Indonesia
Kuei-chou see Guizhou
Kuei-lin see Guilin
Kuei-Yang see Guiyang
Kueyang see Guiyang
Kugluktuk 53 E3 var. Qurlurtuuq prev. Coppermine. Nunavut, NW Canada
Kuhmo 62 E4 Oulu, E Finland
Kühnö see Kihnu
Kuibyshev see Kuybyshevskoye Vodokhranilishche
Kuito 56 B2 Port. Silva Porto. Bié, C Angola
Kuji 108 D3 var. Kuzi. Iwate, Honshū, C Japan
Kukës 79 D5 var. Kukësi. Kukës, NE Albania
Kukësi see Kukës
Kukong see Shaoguan
Kukukhoto see Hohhot
Kula Kangri 113 G3 var. Kulhakangri. Mountain Bhutan/China
Kuldīga 84 B3 Ger. Goldingen. Kuldīga, W Latvia
Kuldja see Yining
Kulhakangri see Kula Kangri
Kullorsuaq 60 D2 var. Kuvdlorssuak. C Greenland
Kulmsee see Chełmża
Kŭlob 101 F3 Rus. Kulyab. SW Tajikistan
Kulu 94 C3 Konya, W Turkey
Kulunda Steppe 92 C4 Kaz. Qulyndy Zhazyghy, Rus. Kulundinskaya Ravnina. Grassland Kazakhstan/Russian Federation
Kum see Qom
Kuma 89 B7 river SW Russian Federation
Kumamoto 109 A7 Kumamoto, Kyūshū, SW Japan
Kumanovo 79 E5 Turk. Kumanova. N FYR Macedonia
Kumasi 53 E5 prev. Coomassie. C Ghana
Kumayri see Gyumri
Kumba 55 A5 Sud-Ouest, W Cameroon
Kumertau 89 D6 Respublika Bashkortostan, W Russian Federation
Kumo 53 G4 Gombe, E Nigeria
Kumon Range 114 B2 mountain range N Myanmar
Kumul see Hami
Kunashiri see Kunashir, Ostrov
Kunashir, Ostrov 108 E1 var. Kunashiri. Island Kuril'skiye Ostrova, SE Russian Federation
Kunda 84 E2 Lääne-Virumaa, NE Estonia
Kunduz 101 E3 var. Kondoz, Kundūz, Qondūz, Per. Kondūz. Kunduz, NE Afghanistan
Kuneitra see Al Qunayţirah
Kunene see Cunene
Kungsbacka 63 B7 Halland, S Sweden
Kungur 89 D5 Permskaya Oblast', NW Russian Federation
Kunlun Mountains see Kunlun Shan
Kunlun Shan 104 B4 Eng. Kunlun Mountains. Mountain range NW China
Kunming 106 B6 var. K'un-ming; prev. Yunnan. Yunnan, SW China
K'un-ming see Kunming
Kununurra 124 D3 Western Australia
Kuopio 63 E5 Itä-Suomi, C Finland
Kupang 117 E5 prev. Koepang. Timor, C Indonesia
Kup"yans'k 87 G2 Rus. Kupyansk. Kharkivs'ka Oblast', E Ukraine
Kura 95 H3 Az. Kür, Geor. Mtkvari, Turk. Kura Nehri. River SW Asia
Kurashiki 109 B6 var. Kurasiki. Okayama, Honshū, SW Japan
Kurasiki see Kurashiki
Kurdistan 95 F4 cultural region SW Asia
Kŭrdzhali 82 D3 var. Kirdzhali. Kŭrdzhali, S Bulgaria
Kure 109 B7 Hiroshima, Honshū, SW Japan
Küre Dağları 94 C2 mountain range N Turkey
Kuressaare 84 C2 Ger. Arensburg; prev. Kingissepp. Saaremaa, W Estonia
Kureyka 90 D2 river N Russian Federation
Kuria Muria Islands see Ḩalāniyāt, Juzur al
Kurile Islands see Kuril'skiye Ostrova
Kurile-Kamchatka Depression see Kurile Trench
Kurile Trench 91 F3 var. Kurile-Kamchatka Depression. Undersea feature NW Pacific Ocean

Maryland – Mitchell, Mount

Maryland 20 D1 Tennessee, S USA
Maryville 23 F4 Missouri, C USA
Masai Steppe 51 C7 grassland NW Tanzania
Masaka 51 B6 SW Uganda
Masallı 95 H3 Rus. Masally. S Azerbaijan
Masasi 51 C8 Mtwara, SE Tanzania
Masawa see Massawa
Masaya 30 D3 Masaya, W Nicaragua
Mascarene Basin 119 B5 undersea feature W Indian Ocean
Mascarene Islands 57 H4 island group W Indian Ocean
Mascarene Plain 119 B5 undersea feature W Indian Ocean
Mascarene Plateau 119 B5 undersea feature W Indian Ocean
Maseru 56 D4 country capital (Lesotho) W Lesotho
Mas-ha 59 D7 W Bank
Mashhad 98 E2 var. Meshed. Khorāsān, NE Iran
Masindi 51 B6 W Uganda
Masīra see Maṣīrah, Jazīrat
Masira, Gulf of see Maṣīrah, Khalīj
Maṣīrah, Jazīrat 99 E5 var. Masīra. Island E Oman
Maṣīrah, Khalīj 99 E5 var. Gulf of Masira. Bay E Oman
Masis see Büyükağrı Dağı
Maskat see Masqaṭ
Mason City 23 F3 Iowa, C USA
Masqaṭ 99 E5 var. Maskat, Eng. Muscat. Country capital (Oman) NE Oman
Massa 74 B3 Toscana, C Italy
Massachusetts 19 G3 off. Commonwealth of Massachusetts; also known as Bay State, Old Bay State, Old Colony State. State NE USA
Massawa 50 C4 var. Masawa, Amh. Mits'iwa. E Eritrea
Massenya 54 B3 Chari-Baguirmi, SW Chad
Massif Central 69 C5 plateau C France
Massif du Makay see Makay
Massoukou see Franceville
Masterton 129 D5 Wellington, North Island, NZ
Masty 85 B5 Rus. Mosty. Hrodzyenskaya Voblasts', W Belarus
Masuda 109 B6 Shimane, Honshū, SW Japan
Masuku see Franceville
Masvingo 56 D3 prev. Fort Victoria, Nyanda, Victoria. Masvingo, SE Zimbabwe
Maṣyāf 96 B3 Fr. Misiaf. Ḥamāh, C Syria
Matadi 55 B6 Bas-Zaïre, W Dem. Rep. Congo
Matagalpa 30 D3 Matagalpa, C Nicaragua
Matale 110 D3 Central Province, C Sri Lanka
Matam 52 C3 NE Senegal
Matamata 128 D3 Waikato, North Island, NZ
Matamoros 28 D3 Coahuila de Zaragoza, NE Mexico
Matamoros 29 E2 Tamaulipas, C Mexico
Matane 17 E4 Quebec, SE Canada
Matanzas 32 B2 Matanzas, NW Cuba
Matara 110 D4 Southern Province, S Sri Lanka
Mataram 116 D5 Pulau Lombok, C Indonesia
Mataró 71 G2 anc. Illuro. Cataluña, E Spain
Mataura 129 B7 river South Island, NZ
Mataura 129 B7 Southland, South Island, NZ
Mata Uta see Matā'utu
Matā'utu 123 E4 var. Mata Uta. Dependent territory capital (Wallis and Futuna) Île Uvea, Wallis and Futuna
Matera 75 E5 Basilicata, S Italy
Matías Romero 29 F5 Oaxaca, SE Mexico
Mato Grosso 41 E4 prev. Vila Bela da Santissima Trindade. Mato Grosso, W Brazil
Mato Grosso do Sul 41 E4 off. Estado de Mato Grosso do Sul. State S Brazil
Mato Grosso, Planalto de 34 C4 plateau C Brazil
Matosinhos 70 B2 prev. Matozinhos. Porto, NW Portugal
Matsue 109 B6 var. Matsuye, Matue. Shimane, Honshū, SW Japan
Matsumoto 109 C5 var. Matumoto. Nagano, Honshū, S Japan
Matsuyama 109 B7 var. Matuyama. Ehime, Shikoku, SW Japan
Matsuye see Matsue
Matterhorn 73 A8 It. Monte Cervino. Mountain Italy/Switzerland see also Cervino, Monte
Matthews Ridge 37 F2 N Guyana
Matthew Town 32 D2 Great Inagua, S Bahamas
Matucana 38 C4 Lima, W Peru
Matue see Matsue
Matumoto see Matsumoto
Maturín 37 E2 Monagas, NE Venezuela
Matuyama see Matsuyama
Mau 113 E3 var. Maunāth Bhanjan. Uttar Pradesh, N India
Maui 25 B8 island Hawaii, USA, C Pacific Ocean
Maulmain see Moulmein
Maun 56 C3 Ngamiland, C Botswana
Maunāth Bhanjan see Mau
Mauren 72 E1 NE Liechtenstein
Mauritania 52 C2 off. Islamic Republic of Mauritania, Ar. Mūrītānīyah. Country W Africa
Mauritius 57 H3 off. Republic of Mauritius, Fr. Maurice. Country W Indian Ocean
Mauritius 119 B5 island W Indian Ocean
Mawlamyine see Moulmein
Mawson 132 D2 Australian research station Antarctica
Maya 30 B1 river E Russian Federation
Mayadin see Al Mayādīn
Mayaguana 32 D2 island SE Bahamas
Mayaguana Passage 32 D2 passage SE Bahamas
Mayagüez 33 F3 W Puerto Rico
Mayamey 98 D2 Semnān, N Iran
Maya Mountains 30 B2 Sp. Montañas Mayas. Mountain range Belize/Guatemala
Maych'ew 50 C4 var. Mai Chio, It. Mai Ceu. N Ethiopia
Maydān Shahr 101 E4 Wardag, E Afghanistan
Mayebashi see Maebashi
Mayfield 129 B6 Canterbury, South Island, NZ
Maykop 89 A7 Respublika Adygeya, SW Russian Federation
Maymana see Meymaneh
Maymyo 114 B3 Mandalay, C Myanmar
Mayo see Maio
Mayor Island 128 D3 island NE NZ
Mayor Pablo Lagerenza see Capitán Pablo Lagerenza
Mayotte 57 F2 French territorial collectivity E Africa
May Pen 32 B5 C Jamaica
Mazabuka 56 D2 Southern, S Zambia
Mazaca see Kayseri
Mazār-e Sharīf 101 E3 var. Mazār-i Sharif. Balkh, N Afghanistan
Mazār-i Sharif see Mazār-e Sharīf
Mazatlán 28 C3 Sinaloa, C Mexico
Mažeikiai 84 B3 Mažeikiai, NW Lithuania
Mazirbe 84 C2 Talsi, NW Latvia
Mazra'a see Al Mazra'ah
Mazury 76 D3 physical region NE Poland
Mazyr 85 C7 Rus. Mozyr'. Homyel'skaya Voblasts', SE Belarus
Mbabane 56 D4 country capital (Swaziland) NW Swaziland
Mbacké see Mbaké
M'Baiki see Mbaïki
Mbaïki 55 C5 var. M'Baiki. Lobaye, SW Central African Republic
Mbaké 52 B3 var. Mbacké. W Senegal
Mbala 56 D1 prev. Abercorn. Northern, NE Zambia
Mbale 51 C6 E Uganda
Mbandaka 55 C5 prev. Coquilhatville. Equateur, NW Dem. Rep. Congo
M'Banza Congo 56 B1 var. Mbanza Congo; prev. São Salvador, São Salvador do Congo. Zaire, NW Angola
Mbanza-Ngungu 55 B6 Bas-Zaïre, W Dem. Rep. Congo
Mbarara 51 B6 SW Uganda
Mbé 54 B4 Nord, N Cameroon
Mbeya 51 C7 Mbeya, SW Tanzania
Mbomou see Bomu
M'Bomu see Bomu
Mbour 52 B3 W Senegal
Mbuji-Mayi 55 D7 prev. Bakwanga. Kasai Oriental, S Dem. Rep. Congo
McAlester 27 G2 Oklahoma, C USA
McAllen 27 G5 Texas, SW USA
McCamey 27 E3 Texas, SW USA
McClintock Channel 15 F2 channel Nunavut, N Canada
McComb 20 B3 Mississippi, S USA
McCook 23 E4 Nebraska, C USA
McKean Island 123 E3 island Phoenix Islands, C Kiribati
McKinley, Mount 14 C3 var. Denali. Mountain Alaska, USA
McKinley Park 14 C3 Alaska, USA
McMinnville 24 B3 Oregon, NW USA
McMurdo Base 132 B4 US research station Antarctica
McPherson see Fort McPherson
McPherson 23 E5 Kansas, C USA
Mdantsane 56 D5 Eastern Cape, SE South Africa
Mead, Lake 25 D6 reservoir Arizona/Nevada, W USA
Mecca see Makkah
Mechelen 65 C5 Eng. Mechlin, Fr. Malines. Antwerpen, C Belgium
Mecklenburger Bucht 72 C2 bay N Germany
Mecsek 77 C7 mountain range SW Hungary
Medan 116 B3 Sumatera, E Indonesia
Medeba see Ma'dabā
Medellín 36 B3 Antioquia, NW Colombia
Médenine 49 F2 var. Madanīyīn. SE Tunisia
Medford 24 B4 Oregon, NW USA
Medgidia 86 D5 Constanţa, SE Romania
Mediaş 86 B4 Ger. Mediasch, Hung. Medgyes. Sibiu, C Romania
Medicine Hat 15 F5 Alberta, SW Canada
Medinaceli 71 E2 Castilla-León, N Spain
Medina del Campo 70 D2 Castilla-León, N Spain
Mediterranean Sea 80 D3 Fr. Mer Méditerranée. Sea Africa/Asia/Europe
Médoc 69 B5 cultural region SW France
Medvezh'yegorsk 88 B3 Respublika Kareliya, NW Russian Federation
Meekatharra 125 B5 Western Australia
Meemu Atoll see Mulaku Atoll
Meerssen 65 D6 var. Mersen. Limburg, SE Netherlands
Meerut 112 D2 Uttar Pradesh, N India
Meghālaya 113 G3 state NE India
Mehdia see Mahdia
Meheso see Mī'ēso
Me Hka see Nmai Hka
Mehrīz 98 D3 Yazd, C Iran
Mehtar Lām see Mehtarlām
Mehtarlām 101 F4 var. Mehtar Lām, Meterlam, Methariam, Metharlam. Laghmān, E Afghanistan
Meiktila 114 B3 Mandalay, C Myanmar
Mejillones 42 B2 Antofagasta, N Chile
Mek'elē 50 C4 var. Makale. N Ethiopia
Mékhé 52 B3 NW Senegal
Mekong 102 D3 var. Lan-ts'ang Chiang, Cam. Mékôngk, Chin. Lancang Jiang, Lao. Mènam Khong, Th. Mae Nam Khong, Tib. Dza Chu, Vtn. Sông Tiên Giang. River SE Asia
Mékôngk see Mekong
Mekong, Mouths of the 115 E6 delta S Vietnam
Melaka 116 B3 var. Malacca. Melaka, Peninsular Malaysia
Melanesia 122 D3 island group W Pacific Ocean
Melanesian Basin 120 C2 undersea feature W Pacific Ocean
Melbourne 127 C7 state capital Victoria, SE Australia
Melbourne 21 E4 Florida, SE USA
Melghir, Chott 49 E2 var. Chott Melrhir. Salt lake E Algeria
Melilla 58 B5 anc. Rusaddir, Russadir. Melilla, Spain, N Africa
Melilla 48 D2 enclave Spain, N Africa
Melita 15 F5 Manitoba, S Canada
Melitopol' 87 F4 Zaporiz'ka Oblast', SE Ukraine
Melle 65 B5 Oost-Vlaanderen, NW Belgium
Mellerud 63 B6 Västra Götaland, S Sweden
Mellieha 80 B5 E Malta
Mellizo Sur, Cerro 43 A7 mountain S Chile
Melo 42 E4 Cerro Largo, NE Uruguay
Melsungen 72 B4 Hessen, C Germany
Melun 68 C3 anc. Melodunum. Seine-et-Marne, N France
Melville Island 124 D2 island Northern Territory, N Australia
Melville Island 15 E2 island Parry Islands, Northwest Territories/Nunavut, NW Canada
Melville, Lake 17 F2 lake Newfoundland and Labrador, E Canada
Melville Peninsula 15 G3 peninsula Northwest Territories, NE Canada
Membidj see Manbij
Memmingen 73 B6 Bayern, S Germany
Memphis 20 C1 Tennessee, S USA
Ménaka 53 F3 Goa, E Mali
Menaldum 64 D1 Fris. Menaam. Friesland, N Netherlands
Mènam Khong see Mekong
Mendaña Fracture Zone 131 F4 tectonic feature E Pacific Ocean
Mende 69 C5 anc. Mimatum. Lozère, S France
Mendeleyev Ridge 133 B2 undersea feature Arctic Ocean
Mendocino Fracture Zone 130 D2 tectonic feature NE Pacific Ocean
Mendoza 42 B4 Mendoza, W Argentina
Menemen 94 A3 İzmir, W Turkey
Menengiyn Tal 105 F2 plain E Mongolia
Menongue 56 B2 var. Vila Serpa Pinto, Port. Serpa Pinto. Cuando Cubango, C Angola
Menorca 71 H3 Eng. Minorca; anc. Balearis Minor. Island Islas Baleares, Spain, W Mediterranean Sea
Mentawai, Kepulauan 116 A4 island group W Indonesia
Meppel 64 D2 Drenthe, NE Netherlands
Merano 74 C1 Ger. Meran. Trentino-Alto Adige, N Italy
Merca see Marka
Mercedes see Villa Mercedes
Mercedes 42 D3 Corrientes, NE Argentina
Mercedes 42 D4 Soriano, SW Uruguay
Meredith, Lake 27 E1 reservoir Texas, SW USA
Merefa 87 G2 Kharkivs'ka Oblast', E Ukraine
Mergui 115 B6 Tenasserim, S Myanmar
Mergui Archipelago 115 B6 island group S Myanmar
Meriç see Maritsa
Mérida 70 C4 anc. Augusta Emerita. Extremadura, W Spain
Mérida 36 C2 Mérida, W Venezuela
Mérida 29 H3 Yucatán, SW Mexico
Meridian 20 C2 Mississippi, S USA
Mérignac 69 B5 Gironde, SW France
Merkinė 85 B5 Varėna, S Lithuania
Merowe 50 B3 desert W Sudan
Merredin 125 B6 Western Australia
Mersen see Meerssen
Mersey 67 D5 river NW England, UK
Mersin 94 C4 İçel, S Turkey
Mērsrags 84 C3 Talsi, NW Latvia
Meru 51 C6 Eastern, C Kenya
Merzifon 94 D2 Amasya, N Turkey
Merzig 73 A5 Saarland, SW Germany
Mesa 26 B2 Arizona, SW USA
Meshed see Mashhad
Mesopotamia 35 C5 var. Mesopotamia Argentina. Physical region NE Argentina
Mesopotamia Argentina see Mesopotamia
Messalo, Rio 57 E2 var. Mualo. River NE Mozambique
Messana see Messina
Messene see Messina
Messina 75 D7 var. Messana, Messene; anc. Zancle. Sicilia, Italy, C Mediterranean Sea
Messina 56 D3 Northern, NE South Africa
Messina, Stretto di 75 D7 Eng. Strait of Messina. Strait SW Italy
Messíni 83 B6 Pelopónnisos, S Greece
Mestghanem see Mostaganem
Mestia 95 F1 var. Mestiya. N Georgia
Mestiya see Mestia
Mestre 74 C2 Veneto, NE Italy
Meta 34 B2 off. Departamento del Meta. Province C Colombia
Metairie 20 B3 Louisiana, S USA
Metán 42 C2 Salta, N Argentina
Metapán 30 B2 Santa Ana, NW El Salvador
Meta, Río 36 D3 river Colombia/Venezuela
Meterlam see Mehtarlām
Methariam see Mehtarlām
Metharlam see Mehtarlām
Metković 78 B4 Dubrovnik-Neretva, SE Croatia
Métsovo 82 B4 prev. Métsovon. Ípeiros, C Greece
Metz 68 D3 anc. Divodurum Mediomatricum, Mediomatrica, Metis. Moselle, NE France
Meulaboh 116 A3 Sumatera, W Indonesia
Meuse 65 C6 Dut. Maas. River W Europe see also Maas
Meuse 68 D3 department NE France
Mexcala, Río see Balsas, Río
Mexicali 28 A1 Baja California, NW Mexico
Mexico 28 C3 off. United Mexican States, var. Méjico, México, Sp. Estados Unidos Mexicanos. Country N Central America
Mexico 23 G4 Missouri, C USA
México 29 E4 var. Ciudad de México, Eng. Mexico City. Country capital (Mexico) México, C Mexico
Mexico City see México
Mexico, Gulf of 29 F2 Sp. Golfo de México. Gulf W Atlantic Ocean
Meyadine see Al Mayādīn
Meymaneh 100 D3 var. Maimāna, Maymana. Fāryāb, NW Afghanistan
Mezen' 88 D3 river NW Russian Federation
Mezőtúr 77 D7 Jász-Nagykun-Szolnok, E Hungary
Mġarr 80 A5 Gozo, N Malta
Miahuatlán 29 F5 var. Miahuatlán de Porfirio Díaz. Oaxaca, SE Mexico
Miahuatlán de Porfirio Díaz see Miahuatlán
Miami 21 F5 Florida, SE USA
Miami 27 G1 Oklahoma, C USA
Miami Beach 21 F5 Florida, SE USA
Mīāneh 98 C2 var. Miyāneh. Āẕarbāyjān-e Khāvarī, NW Iran
Mianyang 106 B5 Sichuan, C China
Miastko 76 C2 Ger. Rummelsburg in Pommern. Pomorskie, N Poland
Mi Chai see Nong Khai
Michalovce 77 E5 Ger. Grossmichel, Hung. Nagymihály. Košický Kraj, E Slovakia
Michigan 18 C1 off. State of Michigan; also known as Great Lakes State, Lake State, Wolverine State. State N USA
Michigan, Lake 18 C2 lake N USA
Michurinsk 89 B5 Tambovskaya Oblast', W Russian Federation
Micoud 33 F2 SE Saint Lucia
Micronesia 122 B1 off. Federated States of Micronesia. Country W Pacific Ocean
Micronesia 122 C1 island group W Pacific Ocean
Mid-Atlantic Cordillera see Mid-Atlantic Ridge
Mid-Atlantic Ridge 44 C3 var. Mid-Atlantic Cordillera, Mid-Atlantic Rise, Mid-Atlantic Swell. Undersea feature Atlantic Ocean
Mid-Atlantic Rise see Mid-Atlantic Ridge
Mid-Atlantic Swell see Mid-Atlantic Ridge
Middelburg 65 B5 Zeeland, SW Netherlands
Middelharnis 64 B4 Zuid-Holland, SW Netherlands
Middelkerke 65 A5 West-Vlaanderen, W Belgium
Middle America Trench 13 B7 undersea feature E Pacific Ocean
Middle Andaman 111 F2 island Andaman Islands, India, NE Indian Ocean
Middlesboro 18 C5 Kentucky, S USA
Middlesbrough 67 D5 N England, UK
Middletown 19 F4 New Jersey, NE USA
Middletown 19 F3 New York, NE USA
Mid-Indian Basin 119 C5 undersea feature N Indian Ocean
Mid-Indian Ridge 119 C5 var. Central Indian Ridge. Undersea feature C Indian Ocean
Midland 18 C3 Michigan, N USA
Midland 16 D5 Ontario, S Canada
Midland 27 E3 Texas, SW USA
Mid-Pacific Mountains 130 C2 var. Mid-Pacific Seamounts. Undersea feature NW Pacific Ocean
Mid-Pacific Seamounts see Mid-Pacific Mountains
Midway Islands 130 D2 US territory C Pacific Ocean
Miechów 77 D5 Małopolskie, S Poland
Międzyrzec Podlaski 76 E3 Lubelskie, E Poland
Międzyrzecz 76 B3 Ger. Meseritz. Lubuskie, W Poland
Mielec 77 D5 Podkarpackie, SE Poland
Miercurea-Ciuc 86 C4 Ger. Szeklerburg, Hung. Csíkszereda. Harghita, C Romania
Mieres del Camín see Mieres del Camino
Mieres del Camino 108 D1 var. Mieres del Camín. Asturias, NW Spain
Mieresch see Mureş
Mī'ēso 51 D5 var. Meheso, Miesso. C Ethiopia
Miesso see Mī'ēso
Miguel Asua 28 D3 var. Miguel Auza. Zacatecas, C Mexico
Miguel Auza see Miguel Asua
Mijdrecht 64 C3 Utrecht, C Netherlands
Mikashevichy 85 C7 Pol. Mikaszewicze, Rus. Mikashevichi. Brestskaya Voblasts', SW Belarus
Mikhaylovka 89 B6 Volgogradskaya Oblast', SW Russian Federation
Míkonos see Mýkonos
Mikre 82 C2 Lovech, N Bulgaria
Mikun' 88 D4 Respublika Komi, NW Russian Federation
Mikuni-sanmyaku 109 D5 mountain range Honshū, N Japan
Mikura-jima 109 D6 island E Japan
Milagro 38 B2 Guayas, SW Ecuador
Milan see Milano
Milange 57 E2 Zambézia, NE Mozambique
Milano 74 B2 Eng. Milan, Ger. Mailand; anc. Mediolanum. Lombardia, N Italy
Milas 94 A4 Muğla, SW Turkey
Milashavichy 85 C7 Rus. Milashevichi. Homyel'skaya Voblasts', SE Belarus
Mildura 127 C6 Victoria, SE Australia
Mile see Mili Atoll
Miles 127 D5 Queensland, E Australia
Miles City 22 C2 Montana, NW USA
Milford Haven 67 C6 prev. Milford. SW Wales, UK
Milford Sound 129 A6 inlet South Island, NZ
Milford Sound 129 A6 Southland, South Island, NZ
Mili Atoll 122 D2 var. Mile. Atoll Ratak Chain, SE Marshall Islands
Mil'kovo 93 H3 Kamchatskaya Oblast', E Russian Federation
Milk River 22 C1 river Montana, NW USA
Milk River 15 E5 Alberta, SW Canada
Milk, Wadi el 88 B4 var. Wadi al Malik. River C Sudan
Milledgeville 21 E2 Georgia, SE USA
Mille Lacs Lake 23 F2 lake Minnesota, N USA
Millennium Island 160 C8 prev. Caroline Island, Thornton Island. Atoll Line Islands, E Kiribati
Millerovo 89 B6 Rostovskaya Oblast', SW Russian Federation
Mílos 83 C7 island Kykládes, Greece, Aegean Sea
Mílos 83 C6 Mílos, Kykládes, Greece, Aegean Sea
Milton 129 B7 Otago, South Island, NZ
Milton Keynes 67 D6 SE England, UK
Milwaukee 18 B3 Wisconsin, N USA
Min see Fujian
Mīnā' Qābūs 118 B3 NE Oman
Minas Gerais 41 F3 off. Estado de Minas Gerais. State E Brazil
Minatitlán 29 F4 Veracruz-Llave, E Mexico
Minbu 114 A3 Magwe, W Myanmar
Minch, The 66 B3 var. North Minch. Strait NW Scotland, UK
Mindanao 117 F2 island S Philippines
Mindanao Sea see Bohol Sea
Mindelheim 73 C6 Bayern, S Germany
Mindello see Mindelo
Mindelo 52 A2 var. Mindello; prev. Porto Grande. São Vicente, N Cape Verde
Minden 72 B4 anc. Minthun. Nordrhein-Westfalen, NW Germany
Mindoro 117 E2 island N Philippines
Mindoro Strait 117 E2 strait W Philippines
Mineral Wells 27 F2 Texas, SW USA
Mingäçevir 95 G2 Rus. Mingechaur, Mingechevir. C Azerbaijan
Mingāora 112 C1 var. Mingora, Mongora. North-West Frontier Province, N Pakistan
Mingora see Mingāora
Minho 70 B2 former province N Portugal
Minho, Rio 70 B2 Sp. Miño. river Portugal/Spain see also Miño
Minicoy Island 110 B3 island SW India
Minius see Miño
Minna 53 G4 Niger, C Nigeria
Minneapolis 23 F2 Minnesota, N USA
Minnesota 23 F2 off. State of Minnesota; also known as Gopher State, New England of the West, North Star State. State N USA
Miño 70 B2 var. Mino, Minius, Port. Rio Minho. River Portugal/Spain see also Minho, Rio
Mino see Miño
Minot 23 E1 North Dakota, N USA
Minsk 85 C6 country capital (Belarus) Minskaya Voblasts', C Belarus
Minskaya Wzvyshsha 85 C6 mountain range C Belarus
Mińsk Mazowiecki 76 D3 var. Nowo-Minsk. Mazowieckie, C Poland
Minto, Lac 16 D2 lake Quebec, C Canada
Minya see El Minya
Miraflores 28 C3 Baja California Sur, W Mexico
Miranda de Ebro 71 E1 La Rioja, N Spain
Miri 116 D3 Sarawak, East Malaysia
Mirim Lagoon 41 E5 var. Lake Mirim, Sp. Laguna Merín. Lagoon Brazil/Uruguay
Mirim, Lake see Mirim Lagoon
Mírina see Mýrina
Mīrjāveh 98 E4 Sīstān va Balūchestān, SE Iran
Mirny 132 C3 Russian research station Antarctica
Mirnyy 93 F3 Respublika Sakha (Yakutiya), NE Russian Federation
Mīrpur Khās 112 B3 Sind, SE Pakistan
Mirtóo Pélagos 83 C6 Eng. Mirtoan Sea; anc. Myrtoum Mare. Sea S Greece
Miskito Coast see Mosquito Coast
Miskitos, Cayos 31 E2 island group NE Nicaragua
Miskolc 77 D6 Borsod-Abaúj-Zemplén, NE Hungary
Misool, Pulau 117 F4 island Maluku, E Indonesia
Miṣrātah 49 F2 var. Misurata. NW Libya
Mission 27 G5 Texas, SW USA
Mississippi 20 B2 off. State of Mississippi; also known as Bayou State, Magnolia State. State SE USA
Mississippi Delta 20 B4 delta Louisiana, S USA
Mississippi River 13 C6 river C USA
Missoula 22 B1 Montana, NW USA
Missouri 23 F5 off. State of Missouri; also known as Bullion State, Show Me State. State C USA
Missouri River 23 E3 river C USA
Mistassini, Lac 16 D3 lake Quebec, SE Canada
Mistelbach an der Zaya 73 E6 Niederösterreich, NE Austria
Misti, Volcán 39 E4 mountain S Peru
Misurata see Miṣrātah
Mitchell 127 D5 Queensland, E Australia
Mitchell 23 E3 South Dakota, N USA
Mitchell, Mount 21 E1 mountain North Carolina, SE USA

Nadi – Niuatobutabu

Nadi *123 E4 prev.* Nandi. Viti Levu, W Fiji
Nadur *80 A5* Gozo, N Malta
Nadvirna *86 C3 Pol.* Nadwórna, *Rus.* Nadvornaya. Ivano-Frankivs'ka Oblast', W Ukraine
Nadvoitsy *88 B3* Respublika Kareliya, NW Russian Federation
Nadym *92 C3* Yamalo-Nenetskiy Avtonomnyy Okrug, N Russian Federation
Náfpaktos *83 B5 var.* Návpaktos. Dytikí Ellás, C Greece
Náfplio *83 B6 prev.* Návplion. Pelopónnisos, S Greece
Naga *117 E2 off.* Naga City; *prev.* Nueva Caceres. Luzon, N Philippines
Nagano *109 C5* Nagano, Honshū, S Japan
Nagaoka *109 D5* Niigata, Honshū, C Japan
Nagara Pathom *see* Nakhon Pathom
Nagara Sridharmaraj *see* Nakhon Si Thammarat
Nagara Svarga *see* Nakhon Sawan
Nagasaki *109 A7* Nagasaki, Kyūshū, SW Japan
Nagato *109 A7* Yamaguchi, Honshū, SW Japan
Nāgercoil *110 C3* Tamil Nādu, SE India
Nagorno-Karabakhskaya Avtonomnaya Oblast *see* Nagornyy Karabakh
Nagornyy Karabakh *95 G3 var.* Nagorno-Karabakhskaya Avtonomnaya Oblast , *Arm.* Lernayin Gharabakh, *Az.* Dağliq Qarabağ. *Former autonomous region* SW Azerbaijan
Nagoya *109 C6* Aichi, Honshū, SW Japan
Nāgpur *112 D4* Mahārāshtra, C India
Nagqu *104 C5 Chin.* Na-ch'ii; *prev.* Hei-ho. Xizang Zizhiqu, W China
Nagykálló *77 E6* Szabolcs-Szatmár-Bereg, E Hungary
Nagykanizsa *77 C7 Ger.* Grosskanizsa. Zala, SW Hungary
Nagykőrös *77 D7* Pest, C Hungary
Nagyszentmiklós *see* Sânnicolau Mare
Naha *108 A3* Okinawa, Okinawa, SW Japan
Nahariya *see* Nahariyya
Nahariyya *97 A5 var.* Nahariya. Northern, N Israel
Nahr al 'Āṣī *see* Orantes
Nahr al Litant *see* Lītani, Nahr el
Nahr an Nīl *see* Nile
Nahr el Aassi *see* Orantes
Nahuel Huapí, Lago *43 B5 lake* W Argentina
Nā'īn *98 D3* Eşfahān, C Iran
Nain *17 F2* Newfoundland and Labrador, NE Canada
Nairobi *47 E5 country capital* (Kenya) Nairobi Area, S Kenya
Nairobi *51 C6 international airport* Nairobi Area, S Kenya
Najaf *see* An Najaf
Najima *see* Fukuoka
Najin *107 E3* NE North Korea
Najrān *99 B6 var.* Abā as Su'ūd. Najrān, S Saudi Arabia
Nakambé *see* White Volta
Nakamura *109 B7* Kōchi, Shikoku, SW Japan
Nakatsugawa *109 C6 var.* Nakatugawa. Gifu, Honshū, SW Japan
Nakatugawa *see* Nakatsugawa
Nakhodka *93 G5* Primorskiy Kray, SE Russian Federation
Nakhon Pathom *115 C5 var.* Nagara Pathom, Nakorn Pathom. Nakhon Pathom, W Thailand
Nakhon Ratchasima *115 C5 var.* Khorat, Korat. Nakhon Ratchasima, E Thailand
Nakhon Sawan *115 C5 var.* Muang Nakhon Sawan, Nagara Svarga. Nakhon Sawan, W Thailand
Nakhon Si Thammarat *115 C7 var.* Nagara Sridharmaraj, Nakhon Sithamnaraj. Nakhon Si Thammarat, SW Thailand
Nakhon Sithamnaraj *see* Nakhon Si Thammarat
Nakorn Pathom *see* Nakhon Pathom
Nakuru *51 C6* Rift Valley, SW Kenya
Nal'chik *89 B8* Kabardino-Balkarskaya Respublika, SW Russian Federation
Nālūt *49 F2* NW Libya
Namakan Lake *18 A1 lake* Canada/USA
Namangan *101 F2* Namangan Wiloyati, E Uzbekistan
Nambala *56 D2* Central, C Zambia
Nam Co *104 C5 lake* W China
Nam Đinh *114 D3* Nam Ha, N Vietnam
Namib Desert *56 B3 desert* W Namibia
Namibe *56 A2 Port.* Moçâmedes, Mossâmedes. Namibe, SW Angola
Namibia *56 B3 off.* Republic of Namibia, *var.* South West Africa, *Afr.* Suidwes-Afrika, *Ger.* Deutsch-Südwestafrika; *prev.* German Southwest Africa, South-West Africa. *Country* S Africa
Namo *see* Namu Atoll
Nam Ou *114 C3 river* N Laos
Nampa *24 D3* Idaho, NW USA
Nampula *57 E2* Nampula, NE Mozambique
Namsos *62 B4* Nord-Trøndelag, C Norway
Nam Tha *114 C4 river* N Laos
Namu Atoll *122 D2 var.* Namo. *Atoll* Ralik Chain, C Marshall Islands
Namur *65 C6 Dut.* Namen. Namur, SE Belgium
Namyit Island *106 C8 island* S Spratly Islands
Nan *114 C4 var.* Muang Nan. Nan, NW Thailand
Nanaimo *14 D5* Vancouver Island, British Columbia, SW Canada
Nanchang *106 C5 var.* Nan-ch'ang, Nanch'ang-hsien. Jiangxi, S China
Nanch'ang-hsien *see* Nanchang
Nan-ching *see* Nanjing
Nancy *68 D3* Meurthe-et-Moselle, NE France
Nandaime *30 D3* Granada, SW Nicaragua
Nānded *112 D5* Mahārāshtra, C India
Nandyāl *110 C1* Andhra Pradesh, E India
Nanjing *106 D5 var.* Nan-ching, Nanking; *prev.* Chianning, Chian-ning, Kiang-ning. Jiangsu, E China
Nanking *see* Nanjing
Nanning *106 B6 var.* Nan-ning; *prev.* Yung-ning. Guangxi Zhuangzu Zizhiqu, S China
Nan-ning *see* Nanning
Nanortalik *60 C5* S Greenland
Nanpan Jiang *114 D2 river* S China
Nanping *106 D6 var.* Nan-p'ing; *prev.* Yenping. Fujian, SE China
Nansei-Shotō *108 A2 var.* Ryukyu Islands. *Island group* SW Japan
Nansei Syotō Trench *see* Ryukyu Trench
Nansen Basin *133 C4 undersea feature* Arctic Ocean
Nansen Cordillera *133 B3 var.* Arctic-Mid Oceanic Ridge, Nansen Ridge. *Undersea feature* Arctic Ocean
Nansen Ridge *see* Nansen Cordillera
Nanterre *68 D1* Hauts-de-Seine, N France
Nantes *68 B4 Bret.* Naoned; *anc.* Condivincum, Namnetes. Loire-Atlantique, NW France
Nantucket Island *19 G3 island* Massachusetts, NE USA
Nanumaga *123 E3 var.* Nanumanga. *Atoll* NW Tuvalu
Nanumanga *see* Nanumaga
Nanumea Atoll *123 E3 atoll* NW Tuvalu
Nanyang *106 C5 var.* Nan-yang. Henan, C China
Napa *25 B6* California, W USA
Napier *128 E4* Hawke's Bay, North Island, NZ
Naples *58 D5 anc.* Neapolis. Campania, S Italy
Naples *21 E5* Florida, SE USA
Napo *34 A3 province* NE Ecuador
Napo, Río *38 C1 river* Ecuador/Peru
Naracoorte *127 B7* South Australia
Naradhivas *see* Narathiwat
Narathiwat *115 C7 var.* Naradhivas. Narathiwat, SW Thailand
Narbada *see* Narmada
Narbonne *69 C6 anc.* Narbo Martius. Aude, S France
Narborough Island *see* Fernandina, Isla
Nares Abyssal Plain *see* Nares Plain
Nares Plain *13 E6 var.* Nares Abyssal Plain. *Undersea feature* NW Atlantic Ocean
Nares Strait *60 D1 Dan.* Nares Stræde. *Strait* Canada/Greenland
Narew *76 E3 river* E Poland
Narmada *102 B3 var.* Narbada. *River* C India
Narowlya *85 C8 Rus.* Narovlya. Homyel'skaya Voblasts', SE Belarus
Närpes *63 D5 Fin.* Närpiö. Länsi-Suomi, W Finland
Narrabri *127 D6* New South Wales, SE Australia
Narrogin *125 B6* Western Australia
Narva *84 E2 prev.* Narova. *River* Estonia/Russian Federation
Narva *84 E2* Ida-Virumaa, NE Estonia
Narva Bay *84 E2 Est.* Narva Laht, *Ger.* Narwa-Bucht, *Rus.* Narvskiy Zaliv. *Bay* Estonia/Russian Federation
Narva Reservoir *84 E2 Est.* Narva Veehoidla, *Rus.* Narvskoye Vodokhranilishche. *Reservoir* Estonia/Russian Federation
Narvik *62 C3* Nordland, C Norway
Nar'yan-Mar *88 D3 prev.* Beloshchel'ye, Dzerzhinskiy. Nenetskiy Avtonomnyy Okrug, NW Russian Federation
Naryn *101 G2* Narynskaya Oblast', C Kyrgyzstan
Năsăud *86 B3 Ger.* Nussdorf, *Hung.* Naszód. Bistriţa-Năsăud, N Romania
Nase *see* Naze
Nāshik *112 C5 prev.* Nāsik. Mahārāshtra, W India
Nashua *19 G3* New Hampshire, NE USA
Nashville *20 C1 state capital* Tennessee, S USA
Näsijärvi *63 D5 lake* SW Finland
Nāsiri *see* Ahvāz
Nasiriya *see* An Nāşirīyah
Nassau *32 C1 country capital* (Bahamas) New Providence, N Bahamas
Nasser, Lake *50 B3 var.* Buhayrat Nasir, Buḥayrat Nāşir, Buḥeiret Nâşir. *Lake* Egypt/Sudan
Nata *56 C3* Central, NE Botswana
Natal *41 G2* Rio Grande do Norte, E Brazil
Natal Basin *119 A6 var.* Mozambique Basin. *Undersea feature* W Indian Ocean
Natanya *see* Netanya
Natchez *20 B3* Mississippi, S USA
Natchitoches *20 A2* Louisiana, S USA
Nathanya *see* Netanya
Natitingou *53 F4* NW Benin
Natsrat *see* Nazerat
Natuna Islands *102 D4 island group* W Indonesia
Naturaliste Plateau *119 E6 undersea feature* E Indian Ocean
Naugard *see* Nowogard
Naujamiestis *84 C4* Panevėžys, C Lithuania
Nauru *122 D2 off.* Republic of Nauru; *prev.* Pleasant Island. *Country* W Pacific Ocean
Nauta *38 C2* Loreto, N Peru
Navahrudak *85 C6 Pol.* Nowogródek, *Rus.* Novogrudok. Hrodzyenskaya Voblasts', W Belarus
Navapolatsk *85 D5 Rus.* Novopolotsk. Vitsyebskaya Voblasts', N Belarus
Navarra *71 E2 cultural region* N Spain
Navassa Island *32 C3 US unincorporated territory* C West Indies
Navojoa *28 C2* Sonora, NW Mexico
Navolat *see* Navolato
Navolato *66 C3 var.* Navolat. Sinaloa, C Mexico
Návpaktos *see* Náfpaktos
Nawabashah *see* Nawābshāh
Nawābshāh *112 B3 var.* Nawabashah. Sind, S Pakistan
Nawoiy *101 E2 Rus.* Navoi. Nawoiy Wiloyati, C Uzbekistan
Naxçıvan *95 G3 Rus.* Nakhichevan'. SW Azerbaijan
Náxos *83 D6 var.* Naxos. Náxos, Kykládes, Greece, Aegean Sea
Náxos *83 D6 island* Kykládes, Greece, Aegean Sea
Nayoro *108 D2* Hokkaidō, NE Japan
Nazca *38 D4* Ica, S Peru
Nazca Ridge *35 A5 undersea feature* E Pacific Ocean
Naze *108 B3 var.* Nase. Kagoshima, Amami-ōshima, SW Japan
Nazerat *97 A5 var.* Natsrat, *Ar.* En Nazira, *Eng.* Nazareth. Northern, N Israel
Nazilli *94 A4* Aydın, SW Turkey
Nazrēt *51 C5 var.* Adama, Hadama. C Ethiopia
N'Dalatando *56 B1 Port.* Salazar, Vila Salazar. Cuanza Norte, NW Angola
Ndélé *54 C4* Bamingui-Bangoran, N Central African Republic
Ndendé *55 B6* Ngounié, S Gabon
Ndindi *55 A6* Nyanga, S Gabon
Ndjamena *54 B3 var.* N'Djamena; *prev.* Fort-Lamy. *Country capital* (Chad) Chari-Baguirmi, W Chad
Ndjolé *55 A5* Moyen-Ogooué, W Gabon
Ndola *56 D2* Copperbelt, C Zambia
Neagh, Lough *67 B5 lake* E Northern Ireland, UK
Néa Moudanía *82 C4 var.* Néa Moudhaniá. Kentrikí Makedonía, N Greece
Néa Moudhaniá *see* Néa Moudanía
Neápoli *82 B4 prev.* Neápolis. Dytikí Makedonía, N Greece
Neápoli *83 D8* Kríti, Greece, E Mediterranean Sea
Neápoli *83 C7* Pelopónnisos, S Greece
Neapolis *see* Nablus
Near Islands *14 A2 island group* Aleutian Islands, Alaska, USA
Néa Zíchni *82 C3 var.* Néa Zíkhni; *prev.* Néa Zíkhna. Kentrikí Makedonía, NE Greece
Néa Zíkhna *see* Néa Zíchni
Néa Zíkhni *see* Néa Zíchni
Nebaj *30 B2* Quiché, W Guatemala
Nebitdag *100 B2* Balkanskiy Velayat, W Turkmenistan
Neblina, Pico da *40 C1 mountain* NW Brazil
Nebraska *22 D4 off.* State of Nebraska; also known as Blackwater State, Cornhusker State, Tree Planters State. *State* C USA
Nebraska City *23 F4* Nebraska, C USA
Neches River *27 H3 river* Texas, SW USA
Neckar *73 B6 river* SW Germany
Necochea *43 D5* Buenos Aires, E Argentina
Neder Rijn *64 D4 Eng.* Lower Rhine. *River* C Netherlands
Nederweert *65 D5* Limburg, SE Netherlands
Neede *64 E3* Gelderland, E Netherlands
Neerpelt *65 D5* Limburg, NE Belgium
Neftekamsk *89 D5* Respublika Bashkortostan, W Russian Federation
Negēlē *51 D5 var.* Negelli, *It.* Neghelli. C Ethiopia
Negelli *see* Negēlē
Neghelli *see* Negēlē
Negomane *57 E2 var.* Negomano. Cabo Delgado, N Mozambique
Negomano *see* Negomane
Negombo *110 C3* Western Province, SW Sri Lanka
Negotin *78 E4* Serbia, E Serbia and Montenegro (Yugo.)
Negra, Punta *38 A3 headland* NW Peru
Negreşti-Oaş *86 B3 Hung.* Avasfelsőfalu; *prev.* Negreşti. Satu Mare, NE Romania
Negro, Río *43 C5 river* E Argentina
Negro, Rio *40 D1 river* N South America
Negro, Río *42 D4 river* Brazil/Uruguay
Negros *117 E2 island* C Philippines
Nehbandān *98 E3* Khorāsān, E Iran
Neijiang *106 B5* Sichuan, C China
Nei Monggol Zizhiqu *see* Inner Mongolia
Nei Mongol *see* Inner Mongolia
Neiva *36 B3* Huila, S Colombia
Nellore *110 D2* Andhra Pradesh, E India
Nelson *15 G4 river* Manitoba, C Canada
Nelson *129 C5* Nelson, South Island, NZ
Néma *52 D3* Hodh ech Chargui, SE Mauritania
Neman *84 A4 Bel.* Nyoman, *Ger.* Memel, *Lith.* Nemunas, *Pol.* Niemen, *Rus.* Neman. *River* NE Europe
Neman *84 B4 Ger.* Ragnit. Kaliningradskaya Oblast', W Russian Federation
Neméa *83 B6* Pelopónnisos, S Greece
Nemours *68 C3* Seine-et-Marne, N France
Nemuro *108 E2* Hokkaidō, NE Japan
Neochóri *83 B5* Dytikí Ellás, C Greece
Nepal *113 E3 off.* Kingdom of Nepal. *Country* S Asia
Nereta *84 C4* Aizkraukle, S Latvia
Neretva *78 C4 river* Bosnia and Herzegovina/Croatia
Neringa *84 A3 Ger.* Nidden; *prev.* Nida. Neringa, SW Lithuania
Neris *85 C5 Bel.* Viliya, *Pol.* Wilia; *prev. Pol.* Wilja. *River* Belarus/Lithuania
Nerva *70 C4* Andalucía, S Spain
Neryungri *93 F4* Respublika Sakha (Yakutiya), NE Russian Federation
Neskaupstadhur *61 E5* Austurland, E Iceland
Ness, Loch *66 C3 lake* N Scotland, UK
Néstos *82 C3 Bul.* Mesta, *Turk.* Kara Su. *River* Bulgaria/Greece *see also* Mesta
Netanya *97 A6 var.* Natanya, Nathanya. Central, C Israel
Netherlands *64 C3 off.* Kingdom of the Netherlands, *var.* Holland, *Dut.* Koninkrijk der Nederlanden, Nederland. *Country* NW Europe
Netherlands Antilles *33 E5 prev.* Dutch West Indies. *Dutch autonomous region* S Caribbean Sea
Netherlands New Guinea *see* Irian Jaya
Nettilling Lake *15 G3 lake* Baffin Island, Nunavut, N Canada
Neubrandenburg *72 D3* Mecklenburg-Vorpommern, NE Germany
Neuchâtel *73 A7 Ger.* Neuenburg. Neuchâtel, W Switzerland
Neuchâtel, Lac de *A7 Ger.* Neuenburger See. *Lake* W Switzerland
Neufchâteau *65 D8* Luxembourg, SE Belgium
Neumünster *72 B2* Schleswig-Holstein, N Germany
Neunkirchen *73 A5* Saarland, SW Germany
Neuquén *43 B5* Neuquén, SE Argentina
Neuruppin *72 C3* Brandenburg, NE Germany
Neusalz an der Oder *see* Nowa Sól
Neusiedler See *73 E6 Hung.* Fertő. *Lake* Austria/Hungary
Neustadt an der Weinstrasse *73 B5 prev.* Neustadt an der Haardt, *hist.* Niewenstat, *anc.* Nova Civitas. Rheinland-Pfalz, SW Germany
Neustrelitz *72 D3* Mecklenburg-Vorpommern, NE Germany
Neu-Ulm *73 B6* Bayern, S Germany
Neuwied *73 A5* Rheinland-Pfalz, W Germany
Neuzen *see* Terneuzen
Nevada *25 C5 off.* State of Nevada; also known as Battle Born State, Sagebrush State, Silver State. *State* W USA
Nevada, Sierra *70 D5 mountain range* S Spain
Nevers *68 C4 anc.* Noviodunum. Nièvre, C France
Neves *54 E2* São Tomé, S Sao Tome and Principe
Nevinnomyssk *89 B7* Stavropol'skiy Kray, SW Russian Federation
Nevşehir *94 C3 var.* Nevshehr. Nevşehir, C Turkey
Nevshehr *see* Nevşehir
Newala *51 C8* Mtwara, SE Tanzania
New Albany *18 C5* Indiana, N USA
New Amsterdam *37 G3* E Guyana
Newark *19 F4* New Jersey, NE USA
New Bedford *19 G3* Massachusetts, NE USA
Newberg *24 B3* Oregon, NW USA
New Bern *21 F1* North Carolina, SE USA
New Braunfels *27 G4* Texas, SW USA
Newbridge *67 B6 Ir.* An Droichead Nua. C Ireland
New Britain *122 B3 island* E PNG
New Brunswick *17 E4 Fr.* Nouveau-Brunswick. *Province* SE Canada
New Caledonia *122 D4 var.* Kanaky, *Fr.* Nouvelle-Calédonie. *French overseas territory* SW Pacific Ocean
New Caledonia *122 C5 island* SW Pacific Ocean
New Caledonia Basin *120 C4 undersea feature* W Pacific Ocean
Newcastle *see* Newcastle upon Tyne
Newcastle *127 D6* New South Wales, SE Australia
Newcastle upon Tyne *66 D4 var.* Newcastle; *hist.* Monkchester, *Lat.* Pons Aelii. NE England, UK
New Delhi *112 D3 country capital* (India) Delhi, N India
Newfoundland *17 G3 Fr.* Terre-Neuve. *Island* Newfoundland, SE Canada
Newfoundland and Labrador *17 F2 Fr.* Terre Neuve. *Province* SE Canada
Newfoundland Basin *44 B3 undersea feature* NW Atlantic Ocean
New Georgia Islands *122 C3 island group* NW Solomon Islands
New Glasgow *17 F4* Nova Scotia, SE Canada
New Goa *see* Pānji
New Guinea *122 A3 Dut.* Nieuw Guinea, *Ind.* Irian. *Island* Indonesia/PNG
New Hampshire *19 F2 off.* State of New Hampshire; also known as The Granite State. *State* NE USA
New Haven *19 G3* Connecticut, NE USA
New Iberia *20 B3* Louisiana, S USA
New Ireland *122 C3 island* NE PNG
New Jersey *19 F4 off.* State of New Jersey; also known as The Garden State. *State* NE USA
Newman *124 B4* Western Australia
Newmarket *67 E6* E England, UK
New Mexico *26 C2 off.* State of New Mexico; also known as Land of Enchantment, Sunshine State. *State* SW USA
New Orleans *20 B3* Louisiana, S USA
New Plymouth *128 C4* Taranaki, North Island, NZ
Newport *18 C4* Kentucky, S USA
Newport *67 D7* S England, UK
Newport *67 C7* SE Wales, UK
Newport *19 G2* Vermont, NE USA
Newport News *19 F5* Virginia, NE USA
New Providence *32 C1 island* N Bahamas
Newquay *67 C7* SW England, UK
Newry *67 B5 Ir.* An tIúr. SE Northern Ireland, UK
New Sarum *see* Salisbury
New Siberian Islands *see* Novosibirskiye Ostrova
New South Wales *127 C6 state* SE Australia
Newton *23 G3* Iowa, C USA
Newtownabbey *67 B5 Ir.* Baile na Mainistreach. E Northern Ireland, UK
New Ulm *23 F2* Minnesota, N USA
New York *19 F4* New York, NE USA
New York *19 F3 state* NE USA
New Zealand *128 A4 abbrev.* NZ. *Country* SW Pacific Ocean
Neyveli *110 C2* Tamil Nādu, SE India
Ngangzê Co *104 B5 lake* W China
Ngaoundéré *54 B4 var.* N'Gaoundéré. Adamaoua, N Cameroon
N'Giva *56 B3 var.* Ondjiva, *Port.* Vila Pereira de Eça. Cunene, S Angola
Ngo *55 B6* Plateaux, SE Congo
Ngoko *55 B5 river* Cameroon/Congo
Ngourti *53 H3* Diffa, E Niger
Nguigmi *53 H3 var.* N'Guigmi. Diffa, SE Niger
Nguru *53 G3* Yobe, NE Nigeria
Nha Trang *115 E6* Khanh Hoa, S Vietnam
Niagara Falls *18 D3 waterfall* Canada/USA
Niagara Falls *19 E3* New York, NE USA
Niagara Falls *16 D5* Ontario, S Canada
Niamey *53 F3 country capital* (Niger) Niamey, SW Niger
Niangay, Lac *53 E3 lake* E Mali
Nia-Nia *55 E5* Orientale, NE Dem. Rep. Congo
Nias, Pulau *116 A3 island* W Indonesia
Nicaragua *30 D3 off.* Republic of Nicaragua. *Country* Central America
Nicaragua, Lago de *30 D4 var.* Cocibolca, Gran Lago, *Eng.* Lake Nicaragua. *Lake* S Nicaragua
Nicaragua, Lake *see* Nicaragua, Lago de
Nicaria *see* Ikaría
Nice *69 D6 It.* Nizza; *anc.* Nicaea. Alpes-Maritimes, SE France
Nicephorium *see* Ar Raqqah
Nicholas II Land *see* Severnaya Zemlya
Nicholls Town *32 C1* Andros Island, NW Bahamas
Nicobar Islands *102 B4 island group* India, E Indian Ocean
Nicosia *80 C5 Gk.* Lefkosía, *Turk.* Lefkoşa. *Country capital* (Cyprus) C Cyprus
Nicoya *30 D4* Guanacaste, W Costa Rica
Nicoya, Golfo de *30 D5 gulf* W Costa Rica
Nicoya, Península de *30 D4 peninsula* NW Costa Rica
Nidzica *76 D3 Ger.* Niedenburg. Warmińsko-Mazurskie, NE Poland
Niedere Tauern *77 A6 mountain range* C Austria
Nieuw Amsterdam *37 G3* Commewijne, NE Suriname
Nieuw-Bergen *64 D4* Limburg, SE Netherlands
Nieuwegein *64 C4* Utrecht, C Netherlands
Nieuw Nickerie *37 G3* Nickerie, NW Suriname
Niğde *94 C4* Niğde, C Turkey
Niger *53 F3 off.* Republic of Niger. *Country* W Africa
Niger *53 F4 river* W Africa
Nigeria *53 F4 off.* Federal Republic of Nigeria. *Country* W Africa
Niger, Mouths of the *53 F5 delta* S Nigeria
Nihon *see* Japan
Niigata *109 D5* Niigata, Honshū, C Japan
Niihama *109 B7* Ehime, Shikoku, SW Japan
Niihau *25 A7 island* Hawaii, USA, C Pacific Ocean
Nii-jima *109 D6 island* E Japan
Nijkerk *64 D3* Gelderland, C Netherlands
Nijlen *65 C5* Antwerpen, N Belgium
Nijmegen *64 D4 Ger.* Nimwegen; *anc.* Noviomagus. Gelderland, SE Netherlands
Nikaria *see* Ikaría
Nikel' *88 C2* Murmanskaya Oblast', NW Russian Federation
Nikiniki *117 E5* Timor, S Indonesia
Nikopol' *87 F3* Pleven, N Bulgaria
Nikšić *79 C5* Montenegro, SW Serbia and Montenegro (Yugo.)
Nikumaroro *123 E3 prev.* Gardner Island, Kemins Island. *Atoll* Phoenix Islands, C Kiribati
Nikunau *123 E3 var.* Nukunau; *prev.* Byron Island. *Atoll* Tungaru, W Kiribati
Nile *46 D3 Ar.* Nahr an Nīl. *River* N Africa
Nile *50 B2 former province* NW Uganda
Nile Delta *50 B1 delta* N Egypt
Nîmes *69 C6 anc.* Nemausus, Nismes. Gard, S France
Nine Degree Channel *110 B3 channel* India/Maldives
Ninetyeast Ridge *119 D5 undersea feature* E Indian Ocean
Ninety Mile Beach *128 C1 beach* North Island, NZ
Ningbo *106 D5 var.* Ning-po, Yin-hsien; *prev.* Ninghsien. Zhejiang, SE China
Ninghsien *see* Ningbo
Ning-po *see* Ningbo
Ningxia *106 B4 off.* Ningxia Huizu Zizhiqu, *var.* Ning-hsia, Ningsia, *Eng.* Ningsia Hui, Ningsia Hui Autonomous Region. Admin. region *autonomous region* N China
Ningxia Huizu Zizhiqu *see* Ningxia
Nio *see* Íos
Niobrara River *23 E3 river* Nebraska/Wyoming, C USA
Nioro *52 D3 var.* Nioro du Sahel. Kayes, W Mali
Nioro du Sahel *see* Nioro
Niort *68 B4* Deux-Sèvres, W France
Nipigon *16 B4* Ontario, S Canada
Nipigon, Lake *16 B3 lake* Ontario, S Canada
Nippon *see* Japan
Niš *79 E5 Eng.* Nish, *Ger.* Nisch; *anc.* Naissus. Serbia, SE Serbia and Montenegro (Yugo.)
Nişab *98 B4* Al Ḥudūd ash Shamālīyah, N Saudi Arabia
Nisibin *see* Nusaybin
Nisiros *see* Nísyros
Nisko *76 E4* Podkarpackie, SE Poland
Nísyros *83 E7 var.* Nisiros. *Island* Dodekánisos, Greece, Aegean Sea
Nitra *77 C6 Ger.* Neutra, *Hung.* Nyitra. *River* W Slovakia
Nitra *77 C6 Ger.* Neutra, *Hung.* Nyitra. Nitriansky Kraj, SW Slovakia
Niuatobutabu *see* Niuatoputapu

O

Porterville – Radviliškis

Porterville 25 C7 California, W USA
Port-Gentil 55 A6 Ogooué-Maritime, W Gabon
Port Harcourt 53 G5 Rivers, S Nigeria
Port Hardy 14 D5 Vancouver Island, British Columbia, SW Canada
Port Harrison see Inukjuak
Port Hedland 124 B4 Western Australia
Port Huron 18 D3 Michigan, N USA
Portimão 70 B4 var. Vila Nova de Portimão. Faro, S Portugal
Port Jackson 126 E1 harbour New South Wales, SE Australia
Port Láirge see Waterford
Portland 19 G2 Maine, NE USA
Portland 24 B3 Oregon, NW USA
Portland 27 G4 Texas, SW USA
Portland 127 B7 Victoria, SE Australia
Portland Bight 32 B5 bay S Jamaica
Portlaoighise see Portlaoise
Portlaoise 67 B6 Ir. Portlaoighise; prev. Maryborough. C Ireland
Port Lavaca 27 G4 Texas, SW USA
Port Lincoln 127 A6 South Australia
Port Louis 57 H3 country capital (Mauritius) NW Mauritius
Port Macquarie 127 E6 New South Wales, SE Australia
Portmore 32 B5 C Jamaica
Port Moresby 122 B3 country capital (PNG) Central/National Capital District, SW PNG
Port Musgrave 127 B9 bay Queensland, N Australia
Port Natal see Durban
Porto 70 B2 Eng. Oporto; anc. Portus Cale. Porto, NW Portugal
Porto Alegre 41 E5 var. Pôrto Alegre. State capital Rio Grande do Sul, S Brazil
Porto Alegre 54 E2 São Tomé, S Sao Tome and Principe
Porto Bello see Portobelo
Portobelo 31 G4 var. Porto Bello, Puerto Bello. Colón, N Panama
Port O'Connor 27 G4 Texas, SW USA
Porto Edda see Sarandë
Portoferraio 74 B4 Toscana, C Italy
Port-of-Spain 33 H5 country capital (Trinidad and Tobago) Trinidad, Trinidad and Tobago
Porto Grande see Mindelo
Portogruaro 74 C2 Veneto, NE Italy
Porto-Novo 53 F5 country capital (Benin) S Benin
Porto Santo 48 A2 var. Ilha do Porto Santo. Island Madeira, Portugal, NE Atlantic Ocean
Porto Torres 75 A5 Sardegna, Italy, C Mediterranean Sea
Porto Velho 40 D2 var. Velho. State capital Rondônia, W Brazil
Portoviejo 38 A2 var. Puertoviejo. Manabí, W Ecuador
Port Pirie 127 B6 South Australia
Port Said 50 B1 Ar. Būr Sa'īd. N Egypt
Portsmouth 19 G3 New Hampshire, NE USA
Portsmouth 18 D4 Ohio, N USA
Portsmouth 67 D7 S England, UK
Portsmouth 19 F5 Virginia, NE USA
Port Stanley see Stanley
Port Sudan 50 C3 Red Sea, NE Sudan
Port Swettenham see Klang
Port Talbot 67 C7 S Wales, UK
Portugal 70 B3 off. Republic of Portugal. Country SW Europe
Portuguese Timor see East Timor
Port-Vila 122 D4 var. Vila. Country capital (Vanuatu) Éfaté, C Vanuatu
Porvenir 43 B8 Magallanes, S Chile
Porvenir 39 E3 Pando, NW Bolivia
Porvoo 63 E6 Swe. Borgå. Etelä-Suomi, S Finland
Posadas 42 D3 Misiones, NE Argentina
Poschega see Požega
Posterholt 65 D5 Limburg, SE Netherlands
Postojna 73 D8 Ger. Adelsberg, It. Postumia. SW Slovenia
Potamós 83 C7 Antikýthira, S Greece
Potenza 75 D5 anc. Potentia. Basilicata, S Italy
P'ot'i 95 F2 W Georgia
Potiskum 53 G4 Yobe, NE Nigeria
Potomac River 19 E5 river NE USA
Potosí 39 F4 Potosí, S Bolivia
Potsdam 72 D3 Brandenburg, NE Germany
Potwar Plateau 112 C2 plateau NE Pakistan
Poŭthĭsăt 115 D6 prev. Pursat. Poŭthĭsăt, W Cambodia
Po Valley 74 C2 It. Valle del Po. Valley N Italy
Považská Bystrica 77 C5 Ger. Waagbistritz, Hung. Vágbeszterce. Trenčiansky Kraj, W Slovakia
Poverty Bay 128 E4 inlet North Island, NZ
Póvoa de Varzim 70 B2 Porto, NW Portugal
Powder River 22 D2 river Montana/Wyoming, NW USA
Powell 22 C2 Wyoming, C USA
Powell, Lake 22 B5 lake Utah, W USA
Požarevac 78 D4 Ger. Passarowitz. Serbia, NE Serbia and Montenegro (Yugo.)
Poza Rica 29 F4 var. Poza Rica de Hidalgo. Veracruz-Llave, E Mexico
Poza Rica de Hidalgo see Poza Rica
Požega 78 D4 prev. Slavonska Požega. Ger. Poschega, Hung. Pozsega. Požega-Slavonija, NE Croatia
Pozsega see Požega
Poznań 76 C3 Ger. Posen, Posnania. Wielkopolskie, C Poland
Pozoblanco 70 D4 Andalucía, S Spain
Pozzallo 75 C8 Sicilia, Italy, C Mediterranean Sea
Prachatice 77 A5 Ger. Prachatitz. Budějovický Kraj, S Czech Republic
Prado del Ganso see Goose Green
Prae see Phrae
Prague 58 D3 Oklahoma, C USA
Praha 77 A5 Eng. Prague, Ger. Prag, Pol. Praga. Country capital (Czech Republic) Středočesky Kraj, NW Czech Republic
Praia 52 A3 country capital (Cape Verde) Santiago, S Cape Verde
Prato 74 B3 Toscana, C Italy
Pratt 23 E5 Kansas, C USA
Prattville 20 D2 Alabama, S USA
Pravda 82 D1 prev. Dogrular. Silistra, NE Bulgaria
Pravia 70 C1 Asturias, N Spain
Prenzlau 72 D3 Brandenburg, NE Germany
Přerov 77 C5 Ger. Prerau. Olomoucký Kraj, E Czech Republic
Presa de la Amistad see Amistad Reservoir
Preschau see Prešov
Prescott 26 B2 Arizona, SW USA
Preševo 79 D5 Serbia, SE Serbia and Montenegro (Yugo.)
Presidente Epitácio 41 E4 São Paulo, S Brazil
Prešov 77 D5 var. Preschau, Ger. Eperies, Hung. Eperjes. Prešouský Kraj, E Slovakia
Prespa, Lake 79 D6 Alb. Liqen i Prespës, Gk. Límni Megáli Préspa, Limni Prespa, Mac. Prespansko Ezero, Serb. Prespansko Jezero. Lake SE Europe
Presque Isle 19 H1 Maine, NE USA
Preston 67 D5 NW England, UK
Prestwick 66 C4 W Scotland, UK
Pretoria 56 D4 var. Epitoli, Tshwane. Country capital (South Africa-administrative capital) Gauteng, NE South Africa
Préveza 83 A5 Ípeiros, W Greece
Pribilof Islands 14 A3 island group Alaska, USA
Priboj 78 C4 Serbia, W Serbia and Montenegro (Yugo.)
Price 22 B4 Utah, W USA
Prichard 20 C3 Alabama, S USA
Priekulė 84 B3 Ger. Prökuls. Gargždai, W Lithuania
Prienai 85 B5 Pol. Preny. Prienai, S Lithuania
Prieska 56 C4 Northern Cape, C South Africa
Prijedor 78 B3 Republika Srpska, NW Bosnia and Herzegovina
Prijepolje 78 D4 Serbia, W Serbia and Montenegro (Yugo.)
Prilep 79 D6 Turk. Perlepe. S FYR Macedonia
Primorsk 84 A4 Ger. Fischhausen. Kaliningradskaya Oblast', W Russian Federation
Primorsko 82 E2 prev. Keupriya. Burgas, E Bulgaria
Prince Albert 15 F5 Saskatchewan, S Canada
Prince Edward Island 17 F4 Fr. Île-du Prince-Édouard. Province SE Canada
Prince Edward Islands 47 E8 island group S South Africa
Prince George 15 E5 British Columbia, SW Canada
Prince of Wales Island 15 F2 island Queen Elizabeth Islands, Nunavut, NW Canada
Prince of Wales Island 126 B1 island Queensland, E Australia
Prince Patrick Island 15 E2 island Parry Islands, Northwest Territories, NW Canada
Prince Rupert 14 D4 British Columbia, SW Canada
Prince's Island see Príncipe
Princess Charlotte Bay 126 C2 bay Queensland, NE Australia
Princess Elizabeth Land 132 C3 physical region Antarctica
Príncipe 55 A5 var. Príncipe Island, Eng. Prince's Island. Island N Sao Tome and Principe
Príncipe Island see Príncipe
Prinzapolka 31 E3 Región Autónoma Atlántico Norte, NE Nicaragua
Pripet 85 C7 Bel. Prypyats', Ukr. Pryp"yat'. River Belarus/Ukraine
Pripet Marshes 85 B7 wetland Belarus/Ukraine
Priština 79 D5 Alb. Prishtinë. Serbia, S Serbia and Montenegro (Yugo.)
Privas 69 D5 Ardèche, E France
Prizren 79 D5 Alb. Prizreni. Serbia, S Serbia and Montenegro (Yugo.)
Probolinggo 116 D5 Jawa, C Indonesia
Progreso 29 H3 Yucatán, SE Mexico
Prokhladnyy 89 B8 Kabardino-Balkarskaya Respublika, SW Russian Federation
Prokuplje 79 D5 Serbia, SE Serbia and Montenegro (Yugo.)
Prome 114 B4 var. Pyè. Pegu, C Myanmar
Promyshlennyy 88 E3 Respublika Komi, NW Russian Federation
Prostějov 77 C5 Ger. Prossnitz, Pol. Prościejów. Olomoucký Kraj, E Czech Republic
Provence 69 D6 cultural region SE France
Providence see Fort Providence
Providence 19 G3 state capital Rhode Island, NE USA
Providencia, Isla de 31 F3 island NW Colombia
Provideniya 172 B1 Chukotskiy Avtonomnyy Okrug, NE Russian Federation
Provo 22 B4 Utah, W USA
Prudhoe Bay 14 D2 Alaska, USA
Prusa see Bursa
Pruszków 76 D3 Ger. Kaltdorf. Mazowieckie, C Poland
Prut 86 D4 Ger. Pruth. River E Europe
Pružany 85 B6 Pol. Prużana. Brestskaya Voblasts', SW Belarus
Prydz Bay 132 D3 bay Antarctica
Pryluky 87 E2 Rus. Priluki. Chernihivs'ka Oblast', NE Ukraine
Prymors'k 87 G4 Rus. Primorsk; prev. Primorskoye. Zaporiz'ka Oblast', SE Ukraine
Przemysl 77 E5 Rus. Peremyshl. Podkarpackie, SE Poland
Psará 83 D5 island E Greece
Psël 87 F2 river Russian Federation/Ukraine
Pskov 92 B2 Ger. Pleskau, Latv. Pleskava. Pskovskaya Oblast', W Russian Federation
Pskov, Lake E3 Est. Pihkva Järv, Ger. Pleskauer See, Rus. Pskovskoye Ozero. Lake Estonia/Russian Federation
Ptsich 85 C7 Rus. Ptich'. River SE Belarus
Ptsich 85 C7 Rus. Ptich'. Homyel'skaya Voblasts', SE Belarus
Ptuj 73 E7 Ger. Pettau; anc. Poetovio. NE Slovenia
Pucallpa 38 C3 Ucayali, C Peru
Puck 76 C2 Pomorskie, N Poland
Pudasjärvi 62 D4 Oulu, C Finland
Puduchcheri see Pondicherry
Puebla 29 F4 var. Puebla de Zaragoza. Puebla, S Mexico
Puebla de Zaragoza see Puebla
Pueblo 22 D5 Colorado, C USA
Puerto Acosta 39 E4 La Paz, W Bolivia
Puerto Aisén 43 B6 Aisén, S Chile
Puerto Ángel 29 F5 Oaxaca, SE Mexico
Puerto Argentino see Stanley
Puerto Ayacucho 36 D3 Amazonas, SW Venezuela
Puerto Baquerizo Moreno 38 B5 var. Baquerizo Moreno. Galapagos Islands, Ecuador, E Pacific Ocean
Puerto Barrios 30 C2 Izabal, E Guatemala
Puerto Bello see Portobelo
Puerto Berrío 36 B2 Antioquia, C Colombia
Puerto Cabello 36 D1 Carabobo, N Venezuela
Puerto Cabezas 31 E2 var. Bilwi. Región Autónoma Atlántico Norte, NE Nicaragua
Puerto Carreño 36 D3 Vichada, E Colombia
Puerto Cortés 30 C2 Cortés, NW Honduras
Puerto Cumarebo 36 C1 Falcón, N Venezuela
Puerto Deseado 43 C7 Santa Cruz, SE Argentina
Puerto Escondido 29 F5 Oaxaca, SE Mexico
Puerto Francisco de Orellana 38 B1 var. Coca. Napo, N Ecuador
Puerto Gallegos see Río Gallegos
Puerto Inírida 36 D3 var. Obando. Guainía, E Colombia
Puerto La Cruz 37 E1 Anzoátegui, NE Venezuela
Puerto Lempira 31 E2 Gracias a Dios, E Honduras
Puerto Limón see Limón
Puertollano 70 D4 Castilla-La Mancha, C Spain
Puerto López 36 C1 La Guajira, N Colombia
Puerto Maldonado 39 E3 Madre de Dios, E Peru
Puerto México see Coatzacoalcos
Puerto Montt 43 B5 Los Lagos, C Chile
Puerto Natales 43 B7 Magallanes, S Chile
Puerto Obaldía 31 H5 San Blas, NE Panama
Puerto Plata 33 E3 var. San Felipe de Puerto Plata. N Dominican Republic
Puerto Princesa 117 E2 off. Puerto Princesa City. Palawan, W Philippines
Puerto Rico 33 F3 off. Commonwealth of Puerto Rico; prev. Porto Rico. US commonwealth territory C West Indies
Puerto Rico 34 B1 island C West Indies
Puerto Rico Trench 34 B1 undersea feature NE Caribbean Sea
Puerto San José see San José
Puerto San Julián 43 B7 var. San Julián. Santa Cruz, SE Argentina
Puerto Suárez 39 H4 Santa Cruz, E Bolivia
Puerto Vallarta 28 D4 Jalisco, SW Mexico
Puerto Varas 43 B5 Los Lagos, C Chile
Puerto Viejo 31 E4 Heredia, NE Costa Rica
Puertoviejo see Portoviejo
Puget Sound 24 B1 sound Washington, NW USA
Puglia 75 E5 Eng. Apulia. Cultural region SE Italy
Pukaki, Lake 129 B6 lake South Island, NZ
Pukekohe 128 D3 Auckland, North Island, NZ
Puket see Phuket
Pukhavichy 85 C6 Rus. Pukhovichi. Minskaya Voblasts', C Belarus
Pula 78 A3 It. Pola; prev. Pulj. Istra, NW Croatia
Pulaski 18 D5 Virginia, NE USA
Pulau Butung see Buton, Pulau
Puławy 76 D4 Ger. Neu Amerika. Lublin, E Poland
Pul-i-Khumri see Pol-e Khomrī
Pullman 24 C2 Washington, NW USA
Pułtusk 76 D3 Mazowieckie, C Poland
Puná, Isla 38 A2 island SW Ecuador
Pune 112 C5 prev. Poona. Mahārāshtra, W India
Punjab 112 C2 prev. West Punjab, Western Punjab. Province E Pakistan
Puno 39 E4 Puno, SE Peru
Punta Alta 43 C5 Buenos Aires, E Argentina
Punta Arenas 43 B8 prev. Magallanes. Magallanes, S Chile
Punta Gorda 31 E4 Región Autónoma Atlántico Sur, SE Nicaragua
Punta Gorda 30 C2 Toledo, SE Belize
Puntarenas 30 D4 Puntarenas, W Costa Rica
Punto Fijo 36 C1 Falcón, N Venezuela
Pupuya, Nevado 39 E4 mountain W Bolivia
Puri 113 F5 var. Jagannath. Orissa, E India
Puriramya see Buriram
Purmerend 64 C3 Noord-Holland, C Netherlands
Purus, Rio 40 C2 Sp. Río Purús. River Brazil/Peru
Pusan 107 E4 off. Pusan-gwangyŏksi, var. Busan, Jap. Fusan. SE South Korea
Püspökladány 77 D6 Hajdú-Bihar, E Hungary
Putorana Mountains see Putorana, Plato
Putorana, Plato 92 D3 var. Gory Putorana, Eng. Putorana Mountains. Mountain range N Russian Federation
Puttalam 110 C3 North Western Province, W Sri Lanka
Puttgarden 72 C2 Schleswig-Holstein, N Germany
Putumayo, Río 36 B5 var. Rio Içá. River NW South America see also Içá, Rio
Putumayo, Río see Içá, Rio
Puurmani 84 D2 Ger. Talkhof. Jõgevamaa, E Estonia
Pyatigorsk 89 B7 Stavropol'skiy Kray, SW Russian Federation
P"yatykhatky 87 F3 Rus. Pyatikhatki. Dnipropetrovs'ka Oblast', E Ukraine
Pyè see Prome
Pyetrykaw 85 C7 Rus. Petrikov. Homyel'skaya Voblasts', SE Belarus
Pyinmana 114 B4 Mandalay, C Myanmar
Pýlos 83 B6 var. Pilos. Pelopónnisos, S Greece
P'yŏngyang 107 E3 var. P'yŏngyang-si, Eng. Pyongyang. Country capital (North Korea) SW North Korea
P'yŏngyang-si see P'yŏngyang
Pyramid Lake 25 C5 lake Nevada, W USA
Pyrenees 80 B2 Fr. Pyrénées, Sp. Pirineos; anc. Pyrenaei Montes. Mountain range SW Europe
Pýrgos 83 B6 var. Pírgos. Dytikí Ellás, S Greece
Pyryatyn 87 E2 Rus. Piryatin. Poltavs'ka Oblast', NE Ukraine
Pyrzyce 76 B3 Ger. Pyritz. Zachodniopomorskie, NW Poland
Pyu 114 B4 Pegu, C Myanmar
Pyuntaza 114 B4 Pegu, SW Myanmar

Q

Qā' al Jafr 97 C7 lake S Jordan
Qaanaaq 60 D1 var. Qânâq, Dan. Thule. N Greenland
Qābis see Gabès
Qacentina see Constantine
Qafşah see Gafsa
Qagan Us see Dulan
Qahremānshahr see Bākhtarān
Qaidam Pendi 104 C4 basin C China
Qal'aikhum 101 F3 Rus. Kalaikhum. S Tajikistan
Qal'at Bīshah 99 B5 'Asīr, SW Saudi Arabia
Qamdo 104 D5 Xizang Zizhiqu, W China
Qamishly see Al Qāmishlī
Qânâq see Qaanaaq
Qaqortoq 60 C4 Dan. Julianehåb. S Greenland
Qara Qum see Garagumy
Qarkilik see Ruoqiang
Qarokŭl 101 F3 Rus. Karakul'. E Tajikistan
Qars see Kars
Qarshi 101 E3 Rus. Karshi; prev. Bek-Budi. Qashqadaryo Wiloyati, S Uzbekistan
Qasigianguit see Qasigiannguit
Qasigiannguit 60 C3 var. Qasigianguit, Dan. Christianshåb. C Greenland
Qasr Farâfra 50 B2 W Egypt
Qaṭanā 97 B5 var. Katana. Dimashq, S Syria
Qatar 98 C4 off. State of Qatar, Ar. Dawlat Qaṭar. Country SW Asia
Qattara Depression see Qaṭṭâra, Monkhafad el
Qaṭṭâra, Monkhafad el 88 A1 var. Munkhafaḍ al Qaṭṭārah, Eng. Qattara Depression. Desert NW Egypt
Qazimämmäd 95 H3 Rus. Kazi Magomed. SE Azerbaijan
Qazvīn 98 C2 var. Kazvin. Qazvin, N Iran
Qena 50 B2 var. Qinā; anc. Caene, Caenepolis. E Egypt
Qeqertarssuaq see Qeqertarsuaq
Qeqertarsuaq 60 C3 var. Qeqertarssuaq, Dan. Godhavn. S Greenland
Qeqertarsuaq 60 C3 island W Greenland
Qeqertarsuup Tunua 60 C3 Dan. Disko Bugt. Inlet W Greenland
Qerveh see Qorveh
Qeshm 98 D4 var. Jazīreh-ye Qeshm, Qeshm Island. Island S Iran
Qeshm Island see Qeshm
Qian see Guizhou
Qilian Shan 104 D3 var. Kilien Mountains. Mountain range N China
Qimusseriarsuaq 60 C2 Dan. Melville Bugt, Eng. Melville Bay. Bay NW Greenland
Qinā see Qena
Qing see Qinghai
Qingdao 106 D4 var. Ching-Tao, Ch'ing-tao, Tsingtao, Tsintao, Ger. Tsingtau. Shandong, E China
Qinghai 104 C4 var. Chinghai, Koko Nor, Qing, Qinghai Sheng, Tsinghai. Admin. region province C China
Qinghai Hu 104 D4 var. Ch'ing Hai, Tsing Hai, Mong. Koko Nor. lake C China
Qinghai Sheng see Qinghai
Qingzang Gaoyuan 104 B4 var. Xizang Gaoyuan, Eng. Plateau of Tibet. Plateau W China
Qinhuangdao 106 D3 Hebei, E China
Qinzhou 106 B6 Guangxi Zhuangzu Zizhiqu, S China
Qiong see Hainan
Qiqihar 106 D2 var. Ch'i-ch'i-ha-erh, Tsitsihar; prev. Lungkiang. Heilongjiang, NE China
Qira 104 B4 Xinjiang Uygur Zizhiqu, NW China
Qitai 104 C3 Xinjiang Uygur Zizhiqu, NW China
Qīzān see Jīzān
Qizil Orda see Kyzylorda
Qizil Qum see Kyzyl Kum
Qizilrabot 101 G3 Rus. Kyzylrabot. SE Tajikistan
Qom 98 C3 var. Kum, Qum. Qom, N Iran
Qomul see Hami
Qondūz see Kunduz
Qorveh 98 C3 var. Qerveh, Qurveh. Kordestān, W Iran
Qostanay see Kostanay
Qoubaïyât 96 B4 var. Al Qubayyāt. N Lebanon
Qoussantîna see Constantine
Quang Ngai 115 E5 var. Quangngai, Quang Nghia. Quang Ngai, C Vietnam
Quangngai see Quang Ngai
Quang Nghia see Quang Ngai
Quanzhou 106 D6 var. Ch'uan-chou, Tsinkiang; prev. Chin-chiang. Fujian, SE China
Quanzhou 106 C6 Guangxi Zhuangzu Zizhiqu, S China
Qu'Appelle 15 F5 river Saskatchewan, S Canada
Quarles, Pegunungan 117 E4 mountain range Sulawesi, C Indonesia
Quarnero see Kvarner
Quartu Sant' Elena 75 A6 Sardegna, Italy, C Mediterranean Sea
Quba 95 H2 Rus. Kuba. N Azerbaijan
Qubba see Ba'qūbah
Québec 17 E4 var. Quebec. Quebec, SE Canada
Quebec 16 D3 var. Québec. Admin. region province SE Canada
Queen Charlotte Islands 14 C5 Fr. Îles de la Reine-Charlotte. Island group British Columbia, SW Canada
Queen Charlotte Sound 14 C5 sea area British Columbia, W Canada
Queen Elizabeth Islands 15 F2 Fr. Îles de la Reine-Élisabeth. Island group Northwest Territories/Nunavut, N Canada
Queensland 126 B4 state N Australia
Queenstown 56 D5 Eastern Cape, S South Africa
Queenstown 129 B7 Otago, South Island, NZ
Quelimane 57 E3 var. Kilimane, Kilmain, Quilimane. Zambézia, NE Mozambique
Quepos 31 E4 Puntarenas, S Costa Rica
Querétaro 29 E4 Querétaro de Arteaga, C Mexico
Quesada 31 E4 var. Ciudad Quesada, San Carlos. Alajuela, N Costa Rica
Quetta 112 B2 Baluchistān, SW Pakistan
Quetzalcoalco see Coatzacoalcos
Quetzaltenango see Quezaltenango
Quezaltenango 30 A2 var. Quetzaltenango. Quezaltenango, W Guatemala
Quibdó 36 A3 Chocó, W Colombia
Quilimane see Quelimane
Quillabamba 38 D3 Cusco, C Peru
Quilon 110 C3 var. Kolam, Kollam. Kerala, SW India
Quimper 68 A3 anc. Quimper Corentin. Finistère, NW France
Quimperlé 68 A3 Finistère, NW France
Quincy 18 A4 Illinois, N USA
Qui Nhon see Quy Nhơn
Quissico 57 E4 Inhambane, S Mozambique
Quito 38 B1 country capital (Ecuador) Pichincha, N Ecuador
Qullai Garmo see Kommunizm, Qullai
Qum see Qom
Qunaytra see Al Qunayṭirah
Qŭqon 101 F2 var. Khokand, Rus. Kokand. Farghona Wiloyati, E Uzbekistan
Qurein see Al Kuwayt
Qŭrghonteppa 101 E3 Rus. Kurgan-Tyube. SW Tajikistan
Qurlurtuuq see Kugluktuk
Qurveh see Qorveh
Quşayr see Al Quşayr
Quy Nhơn 115 E5 var. Quinhon, Qui Nhon. Binh Đinh, C Vietnam
Qyteti Stalin see Kuçovë
Qyzylorda see Kyzylorda

R

Raab 78 B1 Hung. Rába. River Austria/Hungary see also Rába
Raahe 62 D4 Swe. Brahestad. Oulu, W Finland
Raalte 64 D3 Overijssel, E Netherlands
Raamsdonksveer 64 C4 Noord-Brabant, S Netherlands
Raasiku 84 D2 Ger. Rasik. Harjumaa, NW Estonia
Rába 77 B7 Ger. Raab. River Austria/Hungary see also Raab
Rabat 48 C2 var. al Dar al Baida. Country capital (Morocco) NW Morocco
Rabat see Victoria
Rabat 80 B5 W Malta
Rabbah Ammon see 'Ammān
Rabbath Ammon see 'Ammān
Rabinal 30 B2 Baja Verapaz, C Guatemala
Rabka 77 D5 Małopolskie, S Poland
Râbniţa see Rîbniţa
Rabyanāh, Ramlat 49 G4 var. Rebiana Sand Sea, şaḥrā' Rabyanāh. Desert SE Libya
Race, Cape 17 H3 headland Newfoundland, Newfoundland and Labrador, E Canada
Rach Gia 115 D6 Kiên Giang, S Vietnam
Rach Gia, Vinh 115 D6 bay S Vietnam
Racine 18 B3 Wisconsin, N USA
Rădăuţi 86 C3 Ger. Radautz, Hung. Radóc. Suceava, N Romania
Radom 76 D4 Mazowieckie, C Poland
Radomsko 76 D4 Rus. Novoradomsk. Łódzkie, C Poland
Radomyshl' 86 D2 Zhytomyrs'ka Oblast', N Ukraine
Radoviš 79 E6 prev. Radovište. E FYR Macedonia
Radviliškis 84 B4 Radviliškis, N Lithuania

Ruse – San Pedro

Ruse 82 D1 var. Ruschuk, Rustchuk, Turk. Rusçuk. Ruse, N Bulgaria
Rus Krymskaya ASSR see Crimea
Russellville 20 A1 Arkansas, C USA
Russian Federation 90 D2 off. Russian Federation, var. Russia, Latv. Krievija, Rus. Rossiyskaya Federatsiya. Country Asia/Europe
Rustaq see Ar Rustāq
Rust'avi 95 G2 SE Georgia
Rustchuk see Ruse
Ruston 20 B2 Louisiana, S USA
Rutanzige I M, Lake see Edward, Lake
Rutba see Ar Ruṭbah
Rutland 19 F2 Vermont, NE USA
Rutog 104 A4 var. Rutok. Xizang Zizhiqu, W China
Rutok see Rutog
Ruvuma 47 E5 var. Rio Rovuma. River Mozambique/Tanzania see also Rovuma, Rio
Ruvuma see Rovuma, Rio
Ruwenzori 55 E5 mountain range Uganda/Dem. Rep. Congo
Ruzhany 85 B6 Rus. Ruzhany. Brestskaya Voblasts', SW Belarus
Ružomberok 77 C5 Ger. Rosenberg, Hung. Rózsahegy. Žilinsky Kraj, N Slovakia
Rwanda 51 B6 off. Rwandese Republic; prev. Ruanda. Country C Africa
Ryazan' 89 B5 Ryazanskaya Oblast', W Russian Federation
Rybinsk 88 B4 prev. Andropov. Yaroslavskaya Oblast', W Russian Federation
Rybnik 77 C5 Śląskie, S Poland
Rybnitsa see Rîbniţa
Ryde 126 E1 New South Wales, SE Australia
Ryki 76 D4 Lublin, E Poland
Rypin 76 C3 Kujawsko-pomorskie, C Poland
Ryssel see Lille
Rysy 77 C5 mountain S Poland
Ryukyu Islands 103 E3 island group SW Japan
Ryukyu Trench 103 F3 var. Nansei Syotō Trench. Undersea feature S East China Sea
Rzeszów 77 E5 Podkarpackie, SE Poland
Rzhev 88 B4 Tverskaya Oblast', W Russian Federation

S

Saale 72 C4 river C Germany
Saalfeld 73 C5 var. Saalfeld an der Saale. Thüringen, C Germany
Saalfeld an der Saale see Saalfeld
Saarbrücken 73 A6 Fr. Sarrebruck. Saarland, SW Germany
Sääre 84 C2 var. Sjar. Saaremaa, W Estonia
Saaremaa 84 C2 Ger. Oesel, Ösel; prev. Saare. Island W Estonia
Saariselkä 62 D2 Lapp. Suoločielgi. Lappi, N Finland
Sab' Ābār 96 C4 var. Sab'a Biyar, Sa'b Bi'ār. Ḥimṣ, C Syria
Sab'a Biyar see Sab' Ābār
Šabac 78 D3 Serbia, W Serbia and Montenegro (Yugo.)
Sabadell 71 G2 Cataluña, E Spain
Sabah 116 D3 cultural region Borneo, SE Asia
Sabanalarga 36 B1 Atlántico, N Colombia
Sabaneta 36 C1 Falcón, N Venezuela
Sab'atayn, Ramlat as 99 C6 desert C Yemen
Sabaya 39 F4 Oruro, S Bolivia
Sa'b Bi'ār see Sab' Ābār
Şāberī, Hāmūn-e var. Daryācheh-ye Hāmūn, Daryācheh-ye Sīstān. Lake Afghanistan/Iran see also Sīstān, Daryācheh-ye
Sabhā 49 F3 C Libya
Sabi, Rio see Save, Rio
Sabinas 29 E2 Coahuila de Zaragoza, NE Mexico
Sabinas Hidalgo 29 E2 Nuevo León, NE Mexico
Sabine River 27 H3 river Louisiana/Texas, SW USA
Sabkha see As Sabkhah
Sable, Cape 21 E5 headland Florida, SE USA
Sable Island 17 G4 island Nova Scotia, SE Canada
Şabyā 99 B6 Jīzān, SW Saudi Arabia
Sabzawar see Sabzevār
Sabzevār 98 D2 var. Sabzawar. Khorāsān, NE Iran
Sachsen 72 D4 Eng. Saxony, Fr. Saxe. State E Germany
Sachs Harbour 15 E2 Banks Island, Northwest Territories, N Canada
Sacramento 25 B5 state capital California, W USA
Sacramento Mountains 26 D2 mountain range New Mexico, SW USA
Sacramento River 25 B5 river California, W USA
Sacramento Valley 25 B5 valley California, W USA
Şa'dah 99 B6 NW Yemen
Sado 109 C5 var. Sadoga-shima. Island C Japan
Sadoga-shima see Sado
Safad see Ẕefat
Safed see Ẕefat
Säffle 63 B6 Värmland, C Sweden
Safford 26 C3 Arizona, SW USA
Safi 48 B2 W Morocco
Safīd Kūh, Selseleh-ye 100 D4 Eng. Paropamisus Range. Mountain range W Afghanistan
Sagaing 114 B3 Sagaing, C Myanmar
Sagami-nada 109 D6 inlet SW Japan
Sagan see Żagań
Sāgar 112 D4 prev. Saugor. Madhya Pradesh, C India
Saghez see Saqqez
Saginaw 18 C3 Michigan, N USA
Saginaw Bay 18 D2 lake bay Michigan, N USA
Sagua la Grande 32 B2 Villa Clara, C Cuba
Sagunt see Sagunto
Sagunto 71 F3 var. Sagunt, Ar. Murviedro; anc. Saguntum. País Valenciano, E Spain
Saguntum see Sagunto
Sahara 46 B3 desert Libya/Algeria
Sahara el Gharbîya 50 B2 var. Aş Şaḥrā' al Gharbīyah, Eng. Western Desert. Desert C Egypt
Saharan Atlas see Atlas Saharien
Sahel 52 D3 physical region C Africa
Sāḥilīyah, Jibāl as 96 B3 mountain range NW Syria
Sāhīwāl 112 C2 prev. Montgomery. Punjab, E Pakistan
şaḥrā' Rabyanāh see Rabyanāh, Ramlat
Saïda 97 A5 var. Şaydā, Sayida; anc. Sidon. W Lebanon
Saidpur 113 G3 var. Syedpur. Rajshahi, NW Bangladesh
Saigon see Hô Chi Minh
Sai Hun see Syr Darya
Saimaa 63 E5 lake SE Finland
St Albans 67 E6 anc. Verulamium. E England, UK
Saint Albans 18 D5 West Virginia, NE USA
St Andrews 66 C4 E Scotland, UK
Saint Anna Trough see Svyataya Anna Trough
St.Ann's Bay 32 B4 C Jamaica
St.Anthony 17 Gmm3 Newfoundland, Newfoundland and Labrador, SE Canada
Saint Augustine 21 E3 Florida, SE USA
St Austell 67 C7 SW England, UK
St-Brieuc 68 A3 Côtes d'Armor, NW France
St. Catharines 16 D5 Ontario, S Canada
St-Chamond 69 D5 Loire, E France
St.Clair, Lake 18 D3 Fr. Lac à L'Eau Claire. Lake Canada/USA
St-Claude 69 D5 anc. Condate. Jura, E France
Saint Cloud 23 F2 Minnesota, N USA
St Croix 33 F3 island S Virgin Islands (US)
Saint Croix River 18 A2 river Minnesota/Wisconsin, N USA
St David's Island 20 B5 island E Bermuda
St-Denis 57 G4 dependent territory capital (Réunion) NW Réunion
St-Dié 68 E4 Vosges, NE France
St-Egrève 69 D5 Isère, E France
Saintes 69 B5 anc. Mediolanum. Charente-Maritime, W France
St-Étienne 69 D5 Loire, E France
St-Flour 69 C5 Cantal, C France
Saint Gall see Sankt Gallen
St-Gaudens 69 B6 Haute-Garonne, S France
St George 20 B4 N Bermuda
Saint George 127 D5 Queensland, E Australia
Saint George 22 A5 Utah, W USA
St.George's 33 G5 country capital (Grenada) SW Grenada
St-Georges 37 H3 E French Guiana
St-Georges 17 E4 Quebec, SE Canada
St George's Channel 67 B6 channel Ireland/Wales, UK
St George's Island 20 B4 island E Bermuda
Saint Helena 47 B6 UK dependent territory C Atlantic Ocean
St.Helena Bay 56 B5 bay SW South Africa
St Helier 67 D8 dependent territory capital (Jersey) S Jersey, Channel Islands
Saint Ignace 18 C2 Michigan, N USA
St-Jean, Lac 17 E4 lake Quebec, SE Canada
Saint Joe River 24 D2 river Idaho, NW USA
Saint John 19 H1 river Canada/USA
Saint John 17 F4 New Brunswick, SE Canada
St John's 33 G3 country capital (Antigua and Barbuda) Antigua, Antigua and Barbuda
St.John's 17 H3 Newfoundland, Newfoundland and Labrador, E Canada
Saint Joseph 23 F4 Missouri, C USA
St Julian's 80 B5 N Malta
St Kilda 66 A3 island NW Scotland, UK
Saint Kitts and Nevis 33 F3 off. Federation of Saint Christopher and Nevis, var. Saint Christopher-Nevis. Country E West Indies
St-Laurent-du-Maroni 37 H3 var. St-Laurent. NW French Guiana
St.Lawrence 17 E4 Fr. Fleuve St-Laurent. River Canada/USA
St.Lawrence, Gulf of 17 F3 gulf NW Atlantic Ocean
Saint Lawrence Island 14 B2 island Alaska, USA
St-Lô 68 B3 anc. Briovera, Laudus. Manche, N France
St-Louis 68 E4 Haut-Rhin, NE France
Saint Louis 23 G4 Missouri, C USA
Saint Louis 52 B3 NW Senegal
Saint Lucia 33 E1 country SE West Indies
Saint Lucia Channel 33 H4 channel Martinique/Saint Lucia
St-Malo 68 B3 Ille-et-Vilaine, NW France
St-Malo, Golfe de 68 A3 gulf NW France
St Matthew's Island see Zadetkyi Kyun
St.Matthias Group 122 B3 island group NE PNG
St-Maur-des-Fossés 68 E2 Val-de-Marne, N France
St.Moritz 73 B7 Ger. Sankt Moritz, Rmsch. San Murezzan. Graubünden, SE Switzerland
St-Nazaire 68 A4 Loire-Atlantique, NW France
St-Omer 68 C2 Pas-de-Calais, N France
Saint Paul 23 F2 state capital Minnesota, N USA
St-Paul, Île 119 C6 var. St.Paul Island. Island NE French Southern and Antarctic Territories
St Peter Port 67 D8 dependent territory capital (Guernsey) C Guernsey, Channel Islands
Saint Petersburg see Sankt-Peterburg
Saint Petersburg 21 E4 Florida, SE USA
St-Pierre and Miquelon 13 E5 Fr. Îles St-Pierre et Miquelon. French territorial collectivity NE North America
St-Quentin 68 C3 Aisne, N France
Saint Vincent 33 H4 island N Saint Vincent and the Grenadines
Saint Vincent and the Grenadines 33 H4 country SE West Indies
Saint Vincent Passage 33 H4 passage Saint Lucia/Saint Vincent and the Grenadines
Saipan 120 B1 island country capital (Northern Mariana Islands) S Northern Mariana Islands
Sajama, Nevado 39 F4 mountain W Bolivia
Sajószentpéter 77 D6 Borsod-Abaúj-Zemplén, NE Hungary
Sakākah 98 B4 Al Jawf, NW Saudi Arabia
Sakakawea, Lake 22 D1 reservoir North Dakota, N USA
Sakata 108 D4 Yamagata, Honshū, C Japan
Sakhalin see Sakhalin, Ostrov
Sakhalin, Ostrov 93 G4 var. Sakhalin. Island SE Russian Federation
Sakhon Nakhon see Sakon Nakhon
Şäki 95 G2 Rus. Sheki; prev. Nukha. NW Azerbaijan
Sakishima-shotō 108 A3 var. Sakisima Syotô. Island group SW Japan
Sakisima Syotô see Sakishima-shotō
Sakiz see Saqqez
Sakiz-Adasi see Chíos
Sakon Nakhon 114 D4 var. Muang Sakon Nakhon, Sakhon Nakhon. Sakon Nakhon, E Thailand
Saky 87 F5 Rus. Saki. Respublika Krym, S Ukraine
Sal 52 A3 island Ilhas de Barlavento, NE Cape Verde
Sala 63 C6 Västmanland, C Sweden
Salacgrīva 84 C3 Est. Salatsi. Limbaži, N Latvia
Sala Consilina 75 D5 Campania, S Italy
Salado, Río 42 C3 river C Argentina
Salado, Río 40 D5 river E Argentina
Şalālah 99 D6 SW Oman
Salamá 30 B2 Baja Verapaz, C Guatemala
Salamanca 70 D2 anc. Helmantica, Salmantica. Castilla-León, NW Spain
Salamanca 42 B4 Coquimbo, C Chile
Salamīyah 96 B3 var. As Salamīyah. Ḥamāh, W Syria
Salang see Phuket
Salantai 84 B3 Kretinga, NW Lithuania
Salavan 115 D5 var. Saravan, Saravane. Salavan, S Laos
Salavat 89 D6 Respublika Bashkortostan, W Russian Federation
Sala y Gomez 131 F4 island Chile, E Pacific Ocean
Sala y Gomez Fracture Zone see Sala y Gomez Ridge
Sala y Gomez Ridge 131 G4 var. Sala y Gomez Fracture Zone. Tectonic feature SE Pacific Ocean
Šalčininkai 85 C5 Šalčininkai, SE Lithuania
Saldus 84 B3 Ger. Frauenburg. Saldus, W Latvia
Sale 127 C7 Victoria, SE Australia
Salé 48 C2 NW Morocco
Salekhard 92 D3 prev. Obdorsk. Yamalo-Nenetskiy Avtonomnyy Okrug, N Russian Federation
Salem 24 B3 state capital Oregon, NW USA
Salem 110 C2 Tamil Nādu, SE India
Salerno 75 D5 anc. Salernum. Campania, S Italy
Salerno, Golfo di 75 C5 Eng. Gulf of Salerno. Gulf S Italy
Salihorsk 85 C7 Rus. Soligorsk. Minskaya Voblasts', S Belarus
Salima 57 E2 Central, C Malawi
Salina 23 E5 Kansas, C USA
Salina Cruz 29 F5 Oaxaca, SE Mexico
Salinas 25 B6 California, W USA
Salinas 38 A2 Guayas, W Ecuador
Salisbury 67 D7 var. New Sarum. S England, UK
Sallyana see Salyan
Salmon River 24 D3 river Idaho, NW USA
Salmon River Mountains 24 D3 mountain range Idaho, NW USA
Salo 63 D6 Länsi-Suomi, W Finland
Salon-de-Provence 69 D6 Bouches-du-Rhône, SE France
Salonta 86 A3 Hung. Nagyszalonta. Bihor, W Romania
Sal'sk 89 B7 Rostovskaya Oblast', SW Russian Federation
Salt see As Salṭ
Salta 42 C2 Salta, NW Argentina
Saltash 67 C7 SW England, UK
Saltillo 29 E3 Coahuila de Zaragoza, NE Mexico
Salt Lake City 22 B4 state capital Utah, W USA
Salto 42 D4 Salto, N Uruguay
Salton Sea 25 D8 lake California, W USA
Salvador 41 G3 prev. São Salvador. Bahia, E Brazil
Salween 102 C2 Bur. Thanlwin, Chin. Nu Chiang, Nu Jiang. River SE Asia
Salyan 113 E3 var. Sallyana. Mid Western, W Nepal
Salzburg 73 D6 anc. Juvavum. Salzburg, N Austria
Salzgitter 72 C4 prev. Watenstedt-Salzgitter. Niedersachsen, C Germany
Salzwedel 72 C3 Sachsen-Anhalt, N Germany
Šamac see Bosanski Šamac
Samakhixai 115 E5 var. Attapu, Attopeu. Attapu, S Laos
Samalayuca 28 C1 Chihuahua, N Mexico
Samar 117 F2 island C Philippines
Samara 92 B3 prev. Kuybyshev. Samarskaya Oblast', W Russian Federation
Samarang see Semarang
Samarinda 116 D4 Borneo, C Indonesia
Samarqand 101 E2 Rus. Samarkand. Samarqand Wiloyati, C Uzbekistan
Samawa see As Samāwah
Sambalpur 113 F4 Orissa, E India
Sambava 57 G2 Antsirañana, NE Madagascar
Sambir 86 B2 Rus. Sambor. L'vivs'ka Oblast', NW Ukraine
Sambre 68 D2 river Belgium/France
Samfya 56 D2 Luapula, N Zambia
Saminatal 72 E2 valley Austria/Liechtenstein
Samnān see Semnān
Sam Neua see Xam Nua
Samoa 123 E4 off. Independent State of Samoa, var. Sāmoa; prev. Western Samoa. Country W Polynesia
Samoa Basin 121 E3 undersea feature W Pacific Ocean
Samobor 78 A2 Zagreb, N Croatia
Sámos 83 E6 prev. Limín Vathéos. Sámos, Dodekánisos, Greece, Aegean Sea
Sámos 83 D6 island Dodekánisos, Greece, Aegean Sea
Samosch see Someş
Samothráki 82 C4 anc. Samothrace. Island NE Greece
Samothráki 82 D4 Samothráki, NE Greece
Sampit 116 C4 Borneo, C Indonesia
Samsun 94 D2 anc. Amisus. Samsun, N Turkey
Samtredia 95 F2 W Georgia
Samui, Ko 115 C6 island SW Thailand
Samut Prakan 115 C5 var. Muang Samut Prakan, Paknam. Samut Prakan, C Thailand
San 77 E5 river SE Poland
San 52 D3 Ségou, C Mali
Şan'ā' 99 B6 Eng. Sana. Country capital (Yemen) W Yemen
Sana 78 B3 river NW Bosnia and Herzegovina
Sana see Şan'ā'
Sanae 132 B2 South African research station Antarctica
Sanaga 55 B5 river C Cameroon
San Ambrosio, Isla 35 A5 Eng. San Ambrosio Island. Island W Chile
Sanandaj 98 C3 prev. Sinneh. Kordestān, W Iran
San Andrés, Isla de 31 F3 island NW Colombia
San Andrés Tuxtla 29 F4 var. Tuxtla. Veracruz-Llave, E Mexico
San Angelo 27 F3 Texas, SW USA
San Antonio 27 F4 Texas, SW USA
San Antonio 30 B2 Toledo, S Belize
San Antonio 42 B4 Valparaíso, C Chile
San Antonio Oeste 43 C5 Río Negro, E Argentina
San Antonio River 27 G4 river Texas, SW USA
Sanāw 99 C6 var. Sanaw. NE Yemen
San Benedicto, Isla 28 B4 island W Mexico
San Benito 30 B1 Petén, N Guatemala
San Benito 27 G5 Texas, SW USA
San Bernardino 25 C7 California, W USA
San Blas 28 C3 Sinaloa, C Mexico
San Blas, Cape 20 D3 headland Florida, SE USA
San Blas, Cordillera de 31 G4 mountain range NE Panama
San Carlos see Quesada
San Carlos 26 B2 Arizona, SW USA
San Carlos 30 D4 Río San Juan, S Nicaragua
San Carlos de Bariloche 43 B5 Río Negro, SW Argentina
San Carlos del Zulia 36 C2 Zulia, W Venezuela
San Clemente Island 25 B8 island Channel Islands, California, W USA
San Cristobal 122 C4 var. Makira. Island SE Solomon Islands
San Cristóbal see San Cristóbal de Las Casas
San Cristóbal 36 C2 Táchira, W Venezuela
San Cristóbal de Las Casas 29 G5 var. San Cristóbal. Chiapas, SE Mexico
San Cristóbal, Isla 38 B5 var. Chatham Island. Island Galapagos Islands, Ecuador, E Pacific Ocean
Sancti Spíritus 32 B2 Sancti Spíritus, C Cuba
Sandakan 116 D3 Sabah, East Malaysia
Sandanski 82 C3 prev. Sveti Vrach. Blagoevgrad, SW Bulgaria
Sanday 66 D2 island NE Scotland, UK
Sanders 26 C2 Arizona, SW USA
Sand Hills 22 D3 mountain range Nebraska, C USA
San Diego 25 C8 California, W USA
Sandnes 63 A6 Rogaland, S Norway
Sandomierz 76 D4 Rus. Sandomir. Świętokrzyskie, C Poland
Sandoway 114 A4 Arakan State, W Myanmar
Sandpoint 24 C1 Idaho, NW USA
Sand Springs 27 G1 Oklahoma, C USA
Sandusky 18 D3 Ohio, N USA
Sandvika 63 A6 Akershus, S Norway
Sandviken 63 C6 Gävleborg, C Sweden
Sandy Bay 71 H5 bay E Gibraltar
Sandy City 22 B4 Utah, W USA
Sandy Lake 16 B3 lake Ontario, C Canada
San Esteban 30 D2 Olancho, C Honduras
San Felipe 36 D1 Yaracuy, NW Venezuela
San Felipe de Puerto Plata see Puerto Plata
San Félix, Isla 35 A5 Eng. San Felix Island. Island W Chile
San Fernando 70 C5 prev. Isla de León. Andalucía, S Spain
San Fernando 36 D2 var. San Fernando de Apure. Apure, C Venezuela
San Fernando 24 D1 California, W USA
San Fernando 33 H5 Trinidad, Trinidad and Tobago
San Fernando de Apure see San Fernando
San Fernando del Valle de Catamarca 42 C3 var. Catamarca. Catamarca, NW Argentina
San Fernando de Monte Cristi see Monte Cristi
San Francisco 25 B6 California, W USA
San Francisco del Oro 28 C2 Chihuahua, N Mexico
San Francisco de Macorís 33 E3 C Dominican Republic
San Gabriel 38 B1 Carchi, N Ecuador
San Gabriel Mountains 24 E1 mountain range California, W USA
Sangir, Kepulauan 117 F3 var. Kepulauan Sangihe. Island group N Indonesia
Sāngli 110 B1 Mahārāshtra, W India
Sangmélima 55 B5 Sud, S Cameroon
Sangre de Cristo Mountains 26 D1 mountain range Colorado/New Mexico, C USA
San Ignacio 30 B1 prev. Cayo, El Cayo. Cayo, W Belize
San Ignacio 28 B2 Baja California Sur, W Mexico
San Ignacio 39 F3 Beni, N Bolivia
San Joaquin Valley 25 B7 valley California, W USA
San Jorge, Golfo 43 C6 var. Gulf of San Jorge. Gulf S Argentina
San Jorge, Gulf of see San Jorge, Golfo
San José see San José del Guaviare
San Jose 25 B6 California, W USA
San José 30 B3 var. Puerto San José. Escuintla, S Guatemala
San José 39 G3 var. San José de Chiquitos. Santa Cruz, E Bolivia
San José 31 E4 country capital (Costa Rica) San José, C Costa Rica
San José de Chiquitos see San José
San José de Cúcuta see Cúcuta
San José del Guaviare 36 C4 var. San José. Guaviare, S Colombia
San Juan 33 F3 dependent territory capital (Puerto Rico) NE Puerto Rico
San Juan see San Juan de los Morros
San Juan 42 B4 San Juan, W Argentina
San Juan Bautista 42 D3 Misiones, S Paraguay
San Juan Bautista Tuxtepec see Tuxtepec
San Juan de Alicante 71 F4 País Valenciano, E Spain
San Juan del Norte 31 E4 var. Greytown. Río San Juan, SE Nicaragua
San Juan de los Morros 36 D2 var. San Juan. Guárico, N Venezuela
San Juanito, Isla 28 C4 island C Mexico
San Juan Mountains 26 D1 mountain range Colorado, C USA
San Juan River 26 C1 river Colorado/Utah, W USA
San Julián see Puerto San Julián
Sankt Gallen 73 B7 var. St.Gallen, Eng. Saint Gall, Fr. St-Gall. Sankt Gallen, NE Switzerland
Sankt-Peterburg 88 B4 prev. Leningrad, Petrograd, Eng. Saint Petersburg, Fin. Pietari. Leningradskaya Oblast', NW Russian Federation
Sankt Pölten 73 E6 Niederösterreich, N Austria
Sankuru 55 D6 river C Dem. Rep. Congo
Şanlıurfa 95 E4 prev. Sanli Urfa, Urfa, anc. Edessa. Şanlıurfa, S Turkey
San Lorenzo 38 A1 Esmeraldas, N Ecuador
San Lorenzo 39 G5 Tarija, S Bolivia
San Lorenzo, Isla 38 C4 island W Peru
Sanlúcar de Barrameda 70 C5 Andalucía, S Spain
San Luis 28 A1 var. San Luis Río Colorado. Sonora, NW Mexico
San Luis 30 B2 Petén, NE Guatemala
San Luis 42 C4 San Luis, C Argentina
San Luis Obispo 25 B7 California, W USA
San Luis Potosí 29 E3 San Luis Potosí, C Mexico
San Luis Río Colorado see San Luis
San Marcos 30 A2 San Marcos, W Guatemala
San Marcos 27 G4 Texas, SW USA
San Marino 74 D1 off. Republic of San Marino. Country S Europe
San Marino 74 E1 country capital (San Marino) C San Marino
San Martín 132 A2 Argentinian research station Antarctica
San Mateo 37 E2 Anzoátegui, NE Venezuela
San Matías 39 H3 Santa Cruz, E Bolivia
San Matías, Golfo 43 C5 var. Gulf of San Matías. Gulf E Argentina
San Matías, Gulf of see San Matías, Golfo
Sanmenxia 106 C4 var. Shan Xian. Henan, C China
Sânmiclăuş Mare see Sânnicolau Mare
San Miguel 28 D2 Coahuila de Zaragoza, N Mexico
San Miguel 30 C3 San Miguel, SE El Salvador
San Miguel de Ibarra see Ibarra
San Miguel de Tucumán 42 C3 var. Tucumán. Tucumán, N Argentina
San Miguelito 31 G4 Panamá, C Panama
San Miguel, Río 39 G3 river E Bolivia
Sannār see Sennar
Sânnicolaul-Mare see Sânnicolau Mare
Sânnicolau Mare 86 A4 var. Sânnicolaul-Mare, Hung. Nagyszentmiklós; prev. Sânmiclăuş Mare, Sînnicolau Mare. Timiş, W Romania
Sanok 77 E5 Podkarpackie, SE Poland
San Pablo 39 F5 Potosí, S Bolivia
San Pedro 28 D3 var. San Pedro de las Colonias. Coahuila de Zaragoza, NE Mexico
San Pedro 30 C1 Corozal, N Belize

Shantarskiye Ostrova – Somerset Island

Shantarskiye Ostrova 93 G3 Eng. Shantar Islands. Island group E Russian Federation
Shantou 106 D6 var. Shan-t'ou, Swatow. Guangdong, S China
Shantung see Shandong
Shanxi 106 C4 var. Jin, Shan-hsi, Shansi, Shanxi Sheng. Admin. region province C China
Shan Xian see Sanmenxia
Shanxi Sheng see Shanxi
Shaoguan 106 C6 var. Shao-kuan, Cant. Kukong; prev. Ch'u-chiang. Guangdong, S China
Shao-kuan see Shaoguan
Shaqrā see Shuqrah
Shaqrā' 98 B4 Ar Riyāḍ, C Saudi Arabia
Shar 130 D5 var. Charsk. Vostochnyy Kazakhstan, E Kazakhstan
Shari see Chari
Shari 108 D2 Hokkaidō, NE Japan
Shark Bay 125 A5 bay Western Australia
Shashe 56 D3 var. Shashi. River Botswana/Zimbabwe
Shashi see Shashe
Shatskiy Rise 103 G1 undersea feature N Pacific Ocean
Shatt al-Hodna see Hodna, Chott El
Shaṭṭ al Jarīd see Jerid, Chott el
Shawnee 27 G1 Oklahoma, C USA
Shchadryn 85 D7 Rus. Shchedrin. Homyel'skaya Voblasts', SE Belarus
Shchëkino 89 B5 Tul'skaya Oblast', W Russian Federation
Shchors 87 E1 Chernihivs'ka Oblast', N Ukraine
Shchuchinsk 92 C4 prev. Shchuchye. Severnyy kazakhstan, N Kazakhstan
Shchuchyn 85 B5 Pol. Szczuczyn Nowogródzki, Rus. Shchuchin. Hrodzyenskaya Voblasts', W Belarus
Shebekino 89 A6 Belgorodskaya Oblast', W Russian Federation
Shebeli 51 D5 Amh. Wabē Shebelē Wenz, It. Scebeli, Som. Webi Shabeelle. River Ethiopia/Somalia
Sheberghān 101 E3 var. Shibarghān, Shiberghan, Shiberghān. Jowzjān, N Afghanistan
Sheboygan 18 B2 Wisconsin, N USA
Shebshi Mountains 54 A4 var. Schebschi Mountains. Mountain range E Nigeria
Shechem see Nablus
Shedadi see Ash Shadādah
Sheffield 67 D5 N England, UK
Shekhem see Nablus
Shelby 22 B1 Montana, NW USA
Sheldon 23 F3 Iowa, C USA
Shelekhov Gulf see Shelikhova, Zaliv
Shelikhova, Zaliv 93 G2 Eng. Shelekhov Gulf. Gulf E Russian Federation
Shendi 50 C4 var. Shandī. River Nile, NE Sudan
Shengking see Liaoning
Shenking see Liaoning
Shenshi see Shaanxi
Shensi see Shaanxi
Shenyang 106 D3 Chin. Shen-yang, Eng. Moukden, Mukden; prev. Fengtien. Liaoning, NE China
Shepetivka 86 D2 Rus. Shepetovka. Khmel'nyts'ka Oblast', NW Ukraine
Shepparton 127 C7 Victoria, SE Australia
Sherbrooke 17 E4 Quebec, SE Canada
Shereik 50 C3 River Nile, N Sudan
Sheridan 22 C2 Wyoming, C USA
Sherman 27 G2 Texas, SW USA
's-Hertogenbosch 64 C4 Fr. Bois-le-Duc, Ger. Herzogenbusch. Noord-Brabant, S Netherlands
Shetland Islands 66 D1 island group NE Scotland, UK
Shibarghān see Sheberghān
Shiberghān see Sheberghān
Shibetsu 108 D2 var. Sibetu. Hokkaidō, NE Japan
Shibh Jazīrat Sīnā' see Sinai
Shibushi-wan 109 B8 bay SW Japan
Shigatse see Xigazê
Shih-chia-chuang see Shijiazhuang
Shihezi 104 C2 Xinjiang Uygur Zizhiqu, NW China
Shihmen see Shijiazhuang
Shijiazhuang 106 C4 var. Shih-chia-chuang; prev. Shihmen. Hebei, E China
Shikārpur 112 B3 Sind, S Pakistan
Shikoku 109 C7 var. Sikoku. Island SW Japan
Shikoku Basin 103 F2 var. Sikoku Basin. Undersea feature N Philippine Sea
Shikotan, Ostrov 108 E2 Jap. Shikotan-tō. Island NE Russian Federation
Shilabo 51 D5 E Ethiopia
Shiliguri 113 F3 prev. Siliguri. West Bengal, NE India
Shilka 93 F4 river S Russian Federation
Shillong 113 G3 E India
Shimbir Berris see Shimbiris
Shimbiris 50 E4 var. Shimbir Berris. Mountain N Somalia
Shimoga 110 C2 Karnātaka, W India
Shimonoseki 109 A7 var. Simonoseki; hist. Akamagaseki, Bakan. Yamaguchi, Honshū, SW Japan
Shinano-gawa 109 C5 var. Sinano Gawa. River Honshū, C Japan
Shīndand 100 D4 Farāh, W Afghanistan
Shingū 109 C6 var. Singû. Wakayama, Honshū, SW Japan
Shinjō 108 D4 var. Sinzyô. Yamagata, Honshū, C Japan
Shinyanga 51 C7 Shinyanga, NW Tanzania
Shiprock 26 C1 New Mexico, SW USA
Shīrāz 98 D4 var. Shīrāz. Fārs, S Iran
Shivpuri 112 D3 Madhya Pradesh, C India
Shizugawa 108 D4 Miyagi, Honshū, NE Japan
Shizuoka 109 D6 var. Sizuoka. Shizuoka, Honshū, S Japan
Shklow 85 D6 Rus. Shklov. Mahilyowskaya Voblasts', E Belarus
Shkodër 79 C5 var. Shkodra, It. Scutari, SCr. Skadar. Shkodër, NW Albania
Shkodra see Shkodër
Shkubinit, Lumi i 79 C6 var. Shkumbî, Shkumbin. River C Albania
Shkumbî see Shkubinit, Lumi i
Shkumbin see Shkubinit, Lumi i
Sholāpur see Solāpur
Shostka 87 F1 Sums'ka Oblast', NE Ukraine
Show Low 26 B2 Arizona, SW USA
Shpola 87 E3 Cherkas'ka Oblast', N Ukraine
Shreveport 20 A2 Louisiana, S USA
Shrewsbury 67 D6 hist. Scrobesbyrig'. W England, UK
Shu 92 C5 Kaz. Shū. Zhambyl, SE Kazakhstan
Shuang-liao see Liaoyuan
Shumagin Islands 14 B3 island group Alaska, USA
Shumen 82 D2 Shumen, NE Bulgaria
Shumilina 85 E5 Rus. Shumilino. Vitsyebskaya Voblasts', NE Belarus
Shuqrah 99 B7 var. Shaqrā. SW Yemen
Shwebo 114 B3 Sagaing, C Myanmar
Shyichy 85 C7 Rus. Shiichi. Homyel'skaya Voblasts', SE Belarus
Shymkent 92 B5 prev. Chimkent. Yuzhnyy Kazakhstan, S Kazakhstan
Shyshchytsy 85 C6 Rus. Shishchitsy. Minskaya Voblasts', C Belarus
Si see Syr Darya
Siam, Gulf of see Thailand, Gulf of
Sian see Xi'an
Siang see Brahmaputra
Siangtan see Xiangtan
Šiauliai 84 B4 Ger. Schaulen. Šiauliai, N Lithuania
Sibay 89 D6 Respublika Bashkortostan, W Russian Federation
Šibenik 116 B4 It. Sebenico. Šibenik-Knin, S Croatia
Siberia see Sibir'
Siberut, Pulau 116 A4 prev. Siberoet. Island Kepulauan Mentawai, W Indonesia
Sibetu see Shibetsu
Sibi 112 B2 Baluchistān, SW Pakistan
Sibir' 93 E3 var. Siberia. Physical region NE Russian Federation
Sibiti 55 B6 La Lékoumou, S Congo
Sibiu 86 B4 Ger. Hermannstadt, Hung. Nagyszeben. Sibiu, C Romania
Sibolga 116 B3 Sumatera, W Indonesia
Sibu 116 D3 Sarawak, East Malaysia
Sibut 54 C4 prev. Fort-Sibut. Kémo, S Central African Republic
Sibuyan Sea 117 E2 sea C Philippines
Sichon 115 C6 var. Ban Sichon, Si Chon. Nakhon Si Thammarat, SW Thailand
Sichuan 106 B5 var. Chuan, Sichuan Sheng, Ssu-ch'uan, Szechuan, Szechwan. Admin. region province C China
Sichuan Pendi 106 B5 depression C China
Sichuan Sheng see Sichuan
Sicilia 75 C7 Eng. Sicily; anc. Trinacria. Island Italy, C Mediterranean Sea
Sicilian Channel see Sicily, Strait of
Sicily see Sicilia
Sicily, Strait of 75 B7 var. Sicilian Channel. Strait C Mediterranean Sea
Sicuani 39 E4 Cusco, S Peru
Sidári 82 A4 Kérkyra, Iónioi Nísoi, Greece, C Mediterranean Sea
Sidas 116 C4 Borneo, C Indonesia
Siderno 75 D7 Calabria, SW Italy
Sîdi Barrâni 50 A1 NW Egypt
Sidi Bel Abbès 48 D2 var. Sidi bel Abbès, Sidi-Bel-Abbès. NW Algeria
Sidirókastro 82 C3 prev. Sidhirókastron. Kentrikí Makedonía, NE Greece
Sidley, Mount 132 B4 mountain Antarctica
Sidney 22 D1 Montana, NW USA
Sidney 22 D4 Nebraska, C USA
Sidney 18 C4 Ohio, N USA
Sidon see Saïda
Sidra see Surt
Siedlce 76 E3 Ger. Sedlez, Rus. Sesdlets. Mazowieckie, C Poland
Siegen 72 B4 Nordrhein-Westfalen, W Germany
Siemiatycze 76 E3 Podlaskie
Siena 74 B3 Fr. Sienne; anc. Saena Julia. Toscana, C Italy
Sieradz 76 C4 Łódzkie, C Poland
Sierpc 76 D3 Mazowieckie, C Poland
Sierra de Soconusco see Sierra Madre
Sierra Leone 52 C4 off. Republic of Sierra Leone. Country W Africa
Sierra Leone Basin 44 C4 undersea feature E Atlantic Ocean
Sierra Leone Ridge see Sierra Leone Rise
Sierra Leone Rise 44 C4 var. Sierra Leone Ridge, Sierra Leone Schwelle. Undersea feature E Atlantic Ocean
Sierra Leone Schwelle see Sierra Leone Rise
Sierra Madre 30 B2 var. Sierra de Soconusco. Mountain range Guatemala/Mexico
Sierra Madre see Madre Occidental, Sierra
Sierra Nevada 25 C6 mountain range W USA
Sierra Pacaraima see Pakaraima Mountains
Sierra Vieja 26 D3 mountain range Texas, SW USA
Sierra Vista 26 B3 Arizona, SW USA
Sífnos 83 C6 anc. Siphnos. Island Kykládes, Greece, Aegean Sea
Sigli 116 A3 Sumatera, W Indonesia
Siglufjördhur 61 E4 Nordhurland Vestra, N Iceland
Signal Peak 26 A2 mountain Arizona, SW USA
Signan see Xi'an
Signy 132 A2 UK research station South Orkney Islands, Antarctica
Siguatepeque 30 C2 Comayagua, W Honduras
Siguiri 52 D4 Haute-Guinée, NE Guinea
Siilinjärvi 62 E4 Itä-Suomi, C Finland
Siirt 95 F4 var. Sert; anc. Tigranocerta. Siirt, SE Turkey
Sikandarabad see Secunderābād
Sikasso 52 D4 Sikasso, S Mali
Sikeston 23 H5 Missouri, C USA
Sikhote-Alin', Khrebet 93 G4 mountain range SE Russian Federation
Siking see Xi'an
Siklós 77 C7 Baranya, SW Hungary
Sikoku see Shikoku
Sikoku Basin see Shikoku Basin
Šilalė 84 B4 Šilalė, W Lithuania
Silchar 113 G3 Assam, NE India
Silesia 76 B4 physical region SW Poland
Silifke 94 C4 anc. Seleucia. İçel, S Turkey
Siling Co 104 C5 lake W China
Silinhot see Xilinhot
Silistra 82 E1 var. Silistria; anc. Durostorum. Silistra, NE Bulgaria
Silistria see Silistra
Sillamäe 84 E2 Ger. Sillamäggi. Ida-Virumaa, NE Estonia
Šilutė 84 B4 Ger. Heydekrug. Šilutė, W Lithuania
Silvan 95 E4 Dıyarbakır, SE Turkey
Silverek 95 E4 Şanlıurfa, SE Turkey
Simanggang see Sri Aman
Simanichy 85 C7 Rus. Simonichi. Homyel'skaya Voblasts', SE Belarus
Simav 94 B3 Kütahya, W Turkey
Simav Çayı 94 A3 river NW Turkey
Simeto 75 C7 river Sicilia, Italy, C Mediterranean Sea
Simeulue, Pulau 116 A3 island NW Indonesia
Simferopol' 87 F5 Respublika Krym, S Ukraine
Simitli 82 C3 Blagoevgrad, SW Bulgaria
Şimleu Silvaniei 86 B3 Hung. Szilágysomlyó; prev. Şimlăul Silvaniei, Şimleul Silvaniei. Sălaj, NW Romania
Simonoseki see Shimonoseki
Simpelveld 65 D6 Limburg, SE Netherlands
Simplon Pass 73 B8 pass S Switzerland
Simpson see Fort Simpson
Simpson Desert 126 B4 desert Northern Territory/South Australia
Sīnā' see Sinai
Sinai 50 C2 var. Sinai Peninsula, Ar. Shibh Jazīrat Sīnā', Sīnā'. Physical region NE Egypt
Sinaia 86 C4 Prahova, SE Romania
Sinai Peninsula see Sinai
Sinano Gawa see Shinano-gawa
Sincelejo 36 B2 Sucre, NW Colombia
Sind 112 B3 var. Sindh. Admin. region province SE Pakistan
Sindelfingen 73 B6 Baden-Württemberg, SW Germany
Sindh see Sind
Sindi 84 D2 Ger. Zintenhof. Pärnumaa, SW Estonia
Sines 70 B4 Setúbal, S Portugal
Singan see Xi'an
Singapore 116 A1 off. Republic of Singapore. Country SE Asia
Singapore 116 B3 country capital (Singapore) S Singapore
Singen 73 B6 Baden-Württemberg, S Germany
Singida 51 C7 Singida, C Tanzania
Singkang 117 E4 Sulawesi, C Indonesia
Singkawang 116 C3 Borneo, C Indonesia
Singora see Songkhla
Singû see Shingū
Sining see Xining
Siniscola 75 A5 Sardegna, Italy, C Mediterranean Sea
Sinj 78 B4 Split-Dalmacija, SE Croatia
Sinkiang see Xinjiang Uygur Zizhiqu
Sinkiang Uighur Autonomous Region see Xinjiang Uygur Zizhiqu
Sinnamarie see Sinnamary
Sinnamary 37 H3 var. Sinnamarie. N French Guiana
Sînnicolau Mare see Sânnicolau Mare
Sinoie, Lacul 86 D5 prev. Lacul Sinoe. Lagoon SE Romania
Sinop 94 D2 anc. Sinope. Sinop, N Turkey
Sinsheim 73 B6 Baden-Württemberg, SW Germany
Sint Maarten 33 G3 Eng. Saint Martin. Island N Netherlands Antilles
Sint-Michielsgestel 64 C4 Noord-Brabant, S Netherlands
Sint-Niklaas 65 B5 Fr. Saint-Nicolas. Oost-Vlaanderen, N Belgium
Sint-Pieters-Leeuw 65 B6 Vlaams Brabant, C Belgium
Sintra 70 B3 prev. Cintra. Lisboa, W Portugal
Sinujiif 51 E5 Nugaal, NE Somalia
Sinus Aelaniticus see Aqaba, Gulf of
Sinyang see Xinyang
Sinzyô see Shinjō
Sion 73 A7 Ger. Sitten; anc. Sedunum. Valais, SW Switzerland
Sioux City 23 F3 Iowa, C USA
Sioux Falls 23 F3 South Dakota, N USA
Siping 106 D3 var. Ssu-p'ing, Szeping; prev. Ssu-p'ing-chieh. Jilin, NE China
Siple, Mount 132 A4 mountain Siple Island, Antarctica
Siquirres 31 E4 Limón, E Costa Rica
Siracusa 75 D7 Eng. Syracuse. Sicilia, Italy, C Mediterranean Sea
Sir Darya see Syr Darya
Sir Edward Pellew Group 126 B2 island group Northern Territory, NE Australia
Siret 86 C3 var. Siretul, Ger. Sereth, Rus. Seret, Ukr. Siret. River Romania/Ukraine
Siret see Siret
Siretul see Siret
Sirikit Reservoir 114 C4 lake N Thailand
Sīrjān 98 D4 prev. Sa'īdābād. Kermān, S Iran
Sirna see Sýrna
Şırnak 95 F4 Şırnak, SE Turkey
Síros see Sýros
Sirte see Surt
Sirte, Gulf of see Surt, Khalīj
Sisak 78 B3 var. Siscia, Ger. Sissek, Hung. Sziszek; anc. Segestica. Sisak-Moslavina, C Croatia
Siscia see Sisak
Sisimiut 60 C3 var. Holsteinborg, Holsteinsborg, Holstenborg, Holstensborg. S Greenland
Sissek see Sisak
Sistema Penibético see Béticos, Sistemas
Siteía 83 D8 var. Sitía. Kríti, Greece, E Mediterranean Sea
Sitges 71 G2 Cataluña, NE Spain
Sitía see Siteía
Sittang 114 B4 var. Sittoung. River S Myanmar
Sittard 65 D5 Limburg, SE Netherlands
Sittoung see Sittang
Sittwe 114 A3 var. Akyab. Arakan State, W Myanmar
Siuna 30 D3 Región Autónoma Atlántico Norte, NE Nicaragua
Siut see Asyût
Sivas 94 D3 anc. Sebastia, Sebaste. Sivas, C Turkey
Sivers'kyy Donets' see Donets
Siwa 50 A2 var. Sīwah. NW Egypt
Sīwah see Siwa
Six-Fours-les-Plages 69 D6 Var, SE France
Siyăzăn 95 H2 Rus. Siazan'. NE Azerbaijan
Sizuoka see Shizuoka
Sjar see Sääre
Sjælland B8 Eng. Zealand, Ger. Seeland. Island E Denmark
Sjenica 79 D5 Turk. Seniça. Serbia, SW Serbia and Montenegro (Yugo.)
Skadar see Shkodër
Skagerak see Skagerrak
Skagerrak 63 A6 var. Skagerak. Channel N Europe
Skagit River 24 B1 river Washington, NW USA
Skalka 62 C3 lake N Sweden
Skarżysko-Kamienna 76 D4 Świętokrzyskie, C Poland
Skaudvilė 84 B4 Tauragė, SW Lithuania
Skegness 67 E6 E England, UK
Skellefteå 62 D4 Västerbotten, N Sweden
Skellefteälven 62 C4 river N Sweden
Ski 63 B6 Akershus, S Norway
Skíathos 83 C5 Skíathos, Vóreioi Sporádes, Greece, Aegean Sea
Skidal' 85 B5 Rus. Skidel'. Hrodzyenskaya Voblasts', W Belarus
Skierniewice 76 D3 Lodzkie, C Poland
Skiftet 84 C1 Fin. Kihti. Strait Gulf of Bothnia/Gulf of Finland
Skíros see Skýros
Skópelos 83 C5 Skópelos, Vóreioi Sporádes, Greece, Aegean Sea
Skopje 79 D6 var. Üsküb, Turk. Üsküp; prev. Skoplje, anc. Scupi. Country capital (FYR Macedonia) N FYR Macedonia
Skoplje see Skopje
Skovorodino 93 F4 Amurskaya Oblast', SE Russian Federation
Skuodas 84 B3 Ger. Schoden, Pol. Szkudy. Skuodas, NW Lithuania
Skye, Isle of 66 B3 island NW Scotland, UK
Skýros 83 C5 var. Skíros. Skýros, Vóreioi Sporádes, Greece, Aegean Sea
Skýros 83 C5 var. Skíros; anc. Scyros. Island Vóreioi Sporádes, Greece, Aegean Sea
Slagelse 63 B7 Vestsjælland, E Denmark
Slatina 86 B5 Olt, S Romania
Slatina 78 C3 Hung. Szlatina, prev. Podravska Slatina. Virovtica-Podravina, NE Croatia
Slavonska Požega see Požega
Slavonski Brod 78 C3 Ger. Brod, Hung. Bród; prev. Brod, Brod na Savi. Brod-Posavina, NE Croatia
Slavuta 86 C2 Khmel'nyts'ka Oblast', NW Ukraine
Slawharad 85 E7 Rus. Slavgorod. Mahilyowskaya Voblasts', E Belarus
Sławno 76 C2 Zachodniopomorskie, NW Poland
Sléibhte Chill Mhantáin see Wicklow Mountains
Slēmānī see As Sulaymānīyah
Sliema 80 B5 N Malta
Sligeach see Sligo
Sligo 67 A5 Ir. Sligeach. NW Ireland
Sliven 82 D2 var. Slivno. Sliven, C Bulgaria
Slivnitsa 82 B2 Sofiya, W Bulgaria
Slivno see Sliven
Slobozia 86 C5 Ialomiţa, SE Romania
Slonim 85 B6 Pol. Słonim, Rus. Slonim. Hrodzyenskaya Voblasts', W Belarus
Slovakia 77 C6 off. Slovenská Republika, Ger. Slowakei, Hung. Szlovákia, Slvk. Slovensko. Country C Europe
Slovak Ore Mountains see Slovenské rudohorie
Slovenia 73 D8 off. Republic of Slovenia, Ger. Slowenien, Slvn. Slovenija. Country SE Europe
Slovenské rudohorie 77 D6 Eng. Slovak Ore Mountains, Ger. Slowakisches Erzgebirge, Ungarisches Erzgebirge. Mountain range C Slovakia
Slov"yans'k 87 G3 Rus. Slavyansk. Donets'ka Oblast', E Ukraine
Slowakisches Erzgebirge see Slovenské rudohorie
Słubice 76 B3 Ger. Frankfurt. Lubuskie, W Poland
Sluch 86 D1 river NW Ukraine
Słupsk 76 C2 Ger. Stolp. Pomorskie, N Poland
Slutsk 85 C6 Rus. Slutsk. Minskaya Voblasts', S Belarus
Smallwood Reservoir 17 F2 lake Newfoundland and Labrador, S Canada
Smara 48 B3 var. Es Semara. N Western Sahara
Smarhon' 85 C5 Pol. Smorgonie, Rus. Smorgon'. Hrodzyenskaya Voblasts', W Belarus
Smederevo 78 D4 Ger. Semendria. Serbia, N Serbia and Montenegro (Yugo.)
Smederevska Palanka 78 D4 Serbia, C Serbia and Montenegro (Yugo.)
Smila 87 E2 Rus. Smela. Cherkas'ka Oblast', C Ukraine
Smiltene 84 D3 Ger. Smilten. Valka, N Latvia
Smøla 62 A4 island W Norway
Smolensk 89 A5 Smolenskaya Oblast', W Russian Federation
Snake 12 B4 river Yukon Territory, NW Canada
Snake River 24 C3 river NW USA
Snake River Plain 24 D4 plain Idaho, NW USA
Sneek 64 D2 Friesland, N Netherlands
Sněžka 76 B4 Ger. Schneekoppe. Mountain N Czech Republic
Śniardwy, Jezioro 114 D2 Ger. Spirdingsee. Lake NE Poland
Snina 77 E5 Hung. Szinna. Prešovský Kraj, E Slovakia
Snowdonia 67 C6 mountain range NW Wales, UK
Snyder 27 F3 Texas, SW USA
Sobradinho, Represa de 41 F2 var. Barragem de Sobradinho. Reservoir E Brazil
Sochi 89 A7 Krasnodarskiy Kray, SW Russian Federation
Société, Archipel de la 123 G4 var. Archipel de Tahiti, Îles de la Société, Eng. Society Islands. Island group W French Polynesia
Society Islands see Société, Archipel de la
Socorro 26 D2 New Mexico, SW USA
Socorro, Isla 28 B5 island W Mexico
Socotra see Suquṭrā
Soc Trăng 115 D6 var. Khanh. Soc Trăng, S Vietnam
Socuéllamos 71 E3 Castilla-La Mancha, C Spain
Sodankylä 62 D3 Lappi, N Finland
Sodari see Sodiri
Söderhamn 63 C5 Gävleborg, C Sweden
Södertälje 63 C6 Stockholm, C Sweden
Sodiri 50 B4 var. Sawdirī, Sodari. Northern Kordofan, C Sudan
Sofia see Sofiya
Sofiya 82 C2 var. Sophia, Eng. Sofia; Lat. Serdica. Country capital (Bulgaria) Sofiya-Grad, W Bulgaria
Sogamoso 36 B3 Boyacá, C Colombia
Sognefjorden 63 A5 fjord NE North Sea
Sohâg 50 B2 var. Sawhāj, Suliag. C Egypt
Sohar see Ṣuḥār
Sohm Plain 44 B3 undersea feature NW Atlantic Ocean
Sohrau see Żory
Sokal' 86 C2 Rus. Sokal. L'vivs'ka Oblast', NW Ukraine
Söke 94 A4 Aydın, SW Turkey
Sokhumi 95 E1 Rus. Sukhumi. NW Georgia
Sokodé 53 F4 C Togo
Sokol 88 C4 Vologodskaya Oblast', NW Russian Federation
Sokółka 76 E3 Białystok, NE Poland
Sokolov 77 A5 Ger. Falkenau an der Eger; prev. Falknov nad Ohří. Karlovarský Kraj, W Czech Republic
Sokone 52 B3 W Senegal
Sokoto 53 F4 river NW Nigeria
Sokoto 53 F3 Sokoto, NW Nigeria
Sokotra see Suquṭrā
Solāpur 102 B3 var. Sholāpur. Mahārāshtra, W India
Solca 86 C3 Ger. Solka. Suceava, N Romania
Sol, Costa del 70 D5 coastal region S Spain
Soldeu 69 B7 NE Andorra
Solec Kujawski 76 C3 Kujawski-pomorskie, C Poland
Soledad, Isla see East Falkland
Soledad 36 B1 Anzoátegui, NE Venezuela
Solikamsk 92 C3 Permskaya Oblast', NW Russian Federation
Sol'-Iletsk 89 D6 Orenburgskaya Oblast', W Russian Federation
Solingen 72 A4 Nordrhein-Westfalen, W Germany
Sollentuna 63 C6 Stockholm, C Sweden
Solok 116 B4 Sumatera, W Indonesia
Solomon Islands 122 C3 prev. British Solomon Islands Protectorate. Country W Pacific Ocean
Solomon Islands 122 C3 island group PNG/Solomon Islands
Solomon Sea 122 B3 sea W Pacific Ocean
Soltau 72 B3 Niedersachsen, NW Germany
Sol'tsy 88 A4 Novgorodskaya Oblast', W Russian Federation
Solwezi 56 D2 North Western, NW Zambia
Sōma 108 D4 Fukushima, Honshū, C Japan
Somalia 51 D5 off. Somali Democratic Republic, Som. Jamuuriyada Demuqraadiga Soomaaliyeed, Soomaaliya; prev. Italian Somaliland, Somaliland Protectorate. Country E Africa
Somali Basin 47 E5 undersea feature W Indian Ocean
Sombor 78 C3 Hung. Zombor. Serbia, NW Serbia and Montenegro (Yugo.)
Someren 65 D5 Noord-Brabant, SE Netherlands
Somerset 20 A5 var. Somerset Village. W Bermuda
Somerset 18 C5 Kentucky, S USA
Somerset Island 15 F2 island Queen Elizabeth Islands, Nunavut, NW Canada
Somerset Island 20 A5 island W Bermuda

Sýros – Thrissur

Sýros 83 C6 var. Síros. Island Kykládes, Greece, Aegean Sea
Syvash, Zatoka 87 F4 Rus. Zaliv Syvash. Inlet S Ukraine
Syzran' 89 C6 Samarskaya Oblast', W Russian Federation
Szamos see Someş
Szamotuły 76 B3 Wielkopolskie, C Poland
Szczecin 76 B3 Eng./Ger. Stettin. Zachodniopomorskie, NW Poland
Szczecinek 76 B2 Ger. Neustettin. Zachodniopomorskie, NW Poland
Szczeciński, Zalew 76 A2 var. Stettiner Haff, Ger. Oderhaff. Bay Germany/Poland
Szczytno 76 D3 Ger. Ortelsburg. Olsztyn, NE Poland
Szechuan see Sichuan
Szechwan see Sichuan
Szeged 77 D7 Ger. Szegedin, Rom. Seghedin. Csongrád, SE Hungary
Székesfehérvár 77 C6 Ger. Stuhlweissenberg; anc. Alba Regia. Fejér, W Hungary
Szekszárd 77 C7 Tolna, S Hungary
Szenttamás see Srbobran
Szeping see Siping
Sziszek see Sisak
Szlatina see Slatina
Szolnok 77 D6 Jász-Nagykun-Szolnok, C Hungary
Szombathely 77 B6 Ger. Steinamanger; anc. Sabaria, Savaria. Vas, W Hungary
Szprotawa 76 B4 Ger. Sprottau. Lubuskie, W Poland

T

Table Rock Lake 27 G1 reservoir Arkansas/Missouri, C USA
Tábor 77 B5 Budějovický Kraj, S Czech Republic
Tabora 51 B7 Tabora, W Tanzania
Tabrīz 98 C2 var. Tebriz; anc. Tauris. Āžarbāyjān-e Khāvarī, NW Iran
Tabuaeran 123 G2 prev. Fanning Island. Atoll Line Islands, E Kiribati
Tabūk 98 A4 Tabūk, NW Saudi Arabia
Täby 63 C6 Stockholm, C Sweden
Tachov 77 A5 Ger. Tachau. Plzeňský Kraj, W Czech Republic
Tacloban 117 F2 off. Tacloban City. Leyte, C Philippines
Tacna 39 E4 Tacna, SE Peru
Tacoma 24 B2 Washington, NW USA
Tacuarembó 42 D4 prev. San Fructuoso. Tacuarembó, C Uruguay
Tademaït, Plateau du 48 D3 plateau C Algeria
Tadmor see Tudmur
Tadmur see Tudmur
Tādpatri 110 C2 Andhra Pradesh, E India
Taegu 107 E4 off. Taegu-gwangyŏksi, var. Daegu, Jap. Taikyū. SE South Korea
Taejŏn 107 E4 off. Taejŏn-gwangyŏksi, Jap. Taiden. C South Korea
Tafassâsset, Ténéré du 53 G2 desert N Niger
Tafila see Aţ Ţafilah
Taganrog 89 A7 Rostovskaya Oblast', SW Russian Federation
Taganrog, Gulf of 87 G4 Rus. Taganrogskiy Zaliv, Ukr. Tahanroz'ka Zatoka. Gulf Russian Federation/Ukraine
Taguatinga 41 F3 Tocantins, C Brazil
Tagus 70 C3 Port. Rio Tejo, Sp. Río Tajo. River Portugal/Spain
Tagus Plain 58 A4 undersea feature E Atlantic Ocean
Tahat 49 E4 mountain SE Algeria
Tahiti 123 H4 island Îles du Vent, W French Polynesia
Tahlequah 27 G1 Oklahoma, C USA
Tahoe, Lake 25 B5 lake California/Nevada, W USA
Tahoua 53 F3 Tahoua, W Niger
T'aichung 106 D6 Jap. Taichū; prev. Taiwan. C Taiwan
Taieri 129 B7 river South Island, NZ
Taihape 128 D4 Manawatu-Wanganui, North Island, NZ
Tailem Bend 127 B7 South Australia
T'ainan 106 D6 Jap. Tainan; prev. Dainan. S Taiwan
T'aipei 106 D6 Jap. Taihoku; prev. Daihoku. Country capital (Taiwan) N Taiwan
Taiping 116 B3 Perak, Peninsular Malaysia
Taiwan 106 D6 off. Republic of China, var. Formosa, Formo'sa. Country E Asia
T'aiwan Haihsia see Taiwan Strait
Taiwan Haixia see Taiwan Strait
Taiwan Strait 106 D6 var. Formosa Strait, Chin. T'aiwan Haihsia, Taiwan Haixia. Strait China/Taiwan
Taiyuan 106 C4 prev. T'ai-yuan, T'ai-yüan, Yangku. Shanxi, C China
Ta'izz 99 B7 SW Yemen
Tajikistan 101 E3 off. Republic of Tajikistan, Rus. Tadzhikistan, Taj. Jumhurii Tojikiston; prev. Tajik S.S.R. Country C Asia
Tak 114 C4 var. Rahaeng. Tak, W Thailand
Takao see Kaohsiung
Takaoka 109 C5 Toyama, Honshū, SW Japan
Takapuna 128 D2 Auckland, North Island, NZ
Takhiatosh 100 C2 Rus. Takhiatash. Qoraqalpoghiston Respublikasi, W Uzbekistan
Takhtakŭpir 100 D1 Rus. Takhtakupyr. Qoraqalpoghiston Respublikasi, NW Uzbekistan
Takikawa 108 D2 Hokkaidō, NE Japan
Takla Makan Desert see Taklimakan Shamo
Taklimakan Shamo 104 B3 Eng. Takla Makan Desert. Desert NW China
Takow see Kaohsiung
Takutea 123 G4 island S Cook Islands
Talachyn 85 D6 Rus. Tolochin. Vitsyebskaya Voblasts', NE Belarus
Talamanca, Cordillera de 31 E5 mountain range S Costa Rica
Talara 38 B2 Piura, NW Peru
Talas 101 F2 Talasskaya Oblast', NW Kyrgyzstan
Talaud, Kepulauan 117 F3 island group E Indonesia
Talavera de la Reina 70 D3 anc. Caesarobriga, Talabriga. Castilla-La Mancha, C Spain
Talca 42 B4 Maule, C Chile
Talcahuano 43 B5 Bío Bío, C Chile
Taldykorgan 92 C5 Kaz. Taldyqorghan; prev. Taldy-Kurgan. Almaty, SE Kazakhstan
Taldy-Kurgan/Taldyqorghan see Taldykorgan
Ta-lien see Dalian
Taliq-an see Tāloqān
Tal'ka 85 C6 Rus. Tal'ka. Minskaya Voblasts', C Belarus
Tallahassee 20 D3 prev. Muskogean. State capital Florida, SE USA
Tall al Abyaḑ see At Tall al Abyaḑ
Tallinn 84 D2 Ger. Reval, Rus. Tallin; prev. Revel. Country capital (Estonia) Harjumaa, NW Estonia
Tall Kalakh 96 B4 var. Tell Kalakh. Ḩimş, C Syria
Tallulah 20 B2 Louisiana, S USA
Talnakh 92 D3 Taymyrskiy (Dolgano-Nenetskiy) Avtonomnyy Okrug, N Russian Federation
Tal'ne 87 E3 Rus. Tal'noye. Cherkas'ka Oblast', C Ukraine
Taloga 27 F1 Oklahoma, C USA
Tāloqān 101 E3 var. Taliq-an. Takhār, NE Afghanistan
Talsi 84 C3 Ger. Talsen. Talsi, NW Latvia
Taltal 42 B2 Antofagasta, N Chile
Talvik 62 D2 Finnmark, N Norway
Tamabo, Banjaran 116 D3 mountain range East Malaysia
Tamale 53 E4 C Ghana
Tamana 123 E3 prev. Rotcher Island. Atoll Tungaru, W Kiribati
Tamanrasset 49 E4 var. Tamenghest. S Algeria
Tamar 67 C7 river SW England, UK
Tamar see Tudmur
Tamatave see Toamasina
Tamazunchale 29 E4 San Luis Potosí, C Mexico
Tambacounda 52 C3 SE Senegal
Tambov 89 B6 Tambovskaya Oblast', W Russian Federation
Tambura 51 B5 Western Equatoria, SW Sudan
Tamchaket see Tâmchekket
Tâmchekket 52 C3 var. Tamchaket. Hodh el Gharbi, S Mauritania
Tamenghest see Tamanrasset
Tamiahua, Laguna de 29 F4 lagoon E Mexico
Tamil Nādu 110 C3 prev. Madras. State SE India
Tam Ky 115 E5 Quang Nam-Ða Nång, C Vietnam
Tampa 21 E4 Florida, SE USA
Tampa Bay 21 E4 bay Florida, SE USA
Tampere 63 D5 Swe. Tammerfors. Länsi-Suomi, W Finland
Tampico 29 E3 Tamaulipas, C Mexico
Tamworth 127 D6 New South Wales, SE Australia
Tana 62 D2 var. Tenojoki, Fin. Teno, Lapp. Dealnu. River Finland/Norway see also Teno
Tana 62 D2 Finnmark, N Norway
Tanabe 109 C7 Wakayama, Honshū, SW Japan
T'ana Hāyk' 50 C4 Eng. Lake Tana. Lake NW Ethiopia
Tanais see Don
Tanami Desert 124 D3 desert Northern Territory, N Australia
Ţăndărei 86 D5 Ialomiţa, SE Romania
Tandil 43 D5 Buenos Aires, E Argentina
Tanega-shima 109 B8 island Nansei-shotō, SW Japan
Tane Range 114 B4 Bur. Tanen Taunggyi. Mountain range W Thailand
Tanezrouft 48 D4 desert Algeria/Mali
Ţanf, Jabal aţ 96 D4 mountain SE Syria
Tanga 47 E5 Tanga, E Tanzania
Tanga 51 C7 region E Tanzania
Tanganyika, Lake 51 B7 lake E Africa
Tangeh-ye Hormoz see Hormuz, Strait of
Tanger 48 C2 var. Tangiers, Tangier, Fr./Ger. Tangerk, Sp. Tánger; anc. Tingis. NW Morocco
Tangerk see Tanger
Tanggula Shan 104 C4 var. Dangla, Tangla Range. Mountain range W China
Tangier see Tanger
Tangiers see Tanger
Tangla Range see Tanggula Shan
Tangra Yumco 104 B5 var. Tangro Tso. Lake W China
Tangro Tso see Tangra Yumco
Tangshan 106 D3 var. T'ang-shan. Hebei, E China
T'ang-shan see Tangshan
Tanimbar, Kepulauan 117 F5 island group Maluku, E Indonesia
Tanna 122 D4 island S Vanuatu
Tannenhof see Krynica
Tan-Tan 48 B3 SW Morocco
Tan-tung see Dandong
Tanzania 51 C7 off. United Republic of Tanzania, Swa. Jamhuri ya Muungano wa Tanzania; prev. German East Africa, Tanganyika and Zanzibar. Country E Africa
Taoudenit see Taoudenni
Taoudenni 53 E2 var. Taoudenit. Tombouctou, N Mali
Tapa 84 E2 Ger. Taps. Lääne-Virumaa, NE Estonia
Tapachula 29 G5 Chiapas, SE Mexico
Tapajós, Rio 41 E2 var. Tapajóz. River NW Brazil
Tapajóz see Tapajós, Rio
Ţarābulus 49 F2 var. Ţarābulus al Gharb, Eng. Tripoli.Country capital (Libya) NW Libya
Tarābulus see Tripoli
Ţarābulus al Gharb see Ţarābulus
Ţarābulus ash Shām see Tripoli
Taraclia 86 D4 Rus. Tarakilya. S Moldova
Taranaki, Mount 128 C4 var. Egmont, Mount. Mountain North Island, NZ
Tarancón 71 E3 Castilla-La Mancha, C Spain
Taranto 75 E5 var. Tarentum. Puglia, SE Italy
Taranto, Golfo di 75 E6 Eng. Gulf of Taranto. Gulf S Italy
Tarapoto 38 C2 San Martín, N Peru
Tarare 69 D5 Rhône, E France
Tarascon 69 D6 Bouches-du-Rhône, SE France
Tarawa 122 D2 atoll Tungaru, W Kiribati
Taraz 92 C5 prev. Aulie Ata, Auliye-Ata, Dzhambul, Zhambyl. Zhambyl, S Kazakhstan
Tarazona 71 E2 Aragón, NE Spain
Tarbes 69 B6 anc. Bigorra. Hautes-Pyrénées, S France
Tarcoola 127 A6 South Australia
Taree 127 D6 New South Wales, SE Australia
Tarentum see Taranto
Târgovişte 86 C5 prev. Tîrgovişte. Dâmboviţa, S Romania
Târgu Jiu 86 B4 prev. Tîrgu Jiu. Gorj, W Romania
Târgul-Neamţ see Târgu-Neamţ
Târgu Mureş 86 B4 prev. Oşorhei, Tîrgu Mures, Ger. Neumarkt, Hung. Marosvásárhely. Mureş, C Romania
Târgu-Neamţ 86 C3 var. Târgul-Neamţ; prev. Tîrgu-Neamţ. Neamţ, NE Romania
Târgu Ocna 86 C4 Hung. Aknavásár; prev. Tîrgu Ocna. Bacău, E Romania
Târgu Secuiesc 86 C4 Ger. Neumarkt, Szekler Neumarkt, Hung. Kezdivásárhely; prev. Chezdi-Oşorheiu, Târgul-Săcuiesc, Tîrgu Secuiesc. Covasna, E Romania
Tarija 39 G5 Tarija, S Bolivia
Tarīm 99 C6 C Yemen
Tarim Basin 102 C2 basin NW China
Tarim He 104 B3 river NW China
Tarma 38 C3 Junín, C Peru
Tarn 69 C6 cultural region S France
Tarn 69 C6 river S France
Tarnobrzeg 76 D4 Podkarpackie, SE Poland
Tarnów 77 D5 Małopolskie, S Poland
Tarragona 71 G2 anc. Tarraco. Cataluña, E Spain
Tàrrega 71 F2 var. Tarrega. Cataluña, NE Spain
Tarsus 94 C4 İçel, S Turkey
Tartu 84 D3 Ger. Dorpat; prev. Rus. Yurev, Yur'yev. Tartumaa, SE Estonia
Ţarţūs 96 A3 Fr. Tartouss; anc. Tortosa. Ţarţūs, W Syria
Ta Ru Tao, Ko 115 B7 island S Thailand
Tarvisio 74 D2 Friuli-Venezia Giulia, NE Italy
Tashi Chho Dzong see Thimphu
Tashkent see Toshkent
Tash-Kumyr 101 F2 Kir. Tash-Kömür. Dzhalal-Abadskaya Oblast', W Kyrgyzstan
Tashqurghan see Kholm
Tasikmalaya 116 C5 prev. Tasikmalaja. Jawa, C Indonesia
Tasman Basin 120 C5 var. East Australian Basin. Undersea feature S Tasman Sea
Tasman Bay 129 C5 inlet South Island, NZ
Tasmania 127 B8 prev. Van Diemen's Land. State SE Australia
Tasmania 130 B4 island SE Australia
Tasman Plateau 120 C5 var. South Tasmania Plateau. Undersea feature SW Tasman Sea
Tasman Sea 120 C5 sea SW Pacific Ocean
Tassili-n-Ajjer 49 E4 plateau E Algeria
Tatabánya 77 C6 Komárom-Esztergom, NW Hungary
Tathlīth 99 B5 'Asīr, S Saudi Arabia
Tatra Mountains 77 D5 Ger. Tatra, Hung. Tátra, Pol./Slvk. Tatry. Mountain range Poland/Slovakia
Ta-t'ung see Datong
Tatvan 95 F3 Bitlis, SE Turkey
Ta'ū 123 F4 var. Tau. Island Manua Islands, E American Samoa
Tau see Ta'ū
Taukum, Peski 101 G1 desert SE Kazakhstan
Taumarunui 128 D4 Manawatu-Wanganui, North Island, NZ
Taungdwingyi 114 B3 Magwe, C Myanmar
Taunggyi 114 B3 Shan State, C Myanmar
Taunton 67 C7 SW England, UK
Taupo 128 D3 Waikato, North Island, NZ
Taupo, Lake 128 D3 lake North Island, NZ
Tauragė 84 B4 Ger. Tauroggen. Tauragė, SW Lithuania
Tauranga 128 D3 Bay of Plenty, North Island, NZ
Tauris see Tabrīz
Tavas 94 B4 Denizli, SW Turkey
Tavira 70 C5 Faro, S Portugal
Tavoy 115 B5 var. Dawei. Tenasserim, S Myanmar
Tavoy Island see Mali Kyun
Tawakoni, Lake 27 G2 reservoir Texas, SW USA
Tawau 116 D3 Sabah, East Malaysia
Ţawkar see Tokar
Tawzar see Tozeur
Taxco 29 E4 var. Taxco de Alarcón. Guerrero, S Mexico
Taxco de Alarcón see Taxco
Tay 66 C3 river C Scotland, UK
Taylor 27 G3 Texas, SW USA
Taymā' 98 A4 Tabūk, NW Saudi Arabia
Taymyr, Ozero 93 E2 lake N Russian Federation
Taymyr, Poluostrov 93 E2 peninsula N Russian Federation
Taz 92 D3 river N Russian Federation
T'bilisi 95 G2 Eng. Tiflis. Country capital (Georgia) SE Georgia
T'bilisi 90 B4 international airport S Georgia
Tchien see Zwedru
Tchongking see Chongqing
Tczew 76 C2 Ger. Dirschau. Pomorskie, N Poland
Te Anau 129 A7 Southland, South Island, NZ
Te Anau, Lake 129 A7 lake South Island, NZ
Teapa 29 G4 Tabasco, SE Mexico
Teate see Chieti
Tebingtinggi 116 B3 Sumatera, N Indonesia
Tebriz see Tabrīz
Techirghiol 86 D5 Constanţa, SE Romania
Tecomán 28 D4 Colima, SW Mexico
Tecpan 29 E5 var. Tecpan de Galeana. Guerrero, S Mexico
Tecpan de Galeana see Tecpan
Tecuci 86 C4 Galaţi, E Romania
Tedzhen 100 C3 Turkm. Tejen. Akhalskiy Velayat, S Turkmenistan
Tedzhen see Harīrūd
Tees 67 D5 river N England, UK
Tefé 40 D2 Amazonas, N Brazil
Tegal 116 C4 Jawa, C Indonesia
Tegelen 65 D5 Limburg, SE Netherlands
Tegucigalpa 30 C3 country capital (Honduras) Francisco Morazán, SW Honduras
Teheran see Tehrān
Tehrān 98 C3 var. Teheran. Country capital (Iran) Tehrān, N Iran
Tehuacán 29 F4 Puebla, S Mexico
Tehuantepec 29 F5 var. Santo Domingo Tehuantepec. Oaxaca, SE Mexico
Tehuantepec, Golfo de 29 F5 var. Gulf of Tehuantepec. Gulf S Mexico
Tehuantepec, Gulf of see Tehuantepec, Golfo de
Tehuantepec, Isthmus of see Tehuantepec, Istmo de
Tehuantepec, Istmo de 29 F5 var. Isthmus of Tehuantepec. Isthmus SE Mexico
Tejen see Harīrūd
Te Kao 128 C1 Northland, North Island, NZ
Tekax 29 H4 var. Tekax de Álvaro Obregón. Yucatán, SE Mexico
Tekax de Álvaro Obregón see Tekax
Tekeli 92 C5 Almaty, SE Kazakhstan
Tekirdağ 94 A2 It. Rodosto; anc. Bisanthe, Raidestos, Rhaedestus. Tekirdağ, NW Turkey
Te Kuiti 128 D3 Waikato, North Island, NZ
Tela 30 C2 Atlántida, NW Honduras
Telanaipura see Jambi
Tel Aviv-Jaffa see Tel Aviv-Yafo
Tel Aviv-Yafo 97 A6 var. Tel Aviv-Jaffa. Tel Aviv, C Israel
Teles Pirés see São Manuel, Rio
Telish 82 C2 prev. Azizie. Pleven, NW Bulgaria
Tell Abiad see At Tall al Abyaḑ
Tell Abyad see At Tall al Abyaḑ
Tell Kalakh see Tall Kalakh
Tell Shedadi see Ash Shadādah
Telšiai 84 B3 Ger. Telschen. Telšiai, NW Lithuania
Teluk Irian see Cenderawasih, Teluk
Teluk Serera see Cenderawasih, Teluk
Temerin 78 D3 Serbia, N Serbia and Montenegro (Yugo.)
Temirtau 92 C4 prev. Samarkandski, Samarkandskoye. Karaganda, C Kazakhstan
Tempio Pausania 75 A5 Sardegna, Italy, C Mediterranean Sea
Temple 27 G3 Texas, SW USA
Temuco 43 B5 Araucanía, C Chile
Temuka 129 B6 Canterbury, South Island, NZ
Tenasserim 115 B6 Tenasserim, S Myanmar
Ténenkou 52 D3 Mopti, C Mali
Ténéré 53 G3 physical region C Niger
Tenerife 48 A3 island Islas Canarias, Spain, NE Atlantic Ocean
Tengger Shamo 105 E3 desert N China
Tengréla 52 D4 var. Tingréla. N Côte d'Ivoire
Tenkodogo 53 E4 S Burkina faso
Tennant Creek 126 A3 Northern Territory, C Australia
Tennessee 20 C1 off. State of Tennessee; also known as The Volunteer State. State SE USA
Tennessee River 20 C1 river S USA
Teno see Tana
Tenojoki see Tana
Tepelena see Tepelenë
Tepelenë 79 C7 var. Tepelena, It. Tepeleni. Gjirokastër, S Albania
Tepeleni see Tepelenë
Tepic 28 D4 Nayarit, C Mexico
Teplice 76 A4 Ger. Teplitz; prev. Teplice-Šanov, Teplitz-Schönau. Ústecký Kraj, NW Czech Republic
Tequila 28 D4 Jalisco, SW Mexico
Teraina 123 G2 prev. Washington Island. Atoll Line Islands, E Kiribati
Teramo 74 C4 anc. Interamna. Abruzzo, C Italy
Tercan 95 E3 Erzincan, NE Turkey
Terceira 70 A5 var. Ilha Terceira. Island Azores, Portugal, NE Atlantic Ocean
Teresina 41 F2 var. Therezina. State capital Piauí, NE Brazil
Termia see Kýthnos
Términos, Laguna de 29 G4 lagoon SE Mexico
Termiz 101 E3 Rus. Termez. Surkhondaryo Wiloyati, S Uzbekistan
Termoli 74 D4 Molise, C Italy
Terneuzen 65 B5 var. Neuzen. Zeeland, SW Netherlands
Terni 74 C4 anc. Interamna Nahars. Umbria, C Italy
Ternopil' 86 C2 Pol. Tarnopol, Rus. Ternopol'. Ternopil's'ka Oblast', W Ukraine
Terracina 75 C5 Lazio, C Italy
Terrassa 71 G2 Cast. Tarrasa. Cataluña, E Spain
Terre Adélie 132 C4 disputed region SE Antarctica
Terre Haute 18 B4 Indiana, N USA
Territoire du Yukon see Yukon Territory
Terschelling 64 C1 Fris. Skylge. Island Waddeneilanden, N Netherlands
Teruel 71 F3 anc. Turba. Aragón, E Spain
Tervel 82 E1 prev. Kurtbunar, Rom. Curtbunar. Dobrich, NE Bulgaria
Tervueren see Tervuren
Tervuren 65 C6 var. Tervueren. Vlaams Brabant, C Belgium
Teseney 50 C4 var. Tessenei. W Eritrea
Tessalit 53 E2 Kidal, NE Mali
Tessaoua 53 G3 Maradi, S Niger
Tessenderlo 65 C5 Limburg, NE Belgium
Tessenei see Teseney
Testigos, Islas los 37 E1 island group N Venezuela
Tete 57 E2 Tete, NW Mozambique
Teterow 72 C3 Mecklenburg-Vorpommern, NE Germany
Tétouan 48 C2 var. Tetouan, Tetuán. N Morocco
Tetovo 79 D5 Alb. Tetova, Tetovë, Turk. Kalkandelen. Razgrad, N Bulgaria
Tetuán see Tétouan
Tevere 74 C4 Eng. Tiber. River C Italy
Teverya 97 B5 var. Tiberias, Tverya. Northern, N Israel
Te Waewae Bay 129 A7 bay South Island, NZ
Texarkana 20 A2 Arkansas, C USA
Texarkana 27 H2 Texas, SW USA
Texas 27 F3 off. State of Texas; also known as The Lone Star State. State S USA
Texas City 27 H4 Texas, SW USA
Texel 64 C2 island Waddeneilanden, NW Netherlands
Texoma, Lake 27 G2 reservoir Oklahoma/Texas, C USA
Teziutlán 29 F4 Puebla, S Mexico
Thaa Atoll see Kolhumadulu Atoll
Thai Binh 114 D3 Thai Binh, N Vietnam
Thailand 115 C5 off. Kingdom of Thailand, Th. Prathet Thai; prev. Siam. Country SE Asia
Thailand, Gulf of 115 C6 var. Gulf of Siam, Th. Ao Thai, Vtn. Vinh Thai Lan. Gulf SE Asia
Thai Nguyên 114 D3 Băc Thai, N Vietnam
Thakhèk 114 D4 prev. Muang Khammouan. Khammouan, C Laos
Thamarīd see Thamarīt
Thamarīt 99 D6 var. Thamarīd, Thumrayt. SW Oman
Thames 67 B8 river S England, UK
Thames 128 D3 Waikato, North Island, NZ
Thanh Hoa 114 D3 Vinh Phu, N Vietnam
Thanintari Taungdan see Bilauktaung Range
Thar Desert 112 C3 var. Great Indian Desert, Indian Desert. Desert India/Pakistan
Tharthār, Buḩayrat ath 98 B3 lake C Iraq
Thásos 82 C4 island E Greece
Thásos 82 C4 Thásos, E Greece
Thaton 114 B4 Mon State, S Myanmar
Thayetmyo 114 A4 Magwe, C Myanmar
The Crane 33 H2 var. Crane. S Barbados
The Dalles 24 B3 Oregon, NW USA
The Flatts Village see Flatts Village
The Hague see 's-Gravenhage
Theodosia see Feodosiya
The Pas 15 F5 Manitoba, C Canada
Therezina see Teresina
Thérma 83 D6 Ikaría, Dodekánisos, Greece, Aegean Sea
Thermaïkós Kólpos 82 B4 Eng. Thermaic Gulf; anc. Thermaicus Sinus. Gulf N Greece
Thermiá see Kýthnos
Thérmo 83 B5 Dytikí Ellás, C Greece
The Rock 71 H4 E Gibraltar
The Six Counties see Northern Ireland
Thessaloníki 82 C3 Eng. Salonica, Salonika, SCr. Solun, Turk. Selânik. Kentrikí Makedonía, N Greece
The Valley 33 G3 dependent territory capital (Anguilla) E Anguilla
The Village 27 G1 Oklahoma, C USA
Thiamis see Thýamis
Thibet see Xizang Zizhiqu
Thief River Falls 23 F1 Minnesota, N USA
Thienen see Tienen
Thiers 69 C5 Puy-de-Dôme, C France
Thiès 52 B3 W Senegal
Thimbu see Thimphu
Thimphu 113 G3 var. Thimbu; prev. Tashi Chho Dzong. Country capital (Bhutan) W Bhutan
Thionville 68 D3 Ger. Diedenhofen. Moselle, NE France
Thíra 83 D7 prev. Santorin, Santoríni, anc. Thera. Island Kykládes, Greece, Aegean Sea
Thíra 83 D7 Thíra, Kykládes, Greece, Aegean Sea
Thiruvanathapuram see Trivandrum
Thitu Island 106 C8 island NW Spratly Islands
Tholen 64 B4 island SW Netherlands
Thomasville 20 D3 Georgia, SE USA
Thompson 15 F4 Manitoba, C Canada
Thonon-les-Bains 69 D5 Haute-Savoie, E France
Thorlákshöfn 61 E5 Sudhurland, SW Iceland
Thornton Island see Millennium Island
Thouars 68 B4 Deux-Sèvres, W France
Thracian Sea 82 D4 Gk. Thrakikó Pélagos; anc. Thracium Mare. Sea Greece/Turkey
Three Kings Islands 128 C1 island group N NZ
Thrissur see Trichūr

INDEX

U

V

INDEX